LETTERS OF CREDIT AND BANK GUARANTEES UNDER INTERNATIONAL TRADE LAW

SECOND EDITION

Matti S. Kurkela

Docent, University of Helsinki
LL.M., LL.Lic., LL.D, University of Helsinki
LL.M., Harvard Law School
D.S.U. (Paris 2)
Member of Helsinki and Paris Bars
Senior Partner, Hannes Snellman Attorneys At Law Ltd, Helsinki

OXFORD
UNIVERSITY PRESS

OXFORD
UNIVERSITY PRESS

Oxford University Press, Inc., publishes works that further Oxford University's objective of excellence in research, scholarship, and education.

Copyright © 2008 by Oxford University Press, Inc.
Published by Oxford University Press, Inc.
198 Madison Avenue, New York, New York 10016

Oxford is a registered trademark of Oxford University Press
Oceana is a registered trademark of Oxford University Press, Inc.

All rights reserved. No part of this publication may be reproduced, stored in a retrieval system, or transmitted, in any form or by any means, electronic, mechanical, photocopying, recording, or otherwise, without the prior permission of Oxford University Press, Inc.

Library of Congress Cataloging-in-Publication Data

Kurkela, Matti, 1951-
  Letters of credit and bank guarantees under international trade law / by Matti S. Kurkela. — 2nd ed.
    p. cm.
  Rev. ed. of : Letters of credit under international trade law. c 1985.
  Includes bibliographical references and index.
  ISBN 978-0-19-532316-0 (alk. paper)
  1. Conflict of laws—Letters of credit. I. Kurkela, Matti, 1951-
Letters of credit under international trade law.   II. Title.
  K7384.L48K87 2007
  340.9´96—dc22   2007020035

Note to Readers:
This publication is designed to provide accurate and authoritative information in regard to the subject matter covered. It is based upon sources believed to be accurate and reliable and is intended to be current as of the time it was written. It is sold with the understanding that the publisher is not engaged in rendering legal, accounting, or other professional services. If legal advice or other expert assistance is required, the services of a competent professional person should be sought. Also, to confirm that the information has not been affected or changed by recent developments, traditional legal research techniques should be used, including checking primary sources where appropriate.

(Based on the Declaration of Principles jointly adopted by a Committee of the American Bar Association and a Committee of Publishers and Associations.)

You may order this or any other Oxford University Press publication by visiting the Oxford University Press website at www.oup.com

Table of Contents

Preface ix
About the Author xi
List of Abbreviations xiii
Introduction. xv

Chapter I: The Instruments 1

   I.1 The "mechanics" and the simple legal structure
       of the instruments 1
       I.1.1 General. 1
       I.1.2 "Quasi-instruments" or "Mezzanine instruments" 3
       I.1.3 On conditions precedent. 5
   I.2 Comfort letters 7
   I.3 Bonds. 9
   I.4 Traditional guarantees and sureties 11
   I.5 The function of bank guarantees 14
   I.6 On-demand guarantees 18
   I.7 Letters of credit. 24
   I.8 Confirmed letters of credit 28
   I.9 The three main functions of commercial credits 32
   I.10 The function of standby credit 36
   I.11 "Blended" facilities. 40
   I.12 Amendments of the instrument 42
   I.13 The right and remedy of set-off. 45
   I.14 Security interest in the documents or goods. 47
   I.15 Disclaimers 52

   Transferability and Subrogation

   I.16 Transferability. 61
   I.17 No "Bearer" Rights 65
   I.18 Assignability 67
   I.19 Subrogation. 72
       I.19.1 General. 72

TABLE OF CONTENTS

    I.19.2 Subrogation and the UCC........................... 75
    I.19.3 The Niru Case – emphasizing two sources
           for subrogation 76

CHAPTER II: INDEMNITY AGREEMENTS...................... 81

  II.1 Reimbursement, and an introduction to indemnity
       agreements ("services agreements") 81
  II.2 "Good faith" and representations and warranties made
       by the beneficiary....................................... 88
  II.3 Features of the agreement and sample clauses............... 91
      II.3.1 Master agreement................................ 91
      II.3.2 "Umbrella" 91
      II.3.3 Security mechanisms 92
      II.3.4 "Conclusive Evidence" 92
      II.3.5 "Cash Cover" 93
      II.3.6 *Pari Passu* provision.............................. 95
      II.3.7 Covenant as to *Pari Passu* 95
      II.3.8 "Negative Pledge" 95
      II.3.9 Duty to inform as to financial status 97
      II.3.10 Duty to inform as to allegation of
             breach or default 97
      II.3.11 Duty to inform of legal proceedings................. 98
      II.3.12 Duty to give information, and other duties........... 99
      II.3.13 Representations and warranties
             (conditions precedent to agreement)................ 100
      II.3.14 Default.. 101
  II.4 Doctrine of (substantive) independence (autonomy)........ 102

CHAPTER III: BANK-TO-BANK INDEMNITY................ 107

  III.1 General.. 107
  III.2 The role of the underlying agreement and the balance 113
  III.3 Honor and the "moment of death" of the instrument........ 114
  III.4 Strict compliance doctrine 120
  III.5 The requirement of consistency........................... 127
  III.6 The "as tendered" or *è contrario* rule 132

III.7 **Interviews with experts** 137
    III.7.1 Pekka Heino of Nordea Bank 137
    III.7.2 Matti Vainionpää of Sampo Bank 138
    III.7.3 Petri Ikävalko of Svenska Handelsbanken 138
    III.7.4 Mirja Fonck of OKO Bank........................... 139
III.8 **The liability of the banks** 140
    III.8.1 General.. 140
    III.8.2 Bank's duty of care 147
    III.8.3 Duty to whom and for what 154
    III.8.4 Duty to notify and refusal 158
    III.8.5 Reasonable time defined in UCC.................... 162
    III.8.6 Duty to put the documents at the
           disposal of the beneficiary......................... 166
    III.8.7 Duty of confidentiality............................. 168

CHAPTER IV: FRAUD..173
    IV.1 Fraud ("abuse") or *"fraus omnia corrumpit"*,
         generally 173
    IV.2 Establishing that fraud exists – the
         necessary sequence................................... 176
    IV.3 **Duty (right) to refrain from paying.** 178
    IV.4 **Fraud and good faith** 181
    IV.5 **Clear proof** 183
    IV.6 **Whose fraud is relevant?**............................ 187
    IV.7 **Links required and risks assumed** 191
    IV.8 **Who bears the loss?**................................ 193
    IV.9 **Nullity exception**................................... 198
    IV.10 **Illegality**... 201
    IV.11 **Observations and remarks**......................... 206

CHAPTER V: INTERPRETATION OF INSTRUMENTS..........211
    V.1 General... 211
        V.1.1 Multi-party understanding and interpretation? 217
        V.1.2 The substantive independence should not lead to
            disregard of the "facility"........................... 219
        V.1.3 Interpretation of other instruments 229
        V.1.4 Interpretation of applicable rules..................... 232

TABLE OF CONTENTS

V.2 Waiver doctrine: express and implied waivers 234
V.3 Conditions subsequent. 244
    V.3.1 General 244
    V.3.2 "Evergreen clauses" and expiry clause. 247
V.4 "Pay or extend" claims 253
V.5 Contractual patterns. 254
V.6 Sample of use of credits and guarantees in
    a construction contract. 258

Chapter VI: Refusal, Dishonour, and Remedies 259

VI.1 What constitutes refusal? – Teachings from
    Bank of China 259
VI.2 Dishonor. 267
VI.3 Remedies – a substantive or procedural issue? 271
    VI.3.1 General 271
    VI.3.2 Damages as a remedy. 283
    VI.3.3 Dynamics Corporation of America v. The Citizens
           and Southern National Bank and injunction 288
    VI.3.4 United Technologies Corporation v. Citibank
           N.A. and the availability of injunction 290
    VI.3.5 Remedies under the UCC 294
    VI.3.6 Equitable relief. 296
    VI.3.7 Ex parte temporary restraining orders
           or other protective measures 298
    VI.3.8 Declaratory relief 301
    VI.3.9 Various types of injunctions 302
    VI.3.10 Unjust enrichment. 306
VI.4 Duty to mitigate and contributory negligence 309
VI.5 What remains or may remain to be
    governed by national laws 312
VI.6 De lege ferenda. 320

Chapter VII: Jurisdiction and Choice of Law 323

VII.1 Interplay of Lex Mercatoria, Conflict of
    laws and National law. 323

VII.2 Applicable Law 335
    VII.2.1 Uniform law merchant. 335
    VII.2.2 The *Zeevi* case and policy interests 342
VII.3 A Preference for English Law 346
    VII.3.1 General. 346
    VII.3.2 Choice of Law and the *Offshore International* Case... 347
    VII.3.3 Very Little To Do With England: *Power Curber International Ltd. v. National Bank of Kuwait S.A.K.* (Or, The Stay Must Go) 349
    VII.3.4 False conflict? 356
    VII.3.5 Seeking the closest and most real connection: the *Sonali* case. 358
    VII.3.6 Were Performance Bonds Really So New? *Edward Owen Ltd. v. Barclays Bank*. 366
    VII.3.7 The Uniform Commercial Code (UCC) – An American Creature. 368
    VII.3.8 Educating the Adjudicator – the "Burden of Education" 371
VII.4 Jurisdiction 375
    VII.4.1 Forum non conveniens and forum shopping? 386
    VII.4.2 Forum connexitatis. 394
    VII.4.3 Docdex proceedings. 394

APPENDIX A: United Nations Convention on Independent Guarantees and Stand-By Letters of Credit 401

APPENDIX B: Official Comments of Article 5 of the Uniform Commercial Code 431

List of References 473

Index 489

Preface

Letters of credit or documentary credits are very simple in structure: an undertaking, generally a promise to pay a certain amount of money and conditions precedent – nothing else. Naturally the conditions precedent may vary and only imagination is the limit. If, however, these instruments are classified based on the types of conditions precedent used (documentary, non-documentary, substantive, etc.) and their purpose (performance bond, maintenance bond, commercial credit, etc.), one may mistaken be to believe that the instrument is an unidentifiable legal concept, impossible to control and unforeseeable as to its effects, i.e. more than just *sui generis*. That is, the flexibility of conditions precedent may conceal the simplicity of the structure.

The success and survival of these instruments is based on the principle of substantive independence. As long as this principle is respected in practice, understood and applied by courts both in material and procedural ("parole evidence rule") respects, the future of the instrument looks promising. However, one should not let the paramount role of this principle hide the reality that the network of the materially independent agreements, which form the necessary infrastructure of the instrument, form a functional whole which is formally linked together. None of these materially independent contracts have a stand-alone role or function if detached from the infrastructure. The independence, absolute or relative dependence on the conditions precedent, relates to the material scope and defences only, not to the overall function: "the facility".

The instrument is a wonderful creation of commerce, which, thanks to its flexibility, will probably survive any crisis or upheaval. It is estimated to be in use in ten percent of payments in international trade transactions. And, more than any other legal device, it gives us an instrument of supranational character subject to widely accepted universal rules and usages ("lex mercatoria").

My passion for these instruments dates back to 1970s and my first book published in 1980 covered liability issues under letters of credit. In 1985, Oceana Publications, in New York, published the first edition of this book. Much has changed since then and yet, in the final analysis, almost nothing has changed. It has been a great joy to be able to revert to the sins of my youth and live through my passion again – many thanks to Oceana and to Oxford University Press and its wonderful people.

I think with special gratitude of some friends I made and people I met along the road: Professor Detlev F. Vagts of Harvard Law School; Frances Reid (Bank of Boston); Peter K. Ingerman of Chadbourne Parke, New York; John Dolan of Wayne State University; Stephen Doyle (Bank of Boston) and Leena Lehto of the University of Helsinki.

My partners have allowed me and given the facilities to devote a part of my time to research and writing, which I appreciate. My assistant Heidi Lautjärvi is an incurable over-performer and a world-class secretary. In helping me to produce this work she has once again demonstrated unmatched effectiveness and friendliness and kept the "old" man going. Heikki Majamaa, my very talented research assistant, has been a valuable tool in getting it all done on time.

Finally thanks to my family: Pirjo, Jaakko, Tuomo and Saana. They keep me going and make life so worth living.

Matti S. Kurkela
Lappeenranta

About the Author

Matti S. Kurkela is a member of Paris and Helsinki Bars and has been practicing international business law in Finland, France and U.S.A. for over 30 years. He is a senior partner at Hannes Snellman and Docent at Helsinki University Law School. He is a graduate from Harvard and Paris 2 and carries a doctorate from Helsinki University. Besides financial law he has written a number of books and articles on arbitration, contracts and construction law.

List of Abbreviations

DCL	Documentary Credit Law throughout the world. Annotated legislation from more than 35 countries. Professor Dr Rolf A. Schütze and Dr Gabriele Fontane. ICC Publication No 633 (2001)
Docdex	ICC Docdex Rules
Docdex Decision	Collected Docdex Decisions 1997–2003
ICC	International Chamber of Commerce
ICC Opinions	ICC Banking Commission Collected Opinions 1995–2001
ISBP	International Standard Banking Practices (ISBP), ICC Publication No 645 (2003)
ISP	International Standby Practices ISP98, ICC Publication No 590 (1998)
UCC	Uniform Commercial Code (N.Y.)
UNC	United Nations Convention on Independent Guarantees and Stand-by Letters of Credit
UCP 600	Uniform Customs and Practice for Documentary Credits– ICC's New Rules on Documentary Credits, 2007 Revision, ICC Publication No 600LF (2006 ed.)
UNIDROIT	International Institute for the Unification of Private Law (UNIDROIT) Principles of International Commercial Contracts 2004, Rome (2004)
URCB	Uniform Rules for Contract Bonds, ICC Publication No 524 (1994)

List of Abbreviations

URCG	Uniform Rules for Contract Guarantees, ICC Publication No 325 (1994)
URDG	Uniform Rules for Demand Guarantees, ICC Publication No 458 (1994)
URR	ICC Uniform Rules for Bank-to-Bank Reimbursements under Documentary Credits, URR 525, ICC Publication No 525 (1995)

Introduction

Documentary credits and bank guarantees play a very important role in international trade and exchange.[1] The success of these instruments, which both functionally and legally serve the same purposes and to a great extent are governed by similar rules, is based on trust and confidence in banks, and on impeccable predictability: there are no surprises. The trading nations have an immeasurable commercial interest in giving legal protection to the enforceability of these instruments in accordance with the expectations of the parties and in line with the well established practices. The flexibility of these instruments is one of their main advantages as described in Explanatory note to the United Nations Convention on Independent Guarantees and Stand-By Letters of Credit (hereinafter UNC):

> "Independent undertakings covered by the Convention are basic tools of international commerce. They are used in a variety of situations. For example, they are used to secure performance of contractual obligations including construction, supply and commercial payment obligations; to secure repayment of an advance payment in the event that such repayment is required; to secure a winning bidder's obligation to enter into a procurement contract; to ensure reimbursement of payment under another undertaking; to support issuance of commercial letters of credit and insurance coverage; and to enhance creditworthiness of public and private borrowers. Yet familiarity with one or the other instrument covered by the Convention is not universal; there is an absence of legislative provisions dealing with them, practices concerning the two types of instruments have differed in certain respects, and important questions confronting users, practitioners and courts in the daily life of these instruments are beyond the power of the parties to settle contractually."

---

[1] According to some estimates approximately 10% in average of all payments made in international trade are effected by way of commercial letters of credit.

Introduction

Growing international exchange and increasing sophistication of transactions do, however, from time to time cause new problems to emerge. Most of these problems can be solved based on the well established principles.

Common to all these instruments is that none of them is a bearer or holder instrument. In general they are non-transferable or non-assignable.[2]

---

[2] See, e.g., the Uniform Rules for Contract Bonds, ICC Publication No. 524 (1994) (hereinafter URCB) Art. 5.; the Uniform Rules for Contract Guarantees, ICC Publication No. 325 (1994) (hereinafter URCG) Art. 6.

CHAPTER I

THE INSTRUMENTS

I.1 The "mechanics" and the simple legal structure of the instruments

I.1.1 General

The basic structure of these instruments is very, very simple:[1] an undertaking to do something (broadly, to render banking services) at the request of the account party in favor of the beneficiary provided that certain conditions are met (conditions precedent or CP's).[2] Nothing else.

---

[1] UCC 5-103 provides as follows:
"1. Sections 5-102(a)(10) and 5-103 are the principal limits on the scope of Article 5. Many undertakings in commerce and contract are similar, but not identical to the letter of credit. Principal among those are "secondary", "accessory" or "suretyship" guarantees. Although the word "guarantee" is sometimes used to describe an independent obligation like that of the issuer of a letter of credit (most often in the case of European bank undertakings but occasionally in the case of undertakings of American banks), in the United States the word "guarantee" is more typically used to describe a suretyship transaction in which the "guarantor" is only secondarily liable and has the right to assert the underlying debtors defenses. This article does not apply to secondary or accessory guarantees and it is important to recognize the distinction between letters of credit and those guarantees. It s often a defense to a secondary or accessory guarantor's liability that the underlying debt has been discharged or that the debtor has other defenses to the underlying liability. In letter of credit law, on the other hand, the independence principle recognized throughout Article 5 states that the issuer's liability is independent of the underlying obligation. That the beneficiary may have breached the underlying contract and thus have given a good defense on that contract to the applicant against the beneficiary is no defense for the issuer's refusal to honor. Only staunch recognition of this principle by the issuers and the courts will give letters of credit the continuing vitality that arises from the certainty and speed of payment under letters of credit. To that end, it is important that law not carry into letter of credit transactions rules that properly apply only to secondary guarantees or to other forms of engagement."

[2] Unidroit 5.2.1 provides:
"(1) The parties (the "promisor" and the "promisee") may confer by express or implied agreement a right on a third party (the "beneficiary"). (2) The existence and content of the beneficiary's right against the promisor are determined by the agreement of the parties and are subject to any

CHAPTER I

The complexity, if any, arises from the network of agreements forming the transaction as a whole, and the financial facility created to back the instrument up or to support the instrument. The diversity and ambiguity of the conditions precedent often make it hard to tell the forest from the trees. Thus, one can easily make the mistake of treating every type of condition precedent which appears as if the instrument it applies to was a separate category of instrument. There may, of course, be millions of different kinds of conditions precedent, and one or several at the same time may appear in any one instrument. An attempt to identify them all and classify them into "species" is doomed to fail. On the other hand, it sometimes happens that attempts to treat these instruments as ordinary contracts disregard the special characteristics of these agreements. Even so, these attempts perhaps do less violence to these instruments.[3]

Honor

These instruments are not typical contracts. Rather, they are unilateral legally enforceable commitments (contracts/offers) in favour of the beneficiary. The beneficiary's status is unusual, since he has in general no duties under the instrument, (not

---

conditions or other limitations under the agreement."; UCC 5-108 (official comment): "The issuer's obligation to honor runs not only to the beneficiary but also to the applicant. It is possible that an applicant who has made a favorable contract with the beneficiary will be injured by the issuer's wrongful dishonor. Except to the extent that the contract between the issuer and the applicant limits that liability, the issuer will have liability to the applicant for wrongful dishonor under Section 5-111 as a matter of contract law. A good faith extension of the time in Section 5-108(b) by agreement between the issuer and beneficiary binds the applicant even if the applicant is not consulted or does not consent to the extension."

And URCG Art 8 (3) tells us:
"A claim shall not be honoured unless: a. it has been made and received as required by para. 1 of this Article; and b. it is supported by such documentation as is specified in the guarantee or in these Rules; and c. such documentation is presented within the period of time after the receipt of a claim specified in the guarantee, or, failing such a specification, as soon as practicable, or, in the case of documentation of the beneficiary himself, at the latest within six months from the receipt of a claim. In any event, a claim shall not be honoured if the guarantee has ceased to be valid in accordance with its own terms or with these Rules."

and URDG Art 9:
"All documents specified and presented under a Guarantee, including the demand, shall be examined by the Guarantor with reasonable care to ascertain whether or not they appear on their face to conform with the terms of the Guarantee. Where such documents do not appear so to conform or appear on their face to be inconsistent with one another, they shall be refused."

[3] URCG Art 3(3) says: "The guarantor may rely only on those defences which are based on the terms and conditions specified in the guarantee or are allowed under these Rules."

even to present any documents), but he is entitled to receive the benefit of (or proceeds from) the performance of the issuer. (All this is subject, of course, to the beneficiary meeting the conditions precedent.)[4] Meeting the conditions precedent results in "honor", a word which is not often used in a purely legal contract and may therefore cause consternation among non-banking lawyers.

UNC defines honor as follows (Article 2(3)):

> "(3) Payment may be stipulated in the undertaking to be made in any form, including:(a) Payment in a specified currency or unit of account; (b) Acceptance of a bill of exchange (draft); (c) Payment on a deferred basis; (d) Supply of a specified item of value."

The conditions precedent may vary indefinitely from a simple demand to submitting a large number of specified documents. Guarantees do not necessarily require presentation of any document: an oral demand may be sufficient.

I.1.2 "Quasi-instruments" or "Mezzanine instruments"

Another characteristic feature of the conditions precedent in this field is that, under a *genuine* letter of credit or on-demand guarantee, no document or demand, or other condition precedent to be met by the beneficiary, shall require any action from the part of the account party, i.e., they are beyond his control.[5]

If this is not the case, then the instrument does not provide for the certainty and security of a genuine credit. It remains merely a *"quasi-instrument,"* an instrument of no (or very little) practical or real value to the beneficiary. Its value is so small because the account party can render the instrument worthless by not taking the action required, or by not refraining from doing what is required to make the

---

[4] The arrangement can also be construed as an agreement between the issuer and accountant party in favor of a third party (beneficiary).

[5] UNC Art. 3 provides:
"For the purposes of this Convention, an undertaking is independent where the guarantor/issuer's obligation to the beneficiary is not:(a) Dependent upon the existence or validity of any underlying transaction, or upon any other undertaking (including stand-by letters of credit or independent guarantees to which confirmations or counter-guarantees relate); or (b) Subject to any term or condition not appearing in the undertaking, or to any future, uncertain act or event except presentation of documents or another such act or event within a guarantor/issuer's sphere of operations."

CHAPTER I

instrument effective (e.g., by not issuing a certificate of completion that is required to be presented as a condition precedent).

ICC Opinions (1980-1981) of the ICC Banking Commission, R 68: "Soft Confirmations", p. 13 tell us:

> "The Commission agreed that if such undertaking is to be a qualified one, i.e., if payment, etc. is to be subject to the paying bank being reimbursed by a third party, such condition must be clearly made known to the beneficiary in the credit itself, However, such a credit could not be considered to be an irrevocable credit in the terms of Article 3 (c), because one party can cancel the credit without the consent of the beneficiary in the event of such third party reimbursement not being forthcoming. Further any 'confirmation' of such credit is not, therefore, the confirmation envisaged in UCP Article 3 (b)."

The conditions precedent of on-demand instruments may very well include submissions of various documents, just as is the case under letters of credit. If these documents are materially linked to the underlying agreement, or are within the control of the account party, then the instrument is not fully a typical on-demand instrument or a letter of credit in its purest form, but is instead a more or less diluted version, or a secondary guarantee, titled misleadingly as an on-demand instrument.[6]

---

[6] ISBP Preliminary Considerations 4 provides:
"A credit should not require presentation of documents that are to be issued and/or countersigned by the applicant. If a credit is issued including such terms, the beneficiary must either seek amendment or comply with them and bear the risk of failure to do so."

As to a "mezzanine" guarantee, URCG Art. 9 says:
"If a guarantee does not specify the documentation to be produced in support of a claim or merely specifies only a statement of claim by the beneficiary, the beneficiary must submit: in the case of a tender guarantee, his declaration that the principal's tender has been accepted and that the principal has then either failed to sign the contract or has failed to submit a performance guarantee as provided for in the tender, and his declaration of agreement, addressed to the principal, to have any dispute on any claim by the principal for payment to him by the beneficiary of all or part of the amount paid under the guarantee settled by a judicial or arbitral tribunal as specified in the tender documents or, if not so specified or otherwise agreed upon, by arbitration in accordance with the Rules of the ICC Court of Arbitration or with the UNCITRAL Arbitration Rules, at the option of the principal; b. in the case of a performance guarantee or of a repayment guarantee, either a court decision or an arbitral award justifying the claim, or the approval of the principal in writing to the claim and the amount to be paid.".

This could be called a mezzanine guarantee because it is clearly in between the traditional guarantee and an independent instrument.

ISP 4.10 tells us:

> "Applicant Approval. A standby should not specify that a required document be issued, signed, or counter-signed by the applicant. However, if the standby includes such a requirement, the issuer may not waive the requirement and is not responsible for the applicant's withholding of the document or signature."

Such a "mezzanine" instrument may superficially appear to be independent. However, through the control of the account party over the documents, or through their close linkage to the underlying transaction, such an instrument is in essence only secondary in character. Or, in the worst case, it is only just as good as the word or promise of the account party.[7]

I.1.3 On conditions precedent

Here are some examples of what conditions precedent may require:

(i) A demand in writing or notice of default in writing; and/or

---

[7] ISP 1.11 (d) (iv) tells us:
"While the effect of all of these Rules may be varied by the text of the standby, variations of the effect of some of these Rules may disqualify the standby as an independent undertaking under applicable law".

Further, UNC Explanatory note D 17 says:
"While it is widely recognized that undertakings of the type covered by the Convention are "independent", there has been a lack of uniformity internationally in the understanding and recognition of that essential characteristic. The Convention will promote such uniformity by providing a definition of 'independence' (article 3). That definition is phrased in terms of the undertaking not being dependent upon the existence or validity of the underlying transaction, or upon any other undertaking. The latter reference, to other undertakings, clarifies the independent nature of a counter-guarantee from the guarantee that it relates to and of a confirmation from the stand-by letter of credit or independent guarantee that it confirms."

And Note D 18 says:
"In addition, to fall within the scope of the Convention, an undertaking must not be subject to any terms or conditions not appearing in the undertaking. It is specified that, to fall within the Convention, an undertaking should not be subject to any future, uncertain act or event, with the exception of presentation of a demand and other documents by the beneficiary or *of any other such act or event that falls within the "sphere of operations" of the guarantor/issuer*. That is in line with the notion that the role of the guarantor/issuer in the case of independent undertakings is one of paymaster rather than investigator."

CHAPTER I

(ii) Submission of a final court decision or an arbitral award against the account party. (In this case the instrument establishes substantively a secondary liability only, since the liability of the account party must first be established under the transaction, and it is by definition not materially independent therefrom (that is, it is a "mezzanine instrument")); and/or

(iii) Submission of a bank guarantee or a standby credit (e.g., to cover the maintenance period) as a condition precedent (e.g., to payment of the last progress payment); and/or

(iv) Bills of lading; engineer's certificate; expert's opinion; certificate of origin; test results, etc.[8]

The character of the documents to be submitted and the procedure and action required to obtain them determines the character of the instrument regardless of what it is called or how it may have been titled.[9] The wordings are often ambiguous

---

[8] Compare this to URCB Art 7 (j), which says:
"Notwithstanding any dispute or difference between the Principal and the Beneficiary in relation to the performance of the Contract or any Contractual Obligation, a Default shall be deemed to be established for the purposes of these Rules: i. upon issue of a certificate of Default by a third party (who may without limitation be an independent architect or engineer or a PreArbitral referee of the ICC) it the Bond so provides and the service of such certificate or a certified copy thereof upon the Guarantor, ii. if the Bond does not provide for the issue of a certificate by a third party, upon the issue of a certificate of Default by the Guarantor, or iii. by the final judgment, order or award of a court or tribunal of competent jurisdiction, and the issue of a certificate of Default under paragraph (i) or (ii) shall not restrict the rights of the parties to seek or require the determination of any dispute or difference arising under the Contract or the Bond or the review of any certificate of Default or payment made pursuant thereto by a court or tribunal of competent jurisdiction."

[9] ISP Preface p. 7-8 provides:
"Like the UCP and the URDG, the ISP will apply to any independent undertaking issued subject to it. This approach avoids the impractical and often impossible task of identifying and distinguishing standbys from independent guarantees and, in many cases, commercial letters of credit. The choice of which set of rules to select is, therefore, left to the parties as it should be. One may well choose to use the ISP for certain types of standbys, the UCP for others, and the URDG for still others. While the ISP is not intended to be used for dependent undertakings such as accessory guarantees and insurance contracts, it may be useful in some situations in indicating that a particular undertaking which might otherwise be treated as dependent under local law is intended to be independent";

And ISP 1.01 (a-b) says:
"These Rules are intended to be applied to standby letters of credit (including performance, financial, and direct pay standby letters of credit). A standby letter of credit or other similar undertaking, however named or described, whether for domestic or international use, may be made subject to these Rules by express reference to them."

or subject to interpretation; occasionally they are even contradictory. This is sometimes due to hurry, and sometimes due to lack of expertise. And sometimes the ambiguity carries the earmarks of a compromise, with each party hoping that their preferred position would prevail if a conflict arose. However, if the parties' choice of title is an educated one, the choice should be respected to the extent possible and the instrument should be interpreted accordingly.

Unclearness is in most cases subject to the *è contrario* rule, i.e., imposing on the beneficiary only the minimum requirements or the least conditions precedent possible under the express wording of the instrument. In general there is no room to introduce implicit new conditions by way of interpretation. The parties are presumed to have carefully considered the wording prior to the issuance of the instrument.[10]

Generally, the *sui generis* character of the instrument establishes an irrevocable right in the beneficiary, and the instrument may not be cancelled, revoked or even amended without his consent.[11]

I.2 Comfort letters

For various reasons genuine letters of credit or bank guarantees are not always used. This may sometimes be due to the cost of providing such a security, or to the fact that no such security may be obtained by the account party due to lack of a necessary counter-security to be pledged or made available to the issuer under their legal relationship (often defined as an "indemnity agreement"). Sometimes the parties are financially strong enough, or foolish enough, to take a risk, or to

---

[10] If the beneficiary does not accept the instrument because it is not in accordance with the underlying agreement, he may either (1) refuse to deliver or (2) claim that a new instrument is to be issued in accordance with the agreed conditions.

[11] UCP:
"A credit is irrevocable even if there is no indication to that effect." UCP: "A credit constitutes an irrevocable undertaking of the issuing bank – provided that the stipulated documents are presented to the nominated bank or to the issuing bank." UCP: "Except as otherwise provided by sub-article [Transfer], a credit can neither be amended nor cancelled without the agreement of the issuing bank, the confirming bank, if any, and the beneficiary."

justify an expectation that no security, or only a more or less "cosmetic" security, suffices.

Sometimes the parent company or another affiliated entity provides the security. In such cases the security is often a simple letter expressing a vague and often ambiguous commitment of the affiliated entity in favour of the addressee or beneficiary (provided that there is a true benefit) often providing for a "moral" commitment rather than a legally enforceable obligation.[12] At its best comfort letters may take the form of an undertaking "to use the necessary efforts", "ensuring" or "taking whatever measures may be necessary" or something along these lines to provide comfort to the obligee that the issuer will remedy whatever may need to be remedied in the event of a breach or failure of the account party. Often, however, the commitment is so ambiguous and generic that it lacks enough specificity to allow a court order for specific performance. But it may, however, be firm enough to constitute sufficient basis for action for damages, should the issuer fail in its commitment to honor the comfort letter instrument or should the account party simply do nothing.[13] The obligation of the issuer to perform is often directed to the account party ("to use best efforts to cause "A" to be able to . . . .") and not to the beneficiary. This may make it unusually complicated to find the appropriate remedy in case of non-performance by the issuer.

Comfort letters are often worded in a way which creates an indirect obligation. The issuer agrees to assist the account party or, e.g., inject capital or loans to the primary obligor or account party in order to cause this party to be able to perform as agreed in the underlying transaction. In contrast, in genuine guarantees the issuer is under a direct obligation towards the beneficiary in accordance with the terms and conditions of the transaction (bank guarantees and bonds) or in reference to the transaction but independently from its terms and conditions (letters of credit and demand instruments).

---

[12] Philip R. Wood, *Comparative Law of Security and Guarantees*, Sweet & Maxwell, 1995, p. 347:
"Comfort letters also do not usually contain the protective clauses appearing in formal guarantees. In essence, comfort letters are only of use where a shadow of a guarantee is considered better than nothing at all (only just). They are inappropriate for lenders who require a serious legal claim."

[13] Giving comfort letters or (financial) guarantees may be limited by law as, *e.g.*, given guarantee in favor of acquirer of the company in the group.

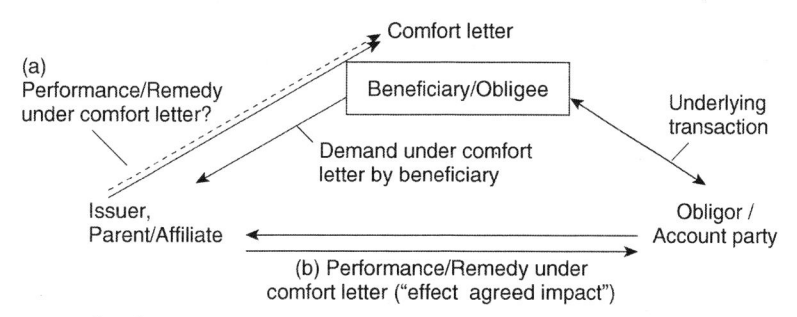

Figure I.1. Comfort letter

I.3 Bonds

Bonds are in common use in some countries. They are not materially independent; in fact they are rather strictly tied into the network of terms and conditions of the underlying transaction.[14]

URCB Art 7 (1) describes the substantive link of a bond and the underlying contract as follows:

> "A claim shall not be honored unless
> i. A Default has occurred; and
> ii. The claim has been made and served in accordance with the provisions of paragraphs (a)-(f) of Article 7 on or before the Expiry Date."

Bonds may cover a large percentage or even over 100% of the value of the contract price of the underlying transaction. They often contain a step-in right (discussed below), or even obligations or rights of the issuer other than mere payment of the balance or cost of remaining performance. In most cases the breach or failure of

---

[14] URCB Art. 7(f):
"Any claim shall state brief details of the Contract to identify the same, state that there has been a breach or default and set out the circumstances of such breach or default and any request for payment, performance or execution." and (h): "The Beneficiary shall, upon written request by the Guarantor, supply to the Guarantor such further information as the Guarantor may reasonably request to enable it to consider the claim, and shall provide copies of any correspondence or other documents relating to the Contract or the performance of any Contractual Obligations and allow the Guarantor, its employees, agents or representatives to inspect any works, goods or services carried out or supplied by the Principal."

Chapter I

the account party needs to be established before the issuer becomes liable under the instrument.

ICC has attempted to codify international bond practices under Uniform Rules for Contract Bonds ("URCB"). There needs to be a reference in the bond for the URCB to apply.[15]

Bonds[16] are often issued by both banks and insurance companies to cover 100% or even more of the value of the contract. They often include a condition under which the issuer may take over the contract and cause the contract to be carried out by third parties, i.e., sub-contractors or suppliers. Such rights are called "step-in rights". As a consequence of the exercise of such step-in rights, the duties of the issuer are often similar or even identical to the obligations of the contractor or account party under the transaction.

URCB Art 3 (b):

> "The liability of the Guarantor to the Beneficiary under the Bond is accessory to the liability of the Principal to the Beneficiary under the Contract and shall arise upon Default. *The Contract is deemed to be incorporated into and form part of the Bond.* The liability of the Guarantor shall not exceed the Bond Amount."

Bonds are usually limited in one way or another and in most cases they are limited to a certain amount of money ("cap"). The limit is often the amount

---

[15] URCB Art 1 (a):
"These Rules shall be known as the 'Uniform Rules for Contract Bonds' and shall apply to any Bond which states that these Rules shall apply, or otherwise incorporates these Rules by reference and, for such purposes, it shall suffice that the Bond incorporates a reference to these Rules and the publication number."

[16] URCB Art 2 Definitions "Bond":
"Any bond, guarantee or other instrument in writing issued or executed by the Guarantor in favour of the Beneficiary pursuant to which the Guarantor undertakes on Default, either: (i) to pay or satisfy any claim or entitlement to payment of damages, compensation or other financial relief up to the Bond Amount: or (ii) to pay or satisfy such claim or entitlement up to the Bond Amount or at the Guarantor's option to perform or execute the Contract or any Contractual Obligation. In either case where the liability of the Guarantor shall be accessory to the liability of the Principal under the Contract or such Contractual Obligation and such expression shall without limitation include Advance Payment Bonds, Maintenance Bonds, Performance Bonds, Retention Bands and Tender Bonds."

contemplated to be sufficient to cover the anticipated cost of executing the contract in case of a breach or failure of the account party or termination or cancellation of the contract or the transaction by the beneficiary. The issuer may have an option to pay the total finishing cost of the beneficiary instead of having the contract carried out by third parties under his control and supervision and at his own risk and cost. The latter may often prove to be a less expensive alternative providing at least a reasonable level of control over costs and expenditures. Bonds are substantively or materially linked to the transaction. There is no element of substantive independence in them.

I.4 Traditional guarantees and sureties

In traditional guarantees the guarantor, most often a bank or an insurance company, guarantees, i.e., assumes an undertaking to pay, (up to) a certain amount of money for and on behalf of the account party to the beneficiary should the account party, i.e., obligor under the transaction, fail in meeting its obligations thereunder.[17] The guarantee may cover one or specific duties of the account party or one or several generic duties of the primary obligor or his performance as a whole under the transaction.[18] The so-called sureties seem to function in similar ways.[19] Dolan writes in *The Law of Letters of Credit* on p. 2-26:

> "Traditionally, a guaranty or surety contract is an undertaking by one party to assure a second party of payment or performance by a third party.

---

[17] Roeland F. Bertrams, *Bank Guarantees in International Trade*, Kluwer Law International, (ICC, 2003), at 290-91:
"If upon construction of the entire text the 'guarantee' is found to be an independent first default, unless clearly stipulated, and the bank does not owe a duty to this effect to the account party. Under German law, however, the submission of a formal statement appears to be required."

[18] URCB Art 3 (a, v.): "Where the Bond does not extend to the whole of the Contract, the precise Contractual Obligation or Obligations to which the Bond relates."

[19] Troy L. Harris, *Good Faith, Suretyship, And The Ius Commune*, 53 Mercer L. Rev. 581, (Winter 2002):
"In the most general terms, suretyship involves three parties: the principal obligor, the creditor to which the principal obligor owes some contractual duty, and the surety which promises the creditor it will perform the underlying duty in the event the principal does not. As others have noted, the law of suretyship affects modern commercial transactions in a variety of ways, and drawing the line between relationships that implicate suretyship principles and those that do not can be difficult and controversial. Perhaps the most familiar context involves accommodation parties on negotiable instruments under Article 3 of the Uniform Commercial Code ("U.C.C."). Because an accommodation party agrees to answer for the debt of another, it is entitled to assert various

CHAPTER I

> The liability of the guarantor is secondary and arises upon non-performance by the third party, the "principal obligor."

A traditional guarantee is *secondary* (and accessory) in the sense that it requires a breach or alleged breach or failure under the transaction as *a condition precedent* to become payable.[20] The word "secondary" describes this substantive dependence (requiring a proved default under the underlying transaction) perhaps better than the word "accessory" does, because all of these instruments are in one way or another accessory.

Dolan writes in *The Law of Letters of Credit* on p. 12-13:

> "The trouble with traditional guaranties or surety contracts lies in the fact that they involve secondary liability. The surety faces two questions. Before undertaking the guaranty, the surety must calculate the chances that the principal will default and, after undertaking the guaranty, must determine whether default has occurred. Neither of these determinations fits the traditional concepts of banking business. The former often involves actuarial judgments; the latter involves factual investigation. Traditionally, these activities are not the business of banking."

Letters of credit and on-demand instruments, however, often create another kind of duty, i.e., a *primary* duty which is not materially, i.e., substantively conditional on *bringing proof* of the breach or failure of the primary obligor under the transaction. They are in this respect materially independent and they may become due

---

defenses traditionally available to sureties. By virtue of their inclusion in Article 3, these defenses have enjoyed substantial scholarly attention. What has received less attention, however, is the relationship between an accommodation party's defenses, its right of reimbursement, and the duty of good faith."

Gao Xiang, Ross P. Buckley, *The Unique Jurisprudence of Letters of Credit: Its Origin and Sources*, 4 San Diego Int'l L.J. 91, (2003):

"While standby letters of credit and independent guarantees may serve the same commercial purpose as accessory guarantees, they are legally different in several aspects . . . . . Because independent guarantees may properly be seen as legal synonyms of standby letters of credit, the United Nations Commission on International Trade Law (UNCITRAL) has regulated both of them together in the Convention on Independent Guarantees and Standby Letters of Credit (UNCITRAL Convention). As accessory guarantees are legally different from letters of credit, they are outside the scope of this work."

[20] URCB uses the word accessory in the meaning of substantive dependence as opposed to substantive independence.

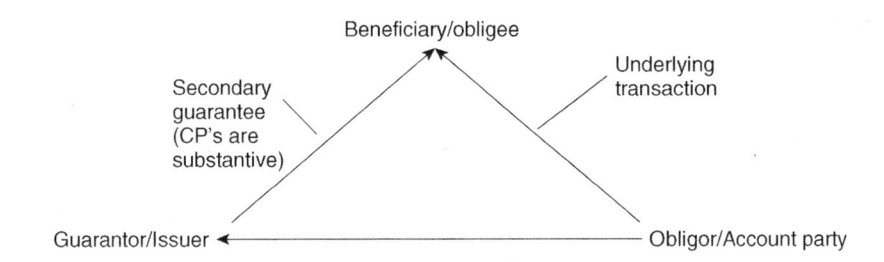

Figure I.2. Traditional guarantee

and payable before any such duty arises under the transaction or even totally regardless of whether or not any such duty matures now or later on.

Traditional guarantees, being under the freedom of contract, may well be drafted to resemble letters of credit requiring presentation of specified documents as a condition precedent for a payment obligation or another obligation to arise. If the documents to be presented relate to the underlying transaction, the guarantee is traditional i.e., materially dependent and, if not, the guarantee is rather abstract, i.e., materially independent and as such similar to letters of credit or on-demand guarantees.

Secondary guarantees may, at least in the absence of agreement to the contrary, be subject to the same substantive law and the same jurisdiction/arbitration clause as the transaction itself is subject to. Indeed, given that the character of secondary guarantees is closely and materially linked to the transaction itself, this seems to be a rational and logical conclusion, and an effective solution in case of a dispute.[21] The guarantor may have the right or duty to take part in the proceedings initiated under the underlying transaction, or the guarantor may intervene in them as a party having an indirect or direct interest in the litigation.[22] In some cases the guarantor may be a party in a straightforward multi-party process. If the beneficiary sues the guarantor, only the primary obligor may be in the same position of having the right of intervention or be under a duty to participate in one form or another in the proceedings depending, however, on the agreements of the parties, the applicable procedural law, and other related procedural rules and practices.

---

[21] URCB Art 8 (a).
[22] URCG Art 11 (2): "If a dispute between the guarantor and the beneficiary which touches upon the rights and obligations of the principal or the instructing party is referred to arbitration, the principal or the instructing party shall have the right to intervene in such arbitral proceedings."

CHAPTER I

ICC has attempted to codify rules which would be applicable to these instruments. URCG was an attempt to this effect, which did not, however, achieve the desired recognition and use.[23] URCG as well as URDG apply only when expressly referred to.[24]

I.5 The function of bank guarantees

The basic mechanism of guarantees is exactly the same as that of credits: there is an undertaking by the guarantor *subject to one or several conditions precedent*. The conditions precedent may vary under national laws or as commercial needs may require.

Since guarantees belong to the realm of commercial law, which in turn is covered by freedom of contract, there may be – at least in theory - such a huge variety of these conditions precedent as to make any effort to list them all fruitless. One may, however, distinguish certain basic situations in which guarantees are used. In most cases the need arises out of one of four factors: (1) insecurity as to "the continued readiness, willingness and ability" of the contracting party to perform as agreed, (2) a lack of confidence between the parties, (3) a lack of confidence in prevailing economic or political circumstances or risks, or (4) a policy. The creditor of the party exposed to risks attempts to reduce or eliminate his own exposure by having a guarantee from a third party as a security instead of, in addition to, or in the absence of, other collateral.

National laws may recognize one or several typical guarantee types, which have their defined characteristics and have their statutory legal effects, such as the right to be subrogated, right to reimbursement, right to call etc. Sometimes the law

---

[23] In introduction to URDG:
"These new Uniform Rules have been introduced because the 1978 ICC Uniform Rules for Contract Guarantees (Publication No. 325) did not gain general acceptance. The new Rules reflect more closely the different interests of the parties involved in a demand guarantee transaction. However, since Publication No. 325 continues to be used to some extent, it will be retained in force for the time being so as to be available for those who may wish to use it in preference to the new Rules. The future of Publication No. 325 will be reviewed at a later date in the light of experience."

This may be partly due to the fact that the substantive dependence was evicted through the front door but admitted re-entry through the kitchen door as a condition precedent resulting in a "mezzanine" guarantee.

[24] URCG Art 1 and URDG Art. 1.

creates a presumption in favour of a type of guarantee over another type ("legal presumption") if the parties have failed to be specific in this respect.

The most common types of *conditions precedent* used in commercial practice domestically or internationally may well be the following:

(a) bankruptcy of the debtor;
(b) insolvency or liquidation of the debtor;

> "BB entered into a subcontract with LL for the placing of rock for a harbour breakwater in Cardiff Bay. A performance bond was entered into by TGG as surety in favour of BB relating to the work undertaken by LL. Work was to be carried out in two phases. BB retained the right to cancel the contract in relation to the second phase and also to determine the subcontract if LL went into liquidation. BB sought to make a claim under the performance bond from TGG after LL, by reason of liquidation, failed to fulfil its obligations under the subcontract. Summary judgment was obtained in favour of BB. TGG appealed, contending that (1) liquidation was not covered by the performance bond when given its proper construction, since liquidation could not be equated with "default", and (2) BB's claim was fraudulent, being made in the knowledge that termination of the subcontract would result in savings to themselves. Summary: Held, dismissing the appeal, that (1) while liquidation was not a breach of contract in most instances, it was not clear whether it was excluded under the construction of this subcontract. It could not be shown that liquidation was not a default under the contract or that BB did not honestly believe that the breach claimed for was in fact a breach, and, (2) there was no clear evidence of fraud either as at the date of the demand or as at the application for summary judgment, Edward Owen Engineering Ltd v Barclays Bank International Ltd [1978] Q.B. 159 considered. None of the evidence before the court indicated that BB had acted dishonestly in making its claim. It was a legitimate expectation that a loss would be suffered by reason of LL going into liquidation."[25]

---

[25] Balfour Beatty Civil Engineering v. Technical & General Guarantee Co Ltd, 1999 WL 852268 (CA (Civ Div)), [2000] C.L.C. 252, 68 Con. L.R. 180.

CHAPTER I

(c) default in payment, breach of agreement or failure to perform (as defined in more detail in most cases or in the underlying agreement) by the debtor;
(d) anticipated default, breach or failure of the debtor ("anticipatory breach") or increased "risk";
(e) change in political, economic or other circumstances;
(f) a mere demand or call by the beneficiary at his will or convenience of the creditor *or beneficiary* in his sole discretion or as may be defined in the instrument or in an agreement.

Some of these conditions precedent may be clear-cut: it either exists or it does not. Some others may need to be substantiated by proof. This depends on the wording of the instrument and on agreement of the parties on the conditions precedent triggering the payment obligation.

Once the condition precedent has been met, the beneficiary may call on the guarantee and the guarantor may of course contest it and refuse to pay, which dispute, if not settled out of court, will be referred to courts of law or arbitration for resolution.

A further issue that arises when a guarantee is called is: what does the undertaking of the guarantor cover. The most common coverage is limited to an amount of money with a cap. The undertaking may, however, be a joint and several liability of the debtor under an agreement to construct a power plant or a guarantee to deliver raw materials, to promote sales or purchase goods.

If the conditions precedent relate to performance other than just paying a monetary debt, the breach may have to be proved and the guarantor may have the same substantive defences available against the beneficiary as the debtor has or at least a number of those. If, however, the guarantee is independent, none of those defences are available to the guarantor as defences, and if the condition precedent is met—at its simplest, a mere demand or "call" by the beneficiary—the guarantor must pay or perform. If the guarantor does not pay or perform, the dispute may be litigated and perhaps, especially if a summary proceeding is available, the beneficiary may relatively soon obtain an enforceable decision against the guarantor and avoid a lengthy process. Moreover there is an additional risk: that a *de jure* on demand instrument will be transformed into a *de facto* traditional guarantee.

Bank guarantees may serve exactly the same purposes as standby credits or commercial credits and they usually do. They may in fact be identical in form and in substance with LC's apart from the name of the instrument. Bank guarantees may or may not require documents as conditions precedent to effecting payment, whereas documentary credits always call for presentation of documents whatever they may be.[26]

Guarantees may back up a specific obligation or constitute a duty similar to (or even identical to) an obligation that the account party has assumed under the transaction towards the beneficiary, e.g., payment of the purchase price under a commercial credit. The commitment of the bank may also be generic or different from the obligation of the account party under the transaction in the sense that one cannot identify a specific or similar duty of the beneficiary under the terms and conditions of the transaction which is being "backed-up" by the guarantee. Some guarantees may require an alleged breach or even an established breach, whereas some may be totally independent from the terms and conditions of the transaction requiring nothing else than a simple demand by the beneficiary to fall due and become payable.[27] The most conservative guarantees may require a certificate of an independent appraiser or engineer as to the existence or non-existence of a breach, a specified fact or a change as *a condition precedent* to effecting payment or even a final court decision or arbitral award to the same effect.[28]

Guarantees are for the most part governed by the freedom of contract in the *inter partes* relationship, but the right and authority of a bank to issue such instruments may be limited or restrained by banking laws and regulations, which often reflect

---

[26] An issuing bank should discourage any attempt by the applicant to include, as an integral part of the credit, copies of the underlying contract, proforma invoice and the like.

[27] So-called on-demand guarantees.

[28] *See, e.g.*, URCG Art. 9. Bertrams writes at 9. 58-59:
"Since the beneficiary is only entitled to payment upon full proof of the account party's liability, as embodied in the arbitral or judicial decision, this type of guarantee is in substance very similar to a traditional accessory suretyship as far as the beneficiary and account party are concerned. The significance of the principle of independence is, in some respects, severely eroded, since any defences relating to the underlying relationship, which the bank could plead, will, no doubt, already have been raised by the principal debtor in the main proceedings and will have been considered by arbitrators or the court. It is, nonetheless, important to distinguish conceptually between the two security devices. In the case of this type of guarantee, the bank must pay, and must only pay if the beneficiary tenders a judicial or arbitral award as specified in the guarantee instrument."

public interests in protecting the creditworthiness of banks and their solidity and liquidity and/or in reducing or eliminating *moral hazard*.[29]

I.6 On-demand guarantees

Under on-demand guarantees or other on-demand instruments, the duty or undertaking of the guarantor or issuer is not secondary but is primary in the sense that there need not be any proven concrete breach or failure under the transaction or any evidence thereof (*in concreto*) and that there is no material link between the two although the instrument is often issued *in abstracto* as a security for such a breach.[30] The independence is material in its nature. UNC defines independent guarantees as follows in Article 2 (1):

> "For the purposes of this Convention, an undertaking is an independent commitment, known in international practice as an independent guarantee or as a stand-by letter of credit, given by a bank or other institution or person ("guarantor/issuer") to pay to the beneficiary a certain or determinable amount upon simple demand or upon demand accompanied by other documents, in conformity with the terms and any documentary conditions of the undertaking, indicating, or from which it is to be inferred, that payment is due because of a default in the performance of an obligation, or because of another contingency, or for money borrowed or advanced, or on account of any mature indebtedness undertaken by the principal/applicant or another person."

The words "on demand" are often followed by words "without condition" and other such provisions attempting to indicate that no substantive defences under the transaction are available to the issuer of the instrument and that there need be

---

[29] The purpose is to eliminate or limit risks. These instruments are "easy" to issue and cause an immediate cash flow into the treasury often in the range of 0.5-2.5% of contract price but no cashflow out or at least none in the ordinary course of events. However, if the account party fails in his performance or the beneficiary acts unfairly there will be a major cash flow out of the bank's treasury and a 100% exposure to credit risk to the bank. By payment to the beneficiary the bank becomes a major creditor of the account party. In addition the risk of insolvency of the account party, if its account is significant in size, may put bank's all the operations in jeopardy. Moral hazard refers most often to the risk of dishonesty of directors, officers and employees of financial or other institutions. Most common of them are perhaps embezzlement, forgery or fraud.

[30] See Wunnicke, Wunnicke, and Turner at 39.

no evidence of acts or omissions under the transaction.[31] Such contractual defences do not qualify as defences under the instrument and are not conditions precedent to the guarantor's obligation to pay or perform.[32] An on-demand instrument may, however, contain conditions precedent of its own, which are not parts of the underlying transaction. These conditions, of course, need to be complied with in order for the issuer's duty to perform to arise and mature.

> "We have been told that all the performance bonds procured by the plaintiffs and issued by Rafidain in favour of Agromark pursuant to those contracts have (mutatis mutandis) taken the same form, namely, that to be found at p. 18 of our Bundle "D". It is addressed by Rafidain to Agromark. It contains both an English and an Arabic text. It states in the English text that Rafidain has issued in favour of Agromark— . . . as beneficiaries *this letter of guarantee* to indemnify you against any damages that you may sustain [— up to a stated amount —] covering a *performance bond* . . . to support a specified contract. It continues: . . . *We undertake to pay you, unconditionally, the said amount on demand, being your claim for damages brought about by the above-named principal.* It goes on to provide that the letter of guarantee is personal to the parties and not assignable. It continues: . . . By this present letter of guarantee we undertake to pay to you any amount or claim not exceeding under any circumstances the above mentioned amount, provided the claim falls within the direct scope of the matter to be indemnified and is irrelevant to any other matter, even if resulting from the subject to be indemnified or relevant thereto, when particular to any other party, whatsoever its origin such as taxes, duties, social security or any other service whatsoever, since this letter of guarantee is in

---

[31] Compare with URCB Art 3 (d):
"All defences, remedies, cross claims, counter-claims and other rights or entitlements to relief which the Principal may have against the Beneficiary under the Contract, or witch may otherwise be available to the Principal in respect of the subject matter thereof, shall be available to the Guarantor in respect of any Default in addition to and without limiting any defence under or arising out of the Bond."

[32] Wunnicke, Wunnicke, and Turner at 40:
"In a typical international demand guarantee, as in many standby letters of Credit, the document presented by the beneficiary is a certificate or statement that the contractor or other obligor has defaulted in its obligations to the beneficiary. Sometimes, however, the document presented under the guarantee is no more than a demand for payment. This kind of guarantee is known as a *simple demand or first demand* guarantee. A simple demand guarantee is functionally similar to a clean letter of credit."

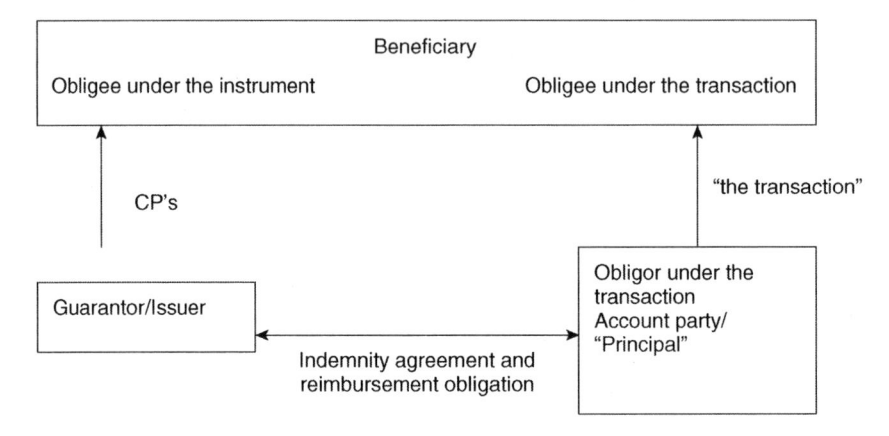

Figure I.3. On-demand instrument

```
                          Beneficiary
Obligee under the instrument          Obligee under the transaction
            ▲                                    ▲
            │                                    │
          CP's                            "the transaction"
            │                                    │
            │                         ┌──────────────────────┐
            │                         │ Obligor under the    │
  ┌──────────────────┐                │ transaction          │
  │ Guarantor/Issuer │                │ Account party/       │
  │                  │                │ "Principal"          │
  └──────────────────┘                └──────────────────────┘
              Indemnity agreement and
              reimbursement obligation
```

your favour as the sole beneficiaries . . . It also provides for the liability of Rafidain to cease if no claim is received by Rafidain by a specified date. *On receipt of the plaintiffs' performance bond Agromark would open an irrevocable letter of credit* in their favour with Rafidain and thus the sale could ordinarily proceed to completion."[33]

There are three separate and substantively independent but formally accessory agreements under an on-demand instrument, namely:

1) The underlying "transaction" or "main" agreement;
2) The Indemnity Agreement between the Account Party or Principal and the Guarantor; and
3) The on-demand instrument between the Guarantor and the Beneficiary.

There is nothing new in an obligation or debt or other performance maturing "on demand". This may, on the contrary, be a legal presumption if nothing else has been agreed.[34] However, when in international exchange in the post-war period in the 1960s through 1980's this on "*demand–condition*" was more and more often incorporated into guarantee undertakings and similar instruments, as a

---

[33] *United Trading Corp v. Allied Arab Bank Ltd*, 1985 WL 311451 (CA (Civ Div)), [1985] 2 Lloyd's Rep. 554 (Note).
[34] *E.g.*, Finnish Act on Promissory Notes and similar acts in other Nordic countries.

replacement to cash deposits or similar "trust" arrangements,[35] it did cause confusion or even panic. When at the same time in the same instruments, the bank's or the issuer's duty to effect payment was made materially independent from the underlying transaction eliminating the account party's rights to intervene in the payment mechanism and both his and the bank's right to invoke any grounds to stop payment, as had traditionally been the case under commercial credits,[36] the international community was sometimes puzzled as to the rules to be applied, and the legal systems strained in their efforts to figure out the "just" balance between demands by the beneficiaries and claims of abuse by the account parties and the *prima facie* independence of the instrument from all such disagreements.[37] A simple demand was sufficient to trigger payment and no evidence was to be submitted or even allowed.[38] This was the case, in particular when these guarantees were simultaneously being called in large numbers in connection with major political or economic changes by *de facto* the same beneficiary.[39]

---

[35] *E.g.*, a bank functioning as an escrow agent.

[36] UCP: A credit by its nature is a separate transaction from the sale or other contract on which it may be based. Banks are in no way concerned with or bound by such contracts, even if any reference whatsoever to such contract is included in the credit. Consequently, the undertaking of a bank to honour, to negotiate or to fulfil any other obligation under the credit is not subject to claims or defences by the applicant resulting from its relationships with the issuing bank or the beneficiary.

[37] Harvard Law Review. *"Fraud in the Transaction": Enjoining Letters of Credit During the Iranian Revolution*, 93 Harv. L. Rev. 992, (March 1980):

"Letter of credit law prior to the Uniform Commercial Code descended from the "Law Merchant" — an amalgam of commercial customs which developed independent of contract law for the convenience of merchants. Both pre-Code case law and article 5 embody a customary allocation of risks primarily geared to the traditional function of the letter of credit: the financing of contracts for the sale of goods across long distances. Absent the use of a letter of credit, a seller who ships to a distant customer on credit risks losing his goods in return for a damage claim in a foreign jurisdiction. If the customer pays in advance, he risks losing his cash in return for a long-distance suit."

[38] See, however, the somewhat "diluted" wording of URDG Art 20 (a):

"Any demand for payment under the Guarantee shall be in writing and shall (in addition to such other documents as may be specified in the Guarantee) be supported by a written statement (whether in the demand itself or in a separate document or documents accompanying the demand and referred to in it) stating: (i) that the Principal is in breach of his obligation(s) under the underlying contract(s) or, in the case of a tender guarantee, the tender conditions; and (ii) the respect in which the Principal is in breach."

[39] Dolan writes in *The Law of Letters of Credit* at 7-48:

"To some extent, American political response to the Iranian revolution interrupted the operation of letter-of-credit law. In November 1979 and in February 1981, the President issued executive orders, first freezing Iranian assets and then directing all claims to these assets to the international arbitration tribunal established under the American-Iranian Hostage Agreement. See Exec. Orders No. 12,170, 44 Fed. Reg. 65,729 (Nov. 14, 1979), No. 12,294, 46 Fed. Reg. 14,111 (Feb. 24, 1981)";

CHAPTER I

The calling was often claimed to be at least "abusive" or fraudulent by a large number of account parties and, in reality, in many cases the calling appeared to have no material grounds whatsoever under the transaction. An issue arose as to the strength and enforceability of this "on-demand" condition and the independence of the instrument in such circumstances.[40] One should, however, note that the *de jure* testing of the enforceability of the condition may in itself result in its unenforceability *de facto*. This is the case if the proceedings take years and all substantive evidence relevant under the transaction is admitted in the proceedings to arrive finally at a conclusion of no abuse or abuse. This substantive litigation should take place in proceedings under the transaction between the parties thereto not under the instrument.

Naming or captioning an instrument as an "on-demand" instrument does not in itself cause the desired effect any more than calling a document a warranty turns an outright disclaimer into an additional benefit to a buyer. Would calling an *inter vivos* gift a "Last Will and Testament" turn it into one?[41] The legal qualification of

---

Harvard Law Review, *"Fraud in the Transaction": Enjoining Letters of Credit During the Iranian Revolution*: "The Iranian letter of credit litigation forced courts interpreting the Code to confront what bank regulators have known for years: standby letters of credit are not the same as traditional letters of credit and should not be treated in the same way. Since 1974, federal banking authorities have subjected standbys to bank lending limits because standbys can contain risks to banks greater than traditional letters of credit. As standbys also present a different allocation of risks to customers, a different interpretation of article 5 — or an amendment to it — is desirable. The Code was from its inception inadequate to handle standby letters of credit, even though it explicitly purports to cover them. Article 5 was a restatement of the law of letters of credit as the law stood in 1952, years before litigation over standbys had brought the problems of these instruments to the fore."

[40] In principle there should be no problem in agreeing on such a term. Compare to United Nations Convention on the Assigned of Receivables in International Trade, Article 19:

"1. The debtor may agree with the assignor in a writing signed by the debtor not to raise against the assignee the defences and rights of set-off that it could raise pursuant to article 18. Such an agreement precludes the debtor from raising against the assignee those defences and rights of set-off. 2. The debtor may not waive defences: (*a*) Arising from fraudulent acts on the part of the assignee; or (*b*) Based on the debtor's incapacity. 3. Such an agreement may be modified only by an agreement in a writing signed by the debtor. The effect of such a modification as against the assignee is determined by article 20, paragraph 2."

This was the case in particular in connection with the Iranian revolution and the Nigerian cement crisis.

[41] See Bertrams, *Bank Guarantees*, at 226. UCC 5-102:

" 6 The label on a document is not conclusive; certain documents labelled 'guarantees' in accordance with European (and occasionally, American) practice are letters of credit. On the other hand, even documents that are labelled [sic] "letter of credit" may not constitute letters of credit under the definition in Section 5-102(a) When a document labelled a letter of credit requires the issuer to pay not upon the presentation of documents, but upon the determination of an extrinsic fact such as applicant's failure to perform a construction contract, and where that condition

The Instruments

an undertaking depends on its contents and wording, not on its right or wrong title.[42] A genuine on-demand condition must render the instrument substantively independent

   (i) from the underlying transaction; and
   (ii) from the account party's will.[43]

Otherwise we are not dealing with a true on-demand instrument.

Further, the obligation to honor i.e., the contingent liability should be

   (iii) irrevocable; and
   (iv) subject to specified conditions precedent only.
   The instrument need not establish a payment on sight; on the contrary, a deferred payment or acceptance does meet the requirements of "honor". There is, however, also a procedural aspect to the enforceability of an on-demand instrument. If the applicable national or arbitral procedural rules do not recognize summary judgement, the "parole evidence rule" or admit evidence which is not materially relevant for the narrow purposes of establishing compliance with the on-demand instrument's conditions precedent, the instrument may not be enforced on demand, but may be subjected to lengthy proceedings beyond the instrument's limited scope transforming the on-demand condition to something resembling traditional guarantees.

---

appears on its face to be fundamental and would, if ignored, leave no obligation to the issuer under the document labelled letter of credit, the issuer's undertaking is not a letter of credit. It is probably some form of suretyship or other contractual arrangement and may be enforceable as such. See Sections 5-102(a)(10) and 5-103(d). Therefore, undertakings whose fundamental term requires an issuer to look beyond documents and beyond conventional reference to the clock, calendar, and practices concerning the form of various documents are not governed by Article 5. Although Section 5-108(g) recognizes that certain nondocumentary conditions can be included in a letter of credit without denying the undertaking the status of letter of credit, that section does not apply to cases where the nondocumentary condition is fundamental to the issuer's obligation. The rules in Sections 5-102(a)(10), 5-103(d) and 5-108(g) approve the conclusion in *Wichita Eagle & Beacon Publishing Co. v. Pacific Nat. Bank*, 493 F.2d 1285 (9th Cir. 1974)."

[42] See Bertrams, *Bank Guarantees*, at 52.
[43] There are "mezzanine" instruments which are *prima facie* independent and subject to presentation of documents but among the documents required as condition precedent to honor are documents subject to will of the account party or his agent or representative or, e.g., on arbitral award. Such an undertaking is not fully an independent instrument.

I.7 Letters of credit

Letters of credit are often defined as contracts *sui generis*. The credits are unilateral undertakings of the issuer to render certain specific services to the beneficiary for and on behalf of the account party and at his request.[44] Dolan gives the following functional definition in *The Law of Letters of Credit* on p. 2-3:

> "It is more accurate to say that credits are sui generis and that the law of contracts supplements the law of credits only to the extent that contract principles do not interfere with the unique nature of credits."

The beneficiary has no explicit and enforceable duties under them. Letters of credit cannot be amended without the consent of the beneficiary. They are irrevocable unless otherwise expressly indicated.[45]

---

[44] UCC 5-102 official comments:
"A letter of credit is an idiosyncratic form of undertaking that supports performance of an obligation incurred in a separate financial, mercantile, or other transaction or arrangement. The objectives of the original and revised Article 5 are best achieved (1) by defining the peculiar characteristics of a letter of credit that distinguish it and the legal consequences of its use from other forms of assurance such as secondary guarantees, performance bonds and insurance policies, and from ordinary contracts, fiduciary engagements, and escrow arrangements; and (2) by preserving flexibility through variation by agreement in order to respond to and accommodate developments in custom and usage that are not inconsistent with the essential definitions and substantive mandates of the statute. No statute can, however, prescribe the manner in which such substantive rights and duties are to be enforced or imposed without risking stultification of wholesome developments in the letter of credit mechanism. Letter of credit law should remain responsive to commercial reality and in particular to the customs and expectations of the international banking and mercantile community. Courts should read the terms of this article in a manner consistent with these customs and expectations."

Greece (DCL) Art. 25:
"1. A Documentary credit is an agreement between a banking corporation (creditor) and another party (debtor) to issue a credit for the benefit of a third party (beneficiary). By this agreement the bank undertakes to pay to such third party the credit amount upon presentation of the bill of lading. Such amount shall be reimbursed by the debtor upon forwarding the bill of lading. 2. By payment of the amount the bank acquires a pledge over the goods referred to in the bill of lading. 3. The agreement on the credit shall be in writing. 4. The agreement on the credit is a commercial transaction for both parties."

[45] UCC Section 5-106:
"Added by Laws 2000, Ch. 471, eff. Nov. 1, 2000. Official comment: 1. This section adopts the position taken by several courts, namely that letters of credit that are silent as to revocability are irrevocable *See, e.g., Weyerhaeuser Co. v. First Nat. Bank*, 27 UCC Rep. Serv. 777 (SD. Iowa 1979); *West Va. Hous. Dev. Fund v. Sroka*, 415 F. Supp. 1107 (W.D. Pa. 1976). This is the position of

UCC Section 5-106:

> "Issuance, Amendment, Cancellation, and Duration. (a) A Letter of credit is issued and becomes enforceable according to its terms against the issuer when the issuer sends or otherwise transmits it to the person requested to advise or to the beneficiary. A letter of credit is revocable only if it so provides. (b) After a letter of credit is issued, rights and obligations of a beneficiary, applicant, confirmer, and issuer are not affected by an amendment or cancellation to which that person has not consented except to the extent the letter of credit provides that it is revocable or that the issuer may amend or cancel the letter of credit without that consent. (c) If there is no stated expiration date or other provision that determines its duration, a letter of credit expires one year after its stated date of issuance or, if none is stated, after the date on which it is issued. (d) A letter of credit that states that it is perpetual expires five years after its stated date of issuance, or if none is stated, after the date on which it is issued."

They are usually materially independent from the transaction and based on documents only — in general nothing else has any relevance.[46] They do not replace any other obligations of the parties.

UCP 600 Article 4:

> "a. A credit by its nature is a separate transaction from the sale or other contract on which it may be based. Banks are in no way concerned with or bound by such contract even if any reference whatsoever to it is included in the credit. Consequently, the undertaking of a bank to honour, to negotiate or to fulfil any other obligation under the credit is not subject to claims

---

the current UCP (500), Given the usual commercial understanding and purpose of letters of credit, revocable letters of credit offer unhappy possibilities for misleading the parties who deal with them."

[46] UCC 5-103 provides:
"Of course, no term in a letter of credit, whether incorporated by reference to practice rules or stated specifically, can free an issuer from a conflicting contractual obligation to its applicant. If, for example, an issuer promised its applicant that it would pay only against an inspection certificate of a particular company but failed to require such a certificate in its letter of credit or made the requirement only a nondocumentary condition that had to be disregarded, the issuer might be obliged to pay the beneficiary even though its payment might violate its contract with its applicant."

or defences by the applicant resulting from its relationships with the issuing bank or the beneficiary. A beneficiary can in no case avail itself of the contractual relationships existing between banks or between the applicant and the issuing bank.

b. An issuing bank should discourage any attempt by the applicant to include, as an integral part of the credit, copies of the underlying contract, proforma invoice and the like."

Documentary credits require submission of documents as conditions precedent whereas bank guarantees may or may not require documents. In the world of developed data transfer and electronic communications, the definition of "document" may present an issue.[47]

Under law merchant, letter of credit law is "black and white". The conditions precedent must be strictly complied with, i.e., the documents to be presented must strictly conform to those specified in the "black letter law" in order for the obligation of the issuer to mature and become payable. However, beyond the express stipulations ("black letter law"), or where the stipulations are vague or ambiguous, the documents must be accepted "as presented".[48] This is the "white law". There is no grey law area in between except perhaps the requirement of consistency.

When the conditions precedent have been met, the payment mechanism or "honor" matures.

---

[47] UCC 5-102 official comment:
"2. The definition of "document" contemplates and facilitates the growing recognition of electronic and other nonpaper media as "documents" however, for the time being, data in those media constitute documents only in certain circumstances. For example a facsimile received by an issuer would be a document only if the letter of credit explicitly permitted it, if the standard practice authorized it and the letter did not prohibit it, or the agreement of the issuer and beneficiary permitted it. The fact that data transmitted in a nonpaper (unwritten) medium can be recorded on paper by a recipient's computer printer, facsimile machine, or the like does not under current practice render the data so transmitted a "document." A facsimile or S.W.I.F.T. message received directly by the issuer is in an electronic medium when it crosses the boundary of the issuer's place of business. One wishing to make a presentation by facsimile (an electronic medium) will have to procure the explicit agreement of the issuer (assuming that the standard practice does not authorize it). Where electronic transmissions are authorized neither by the letter of credit nor by the practice, the beneficiary may transmit the data electronically to its agent who may be able to put it in written form and make a conforming presentation"

[48] UCP Art.

UCC 5-102 official comment:

> "4. Payment and acceptance are familiar modes of honor. A third mode of honor, incurring an unconditional obligation, has legal effects similar to an acceptance of a time draft but does not technically constitute an acceptance."

Payment does not always mean cash payment; what it means is the arising of an unconditional obligation.[49] When the conforming tender meets the acceptance or honor of the bank, the credit is consummated ("the moment of death") and the credit expires.[50] Thereafter the relationships of the parties are governed by other rules.

There is lot to be said about the strict compliance doctrine versus the substantial compliance doctrine applicable in some national laws. Should substantial compliance be the rule to determine what would constitute substantial in any individual case, it would become a tedious exercise for the banks. The banks do not necessarily have any expertise as to what objectively may or may not be an essential discrepancy and what the parties would or would have subjectively deemed as such. This might cause the examination of documents to become a time-consuming exercise and would increase costs. In the worst case parties and experts would have to be heard and what was meant to be expeditious would start to resemble litigation, with the banker being the judge — most inconvenient and inappropriate for bank officers and banking business. The courts would then start to second-guess the bank's judgement as to substantiality and according to what criteria? At the same time the instrument would dilute

---

[49] UCC 5-102 official comment:
"4. The practice of making letters of credit available by 'deferred payment undertaking' as now provided in UCP 500 has grown up in other countries and spread to the United States. The definition of 'honor' will accommodate that practice." 5-102 official comment: "In almost all cases the ultimate performance of the issuer under a letter of credit is the payment of money. In rare cases the issuer's obligation is to deliver stock certificates or the like. The definition of letter of credit in Section 5-102(a)(10) contemplates those cases."

[50] One could argue that the fraud rule is stronger than the doctrine of independence only when by enjoining the payment may still prevent a fraudulent partly from receiving the funds. See Xiang Gao *Presenters immune from the fraud rule in the law of letters of credit*, Lloyd's Maritime Commercial Law Quarterly 10-38 (2002, 1 (Feb)),:
"To determine who should be immune from the fraud rule can be one of the most challenging areas for the courts. In many cases, it involves two branches of commercial law: the law of letters of credit and the law of negotiable instruments. As has been revealed, rules of these laws do not always accord with each other. However, it is submitted that, when deciding a case of letters of credit, the controlling basis should be the law of letters of credit."

from having been cast in concrete into a "maybe, maybe not – who knows" speculative promise and would lose its real commercial value, resulting in an increase in costs and a reduction in or loss of value.

Apart from UCP, the letter-of-credit law has been allowed to develop under the umbrella of another great statute, namely that of Uniform Commercial Code Article 5. UCP and UCC are in this field closely related and have made progress in facilitating the use of these instruments and allowing them to develop, without imposing a straight jacket on them, already for many decades.

There are three separate and materially independent but formally accessory agreements under a commercial letter of credit, namely:

1) The underlying transaction or "main" agreement;
2) The Indemnity Agreement between the Account Party or Principal and the Issuer; and
3) The letter of credit between the Issuer and the Beneficiary.

I.8 Confirmed letters of credit

In a letter-of-credit transaction there may be and often is a need to engage another bank in addition to the issuer. Or there may be a benefit in doing so.[51] Sometimes the other bank or banks play a simple role of advising the credit (advising bank) or simply facilitating the carrying out of the payment and negotiation and transfer of documents (nominated bank).[52]

---

[51] UCC 5-102 (official comment):
"7. A restricted negotiation credit might be "available with x bank by negotiation or the like. Several legal consequences may attach to the status of nominated person. First, when the issuer nominates a person, it is authorizing that person to pay or give value and is authorizing the beneficiary to make presentation to that person. Unless the letter of credit provides otherwise, the beneficiary need not present the documents to the issuer before the letter of credit expires; it need only present those documents to the nominated person. Secondly, a nominated person that gives value in good faith has a right to payment from the issuer despite fraud. Section 5-109(a)(1)."

[52] UCP Art. UCC 5-107 (official comment):
"When the issuer nominates another person to "pay," "negotiate," or otherwise to take up the documents and give value, there can be confusion about the legal status of the nominated person. In rare cases the person might actually be an agent of the issuer and its act might be the act of the issuer itself. In most cases the nominated person is not an agent of the issuer and has no authority to act on the issuer's behalf. Its 'nomination' allows the beneficiary to present to it and earns it certain rights to payment under Section 5-109 that others do not enjoy. For example, when an issuer

```
                        Beneficiary
Obligee under the letter of credit      Obligee under
                                         the transaction
```

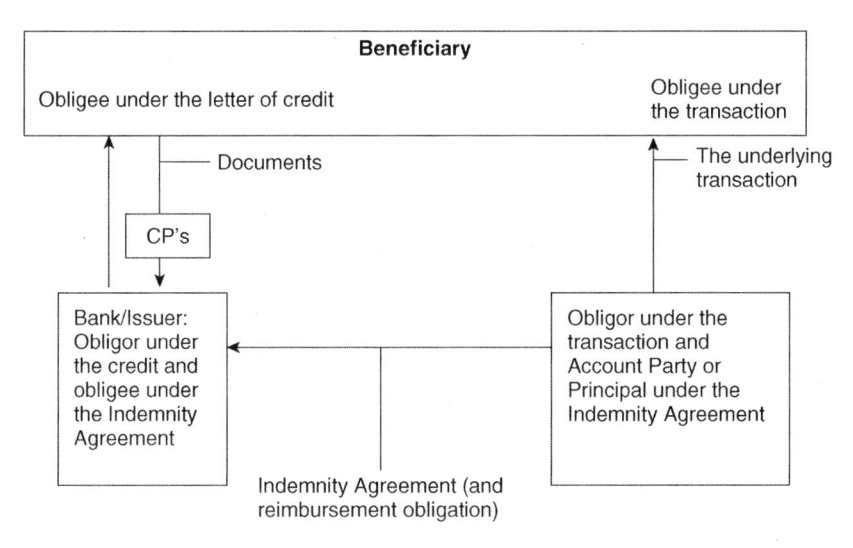

Figure I.4. Commercial letter of credit

UCC 5-102 (official comment):

> "7. Under the UCP any bank is a nominated bank where the letter of credit is "freely negotiable." A letter of credit might also nominate by the following: "We hereby engage with the drawer, indorsers, and bona fide holders of drafts drawn under and in compliance with the terms of this credit that the same will be duly honored on due presentation" or "available with any bank by negotiation."

In these cases the banks do not give any legally binding undertaking of their own.[53]

---

issues a "freely negotiable credit," it contemplates that banks or others might take up documents under that credit and advance value against them, and it is agreeing to pay those persons but only if the presentation to the issuer made by the nominated person compiles with the credit. Usually there will be no agreement to pay, negotiate, or to serve in any other capacity by the nominated person, therefore the nominated person will have the right to decline to take the documents. It may return them or agree merely to act as a forwarding agent for the documents but without giving value against them or taking any responsibility for their conformity to the letter of credit."

[53] UCP 600 Article 9:
"An advising bank may utilize the services of another bank ("second advising bank) to advise the credit and any amendment to the beneficiary By advising the credit or amendment, the second advising bank signifies that it has satisfied itself as to the apparent authenticity of the advice it has received and that the advice accurately reflects the terms and conditions of the credit or amendment received."

UCP 600 Article 12:
"a. Unless a nominated bank is the confirming bank, an authorization to honour or negotiate does not impose any obligation on that nominated bank to honour or negotiate, except when expressly

UCP 600 Article 9:

> "A credit and any amendment may be advised to a beneficiary through an advising bank. An advising bank that is not a confirming bank advises the credit and any amendment without any undertaking to honour or negotiate."

However, when another bank *confirms* the credit, it assumes a direct duty and liability towards the beneficiary identical with that of the issuing bank. In addition the confirming bank also assumes the original undertaking of the obligor under the transaction and not in replacement thereof.[54]

UCP 600 provides as follows in Article 8:

> "b. A confirming bank is irrevocably bound to honour or negotiate as of the time it adds its confirmation to the credit.
> c. A confirming bank undertakes to reimburse another nominated bank that has honoured or negotiated a complying presentation and forwarded the documents to the confirming bank. Reimbursement for the amount of

---

> agreed to by that nominated bank and so communicated to the beneficiary. b. By nominating a bank to accept a draft or incur a deferred payment undertaking, an issuing bank authorizes that nominated bank to prepay or purchase a draft accepted or a deferred payment undertaking incurred by that nominated bank. c. Receipt or examination and forwarding of documents by a nominated bank that is not a confirming bank does not make that nominated bank liable to honour or negotiate, nor does it constitute honour or negotiation."

[54] UCC 5-107 (official comment):
"A confirmer that has paid in accordance with the terms and conditions of the letter of credit is entitled to reimbursement by the issuer even if the beneficiary committed fraud (see Section 5-109(a)(1)(ii)) and, in that sense, has greater rights against the issuer than the beneficiary has. To be entitled to reimbursement from the issuer under the typical confirmed letter of credit, the confirmer must submit conforming documents, but the confirmer's presentation to the issuer need not be made before the expiration date of the letter of credit.

A letter of credit confirmation has been analogized to a guarantee of issuer performance, to a parallel letter of credit issued by the confirmer for the account of the issuer or the letter of credit applicant or both, and to a back-to-back letter of credit in which the confirmer is a kind of beneficiary of the original issuer's letter of credit. Like letter of credit undertakings, confirmations are both unique and flexible, so that no one of these analogies is perfect, but unless otherwise indicated in the letter of credit or confirmation a confirmer should be viewed by the letter of credit issuer and the beneficiary as an issuer of a parallel letter of credit for the account of the original letter of credit issuer. *Absent a direct agreement between the applicant and a confirmer,* normally the obligations of a confirmer are to the issuer not the applicant, but the applicant might have a right to injunction against a confirmer under Section 5-109 or warranty claim under Section 5-110, and either might have claims against the other under Section 5-117."

a complying presentation under a credit available by acceptance or deferred payment is due at maturity, whether or not another nominated bank prepaid or purchased before maturity. A confirming bank's undertaking to reimburse another nominated bank is independent of the confirming bank's undertaking to the beneficiary.

d. If a bank is authorized or requested by the issuing bank to confirm a credit but is not prepared to do so, it must inform the issuing bank without delay and may advise the credit without confirmation."

and UCC 5-107 (a) reads as follows:

"A confirmer *is directly obligated on a letter of credit* and has the rights and obligations of an issuer to the extent of its confirmation. The confirmer also has rights against and obligations to the issuer *as if the issuer were an applicant* and the confirmer had issued the letter of credit at the request and for the account of the issuer."

The role of the issuer in a confirmed credit resembles *mutatis mutandis* the role of applicant. The issuing bank is under an obligation of reimbursement to the confirming bank and the other banks involved.

UCC 5-108 (official comment):

"A confirmer that has paid in accordance with the terms and conditions of the letter of credit is entitled to reimbursement by the issuer even if the beneficiary committed fraud (see Section 5-109(a)(1)(ii)) and, in that sense, *has greater rights against the issuer than the beneficiary has*. To be entitled to reimbursement from the issuer under the typical confirmed letter of credit, the confirmer must submit conforming documents, but the confirmer's presentation to the issuer *need not be made before the expiration date of the letter of credit*. A letter of credit confirmation has been analogized to a guarantee of issuer performance, to a parallel letter of credit issued by the confirmer for the account of the issuer or the letter of credit applicant or both, and to a back-to-back letter of credit in which the confirmer is a kind of beneficiary of the original issuer's letter of credit."

As a consequence of confirmation, the beneficiary may at his choice demand payment from either the issuing bank or the confirming bank, and of course from the original obligor under the agreement: there are three obligors.

Chapter I

The structure of confirmed letters of credit is only somewhat more complicated than that of "simple" letters of credit. The confirmed letter of credit may form a three-party agreement between the two banks and the beneficiary, or two identical agreements between a bank on the one hand and the beneficiary on the other hand with identical conditions precedent in both letters of credit.

UCC 5-108 official comment:

> "Like letter of credit undertakings, confirmations are both unique and flexible, so that no one of these analogies is perfect, but unless otherwise indicated in the letter of credit or confirmation a confirmer *should be viewed by the letter of credit issuer and the beneficiary as an issuer of a parallel letter of credit for the account of the original letter of credit issuer.* Absent a direct agreement between the applicant and a confirmer, normally the obligations of a confirmer are to the issuer not the applicant, but the applicant might have a right to injunction against a confirmer under Section 5-109 or warranty claim under Section 5-110, and either might have claims against the other under Section 5-117."

There may be several separate and substantially independent but formally accessory agreements under a confirmed letter of credit, namely:

1) The underlying transaction or "main" agreement;
2) The Indemnity Agreement between the Account Party or Principal and the Issuing Bank;
3) The Indemnity Agreement between the Issuing Bank and the Confirming Bank (and the Account Party);
4) The letter of credit between the Issuing Bank and the Beneficiary (and the Confirming Bank);
5) The letter of credit between the Confirming Bank and the Beneficiary; and
6) The Indemnity Agreement, if any, between the Confirming Bank and the Account Party.

I.9 The three main functions of commercial credits

Commercial letters of credit serve three primary functions. These are:

(i) an instrument or method for the payment of the contract price (credit available by sight, payment by deferred payment or by acceptance);

```
                                    Beneficiary
         Obligee under the LC                  Obligor or obligee under the
         transaction                           underlying transaction

                                                          ── The underlying
              CPs    =    CPs                                transaction

                                                 Account party:
         Other    Issuing
         banks    bank:          Confirming Bank  Obligee or obligor
                  obligor                         under the transaction/
                  under the                       account party and
                  credit and                      obligor under the
                  obligee                         indemnity agreement
                  under the
                  indemnity

                                 Indemnity
                                 Agreement and
                                 reimbursement
                                 obligation
```

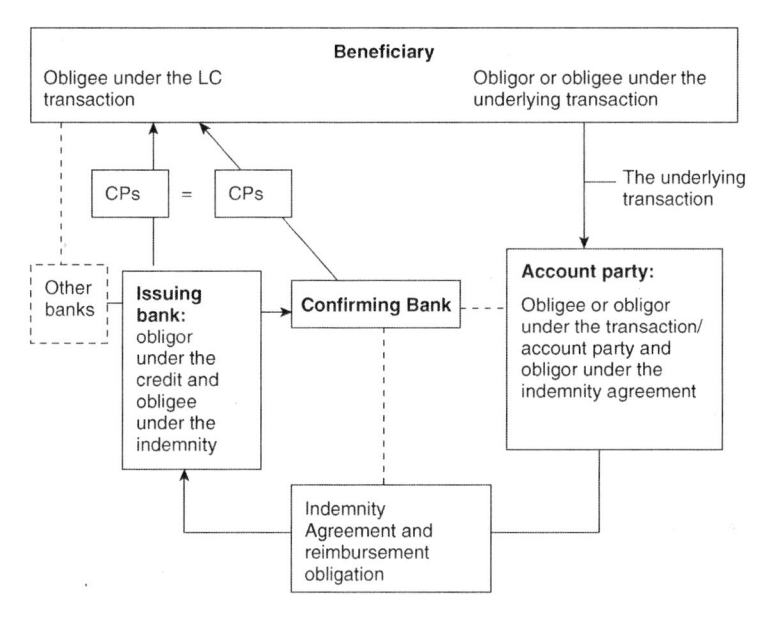

Figure I.5. Confirmed letter of credit

(ii) a security to the beneficiary for honor[55] when the conditions agreed upon have been met and "a security" to the account party[56] at the same

---

[55] Under UCP honour means
"a. to pay at sight if the credit is available by sight payment. b. to incur a deferred payment undertaking and pay at maturity if the credit is available by deferred payment. c. to accept a bill of exchange ("draft") drawn by the beneficiary and pay at maturity if the credit is available by acceptance." One should note that a security interest is often created by force of law in the letter of credit transaction itself.

UCC 5-118:
"(a) An issuer or nominated person has a security interest in a document presented under a letter of credit and any identifiable proceeds of the collateral to the extent that the issuer or nominated person honors or gives value for the presentation. (b) Subject to subsection (a), as long as and to the extent that an issuer or nominated person has not been reimbursed or has not otherwise recovered the value given with respect to a security interest in a document under subsection (a), the security interest continues and is subject to Article 9, but: (1) a security agreement is not necessary to make the security interest enforceable under Section 9-203(b)(3); (2) if the document is presented in a medium other than a written or other tangible medium, the security interest is perfected; and (3) if the document is presented in a written or other tangible medium and is not a certificated security, chattel paper, a document of title, an instrument, or a letter of credit, so long as the debtor does not have possession of the document, the security interest is perfected and has priority over a conflicting security interest in the document."

[56] UCC 5-108 (a):
"Except as Otherwise provided in Section 5-109, an issuer shall honor a presentation that, as determined by the standard practice referred to in subsection (e) of this section, *appears on its face*

time providing an incentive to the beneficiary to perform as agreed i.e., to solicit and to monitor the agreed performance by the beneficiary;[57] and *Niru v. Milestone* demonstrates well some of the most fundamental security aspects:

"The documents, including the bill of lading and the inspection certificate, were presented to Bank Sepah under the letter of credit by CAI, which presented them as a principal. After some minor discrepancies had been corrected, the documents were accepted by Bank Sepah, but it was unable to make payment because the authorities in Iran failed to make the necessary foreign currency available. *The price of lead began to fall causing CAI to become concerned about the adequacy of its security and eventually, after consulting Mr Mahdavi but without telling Bank Sepah or Niru, it sold the goods to reimburse itself.* Then, somewhat to everyone's surprise, funds were made available to enable Bank Sepah to honour the letter of credit and a sum of about US$5.8 million was remitted to CAI for payment to Milestone. The officer responsible for Milestone's account, Mr Francis, knew that the bank had sold the lead that was to have been delivered under the contract and had assumed that the transaction was dead. He was unsure, therefore, how to respond to the receipt of the funds, but having spoken to Mr Mahdavi he was persuaded to release them to another company in the Woralco group, Nikam Metal Finance Ltd. Needless to say (as the judge put it) they were subsequently lost. In the result no goods were delivered to Niru by Milestone, or by any other company under the Mahdavi umbrella. *Niru was, however, out of pocket because, pursuant to its counter-indemnity, Bank Sepah had debited its account with the full amount of the payment.* In short, Niru had been induced to part with the sum of US$5.8 million and received nothing in return other than the sum of US$116,760, which was

---

strictly to comply with the terms and conditions of the letter of credit. Except as otherwise provided in Section 5-113 and unless otherwise agreed with the applicant, an issuer shall dishonor a presentation that does not appear so to comply."

[57] Standby letters of credit do not solicit performance or provide a directive incentive therefor. They rather provide a security for non-performance and thus they rather function as a primary source of funds to be set-off against claim for damages and operate to change the balance of payments between the beneficiary and the account party under the transaction in favor of the beneficiary.

> paid under a performance guarantee provided by Milestone under the contract."[58]
>
> (iii) an instrument of *financing* when credit provides for deferred payment or is available by negotiation or acceptance of drafts.[59]

Besides providing direct financing by way of deferred payment or negotiation or acceptance of drafts, letters of credit are used as collateral and as back-up for financing. For instance they may provide a basis for post-financing, in which the LC is in essence only an instrument to establish the availability of foreign currency, which facility is then used to back-up a credit given to an importer (account party) by the issuing bank.[60]

As an instrument or method for the payment of the contract price the credit is self-explanatory. In export trade the need to use credits as payment instruments arises also from the geographic distance between the account party and the seller.

The second function provides a "double" security. The credit provides the beneficiary a security for honor of his claims for the agreed price provided that he meets the conditions precedent set forth in the credit: he may rest assured that payment will be effected and that the commitment remains firm and irrevocable despite changes at the marketplace and in particular beyond the will of the account party and his possible change of mind.[61]

---

[58] *Niru Battery Mfg Co, Bank Sepah Iran v. Milestone Trading, Ltd*, Case No: A3/2003/1167, Neutral Citation Number: [2004] EWCA Civ 487, Court of Appeal (Civil Division).

[59] This applies to some extent to all these instruments. Bertrams, *Bank Guarantees*, at 459:
"Bank guarantees, and especially first demand guarantees, are useful instruments in order to accomplish such a mutually agreeable re-allocation of the burden of financing projects. In fact, construction firms and employers tend to view bank guarantees as a financing instrument no less than as a security instrument. This tallies with the fact that guarantees are only called in a small number of cases, while the financing aspect is nearly always present. For example, an employer or importer of capital goods might prepared to make an advance payment against a first demand repayment guarantee. Certain interim payments, as the work progresses, can be made by the employer if a first demand performance guarantee is furnished. The full percentage of interim installments and/or the last installment can be released if a retention and/or a maintenance guarantee is made available."

[60] This financing is in use in export to Turkey and Russia by banks in these countries when opening credits in favor of foreign importers. The letter of credit is not primarily for the purposes of payment but for the granting of credit.

[61] Irrevocability is also rule under URDG Art 5: "All guarantees and Counter-Guarantees are irrevocable unless otherwise indicated."

Chapter I

By the payment commitment of the bank, the payment obligation of the account party is assumed by the bank jointly and severally with the account party, i.e., in addition to his agreement, but not in replacement thereof. The buyer remains liable under the transaction. At its simplest, this is a classic cash transaction: goods (represented by documents) against payment in cash ("Zug um Zug").[62]

At the same time the credit provides a security for the account party, to a degree of certainty that the seller has performed as agreed at least as may be reflected in the documents submitted by him and required by the credit.[63] The account party may impose such conditions in the credit as he may deem necessary and as his leverage may allow thereby achieving a level of risk acceptable to him.

Finally, the beneficiary may use the deferred payment undertaking or the drafts accepted by the bank to finance its operations by negotiating, i.e., selling them with or without recourse or using them as a security to obtain credit.

I.10 The function of standby credit

When a commercial letter of credit is established for the purpose of effecting payment in accordance with the terms and conditions of the transaction in question, a standby letter is opened and issued as an instrument to be resorted to by the beneficiary only in the event of breach of agreement or otherwise when the course of events deviates from what was agreed upon or anticipated under the transaction to the detriment of the beneficiary.[64]

---

[62] Unidroit Art 7.1.3:
"(1) Where the parties are to perform simultaneously, either party may withhold performance until the other party tenders its performance.(2) Where the parties are to perform consecutively, the party that is to perform later may withhold its performance until the first party has performed."

[63] UCP: "Banks deal with documents and not with goods, services or other performances to which the documents may relate."

[64] ISP, Preface:
"Standbys are issued to support payment, when due or after default, of obligations based on money loaned or advanced, or upon the occurrence or non-occurrence of another contingency. For convenience, standbys are commonly classified descriptively (and without operative significance in the application of these Rules) based on their function in the underlying transaction or other factors not necessarily related to the terms and conditions of the standby itself. For example: - A "Performance Standby" supports an obligation to perform other than to pay money including

ISP 1.10:

"a. A standby *should not or need not state* that it is: i. *unconditional* or *abstract* (if it does, it signifies merely that payment under it is conditioned solely on presentation of specified documents); ii. *absolute* (if it does, it signifies merely that it is irrevocable); iii. *primary* (if it does, it signifies merely that it is the independent obligation of the issuer); iv. *payable from the issuer's own funds* (if it does, it signifies merely that payment under it does not depend on the availability of applicant funds and is made to satisfy the issuer's own independent obligation); v. *clean* or *payable on demand* (if it does, it signifies merely that it is payable upon presentation of a written demand or other documents specified in the standby). b. A standby should not use the term "*and/or*" (if it does it means either or both). c. The following terms have no single accepted meaning: i. and shall be disregarded: "*callable*", "*divisible*", "*fractionable*" "*indivisible*", and "*transmissible*", ii. and shall be disregarded unless their context gives them meaning: "*assignable*", "*evergreen*", "*reinstate*", and "*revolving*"."

Payment under a commercial letter of credit is anticipated in the ordinary course of transaction whereas payment under a standby letter of credit is anticipated not to be effected in the ordinary course of the transaction but only in exceptional cases of breach or other failure.[65]

---

for the purpose of covering losses arising from a default of the applicant in completion of the underlying transactions. - An "Advance Payment Standby" supports an obligation to account for an advance payment made by the beneficiary to the applicant. - A "Bid Bond/Tender Bond Standby" supports an obligation of the applicant to execute a contract if the applicant is awarded a bid. - A "Counter Standby" supports the issuance of a separate standby or other undertaking by the beneficiary of the counter standby. - A "Financial Standby" supports an obligation to pay money, including any instrument evidencing an obligation to repay borrowed money. - A "Direct Pay Standby" supports payment when due of an underlying payment obligation typically in connection with a financial standby without regard to a default. - An "Insurance Standby" supports an insurance or reinsurance obligation of the applicant. - A "Commercial Standby" supports the obligations of an applicant to pay for goods or services in the event of non-payment by other methods."

[65] The use of standbys has become more diversified. Wunnicke, Wunnicke, and Turner at 50: "As part of the regulations related to risk-based Capital requirements and direct credit substitutes, the Office of the Controller of the Currency (OCC) has amended 12 C.F.R. Appendix A to Part 3 (1994) to include the following definition; please note in this definition that account party is the applicant as defined in New UCC Article 5: *Financial guarantee-type standby letter of credit* means any letter of credit or similar arrangements, however named or described, which represents an irrevocable obligation to the beneficiary on the part of the issuer (1) to repay money borrowed by or advanced to or for the account of the account party, or (2) to make payment on account of any

Bertrams writes on p. 7:

> "There is a widespread belief that American standby letters of credit are different from the European independent guarantee. This is a fallacy. As is apparent from the above description, its function, i.e., the furnishing of security, and its mechanics, notably the rule of independence and the documentary nature of the conditions of payment, are the same as those of the European independent guarantee. They can be used for the same purposes (see Chapter 3), and they may contain the same conditions of payment (payment mechanism) (see Chapter 4). Accordingly, the American standby letter of credit and the European independent guarantee represent conceptually and legally the same device."

As a consequence of such an adverse change in the performance of the account party under the transaction, the beneficiary may be partly or wholly exposed to an increased risk. This increased risk may either be an established fact or only anticipatory non-performance by the account party or other such change of circumstances deemed detrimental to the beneficiary. When commercial credit is used by the beneficiary, the transaction proceeds as agreed, but when standby credit is called, something exceptional has allegedly happened to cause the beneficiary to resort to his defensive financial instrument. In the absence of such an exceptional course of event or a breach of agreement by the account party, the calling of the standby credit by the beneficiary may be unfounded and unfair. This may in its turn constitute an abuse of the instrument by the beneficiary and thereby a breach of the duty of good faith and fair dealing implicit in every transaction under the underlying transaction or the instrument itself.[66] One could conclude that when a standby letter of credit is called, there is always a breach under the transaction committed either by the account party or by the beneficiary.[67]

---

    indebtedness undertaken by the account party, in the event that the account party fails to fulfill its obligation to the beneficiary."

[66] Unidroit 1.7: "(1) Each party must act in accordance with good faith and fair dealing in international trade. (2) The parties may not exclude or limit this duty."

[67] Dolan describes in *The Law of Letters of Credit*, 1993 Cum Supp No. 2, another kind of use of standby at 2.02, as follows:
"Many fraud claims have arisen out of syndicated loan transactions in which the letter of credit can play a quite essential and efficient role. An enterprise needing credit for what is typically a risky venture, being unable to obtain capital from commercial lenders, may package the investment part of the transaction as a general partnership with the investors as limited partners. The limited partners provide the capital under a standby credit arrangement that generates credit for the partnership by permitting it to borrow from a commercial lender."

Standby credits have emerged as a brother-in-law to commercial credits and have earned their own codification referred to as ISP. In the foreword to ISP, Maria Cattaui describes the development of the instrument and the birth of ISP as follows:

> "ISP98 embodies the commitment of ICC, through its Commission on Banking Technique and Practice, to provide global leadership in the formulation of standard banking practice for letters of credit and related independent undertakings such as standby letters of credit. In the tradition of ICC's *Uniform Customs and Practice for Documentary Credits* (UCP), which is recognized worldwide as the code of practice governing commercial letters of credit, endorsement of the ISP98 by ICC assures that these rules will assume a global character as well. As standbys came into their own under the UCP, it nevertheless became clear that issues of practice had emerged which required different solutions than those provided by the UCP. ISP98, in a sense, is an evolutionary product of the application of the UCP to standbys, as can be seen in the similarities between the two sets of rules. It is important to note that standbys can still be issued subject to UCP, if the parties determine it is their wish to do so."

There are three separate and materially independent but formally accessory agreements under a stand-by letter of credit, namely:

1) The underlying transaction or "main" agreement;
2) The Indemnity Agreement between the Account Party or Principal and the Issuer; and
3) The letter of credit between the Issuer and the Beneficiary.

When a correspondent bank or other financial institution is required under a commercial credit to confirm the undertaking of the issuing bank, the position of the beneficiary is strengthened by the introduction of a new obligor in addition to the issuing entity and the undertaking of the contracting party under the transaction. This may result in the creation of a multi-party agreement or in two separate almost identical beneficiary-bank agreements.

Under standby credits, another bank or financial entity is not necessarily engaged as a confirming entity but directly as an issuing entity, whose credit is being

CHAPTER I

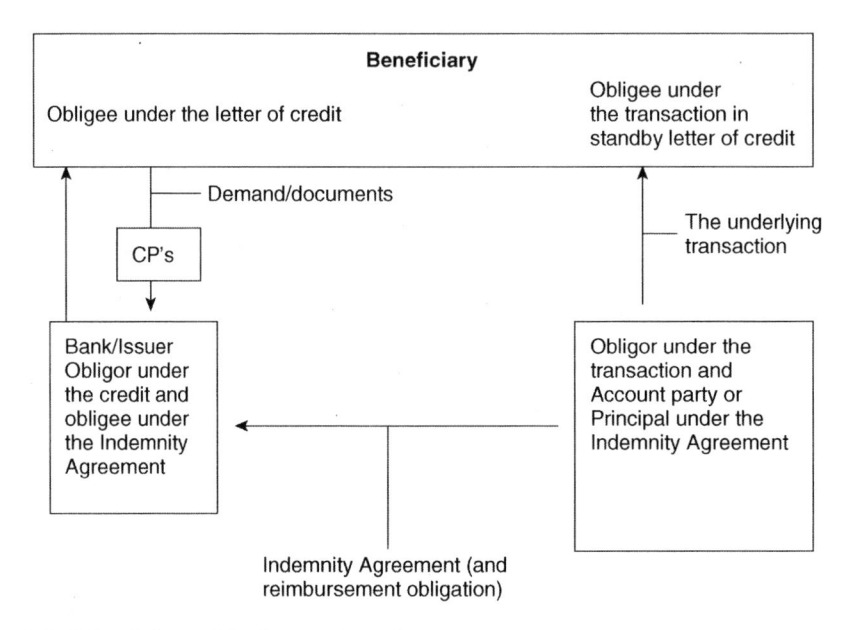

```
                         Beneficiary
                                        Obligee under
   Obligee under the letter of credit   the transaction in
                                        standby letter of credit

           ─── Demand/documents ───
                                              The underlying
                                              transaction
        CP's

   Bank/Issuer              Obligor under the
   Obligor under            transaction and
   the credit and           Account party or
   obligee under    ◄────   Principal under the
   the Indemnity            Indemnity Agreement
   Agreement

              Indemnity Agreement (and
              reimbursement obligation)
```

Figure I.6. "Simple" stand-by letter of credit

backed-up by a stand-by credit of the instructing bank, which does not give any direct undertakings to the beneficiary.[68]

I.11 "Blended" facilities

A letter of credit or a guarantee is on one hand a substantively independent agreement and on the other hand a component of a network forming a facility or a function. This facility may consist of similar or even almost identical parts like, e.g., a back-to-back credit forming a chain of commercial letters of credit. Such a chain is illustrated in Figure I.8, where LC means letter of credit and CP means conditions precedent:

In the transaction illustrated in Figure I.8, the conditions precedent are identical except that Beneficiary No 1 will replace the invoices of Beneficiary 2 by his own invoices.

---

[68] See *United Technologies Corp v. Citibank*, 469 F.Supp 662 (1978).

THE INSTRUMENTS

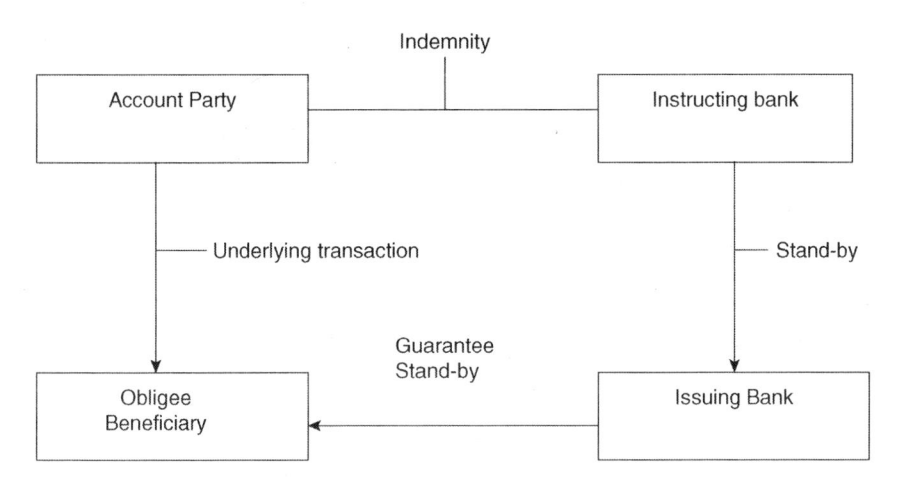

Figure I.7. Multi-party stand-by

A typical stand-by credit facility or a bank guarantee, illustrated in Figure I.9, is a simple "brokerage" of credit with no confirmations.

In this brokerage the facility is generated by the instructions of the account party to the issuing bank, which (i) "lends" into credit to the account party under an indemnity agreement or against a collateral and (ii) asks another bank to issue the instrument (bank guarantee or letter of credit) in favor of the beneficiary against a standby or guarantee of the issuing bank, which does not establish any contractual relationship with the ultimate beneficiary. In such "blended" facilities bank guarantees and letters of credit are both used and appear to be fully acceptable and interchangeable as instruments subject to applicable banking laws and regulations.

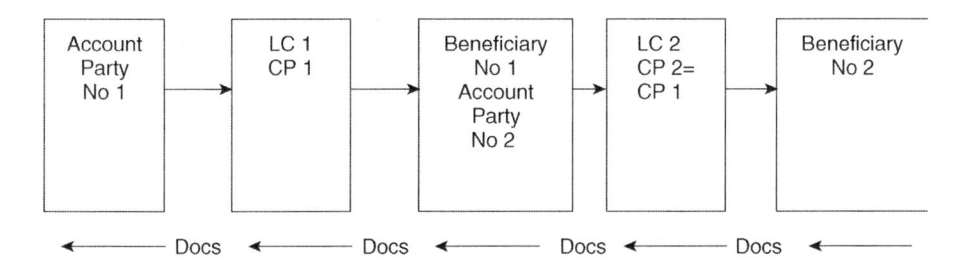

Figure I.8. A back-to-back credit forming a chain of commercial letters of credit

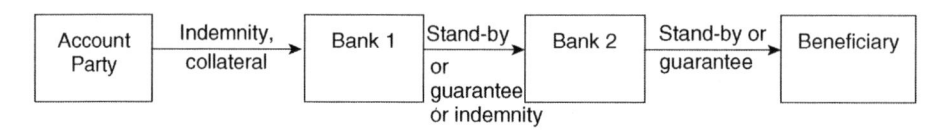

```
Account      Indemnity,    Bank 1   Stand-by   Bank 2   Stand-by or   Beneficiary
Party        collateral  ─────────> or       ─────────> guarantee    ─────────>
                                    guarantee
                                    or indemnity
```

Figure I.9. Stand-by credit facility

"For the purpose of procuring the requisite performance bond, the plaintiffs did not themselves make the direct approach to Rafidain. They requested their own bankers, Allied Arab Bank Ltd. ("Allied"), Arab Bank Ltd. ("Arab Bank") or the Fidelity Bank ("Fidelity") to instruct Rafidain to issue the performance bond. In consideration of Allied, Arab Bank or Fidelity complying with this request, the plaintiffs would give them a written indemnity. A typical indemnity is to be found at p. 6 of our bundle "C", by which United agreed to indemnify Arab Bank against all losses, etc. which it might incur by reason of giving such instructions and agreed that— . . . any demand made upon you by [Rafidain] for the payment of any sums of money in pursuance of your having instructed them as aforesaid shall be a sufficient authority to you for your making any such payment and it shall not be incumbent upon you to enquire whether any such amount is in fact due. The indemnity also provides that all matters arising out of it shall be construed and determined according to English law. Rafidain itself always required a counter-indemnity from the bank at whose request it issued the performance bond. One of the standard terms of such counter-indemnity provided (see, e.g.,p. 28 of Bundle B): In case of implementation, any claim or claims will be paid to us on first demand, despite of any contestation between principals and the beneficiaries. In the case of some contracts, Allied, on receiving instructions, coupled with an indemnity, from one or other of the plaintiffs, itself instructed Barclays Bank International Ltd. ("B.B.I.") to procure that Rafidain should issue the requisite performance bond, which B.B.I. did on receiving an appropriate counter-indemnity from Allied. The following contracts fall into this category."[69]

I.12 Amendments of the instrument

In a traditional contract there are two parties. The contract cannot be amended except with the consent of both. When a contract is backed up by an undertaking

---

[69] United Trading Corp v. Allied Arab Bank,1985 WL 311451 (CA (Civ Div)), [1985] 2 Lloyd's Rep. 554 (Note).

of a third party by way of guarantee or letter of credit, the issue of amendment becomes more complicated. On the one hand the parties to the contract may not amend, reduce or expand the duties of the guarantor or issuer by their mutual agreement only; rather the consent of the issuer or guarantor is required. If no consent is given, the duties remain to be backed-up under the instrument in their original contents or, alternatively, the instrument becomes ineffective or unenforceable depending on the amendments which were made.

On the other hand the issuer or the guarantor and the beneficiary can neither agree effectively on any amendment without the consent of the account party or other undertakers to the facility, like, e.g., the confirming bank.

A simple and straightforward matter becomes somewhat confusing due to the multiparty character of the facility, in particular if the doctrine of independence applicable to some of these instruments is overemphasized as if there were no links at all between the agreements, no facility but just stand-alone isolated undertakings. The substantive independence does not, however, mean this. It only bars or restricts substantive agreements or conditions from being "transferred" from the underlying contract to the instrument side, where they do not belong. The formal lines and accessory character remain and stay there requiring consent of all concerned when amendments are made; there is no doubt about it.

Credits and guarantees are parts of a network of agreements, i.e., the facility. The agreements are accessory to each other, i.e., functionally dependent but substantively independent from each other. In order for the instrument issued to be effectively amended, all the parties thereto must consent to the amendment ("multi-party consent"). This means in particular that the consent of the beneficiary is required but so are the agreement of the issuing entity, the confirming entity and the principal or the account party.

The only major exception is a revocable credit, which by its very nature is revocable at the convenience of the issuing entity or the account party or the confirming bank. Revocable instruments are very uncommon. Revocability by the beneficiary would be an absurdity, because the beneficiary has no duties under the instrument and may, in his sole discretion, and without exposure to any liability, decide not to make any demand or present any documents as a tender under the instrument. The beneficiary may, however, waive his right or release other parties from their duties.

Chapter I

If any of the agreements constituting the network is amended without the consent of the beneficiary, the amendment is not effective with respect to him or anyone else not having given his consent, and the instrument as originally issued will stay in force and intact as it was when issued between all parties thereto.

This fundamental rule has been expressed in UCP 600 Article 10 as follows:

> "a. Except as otherwise provided by article 38, a credit can neither be amended nor cancelled without the agreement of the issuing bank, the confirming bank, if any, and the beneficiary.
> b. An issuing bank is irrevocably bound by an amendment as of the time it issues the amendment. A confirming bank may extend its confirmation to an amendment and will be irrevocably bound as of the time it advises the amendment. A confirming bank may, however, choose to advise an amendment without extending its confirmation and, if so, it must inform the issuing bank without delay and inform the beneficiary in its advice.
> c. The terms and conditions of the original credit (or a credit incorporating previously accepted amendments) will remain in force for the beneficiary until the beneficiary communicates its acceptance of the amendment to the bank that advised such amendment. The beneficiary should give notification of acceptance or rejection of an amendment If the beneficiary fails to give such notification, a presentation that complies with the credit and to any not yet accepted amendment will be deemed to be notification of acceptance by the beneficiary of such amendment. As of that moment the credit will be amended.
> d. A bank that advises an amendment should inform the bank from which it received the amendment of any notification of acceptance or rejection.
> e. Partial acceptance of an amendment is not allowed and will be deemed to be notification of rejection of the amendment.
> f. A provision in an amendment to the effect that the amendment shall enter into force unless rejected by the beneficiary within a certain time shall be disregarded."

UCC 5-106 (a) (b) approaches the issue of amendment from another point of view declaring non-consented-to amendments unenforceable:

> "(a) A Letter of credit is issued and becomes enforceable according to its terms against the issuer when the issuer sends or otherwise transmits it to the person requested to advise or to the beneficiary. A letter of credit is

revocable only if it so provides. (b) After a letter of credit is issued, *rights and obligations of a beneficiary, applicant. confirmer, and issuer are not affected by an amendment or cancellation* to which that person has not consented except to the extent the letter of credit provides that it is revocable or that the issuer may amend or cancel the letter of credit without that consent."

In UNC in Article 8 the same rules govern the interbank relationships:

> "(1) An undertaking may not be amended except in the form stipulated in the undertaking or, failing such stipulation, in a form referred to in paragraph (2) of article 7. (2) Unless otherwise stipulated in the undertaking or elsewhere agreed by the guarantor/issuer and the beneficiary, an undertaking is amended upon issuance of the amendment *if the amendment has previously been authorized by the beneficiary*.
>
> (3) Unless otherwise stipulated in the undertaking or elsewhere agreed by the guarantor/issuer and the beneficiary, where any amendment has not previously been authorized by the beneficiary, the undertaking is amended only when the guarantor/issuer receives a notice of acceptance of the amendment by the beneficiary in a form referred to in paragraph (2) of article 7. (4) An amendment of an undertaking has no effect on the rights and obligations of the principal/applicant (or an instructing party) or of a confirmer of the undertaking unless such person consents to the amendment."

I.13 The right and remedy of set-off

The right of set-off is one of the most important rights both in commercial law in general and in particular in sale of goods and also in financial and banking law. Set-off is a right or a "remedy" which most often becomes a critical or main issue in connection with a default or a breach of a party under a transaction exposing the other parties or trading partners to increased risk of credit loss.

Unidroit 8.1:

> "(1) Where two parties owe each other money or other performances of the same kind, either of them ("the first party") may set off its obligation against that of its obligee ("the other party") if at the time of set-off, (a) the first party is entitled to perform its obligation; (b) the other party's

obligation is ascertained as to its existence and amount and performance is due. (2) If the obligations of both parties arise from the same contract, the first party may also set off its obligation against an obligation of the other party which is not ascertained as to its existence or to its amount."[70]

The default or breach may be a prelude to bankruptcy and insolvency or reorganization and, should this happen, the right to set off may have to be scrutinized on the basis of mandatory and strict rules of national laws. In sum, right to set-off, while not formally a security, carries some features of a security.

The right of set-off may, under the instruments discussed, materialize in connection with honor and payment. There is no law merchant on the issue and it remains to be covered by national law.[71] On the other hand, there is no law merchant or policy against set-off either. The doctrine of independence relates to substantive independence of the credit itself from the underlying agreement and is meant to protect the instrument issued. It is unclear whether it extends to the payor's and the beneficiary's relationship beyond the letter of credit to any degree. [72]

The same issue arises in connection with subrogation. Is the payment insulated from the commercial reality beyond the facility after the moment of death? If it is not, the payor may have a right to set off its receivable from the beneficiary against payment under the instrument. Such set-off is subject to such terms and conditions as the applicable law may provide. However, if this receivable has been assigned to the payor by the account party or another entity engaged in the facility, set-off should not be permissible in such circumstances. To allow set-off in such a case would violate the doctrine of independence and introduce such

---

[70] Unidroit 8.2:
"Where the obligations are to pay money in different currencies, the right of set-off may be exercised, provided that both currencies are freely convertible and the parties have not agreed that the first party shall pay only in a specified currency."; 8.3: "The right of set-off is exercised by notice to the other party."; 8.4: "(1) The notice must specify the obligations to which it relates. (2) If the notice does not specify the obligation against which set-off is exercised, the other party may, within a reasonable time, declare to the first party the obligation to which set-off relates. If no such declaration is made, the set-off will relate to all the obligations proportionally."; 8.5: "(1) Set-off discharges the obligations. (2) If obligations differ in amount, set-off discharges the obligations up to the amount of the lesser obligation. (3) Set-off takes effect as from the time of notice."

[71] Ellinger writes: "Another issue considered in *Frid* concerned the availability of a set off where a debt is contingent."

[72] See Bertrams, *Bank Guarantees*, at 108.

implicit conditions precedent to the instrument which do not *expressis verbis* form part of the facility.[73]

To allow set-off under such circumstances would render these facilities in many circumstances worthless and cause them to become a source of dispute and litigation contrary to the basic policies and could cause many problems to arise in particular in connection with bankruptcy or reorganization.[74]

The same principle should apply regardless of the sequence of events, i.e., whether the receivable was assigned prior to or after the setting-up of the facility (or any part thereof). To rule otherwise would seem to endorse bad faith in the transaction or fraudulent behavior except in cases where the arrangement is openly disclosed and accepted by the beneficiary.

These basic rules are codified in UNC providing for the right to set-off. The final analysis will, however, as stated, depend on the applicable national law.

UNC Art 18:

> "Unless otherwise stipulated in the undertaking or elsewhere agreed by the guarantor/issuer and the beneficiary, the guarantor/issuer may discharge the payment obligation under the undertaking by availing itself of a right of set-off, except with any claim assigned to it by the principal/applicant or the instructing party."

I.14 Security interest in the documents or goods

Commercial letters of credit are based on the goods purchased represented by the documents to be tendered as required by the conditions precedent. In traditional

---

[73] Dolan writes in *The Law of Letters of Credit* at 9-43: "An issuer's attempt to use the doctrine of setoff poses serious questions and may violate the independence principle."

[74] Gerard McMeel, *Pay now, argue later*, Lloyd's Maritime and Commercial Law Quarterly (1999, 1(Feb)), 5-9: "Letters of credit, bills of exchange and performance bonds oil the wheels of international commerce. English courts, which routinely deal with summary judgment applications in respect of such, are reluctant to allow the commercial perception of such mechanisms as the equivalent of cash to be "dashed by an over-zealous application of set-off. Accordingly, in the absence of cogent evidence of fraud, such undertakings are enforced by way of R.S.C., Ord. 14 without permitting any stay of execution, where a set-off or counterclaim of an unliquidated nature is argued for."

CHAPTER I

trade, some of the documents establish a right of ownership or title to the goods or at least require their surrender in order to again possession thereof. Other documents establish a contingent liability often equaling the price of the goods plus profit like, e.g., an insurance policy entitling the holder to receive a payment in lieu of perished or deteriorated merchandise purchased and sold. Some of the documents tendered by the beneficiary may thus be very valuable. In the case of standby credits or guarantees, this is not usually the case; a simple payment demand by the beneficiary has no value nor does an arbitral award tendered by the beneficiary to the guarantor under traditional guarantee undertakings.[75]

Valuable property may, either by operation of law, trade usage or agreement, be subject to security rights. Such a right may be created by mere possession of the document. The security interest may arise by operation of law very much like subrogation or it may require a specific legal act to be perfected.[76] A perfected security interest may arise by operation of trade usage or custom of the trade or by implicit agreement in the absence of a specific act. These issues are mainly covered by national laws and the role and enforceability of trade usages may be subject to the status given by the applicable law.[77] In some cases it may be difficult to establish which national law covers the creation and perfection of a security interest in movable property since in international trade the goods and the documents keep crossing national borders in the ordinary course of things.[78] Under the majority of conflict-of-laws rules, movable property

---

[75] See Dolan in *The Law of Letters of Credit* at 8-17 – 8-18.

[76] Dolan writes in *The Law of Letters of Credit* at 8-25:
"In many cases, the credit will call for nonnegotiable documents of title, and the issuing bank must then perfect its security interest under Section 9-304(3), which covers perfection of security interests in goods not subject to a negotiable document. That provision sets out three ways to perfect the security interest: (1) causing the nonnegotiable document to be issued in the bank's name; (2) notifying the carrier of the bank's security interest; or (3) filing a financing statement describing the goods. In no event can the holder of a nonnegotiable document of title look to Section 9-309 for protection. A holder of a nonnegotiable document cannot rise to the level of a qualified holder who must hold a negotiable document."

[77] Carlo Lombardini, *Switzerland: Letters of Credit - Letters of Indemnity*, Case Comment, J Int'l Busn L (1997) 12(1), N12-13:
"In the opinion of the courts, it was obvious that if Bank Y had insisted that the bills of lading be made payable to its order, it meant to retain control over the merchandise, the purchase of which it was financing, either by a lien or by obtaining ownership of the goods. It was obvious to all the parties, including C, that Bank Y intended, in case of need, to be able to seize the wheat. By issuing l.o.i.s without informing Bank Y, C was preventing it from taking possession of the wheat and was thus responsible for the damage suffered by Bank Y."

[78] Compare to UNC Article 30:

(chattel) is governed by the law of the place where it is located and, as a consequence, the property may be subject to different local laws when moving from hand to hand in a transaction. In addition, there may be several creditors claiming a security interest in the same goods and in the same documents and their internal priority may become a complex issue to be resolved, even in the absence of a bankruptcy in the network of players.

One could perhaps support the idea of a security interest being created in the documents in favor of the paying bank or issuing bank by mere possession and payment even in the absence of express agreement.[79] When honoring the instrument and making payment, the bank gains possession of the documents and, simultaneously, as a main rule, acquires the right to reimbursement against the account party, often the assignee or purchaser of the goods. This may create *a right* and even *a duty* to the payor to sell the goods for and on behalf of the account party and to setoff the proceeds against the right of reimbursement in the event of the account party failing to reimburse the payor. The proceeds of such sale can either be used to set off the debt, by right created under the applicable law and/or by that created under the indemnity agreement.

In addition to the indemnity agreement and the security perhaps provided thereunder, the document may serve as a secondary security in favor of the payor. One may arrive at the same conclusion by way of applying the doctrine of subrogation if it is applicable. By payment to the beneficiary or by payment to the payor by the issuer, the payor is subrogated to the right of the beneficiary

---

"1. The law of the State in which the assignor is located governs the priority of the right of an assignee in the assigned receivable over the right of a competing claimant. 2. The rules of the law of either the forum State or any other State that are mandatory irrespective of the law otherwise applicable may not prevent the application of a provision of the law of the State in which the assignor is located. 3. Notwithstanding paragraph 2 of this article, in an insolvency proceeding commenced in a State other than the State in which the assignor is located, any preferential right that arises, by operation of law, under the law of the forum State and is given priority over the rights of an assignee in insolvency proceedings under the law of that State may be given priority notwithstanding paragraph 1 of this article."

[79] Dolan writes in *The Law of Letters of Credit* at 8-19:
"The mere taking of the bill by due negotiation would be sufficient to give the issuer a security interest. The careful issuer, nevertheless, usually provides in the credit application for security agreement language giving the issuer a security interest in both the document of title and the goods covered by it."

CHAPTER I

to receive payment for "the goods", and the goods, which are in his possession represented by the documents, may be sold for the account of the account party or purchaser should the latter refuse or fail to make the required payment, i.e., reimbursement. In any case the possession gives the bank a strong position *de facto* if not also *de jure*. Most of the discussion above has hardly any relevance at all to standby credits or on-demand type of guarantees. Under those substantively independent instruments, the claim, the documents or the tender required to meet the conditions precedent have in general no commercial or other value and cannot be sold at a market.

The UCC addresses both the issue of the creation of a security interest and its perfection. The UCC is a national (U.S.) statute and does not reflect lex mercatoria or international trade usage as such in this respect. The security interest covers both the documents presented and the proceeds of the collateral, provided that the tender is accepted and payment made. A security agreement is not necessary and the security interest may create priority rights over conflicting interests in the document.

UCC 5-118:

> "(a) An issuer or nominated person has a security interest in a document presented under a letter of credit and any identifiable proceeds of the collateral to the extent that the issuer or nominated person honors or gives value for the presentation. (b) Subject to subsection (a), as long as and to the extent that an issuer or nominated person has not been reimbursed or has not otherwise recovered the value given with respect to a security interest in a document under subsection (a), the security interest continues and *is* subject to Article 9, but:
> (1) a security agreement is not necessary to make the security interest enforceable under Section 9-203(b)(3);
> (2) if the document is presented in a medium other than a written or other tangible medium, the security interest is perfected; and
> (3) if the document is presented in a written or other tangible medium and is not a certificated security, chattel paper, a document of title, an instrument, or a letter of credit, so long as the debtor does not have possession of the document, the security interest is perfected and has priority over a conflicting security interest in the document."

There are national statutes which entitle the payor to sell the goods should the account party fail to meet his reimbursement obligations as if the goods had been pledged as a security:

The statue of Bahrain (DCL) Art 327 provides:

> "If the applicant does not pay to the bank the value of the consignment documents according to the terms of the credit within three months running from the date of notification to the applicant that the documents have been presented, the bank may sell the goods in accordance with the execution proceedings applicable to commercially pledged property."

Egypt's statute (DCL) 350 says:

> "If the applicant does not reimburse the bank for the value of the documents conforming to the credit's conditions within six months from the date of notification that the documents were received, the bank may execute the goods according to the procedures of execution of commercially pledged objects."

In contrast to the somewhat laconic provisions in the countries referred to above, in the UAE the laws deal with the issue with more detail and sophistication. The provisions protect the bank and reduce its exposure to credit risk as to the account party in many respects:

The UAE statute, (DCL) Art 439 provides:

> "1. The applicant shall reimburse the bank for any amounts paid to the beneficiary according to the terms of the credit and compensate all expenses that have been incurred by the bank.
> 2. The bank shall be *entitled to foreclose* the documents that it received from the seller and to obtain a pledge over the goods that are represented by the documents as collateral for the bank's claims.
> 3. If the applicant fails to pay the bank the value of the transport documents that are in compliance with the credit within one month running from the date of the notification that such documents have been presented, *the bank is entitled to sell the goods* according to the provisions applicable to the execution of commercially pledged property.

4. If the goods have perished or been damaged *the pledge shall apply to any amounts held in deposit*.

5. After presentation of the documents the bank and its customer may agree that the customer transfers the goods that are subject to the credit in whole or in part to the bank as total or partial settlement of the customer's debt to the bank. The bank shall then authorize the customer to receive the goods and *hold them in trust* and sell them on behalf and for the account of the bank, at the terms and conditions agreed on between the parties. The customer shall be responsible as a commission agent and the bank shall have the rights of a trustee of the goods or their value."

I.15 Disclaimers

Since World War II, a huge expansion has taken place in the use of exemption clauses or disclaimers. The rules of *Hadley v. Baxendale* (1854) and the foreseeability element, in particular, may, indeed, expand the scope of potential liability in the event of breach to amounts which may put a party's business or existence in jeopardy or at least seriously damage its business prospects or reduce its profits. On the other hand, limitation of liability by dominant players in the market may equally cause considerable problems to those dependent on transacting business with them. This development has been one of the most serious threats to fair trade, causing problems in contracting. The disclaiming of liability has spread from shipping and transportation to practically every market and industry. The legislatures have taken some countermeasures by way of statutes which set forth a minimum or a fixed liability which cannot be excluded by contract, or by introducing general provisions allowing court intervention if the terms and conditions prove to be unreasonably harsh or unconscionable. The courts have responded with equitable remedies or by applying new statutes, broadening the powers of the courts to deviate from the *pacta sunt servanda* principle and to disregard disclaimers altogether in the event of gross negligence or deliberate acts.

Unidroit 7.1.6 tells us:

"A clause which limits or excludes one party's liability for non-performance or which permits one party to render performance substantially different from what the other party reasonably expected may not be invoked if it would be grossly unfair to do so, having regard to the purpose of the contract."

There are a number of disclaimers in UCP. Some of them serve a useful purpose in ordinary circumstances.[80] Sometimes they should not be understood or interpreted literally. They do not necessarily mean what they state, as if the words "in the absence of negligence" had been omitted by negligence.[81] Some of them are natural in the context of services agreements: there is no liability for a specific result, but a liability for services and their performance according to good banking standards (*culpa*/negligence-based liability). From the policy point of view, the applicant should bear certain risks and costs instead of banks. To do otherwise might allocate risks to the banks which they are not in the best position to carry, or expose the banks to liability which would then be reflected in increased costs and reduced expediency in clearing these instruments.[82]

---

[80] UCP 600 Article 34:
"A bank assumes no liability or responsibility for the form, sufficiency, accuracy, genuineness, falsification or legal effect of any document or for the general or particular conditions stipulated in a document or superimposed thereon; nor does it assume any liability or responsibility for the description, quantity, weight, quality, condition, packing, delivery, value or existence of the goods, services or other performance represented by any document or for the good faith or acts or omissions, solvency, performance or standing of the consignor, the carrier, the forwarder, the consignee or the insurer of the goods or any other person."

[81] ICC Decisions (1975-1979) of the ICC Banking Commission, R 17, p. 30:
"The Commission stated that Article 12 established a principle according to which the issuing bank was exonerated from all liability for the errors of the advising bank – whether this bank had been chosen by the issuing bank or by the credit-applicant – but that this immunity did not apply where the issuing bank had been guilty of negligence."

[82] UCP 600 Article 35-37:
"*Article 35 Disclaimer on Transmission and Translation* A bank assumes no liability or responsibility for the consequences arising out of delay, loss in transit, mutilation or other errors arising in the transmission of any messages or delivery of letters or documents when such messages letters or documents are transmitted or sent according to the requirements stated in the credit, or when the bank may have taken the initiative in the choice of the delivery service in the absence of such instructions in the credit. If a nominated bank determines that a presentation is complying and forwards the documents to the issuing bank or confirming bank, whether or not the nominated bank has honoured or negotiated, an issuing bank or confirming bank must honour or negotiate, or reimburse that nominated bank, even when the documents have been lost in transit between the nominated bank and the issuing bank or confirming bank, or between the confirming bank and the issuing bank. A bank assumes no liability or responsibility for errors in translation or interpretation of technical terms and may transmit credit terms without translating them.

Article 36 Force Majeure A bank assumes no liability or responsibility for the consequences arising out of the interruption of its business by Acts of God, riots, civil commotions, insurrections, wars, acts of terrorism, or by any strikes or lockouts or any other causes beyond its control. A bank will not, upon resumption of its business, honour or negotiate under a credit that expired during such interruption of its business.

CHAPTER I

There are often similar or even wider disclaimers in indemnity agreements. The *Credit Agricole* case, *infra*, deals with the issues of interpreting and understanding disclaimers in UCP and indemnity agreements and the liability of the examiner for the end result: discrepant documents. The disclaimers could be read to eliminate or exclude all liability except acts or omissions done in bad faith.

Disclaimers under the Credit Agricole case:

> "INDEMNITY It was [defendant bank] Generale's case that even if the documents were discrepant, nonetheless *it was entitled to reimbursement by Seco/Considar*. First, reliance was placed on cl. 5 of the letter of credit agreement which ends with this sentence: Borrower further agrees that *any action, inaction or omission* by the Bank or any of Bank's correspondence under or in connection with any credit or documents *if done in good faith*, shall be binding on borrower and shall not put Bank or Bank's correspondence under any liability to borrower.
>
> Leaving aside the fact that Seco were not parties to that agreement, the reliance placed on the apparent broad scope of this provision by Generale wholly ignores its context in both the narrow and the broad sense. In the narrow sense, the overall thrust of cl. 5 was to excuse the bank from liability arising from the underlying transaction. By the same token the bank's activities qua bank are not to expose it to liability to the borrower. These provisions are not material on the face of it to the right of reimbursement or otherwise in the event of rejection of the documents by the bank. The broader context was *the express incorporation of UCP by virtue of cl. 12 of the agreement*. The contract has to be construed, if possible, in a manner consistent with UCP and the banker's duty of strict compliance: see *Forestal Mimosa Ltd. v. Oriental Credit Ltd., [1986] 1 Lloyd's Rep. 329; [1986] 1 W.L.R. 631.* To that end the provisions of cl. 5 are comfortably consistent to the construction urged by Seco/Considar.
>
> In the alternative, Generale relied upon art. 18(a) of UCP: Banks utilising the services of another bank or other banks for the purpose of giving effect

---

Article 37 Disclaimer for Acts of an Instructed Party a. A bank utilizing the services of another bank for the purpose of giving effect to the instructions of the applicant does so for the account and at the risk of the applicant b. An issuing bank or advising bank assumes no liability or responsibility should the instructions it transmits to another bank not be carried out, even if it has taken the initiative in the choice of that other bank."

to the instructions of the applicant *do so for the account and at the risk of such applicant*. It was Generale's case that the effect of art. 18(a) was that, if the documents were discrepant, *then Indosuez's acceptance of them was at the risk of Seco/Considar*. This approach received some support from a passage in Benjamin, Sale of Goods, 5th ed., par. 23-158. I unhesitatingly prefer the contrary view expressed in Jack, Documentary Credit, 2nd ed., par. 4.18 to the effect that *art. 18 does not require an applicant to accept and pay for documents which do not comply with his instructions*. The sole effect of art. 18 is to prevent an applicant holding an issuing bank liable for damage caused to the applicant by the action of the bank instructed by the issuing bank. Any other construction would, to put it at its lowest, be surprising in that it would be relieving the issuing bank of any need to determine compliance pursuant to art. 14 of the UCP."[83]

Where does the borderline between an acceptable disclaimer and a non-acceptable disclaimer belong? In general, liability for gross negligence or for willful acts cannot be excluded or, if liability is excluded then the disclaimer is unenforceable. Nor can good faith be disclaimed. Under URDG, reasonable care cannot be excluded either, but if this is adopted as a general rule, have we come all the way back to where we started?

URDG 15 says:

> "Guarantors and Instructing Parties shall not be excluded from liability or responsibility under the terms of Articles 11, 12 and 14 above for their failure to act in good faith and with reasonable care."

Disclaimers have been found to be critical, in particular in areas where the sophistication or bargaining power of the parties is not on an equal footing, or where a few players dominate the playground ("joint dominance"). Likewise, industry-wide collaboration or collusion may lead to standardized terms and conditions and, in order to trade, one must accept these standard terms or not trade at all. Restraints on competition often have very harmful effects, not just perhaps in an individual transaction, or on the business of those who have no market power, but on industries in the aggregate.

---

[83] *Credit Agricole Indosuez v. Generale Bank & Seco Steel Trading Inc. & Considar Inc.*, Queen's Bench Division (Commercial Court) Sept. 30, 1999.

Chapter I

Some of this may have some relevance with respect to the instruments at hand. As to some instruments like, e.g., commercial credits, the terms and conditions are practically read the same no matter where or with whom one is dealing. With respect to other instruments, a similar development is already in progress or may be anticipated: law merchant is making progress. On the other hand, these standardized rules contain a number of far-reaching disclaimers and exemption clauses and, in addition, their contents and development have taken place under a strong influence of the international banking community and other financial institutions in close collaboration. Might we be dealing with industry-wide restraints of trade?

What would then be a balanced approach? Should one expand the liability and force the financial industry to carry the risks on a larger scale? What would the outcome be? The fees would increase dramatically and the whole process would, instead of being expeditious, be weighted down and plagued by caution. Would anybody win? I do not think so. The other parties to the transaction should carry the risks and are often in a better position to assess them. They can have the risks insured, or take other actions as a guard against them.

What about *collusive elements*? This competition-law concern is a tougher nut to crack. On the one hand, there are no direct price-fixing issues. Law merchant is not about pricing. The concern about potential for collusion can perhaps be answered by way of a question: is there a better alternative or a less harmful alternative? It may be hard to figure out. The safe and sound alternative is the court system. Courts are used to providing protective measures. They are used to ruling out unreasonable or unconscionable behavior. The principle that gross negligence and a deliberate (willful) act nullifies or renders unenforceable all disclaimers is a well-established and effective measure. On balance, the risks of introducing something revolutionary may well outweigh the benefits those changes might bring; in fact, the risks might outweigh the benefits by an overwhelming margin: if it works, don't fix it. If the instrument is found to be non-acceptable, new and better products will be developed. There will, however, always be room for instruments which give you a 99.9% certainty of what you are getting, which is far preferable to a bagful of court rulings. When it comes to interbank relationships the above concerns do not appear well-founded.

One should in particular note that law merchant is similar to law as to its function. Why would uniform laws be harmful? Is the policy and common belief not the contrary?

Simple disclaimers in standardized conditions

The URDG disclaims liability for matters which do not catch the eye in the examination of documents and their legal effects. The first part of the clause resembles disclaimers in legal opinions: the examiner or the opiner cannot and need not investigate whether the submission is genuine, etc. But whereas legal opinions are meant to cover the legal effects, the URDG disclaimer excludes that liability also. Nor do the banks assume liability for the substantive statements made therein or for the good faith of anyone else, i.e., fraud or dishonesty. This disclaimer is to a great extent compatible with the "on their face" criterion and as such not objectionable. If, however, these discrepancies are apparent, the disclaimer may be unenforceable.

URDG Art 11:

> "Guarantors and Instructing Parties *assume no liability or responsibility* for the form, sufficiency, accuracy, genuineness, falsification, or legal effect of any document presented to them or for the general and/or particular statements made therein, nor for the good faith or acts or omissions of any person whomsoever."

URDG Art 12 disclaims liability for delay or errors in communications. The same applies to translations. To the extent banks and instructing parties utilize their own communication system and personnel, the disclaimer may be too far-reaching whereas in cases where the errors occur in using public or outside services which are of recognized quality, and in particular, if there is no negligence on the part of the banks, the disclaimer appears fully plausible. Translations and their correctness or accuracy are often totally beyond the competence of the examiner and in this case the disclaimer is wholly warranted.

URDG Art 12:

> "Guarantors and Instructing Parties *assume no liability or responsibility* for the consequences arising out of delay and/or loss in transit of any messages, letters, demands or documents, or for delay, mutilation or other errors arising in the transmission of any telecommunication. Guarantors and Instructing Parties assume no liability for errors in translation or interpretation of technical terms and reserve the right to transmit Guarantee texts or any parts thereof without translating them."

CHAPTER I

At first reading, URDG 13 carries all the appearances of a classic *force majeure* clause. Besides listing some of the most common events referred to in *force majeure* clauses like acts of God, and wars, the clause contains the "magic" expression "beyond their control". Even a most sophisticated practitioner may fully underwrite the right of existence of this clause, perhaps with some reservations as to some events or expressions like "of whatever nature". At the same time under some legal systems and their structure of contractual liability, the clause may be superfluous in the sense that it does not really add anything or change anything under the applicable law. If the performance is characterized as a services agreement, the liability is in general based on negligence (*culpa*) and the performer of the services may always exculpate himself and, as a consequence of successful exculpation, be released from liability by providing that the non-performance was beyond his control, i.e., not due to his acts or omissions or negligence (*culpa*). Moreover, even this conclusion may be misleading in the light of risk assessment and allocation of risks, since the exculpation, even when successful, may become ineffective as a defence if the banks are deemed to have assumed the risk. The risk may be deemed to have been assumed by a party if it is foreseeable and the party in question and his performance is in the natural course of events directly exposed to that risk and he is in the best position to foresee or avoid or take other measures to reduce or eliminate its effects.

There are thus a great number of complex issues behind the clause which *per se* appears classic and "innocent". These complexities may arise or may not arise depending on the substantive law applicable to the issue of liability and the rules therein relating to the basis for liability, and allocation of risks.

URDG Art 13:

> "Guarantors and Instructing Parties *assume no liability or responsibility* for consequences arising out of the interruption of their business by acts of God, riots, civil commotions, insurrections, wars or any other causes beyond their control or by strikes, lock-outs or industrial actions of whatever nature."

In ISP the disclaimers have been worded differently. The first disclaimer relates to any performance under the transaction. Although the principle is uncontested, it is certainly beneficial to have clarity and no doubt with respect to this issue. It is the other side of the doctrine of independence.

The second disclaimer relates to the genuineness of sufficiency or effect of documents submitted. This disclaimer relates to the nature of these instruments and the application of the strict compliance rule. Banks do not operate as legal or commercial advisers or surveyors; all they do is to check if the documents as presented comply with the conditions precedent. If, however, the documents presented are not merely suspicious but apparently forged or fraudulent, the banks may not enjoy the protection contemplated under this disclaimer. Gross negligence, willful acts and bad faith may be exceptions to any disclaimers.

The third exemption clause disclaims liability for acts or omissions of others even when they have been chosen or retained by the bank ("*culpa in eligendo*"). Liability may arise in gross negligence in the choice or control of those others. What is discussed above applies here, too. Here, in particular, the assessment of liability may relate to various types of situations. The other person may have been chosen or recommended by the bank or by the customer of the bank. The other person may have been (i) retained by the bank on its own behalf or (ii) for and on behalf of the customer only or (iii) both. In these cases different structures may be formed. Figure I.10 here illustrates the situations.

In the latter case there may be a three-party agreement or three separate agreements or a combination of those.

The last exemption clause relates to liability or effects of laws other than the law chosen in the instrument or the law applicable in the place of issuance of the bank. It is a sound basic rule that the bank involved must assume liability for compliance with the law applicable to its own operations at the place of issuance of the instrument. The same applies, but to a lesser extent, to the law chosen by the parties to the instrument (including of course the bank itself), even when the law chosen is foreign to the bank. The foreign law is then an agreed and known risk and liability and its rules and substance may be investigated in advance by the bank to the extent deemed necessary or, e.g., by requesting a legal opinion. In international banking this is a standard procedure in major financing.

As to other laws which may apply, it is natural to place the "burden of education" on the parties, because they are better equipped and perhaps already experienced and educated in these respects. There would be little or no point in imposing on the banks a role of "multinational research centers in law" although over the years a data bank of information may accumulate at the offices or be acquired by executives. Even in such cases, the data is neither consistently updated or verified, and

CHAPTER I

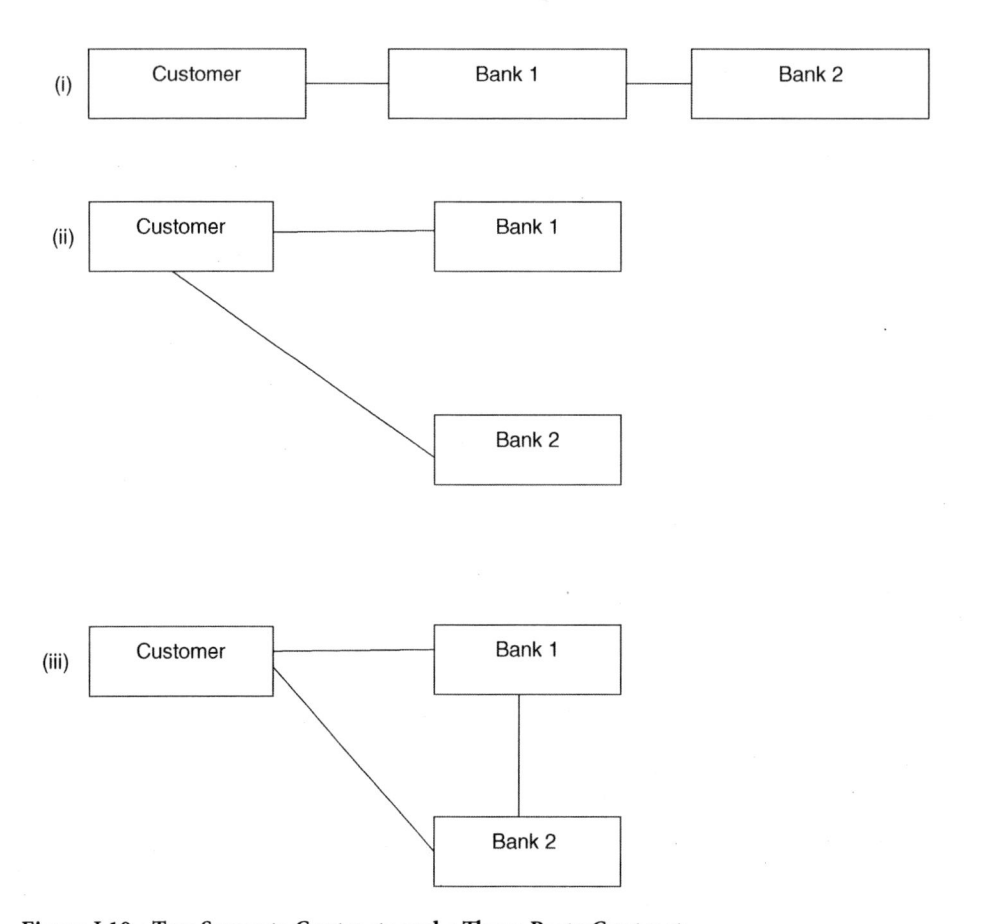

Figure I.10. Two Separate Contracts and a Three-Party Contract

it is not usually recorded or organized in a professional manner, such operations being clearly beyond the business of banking.

ISP 1.08:

> "An issuer is *not responsible* for:
> a. performance or breach of any underlying transaction;
> b. accuracy, genuineness, or effect of any document presented under the standby;
> c. action or omission of others even if the other person is chosen by the issuer or nominated person; or

d. observance of law or practice other than that chosen in the standby or applicable at the place of issuance."

The official comments of the UCC reflect some of these concerns highlighted in this work. The revised text reflects, on the one hand, the sophistication of the hierarchy of rules. The revised UCC no longer permits categoric contracting out: certain parts of the UCC are "hard core" and will apply despite the parties' express choice of another law, UCP or other sets of rules. To the extent that the UCC and UCP do not conflict, both may apply simultaneously and in parallel.

On the other hand, "the hard core" relates in particular to disclaimers of liability. "Depending upon the circumstances" disclaimers, may become unenforceable or "ineffective".

UCC 5-116 (Official Comment) 3:

> "This section does not permit what is now authorized by the nonuniform Section 5-102(4) in New York. Under the current law in New York a letter of credit that incorporates the UCP is not governed in any respect by Article 5. Under revised Section 5-116 letters of credit that incorporate the UCP or similar practice *will still be subject to Article 5 in certain respects*. First, incorporation of the UCP or other practice does not override the nonvariable terms of Article 5. Second, where there is no conflict between Article 5 and the relevant provision of the UCP or other practice, both apply. Third, practice provisions incorporated in a letter of credit will not be effective if they fail to comply with Section 5-103(c) Assume, for example, *that a practice provision purported to free a party from any liability unless it were "grossly negligent" or that the practice generally limited the remedies that one party might have against another. Depending upon the circumstances, that disclaimer or limitation of liability might be ineffective because of Section 5-103(c)*."

Transferability and Subrogation

I.16 Transferability

Letters of credit and bank guarantees and similar instruments are cast in concrete in many respects. In general they are irrevocable, non-amendable and allow no changes in the parties which originally were engaged in it and assumed responsibilities thereunder. In particular this applies to the banks, but also to the beneficiary. As a rule, it is of vital interest and of essence to the account party that the claim or demand is presented by the beneficiary and by no one else. This applies to commercial credits, where the beneficiary needs to submit documents to meet the conditions precedent to receive payment. It applies equally to standby credits and on-demand bonds, where nobody else is entitled to make the claim and "pull the trigger". There is plenty of trust and confidence in play. For the same reason and as an accessory instrument the credit cannot be negotiated or transferred to a third party detached from non-visible conditions: it is not a stand-alone (conditional) receivable or negotiable.[84]

UCC 5-112 official comment:

> "1. In order to protect the applicant's reliance on the designated beneficiary, letter of credit law traditionally has forbidden the beneficiary to convey to third parties its right to draw or demand payment under the letter of credit. Subsection (a) codifies that rule. The term "transfer" refers to the beneficiary's conveyance of that right. Absent incorporation of the UCP (which make elaborate provision for partial transfer of a commercial letter of credit) or similar trade practice and absent other express indication in the letter of credit that the term is used to mean something else, a term in the letter of credit indicating that the beneficiary has the right to transfer should be taken to mean that the beneficiary may convey to a third party its right to draw or demand payment. Even in that case, the issuer or other person controlling the transfer may make the beneficiary's right to transfer subject to conditions, such as timely notification, payment of a fee, delivery of the letter of credit to the issuer or other person controlling the transfer, or execution of appropriate forms to document the transfer. A nominated person who is not a confirmer has no obligation to recognize a transfer."

The substantively independent instruments may, however, be made transferable if all the parties agree to this. A non-independent instrument cannot be made

---

[84] Bertrams, *Bank Guarantees*, at 274-5:
"Genuine standby letters of credit and bank guarantees are on-balance activities and they are only payable in relation to default in a particular underlying transaction. This also explains why genuine instruments are ordinarily not freely negotiable or transferable. As a consequence, a secondary market in these instruments does not and cannot exist. Several government agencies, many banks as well as the ICC have repeatedly warned against these fraudulent schemes."

transferable because the underlying agreement and the instrument are materially inseparable. Both may be transferred together subject to consent of the other parties with or without discharge of the assignor or transferor and, subject to material law, the instrument may follow transfer or assignment of the underlying agreement unamended.

ISP provides as follows in Article 6.02 (a):

"A standby is not transferable unless it so states."

and in UCP 600 Article 38 a-b:

"a. A bank is under no obligation to transfer a credit except to the extent and in the manner expressly consented to by that bank.
b. For the purpose of this article:
Transferable credit means a credit that specifically states it is "transferable". A transferable credit may be made available in whole or in part to another beneficiary ("second beneficiary") at the request of the beneficiary ("first beneficiary").
Transferring bank means a nominated bank that transfers the credit or, in a credit available with any bank, a bank that is specifically authorized by the issuing bank to transfer and that transfers the credit. An issuing bank may be a transferring bank.
Transferred credit means a credit that has been made available by the transferring bank to a second beneficiary."

An instrument may be expressly made transferable as it may be made revocable as provided in Article 6.02 (b) of ISP and in the UCP provision quoted above.

UCC is fully in line with the above but addresses the issue from another perspective and larger coverage. The issuer may refuse the transfer if it violates the applicable law or if any usage of trade or otherwise a reasonable (implicit) condition has not been met:

UCC 5-112:

"(a) Except as otherwise provided in Section 5-113, unless a letter of credit provides that it is transferable, the right of a beneficiary to draw or otherwise demand performance under a letter of credit may not be transferred.

(b) Even if a letter of credit provides that it is transferable, *the issuer may refuse to recognize or carry out a transfer* if:
(1) the transfer *would violate applicable* law; or
(2) the transferor or transferee has failed to comply with any requirement stated in the letter of credit or any other requirement relating to transfer imposed by the issuer which is *within the standard practice* referred to in subsection (e) of Section 5-108 or is *otherwise reasonable* under the circumstances."

A transfer may take place in the event of legal succession or by operation of law. [85]

UCC 5-113:

"Except as otherwise provided in subsection (e) of this section, an issuer shall recognize a disclosed successor of a beneficiary as beneficiary in full substitution for its predecessor upon compliance with the requirements for recognition by the issuer of a transfer of drawing rights by operation of law

---

[85] UCC 5-113:
"(a) A successor of a beneficiary may consent to amendments, sign and present documents, and receive payment or other items of value in the name of the beneficiary without disclosing its status as a successor. (b) A successor of a beneficiary may consent to amendments, sign and present documents, and receive payment or other items of value in its own name as the disclosed successor of the beneficiary. (c) An issuer is not obliged to determine whether a purported successor is a successor of a beneficiary or whether the signature of a purported successor is genuine or authorized. (d) Honor of a purported successor's apparently complying presentation under subsection (a) or (b) of this section has the consequences specified in subsection (i) of Section 5-108 even if the purported successor is not the successor of a beneficiary. Documents signed in the name of the beneficiary or of a disclosed successor by a person who is neither the beneficiary nor the successor of the beneficiary are forged documents for the purposes of Section 5-109. (e) An issuer whose rights of reimbursement are not covered by subsection (d) of this section or substantially similar law and any confirmer or nominated person may decline to recognize a presentation under subsection (b) of this section. (f) A beneficiary whose name is changed after the issuance of a letter of credit has the same rights and obligations as a successor of a beneficiary under this section."

Transfer by operation of law: UCC 5-102 (official comment):
"10. Although a successor of a beneficiary is one who succeeds "by operation of law", some of the successions contemplated by Section 5-102(a)(15) will have resulted from voluntary action of the beneficiary such as merger of a corporation. Any merger makes the successor corporation the "successor of a beneficiary" even though the transfer occurs partly by operation of law and partly by the voluntary action of the parties. The definition excludes certain transfers, where no part of the transfer is "by operation of law" - such as the sale of assets by one company to another."

under the standard practice referred to in subsection (e) of Section 5-108 or, in the absence of such a practice, compliance with other reasonable procedures sufficient to protect the issuer."

This applies in particular to mergers or liquidations of a corporation.

UNC covers the same issue in a like manner in more generic terms avoiding any "trespassing" into areas traditionally left for coverage by national laws.

UNC Art 9 provides:

> "(1) The beneficiary's right to demand payment may be transferred only if authorized in the undertaking, and only to the extent and in the manner authorized in the undertaking. (2) If an undertaking is designated as transferable without specifying whether or not the consent of the guarantor/issuer or another authorized person is required for the actual transfer, neither the guarantor/issuer nor any other authorized person is obliged to effect the transfer except to the extent and in the manner expressly consented to by it."

I.17 No "Bearer" Rights

These instruments are not bearer instruments and the possession of a guarantee or a letter of credit does not serve any other than evidentiary purposes.

Once the instrument has expired, the bearer or holder of the instrument does not have any rights thereunder. After expiry, no holder in due course may be constituted under any circumstances. These instruments are not bearer instruments and are in general not assignable or transferable although the proceeds may be assigned. [86]

---

[86] URCB Art. 4(d):
"A Bond shall terminate and, without prejudice to any term, provision, agreement or stipulation of the Bond, any other agreement or the Applicable Law providing for earlier release or discharge, the liability of the Guarantor shall be discharged absolutely and the Guarantor shall be released upon the Expiry Date whether or not the Bond shall be returned to the Guarantor, save in respect of any claim served in accordance with Article 7."

CHAPTER I

URDG Art 24

> "Where a Guarantee has terminated by payment, expiry, cancellation or otherwise, retention of the Guarantee or of any amendments thereto shall not preserve any rights of the Beneficiary under the Guarantee."

In general, return of the instrument, although often stated in the document, is not required to take place for the instrument to expire by payment or at the expiry date. UNC also deals with expiry by release by the beneficiary, agreement on termination and payment. In addition, it deals with automatic extension clauses, which are exceptions to expiry by payment rule.

UNC Art 11 (1):

> "(1) The right of the beneficiary to demand payment under the undertaking ceases when:
> (a) The guarantor/issuer has received a statement by the beneficiary of *release from liability* in a form referred to in paragraph (2) of article 7;
> (b) The beneficiary and the guarantor/issuer have agreed on the *termination of the undertaking* in the form stipulated in the undertaking or, failing such stipulation, in a form referred to in paragraph (2) of article 7;
> (c) The amount available under the *undertaking has been paid, unless the undertaking provides for the automatic renewal or for an automatic increase of the amount available or otherwise provides for continuation of the undertaking*;
> (d) *The validity period of the undertaking expires* in accordance with the provisions of article 12."

UNC Art 11 (2):

> "The undertaking may stipulate, or the guarantor/issuer and the beneficiary may agree elsewhere, that
> *return of the document embodying* the undertaking to the guarantor/issuer, or a procedure functionally equivalent to the return of the document in the case of the issuance of the undertaking in non-paper form, *is required for the cessation of the right to demand payment*, either alone or in conjunction

with one of the events referred to in subparagraphs (a) and (b) of paragraph (1) of this article. *However, in no case shall retention of any such document by the beneficiary after the right to demand payment ceases in accordance with subparagraph (c) or (d) of paragraph (1) of this article preserve any rights of the beneficiary under the undertaking."*

However, under drafts drawn and accepted by the issuer or confirming bank prior to the expiry of the instrument, a holder in due course may be constituted even after expiry.[87] These instruments are and remain independent from the letter of credit under which they were drawn.

I.18 Assignability

As a main rule, rights are assignable, e.g., receivables, claims and rights under contracts whereas obligations or duties are not. When rights are assigned, the assignee shall not in general have wider or better rights than the assignor had: the rights remain to be subject to the same conditions and defences. By assignment one cannot detach the right from the terms and conditions of the underlying agreement. Traditional guarantees, bonds and other substantively dependent instruments thus remain part of the transaction; one cannot separate one from the other or cut the links of interdependence between the two. However, the right to the funds under the instruments may be assigned. For example, if there is a right to funds or other performance, this may be paid to the assignee subject to the defences of the original obligor.

In exceptional circumstances certain rights may be assigned or transferred (via negotiable instrument) so that the assignee receives the right "as it is" on the face thereof free from any other defences or conditions (except those known to the assignee or transferee (i.e., in situations where there is bad faith)).

---

[87] UCC 5-109 (a) (1):
"the issuer shall honor the presentation, if honor is demanded by: (i) a nominated person who given value in good faith and without notice of forgery or material fraud, (ii) a confirmer who has honored its confirmation in good faith, (iii) a holder in due course of a draft drawn under the letter of credit which was taken after acceptance by the issuer or nominated person, or (iv) an assignee of the issuer's or nominated person's deferred obligation that was taken for value and without notice of forgery or material fraud after the obligation was incurred by the issuer or nominated person."

Chapter I

Assignment, as opposed to transfer, does not replace the original beneficiary by a new party.[88]

UCC 5-113 (official comment):

> ""Transfer" of a letter of credit should be distinguished from "assignment of proceeds." The former is analogous to a novation or a substitution of beneficiaries. It contemplates not merely payment to but also performance by the transferee. For example, under the typical terms of transfer for a commercial letter of credit, a transferee could comply with a letter of credit transferred to it by signing and presenting its own draft and invoice. An assignee of proceeds, on the other hand, is wholly dependent on the presentation of a draft and invoice signed by the beneficiary."

When rights are assigned, the original beneficiary remains in its original legal position and the payment continues to be subject to same conditions precedent including applicable law and jurisdiction clauses but the demand or claim may be made by the assignee.

---

[88] UNC Article 2:
"*Assignment of receivables* For the purposes of this Convention: (*a*) "Assignment" means the transfer by agreement from one person ("assignor") to another person ("assignee") of all or part of or an undivided interest in the assignor's contractual right to payment of a monetary sum ("receivable") from a third person ("the debtor"). The creation of rights in receivables as security for indebtedness or other obligation is deemed to be a transfer; (*b*) In the case of an assignment by the initial or any other assignee ("subsequent assignment"), the person who makes that assignment is the assignor and the person to whom that assignment is made is the assignee."

Unidroit Art. 9.1.1:
"Assignment of a right" means the transfer by agreement from one person (the "assignor") to another person (the "assignee"), including transfer by way of security, of the assignor's right to payment of a monetary sum or other performance from a third person ("the obligor")."

Art. 9.1.2:
"This Section does not apply to transfers made under the special rules governing the transfers: (a) of instruments such as negotiable instruments, documents of title or financial instruments, or (b) of rights in the course of transferring a business."; Art. 9.1.13: "(1) The obligor may assert against the assignee all defences that the obligor could assert against the assignor. (2) The obligor may exercise against the assignee any right of set-off available to the obligor against the assignor up to the time notice of assignment was received."

and Art 9.1.14:
"The assignment of a right transfers to the assignee: (a) all the assignor's rights to payment or other performance under the contract in respect of the right assigned, and (b) all rights securing performance of the right assigned."

UNC Article 15:

> "*Principle of debtor protection* 1. Except as otherwise provided in this Convention, an assignment does not, without the consent of the debtor, affect the rights and obligations of the debtor, including the payment terms contained in the original contract. 2. A payment instruction may change the person, address or account to which the debtor is required to make payment, but may not change: (*a*) The currency of payment specified in the original contract; or (*b*) The State specified in the original contract in which payment is to be made to a State other than that in which the debtor is located."[89]

Under substantively independent instruments, only the original beneficiary may make the claim or demand. The tender of documents may be made by him only. This is due to the fact that the right to "pull the trigger" is highly personal and no one else can be vested with that right.

UCP 600 Article 39:

> "The fact that a credit is not stated to be transferable shall not affect the right of the beneficiary to assign any proceeds to which it may be or may

---

[89] UNC Article 18:
"*Defences and rights of set-off of the debtor* 1. In a claim by the assignee against the debtor for payment of the assigned receivable, the debtor may raise against the assignee all defences and rights of setoff arising from the original contract, or any other contract that was part of the same transaction, of which the debtor could avail itself as if the assignment had not been made and such claim were made by the assignor. 2. The debtor may raise against the assignee any other right of set-off, provided that it was available to the debtor at the time notification of the assignment was received by the debtor. 3. Notwithstanding paragraphs 1 and 2 of this article, defences and rights of set-off that the debtor may raise pursuant to article 9 or 10 against the assignor for breach of an agreement limiting in any way the assignor's right to make the assignment are not available to the debtor against the assignee."

Bertrams, *Bank Guarantees*, writes at 107:
"As a general rule the beneficiary can assign his rights pursuant to the guarantee to a third party, with or without a specific stipulation to this effect. This rule is also endorsed in Art. 4 URDG, Rule 6.06 ISP98 and Art. 10 UNCITRAL Convention. It is expressly noted that assignment of the rights of the guarantee means assignment of the proceeds only, and that the assignee cannot call the guarantee without the cooperation of the beneficiary. This only differs if the guarantee contains explicit provisions to the contrary. Such a stipulation would be extremely dangerous for the account party, since it virtually turns the guarantee into a negotiable instrument and the risk of a call, including a fraudulent call, will increase significantly."

Chapter I

become entitled under the credit, in accordance with the provisions of applicable law. This article relates only to the assignment of proceeds and not to the assignment of the right to perform under the credit."

Assignment of proceeds constitutes a new party to the relationship, who is entitled to receive the payment or funds under the instrument *after a conforming tender by the original beneficiary* or claim or demand made by him or by the assignee if this is permissible under the instrument as is the case under substantively dependent instruments. Apart from this, the assignee has no right to claim payment from the guarantor or issuer and no legal position under the contractual network or the instrument except that payment shall be effected to the assignee by the original obligor.

Assignment of Proceeds under UCC 5-114

The right to proceeds may be assigned under UCC subject to the issuer's consent, which shall not be unreasonably withheld.

> "(a) In this section, "proceeds of a letter of credit" means the cash, check, accepted draft, or other item of value paid or delivered upon honor or giving of value by the issuer or any nominated person under the letter of credit. The term does not include a beneficiary's drawing rights or documents presented by the beneficiary.
> (b) *A beneficiary may assign its right to part or all of the proceeds of a letter of credit.* The beneficiary may do so before presentation as a present assignment of its right to receive proceeds contingent upon its compliance with the terms and conditions of the letter of credit.
> (c) An issuer or nominated person need not recognize an assignment of proceeds of a letter of credit until it consents to the assignment.
> (d) An issuer or nominated person has no obligation to give or withhold its consent to an assignment of proceeds of a letter of credit, but *consent may not be unreasonably* withheld if the assignee possesses and exhibits the letter of credit and presentation of the letter of credit is a condition to honor.

The rights transferred, if the instrument is transferable, cause the original beneficiary to be replaced by the transferee. The claim may be made or the tender submitted by the new beneficiary but the instrument remains naturally subject to unamended conditions precedent as originally agreed. A transfer does not require the issuer's consent; this was already given when the transferable instrument was issued by him. Transfer establishes rights superior to assignment. Neither assignment nor transfer operates as such as a security, or amounts to perfection of a security interest.

> "(e) Rights of a transferee beneficiary or nominated person are independent of the beneficiary's assignment of the proceeds of a letter of credit and *are superior to the assignee's right to the proceeds.*
> (f) Neither the rights recognized by this section between an assignee and an issuer, transferee beneficiary, or nominated person nor the issuer's or nominated person's payment of proceeds to an assignee or a third person affect the rights between the assignee and any person other than the issuer, transferee beneficiary, or nominated person. The mode of creating and perfecting a security interest in or granting an assignment of a beneficiary's rights to proceeds is governed by article 9 or other law. Against persons other than the issuer, transferee beneficiary, or nominated person, the rights and obligations arising upon, the creation of a security interest or other assignment of a beneficiary's right to proceeds and its perfection are governed by article 9 or other law."

Under UNC proceeds are assignable unless otherwise agreed. The words "to which he may be or may become entitled" indicate the conditional character of the rights assigned. Should an assignment take place and be notified to the original obligor, the latter is released from his obligation by payment to the assignee so notified.

UNC Art 10 provides:

> "(1) *Unless otherwise stipulated* in the undertaking or elsewhere agreed by the guarantor/issuer and the beneficiary, the beneficiary may assign to another person any proceeds to which it may be, or may become, entitled under the undertaking. (2) If the guarantor/issuer or another person obliged to effect payment has received a notice originating from the beneficiary, in a form referred to in paragraph (2) of article 7, of the beneficiary's irrevocable assignment, payment to the assignee discharges the obligor, to the extent of its payment, from its liability under the undertaking."[90]

---

[90] Bahrain Art 326:

I.19 Subrogation

I.19.1 General

After the moment of death of the instrument the clearing of the rights and obligations created to establish the facility will begin ("the domino effect"). The main and immediate consequence is the arising of the payor's right to reimbursement. The payor under a credit facility or guarantor is entitled to recover from the issuing entity and/or the account party his fee and costs and the amount of the payment effected under the indemnity agreement.

If the dominos keep falling as agreed and contemplated, there is no problem, and this is the case in the overwhelming majority of transactions. However, should the account party or another party in the network or facility fail to meet his reimbursement duty or be prevented from doing it as a consequence of court order (injunction), bankruptcy, reorganization or insolvency, the legal position of the payor in this new situation of increased risk to credit loss may be unclear in many respects, in particular in the absence of a clear and watertight security arrangement. In the everyday flow of banking, exchange and trade, such

---

"The documentary credit may not be assigned in part or in whole unless the issuing bank is authorized by the applicant to make payment on the credit in accordance with the applicant's instructions in part or in full to one or several third parties. The credit may not be assigned unless the concerned bank agrees to the assignment. The credit may be assigned only once unless otherwise agreed upon."

UCC 5-107 (official comment):
"In general the right of a recognized transferee beneficiary cannot be altered without the transferee's consent, but the same is not true of the rights of assignees of proceeds from the beneficiary. When the beneficiary makes a complete transfer of its interest that is effective under the terms for transfer established by the issuer, adviser, or other party controlling transfers, the beneficiary no longer has an interest in the letter of credit, and the transferee steps into the shoes of the beneficiary as the one with rights under the letter of credit. Section 5-102(a)(3). When there is a partial transfer, both the original beneficiary and the transferee beneficiary have an interest in performance of the letter of credit and each expects that its rights will not be altered by amendment unless it consents.

The assignee of proceeds under a letter of credit from the beneficiary enjoys no such expectation. Notwithstanding an assignee's notice to the issuer of the assignment of proceeds, the assignee is not a person protected by subsection (b). An assignee of proceeds should understand that its rights can be changed or completely extinguished by amendment or cancellation of the letter of credit. An assignee's claim is precarious, for it depends entirely upon the continued existence of the letter of credit and upon the beneficiary's preparation and presentation of documents that would entitle the beneficiary to honor under Section 5-108."

arrangements are seldom in place since they would increase the transaction costs and slow down the process intolerably. In addition, bankruptcy and reorganization often supersede agreements as part of mandatory law.

When things have develop in a way not contemplated or expected the right to subrogation along with set-off or security or title to document may arise. These issues are covered by national laws and, in particular bankruptcy and related proceedings governed by mandatory law, and they are are often a part of the *ordre public* of the jurisdiction in question.

The payor, since he paid a "debt" of another person for and on behalf of the account party, *may*, subject to the applicable law, be subrogated into the rights of the payee against the account party as well as to the right of the issuing entity or the account party including the rights to security given.[91]

Wunnicke, Wunnicke, and Turner write on p. 231:

> "The effect of subrogation is that the subrogee "stands in the shoes" of the subrogor. Subrogation is an equitable remedy. . . . The two types of

---

[91] Wunnicke, Wunnicke, and Turner at 86:
"*Subrogation* is a legal doctrine under the laws of suretyship. Subrogation occurs when a surety—such as a guarantor, the issuer of a performance bond, or an insurance company—pays another person it is obligated as a surety to pay and thereby acquires the rights of the payee against a third party. An insurance company, for example, that pays property damage insurance to its insured acquires the rights of the insured against a person who caused the damage."

Philip R Wood, p. 326:
"*Guarantor's right of subrogation* As soon as the guarantor has paid his guarantee in full, he acquires an immediate right to seek reimbursement from the borrower. He can also take over all the securities for the loan and claims against co-guarantors even though the guarantor did not know of the existence of the security or the security was given after the guarantee was entered into. He can claim rateable contribution from co-guarantors. If the liability of the guarantor does not cover the whole claim, the guarantor acquires a proportionate interest in the securities and the claims against the co-guarantors: *Goodwin v Gray* (1874) 22 WR 312.".

Bertrams writes p. 157:
"Just as the surety does, the independent guarantor satisfies both his own debt and the debt of the account party. Independence has no bearing on the issue of subrogation. A significant number of German writers, therefore, correctly advocates the analogous application of the suretyship provisions relating to subrogation. This is also the view under English law. In France, legal writing derives the bank's right to invoke subrogation from two decisions by the French Cour de Cassation."

subrogation are conventional and equitable. *Conventional subrogation* arises through an agreement among the parties. *Equitable subrogation* is a right that does not arise through contract but instead by operation of law."

Dolan writes with respect to US law and UCC and also universally:

"It ought to be abundantly clear that mechanical denial of the subrogation remedy conflicts with the law of equity and yields pernicious results. Thus, courts should not deny equity on the basis of rhetorical analysis. Section 5-117 indorses this view. This Article attempts to show, however, that *mechanically granting the remedy is equally harmful*. In short, whether subrogation should be granted or denied must turn on the equities of a particular case. The illustration of that analysis in the abstract obligation setting makes the case with some clarity. One must admit that the case against subrogation in the abstract obligation context is not all embracing. There will undoubtedly arise cases in which it would be unjust to leave the parties where they have left themselves. The critical point this Article makes is that before they start altering commercial relationships that the parties themselves confected, courts should engage in full unjust enrichment analysis. That analysis is not complete when the court observes that one party has paid money that permits another party to be enriched. Courts must look to the entire transaction; and, when they do, they should not forget that permitting subrogation will damage what has been a successful commercial product: the abstract obligation. When they conduct that analysis, moreover, they are not violating Section 5-117 of Revised Article 5. They are only engaging in traditional subrogation inquiry, a staple of subrogation law that Section 5-117 denies any intention to alter. Finally, this Article attempts to show that *the lesson from the abstract obligation setting has universal application, that courts have been far too generous in according the remedy*, and that the result has been the externalization of costs that guarantors should bear. Usually, though not always, guarantors and issuers that are present at the beginning of the underlying transaction are in a position to protect themselves, while those who appear later are not. The former are poor candidates for the remedy; the latter are prime candidates."[92]

---

[92] John F. Dolan, *A study of subrogation mostly in letter of credit and other abstract obligation transactions*, Mo L Rev, (Fall 1999).

As to the right of subrogation, one may have to draw a distinction as to the obligations of issuer or payor under the instrument, which are similar to or identical with those of the account party under the underlying transaction, and those which are generic, non-specific and abstract in that sense.

It would seem to be justified to set a presumption in favor of subrogation under substantively dependent instruments but a presumption against subrogation under substantively independent ones.[93]

I.19.2 Subrogation and the UCC

The UCC takes a position in favor of subrogation. The right of subrogation arises by force of Section 5-117 as a consequence of payment or reimbursement as if the payor were a secondary obligor under the underlying obligation: this is only national US law and does not even purport to be part of international trade usages but serves as a good example of addressing the issue. One could argue that a favourable position as to the right of subrogation is justified since there is no reason or policy to deny this right. In substantively independent instruments, except commercial letters of credit, identifying the underlying specific obligation and rights to be subrogated may, however, be problematic reducing the plausibility of such an argument.

UCC 5-117 provides:

> "(a) An issuer that honors a beneficiary's presentation is *subrogated to the rights of the beneficiary to the same extent as if the issuer were a secondary obligor of the underlying obligation* owed to the beneficiary and of the applicant to the same extent as if the issuer were the secondary obligor of the underlying obligation owed to the applicant.
> (b) An applicant that reimburses an issuer is subrogated to the rights of the issuer against any beneficiary, presenter, or nominated person to the same extent as if the applicant were the secondary obligor of the

---

[93] Dolan writes in *The Law of Letters of Credit* at 7-55:
"It is difficult to see what issuers would gain in the aggregate by a subrogation theory. They do stand to lose something. Subrogation is a creature of equity, and it has a sibling, the injunction, whose career in letter-of-credit cases suggests that creatures of equity (subrogation and injunction) and creatures of the law merchant (letters of credit) do not mesh well."

CHAPTER I

obligations owed to the issuer and has the rights of subrogation of the issuer to the rights of the beneficiary stated in subsection (a) of this section.
(c) A nominated person who pays or gives value against a draft or demand presented under a letter of credit is subrogated to the rights of:
(1) the issuer against the applicant to the same extent as if the nominated person were a secondary obligor of the obligation owed to the issuer by the applicant;
(2) the beneficiary to the same extent as if the nominated person were a secondary obligor of the underlying obligation owed to the beneficiary; and
(3) the applicant to the same extent as if the nominated person were a secondary obligor of the underlying obligation owed to the applicant. (d) Notwithstanding any agreement or term to the contrary, *the rights of subrogation* stated in subsections (a) and (b) of this section do not arise *until the issuer honors the letter of credit or otherwise pays and the rights* in subsection (c) of this section do not arise until the nominated person pays or otherwise gives value. Until then, the issuer, nominated person, and the applicant do not derive under this section present or prospective rights forming the basis of a claim, defense, or excuse."

I.19.3 The Niru Case – emphasizing two sources for subrogation

The *Niru* case discusses at some length the right of subrogation under English law, emphasizing that there are in principle two kinds of subrogation: one based on agreement, and the other arising by force of law under special circumstances to prevent unjust enrichment. The contractual right of subrogation is very common in the insurance industry and in property law. In some circumstances such a right of the insurer would arise even in the absence of agreement, e.g., if property damage has been caused through unlawful or illegal acts or omissions of a third party.

In *Niru* the unjust enrichment resulted in release of a payment duty. *CAI* was unjustly enriched and the payment of the funds in bad faith did not release it from liability under the doctrine.

"Before considering these particular situations, it is appropriate to refer to what I agree with the judge is the leading modern authority on the equitable remedy of subrogation, namely the Banque Financière case. In that case, as the judge observed in paragraph 29 of his judgment, Lord Hoffman, with whom the majority of the other members of the House agreed, drew a distinction between *contractual subrogation* of the kind most commonly encountered in connection with contracts of insurance and *subrogation in equity*. He pointed out that the former is founded upon the common intention of the parties whereas the latter is an equitable remedy *designed to reverse or prevent unjust enrichment. It does not depend on agreement between the party enriched and the party deprived but upon principles of restitution.* Lord Hoffmann summarised the principles governing the availability of the equitable remedy in the following terms at page 234C-D: "I think it should be recognised that one is here concerned with a restitutionary remedy and that the appropriate questions are therefore, first, whether the defendant would be enriched at the plaintiff's expense; secondly, whether such enrichment would be unjust; and thirdly, whether there are nevertheless reasons of policy for denying a remedy."[94]

"Mr Bloch placed some reliance upon the speech of Lord Diplock in *Orakpo v Manson Investments [1978] AC 95* at page 104 and upon the judgment of Millett LJ in *Boscawen v Bajwa [1996] 1 WLR 328*. In the Orakpo case Lord Diplock said that some rights of subrogation "are in no way based on contract and appear to defeat classification except as an empirical remedy to prevent a particular kind of unjust enrichment. This makes particularly perilous any attempt to rely upon analogy to justify applying one set of circumstances which would otherwise result in unjust enrichment a remedy of subrogation which has been held to be available for that purpose in another and different set of circumstances."

Nothing in the conclusions which I have reached seems to me to be inconsistent with those views. The same is true of the statements of Millett LJ in Boscawen v Bajwa, where he said at page 335: "Subrogation, therefore, is a remedy not a cause of action . . . *It is available in a wide variety of different factual situations in which it is required in order to reverse the defendant's unjust enrichment.* Equity lawyers speak of a right of subrogation or of an equity of subrogation, but this merely reflects the fact that it is not a remedy

---

[94] Niru Battery Manf'g Co, Bank Sepah Iran v. Milestone Trading, Ltd Case No: A3/2003/1167, Neutral Citation Number: [2004] EWCA Civ 487, Court of Appeal (Civil Division).

which the court has a general discretion to impose whenever it thinks it just to do so. The equity arises from the conduct of the parties on well-settled principles and in defined circumstances which make it unconscionable for the defendant to deny the proprietary interest claimed by the plaintiff."

Lord Hutton said much the same in the Banque Financière case at page 245, where he stressed the wide variety of different circumstances in which the remedy of subrogation may be appropriate. He quoted with approval the statement from the then edition of *Goff & Jones* on *The Law of Restitution* at page 593 that: "subrogation is essentially a remedy, which is fashioned to the facts of the particular case and which is granted in order to prevent the defendant's unjust enrichment." Lord Hutton also referred with approval to parts of the passages from the Orakpo case and Boscawen v Bajwa which I have quoted above.

In these circumstances, it is I think clear that the remedy of subrogation is appropriate in much wider circumstances than was submitted by Mr Bloch. As I see it, and as stated in the Coys case, the correct approach today is to ask the questions posed by Lord Hoffmann and Lord Steyn in the Banque Financière case. The judge answered Lord Hoffmann's questions one and two yes and his third question no. For the same reasons he would have answered Lord Steyn's first three questions yes and his fourth question no.

In my opinion the judge answered those questions correctly for the reasons which he gave. The judge held *that if subrogation were refused, that is if CAI were not ordered to repay SGS, CAI would be benefited or enriched at the expense of SGS and thus* answered Lord Hoffmann's first question and Lord Steyn's first two questions yes. His reason was that by *satisfying the judgment in full SGS had relieved CAI of liability to Niru. That is plainly correct.*

Lord Hoffmann's second question and *Lord Steyn's third question ask whether such enrichment would be unjust.* The judge held that it would. In deciding that question he considered all the circumstances of the case and for that purpose he looked behind the judgment. He was in my opinion right to do so for the reasons which he gave in paragraph 39 of his judgment, which it is not necessary to repeat here.

I have already set out in some detail my reasons for concluding that CAI would be unjustly enriched if SGS could not recover the amount it paid to Niru under the judgment. In short, if *CAI retained the monies there can be no doubt that continued retention of them would leave it unjustly enriched. It paid them away on the instructions of Mr Mahdavi in bad faith.* I have already expressed my view that CAI should not be in any better position by paying the monies away in bad faith than if it had retained them. It would be unjustly enriched in either case: see paragraphs 34 to 49 above."[95]

---

[95] Id.

CHAPTER II

INDEMNITY AGREEMENTS

II.1 Reimbursement, and an introduction to indemnity agreements ("services agreements")

The agreement between the issuing bank and the account party or Principal has two distinct sides: on one hand it is an agreement by the bank to render certain special services at the request of the account party against a fee including an authorization ("mandate") by the Principal to the bank to do so.[1] On the other hand,

---

[1] Bertrams writes p. 116:
"In the Netherlands and the Germanic legal family the relationship between the account party and bank has been labelled as one of mandate *(lastgeving, Geschäftsbesorgungsvertrag gerichtet auf Werkleistung,* and *Mandat).* English law also classifies the relationship as a mandate." UCC 5-108 official comment:

"In some circumstances standards may be established between the issuer and the applicant by agreement or by custom that would free the issuer from liability it might otherwise have. For example, an applicant might agree that the issuer would have no duty whatsoever to examine documents on certain presentations (e.g., those below a certain dollar amount). Where the transaction depended upon the issuer's payment in a very short time period (e.g., on the same day or within a few hours of presentation), the issuer and the applicant might agree to reduce the issuer's responsibility for failure to discover discrepancies. By the same token, an agreement between the applicant and the issuer might permit the issuer to examine documents exclusively by electronic or election-optical means. Neither those agreements nor others like them explicitly made by issuers and applicants violate the terms of Section 5-108(a) or (b) or Section 5-103(c)."

Bolivia (DCL) Art 1401:
"1. To accept the documents, which evidence that the goods have been loaded on board, promptly after notification by the issuing bank or at the latest within the subsequent three days; 2. To reimburse the bank for the amount paid during the periods as set forth in the agreement which the bank has paid for the benefit of the beneficiary unless the applicant deposits such amount prior to payment, provided that the payment is made in compliance with the instructions given to the bank (Articles 1400, 1428, Commercial Code); 3. To pay the expenses, interest and commission for the issuance of the credit regardless of whether the credit has been used or not except in the case that the bank has unliterary revoked the credit; and 4. Upon request of the bank to provide personal or real collateral to secure the transaction."

CHAPTER II

an inseparable act or agreement is the bank's right to be reimbursed by the Principal: "indemnification" in the event the bank effects payment under the instrument as agreed and incurs costs or is exposed to liability when doing so.[2]

No specific agreement needs to be made in order for the right of reimbursement to arise, since the bank is acting at the request of the applicant and under his mandate. The payment effected is made for and on behalf of the Principal and not on the bank's own account: this is evident and the very purpose of the arrangement. However, certain jurisdictions may require that the agreement be in written form in order for it to be enforceable.

Indemnity agreements resemble loan agreements or credit facility agreements and may include similar conditions and covenants. The instructions of the

---

Greece (DCL) Art. 29:
"1. If the applicant hands over to the issuing bank moneys or securities as collateral for the issuance of the credit the bank shall acquire a pledge at the time of accepting such moneys or securities even if the formalities for creating a pledge are not complied with. 2. The provisions on the sale of pledged property shall apply to the forced sale of the handed-over securities."

And Art. 31:
"1. The bank is authorized to sell the goods according to the provisions on the sale of pledged property if after receipt of the bills of lading at the final destination the applicant does not meet its obligation to pay its debts and to take over the goods despite request to do so. 2. Such sale may only be carried out after expiry of a period of 24 hours for perishable goods or a period of 10 days for all other goods. The period shall run from the time of the request. The type of goods shall be determined by the presiding judge of the District Court based on an opinion by the President of the Chamber of Commerce if there is a Chamber of Commerce at the place of the District Court. Such opinion shall be completed within 24 hours after the time of the request. 3. If the bank carries out the sale upon permission by the presiding judge the bank shall not be liable to the debtor or a third party unless the bank acts intentionally or with gross negligence in the sale."

And Art. 32:
"If the proceeds from the sale are not sufficient to cover the bank's claims the applicant shall be liable for the remaining amount."; Libya (DCL) Art. 255: "Pledges, attachments, seizures and any other charges on the rights arising from a credit or on the goods represented thereby are invalid unless they are registered in the document."

[2] See Bertrams p. 118-119. ISP 8.01: "a. Where payment is made against a complying presentation in accordance with these Rules, reimbursement must be made by: i. an applicant to an issuer requested to issue a standby; and ii an issuer to a person nominated to honour or otherwise give value. b. An applicant must indemnify the issuer against all claims, obligations and responsibilities (including attorney's fees) arising out of: i. the imposition of law or practice other than that chosen in the standby or applicable at the place of issuance; ii. the fraud, forgery, or illegal action of others; or iii. the issuer's performance of the obligations of a confirmer that wrongfully dishonours a confirmation. c This Rule supplements any applicable agreement, course of dealing, practice custom or usage providing for reimbursement or indemnification on lesser or other grounds."

applicant may be specified therein, as well as the security given to the bank which may take various forms ranging from cash deposit to third party guarantees or mortgages which are not covered by *lex mercatoria* but may be more or less covered by the statutes and case law of national jurisdictions. Since it may be unclear which national law is to be applied, a clause specifying which law is to be applied may be in place. It has become a common practice to use so called "master agreements" under which a group of financial institutions agree to issue guarantees, bonds, letters of credit and the like on global or wide international basis to a group of companies operating worldwide, as is discussed in more depth later on.

Docdex Decisions No 217, p. 67:

> "*1. Issuing bank's refusal to accept documents timely received* When conforming documents are received by the issuing bank, that bank has an obligation to examine them and to decide whether they comply (sub-Article 13 (a)). If they are not in compliance, the issuing bank can refuse the documents and serve notice in accordance with sub-Article 14(d). Otherwise, the issuing bank must pay. *2. Issuing bank's statement that it did not receive a timely authenticated reimbursement claim* As stated under "Analysis", the reimbursement instruction is a facility providing for prompt payment to the presenter (nominated bank). If no reimbursement claim had been received (and if no documents had been received), then the issuing bank would not be obliged to pay. However, in accordance with the reimbursement instructions, upon receipt of a reimbursement claim from the nominated bank stating that conforming documents have been timely presented, the issuing bank must pay (whether or not by that time the credit has expired). If it is necessary to have an "authenticated reimbursement message" and the message is not so authenticated, the issuing bank should go back to the sender of the message in order to clarify the authentication. We there conclude that:
>
> 1. Conforming documents were timely presented and the issuing bank had no reason to refuse payment.
> 2. The payment should have been effected or receipt of a reimbursement claim or on receipt of the documents, whichever occurred first."

The issuing bank's position and its right to be reimbursed by the account party is defined in UCC 5-108 (1) as follows:

> "(i) An issuer that has honored a presentation as permitted or required by this Article:
> (1) is entitled to be reimbursed by the applicant in immediately available funds not later than the date of its payment of funds;
> (2) takes the documents free of claims of the beneficiary or presenter;
> (3) *is precluded from asserting a right of recourse on a draft under Sections 3-414 and 3-415;*
> (4) except as otherwise provided in Sections 5-110 and 5-117, *is precluded from restitution of money paid* or other value given by mistake to the extent the mistake concerns discrepancies in the documents or tender which are apparent on the face of the presentation; and
> (5) is discharged to the extent of its performance under the letter of credit unless the issuer honored a presentation in which a required signature of a beneficiary was forged."

In most banking transactions there is an indemnity agreement in writing. Here, for example, is a clause used by banks in their agreements to specify what is to be paid, and when, and to create an obligation to indemnify the bank against loss, It also authorizes the bank to pay on demand, without any further confirmation.

sample clause: Each Principal (in relation to Guarantees issued for that Principal's account) irrevocably and unconditionally: (i) agrees to pay to the Bank any and all amounts paid by the Bank from time to time on or after the date hereof under a Guarantee, provided that any claim honored has been made in accordance with and met the stipulations in the Guarantee; (ii) agree to indemnify and hold harmless the Bank from any direct loss or damage, reasonable costs and expenses or exchange rate losses and interest which may be incurred or suffered by the Bank under, or as a result of the Bank issuing or amending or extending, a Guarantee; (iii) authorise and direct the Bank to pay any sums on demand under a Guarantee so requested or extended in accordance with the term of such Guarantee without any confirmation or verification by the Principal.

In civil law countries the indemnity agreement does not always need to be in writing. The account party's obligation to reimburse the bank arises even in the absence of an agreement in writing because to presume anything else would be plain absurdity: the banks are in the business of banking and anything else would constitute a donation, unjust enrichment and an *ultra vires* transaction.[3]

---

[3] Troy L. Harris: "The Restatement, unlike its predecessor, the Restatement of Security, divides the surety's indemnification rights between a right of reimbursement and one of restitution. There are two basic differences between reimbursement and restitution under the Restatement. The first goes to liability: a surety is entitled to reimbursement to the extent that it either performs the secondary obligation or settles with the obligee so as to discharge the principal, in whole or in part, from the underlying obligation. The surety is entitled to restitution to the extent that its performance or settlement of the secondary obligation relieves the principal from its duty under the underlying obligation. Thus, the right of reimbursement is slightly broader than the right to restitution: a surety is entitled to reimbursement when it performs the secondary obligation, even if doing so does not relieve the principal from any obligation pursuant to the underlying obligation."

2004 WL 960993 (CA (Civ Div)), [2004] 1 C.L.C. 882, [2004] 2 Lloyd's Rep. 319, (2004) 148 S.J.L.B. 538, [2004] 2 All E.R. (Comm) 289, [2004] EWCA Civ 487. Niru Battery Manufacturing Company, Bank Sepah Iran v. Milestone Trading, Limited, Maritime Freight Services Limited, Ali Akhbar Mahdavi, Credit Agricole Indosuez, SGS United Kingdom Limited, Case No: A3/2003/1167, Neutral Citation Number: [2004] EWCA Civ 487, Court of Appeal (Civil Division), CA, Before: The President Lord Justice Clarke and Lord Justice Sedley, Wednesday 28th April 2004, On Appeal from the High Court of Justice Queen's Bench Division Commerical Court, Mr Justice Moore-Bick [2003] EWHC 1032 (Comm): "Miss Andrews submits that the judge was wrong to hold that SGS' claim against CAI does not satisfy the principles of recoupment. Although, in the light of my conclusions on subrogation, it is not necessary to decide this question, I will shortly state my opinion on it since it was the subject of argument. The relevant principles were stated by Cockburn CJ in Moule v Garrett (1872) LR 7 Ex 101 as follows: "Where the plaintiff has been compelled by law to pay, or, being compellable by law, has paid, money which the defendant was ultimately liable to pay, so that the latter obtains the benefit of the payment by the discharge of his liability: under such circumstances the defendant is held indebted to the plaintiff in the account". The judge set out that passage and added that the principle depends upon the compulsory discharge of a liability which rested *primarily* on the defendant (my emphasis). He referred to paragraph 15-001 of the 6th edition of *Goff & Jones* on *The Law of Restitution*, where the position was put as follows: "In general, anybody who has under compulsion of law made a payment whereby he has discharged the primary liability of another is entitled to be reimbursed by that other. . . . To succeed in his claim for recoupment, the plaintiff must satisfy certain conditions. He must show: (1) that he was compelled, or was compellable, by law to make the payment; (2) that he did not officiously expose himself to the liability to make the payment; and (3) that his payment discharged a liability of the defendant.""

Hemmo, Mika: Pankkioikeus. Talentum Media Oy, Jyväskylä 2001., p. 324-5; Lehtinen, Tuomas, First demand -takuu, Tampere 1994, p. 15.

Chapter II

The words "indemnity agreement" are used in this book as an expression common to a multitude of arrangements or rights and duties between a bank and its customer.[4]

> "All the contracts provided that the plaintiffs were to establish a guarantee confirmed by a bank of 5 per cent of the price in favour of the buyers. These were in effect to be performance bonds. They were called *guarantees simpliciter*, but their purpose was to provide security to the buyers for the fulfilment by the plaintiffs of their obligations under the contracts. They were to be established with the respective Egyptian banks.
>
> The machinery was that the plaintiffs instructed the bank to confirm the guarantees to the respective Egyptian bank, which therefore became the bank's correspondent in Egypt for this purpose. The Egyptian banks in turn confirmed the guarantees to the buyers. *The guarantees were backed by counter-indemnities by the plaintiffs to the bank.*
>
> The plaintiffs agreed to indemnify the bank in the widest terms and gave authority for payment under the guarantees and to debit the plaintiffs' account accordingly. In the first and second cases this part of the counter-indemnity was in the following terms: "You are hereby irrevocably authorised and directed to pay forthwith on any demand appearing or purporting to be made by or on behalf of the beneficiary (i.e. the buyers) any sums up to the limit of your liability which may be demanded of you from time to time *without any reference to or any necessity for confirmation or verification on the part of the undersigned*, it being expressly agreed that any such demand shall as between the undersigned and you *be conclusive evidence* that the sum stated therein is properly due and payable, and *you are further authorised to debit any account of the undersigned . . .*"
>
> In the third case the authority was more restricted. It was not stated to be irrevocable, but nothing turns on this. It also contained no exclusive

---

[4] UCC 5-103 Official comment P10: "Neither the obligation of an issuer under Section 5-108 nor that of an adviser under Section 5-107 is an obligation of the kind that is invariable under Section 1-102(3). Section 5-103(c) and Comment 1 to Section 5-108 make it clear that the applicant and the issuer may agree to almost any provision establishing the obligations of the issuer to the applicant. The last sentence of subsection (c) limits the power of the issuer to achieve that result by a nonnegotiated disclaimer or limitation of remedy."

evidence provision but merely provided: "You are further authorised to debit any account of the undersigned . . . with the whole or any part of the amount of any payment which you may make thereunder . . ."."[5]

This relationship is in most cases domestic or national in character, generally not crossing any borders. Hence, there is usually no issue as to which law applies, and the Indemnity Agreement is not of supranational character as such.

The Indemnity Agreement is to a great extent similar to loan agreements (or "facility agreements") although the issuer's obligation or liability to effect payment is contingent, i.e., subject to conditions precedent, and the payee is not the customer himself but a third-party beneficiary. However, since the customer or account party is liable to reimburse the bank (not the beneficiary) once payment to the beneficiary has been effected,[6] the arrangement has all the essential features of giving loans under a facility or credit line. Under commercial letters of credit, "the loan" is given in the ordinary course of the transaction, but under standby credits "the loan" is given only in exceptional cases, that is, where something has gone wrong on either side.

For these reasons, as in bank-customer relationships in generally, the agreement reflects the risk the bank is willing or allowed to take with respect to this particular customer. Therefore the customer's creditworthiness, reflected in the credit rating, determines both the price of the bank's commitment and the risk it assumes. If there is a risk, a security may be required for this particular purpose or in general covering all loans given or exposure to liability by the bank. Sometimes a cash deposit in advance is deemed necessary by a bank, in which case the customer is paying a "royalty" for having the right to use the bank's good name and creditworthiness, in addition to its own, in order to inspire the necessary confidence of its contracting party and as may be required under the underlying transaction. In the best of circumstances, based on the excellent credit rating of the bank's customer, no security is required by the bank.

---

[5] 1977 WL 59355 (QBD), [1978] Q.B. 146, [1977] 2 All E.R. 862, [1977] 3 W.L.R. 752, (1977) 121 S.J. 745. R. D. Harbottle (Mercantile) Ltd. v. National Westminster Bank Ltd. and Others, Same v. Same and Others, Harbottle Coal Co. Ltd. and Another v. Same and Others, [1976 R. No. 3861][1976 R. No. 4314][1976 H. No. 7364]; [1977] 3 W.L.R. 752, Queen's Bench Division, QBD, Kerr J., 1977 Jan. 26, 27, 31 Feb. 3.

[6] Except perhaps in cases of fraud, unjust enrichment, bankruptcy etc.

Chapter II

Being subject to national laws as to loans, credits, security interests and banking laws and in the light of the great diversity of banks and their customers, the flora of how the Indemnity Agreement is structured and worded is certainly impressive. However, at least one thing is common to all Indemnity Agreements: the bank is entitled to be reimbursed save for exceptional cases of *mala fide* or negligence.[7]

II.2 "Good faith" and representations and warranties made by the beneficiary

A common feature of letters of credit and bank guarantees is that they do not impose any express obligations or duties on the beneficiary except the duties that are implicit in every transaction[8]. Once issued, the instruments cannot be amended or cancelled without the beneficiary's consent. However, if the beneficiary calls on the instrument, the demand must meet the express conditions of the instrument in order for the beneficiary to receive the economic benefit. In most cases, receiving the economic benefit means receiving the funds.

The United Nations Convention on Independent Guarantees and Standby Letters of Credit (hereinafter UNC) Art 15 provides:

> "(1) Any demand for payment under the undertaking shall be made in a form referred to in paragraph (2) of article 7 and in conformity with the terms and conditions of the undertaking.

---

[7] UCC 5-102 official comment: "A financial institution may be both the issuer and the applicant or the issuer and the beneficiary. Such letters are sometimes issued by a bank in support of the bank's own lease obligations or on behalf of one of its divisions as an applicant or to one of its divisions as beneficiary, such as an overseas branch. Because wide use of letters of credit in which the issuer and the applicant or the issuer and the beneficiary are the same would endanger the unique status of letters of credit, only financial institutions are authorized to issue them." Honduras (DCL) Art. 907: "The banks shall be responsible for the formal regularity and compliance of the documents with the terms of the issuance of the credit which was required by the applicant."; and Art. 908: "Banks do not assume any liability a. with regard to the holder and the authenticity of the documents which are presented to the banks; b. with regard to the conditions, the quality, the quantity or the price of the goods referred to in the documents; c. with regard to the precision of the translation of the credit's terms and conditions; d. in case of a loss of the documents during transport, in case of delay, expiry, error or defaults in the transmission of wire transfers or telegrams; and e. in case of non-compliance with further instructions by the banks whose services were used unless the bank elected the correspondent bank at its own initiative."

[8] Unidroit Article 1.7 says: "(1) Each party must act in accordance with good faith and fair dealing in international trade.(2) The parties may not exclude or limit this duty."

INDEMNITY AGREEMENTS

> (2) Unless otherwise stipulated in the undertaking, the demand and any certification or other document required by the undertaking shall be presented, within the time that a demand for payment may be made, to the guarantor/issuer at the place where the undertaking was issued.
>
> (3) The beneficiary, when demanding payment, *is deemed to certify that the demand is not in bad faith and that none of the elements referred to in subparagraphs (a), (b) and (c) of paragraph (1) of article 19 are present.*"

In addition, the beneficiary may be deemed to have given certain good faith representations and warranties, or the beneficiary may have warranted absence of bad faith and fraud, as provided in UCC Section 5-110:

> "Warranties. (a) If its presentation is honored, the beneficiary warrants: (1) to the issuer, any other person to whom presentation is made, and the applicant that *there is no fraud or forgery* of the kind described in subsection (a) of Section 5-109; and (2) to the applicant that the drawing *does not violate any agreement* between the applicant and beneficiary or any other agreement intended by them to be augmented by the letter of credit. (b) The warranties in subsection (a) of this section are in addition to warranties arising under articles 3, 4, 7 and 8 because of the presentation or transfer of documents covered by any of those articles."

UCC 5-110 (official comment) provides:

> "2. The warranty in Section 5-110(a)(2) assumes that payment under the letter of credit is final. It does not run to the issuer, only to the applicant. In most cases the applicant will have a direct cause of action for breach of the underlying contract. This warranty has primary application in standby letters of credit or other circumstances where the applicant is not a party to an underlying contract with the beneficiary. It is not a warranty that the statements made on the presentation of the documents presented are truthful nor is it a warranty that the documents strictly comply under Section 5-108(a). *It is a warranty that the beneficiary has performed all the acts expressly and implicitly necessary under any underlying agreement to entitle the beneficiary to honor.* If, for example, an underlying sales contract authorized the beneficiary to draw only upon "due performance" and the beneficiary drew even though it had breached the underlying contract by

delivering defective goods, honor of its draw would break the warranty. By the same token, if the underlying contract authorized the beneficiary to draw only upon actual default or upon its or a third party's determination of default by the applicant and if the beneficiary drew in violation of its authorization, then upon honor of its draw the warranty would be breached. In many cases, therefore, the documents presented to the issuer will contain inaccurate statements (concerning the goods delivered or concerning default or other matters), but the breach of warranty arises not because the statements are untrue but because the beneficiary's drawing violated its express or implied obligations in the underlying transaction."

Good faith, unreasonableness and unconscionability as terms may partly overlap.[9] Good faith or bad faith may equally, but more often, be relevant in other relationships as well.[10]

---

[9] Quentin Loh; Tang Hang Wu: *Injunctions* restraining calls on performance bonds – is fraud the only ground in Singapore? Lloyds Maritime and Commercial Law Quarterly 2000, 3 (Aug), 348-363: "Both these cases were considered in detail by the Singapore Court of Appeal in the landmark *Bocotra* case in a judgment written by Karthigesu, J.A., who, after citing *Royal Design* and *Kvaerner,* said:

In our opinion, whether there is fraud or unconscionability is the sole consideration in applications for injunctions restraining payment or calls on bonds to be granted. Once this can be established, there is no necessity to expend energies in addressing the superfluous question of "balance of convenience".

It does not lie in the mouth of the defendant to claim that damages would still somehow be an adequate remedy. . . . This new and amorphous "unconscionable" ground in *Bocotra* was seized upon by Lai Kew Chai, J., in *Raymond Construction Pte Ltd v. Low Ya Tong & Another.* Lai Kew Chai, J., had no difficulty in attempting to define the ambit of "unconscionability". Lai Kew Chai, J., observed that:

The concept of "unconscionability" to me involves unfairness, as distinct from dishonesty or fraud or conduct of a kind so reprehensible or lacking in good faith that a court of conscience would either restrain the party or refuse to assist the party. Mere breaches of contract by the party in question. . . .would not by themselves be unconscionable."

[10] John F. Dolan writes in The Law of Letters of Credit, Commercial and Standby Credits, Warren, Gorham & Lamont 1984 on p. 8-15:

"The *Intraworld* court appears to favor the pure-heart definition of good faith over the objective rule. *Lustrelon, Ine. v. Prutscher* explicitly adopts the pure-heart rule and holds that good faith for the purposes of Section 5-114(2) (b) means honesty in fact. *Philadelphia Gear Corp. v. Central Bank* also adopts the pure-heart test. In that case, the court holds that it is not dishonest, and therefore not bad faith, for the issuer to reject a nonconforming presentation by the beneficiary without first soliciting the view of the account party."

II.3 Features of the agreement and sample clauses

II.3.1 Master agreement

When a customer of a bank or insurance company is, its ordinary business, frequently in need of bonds, guarantees, letters of credit, and other such instruments, the financial institution may offer a Master Agreement as an umbrella under which such instruments are issued by the Guarantor or "Surety" globally when and where the customer may need them. This section contains examples of clauses meant to protect the sound basis of the overall relationship and to eliminate excessive credit risk and exposure to liability.

II.3.2 "Umbrella"

Here is a sample clause that a bank or insurance company might use to effect such a Master Agreement, or "umbrella". Note that it carries a time limit and that it limits the amount of funds available, and the other terms and conditions and wording must be acceptable to the issuer:

sample clause: "Subject to the other terms of this Agreement the Bank shall issue a Guarantee in EUR or in an Optional Currency, provided that: (i) the Bank having received a Request, duly filled in and signed by an Authorised Signatory of the Principal and approved by the Parent, not later than on the fifth (5) Banking Day prior to the proposed date for the issuance of the Guarantee; (ii) the Guaranteed Amount of all Guarantees issued and still valid and the proposed Guarantee to be issued under the Facility does not exceed the Commitment; (iii) the form of the proposed Guarantee is attached to the Request (iv) the proposed Guarantee has terms and conditions which are consistent with usual market practice or otherwise acceptable to the Bank and authorizes payment of any calls thereunder in a manner that is acceptable to the Bank; (v) the proposed wording of the Guarantee is not in breach of any applicable agreement, contravene any applicable law or public policy."[11]

---

[11] This resembles lending in general. Dolan writes from the banking law perspective. Dolan in The Law of Letters of Credit on p. 12-19: "The National Bank Act establishes in Section 84 maximum amounts that a nationally chartered bank may loan to a single entity. States have adopted similar rules. It makes sense that banks include the amounts of outstanding standby letters of credit in determining the loan limit for a borrower."

II.3.3 Security mechanisms

In such a Master Agreement various security mechanisms are put in place in the form of representations and warranties and covenants. Here is a Sample Clause that incorporates such security mechanisms:

sample clause: "Each Principal agrees to be bound by the covenants in this clause and shall, unless the Bank's prior written consent thereof is obtained: *(a) Ranking Pari Passu:* ensure that at all times the claims of the Bank against it hereunder rank at least *pari passu* with the claims of all its other unsecured and unsubordinated creditors except for Excepted Debts; (b) *M&A Transactions:* not enter into any merger or consolidation or sell, assign, grant a lease over or otherwise dispose of a substantial part of its assets or business save in the ordinary course of its business; (c) *Compliance with law:* at all times procure, maintain in effect and comply with all the terms and conditions of all governmental and other resolutions, environmental or other laws and regulations, approvals, authorisations, consents and registrations to which it may be subject; and (d) *New Business:* not to make any material change in the overall nature of its business or commence any new type of business materially different from its business as the date of this Agreement."

II.3.4 "Conclusive Evidence"

sample clause: "If the Surety (a) shall be required or obligated to make any payment in respect of any Damages; or (b) becomes aware of any potential or threatened claim; under or by virtue of or in connection with any Bond or Bonds the Indemnitors shall pay to the Surety a sum equal to the full amount thereof immediately upon written demand therefor (whether before or after the date of payment of such Damages by the Surety). It is expressly agreed that any demand by the Surety in respect of any such payment or potential or threatened claim shall as between the Indemnitors and the Surety be conclusive evidence (in the absence of fraud or manifest error) that the

---

sample clause: "In consideration of the Surety executing or procuring the execution of any Bond or Bonds the Indemnitors shall indemnify and keep indemnified the Surety from and against any and all Damages incurred by the Surety under or by virtue of or in connection with any Bond or Bonds and whether before or after the date of this Deed. The obligations of the Indemnitors under this Clause are not to be reduced or qualified in any way by the following provisions of this Deed."

amount demanded by the Surety is payable forthwith by the Indemnitors to the Surety."

II.3.5 "Cash Cover"

sample clause: "Any payments to be made by a Principal under this General Counter Indemnity shall be made on the Bank's first demand specifying the amount paid by the Bank under any Guarantee and any other amount the Principal is obliged to pay under this General Counter Indemnity. Any such a demand shall be conclusive evidence for payment purposes of the facts specified or referred to in it. Any payments under this General Counter Indemnity shall be payable within five (5) Banking Days of the Principal's receipt of the Bank's demand."

sample clause: "The Indemnitors shall *forthwith deposit with the Guarantor a sum in immediately available funds* or, in each case at the sole option and in the absolute discretion of the Guarantor, *an unconditional irrevocable letter of credit* from a bank in all respects acceptable to the Guarantor and in a form acceptable to the Guarantor or other collateral in all respects acceptable to the Guarantor in an amount or to a value, equal to the full amount of the Bonds (being the aggregate sum of the amounts set out in each Bond as the maximum aggregate liability of the Guarantor thereunder) *upon written demand* by the Guarantor in any of the following circumstances:
  (i) if the Indemnitors, the Subsidiaries, the Associated Companies or any of them shall without the prior written consent of the Guarantor *cease or resolve to cease to carry on business* or shall dispose or resolve to *dispose of the whole or a mater ial part of its or their Assets* (with the exception of a disposal of trading assets in the ordinary course of business) or *shall stop or resolve to stop payments* generally or be *unable to pay its or their debts*; or
  (ii) if an encumbrancer takes possession or a receiver, administrative receiver or manager is appointed in respect of the whole or any material part of the undertaking, property or assets of the Indemnitors, the Subsidiaries, the Associated Companies or any of them; or
  (iii) if a petition is presented for the appointment of an administrator in respect of the Indemnitors, the Subsidiaries, the Associated Companies or any of them; or

(iv) if a meeting is convened or a petition presented or an resolution is passed or an order made for the winding up of all or any of the Indemnitors, the Subsidiaries or the Associated Companies except for the purposes of amalgamation or reconstruction without insolvency on terms previously approved by the Surety in writing, which approval shall not be unreasonably withheld or delayed; or

(v) if in relation to all or any of the Indemnitors, the Subsidiaries or the Associated Companies (i) any proposal is made for a voluntary arrangement or (ii) a petition is presented or an order is made for the appointment of an administrator; or

(vi) upon an interim moratorium taking effect in respect of any Indemnitor, Subsidiary or Associated Company; or

(vii) if all or any of the Indemnitors, the Subsidiaries, the Associated Companies enter into any general arrangement or composition for the benefit of its or their creditors or the creditors of any of them; or

(viii) if all or any of the Indemnitors, the Subsidiaries, the Associated Companies *are in breach or default of the terms under any loan agreement or analogous documentation* to which they or it are a party where such breach or default entitles the lender, or the lender under any other loan agreement or analogous documentation to which the Indemnitors, the Subsidiaries or the Associated Companies or any of them are party, *to accelerate* payment provided that the Surety shall not be entitled to issue a demand if the breach or default referred to therein is remedied (where capable of being so remedied) within any period of grace permitted in respect of the breach or default under the loan agreement or analogous documentation, whichever period shall be the shorter; or

(ix) if documents are filed with a court of competent jurisdiction for the appointment of an administrator of all or any of the Indemnitors, the Subsidiaries or the Associated Companies or notice of intention to appoint an administrator is given by all or any of the Indemnitors, the Subsidiaries or the Associated Companies or its directors or by a qualifying floating charge holder; or

(x) if there shall or in any jurisdiction in relation to all or any of the Indemnitors, Subsidiaries or the Associated Companies any event which is analogous to those set out in therein; or

(xi) if the Indemnitors, the Subsidiaries or the Associated Companies or any of them *shall be in breach of their obligations* provided herein; or

(xii) if there shall be a *change of Control* of any of the Indemnitors, the Subsidiaries or the Associated Companies; or

(xiii) if the Guarantor shall certify that there has occurred any event or circumstance which has or *may reasonably be expected to have* (with the passage of time or the fulfillment of any condition) *a Material Adverse Effect upon the Indemnitors.*"

II.3.6 *Pari Passu* provision

Here is a clause designed to prevent the bank (or insurance company) from sliding down the chain of creditors who will have to be paid in the event that things go bad:

sample clause: "Each of the Indemnitors covenants and agrees that its obligations hereunder do and will rank at least pari passu with all present and future unsecured obligations of the Indemnitors other than those mandatorily preferred by law."

II.3.7 Covenant as to *Pari Passu*

Here is a clause designed to ensure that the bank is on at least equal footing with other creditors, going so far as to, if necessary, re-write the existing agreement to bring it level with any future agreement that the indemnitor enters into:

sample clause: "The Indemnitors further covenant with the Surety that in the event that they (or any of them) enter into any arrangements with any provider(s) of Borrowings which are similar or analogous to the Counter Indemnity arrangements comprised herein, they will ensure either that the terms of such arrangements to be entered into *are not at any time any more favourable than those comprised herein* (other than to the extent of security to be granted in respect of such Borrowings) or that, where the terms of such arrangements are to be more favourable (other than as aforesaid), *the terms comprised herein shall* (prior to the entry into such proposed arrangements) *be aimed or varied so* that they shall be no less favourable."

II.3.8 "Negative Pledge"

Here is a sample clause that carries a "negative pledge", that is a pledge that the indemnitor will not create any encumbrance over its revenues or assets (with stated exceptions), or sell, etc., its assets. Thus, an indemnitor who signed such a pledge could not, for example, go out the next day and sell its headquarters building (or get a mortgage on it).

sample clause: "Each of the Indemnitors covenants and agrees that it shall not and shall procure that each of the Subsidiaries and Associated Companies shall not (except with the prior written consent of the Surety) at any time whilst any Bond or Bonds shall be outstanding and shall not have been released or discharged in full or otherwise to the satisfaction of the Surety:

(a) *create, assume or permit to exist any encumbrance on or over any of its or their present or future revenues, assets or properties except for the following:*

  (i) in the case of any company or corporation becoming a Subsidiary or an Associated Company after the date hereof, any encumbrance existing over the Assets of such Subsidiary or Associated Company provided that such Encumbrance is not created in contemplation or in connection with it becoming a Subsidiary or an Associated Company and provided further that the terms thereof shall not be amended and the sums secured thereby shall not be materially amended; and

  (ii) liens arising by operation of law or by order of a court or tribunal or in the ordinary course of business securing amounts not more than 30 days overdue;

  (iii) any Encumbrances over any Assets arising out of title, retention provisions in a supplier's standard conditions of supply of goods and securing only the purchase price of such Assets, but only if the Assets are purchased by a Member of the Indemnitor Group in the ordinary course of trading;

  (iv) pledges over and assignments of documents of title insurance policies and sale contracts in relation to commercial goods created or made in the ordinary course of business to secure the purchase price of such goods. (b) either in a single transaction or in a series of transactions, whether related or not and whether voluntarily or involuntarily, sell, transfer, lease or otherwise dispose of the Assets of the Indemnitors, the Subsidiaries or the Associated Companies or any of them."

II.3.9 Duty to inform as to financial status

Here is a clause that imposes upon the Indemnitor a duty to give the bank its financial statements and auditors' reports in a timely fashion, and to promptly inform the bank of any event likely to have a "material adverse effect". "Material adverse effect" is a term of art in the accounting profession and such an event is clearly identifiable by a financial analyst or auditor.

> **sample clause:** The Parent and each Principal shall furnish the Bank with the following information: (i) at the reasonable request of the Bank, as soon as available, and in any event within 120 days after the end of its fiscal year, its financial statements together with the auditors' reports and any public financial information relevant for the evaluation of the financial condition of the Principal; and (ii) promptly upon becoming aware thereof, information of any occurrence or circumstance which has or is reasonably likely to have a Material Adverse Effect and the steps (if any) being taken or proposed to be taken to remedy it.

II.3.10 Duty to inform as to allegation of breach or default

Here is a clause that imposes upon the Indemnitor a duty to give the surety bank notice if the indemnitor receives a written allegation made by a third party against it of any substantial breach or default. Further, the Indemnitor agrees not to sign any admission of liability that would give rise to liability on the part of the surety bank.

> **sample clause:** Each of the Indemnitors covenants with and undertakes to the Surety that: it shall notify the Surety in writing within 10 days of receipt of any written allegation of breach or default made against it where there is any likelihood of the alleged breach or default giving rise to a material liability on the part of the Surety (other than in relation to the rectification of defects or any minor or insubstantial breach or default from time to time which are not in either case capable of giving rise to any material liability on the part of the Surety) pursuant to any of its obligations or liabilities under any Contract or obligation secured by a Bond (a "Bonded Obligation") upon becoming aware of the same; where there has occurred and is subsisting any alleged default, it shall not without the prior written consent of the Surety, at any time sign or provide any admission of liability in relation to any claim or default alleged

by an employer or beneficiary under or in respect of a Bonded Obligation save where the liability admitted would not in any circumstances give rise to a liability on the part of the Surety.

II.3.11 Duty to inform of legal proceedings

Here is a sample clause wherein the indemnitor agees to let the surety know if there are legal proceedings brought against the indemnitor by an employer of beneficiary of a bond, and to keep the surety informed of how proceedings are going. In fact, the surety gets the opportunity, if it wants, to step into the indemnitor's shoes and conduct the litigation.

sample clause: "If an employer or beneficiary of any Bond shall send a formal letter before action to or shall bring proceedings of any description against an Indemnitor or (including adjudication, arbitration or litigation in any court) arising out of or in respect of a Bonded Obligation which might give rise to a material liability on the part of the Surety
  (i) the Indemnitor shall keep the Surety fully informed as to the conduct of such proceedings and authorise and instruct its solicitors or other representatives to provide copies of all pleadings, orders, documents and statements prepared or received for the purposes thereof or in connection therewith to the Surety at the expense of the Indemnitors; and
  (ii) permit the Surety to take over and conduct any such proceedings in its name and at the cost of the Indemnitors and for such purposes co-operate with the Surety in the provision of information and full and unrestricted access to documents and records required for such purpose; and the Surety is appointed irrevocably as its attorney for the purposes
  (iii) the Surety hereby acknowledging that it will only exercise its rights under this Clause upon the occurrence of any Alleged default. The Surety shall be entitled to appoint solicitors, counsel or other representatives (having regard to the nature of the relevant proceedings) and to appoint such experts and to commission such reports as it shall deem necessary or requisite for such purposes; and any costs, expenses and liabilities incurred by the Surety in consequence of the exercise of any right or power under this Clause shall be recoverable from the Indemnitors."

II.3.12 Duty to give information, and other duties

Here is a clause that imposes a duty on the surety to inform other parties that it deals with that the indemnity Deed exists. In particular, the indemnitor must inform others who provide loans to the indemnitor.

sample clause: "The Indemnitor hereby undertakes to deliver to the Surety a copy of the annual and interim audited consolidated accounts of the Indemnitor within 2 months of the end of the period to which such accounts relate; and hereby undertakes to:
  (i) *deliver a copy of this Deed* to each person, bank, company or other financial institution which shall from time to time provide any loan or other financial facility whatsoever to the Indemnitors, the Subsidiaries or the Associated Companies or any of them (and, in case of any loan or other financial facility provided to the Indemnitors after the date hereof, before utilisation or drawdown thereof) and produce to the Surety a copy duly certified by an authorised officer of the relevant Indemnitor or Indemnitors of the acknowledgement of the receipt of such notice by each such person, bank, company or financial institution
  (ii) where any or all of the Indemnitors are required at the request of any bank or financial institution to confirm compliance with all or any of the terms of any loan, guarantee or similar financial facility, *provide a copy of any certificate of compliance* given to any such bank or financial institution showing the calculations necessary to determine compliance with any such loan, guarantee or similar financial facility and *stating that no default or unmatured default exists* or, if any default or unmatured default exists, stating the nature and status thereof; within twenty (20) Business Days of the date of issue by the relevant Indemnitor.
  (iii) *give notice to the Surety of any technical or other default under any loan*, guarantee or similar financial facility within ten (10) Business Days of the occurrence thereof, whether or not such default has been waived or cured;
  (iv) *provide to the Surety on request* such financial, operational and other information and documents concerning each of the Indemnitors as the Surety may from time to time request;
  (v) if any bank or other financial institution shall request or demand the creation of any Encumbrance in its favour, then the indemnitors shall forthwith: (i) *inform the Surety* of such request or demand; and (ii) *produce to the Surety* evidence in writing satisfactory to them of the

receipt or acknowledgement of each such bank or institution of copies of this Deed provided to them."

II.3.13 Representations and warranties (conditions precedent to agreement)

Here is a sample clause in which the indemnitor must recite that it has fulfilled all of the conditions precedent to the agreement:

sample clause: "Each of the indemnitors represents and warrants to the Surety that:

it has taken all actions, fulfilled all conditions and obtained and maintained all such consents as are necessary to enable it to enter into this Deed and perform the obligations herein set out;

this Deed creates *valid* and *binding* obligations on its part, which are fully enforceable in accordance with their terms; *the execution, delivery and performance* of the terms of this Deed do not and will not:

(i) *contravene* any law or any order or regulation binding upon it; or
(ii) conflict with or cause any breach or default under any other deed, instrument or agreement binding upon it or any of its assets; or
(iii) contravene or conflict with its memorandum and articles of association; It is *lawfully empowered* by its memorandum of association or otherwise to enter into this Deed, and that it is duly authorised to execute the same in the manner appearing below;

and Each of the Indemnitors represents and warrants to the Surety that it *has made and will make independently* and without reliance on any representation or advice from the Surety and/or its agents or advisers, its *own independent investigation and assessment* of the contractual and all other liabilities secured and guaranteed by any Bond or Bonds and has reached its own decision in relation to the effect and import of and the desirability of any Member or Members of the Indemnitor Group entering into any Contract(s) and/or any Bond or Bonds and/or any other agreements."

II.3.14 Default

Here is a clause which sets forth a number of events, the occurrence of which constitutes default. That is, each event alone is enough to constitue default. The events include non-payment, breach of other obligations, mis-representation, cross-default, and insolvency.

sample clause: **Events of Default**

Each of the events set out in this clause is an Event of Default.

Non-payment

The Parent or a Principal does not pay on the due date any amount payable by it under this Agreement in the manner required hereunder, unless the non-payment: (a) is caused by technical or administrative error in each case outside the control of the Parent or the Principal; and (b) is remedied within five (5) Banking Days of the due date.

Breach of other obligations

A Principal does not comply in any material respect with any other provisions of this Agreement not already referred to in this clause, unless the non-compliance: (a) is capable of remedy; and (b) is remedied within twenty-one (21) days of the earlier of the Bank giving notice and the Principal becoming aware of the non-compliance.

Misrepresentation

Any representation or warranty made or deemed to be made hereunder shall prove to be or shall become incorrect in any material respect as at the date it is made or deemed to be repeated and the occurrence of the event giving rise to the non-compliance or incorrect representation or warranty has a Material Adverse Effect, unless the underlying circumstances are remedied within fourteen (14) days of that date.

Cross default

The Parent or a Principal fails in making payment in respect of any indebtedness (not being immaterial) towards the Bank (other than payment obligations under this Agreement) on the due date for such payment or within any applicable grace period, or should any such indebtedness become due, or become capable of being declared due, prior to its stated maturity by reason of an event of default (howsoever described).

Insolvency

(a) Insolvency: any of the Principals or the Parent is (or is held by a court of competent jurisdiction to be) insolvent or unable to pay its debts as they become due, or becomes the subject of an insolvency proceeding. (b) Winding-up: any step is taken by any person with a view to the winding-up of any of the Principals or the Parent or the Parent or any of the Principals ceases or threatens to cease to carry on all or a substantial part of its business, except for the purpose of a solvent intra-Group reconstruction, amalgamation, reorganization, merger or consolidation, or otherwise where such winding-up is vexatious or frivolous and is discharged within thirty (30) days of such step being taken.

Material adverse change

Save as may be disclosed to the Bank by the Parent and/or a Principal prior to the date of this Agreement, any event or series of events occur(s) which give(s) reasonable grounds to the Bank to believe that a Material Adverse Effect has occurred since the date of this Agreement and is continuing

II.4 Doctrine of (substantive) independence (autonomy)

The doctrine of "substantive" independence applies to practically taken all genuine credits and genuine on-demand guarantees.

UNC Art 3:

"For the purposes of this Convention, an undertaking is independent where the guarantor/issuer's obligation to the beneficiary is not: (a) Dependent upon the existence or validity of any underlying transaction, or upon any other undertaking (including stand-by letters of credit or independent guarantees to which confirmations or counter-guarantees relate); or (b) Subject to any term or condition not appearing in the undertaking, or to any future, uncertain act or event except presentation of documents or another such act or event within a guarantor/issuer's sphere of operations."

Whereas, in the domain of commercial credits, the doctrine has been well established, the same concept, when introduced by way of stipulations under standby credits and on-demand bank guarantees, did cause some confusion at the time. By now the dust seems to have settled for the most part and the recognition that these instruments have essentially the same function and are subject to the same rules of law as commercial letters of credit, despite their different names, seems to have been making progress and gained recognition even if perhaps not yet fully acknowledged by everyone in the trading community.

The substantive independence depends on the type of conditions precedent agreed to. If the conditions precedent agreed to *in casu* or incorporated by reference create the independence (as, e.g., in ISP 1.06 quoted below) of the instrument from other legal relationships constituted under the facility and in particular the underlying agreement, the instrument is substantively independent regardless of what it is called, and vice versa; naming an instrument a stand-by credit or on-demand guarantee does not turn it into one if the conditions precedent create substantive links between the two in the performance of the parties or in other respects or in general.

The core of the doctrine of substantive independence is *the limitation or elimination of the account party's and the issuer's right to invoke terms and conditions* or any actions or omissions of the account party or obligor under the transaction as if it were wholly irrelevant.[12] The substantive independence is, however, relative, since for instance the fraud rule, invalidity or illegality of the transaction may pierce or penetrate not the "veil" but "the armour of independence". Nor can fundamental principles of law merchant or *ordre public* rules be contracted away. They are there to protect you or your partners in good and evil whether you desire it or not.

ISP 1.06 provides:

"a. A standby is an irrevocable, *independent*, documentary, and binding undertaking when issued and need not so state.

---

[12] See Bertrams, *Bank Guarantees*, at 232-233.

  b. Because a standby is irrevocable, an issuer's obligations under a standby cannot be amended or cancelled by the issuer except as provided in the standby or as consented to by the person against whom the amendment or cancellation is asserted.
  c. Because a standby is independent, the enforceability of an issuer's obligations under a standby does not depend on:
   i. the issuer's right or ability to obtain reimbursement from the applicant;
   ii. the beneficiary's right to obtain payment from the applicant;
   iii. *a reference in the standby to any reimbursement agreement or underlying transaction;* or
   iv. the issuer's knowledge of performance or breach of any reimbursement agreement or underlying transaction.
  d. Because a standby is documentary, an issuer's obligations depend on the presentation of documents and an examination of required documents on their face."

The doctrine of substantive independence does not mean total or absolute independence. The instrument is and remains *functionally* dependent.

Payment under the instrument against a conforming tender releases the issuer from its obligation towards the beneficiary. At the same time the payment constitutes a payment on account (*à conto*) by the principal to the beneficiary under the underlying transaction. The payment does thus in the ordinary course of business have a "double effect" i.e., two debts are settled by one payment: payment under the instrument is also payment under the facility (a "double effect" payment). The balance (debts) of the principal or account party under the underlying agreement is credited by that payment in the principal's favor. The payment may result in reduction of his actual or contingent debt or liability or payment in excess of his debt or liability thereunder resulting in credit in his favor which he is entitled to recover from the beneficiary in accordance with the provisions of the underlying agreement. Should the payment, however, have been effected by the bank against a non-confirming tender, contested or challenged by the account party, the payment by the bank may or may not constitute payment under the underlying agreement and the bank may have to recover the payment made from the beneficiary either by way of remedies generally available under the applicable law and/or possibly by rights of subrogation if the account party enjoys the benefits of the payment in mistake.

Independence does not mean that the instrument would be a stand-alone undertaking and, as such, a truly independent and non-accessory, negotiable or other (credit) instrument. A letter of credit or guarantee remains always formally accessory to the underlying transaction and its right of existence is based on serving the purpose of the "main" transaction: forming a facility or "function".[13] If the instrument were totally independent, it would not be a letter of credit or guarantee anymore, but another kind of credit or security instrument.[14]

The substantive independence should also be reflected in *the procedural "independence"*, as stated by Dolan in "The Law of Letters of Credit" on p. 2-21:

> "The opinion holds that the "intention of paragraph 6 of the letter of credit, read in conjunction with clause XV of the building contract," was to give the beneficiary an opportunity to cure any such defect. The court's own language belies the idea, although the court expressed it elsewhere, that the credit in the *Fair Pavilions* case was independent of the underlying contract. *The error of the case is one that appears to be common among courts—that of construing the credit by referring to the underlying agreement.*"

The relative independence may have some other consequences as well, in particular when the substantively dependent instruments are in question. For instance the jurisdiction clause, arbitration clause and the choice-of-law clause of the main agreement may "attach" and become applicable to the credit or guarantee as well. This is of course an issue of interpretation of the facility and the purpose of the parties and structure of the deal and its documentation. An arbitration clause in the transaction documents tends to be "contagious" especially in international transactions and it is more likely to "attach" to cover the instrument in the beneficiary-account party relationship and less likely to attach to the banks involved only in the credit or guarantee instrument as parties. These issues will be discussed in more depth later on in this work.

---

[13] The doctrine of independence may be over emphasized, which may result in disregarding the reality and lead to extreme conclusions.

[14] In such a case a secondary market would be created and the risk of a (bona fide) holder presenting a demand would either lead to dramatically increased fees or withdrawal of many banks or other issuers from this business.

CHAPTER III

BANK-TO-BANK INDEMNITY

III.1 General

An Indemnity Agreement between two banks involved is of a somewhat different character. In most cases it is a cross-border agreement, which causes a conflict-of- law issue to arise.[1]

---

[1] Russia (DCL) Art. 867 (2):
"If a covered (deposited) letter of credit is opened, the issuing bank is obligated upon the opening of the letter of credit to transfer the amount of the letter of credit (coverage), at the payer's expense or of the credit provided to the payer, to the executing bank for the entire term of the issuing bank's obligation. If a non-covered (guaranteed) letter of credit is opened, the executing bank is entitled to deduct the total amount of the letter of credit from the account of the issuing bank held by the executing bank."

and (3):
"The procedure for making settlements under a letter of credit shall be governed by a statute and also by bank rules set up in accordance with such statute and rules and by customs of trade applied in banking practice."

and Art 870 (2):
"If the executing bank has made payment of another operation in connection with the terms of the letter of credit, the issuing bank shall compensate it for the incurred expenditures. These expenses and all of the issuing bank's other expenditures related to the execution of the letter of credit shall be compensated by the payer."

and 871(2):
"If the issuing bank, after receipt of the documents accepted by the executing bank, concludes that they do not correspond by evident features to the terms of the letter of credit, it is entitled to refuse acceptance and to demand repayment of the amount paid to the beneficiary from the executing bank as a violation of the terms of the letter of credit and, in case of an uncovered letter of credit, to refuse compensation of the disbursed amounts."

and Art 873 (2):
"The unused amount of a covered letter of credit shall be returned to the issuing bank promptly at the time of the termination of the letter of credit. The issuing bank is obligated to transfer the returned amount to the payer's account from which the funds were debited."

Chapter III

URR Art. 13:

> "The Issuing Bank shall be bound by and shall indemnify the Reimbursing Bank against all obligations and responsibilities imposed by foreign laws and usages."

Further, the bank-to-bank relationship is of special character because both parties are experts in their own business and both usually enjoy a high credit rating.

Substantive issues may also arise in connection with the examination of the documents. For example: did the confirming bank wrongfully accept, or wrongfully refuse, the documents? The conditions precedent in this relationship must be the same as under the letter of credit itself. Are the criteria for liability the same, too? Is the confirming bank entitled to be reimbursed by the issuing bank? If so, under what conditions?

This cross-border *inter-bank* relationship is international or supranational and covered by many rules which may be regarded as law merchant.

The inter-bank relationship is the often the invisible foundation of international letter of credit – and bank-guarantee – banking practice. The relationship is in principle covered by UCP, but UCP's coverage was not found to be sufficient to safeguard a frictionless inter-bank relationship. Therefore URR was developed as a spin-off of UCP.[2] URR is subsidiary in its relationship to UCP.[3]

---

[2] URR Preface:
"During the past 30 years, specific practices have developed around bank-to-bank reimbursements under documentary credits. These practices, while covered in the Uniform Customs and Practice (UCP), have developed into more sophisticated procedures followed by banks, not a party to the credit, which provide reimbursement for payments made under another bank's credit and help provide prompt payment to beneficiaries. These practices, however, have "outgrown" what is contained in the UCP on this subject. In 1993, the ICC Banking Commission authorised a Working Party to develop rules specific to the bank-to-bank reimbursement process. This publication is a result of that process. The work in creating new rules is often difficult. Unlike the revision of prior publications, creation of new rules requires an in-depth look at practices and procedures of banks from every part of the world which are involved in the transaction. Thanks to the comprehensive comments of the ICC National Committees and banking organisations around the world, the Working Party creating these rules has had a wealth of information to work from."

[3] URR Article 1 (3):
"These rules are not intended to override or change the provisions of the ICC Uniform Customs and Practice for Documentary Credits."

UCP 600 provides as follows:

> "Article 13 Bank-to-Bank Reimbursement Arrangements a. If a credit states that reimbursement is to be obtained by a nominated bank ("claiming bank") claiming on another party ("reimbursing bank"), the credit must state if the reimbursement is subject to the ICC rules for bank-to-bank reimbursements in effect on the date of issuance of the credit. b. If a credit does not state that reimbursement is subject to the ICC rules for bank-to-bank reimbursements, the following apply:
> i. An issuing bank must provide a reimbursing bank with a reimbursement authorization that conforms with the availability stated in the credit. The reimbursement authorization should not be subject to an expiry date.
> ii. A claiming bank shall not be required to supply a reimbursing bank with a certificate of compliance with the terms and conditions of the credit.
> iii. An issuing bank will be responsible for any loss of interest, together with any expenses incurred, if reimbursement is not provided on first demand by a reimbursing bank in accordance with the terms and conditions of the credit.
> iv. A reimbursing bank's charges are for the account of the issuing bank. However, if the charges are for the account of the beneficiary, it is the responsibility of an issuing bank to so indicate in the credit and in the reimbursement authorization. If a reimbursing bank's charges are for the account of the beneficiary, they shall be deducted from the amount due to a claiming bank when reimbursement is made. If no reimbursement is made, the reimbursing bank's charges remain the obligation of the issuing bank.
> c. An issuing bank is not relieved of any of its obligations to provide reimbursement if reimbursement is not made by a reimbursing bank on first demand."

URR operates with such terms as "Reimbursement Authorization,"[4] "Reimbursement Undertaking"[5] and "Reimbursement Claim". The Reimbursement relationship is a

---

[4] URR Article 2 (c):
"'Reimbursement Authorization' shall mean an instruction and/or authorization, independent of the Credit, issued by an Issuing Bank to a Reimbursing Bank to reimburse a Claiming Bank, or, if so requested by the Issuing Bank, to accept and pay a time draft(s) drawn on the Reimbursing Bank."

[5] URR Article 2 (g):
"'Reimbursement Undertaking' shall mean a separate irrevocable undertaking of the Reimbursing Bank, issued upon the authorisation or request of the Issuing Bank, to the Claiming Bank named

CHAPTER III

separate and independent agreement between the banks not part or directly linked to the credit.

URR Article 3

> "A Reimbursement Authorisation is separate from the Credit to which it refers, and a Reimbursing Bank is not concerned with or bound by the terms and conditions of the Credit, even if any reference whatsoever to the terms and conditions of the Credit is included in the Reimbursement Authorisation."

The Claiming Bank is the bank which effects payment under the letter of credit to the beneficiary.[6]

The URR is meant to insulate the inter-bank payment mechanism from any disputes or reservations in any relationships under the letter of credit.[7] The Reimbursement Authorizations and Undertakings are irrevocable and cannot be amended in line with the established practice of letter of credit.[8]

---

in the Reimbursement Authorisation, to honour that bank's Reimbursement Claim provided the terms and conditions of the Reimbursement Undertaking have been complied with."

[6] URR Article 2 (f): "'Reimbursement Claim' shall mean a request for reimbursement from the Claiming Bank to the Reimbursing Bank."

[7] URR Art 10 (c): "Claiming Banks must not indicate in a Reimbursement Claim that a payment, acceptance or negotiation was made under reserve or against an indemnity."

[8] URR Art. 9:

"It must (in addition to the requirement of Article 1 for incorporation of reference to these Rules) contain the following: i. Credit number; ii. currency and amount; iii. additional amounts payable and tolerance, if any; iv. full name and address of the Claiming Bank to whom the Reimbursement Undertaking should be issued; v. latest date for presentation of a claim including any usance period; vi. parties responsible for charges (Claiming Bank's and Reimbursing Bank's charges and Reimbursement Undertaking fee) in accordance with Article 16 of these Rules.

c. If the Reimbursing Bank is requested to accept and pay a time draft(s), the Irrevocable Reimbursement Authorisation must also indicate the following, in addition to the information contained in (b) above: i. tenor of draft(s) to be drawn; ii. drawer; iii. party responsible for acceptance and discount charges, if any. Issuing Banks should not require a sight draft(s) to be drawn on the Reimbursing Bank.

d. If the Reimbursing Bank is authorised or requested by the Issuing Bank to issue its Reimbursement Undertaking to the Claiming Bank but is not prepared to do so, it must so inform the Issuing Bank without delay.

e. A Reimbursement Undertaking must indicate the terms and conditions of the undertaking and: i. Credit number and Issuing Bank; ii. currency and amount of the Reimbursement Authorisation; iii. additional amounts payable and tolerance, if any; iv. currency and amount of the Reimbursement

Bank-to-Bank Indemnity

```
┌──────────────┐  Reimbursement      ┌──────────────────┐
│ Issuing Bank │──Authorization────→ │ Reimbursing Bank │
└──────┬───────┘                     └──────────────────┘
       │            Reimbursement    ↗↙
       │            Undertaking ────     Payment under
       │           ┌──────────────┐ ──── Reimbursement
       │           │ Claiming Bank│      Undertaking
       │           └──────────────┘
       │  LC                              Payment under Credit
       │                                 
       ↓           ┌──────────────┐
                   │  Beneficiary │
                   └──────────────┘
```

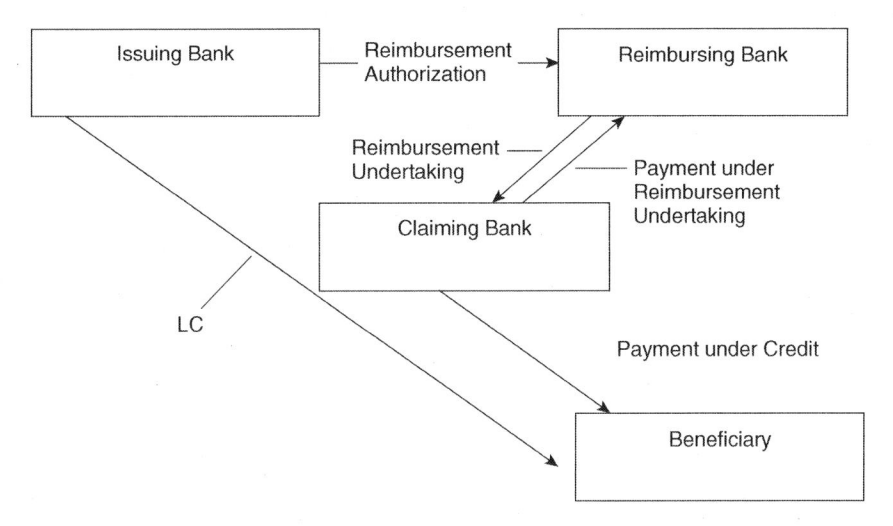

Figure III.1. Claiming bank under letter of credit to the beneficiary

URR Art. 9

"An authorisation or request by the Issuing Bank to the Reimbursing Bank to issue a Reimbursement Undertaking is irrevocable ('Irrevocable Reimbursement Authorisation'). . . . . .

Undertaking; v. latest date for presentation of a claim including any usance period; vi. party to pay the Reimbursement Undertaking fee, if other than the Issuing Bank. The Reimbursing Bank must also include its charges, if any, that will be deducted from the amount claimed.

f. If the latest date for presentation of a claim falls on day on which the Reimbursing Bank is closed for reasons other than those mentioned in Article 15, the latest date for presentation of a claim shall be extended to the first following day on which the Reimbursing Bank is open.

g. i. An irrevocable Reimbursement Understanding cannot be amended or cancelled without the agreement of the Reimbursing Bank. ii. When an Issuing Bank has amended its Irrevocable Reimbursement Authorisation, a Reimbursing Bank which has issued its Reimbursement Undertaking may amend its undertaking to reflect such amendment, If a Reimbursing Bank chooses not to issue its Reimbursement Undertaking Amendment it must so inform the Issuing Bank without delay. iii. An Issuing Bank which has issued its Irrevocable Reimbursement Authorisation Amendment, shall be irrevocably bound as of the time of its advice of the Irrevocable Reimbursement Authorisation Amendment. iv. The terms of the original Irrevocable Reimbursement Authorisation (or an Authorisation incorporating previously accepted Irrevocable Reimbursement Authorisation Amendments) will remain in force for the Reimbursing Bank until it communicates its acceptance of the amendment to the Issuing Bank. v. A Reimbursing Bank must communicate its acceptance or rejection of an Irrevocable Reimbursement Authorisation Amendment to the issuing bank. A Reimbursing Bank is not required to accept or reject an Irrevocable Reimbursement Authorisation Amendment until it has received acceptance or rejection from the Claiming Bank to its Reimbursement Undertaking Amendment."

> h. i. A Reimbursement Undertaking cannot be amended or cancelled without the agreement of the Claiming Bank. ii. A Reimbursing Bank which has issued its Reimbursement Undertaking Amendment shall be irrevocably bound as of the time of its advice of the Reimbursement Undertaking Amendment. iii. The terms of the original Reimbursement Undertaking (or a Reimbursement Undertaking incorporating previously accepted Reimbursement Amendments) will remain in force for the Claiming Bank until it communicates its acceptance of the Reimbursement Undertaking Amendment to the Reimbursing Bank. iv. A Claiming Bank must communicate its acceptance or rejection of a Reimbursement Undertaking Amendment to the Reimbursing Bank.

The Reimbursing Bank does not carry the risks or assume any major significant liability.[9]

As URR Art. 10 (d) says:

> "Reimbursing Banks assume no liability or responsibility for any consequences that may arise out of any non-acceptance or delay of processing should the Claiming Bank fail to follow the provisions of this Article."

And URR Art. 11 (e) further provides that:

> "Reimbursing Banks assume no liability or responsibility if they honor a Reimbursement Claim that indicates that a payment, acceptance or negotiation was made under reserve or against an indemnity and shall disregard such indication. Such reserve or indemnity concerns only the relations between the Claiming Bank and the party towards whom the reserve was made, or from whom, or on whose behalf, the indemnity was obtained."

---

[9] URR Art. 15:
"Reimbursing Banks assume no liability or responsibility for the consequences arising out of the interruption of their business by Acts of God, riots, civil commotions, insurrections, wars or any other causes beyond their control, or by any strikes or lockouts.", Art. 17: "All claims for loss of interest, loss of value due to any exchange rate fluctuations, revaluations or devaluations are between the Claiming Bank and the issuing Bank, unless such losses result from the non-performance of the Reimbursing Banks obligation under a Reimbursement Undertaking."

The relationship may also be *intra-bank*, i.e., between two offices or branches of the same bank, in which case it is not a true agreement but an internal arrangement only.

III.2 The role of the underlying agreement and the balance

The facility is created to support the underlying agreement in accordance with its terms and conditions. The two have formal links and in some instances and in some cases they also have substantive links. There may or may not be procedural links between them. The facility matures to cause the required instrument to be issued in favor of the beneficiary.

If the instrument issued under the facility is a substantively independent one, the links are functional or formal only. The purpose of such an instrument is often similar to a cash cover clause: the balance of payments is changed in favor of the beneficiary. There is no assessment of the justification of the demand in the light of the underlying agreement, either materially or (should there be any such issue) procedurally ("pay now, litigate later"). The instrument is independent, and there are hardly any other indispensable parties to the proceedings under the facility than the issuer/confirmer and the beneficiary.

The balance of payments under the underlying agreement remains open even after payment under the instrument. The beneficiary may or may not be entitled to further payments or the balance may even be in favor of the account party. This issue remains to be settled under the mechanism provided for in the underlying agreement.

If, however, the instrument issued is a substantively dependent one, the question of the issuer's/confirmer's duty to make payment is subject to an assessment of the account party's material liability under the underlying agreement. Making this assessment may require extensive evidence and the involvement of several parties to the process.[10]

---

[10] Once this process has been completed payment may be made and once made should result in zero balance as to the issues covered.

CHAPTER III

If the instrument issued is a mezzanine instrument requiring, e.g., submission of an arbitral award on the account party's liability under the underlying agreement as a condition precedent for payment, the justification analysis has already been made and the issuer may proceed with the payment at his earliest convenience without exposure to risk for wrongful payment, provided, however, that the other conditions have been met. The aggregate balance after the payment between the parties to the transaction need not be zero but, with respect to the duties covered by the instrument, this should be the case. There are no outstanding or other procedural links, once the proceedings have been closed and resulted in the award.

III.3 Honor and the "moment of death" of the instrument

Bank guarantees and letters of credit, broadly understood, are a network of materially independent contracts, one "dependent" on or accessory to another in function forming together "a facility" to perform "services": none of these contracts are stand-alone instruments although each of them also has a purpose of its own. They are *functionally* dependent: they support one another to form the letter of credit or bank guarantee. The main objective and the focus is, however, one single thing: payment to the beneficiary. The network is constructed to enable the beneficiary to demand payment when the circumstances call for it under the underlying agreement. When the beneficiary presents conforming documents ("tender") or meets substantive conditions precedent and the bank honors its commitment by making payment, accepting drafts or by assuming a deferred-payment undertaking, when all this has been accomplished, the instrument has been consummated ("the moment of death").

Figure III.2 demonstrates how this works.

UCP 600 describes honor as follows in article 15:

> "a. When an issuing bank determines that a presentation is complying, it must honour. b. When a confirming bank determines that a presentation is complying, it must honour or negotiate and forward the documents to the issuing bank. c. When a nominated bank determines that a presentation is complying and honours or negotiates, it must forward the documents to the confirming bank or issuing bank."

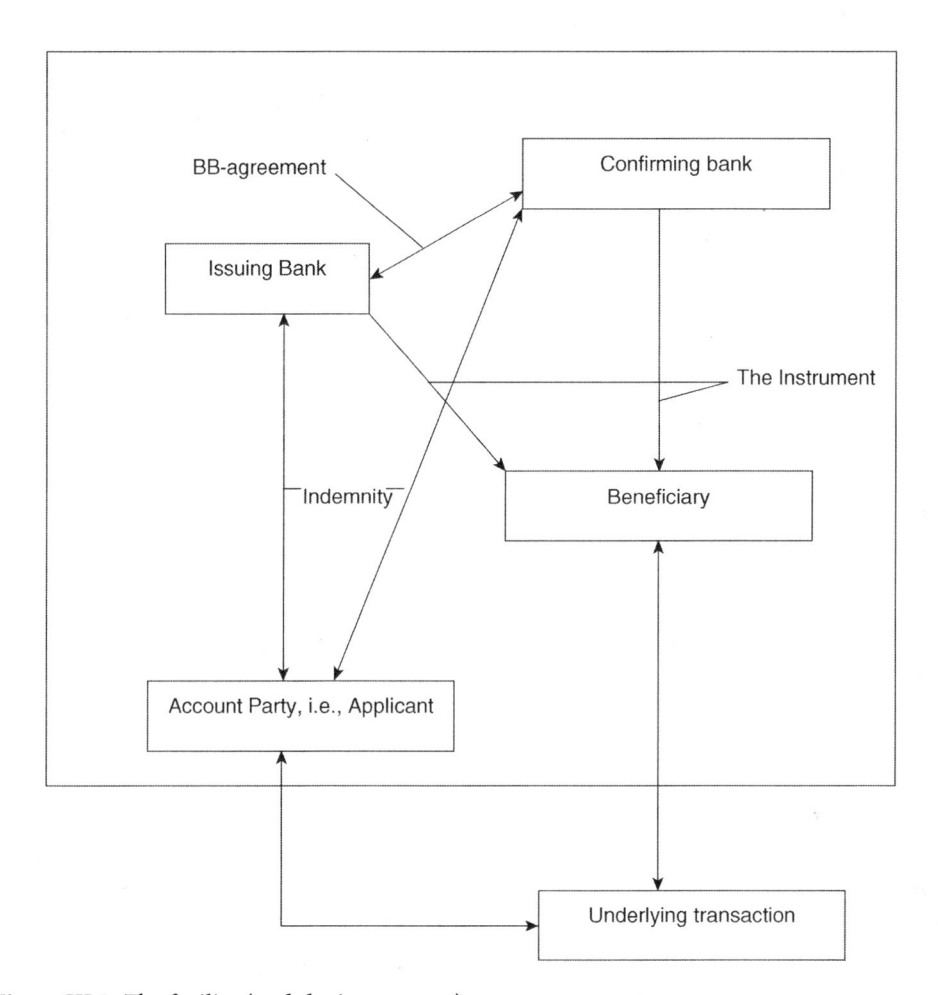

Figure III.2 The facility (and the instrument).

Once payment to the beneficiary has been made, deferred undertaking accepted or drafts have been purchased, this should cause a "domino effect" by causing further payments to be effected under reimbursement obligations and by transfer of documents in the opposite direction. In most cases, the "dominos" keep falling until all parts of the facility have been consummated and all obligations have been fulfilled and requirements met causing the consummation of the facility: this is the "death of the facility". Sometimes the domino effect will be interrupted and the dismantling of the facility fails, when one of the parties to the facility either refuses to pay or reimburse challenging the compliance of the tender of documents or claim made.

CHAPTER III

After the moment of death, the fraud rule will, however, continue to apply when its application may prevent the fraudulent partly from receiving the funds. The fraud rule is a general principle applying whenever its enforcement may prevent a fraudulent party from receiving the unlawful or illegal benefits of the fraud.[11]

Gustavsberg v. CCRB-Bank, a Hong Kong case, describes the rules applicable to the death of the instrument as follows:

> "Article 13a. of the UCP 500 states: "Documents which appear on their face to be inconsistent with one another will be considered as not appearing on their face to be in compliance with the terms and conditions of the Credit." 50. In *Banque De L' Indochine v. JH Rayner [1983].1 QB.711*, 729-730, Donaldson MR stated:
> "I approach this aspect of the appeal on the same basis as did the judge, namely, that the banker is not concerned with why the buyer has called for particular documents *(Commercial Banking Co. of Sydney Ltd. v. Jalsard Pty. Ltd. [1973] A.C. 279)*, that there is no room for documents which are almost the same, or which will do just as well, as those specified *(Equitable Trust Co. of New York v. Dawson Partners Ltd. (1926) 27 Ll.L.Rep..49)*, that whilst the bank is entitled to put a reasonable construction upon any ambiguity in its mandate, if the mandate is clear, there must be strict compliance with that mandate *(Jalsard's case [1973] A.C..279)*, that documents have to be taken up or rejected promptly and without opportunity for prolonged inquiry *(Hansson v. Hamel and Horley Ltd. [1922].2 A.C. 36)* and that a

---

[11] See Bertrams, *Bank Guarantees*, at 315-316. Charles Proctor, "Confirmed Letters of Credit – A New Twist", *Butterworths Journal of International Banking and Financial Law*, (April 2000):
"What conclusions can be drawn from this analysis? First of all, it may be that the *Banco Santander* decision will tend to promote the use of acceptance credits - in preference to deferred payment credits - because (i) the confirming bank's right to reimbursement is crystallised upon acceptance of the bill and (ii) that right cannot be affected by the subsequent discovery of a fraud on the part of the beneficiary."

Daniel Aharoni and Adam Johnson. "Fraud and Discounted Deferred Payment Documentary Credits: The Banco Santander Case", *J.I.B.L. 2000, 15(1)*, (2000, 22-25):

"The basic authority given by the issuing bank to the confirming bank in a deferred payment letter of credit is to pay at maturity. The consequent obligation to reimburse is to reimburse on payment being made at maturity. If at that time there is established fraud, there is no obligation on the confirming bank to pay nor on the issuing bank to reimburse. This is to be distinguished from the position under a negotiation credit. In European Asian Bank A.G. v. Punjab and Sind Bank, the Court of Appeal held that, in the case of a negotiation credit, the issuing bank must bear the risk of fraud discovered after the date of payment of the discounted value but prior to the maturity date."

tender of documents which properly read and understood calls for further inquiry or are such as to invite litigation are a bad tender (*M. Golodetz & Co. Inc. v. Czarnikow-Rionda Co. Inc. [1980].1 W.L.R..495).*" "[12]

The classic *Sztejn* case discusses the fraud rule:

"*No hardship will be caused by permitting the bank to refuse payment* where fraud is claimed, where the merchandise is not merely inferior in quality but consists of worthless rubbish, *where the draft and the accompanying documents are in the hands of one who stands in the same position as the fraudulent seller*, where the bank has been given notice of the fraud before being presented with the drafts and documents for payment, and *where the bank itself does not wish to pay pending an adjudication of the rights and obligations of the other parties.*
While the primary factor in the issuance of the letter of credit is the credit standing of the buyer, the security afforded by the merchandise is also taken into account. In fact, *the letter of credit requires a bill of lading made out to the order of the bank and not the buyer.* Although the bank is not interested in the exact detailed performance of the sales contract, it is vitally interested in assuring itself that there are some goods represented by the documents. Finkelstein, Legal Aspects of Commercial Letters of Credit, p. 238; *O'Meara v. National Park Bank of New York*, 239 N.Y. 386, 401, 146 N.E. 636, 39 A.L.R. 747, opinion of Cardozo, J., dissenting; Thayer, Irrevocable Credits in International Commerce, 37 C.L.R. 1326, 1335.
On this motion only the complaint is before me and I am bound by its allegation that the Chartered Bank is not a holder in due course but is a mere agent for collection for the account of the seller charged with fraud. Therefore, the Chartered Bank's motion to dismiss the complaint must be denied. If it had appeared from the face of the complaint that the bank presenting the draft for payment was a holder in due course, its claim against the bank issuing the letter of credit would not be defeated even though the primary transaction was tainted with fraud. This I believe to be the better rule despite some authority to the contrary. See *Old Colony Trust Co. v. Lawyers' Title & Trust Co.*, 2 Cir., 297 F. 152, certiorari denied 265 U.S. 585, 44 S.Ct. 459, 68 L.Ed. 1192; Thayer, Irrevocable Credits in International

---

[12] NV Koninklijke Sphinx Gustavsberg v Cooperatieve Centrale-Raiffeisen-Boerenleenbank BA, 24 November 2005, Court of Appeal, Civil Appeal No 161 of 2004.

CHAPTER III

> Commerce, 37 C.L.R. 1326, 1344; Campbell, Guaranties & The Suretyship Phases of Letters of Credit, 85 U. of Pa.L.R. 261, 272; but see Finkelstein, Legal Aspects of Commercial Letters of Credit, p. 248; *O'Meara Co. v. National Park Bank of New York*, 239 N.Y. 386, 401, 146 N.E. 636, 39 A.L.R. 747."[13]

After *the moment of death* the relationships are governed by the laws and rules applicable to the other "supporting" agreements or instruments for clearing purposes. Once the beneficiary has either received the funds or drafts ("bills of exchange") or other payment undertakings, its relationship with the bank(s) is thereafter governed by material law applicable to those instruments provided that this has been effected at original maturity and not prior thereto.

The Sztejn opinion continues:

> "However, I believe that a different situation is presented in the instant action. This is not a controversy between the buyer and seller concerning a mere breach of warranty regarding the quality of the merchandise; on the present motion, it must be assumed that the seller has intentionally failed to ship any goods ordered by the buyer. *In such a situation, where the seller's fraud has been called to the bank's attention before the drafts and documents have been presented for payment, the principle of the independence of the bank's obligation under the letter of credit should not be extended to protect the unscrupulous seller.* It is true that even though the documents are forged or fraudulent, if the issuing bank has already paid the draft before receiving notice of the seller's fraud, it will be protected if it exercised reasonable diligence before making such payment. *Bank of New York & Trust Co. v. Atterbury Bros., Inc.*, 226 App.Div. 117, 234 N.Y.S. 442, affirmed 253 N.Y. 569, 171 N.E. 786; *Brown v. C. Rosenstein Co.*, 120 Misc. 787, 200 N.Y.S. 491, affirmed 208 App.Div. 799, 203 N.Y.S. 922.
>
> However, in the instant action Schroder has received notice of Transea's active fraud before it accepted or paid the draft. The Chartered Bank, which under the allegations of the complaint stands in no better position than Transea, should not be heard to complain because *Schroder is not forced to pay the draft* accompanied by documents covering a transaction which it has reason to believe is fraudulent. Although our courts have used broad language to the effect that a letter of credit is independent of the primary contract between the buyer and seller, that language was used in cases

---

[13] *Sztejn v J. Henry Schroeder Banking Corp*, 177 Misc. 719, 31 N.Y.S.2d 631 (SC NY 1941).

concerning alleged breaches of warranty; no case has been brought to my attention on this point involving *an intentional fraud on the part of the seller* which was brought to the bank's notice with the request that it withhold payment of the draft on this account. *The distinction between a breach of warranty and active fraud on the part of the seller is supported by authority and reason.* As one court has stated: 'Obviously, when the issuer of a letter of credit knows that a document, although correct in form, is, in point of fact, false or illegal, he cannot be called upon to recognize such a document as complying with the terms of a letter of credit.' *Old Colony Trust Co. v. Lawyers' Title & Trust Co., 2 Cir., 297 F. 152 at page 158*, certiorari denied *265 U.S. 585, 44 S.Ct. 459, 68 L.Ed. 1192.*"[14]

Once the payment has been made, the paying bank has the right to be reimbursed by the issuing bank and perhaps also by the account party against the tendered documents. The issuing bank has the right to be reimbursed by the account party ("principal") against surrender of documents. The "clearing" of the facility may thus continue although the instrument itself has served its purpose and is "dead". At the end all parties have been satisfied and the buyer has the documents agreed upon. Under stand-bys, the document route does not represent any real value or security but may still cause a challenge to be raised due to non-compliance or fraud (abuse). When stand-bys are called, paid and cleared litigation is likely to follow under the underlying agreement. As to dependent instruments like bonds and tradition guarantees, once the payment has been made, the right to reimbursement arises, but since the substantive justification was cleared prior to payment and the substantive conditions precedent were met, there should not be further "laundry" as to those issues between the parties to the underlying agreement.

The payment to the beneficiary is a non-recourse payment, i.e., under a letter of credit the bank, when making the payment or accepting or negotiating drafts, has no right to demand repayment, not even in the event of error in reviewing the tendered documents. This rule, often disregarded, is a very important element of providing the security to the beneficiary.[15]

"It has, so far as I know, never been disputed that, as between confirming bank and issuing bank and as between issuing bank and the buyer, the

---

[14] Id.
[15] UCC 5-108 i (1): "is entitled to be reimbursed by the applicant in immediately available funds not later than the date of its payment of funds."

CHAPTER III

contractual duty of each bank under a confirmed irrevocable credit is to examine with reasonable care all documents presented in order to ascertain that they appear *on their face* to be in accordance with the terms and conditions of the credit, and, if they do so appear, to pay to the seller/beneficiary by whom the documents have been presented the sum stipulated by the credit, or to accept or negotiate *without recourse to drawer drafts* drawn by the seller/beneficiary if the credit so provides. It is so stated in the latest edition of the Uniform Customs. It is equally clear law, and is so provided by article 9 of the Uniform Customs, that confirming banks and issuing banks assume no liability or responsibility to one another or to the buyer "for the form, sufficiency, accuracy, genuineness, falsification or legal effect of any documents." This is well illustrated by the Privy Council case of *Gian Singh & Co. Ltd. v. Banque de l'Indochine [1974] 1 W.L.R. 1234*, where the customer was held liable to reimburse the issuing bank for honouring a documentary credit upon presentation of an apparently conforming document which was an ingenious forgery, a fact that the bank had not been negligent in failing to detect upon examination of the document."[16]

III.4 Strict compliance doctrine

The strict compliance doctrine refers in general to the examination of documents under both stand-by and commercial letters of credit. The documentary conditions precedent must be strictly met in order for the duty of honor to arise. The strict compliance requirement, as applied these instruments means formal or literal compliance, and the reality existing or even known beyond the documents is not relevant at all. The formal test is merciless: discrepancy leads to dishonor regardless of its substance or significance.

URDG Art 2 (b)

"Guarantees by their nature are separate transactions from the contract(s) or tender conditions on which they may be based, and Guarantors are in no way concerned with or bound by such contract(s), or tender conditions,

---

[16] United City Merchants (Investments) Ltd v. Royal Bank of Canada,1982 WL 221777 (HL), [1983] 1 A.C. 168, [1982] 2 All E.R. 720, [1982] 2 Lloyd's Rep. 1, [1982] 2 W.L.R. 1039, [1982] Com. L.R. 142., [1982] 2 W.L.R. 1039.

despite the inclusion of a reference to them in the Guarantee. The duty of a Guarantor under a Guarantee is to pay the sum or sums therein stated on the presentation of a written demand for payment and other documents specified in the Guarantee which appear on their face to be in accordance with the terms of the Guarantee."

When the instrument is substantively independent, what *de facto* has taken place or may take place under the transaction is irrelevant and the reality has no relevance *de jure* to the rights of the beneficiary or the duties of the issuer under the instrument: only the conditions precedent, specified as to the documents to be presented therein, are to be met strictly by the beneficiary in order for him to be entitled to performance under the instrument.[17]

ISP 4.01

"a. Demands for honour of a standby must comply with the terms and conditions of the standby. b. Whether a presentation appears to comply is determined by examining the presentation on its face against the terms and conditions stated in the standby as interpreted and supplemented by these Rules which are to be read in the context of standard standby practice."

CAI v. GB et al.

This well-established rule was expressed as follows:

"I was not addressed at any length as to the proper approach to the question of discrepancy. Indeed, the principles are well established and were

---

[17] ISP 4.02:
"Documents presented which are not required by the standby need not be examined and, in any event, shall be disregarded for purposes of determining compliance of the presentation. They may without responsibility be returned to the presenter or passed on with the other documents presented." 4.03: "An issuer or nominated person is required to examine documents for inconsistency with each other only to the extent provided in the standby."; 4.09 (c): "Specified wording by the use of quotation marks, blocked wording, or an attached exhibit or form, and also provides that the specified wording be "exact" or "identical", then the wording in the documents presented, including typographical errors in spelling, punctuation, spacing and the like, as well as blank lines and spaces for data, must be exactly reproduced.". Russia (DCL) Art. 870: "In order to execute a letter of credit the beneficiary shall present to the executing bank documents evidencing due performance of all conditions of the letter of credit. If any — even if only one — condition of the letter of credit is not met, the letter of credit shall not be executed".

recently re-emphasized by the Court of Appeal in both Seaconsar Far East Ltd. v. Bank Markazi Jomhouri Islami Iran, [1993] 1 Lloyd's Rep. 236 and in Glencore International A.G. v. Bank of China, [1996] 1 Lloyd's Rep. 135. For present purposes it is sufficient to state as follows:

(1) The basic principle is that documents must comply strictly with the terms and conditions of the letter of credit: Equitable Trust Co. New York v. Dawson Partners Ltd., (1927) 27 Ll.L.Rep. 49.
(2) The banker is under no duty to consider the legal effect of the documents or their purpose; Midland Bank Ltd. v. Seymour, [1955] 2 Lloyd's Rep. 147 and Commercial Banking Co. of Sydney v. Jalsard Pty. Ltd., [1973] A.C. 279.
(3) It is not enough to check each document individually against the wording of the credit. Each document must be compared with the other documents to ensure that they are consistent. See Glencore v. Bank of China (sup.).
(4) The documents have to be taken up or rejected promptly and without any opportunity for prolonged enquiry so that a tender of documents which, properly read and understood, invites litigation or calls for further enquiry is a bad tender: Golodetz & Co. Inc. v. Czarnikow-Rionda Co. Inc., [1980] 1 Lloyd's Rep. 453; [1980] 1 W.L.R. 495."[18]

The strict compliance rule demonstrates the special character of these instruments: they do not operate as ordinary contracts. Under contract law a breach must in general be material in order to justify cancellation or termination for cause, whereas under these instruments *any* insignificant deviation or discrepancy entitles the bank to refuse payment.[19] However, once accepted, the bank is entitled to be reimbursed if the documents "appeared *prima facie*" to be strictly conforming i.e., they do not have to be *de facto* strictly conforming. If the tender is, on the other hand, refused, the discrepancies must be identified and specified to the beneficiary, and the documents returned to him, and the bank is precluded from raising new objections as to the documents tendered. The beneficiary may

---

[18] Credit Agricole Indosuez v. Generale Bank and Seco Steel Trading Inc. and Considar Inc., 1999 WL 1319093 (QBD (Comm Ct)), [2000] C.L.C. 205, [2000] 1 Lloyd's Rep. 123, [1999] 2 All E.R. (Comm) 1016.

[19] Pifer presents various theories of strict compliance doctrine on p. 4: Flexible strict compliance, substantial compliance and reasonable compliance in addition to classic strict compliance rule (Tom Pifer, "The ICC Publication of International Standard Banking Practice (ISBP) and the Probable Effect on United States Letter of Credit Law", *Texas Wesleyan Law Review*, (Spring 2006).)

thus tender again, until expiry of the instrument. The bank may raise new objectives as to documents not tendered earlier, but not to the ones already tendered and not objected to.

There is nothing unconscionable in the strict compliance rule: *primo*: the conditions precedent are given in advance in writing allowing the beneficiary to be prepared; *secondo*: if refused, the beneficiary may try again since the bank will identify and indicate the discrepancies to him; and *terzo*: if the instrument is not used, the primary obligor remains liable under the transaction like before.[20]

The same "appear on their face" rule applies to indemnity agreements and reimbursement obligations.[21]

Since the above expressly deals with substantively independent documents, what are the criteria to be applied to instruments which are not substantively independent like, e.g., traditional guarantees or bonds? In essence, the criteria are the

---

[20] Goode writes in *Abstract Payment Undertakings in International Transactions*:
"There is another, and potentially more serious, challenge to the principle of strict compliance, namely the concept of good faith. A general concept of good faith has long been a tenet of the civil law and has been spreading rapidly to other legal families. It is featured, for example, in the American Uniform Commercial Code, the Vienna Sales Convention, the EC Directives on self-employed commercial agents and unfair terms in consumer contracts, the UNCITRAL Convention, and the UNIDROIT Conventions on International Factoring and International Financial Leasing, as well as in the UNIDROIT Principles for International Commercial Contracts and the separate Principles of European Contract Law issued by the Commission on European Contract Law."

Jean Stoufflet, *Fraud in Documentary Credit, Letter of Credit and Demand Guaranty*, 10th Biennial Conference of the International Academy of Commercial and Consumer Law International Banking Development, 21 Dick. L. Rev. 106, (Summer 2001):
"In my opinion, fraud should not to be considered an ethical matter in the area of documentary credits, letters of credit and guaranties. Rather, fraud is really a technical issue. Under this formulation, it is difficult to understand why fraud in the underlying obligation has no effect on the right to payment by the credit beneficiary."

[21] Compare to URDG Art. 2 (c):
"For the purpose of these Rules, "Counter-Guarantee" means any guarantee, bond or other payment undertaking of the Instructing Party, however named or described, given in writing for the payment of money to the Guarantor on presentation in conformity with the terms of the undertaking of a written demand for payment and other documents specified in the Counter-Guarantee which *appear on their face* to be in accordance with the terms of the Counter Guarantee. Counter-Guarantees are by their nature separate transactions from the Guarantees to which they relate and from any underlying contract(s) or tender conditions, and Instructing Parties are in no way concerned with or bound by such Guarantees, contract(s) or tender conditions, despite the inclusion of a reference to them in the Counter-Guarantee."

CHAPTER III

same, but compliance is not a formal analysis. Instead, there is a fact or evidence analysis, where oral and other non-documentary material plays a significant role. Not only does the "examiner" have to assess the weight of the evidence, the examiner also has to evaluate its significance, often according to terms and conditions which are those of traditional contract law reflected on the instrument by the conditions precedent.

This analysis is very difficult and most unsuitable for a bank to do. The only comfort is that the bankers do not usually have to be involved in the process: the court or arbitrators do it.

The so-called mezzanine instruments fall in between the two: the arbitral award is to be strictly conforming, but the assessment and the decision is taken by the panel, not by the banks.

In general there is no room for any deviation, discretion or reasonableness to be allowed in the documents presented by the beneficiary, no matter how immaterial or insignificant or formal the discrepancies or deviations may appear to be.[22] The documents tendered by the beneficiary which are not strictly confirming *may always be refused*. The right of the confirming bank or nominated bank against the issuing bank and the issuing bank's right to reimbursement from the account party may, however, differ from the beneficiary's right to honor.

The whole mechanism of letters of credit would be endangered if the documents to be tendered by the beneficiary would not have to be in strict conformity with the credit. Whereas the *Szteijn case* as a classical fraud case is the main export product of American letter of credit law, the opinion of Lord Summer in *Equitable Trust Company of New York v. Dawson Partners Ltd.*

---

[22] Tom Pifer, *The ICC Publication of International Standard Banking Practice (ISBP) and the Probable Effect on United States Letter of Credit Law*, Texas Wesleyan L Rev, (Spring 2006):
"To review the current status of LC law, the standard of compliance applied to the review of an LC presentation has historically been an issue of inconsistency among United States courts. Fortunately, the 1993 publication of the UCP 500 and the 1995 publication of the revised UCC 5 have produced substantial advancement in fixing the standard at flexible strict compliance. The stringency of application of this strict compliance standard should be greater when a discrepancy is related to a commercial issue for which the bank is ill equipped to determine the degree of significance. On the other hand, a more flexible standard can be applied in waiving banking discrepancies which the bank can determine to be insubstantial."

is quoted by many U.S. courts and scholars as well as other commentators everywhere.

> "It is both common ground and common sense that in such a transaction the accepting bank can only claim indemnity if the conditions on which it is authorised to accept are in the matter of the accompanying documents strictly observed. There is no room for documents which are almost the same, or which will do just as well. Business could not proceed securely on any other lines."[23]

There is no doubt that letter of credit law lives or dies with the doctrine of strict compliance. It is a cornerstone of classical lex mercatoria. There are some limitations to the requirement of strict compliance which could be defined as a rule of common sense. The rule applies to both commercial and standby credits. It is certain that the doctrine of strict compliance applies and must apply to the first tender. Since the beneficiary often has plenty of time (or the time he has seems sufficient) to collect and tender the documents, the doctrine seems most justified. We have to remember that the beneficiary also has the right to remedy any discrepancies in the documents within the validity of the credit. Any deviation from this principle as to the first tender would be equal to denying the customer's right to reasonable expectations and protection given by this doctrine.

It is, however, not as clear whether the doctrine of strict compliance applies to the paying bank, which is in a different position than the beneficiary. The paying bank can seldom, if ever, itself obtain the required documents. It has to make the decision as to their conformity within a limited period of time. The commission and fee collected by it would not economically allow any major investigation. Very often the credit has expired when it tenders the documents to the customer or the issuing bank and there are no possibilities to remedy any discrepancies. Regardless of this, most scholars seem to apply the doctrine of strict compliance to the second tender as well.

---

[23] Strict compliance. *Equitable Trust Company of New York v. Dawson Partners, Ltd.*
"The bank's branch abroad, which knows nothing officially of the details of the transaction thus financed, cannot take upon itself to decide what will do well enough and what will not. If it does as it is told, it is safe; if it declines to do anything else, it is safe; if it departs from the conditions laid down, it acts at its own risk. The documents tendered were not exactly the documents which the defendants had promised to take up, and prima facie they were right in refusing to take them."

This interpretation is not in conformity with the practical realities and the provisions of the UCP (URC 14): The terms "reasonable care" and "appear on their face" clearly describe something other than strict compliance. The "appear on their face" criterion limits the scope of examination and clearly demonstrates that no legal or other analysis of the documents is necessary. The documents will be accepted as tendered if they appear to be conforming. *De facto* they do not have to be such. If the documents have been "substantially" conforming, the paying bank has the right to reimbursement. The beneficiary could not, however, invoke the doctrine of substantial compliance for reasons given above and because "a beneficiary can in no case avail himself of the contractual relationships existing between banks or between the applicant for the credit and the issuing bank".

There may, however, be situations where the bank's duty of reasonable care is heightened to a more strict standard. This is the principle of the "red flag". The relationship of strict compliance and custom is sometimes problematic.

The UCC describes the strict compliance rule as follows:

> "The standard of strict compliance governs the issuer's obligation to the beneficiary and to the applicant. By requiring that a "presentation" appear strictly to comply, the section requires not only that the documents themselves *appear on their face strictly to comply, but also that the other terms of the letter of credit such as those dealing with the time and place of presentation are strictly complied with.* Typically, a letter of credit will provide that presentation is timely if made to the issuer, confirmer, or any other nominated person prior to expiration of the letter of credit.
> Accordingly, a nominated person that has honored a demand or otherwise given value before expiration will have a right to reimbursement from the issuer even though presentation to the issuer is made after the expiration of the letter of credit. Conversely, where the beneficiary negotiates documents to one who is not a nominated person, the beneficiary or that person acting on behalf of the beneficiary must make presentation to a nominated person, confirmer, or issuer prior to the expiration date."

If the conditions are met, the issuer is entitled to effect payment. In case of fraud or other exceptional circumstances, *the issuer's duty* to honor may "disappear", but the issuer's *right* to honor may remain regardless of the disappearance of his duty to do so subject, however, to orders of courts of law. If the conditions precedent are not met, the demand must be refused and no payment be effected. The account party may of course waive the discrepancies at his convenience and in his sole discretion, but is under no duty to do so. In letter of credit practice there are discrepancies in over 50% of documents tendered. This leaves plenty of room for the account party's waiver and it is often given for various reasons.[24]

The strict compliance rule allows certain tolerance at least when expressly provided in the applicable rules as, e.g., in UCP 600 Article 30:

> "a. The words "about" or "approximately" used in connection with the amount of the credit or the quantity or the unit price stated in the credit are to be construed as allowing a tolerance not to exceed 10% more or 10% less than the amount, the quantity or the unit price to which they refer.
> b. A tolerance not to exceed 5% more or 5% less than the quantity of the goods is allowed, provided the credit does not state the quantity in terms of a stipulated number of packing units or individual items and the total amount of the drawings does not exceed the amount of the credit.
> c. Even when partial shipments are not allowed, a tolerance not to exceed 5% less than the amount of the credit is allowed, provided that the quantity of the goods, if stated in the credit, is shipped in full and a unit price, if stated in the credit, is not reduced or that sub-article 30 (b) is not applicable. This tolerance does not apply when the credit stipulates a specific tolerance or uses the expressions referred to in sub-article 30 (a)."

III.5 The requirement of consistency

Strict compliance requires that, to the extent specified, the documents presented must match the specifications. If this is the case, there is, however, an additional requirement, namely, that of *consistency* of the tender as a whole.[25] In practice this

---

[24] According to Pekka Heino, a trade finance director and expert at Nordea Bank, the reasons for such huge numbers of discrepancies is due to failures in drafting and negotiating the transaction. These failures include poor drafting and instructions, inaccurate guidance and advice by the issuing bank, and finally lack of diligence in preparing the tender to comply with the credit by the beneficiary.

[25] Lars Gorton, *Remburs, dokumentgranskning och doktrinen om strikt uppfyllelse*, Svensk Juristtidning No. 9 (2003):
"En av de centrala frågorna när det gäller inriktningen på och omfattningen av rembursbankens granskningsskyldighet rör sålunda bedömningen av de dokument som presenteras. Vilka omständigheter skall beaktas, hur skall dokument samläsas, vad behövs för att dokument skall anses

means that the data in the tender beyond the area specified must not be inconsistent with the specifications or internally, i.e., the data in the tender should not be internally contradictory but form a consistent whole.

In an "old" decision the ICC Banking Commission (florissant 1975-1979) gave the following definition:

> "The Commission decided that the notion of "consistency" referred to in Article 7 should be understood as meaning that the whole of the documents must obviously relate to the same transaction, that is to say, that each should bear a relation (link) with the others on its face, and the documents should not be inconsistent with one another"

UNC Article 16(1) provides:

> "In determining whether documents are in facial conformity with the terms and conditions of the undertaking, and *are consistent with one another*, the guarantor / issuer shall have. . . "

UCP 600 provides in Article 14 as follows:

> "d. Data in a document, when read in context with the credit, the document itself and international standard banking practice, need not be identical to, but must not conflict with, data in that document, any other stipulated document or the credit.
> e. In documents other than the commercial invoice, the description of the goods, services or performance, if stated, may be in general terms not conflicting with their description in the credit."

The requirement of consistency is not a "mechanical" analysis as the strict compliance requirement is. It does not extend to documents tendered by the beneficiary but not required by the credit, which are to be disregarded and returned

---

avvika från remburskraven, vilka åtgärder förväntas rembursbanken vidta? Banken skall granska dokumenten vart och ett för sig men också i förhållande till övriga dokument. Dokumenten skall granskas i förhållande till vad som bestämts i rembursen men också i förhållande till rembursreglerna. Därigenom kan flera olika mer eller mindre svårbedömda problem uppkomma."

to the presenter.[26] In certain cases the inconsistency may be obvious, hinting to fraud, and in some other cases it may appear insignificant.

The consistency requirement may put the examiner in a difficult position. One may perhaps deem the consistency requirement to be a rule subsidiary to the main principle of "appearing on their face to be compliant". If this is accepted as the starting point, as it would seem justified, *in dubio* the examiner may presume that there is no inconsistency unless this is obvious (*"prima facie"*) and appears to be material and significant. The rules and practice seem to indicate, however, that the criterion of consistency may have an independent value creating a grey area in between the otherwise very clear rules.

The *CIC v. CMB case*, where the consistency criterion appears to be a sub-rule of the "facial conformity", illustrates the issues as follows:

There was inconsistency between the commercial invoice and the packing list, one showing 38,64% and the other 40,00% percentage.

> *"The defendant maintained that the commercial invoice and the packing list were mutually inconsistent.* This reflected the outcome of a calculation made by CMB by reference to the packing list that the percentage of, for example, CI logs in the entire Okoume log parcel was 38.64% whilst the commercial invoice, reciting the terms of the L/C, recorded a percentage of 40%. Whilst I reject the submission that the objection was not put forward with sufficient clarity (indeed CIC's immediate response demonstrates that it had hoisted in the point), I unhesitatingly hold that the documents were not thereby rendered discrepant.

The issue was: what action must the examiner take to establish or discover a possible inconsistency? The decision was based on provisions of UCP 500 as cited by the judge:

> The first point to be made is that I am not remotely persuaded that reasonable care on the part of CMB (or for that matter, CIC) required any such

---

[26] UCP 600 in Article 14:
"g. A document presented but not required by the credit will be disregarded and may be returned to the presenter. h. If a credit contains a condition without stipulating the document to indicate compliance with the condition, banks will deem such condition as not stated and will disregard it."

calculation to be made. The governing provision of UCP 500 is Article 13 (a):— "Banks must examine all documents stipulated in the Credit with reasonable care, to ascertain whether or not they appear, on their face, to be in compliance with the terms and conditions of the Credit. Compliance of the stipulated documents on their face with the terms and conditions of the Credit, shall be determined by international standard banking practice as reflected in these Articles. Documents which appear on their face to be inconsistent with one another will be considered as not appearing on their face with being in compliance with the terms and conditions of the Credit. . . ." This is supplemented by Article 21, which reads: "When documents other than transport documents, insurance documents and commercial invoices are called for, the Credit should stipulate by whom such documents are to be issued and their wording or data content. If the Credit does not so stipulate, *banks will accept such documents as presented, provided that their data content is not inconsistent with any other stipulated document presented.*"

The court described the test by two steps, ruling expressly that no action is required to discover inconsistencies: the inconsistency must be apparent.

Against that background, my approach is as follows:—
i) The obligation on the bank is to exercise reasonable care, as determined in accordance with international standard banking practice.
ii) The obligation *is a passive one*, in the sense of using reasonable care to assess the absence of any apparent inconsistency on the face of the documents *as opposed to an active obligation to establish the existence of complete consistency on the basis of the material contained on the face of the document.*

It follows in my judgment, that the checker of the documents was not required, in the exercise of reasonable care, to embark on the calculations relied upon. It is common ground that, absent those calculations, there was no inconsistency between the packing list, the commercial invoice and the L/C. In any event, the commercial invoice complied with the terms of Article 37(c):— "The description of the goods in the commercial invoice must correspond with the description in the Credit. In all other documents, the goods may be described in general terms not inconsistent with the description of the goods in the Credit." This it did. The description in the commercial invoice expressly matched that in the letter of credit. The packing list set out the exact number and volume of logs shipped, matching the totals in the Bills of Lading. There was no percentage grade shown on the face of the packing list and no requirement that there should be. Absent further calculations, there was thus no inconsistency.

The test set forth was compatible with the opinion of ICC banking commission:

> This conclusion is fortified by the opinion of the ICC dated 6th September 1999 in response to a query from another Chinese bank relating to packing lists: "In previous opinions the ICC Banking Commission has stated *that banks do not have a duty to carry out mathematical calculations or complete lists of individual items, weights or measurements to ensure consistency with other documents.* If totals are declared on documents, then these should be in agreement with those shown on other documents presented. If the Credit did not specify the manner in which packing details were to be expressed, the packing list may show the individual or collective information of the packages shipped, subject to any totals agreeing with those shown on other documents."

CMB argued that although there is no duty to engage in active discovery, the bank has the right to do so and invoke the inconsistency so established. The court did not agree. In addition there was a permitted tolerance of 10% and thus no inconsistency at all.

> The defendant sought to ague in accordance with the views of their expert, Mr Claude Mifsud, that CMB were nonetheless entitled to perform the calculations if such was their own practice and then to rely on any inconsistency thus unearthed. *I reject this submission. The issue of discrepancy cannot depend upon the degree of inquisitiveness within the bank. The identification of any inconsistency must flow from a consistency of approach, i.e., steps that no reasonable bank would fail to take.* In any event, the outcome of the calculations does not establish any inconsistency. The description of the goods in the L/C specifies various percentages for each grade, subject to a tolerance of plus or minus 10%. It was common ground that this tolerance applied to each grade as well as to the total (not surprisingly, since the task of shipping the precise percentages can be treated as physically impossible). The calculations based on the packing list revealed that the number of logs in each grade was *within the permitted 10% tolerance.* Accordingly, the suggestion of inconsistency (even if reasonable care called for the calculations actually to be conducted) is, in my judgment, based upon a misconception.

CMB argued also that the drafts were not in the right language i.e., they were in French in lieu of English. The court held that the drafts were not at all in this case included in the documents to be examined.

The drafts

The objection taken to the drafts was that printed parts were in the French language contrary, it is contended, to the terms of the L/C. On the assumption that these documents were within the compass of field 47A in the L/C, I reject the claimant's submission that they were nonetheless "in English". The fact that the checkers at CMB were aware of the nature of the documents and able to comprehend the significance of the entries is not to the point. The short answer to the point, in my judgment, is that on a proper construction of the L/C, the documents required to be in English by virtue of Field 47A are those documents required for negotiation by virtue of Field 46A. *They do not include the drafts.* This distinction is made clear by Field 78 whereby the bank undertook that, on receipt of the "documents", it would accept the draft. *This approach reflects the function of the drafts. They were not part of the commercial documentation, which, following negotiation, was to be passed on to the applicant Jiangsu.* They were simply part of the process whereby CMB's obligations to pay could be put in a form in which they could be readily discounted. Non-acceptance of the draft would not relieve CMB of its obligation to pay at maturity. It merely deprived CIC of the opportunity of going into the market."[27]

III.6 The "as tendered" or *è contrario* rule

The strict compliance rule and the doctrine of substantive independence are the cornerstones of international letter of credit law. Should they erode or not be enforced by the courts, the whole existence of this valuable instrument, often described as the "life blood" of international exchange, would be put in jeopardy. The strict compliance doctrine must be maintained at any cost if we wish the instrument to survive as a useful tool of international exchange. From the theoretical point of view one could say that what the parties have agreed as to the

---

[27] *Credit Industriel et Commercial v. China Merchants Bank,* 2002 WL 819936 (QBD (Comm Ct)), [2002] C.L.C. 1263, [2002] 2 All E.R. (Comm) 427, [2002] EWHC 973, Case No: 2000/738, Neutral citation number: [2002] EWHC 973 (Comm).

conditions precedent is to be deemed crucial and "of essence" and no one else has the right to question it or construe it otherwise than what has been expressly agreed ("expressis verbis").[28]

The *pacta sunt servanda* rule prevails as cast in reinforced concrete and the interpretation follows *mutatis mutandis* the principle of *parole evidence* or extrinsic evidence: nothing else matters or is relevant other than the wording of the instrument. Consequently, the courts should not admit any evidence to demonstrate or prove an intention not expressed or a meaning different from the one expressed, simply because it is materially irrelevant. This is called "objective interpretation". Moreover, what is objective becomes less flexible than in contract law in general because the instrument is often an expression of several parties: the account party, the issuing bank and the confirming bank and perhaps also the beneficiary.

Under letters of credit, non-documentary conditions may be simply disregarded.[29]

---

[28] Bulgaria (DCL) Art 435 (4): "For payment of the credit's amount only such conditions shall be relevant which are named in the credit."

[29] UCC 5-108 (official comment):
"In requiring that nondocumentary conditions in letters of credit be ignored as surplusage, Article 5 remains aligned with the UCP (see UCP 500 Article 13c), approves cases like *Pringle-Associated Mortgage Corp. v. Southern Nat'l Bank*, 571 F.2d 871, 874 (5th Cir. 1978), and rejects the reasoning in cases such as *Sherwood & Roberts, Inc. v. First Sec. Bank*, 682 P.2d 149 (Mont. 1984). Subsection (g) recognizes that letters of credit sometimes contain nondocumentary terms or conditions. Conditions such as a term prohibiting "shipment on vessels more than 15 years old," are to be disregarded and treated as surplusage. Similarly, a requirement that there be an award by a "duly appointed arbitrator" would not require the issuer to determine whether the arbitrator had been "duly appointed." Likewise a term in a standby letter of credit that provided for differing forms of certification depending upon the particular type of default does not oblige the issuer independently to determine which kind of default has occurred. These conditions must be disregarded by the issuer. Where the nondocumentary conditions are central and fundamental to the issuer's obligation (as for example a condition that would require the issuer to determine in fact whether the beneficiary had performed the underlying contract or whether the applicant had defaulted) their inclusion may remove the undertaking from the scope of Article 5 entirely. See Section 5-102(a)(10) and Comment 6 to Section 5-102. Subsection (g) would not permit the beneficiary or the issuer to disregard terms in the letter of credit such as place, time, and mode of presentation. The rule in subsection (g) is intended to prevent an issuer from deciding or even investigating extrinsic facts but not from consulting the clock, the calendar the relevant law and practice, or its own general knowledge of documentation or transactions of the type underlying a particular letter of credit. Even though nondocumentary conditions must be disregarded in determining compliance of a presentation (and thus in determining the issuer's duty to the beneficiary), an issuer that has promised its applicant that it will honor only on the occurrence of those nondocumentary conditions may have liability to its applicant for disregarding the conditions."

Chapter III

UCP 600 Article 14 (h) says:

> "If a credit contains a condition without stipulating the document to indicate compliance with the condition, banks will deem such condition as not stated and will disregard it."

ISP 4.11 (a-b) provides:

> "A standby term or condition which is non-documentary must be disregarded whether or not it affects the issuer's obligation to treat a presentation as complying or to treat the standby as issued, amended, or terminated. Terms and conditions are non-documentary if the standby does not require presentation of a document in which they are to be evidenced and if their fulfillment cannot be determined by the issuer from the issuer's own records or within the issuer's normal operations."

UCC 5-108 (official comment) tells us:

> "9. The responsibility of the issuer under a letter of credit is to examine documents and to make a prompt decision to honor or dishonor based upon that examination Nondocumentary conditions have no place in this regime and are better accommodated under contract or suretyship law and practice."

In other instruments they may play a role but are subject to narrow interpretation. Documents tendered but not required will also be disregarded, and some undefined words will be disregarded too.[30]

UCP 600 Article 14 (g) says:

> "A document presented but not required by the credit will be disregarded and may be returned to the presenter."

---

[30] UCP 600 Article 3: "Unless required to be used in a document, words such as "prompt", "immediately" or "as soon as possible" will be disregarded."
UCP 600 Article 17: "c. Unless a document indicates otherwise, a bank will also accept a document as original if it:
    i. appears to be written, typed, perforated or stamped by the document issuer's hand; or
    ii. appears to be on the document issuer's original stationery; or
    iii. states that it is original, unless the statement appears not to apply to the document presented."

What rules, if any, then remain to be applied beyond the border of clearly expressed conditions precedent? May one introduce new rules or implicit conditions in the area not covered by the express stipulations of the parties? Beyond the strict compliance rule of "what you see is what you have", the legal environment changes and changes totally. Right beyond the express conditions precedent of an instrument the territory of the "*as tendered* "- or "*as presented*" begins.[31]

ISP 4.17 tells us:

> "If a standby requires a statement, certificate, or other recital of a default or other drawing event and does not specify content, the document complies if it contains: a. a representation to the effect that payment is due because a drawing event described in the standby has occurred; b. a date indicating when it was issued; and c. the beneficiary's signature."

ISP 4.20 (a) goes on to say:

> "If a standby requires a document other than one whose content is specified in these Rules without specifying the issuer, data content, or wording, a document complies if it appears to be appropriately titled or to serve the function of that type of document under standard standby practice."

---

[31] Collected Docdex Decisions 1997-2003, No 210, p. 45. See also Collected Docdex Decisions 1997-2003, No 211, p. 47: "UCP 500 sub-Article 13(a), Articles 2, 20 and 38. Whether an issuing bank is required to accept the combination in one document of individual independent document stipulated in the letter of credit; whether by having taken up previously a set of documents with a specific discrepancy, an issuing bank is prejudiced to take up a further presentation of documents with the same specific discrepancy under the same credit."

ISP "a. 4.12: ("9. 4.12:)
A required statement need not be accompanied by a solemnity, officialization, or any other formality. b. If a standby provides for the addition of a formality to a required statement by the person making it without specifying form or content, the statement complies if it indicates that it was declared, averred, warranted, attested, sworn under oath, affirmed, certified, or the like. c. If a standby provides for a statement to be witnessed by another person without specifying form or content, the witnessed statement complies if it appears to contain a signature of a person other than the beneficiary with an indication that the person is acting as a witness. d. If a standby provides for a statement to be counter-signed, legalized, visaed, or the like by a person other than the beneficiary acting in a governmental, judicial, corporate, or other representative capacity without specifying form or content, the statement complies if it contains the signature of a person other than the beneficiary and includes an indication of that person's representative capacity and the organization on whose behalf the person has acted."

CHAPTER III

This is the Wild West of letter of credit law.[32] The theory is that if the condition was not important enough to the parties to be incorporated into the express provisions of the credit, it is deemed to be irrelevant and cannot be introduced by way of "implied" terms, much less by the subjective assessment of the interpreter or examiner.[33]

The "as tendered rule" is expressed in UCP 600 also, as follows, in Article 3 and 14:

> "A requirement for a document to be legalized, visaed, certified or similar will be satisfied *by any signature*, mark, stamp or label on the document which appears to satisfy that requirement." . . . . "Terms such as "first class", "well known", "qualified", "independent", "official", "competent" or "local" used to describe the issuer of a document allow *any issuer* except the beneficiary to issue that document"
> "f. If a credit requires presentation of a document other than a transport document, insurance document or commercial invoice, without stipulating

---

[32] Opinions of the ICC Banking Commission 1984-1986, R 111: "The Commission stressed that in accordance with Article 23 of the Uniform Customs and Practice (1983 Revision) credits should stipulate by whom certain documents are to be issued and their wording or data content. If the credit does not so stipulate, banks will accept such documents as presented, provided that their data content makes it possible to relate the goods and/or services referred to therein to those referred to in the commercial invoice(s) presented, or to those referred to in the credit if the credit does not stipulate presentation or a commercial invoice."

[33] Credit Industriel et Commercial v. China Merchants Bank, Case No: 2000/738, Neutral citation number: [2002] EWHC 973 (Comm):
"General Approach. Banks examine documents presented under a letter of credit to determine, among other things, whether on their face they appear to be original. Banks treat as original any document bearing an apparently original signature, mark, stamp, or label of the issuer of the document, unless the document itself indicates that it is not original. Accordingly, unless a document indicates otherwise, it is treated as original if it: 1. appears to be written, typed, perforated, or stamped by the document issuer's hand; or 2. appears to be on the document issuer's original stationery; or 3. states that it is original, unless the statement appears not to apply to the document presented (e.g. because it appears to be a photocopy of another document and the statement of originality appears to apply to that other document). Hand signed documents. Consistent with sub-paragraph (A) above, banks treat as original any document that appears to be hand signed by the issuer of the document. For example, a hand signed draft or commercial invoice is treated as an original document, whether or not some or all other constituents of the document are preprinted, carbon copied or produced by reprographic, automated or computerised systems. . . . 4. What is not an "Original"? A document indicates that it is not an original if it 1. appears to be produced on a telefax machine: 2. appears to be a photocopy of another document which has not otherwise been completed by hand marking the photocopy or by photocopying it on what appears to be original stationery; or 3. states in the document that it is a true copy of another document or that another document is the sole original."

by whom the document is to be issued or its data content, banks will accept the document *as presented* if its content appears to fulfil the function of the required document and otherwise complies with sub-article 14 (d)."

There is an iron curtain between the domain of strict compliance and "the territory of *as presented*" where "anything goes". The smooth running of international exchange and banking requires this and tolerates no surprises or new conditions. The only exceptions are the hard core of *lex mercatoria* and the international *ordre public* like, e.g., the principle of good faith or the maxim of "*fraus omnia corrumpit*."

III.7 Interviews with experts

III.7.1 Pekka Heino of Nordea Bank

Pekka Heino, Head of Trade Finance at Nordea Bank, who has years of experience in the area, confirms that proportionally the use of different instruments has remained more or less the same although he believes that the share of bank guarantees will grow also in the future.[34] Basel II (regulations on banking laws) will probably lead to a growth in number of documentary credits although its proportionate share of foreign trade payments will diminish due to the growing use of bank transfers. In trade with Russia there are less advance payments, but letters of credit are used more and more often.

Nordea has not received any letter of credit requests or applications which would not refer to or incorporate UCP, and the bank would probably not agree to issue a letter of credit without such a reference. In the field of bank guarantees, there are a number of diverse rules, none of which has risen to a status comparable to that of UCP.

Since the 1970s and 1980s there have been no revocable credits. They were used at one time to pay the salaries and related costs of expatriate persons.

The electronic letter of credit is not yet truly practical to use, which is partly due to the poor acceptance of electronic transport documents like, e.g., bills of lading and a lack of sufficient infrastructure in certain parts of the world.

---

[34] He estimates the Nordic market to range clearly over 2 billion EUR.

He points out that the most serious and common problems relate to poor expertise or attention to these issues when negotiating the underlying agreement, which may accumulate in connection with the banking procedures if the banks are not sufficiently instructed as to the particularities of the industry or transaction in question.

In almost 100% of discrepancies, which are very common, the issues are settled by way of express waiver.

III.7.2 Matti Vainionpää of Sampo Bank

Matti Vainionpää, Head of Financial Institutions and Trade Finance at Sampo Bank believes that the use of letters of credit will continue to grow, but that their share of payments will decrease. The main countries involved are China, Russia, Taiwan and India on the import side and China, Russia, Turkey, Korea and India on the export side. Close to 70-80% of the documents presented are discrepant, but the discrepancies are usually waived. Over 90% of the documents are examined on the very same day.

Guarantee instruments are in growing use in Europe, most of which are on-demand guarantees or joint-and-several type guarantees. In trade with Russia and Turkey, letters of credit are used for post-financing, where the instrument is a security for foreign exchange credits. There are fewer than ten claims per year under guarantees.

His estimate of the Finnish market (domestic and foreign) in all these instruments including guarantees is in the range of 40 billion EUR, and that letters of credit make up approximately 50% of that total.

III.7.3 Petri Ikävalko of Svenska Handelsbanken

Petri Ikävalko is in charge of documentary credits, collections and guarantees at Svenska Handelsbanken and he has a long experience in the field. He emphasizes the role played by these instruments in export transactions. The main area of use is the Middle East and Asia, but there is still some limited use within Europe, too.

Among these instruments, bank guarantees play a dominant role. The bank recommends their use in transactions to cover the payments and risks from advance payment to completion and maintenance/warranty period by way of a chain of instruments.

UCP forms an unchanged foundation of the letter of credit operations of the bank and the bank refuses to transact without having it incorporated. As to bank guarantees, there is no such generally accepted set of reference rules.

He points out that sometimes documents are to be tendered which are subject to the account party's will or action although the bank attempts to polish them in the course of the application process. They often relate to excessive attempts to control payments by the account party and, if incorporated, sometimes result in delays in payment.

On the other hand, most of the problems are due to discrepant documents, which discrepancies are usually waived by the account party.

III.7.4 Mirja Fonck of OKO Bank

Mirja Fonck, Vice President of OKO Bank, is in charge of international payments in Finland's largest banking group.

Bank guarantees and letters of credit have almost equal shares of the product market. The main geographic areas are China, India, Korea and Eastern Europe and Russia. The use of letters of credit is growing, in particular to finance the transaction. Deferred payments, credits and forfeiting financing are growing as well. She points out that discrepancies are the most common problem and that the bank has a good experience from using the ICC's DOCDEX panel. The bank also warns clients against instruments which require the account party's acts as a condition precedent.

The role of UCP is very strong and its incorporation into the letter-of-credit documents is a must. As to guarantees, the situation is different. Less than 10% of the bank guarantee instruments issued refer to ICC rules. She is, however, expecting a positive development in the area, referring to World Bank's adoption of ICC Rules.

Chapter III

III.8 The liability of the banks

III.8.1 General

How is the strict compliance doctrine to be applied in the heat of a banking day?

UCC 5-108 (official comment) tells us:

> "2. Section 5-108(a) balances the need of the issuer for time to examine the documents against the possibility that the examiner (at the urging of the applicant or for fear that it will not be reimbursed) will take excessive time to search for defects. What is a "reasonable time" is not extended to accommodate an issuer's procuring a waiver from the applicant. See Article 14c of the UCP. Under both the UCC and the UCP the issuer has a reasonable time to honor or give notice. The outside limit of that time is measured in business days under the UCC and in banking days under the UCP, a difference that will rarely be significant.
> Examiners must note that the seven-day period is not a safe harbor. The time within which the issuer must give notice is the lesser of a reasonable time or seven business days. Where there are few documents (as, for example, with the mine run standby letter of credit), the reasonable time would be less than seven days. If more than a reasonable time is consumed in examination, no timely notice is possible. What is a "reasonable time" is to be determined by examining the behavior of those in the business of examining documents, mostly banks. Absent prior agreement of the issuer, one could not expect a bank issuer to examine documents while the beneficiary waited in the lobby if the normal practice was to give the documents to a person who had the opportunity to examine those together with many others in an orderly process. That the applicant has not yet paid the issuer or that the applicant's account with the issuer is insufficient to cover the amount of the draft is not a basis for extension of the time period."

Transactions pending may be numerous and the documentary requirements may vary across a wide spectrum.[35] The time available to examine the

---

[35] UCC 5-108:
"This section does not impose a bifurcated standard under which an issuer's right to reimbursement might be broader than a beneficiary's right to honor. However, the explicit deference to standard practice in Section 5-108(a) and (e) and elsewhere expands issuers' rights of reimbursement

documents tendered by the beneficiary is limited to five banking days or seven business days.

UCP 600 Article 14 b:

> "A nominated bank acting on its nomination, a confirming bank, if any, and the issuing bank shall each have a maximum of five banking days following the day of presentation to determine if a presentation is complying. This period is not curtailed or otherwise affected by the occurrence on or after the date of presentation of any expiry date or last day for presentation."

What does it mean in the practice of banking? There may also be issues which are expressly excluded from examination.[36]

In case law the rules were summarized by the court as follows:

Time needed and available to the examiner:

This Hong Kong case demonstrates the duties of the examining bank in the process:

> "Issue (3) - law on reasonable time and delay.
> On the law relating to the reasonable time referred to in article 13b. and article.14d.i. of UPC.500, Mr. Sussex referred us to *Seaconsar v. Bank Markazi [1999].1 Lloyd's Rep 36* where Sir Christopher Staughton stated at pages 41-42: "*The time needed for checking documents must necessarily be*

---

where that practice so provides. Also, issuers can and often do contract with their applicants for expanded rights of reimbursement. *Where that is done, the beneficiary will have to meet a more stringent standard of compliance as to the issuer than the issuer will have to meet as to the applicant.* Similarly, a nominated person may have reimbursement and other rights against the issuer based on this article, the UCP, bank-to-bank reimbursement rules, or other agreement or undertaking of the issuer. *These rights may allow the nominated person to recover from the issuer even when the nominated person would have no right to obtain honor under the letter of credit.*"

[36] UCP 600 Article 19:
"v. contain terms and conditions of carriage or make reference to another source containing the terms and conditions of carriage (short form or blank back transport document). Contents of terms and conditions of carriage) will not be examined".

UCP 600 Article 22:
"b. A bank will not examine charter party contracts, even if they are required to be presented by the terms of the credit."

somewhat vague; it depends how many documents are required by the credit, what detail they must contain, and how clearly or (as the case may be) obscurely that is spelt out. But once that is done and the decision taken, it will ordinarily be a fairly simple task to give notice to the beneficiary. We can see no reason why the bank, if it has checked the documents with greater dispatch than normal, should be allowed to carry forward a period of time as a credit against its next obligation. The Judge thought they could but we cannot agree. If this seems stern doctrine, the answer is that the letter of credit law is and has to be precise; it is not concerned with merits."

The meaning of "without delay":

"The words 'without delay' mean what they say, and nothing is to be gained by paraphrasing them. Where a decision to reject documents is made at or about the close of business on a Friday, as may have happened in this case, we would expect the obligation to give notice without delay to require that it be given on the Monday, which was the next banking day; Mr. Mansouri appears to have accepted that in cross-examination. It may well be that, *in other cases the obligation requires notice to be given on the same day as the decision is taken.* But the difficulty that we face is that we have no precise information as to what was done on Monday Dec. 7, 1987; and the reason why we have no such information is not the fault of Bank Melli but of Seaconsar, who did not take any point on the words 'without delay' until years afterwards."

In *Bankers Trust Co. v. State Bank of India [1991].1 Lloyd's Rep 587*, Hirst.J had this to say on the "reasonable time" to be taken for examination of documents presented at page 600: "I do not think the requirement of 'a reasonable time' in art. 16c [c.f. article 13b. of UCP 500] was intended to allow, let alone encourage, an intricate minute-by-minute examination of the issuing bank's work of the kind undertaken here, but rather *to require consideration in broad terms whether the issuing bank set about its work conscientiously and, viewed overall, handled the matter with reasonable promptness, either by reference to an appropriate fixed time-limit or generally.*

The special requirements and features of any individual case are to be taken into account:

This was an unusually (though not uniquely) onerous checking exercise. Having seen BT's witnesses, I am satisfied that they fully complied with these requirements during stage (1), and consequently reject all the above criticisms."

The notice of rejection must specify the discrepancies.

Regarding the notice of rejection to be sent to the beneficiary of the LC "without delay", Hirst.J continued at page 601: "That telex did not, however, comply with art. 16d [c.f. article 14d.i. of UCP 500], since it did not specify the discrepancies, an essential requirement since it enables the presenting bank to decide for themselves whether the items relied upon by the issuing bank are in fact discrepant; I reject Mr. Goldsmith' s suggestion that this telex can be read together with the later telex in order to surmount this problem. Mr. Scott submits that, in consequence, the issuing bank failed to give notice of its decision to refuse the documents 'without delay' in breach of art. 16d. Mr. Goldsmith submits that the words 'without delay' relate both to decision and its basis, and that therefore until BT had the opportunity to check H & J's discrepancies, they were not guilty of delay. I am unable to accept Mr. Goldsmith's construction, which does not accord with the clear language of art. 16d, and I therefore hold that BT failed to give notice of their decision to refuse the documents without delay, and therefore infringed the first part of art. 16d."
In *Hing Yip Hing Fat Co. Ltd v. Daiwa Bank Ltd [1991].2 HKLR.35,* Kaplan. J observed at page 58C-E as follows: "There are two points which I believe are important to bear in mind. Firstly Daiwa are not, on the evidence before me, a large bank and Hirst.J specifically stated that 'for a smaller bank with smaller resources a reasonable time limit might be longer'. That is longer than the three days that Barclays set themselves generally and contended for in the Bankers Trust case. Secondly and I think more importantly it has to be borne in mind that most checkers of documentary credits in Hong Kong will not have English as their mother tongue. This must add time to the checking process and must justify a fairly rigorous checking procedure and hierarchy." "[37]

---

[37] *NV Koninklijke Sphinx Gustavsberg v Cooperatieve Centrale-Raiffeisen-Boerenleenbank* BA, 24 November 2005, Court of Appeal, Civil Appeal No 161 of 2004.

In another Hong Kong case, *Hing Yip v. Daiwa Bank*, the court discussed the appropriate means of communicating the discrepancy both from the practical point of view and for evidentiary purposes:

> "Article 16(d) simply says "without delay by telecommunication, or if that is not possible by other expeditious means". *No one suggested that telecommunication, which, both sides concede, include a telephone call, was not possible but only that it was hard to prove.* I am not impressed with this argument. If telecommunication whether by phone, fax or telex is possible then *it ought to be used so that the beneficiary knows as soon as possible* that a problem exists and so the beneficiary has as much time as possible before the expiration of the credit to get the alleged *discrepancies accepted or to consider giving an indemnity.*

Telephone call combined with a written record would be an ideal way of communication:

> In this case a telephone call could have been made setting out the discrepancies and following this up with *a written notice as was in fact done.* Alternatively Mrs. Wong could have complied with the requirement by giving the grounds to the caller from NCB. If the relevant parties had a fax then that could have been sent with the original taken round by hand or by mail. A messenger would arrive somewhat after the fax had been sent and received. So it follows that whereas I am satisfied as a question of fact on the evidence before me that Daiwa acted without delay I find that *they did not give notice by telecommunication*, which I find, in one form or another and certainly by phone, was possible in September 1988.
>
> I do not believe that my conclusion will place a great burden on the banking community. Once documents are checked and discrepancies found which justify rejection *a phone call should be made to the remitting bank in which the discrepancies are explained and this should be followed up by a written* advice of discrepancies, confirming the telephone call, which should be sent by messenger, courier or, if not possible, by mail. No doubt the rejecting bank will ask to identify the person to whom they are speaking at the remitting bank and no doubt they will recall this fact and the time of the telephone call. If an issue should ever arise as to whether such a call was made, it would be resolved by the court in the usual way. The fact that a telephone call cannot be proved in the same way as a SWIFT message is, in my judgment, not relevant because the same argument applies to

a letter which is not sent by registered post. A receipt in the messenger's delivery book will usually be conclusive. Banks in Hong Kong have relied upon letters and in so far as they have been sent by ordinary mail there is always a possibility of arguments about non-receipt. Yet the practice has continued for some time and I do not see why a telephone call and a letter cannot be used as this would fulfill the requirements of Article 16(d). It goes without saying that Article 16(d) can also be complied with by sending a fax or telex where it is possible and sending the original or a letter containing the same information by hand, courier or post."[38]

In *Bankers Trust v. State Bank of India* the case dealt with exceptionally heavy documentation to be checked by the bank:

"When asked in cross-examination how often he would meet with documents as bulky as these, he answered about two or three times a year. *With one exception he had never come across a set of documents which had taken more than three days to check.* In re-examination he was asked: Can you envisage, in the whole of your experience, any set of documents which would require more than three days between receipt and despatch of an Article 16 telex if an Article 16 telex was called for? He replied that he could not. Mr. Procter himself checked the documents in the present case *in four hours*, although admittedly *he had prior knowledge of the alleged discrepancies*, and *was working at his home, without office interruptions.*
It is a standing instruction at Barclays Bank that all documents must be checked, and, *if there are discrepancies, a rejection telex sent, within three days of the receipt of the documents.* According to Mr. Procter, the same practice applies at all four clearing banks.
According to Judge Raymond Jack's very recent book on Documentary Credits, to which I will return later, the period allowed by the U.S. Uniform Commercial Code (with which the plaintiffs are presumably familiar) is three clear banking days. But we were told that the U.S. Code is not exactly analogous, since documents are deemed to be rejected, unless they are accepted within three clear banking days, not the other way round.
Mr. Barlow, the other expert witness called on behalf of the defendants, was head of the documentary credit department at Williams and Glyns

---

[38] *Hing Yip Hing Fat Co Ltd v Daiwa Bank Ltd*, 1991 WL 1124851 (HC), [1991] 2 HKLR 35, [1991] HKLY 70.

Chapter III

Bank until he retired in 1982. He acted as U.K. representative on the ICC Banking Commission, and was directly concerned in that capacity with revisions to the Code. He gave evidence to the same effect as Mr. Procter. In cross-examination he accepted that it was a large set of documents, but his bank would have completed the check in one and a half days. He said that his personal check of the documents took three and a half hours. Finally it is to be noted that Mr. Cormack himself took only a day to check the documents, once he had got them sorted; and Miss Leung took about the same time. . . . . . .

The court applied the following test to measure reasonable time:

> I start with the language of art. 16(c) itself. *The reasonable time allowed to the issuing bank is composed of two components*, namely,
> (i) time for the bank to examine the documents and
> (ii) time for the bank to determine whether to accept or reject the documents.
>
> Clearly the time taken to consult the buyers cannot be included under (i). Can it be included under (ii)? Mr. Goldsmith submits that it can. He relies on two main arguments, and a third which was suggested to him by the Court. I take them in descending order of merit. . . . .
>
> The answer to this ingenious argument, if I have stated it correctly, is quite simple. *There is nothing in the Code, as I have said, to prohibit the bank asking the customer whether he is willing to waive any discrepancies.* But if the customer does so, he is not exercising a right conferred by the Code. He is exercising his ordinary right, independent of the Code, to waive a contractual provision which is exclusively for his benefit. *The bank's determination to reject the documents remains a determination made by the bank on the basis of the documents alone. But the customer's waiver overrides the bank's determination.*
>
> I am not persuaded by any of these three arguments to depart from what seems to me to be the plain meaning of the Code, namely, that the reasonable time allowed under art. 16(c) is a reasonable time for the *bank* to examine the documents, and for the *bank* to determine, on the basis of the documents alone, whether to accept them or not. If it had been intended that the bank should also be allowed time to consult its customer whether the customer was willing to waive any discrepancies, it would have been easy enough to say so, by the insertion of "after consulting the applicant" in art. 16(b). But I see no reason to read in those words, whether as a

matter of construction, or, as Mr. Justice Gatehouse thought, as a matter of implication."[39]

There is no unanimity as to whether or not the "reasonable time" allows such a consultation.

III.8.2 Bank's duty of care

What if all discrepancies or deviations are not discovered by bank officers – what criteria are to be applied to the bank's duty of care in the examination of the documents?[40] Does strict compliance lead to strict liability for failure or error? Is the examiner's liability based on the result or on best efforts?[41]

Unidroit Art 5.1.4 tells us:

> "(1) To the extent that an obligation of a party involves a duty to achieve a specific result, that party is bound to achieve that result. (2) To the extent that an obligation of a party involves a duty of best efforts in the performance of an activity, that party is bound to make such efforts as would be made by a reasonable person of the same kind in the same circumstances."

---

[39] *Bankers Trust Co. v. State Bank of India*, 1991 WL 837888 (CA (Civ Div)), [1991] 2 Lloyd's Rep. 443, 6-25-1991 Times 837, 888, 8-14-1991 Independent 837, 888, 6-28-1991 Financial Times 837, 888.

[40] Russia (DCL). Art 872:
"1. The issuing bank shall be liable to the payer and the executing bank to the issuing bank for a violation of the terms of the letter of credit, except for the cases provided in this Article. 2. In case of unjustified refusal by the executing bank to make payment under' covered or guaranteed letter of credit the executing bank shall be liable to the beneficiary 3. In case of making an incorrect payment by the executing bank under a covered or guaranteed letter of credit as a result of violations of the terms of the letter of credit, the payer shall be liable to the executing bank."

See also Jason C.T. Chuah, *International standard banking practice for the examination of documents under documentary credits*, 39 Student L Rev, 46-48 (Sum 2003).

[41] Bolivia (DCL) Art. 1405:
"The issuing bank is liable to the applicable according to the provisions of professional mandates and shall ensure that the documents presented by the beneficiary precisely comply with the contents of the credit document."

Greece. *See, e.g.*, UAE (DCL) Art. 30:
"1. The bank shall not be liable a. for accidental loss of the goods, b. for failure of any telegraph service in the transmission of telegraphs. 2. The bank shall be liable for intentional or negligent acts including negligence in the choice of the correspondent bank."

Chapter III

> and Art 5.1.5: "In determining the extent to which an obligation of a party involves a duty of best efforts in the performance of an activity or a duty to achieve a specific result, regard shall be had, among other factors, to (a) the way in which the obligation is expressed in the contract; (b) the contractual price and other terms of the contract; (c) the degree of risk normally involved in achieving the expected result; (d) the ability of the other party to influence the performance of the obligation."

The banks have only a limited time to examine the documents and from time to time the exercise may be quite tedious.

UCP 600 provides in Article 14:

> "a. A nominated bank acting on its nomination, a confirming bank, if any, and the issuing bank must examine a presentation to determine, on the basis of the documents alone, whether or not the documents appear on their face to constitute a complying presentation.
> b. A nominated bank acting on its nomination, a confirming bank, if any, and the issuing bank shall each have a maximum of five banking days following the day of presentation to determine if a presentation is complying. This period is not curtailed or otherwise affected by the occurrence on or after the date of presentation of any expiry date or last day for presentation."

Article 14(d) refers to generally accepted "standards of international practice". The standard shall not be local or parochial. It must be generally accepted and apply to instruments of international character. In addition, the standard is expressly made subject to good faith.

UNC gives the following guidance as to the criteria to be applied:

> UNC Article 16 (1) provides: "The guarantor/issuer shall examine the demand and any accompanying documents *in accordance with the standard of conduct referred to in paragraph* (1) of article 14.
> In determining whether documents are in facial conformity with the terms and conditions of the undertaking, and are consistent with one another, the guarantor/issuer shall have due regard to the applicable international standard of independent guarantee or stand-by letter of credit practice."

UCC (5-108) answers these questions as follows:

> "(e) An issuer shall observe standard practice of financial institutions that regularly issue letters of credit."[42]

ICC published "International Standard Banking Practice" (ISBP) in 2003. This document and rules codified existing banking practices.[43] The codification will guide to even greater uniformity and will maintain and enhance the prevailing confidence in these instruments and of course contribute to making the process more expedient and frictionless.

ISBP Foreword 2 and 3 says:

> "The ISBP, as it is more commonly called, is a practical complement to UCP 500, ICC's universally used rules on documentary credits. The ISBP does not amend the UCP. It explains, in explicit detail, how the rules are to be applied on a day-to-day basis. As such, it fills a needed gap between the general principles announced in the rules and the daily work of the documentary credit practitioner."

It may appear to be somewhat like playing with words, since the examination process in a bank, when applying the strict compliance standard to the

---

[42] UCC 5-108 (official comment):
"Identifying and determining compliance with standard practice are matters of interpretation for the court, not for the jury. As with similar rules in Sections 4A- 202(c) and 2-302, it is hoped that there will be more consistency in the outcomes and speedier resolution of disputes if the responsibility for determining the nature and scope of standard practice is granted to the court, not to a jury. Granting the court authority to make these decisions will also encourage the salutary practice of courts' granting summary judgment in circumstances where there are no significant factual disputes. The statute encourages outcomes such as American Coleman Co. v. Intrawest Bank, 887 F.2d 1382 (10th Cir. 989) where summary judgment was granted."

[43] ISBP Foreword 2 and 3:
"The task force that developed the ISBP was meticulous in seeking to document international practice in the field. It started by asking ICC national committees and members to send checklists on how documents were examined in their banks. Some 39 national committees and a substantial number of individual banks responded. Culling these comments required 14 task force meetings and four different drafts before the ISBP was finally in a shape to be approved."

examination of the documents, is not subject to strict liability but subject to the standard of *reasonable care*.[44]

URDG Art 9 provides:

> "All documents specified and presented under a Guarantee, including the demand, shall be examined by the Guarantor with reasonable care to ascertain whether or not they appear on their face to conform with the terms of the Guarantee. Where such documents do not appear so to conform or appear on their face to be inconsistent with one another, they shall be refused."

This comes close to the *bonus pater familias* standard. The bank has no liability for not reaching an impeccable result, but only for its own *culpa* defined on the basis of international banking practice.[45]

---

[44] Dolan writes in *The Law of Letters of Credit* at 9-23:
"It may well be better to rationalize the bifurcated standard by saying that the strict-compliance rule applies in actions on the letter of credit because such a rule serves the ministerial role issuers play. The substantial compliance test (the normal contract rule) is appropriate in suits on the contract between the issuer and the account party. The strict-compliance standard recognizes the unique nature of credits; the substantial compliance standard recognizes that the credit application is just another contract."

See e.g. UAE (DCL) Art. 436:
"The bank shall only be liable to examine the documents and to verify that they comply on their face with the documents stipulated in the credit. The bank shall not be liable for examining whether the goods themselves comply with the documents that represent them."; Tunisia (DCL) Art. 725: "The bank shall assure that the documents strictly comply with the applicant's instructions. If the bank refuses the documents it shall as soon as possible inform the applicant thereof and inform him of the detected discrepancies."

and Art. 726:
"The bank does not assume any responsibility if the documents on their face appear to comply with the received instructions. The bank does not assume any responsibility regarding the goods which are subject to the issued credit"; Libya (DCL) Art 249: "The holder of a documentary credit is entitled to the rights provided for in the documentary credit upon presentation of the documents on the condition that he is in the lawful possession thereof. A debtor who performs under the documentary credit in good faith or without gross negligence is discharged even if the holder is not the owner of the right."

[45] UCP 500: "Banks deal with documents and not with goods, services or other performances to which the documents may relate."

UCP 500 tells us:

> "A bank must examine all documents stipulated in the credit with reasonable care to determine, on the basis of the documents alone, whether or not they appear on their face to be in compliance with the terms and conditions of the credit ("compliance"). Compliance is determined in accordance with international standard banking practice."

The compliance test as to the examination is not that of strict compliance but of appearance, i.e., *prima facie* impression ("appear on their face")[46].

One could say that it is a mixed standard of liability.

On one hand it establishes a duty of care i.e., (i) the bank must examine the documents with such care as is required to meet international banking practice. On the other hand there is a modified "results liability", i.e., (ii) in such an examination the documents *must appear* to be strictly conforming but they do not have to be that in fact (after in-depth analysis). Should the examiner prove that (i) the examination was carried out with due care (diligence) and that (ii) the documents or demand appear to be strictly conforming although it is not to in fact, the examiner has exculpated and cannot be held liable for the deviation or discrepancy and is entitled to be reimbursed.

---

[46] UCC 5-108:
"The section adopts strict compliance, rather than the standard that commentators have called "substantial compliance," the standard arguably applied in *Banco Espanol de Credito v. State Street Bank and Trust Co.*, 385 F.2d 230 (1st Cir. 1967) and *Flagship Cruises Ltd. v. New England Merchants Nat. Bank*, 569 F2d 699 (1st Cir. 1978). Strict compliance does not mean slavish conformity to the terms of the letter of credit. For example, standard practice (what issuers do) may recognize certain presentations as complying that an unschooled layman would regard as discrepant. By adopting standard practice as a way of measuring strict compliance, this article indorses the conclusion of the court in *New Braunfels Nat. Bank v. Odiorne*, 780 S.W. 2d 313 (Tex. Ct. App. 1989) (beneficiary could collect when draft requested payment on "Letter of Credit No. 86-122-5" and letter of credit specified Letter of Credit No. 86-122-S" holding strict compliance does not demand oppressive perfectionism). The section also indorses the result in *Tosco Corp. v. Federal Deposit Ins. Corp.*, 723 F.2d 1242 (6th Cir. 1983). The letter of credit in that case called for "drafts Drawn under Bank of Clarksville Letter of Credit Number 105" The draft presented stated "drawn under Bank of Clarksville, Clarksville, Tennessee letter of Credit No. 105." The court correctly found that despite the change of upper case "L" to a lower case "l" and the use of the word "No." instead of "Number," and despite the addition of the words "Clarksville, Tennessee," the presentation conformed. Similarly a document addressed by a foreign person to General Motors as "Jeneral Motors" would strictly conform in the absence of other defects."

Should the reimbursing party prove that due care was not exercised, it will be released from the reimbursement obligation.

The bank is, however, always right when refusing documents which are not strictly in compliance although they might "appear" to be so.[47]

The examination must be carried out on the basis of the documents only and any information obtained or received should have no bearing on this analysis in the light of the doctrine of independence.[48] This is "the *parole evidence rule* of letter of credit law".

Under UNC, the standard of conduct and liability of the issuer has been defined in the following "constitution" in Article 14:

> "(1) In discharging its obligations under the undertaking and this Convention, the guarantor/issuer shall act in good faith and exercise reasonable care having due regard *to generally accepted standards of international practice* of independent guarantees or stand-by letters of credit.
> (2) *A guarantor/issuer may not be exempted from liability for its failure to act in good faith or for any grossly negligent conduct.*"[49]

---

[47] See however Margaret L. Moses, *Letters of Credit and the Insolvent Applicant, A Recipe for Bad Faith Dishonor*, Alabama L Rev, (Fall 2005):
"Bankers will argue that once you diminish the strict compliance obligation, then the letter of credit will lose its characteristics of swiftness and certainty that are made possible by focusing strictly on the compliance of documents. In the case of the opportunistic bank, however, it is already focused on something other than the documents — the financial status of the party from whom it will seek reimbursement. Its decision to deny payment is therefore not made on the documents alone, but rather on the basis of another contract, the reimbursement agreement, which according to the independence principle, should have no impact on the bank's obligations under the letter of credit. The argument for heightened scrutiny of a bank's conduct when the bank's customer is insolvent is an argument for courts and juries to consider the letter of credit transaction with the broader lens required by honesty in fact. It is only by considering the banks conduct in light of its obligations that a fact-finder can determine whether the bank acted with a proper or an improper motive."

[48] UCP 600 Art. 14 (a).

[49] Tom Pifer, p. 7. The UCC 5 directs that sources of standard practice include: (1) the UCP 500; (2) other practice rules published by banking associations; and (3) local and regional practice—presumably to be established by expert testimony. Because the UCP 500 is the most recognized source of standard practice "it applies to the vast majority of LCs by incorporation; and its express terms state that standard practice is as reflected in these articles," the UCP 500 itself is a logical first source to consult. Unfortunately, only some standard practices are specified in the UCP 500. Given the nearly unlimited number of discrepancies that a bank may encounter, there results a large area of practice with no guidance" where such areas

The standard is that of *reasonable care*, i.e., the examiner is not responsible for achieving the result of strict compliance. It is only liable for rendering the services required and for due diligence in the examination of the documents submitted. This is fully in line with the character of the contract for rendering services.

There are a number of express disclaimers in many applicable laws or in the commonly used sets of rules.[50]

For example, UCC 5-108 (official comment) (f) says:

> "An issuer is not responsible for: (1) the performance or nonperformance of the underlying contract, arrangement, or transaction, (2) an act or omission of others, or (3) observance or knowledge of the usage of a particular trade other than the standard practice referred to in subsection (e) of this section."

On one hand disclaimers are in general beneficial, since they reduce the costs of these instruments; on other hand they may be unreasonable and as such unenforceable under exceptional circumstances.[51]

URDG Art. 11 provides:

> "Guarantors and Instructing Parties assume no liability or responsibility for the form, sufficiency, accuracy, genuineness, falsification or legal effect

---

exist litigation will often result. . . . The ICC responded with the publication of the International Standard Banking Practice for the Examination of Documents under Documentary Credits."

[50] Bahrain (DCL) Art. 325:
"1. The bank does not assume any liability if the presented documents on their face appear to comply with the applicant's instructions. 2. The bank shall neither be liable for the performance of consignors and insurers of the goods for which payment the credit has been issued, their quality, weight, condition, packaging or value."

[51] See e.g. URDG Art. 12:
"Guarantors and Instructing Parties assume no liability or responsibility for the consequences arising out of delay and/or loss in transit of any messages, letters, demands or documents, or for delay, mutilation or other errors arising in the transmission of any telecommunication, Guarantors and Instructing Parties assume no liability for errors in translation or interpretation of technical terms and reserve the right to transmit Guarantee texts or any parts thereof without translating them.", Art. 13 "Guarantors and Instructing Parties assume no liability or responsibility for consequences arising out of the interruption of their business by acts of God, civil commotions, insurrections, wars or any other causes beyond their control or by strikes, lock-outs or industrial actions of whatever nature."

of any document presented to them or for the general and/or particular statements made therein, nor for the good faith or acts or omissions of any person whomsoever."

The UNC article quoted above catches this trend by providing that in no circumstances may the guarantor or issuer be exempted from liability for gross negligence or be released from the duty of good faith.

III.8.3 Duty to whom and for what

The banks have a number of standard duties when rendering services under these instruments.[52] Banks owe primarily duties to the account party but the latter bears the risk of demand and payment by the beneficiary.

The banks assume in general no risks other than the risk with respect to the account party i.e., the bank's customer. The bank is in good position to guard against this risk by way of security and indemnity agreement.

The banks also owe duties to other parties. These may include other banks and of course its principal duty is to the beneficiary to honor its complying demand for payment under the instrument.

The basic structure of the instrument is very, very simple: payment when the conditions precedent have been met. This is, however, only the tip of the facility. In order to establish the facility, other agreements have to be established to create the network culminating in the issuing of the instrument. Likewise, once triggered by the beneficiary, a number of steps and actions are required to dismantle the network constituting the facility. Upon death of the instrument the duties owed to the beneficiary have been cleared, but duties to other parties arise which, when executed, finally dismantle the facility as a whole.

Although the emphasis and legal focus is in the execution of payment, acceptance or negotiation, there are some duties that relate to the drafting and creation of the instrument. A bank issuing a letter of credit *has to actively contribute to the drafting and issuing* of a letter of credit which is clear and unambiguous and

---

[52] See Bertrams, *Bank Guarantees*, at 83.

protects the customer adequately and is suitable for the underlying transaction. The bank must actively participate in every instance to protect the credit undertaking and the rights of the parties thereunder including those of intermediary banks and the beneficiary.[53] This duty is emphasized since banks are often to be deemed to be experts in this business which, in particular with respect to clients unsophisticated in this field, may require the banks to draw the client's attention to risks and issues that the client may be unaware of.

One of the main duties of the bank is to put the beneficiary on notice of discrepancies in the tender, if any, within the period of time provided without undue delay at the risk of the bank losing its right to invoke those discrepancies. This duty serves the basic function of the instrument to provide expedient clearing of the payment obligation and allowing the beneficiary to remedy the defects at the same time eliminating the risk of speculation by the bank (in bad faith) and compelling the banks to be duly and adequately organized.

The banks may also be under a contractual or other duty to notify the applicant of a demand under the instrument received by the bank to allow the applicant to take any action or form a position should the demand be unjustified. Such an action may include direct contract with the beneficiary or in the extreme legal action by the applicant to eliminate fraudulent practices or guard against its consequences.

Here is a sample clause that puts the bank in the position of helping the beneficiary to take an action or form a position where the demand is unjustified.

sample clause: *placing documents at the disposal of the beneficiary*

"The Bank shall be entitled at its own discretion, after receipt of a demand for payment under an on demand Guarantee, to pay the amounts demanded without the Bank being obliged to examine the validity, justification or authenticity of the demand within the absence of manifest error. However in respect of on demand Guarantees the Bank shall, subject to any law and/or the conditions for the on demand Guarantee in question, use all reasonable efforts to act

---

[53] Bertrams, *Bank Guarantees*, at 133-134, writes:
"A certain duty to advise its customer may, however, exist in special situations, for instance where the bank is aware of the inexperience of the account party, where the bank has actual knowledge of a particular piece of information which it knows to be vital to its customer, or where the bank insists that significant alterations be made to the terms or the type of guarantee."

according to the following: No payment shall provided that the Bank will not thereby be exposed to liability, be made by the Bank less than two (2) Banking Days after a demand for payment has been made by or on behalf of the beneficiary and the Bank shall, without delay, deliver by telefax or messenger a copy of the original demand for payment to the relevant Principal, with the Bank´s notice of the date when the demand was received by the Bank.

These duties include the duty *to put the documents at the disposal of the beneficiary* when the tender has failed and payment has been refused resulting in dishonor. If the beneficiary does not remedy the discrepancies in a new tender, the facility will be dismantled as unconsummated upon expiry. The duty to put the documents at the disposal of the beneficiary *and the duty of the examiner to indicate the reasons for dishonor* are *sui generis* since they do not lead to an immediate death of the instrument, but allow and encourage new attempts by the beneficiary until the expiry of the instrument.

When honor has taken place and the facility will be dismantled after payment, *the documents need to be delivered* "down the chain" against reimbursement. The documents will then be *re-examined* and may be refused by the issuing bank and finally by the account party. If discrepancies are found, notice must be given unless the account party waives them as is often the case. The process is described in *Credit Industriel et Commercial v. China Merchants Bank* as follows:

> "The governing Article in respect of this issue is Article 14:
> "c. If the Issuing Bank determines that the documents appear on their face not to be in compliance with the terms and conditions of the Credit, it may in its sole judgment approach the Applicant for a waiver of the discrepancy(ies). This does not, however, extend the period mentioned in sub-Article 13 (b).
> d.i. If the Issuing Bank and/or Confirming Bank, if any, or a Nominated Bank acting on their behalf, decides to refuse the documents, it must give notice to that effect by telecommunication or, if that is not possible, by other expeditious means, without delay but no later than the close of the seventh banking day following the day of receipt of the documents. *Such notice shall be given to the bank from which it received the documents,* or to the Beneficiary, if it received the documents directly from him.
>
> ii. Such notice must state all discrepancies in respect of which the bank refuses the documents and must also state whether it is holding the documents at the disposal of, or is returning them to, the presenter.

iii. The Issuing Bank and/or Confirming Bank, if any, shall then be entitled *to claim from the remitting bank refund*, with interest, of any reimbursement which has been made to the bank.

If the Issuing Bank and/or Confirming Bank, if any,
fails to act in accordance with the provision of this Article and/or
fails to hold the documents at the disposal of, or
return them to the presenter, the Issuing Bank and/or Confirming Bank, if any, shall be precluded from claiming that the documents are not in compliance with the terms and conditions of the Credit."

The procedure is accordingly as follows:

i) The bank must examine the documents for compliance with reasonable care — Article 13 (a).

ii) The bank has a reasonable time to determine whether to take them up or refuse them, such time not to exceed seven days — Article 13 (b).

iii) Prior to deciding whether to accept or reject, it is permissible to approach the applicant for a waiver in the event of any discrepancies — Article 14 (c).

iv) If in the light of its own examination of the documents (and the outcome of any approach to the applicants) the bank decides to refuse, it *must give immediate notice within the seven day period identifying the discrepancies and stating that the documents are being returned or held to order* — Article 14 (d).

v) Failure to comply with Article 14 (d) precludes reliance on the discrepancies — Article 14 (e).

It follows inexorably, in my judgment, that the rejection notice in this case was not in accordance with Article 14 (d) and that CMB cannot rely on any discrepancies. The SWIFT message ended:— "*Should the disc. being accepted by the applicant, we shall release the docs to them without further notice to you unless yr instructions to the contrary received prior to our payment.*" It follows that the documents were not to be returned to CIC or held to their order. They were to be released to the applicant, within some indefinite period, in the event of the applicant accepting the discrepancies, without any notice to CIC. *The conditional nature of this rejection is not saved by the potential for acceptance of contrary instructions* prior to payment, particularly where no notice is to be given. In short, the message constitutes a continuing threat of conversion of CIC's documents."[54]

---

[54] Credit Industriel et Commercial v. China Merchants Bank, Case No: 2000/738, Neutral citation number: [2002] EWHC 973 (Comm).

In addition, banks may assume special duties as may be agreed beyond those established in UCP or other reference documents or by law. For instance, banks sometimes agree to examine the documents in less than 48 hours. As discussed, the banks often disclaim their liability for any failure in services rendered or breach of agreement and the account party or Principal must carry the risk.

UCC 5-103 tells us:

> "What the issuer could achieve by an explicit agreement with its applicant or by a term that explicitly defines its duty, it cannot accomplish by a general disclaimer. The restriction on disclaimers in the last sentence of subsection (c) is based more on procedural than on substantive unfairness. Where, for example, the reimbursement agreement provides explicitly that the issuer need not examine any documents, the applicant understands the risk it has undertaken. A term in a reimbursement agreement which states generally that an issuer will not be liable unless it has acted in "bad faith" or committed "gross negligence" is ineffective under Section 5-103(c). On the other hand, less general terms such as terms that permit issuer reliance on an oral or electronic message believed in good faith to have been received from the applicant or terms that entitle an issuer to reimbursement when it honors a "substantially" though not 'strictly' complying presentation, are effective. In each case the question is whether the disclaimer or limitation is sufficiently clear and explicit in reallocating a liability or risk that is allocated differently under a variable Article 5 provision."

III.8.4 Duty to notify and refusal

As discussed above the banks may be under an obligation to actively notify or advise the parties.[55]

---

[55] UNC Art. 16 (2):
"Unless otherwise stipulated in the undertaking or elsewhere agreed by the guarantor/issuer and the beneficiary, the guarantor/issuer shall have reasonable time, but not more than seven business days following the day of receipt of the demand and any accompanying documents, in which to: (a) Examine the demand and any accompanying documents; (b) Decide whether or not to pay; (c) *If the decision is not to pay, issue notice thereof to the beneficiary.* The notice referred to in subparagraph (c) above shall, unless otherwise stipulated in the undertaking or elsewhere agreed by the guarantor/issuer and the beneficiary, be made by teletransmission or, if that is not possible, by other expeditious means and indicate the reason for the decision not to pay."

This applies in particular to refusal. UCP 600 provides in Article 16:

> "c. When a nominated bank acting on its nomination, a confirming bank, if any, or the issuing bank decides to refuse to honour or negotiate, it must give a single notice to that effect to the presenter. The notice must state:
> i. that the bank is refusing to honour or negotiate; and
> ii. each discrepancy in respect of which the bank refuses to honour or negotiate; and
> iii. a) that the bank is holding the documents pending further instructions from the presenter; or
> b) that the issuing bank is holding the documents until it receives a waiver from the applicant and agrees to accept it, or receives further instructions from the presenter prior to agreeing to accept a waiver; or
> c) that the bank is returning the documents; or
> d) that the bank is acting in accordance with instructions previously received from the presenter."

The duty to give notice may extend to those parties of the instrument or facility which have a direct interest at stake.

UCC 5-108 (official comment) says:

> "5. Confirmers, other nominated persons, and collecting banks acting for beneficiaries can be presenters and, when so, are entitled to the notice provided in subsection (b). Even nominated persons who have honored or

---

Czech Republic (DCL) Art 688:
"If the issuance of the credit is accomplished though another bank such bank is liable for the damage that results from the incorrectness of the notification. However, such bank is not liable for the credit itself."

and Art 690(2):
"The bank shall be liable to the applicant for the loss or destruction of the documents taken over by the beneficiary unless the damage could not have been avoided if adequate diligence was applied."

Egypt (DCL) Art 347:
"1. The bank shall ascertain the compliance of the documents with the applicant's instructions for opening the credit. 2. If the bank refuses the documents it shall promptly inform the applicant and indicate the reason thereof."

and Art 348: "1. No liability of the bank shall be incurred if the documents appear to be in compliance with the instructions by the applicant. 2. The bank shall not have any liability for the goods that are paid by the credit."

CHAPTER III

given value against an earlier presentation of the beneficiary and are themselves seeking reimbursement or honor need notice of discrepancies in the hope that they may be able to procure complying documents, The issuer has the obligations imposed by this section whether the issuer's performance is characterized as "reimbursement" of a nominated person or as "honor."

The duty to notify applies in particular to discrepancies but also to other issues.[56]

"In respect of notices of refusal sent by an issuing bank to the presenter sub-Article 14(d)(ii) states "Such notice must state all discrepancies in respect of which the bank refuses the documents and must also state whether it is holding the documents at the disposal of, or is returning them to, the presenter." Sub-Article 14 (e) then goes on to state: "If the Issuing Bank and/or Confirming Bank, if any, fails to act in accordance with the provisions of this Article and/or fails to hold the document at the disposal

---

[56] ISP 5.01:
"a. Notice of dishonour must be given within a time after presentation of documents which is not unreasonable. i. Notice given within three business days is deemed to be not unreasonable and beyond seven business days is deemed to be unreasonable. ii. Whether the time within which notice is given is unreasonable does not depend upon an imminent deadline for presentation. iii. The time for calculating when notice of dishonour must be given begins on the business day following the business day of presentation. iv. Unless a standby otherwise expressly states a shortened time within which notice of dishonour must be given, the issuer has no obligation to accelerate its examination of a presentation. b.i. The means by which a notice of dishonour is to be given is by telecommunication, if available, and, if not, by another available means which allows for prompt notice. ii. If notice of dishonour is received within the time permitted for giving the notice, then it is deemed to have been given by prompt means. c. Notice of dishonour must be given to the person from whom the documents were received (whether the beneficiary, nominated person, or person other than a delivery person) except as otherwise requested by the presenter." See e.g. URDG Art. 7 (a) "Where a Guarantor has been given instructions for the issue of a Guarantee but the instructions are such that, if they were to be carried out, the Guarantor would by reason of law or regulation in the country of issue be unable to fulfil the terms of the Guarantee, the instructions shall not be executed and the Guarantor shall immediately inform the party who gave the Guarantor his instructions by telecommunication, or, if that is not possible, by other expeditious means, of the reasons for such inability and request appropriate instructions from that party". URDG Art. 10 (b): "If the Guarantor decides to refuse a demand, he shall immediately give notice thereof to the Beneficiary by teletransmission, or, if that is not possible, by other expeditious means. Any documents presented under the Guarantee shall be held at the disposal of the Beneficiary." URDG Art 17: "Without prejudice to the terms of Article 10, in the event of a demand the Guarantor shall without delay so inform the Principal or, where applicable, his instructing Party, and in that case the Instructing Party shall so inform the Principal" URDG Art. 25: "Where to the knowledge of the Guarantor the Guarantee has terminated by payment, expiry, cancellation or otherwise, or there has been a reduction of the total amount payable thereunder, the Guarantor shall without delay so notify the Principal or, where applicable, the Instructing Party and, in that case, the Instructing Party shall so notify the Principal."

of, or return them to the presenter the Issuing Bank and or Confirming Bank if any, shall be precluded from claiming that the documents are not in compliance with the terms and conditions of the Credit. An issuing bank that releases documents to an applicant upon receipt of a waiver having stated that it is holding the documents at the disposal of the presenter, without receiving corresponding instructions from the presenter and which then effects settlement, *may find that it is liable if the presenter/beneficiary did not require settlement but the return of the documents. Such action is a business decision that the issuing bank would make.* Previously approved, but not yet published, opinions under references TA 368, TA 428rev and TA 449 also refer to this issue."[57]

One of these issues is the duty to notify the account party prior to making payment to the beneficiary.

Bertrams writes on pp. 150-151:

> "Among legal writers on the Continent the question of a legal duty to notify the customer prior to payment has been much debated, but a unanimous view has not emerged. A vast majority favours such a duty, while a small, but forceful minority opposes the proposition. The issue has not been settled conclusively by case law, at least not in each of the several jurisdictions concerned"

UCC describes the process of examination and the resulting honor or dishonor as follows, in UCC 5-108 (a) (b):

> "(a) Except as otherwise provided in Section 5-109, an issuer shall honor a presentation that, as determined by the standard practice referred to in subsection (e) of this section, *appears on its face strictly to comply with the terms and conditions of the letter of credit.* Except as otherwise provided in Section 5-113 and unless otherwise agreed with the applicant, *an issuer shall dishonor* a presentation that does not appear so to comply. (b) An issuer has a reasonable time after presentation, but not beyond the end of the seventh business day of the issue after the day of its receipt of documents: (1) to honor, (2) if the letter of credit provides for honor to be completed

---

[57] ICC Banking Commission Collected Opinions 1995-2001, R 430.

Chapter III

more than seven business days after presentation, to accept a draft or incur a deferred obligation, or (3) *to give notice to the presenter of discrepancies in the presentation.*"

The bank must either honor or reject the tendered documents. In the latter case notice must be given to the beneficiary without undue delay. This is important to allow the beneficiary to remedy the defect. These instruments remain open until conditions subsequent are met allowing many attempts to meet the conditions precedent.

III.8.5 Reasonable time defined in UCC

UCC 5-108(b) defines reasonable time as follows:

"An issuer has a reasonable time after presentation, but not beyond the end of the seventh business day of the issue after the day of its receipt of documents: (1) to honor: (2) if the letter of credit provides for honor to be completed more than seven business days after presentation, to accept a draft or incur a deferred obligation, or (3) to give notice to the presenter of discrepancies in the presentation."

What is reasonable under the circumstances is a flexible standard. The applicable rules fix the outer limit of reasonable time to 5 or 7 days but in many cases the reasonable time is considerably less perhaps only a day or two or a few hours only.

UCC 5-108 (official comment) tells us further:

"2. Section 5-108(a) balances the need of the issuer for time to examine the documents against the possibility that the examiner (at the urging of the applicant or for fear that it will not be reimbursed) will take excessive time to search for defects. *What is a "reasonable time" is not extended to accommodate an issuer's procuring a waiver from the applicant.* See Article 14c of the UCP.
Under both the UCC and the UCP the issuer has a reasonable time to honor or give notice. The outside limit of that time is measured in business days under the UCC and in banking days under the UCP, a difference that will rarely be significant. Neither business nor banking days are defined

in Article 5, but a court may find useful analogies in Regulation CC, 12 CFR 229.2, in state law outside of the Uniform Commercial Code, and in Article 4. Examiners must note that the seven-day period is not a safe harbor. *The time within which the issuer must give notice is the lesser of a reasonable time or seven business days. Where there are few documents (as, for example, with the mine run standby letter of credit), the reasonable time would be less than seven days.* If more than a reasonable time is consumed in examination, no timely notice is possible.

What is a "reasonable time" is to be determined by examining the behavior of those in the business of examining documents, mostly banks. Absent prior agreement of the issuer, one could not expect a bank issuer to examine documents while the beneficiary waited in the lobby if the normal practice was to give the documents to a person who had the opportunity to examine those together with many others in an orderly process. That the applicant has not yet paid the issuer or that the applicant's account with the issuer is insufficient to cover the amount of the draft is not a basis for extension of the time period."

The duty to honor or refuse does not extend to nominated banks as such.[58]

The duty to give notice within reasonable time is a fundamental duty. The failure to give notice will in general constitute acceptance. Under the UCC, the absence of such a notice or honor constitutes dishonor, which, when unjustified, will result in liability for damages: one could thus almost equally well argue that it constitutes honor of conforming documents and refusal of non-conforming ones.

---

[58] UCC 5-107 (official comment):
"When the issuer nominates another person to "pay," 'negotiate," or otherwise to take up the documents and give value, there can be confusion about the legal status of the nominated person. In rare cases the person might actually be an agent of the issuer and its act might be the act of the issuer itself. In most cases the nominated person is not an agent of the issuer and has no authority to act on the issuer's behalf. Its 'nomination' allows the beneficiary to present to it and earns it certain rights to payment under Section 5-109 that others do not enjoy. For example, when an issuer issues a "freely negotiable credit," it contemplates that banks or others might take up documents under that credit and advance value against them, and it is agreeing to pay those persons but only if the presentation to the issuer made by the nominated person compiles with the credit. *Usually there will be no agreement to pay, negotiate, or to serve in any other capacity by the nominated person, therefore the nominated person will have the right to decline to take the documents. It may return them or agree merely to act as a forwarding agent* for the documents but without giving value against them or taking any responsibility for their conformity to the letter of credit."

Chapter III

UCC 5-108 (official comment) has this to say:

> "Failure of the issuer to act within the time permitted by subsection (b) *constitutes dishonor*. Because of the preclusion in subsection (c) and the liability that the issuer may incur under Section 5-111 for *wrongful dishonor*, the effect of such a silent dishonor *may ultimately be the same as though the issuer had honored*, i.e., it may owe damages in the amount drawn but unpaid under the letter of credit."[59]

And UCC 5-108 (official comment) says further:

> "3 The requirement that the issuer send notice of the discrepancies or be precluded from asserting discrepancies is new to Article 5. It is taken from the similar provision in the UCP and is intended to promote certainty and finality. The section thus substitutes a strict preclusion principle for the doctrines of waiver and estoppel that might otherwise apply under Section 1-103."

The notice must identify the discrepancies to the beneficiary to allow him to remedy them. To invoke a discrepancy not expressly indicated in the notice after lapse of reasonable time does not give the bank a right to refuse. The right to refuse is extinguished after the reasonable time.

The next part of the UCC 5-108 (official comment) says:

> "4. To act within a reasonable time, the issuer must normally give notice without delay after the examining party makes its decision. If the examiner

---

[59] UCC 5-108:
"It rejects the reasoning in *Flagship Cruises Ltd. e New England Merchants' Nat'l Bank*, 569 F.2d 699 (1st Cir. 1978) and *Wing On Bank Ltd. v. American Nat'l Bank & Trust Co.*, 457 F.2d 328 (5th Cir. 1972) where the issuer was held to be estopped only if the beneficiary relied on the issuer's failure to give notice. Assume, for example, that the beneficiary presented documents to the issuer shortly before the letter of credit expired, in circumstances in which the beneficiary could not have cured any discrepancy before expiration. Under the reasoning of Flagship and Wing On, the beneficiary's inability to cure, even if it had received notice, would absolve the issuer of its failure to give notice. The virtue of the preclusion obligation adopted in this section is that it forecloses litigation about reliance and detriment. Even though issuers typically give notice of the discrepancy of tardy presentation when presentation is made after the expiration of a credit, they are not required to give that notice and the section permits them to raise late presentation as a defect despite their failure to give that notice."

decides to dishonor on the first day, it would be obliged to notify the beneficiary shortly thereafter, perhaps on the same business day. This rule accepts the reasoning in cases such as *Datapoint Corp. v. M & I Bank*, 665 F. Supp. 722 (W.D. Wis. 1987) and *Esso Petroleum Canada, Div. of Imperial Oil, Ltd. v. Security Pac. Bank.* 710 F. Supp. 275 (D. Ore. 1989). The section deprives the examining party of the right simply to sit on a presentation that is made within seven days of expiration. The section requires the examiner to examine the documents and make a decision and, having made a decision to dishonor, *to communicate promptly with the presenter*. Nevertheless, a beneficiary who presents documents shortly before the expiration of a letter of credit *runs the risk that it will never have the opportunity to cure any discrepancies.*"

III.8.6 Duty to put the documents at the disposal of the beneficiary

The banks also have obligations as to the transmission of documents.[60] If the tender is rejected and dishonored, besides giving notice of discrepancies within a reasonable time the examining bank time has a duty to put the documents at the disposal of the beneficiary or another bank.

UCP 600 provides in Article 16 (c):

> "iii. a) that the bank is holding the documents pending further instructions from the presenter; or
> b) that the issuing bank is holding the documents until it receives a waiver from the applicant and agrees to accept it, or receives further instructions from the presenter prior to agreeing to accept a waiver; or
> c) that the bank is returning the documents; or
> d) that the bank is acting in accordance with instructions previously received from the presenter"

---

[60] See, e.g., URDG Art. 21: "The Guarantor shall without delay transmit the Beneficiary's demand and any related documents to the Principal or, where applicable, to the Instructing Party for transmission to the Principal." URCB Art 7 (e): "The Beneficiary shall, when giving notice of any claim by telefax or other tele-transmission or EDI, also send a copy of such claim by post."

The failure to do this will amount to the preclusion of the right to refuse the tender. Putting the documents at the disposal of the presenter must be unambiguous and without reservation.

> "ANALYSIS AND CONCLUSION QUESTION 1 The content of UCP Article 14 requires the issuing bank to provide a valid notice of rejection within a reasonable time not to exceed seven banking days following the day of receipt of the documents. As part of that advice, the issuing bank is required to confirm that documents are being held at the disposal of the presenter or being returned. If the issuing bank has told the presenter that it is holding documents at his disposal, when the applicant provides a waiver (in an acceptable form to the issuing bank) of those discrepancies, the issuing bank should approach the presenters and request their approval to continue with the payment. If the bank chooses to make settlement without any communications having taken place, then the issuing bank will bear the risk(s) associated with that action. QUESTION 2 There is no "international practice" with regard to the amount of time that an issuing bank has before the documents should be returned. The issuing bank's responsibility is to provide a valid notice of rejection in accordance with sub-Article 14(d) of UCP 500. By stating that documents are held at the disposal of the presenter, it is for the presenter to provide fresh instructions to the issuing bank. Normally, it would be the issuing bank that would decide that the amount of time it has held documents is considered to be excessive (without further instructions from the presenter) and that with a reasonable amount of notice — for the presenter to provide fresh instructions — it would be returning the documents unless fresh instructions were received. An issuing bank is only responsible for the return of the documents that it received from the presenter. If part of the L/C terms were that one or more of the original documents were to be sent to a party other than the issuing bank, then this is outside the control of the issuing bank. The issuing bank's responsibility is merely to return the documents in its possession."[61]

In commercial letters of credit the documents tendered often have considerable commercial value. They are often documents of title or other documents which

---

[61] ICC Banking Commission Collected Opinions 1995-2001, R 429.

give the holder the right of possession or delivery. Security interests may also be attached to the documents and their possession. If the tender is rejected, the presenter may then proceed to remedy the tender. Should this be impossible, the presenter may then sell or deliver the goods in another practical manner.

In this ICC expertise case the issue was whether or not the documents had been accepted despite discrepancies in them. The exchange of messages was subject to interpretation but there never was an express acceptance:

> "A documentary credit undertaking binds the issuing bank on the condition that the documents presented comply with the terms and conditions of the credit; the same applies to the undertaking of the confirming bank. The obligation of the issuing/confirming bank is undertaken when the credit is issued, and the beneficiary needs no further engagement to be sure to be paid; *he only needs the declaration of acceptance* of the documents by the issuing/confirming bank, this being the sole condition allowing him to exercise his right to be paid. In the case at hand, the Initiator and the Respondent continued through several messages to deal with requests of "engagement of payment", in an obvious attempt to match the value date of the expected deferred payment, but *neither the confirming bank nor the issuing bank informed the Initiator (beneficiary) of their acceptance of the documents*. The confirming bank rejected the documents and held its position. The issuing bank never examined the documents, as the Initiator instructed the Respondent to keep the documents at its counters and to ask the issuing bank's acceptance notwithstanding the discrepancies. The issuing bank simply answered that the applicant did not accept documents.
> Subsequently, Bank G's SWIFT message to the Respondent dated 25/08/98, faxed to the Initiator by the beneficiary does not state that the documents would be accepted despite the discrepancies on the condition that the beneficiary agreed to a new maturity date (02 11 98). It simply states: "We authorise you to take documents [despite] discrepancies but only under condition that beneficiary agrees with new maturity date as November 2 1998." In its message to the Respondent dated 27/08/98, the Initiator "translated" these words as: "We understand that you received from Bank G its Swift authorisation to accept the documents presented despite the discrepancies pointed out," which is inaccurate.
> The wording given by the issuing bank was the best it could give, *given that it had not seen the documents at the point the message was sent*. The issuing bank was only liable for payment once it had reviewed the documents and

accepted them. If the issuing bank had found additional discrepancies, then it would have been entitled to rescind its approval to accept.

Moreover, in its message to the Respondent dated 28/08/98 — which was sent to the Initiator by the beneficiary — the issuing bank stated: "We irrevocably confirm that we will credit your account with Bank Z for the value of the documents (USD 1,308,371.12 plus USD 9.000.000, being interest for period 23.09- 02.11.1998)", *but once again the issuing bank was silent about the acceptance of documents*, which is the only binding condition to execute the payment under a documentary credit. The investigation about the possibility of obtaining a court judgement concerning the damages suffered by parties following the non-fulfilment of the engagement undertaken by the issuing bank in its message to the Respondent dated 28/08/98, is out of the scope of this expertise. For the above reasons, the Panel of Experts holds that the Respondent was not bound to its undertaking as confirming bank of the documentary credit in its hands. The issuing bank and the Respondent never accepted the documents presented by the Initiator (beneficiary)."[62]

III.8.7 Duty of confidentiality

Banks in particular, but also insurance companies and other financial institutions and commercial operators, are subject to general duties of confidentiality and secrecy and may be held liable for the breach of such duties. Such general duties based on national legislations applicable to the banks in the countries of incorporation, registration or branch operations, extend presumably to their undertakings and operations in the field of letter of credit and bank guarantees as well. Breach of these duties may expose the bank to liability to those customers or to private parties to whom the institutions owe these duties and may subject them to other sanctions as well. Sometimes such rules reflect national policies and may even have an *ordre public* character when creating measures which form a foundation of an internationally attractive banking business.

---

[62] Collected Docdex Decisions 1997-2003, No 210, p. 45. See also Collected Docdex Decisions 1997-2003, No 210, p. 42: "UCP 500 sub-Articles 14(e), 9(a) and (b). Implications of failing to hold documents at the disposal of the beneficiary or to send them back; indication of intention to deal with non-complying documents; effect of instruction from the issuing bank authorizing acceptance of discrepancies."

Duty of confidentiality may arise in other commercial transactions even in the absence of express statutory basis or agreement to such an effect. This may be implicit or be a natural or customary consequence of the overall commercial framework as demonstrated by Unidroit:

Unidroit 2.1.16 tells us:

> "Where information is given as confidential by one party in the course of negotiations, the other party is under a duty not to disclose that information or to use it improperly for its own purposes, whether or not a contract is subsequently concluded. Where appropriate, the remedy for breach of that duty may include compensation based on the benefit received by the other party."[63]

As to letters of credit, there are, in addition specific obligations of confidentiality as provided in UCP 600 in Article 38 (i):

> "i. If the first beneficiary is to present its own invoice and draft, if any, but fails to do so on first demand, or if the invoices presented by the first beneficiary create discrepancies that did not exist in the presentation made by the second beneficiary and the first beneficiary fails to correct them on first demand, the transferring bank has the right to present the documents as received from the second beneficiary to the issuing bank, without further responsibility to the first beneficiary."

As such, there are no public policy interests behind this rule. They relate only to the protection of trade secrets, which may form a basis for a successful private business.

---

[63] Unidroit 2.1.16 Comment 2:
"A party may have an interest in certain information given to the other party not being divulged or used for purposes other than those for which it was given. As long as that party expressly declares that such information is to be considered confidential, the situation is clear, for by receiving the information the other party implicitly agrees to treat it as confidential. The only problem which may arise is that if the period during which the other party is not to disclose the information is too long, this might contravene the applicable laws prohibiting restrictive trade practices. Yet even in the absence of such an express declaration the receiving party may be under a duty of confidentiality. This is the case where, in view of the particular nature of the information or the professional qualifications of the parties, it would be contrary to the general principle of good faith and fair dealing for the receiving party to disclose it, or to use it for its own purposes after the breaking off of negotiations."

Chapter III

The liability to customers or private parties does probably in most, if not all, cases, result in damages

Unidroit 2.1.16 Comment 3 provides:

> "The breach of confidentiality implies first liability in damages. The amount of damages recoverable may vary, depending on whether or not the parties entered into a special agreement for the non-disclosure of the information. Even if the injured party has not suffered any loss, it may be entitled to recover from the non-performing party the benefit the latter received by disclosing the information to third persons or by using it for its own purposes. If necessary, for example when the information has not yet been disclosed or has been disclosed only partially the injured party may also seek an injunction in accordance with the applicable law."

This is demonstrated in *Jackson v. Royal Bank of Scotland*:

> "The judge, Judge Kershaw QC, held that the bank was in breach of an obligation of confidence under its contract with Samson not to disclose to Economy Bag any of the documents relating to its purchase of goods from Pet Products. These documents included the invoice by Pet Products to Samson. *It was the disclosure of this document to Economy Bag that revealed the amount of the profit that Samson was making on the transaction.* There was no appeal against that part of his judgment. It was common ground in the Court of Appeal that the bank was in breach of its contract with Samson when it disclosed the invoice to Economy Bag.

The bank did violate its confidentiality obligation and the profit the customer was making was revealed, leading to termination of his lucrative back-to-back trading operations. Assessing damages for lost business relationships is not an easy task as demonstrated by the case.

> The judge then found that *Samson was entitled to damages for loss of the opportunity to earn profits from its trading relationship*. He held that there was a significant chance that Samson's trading relationship with Economy Bag would have continued for a further four years. But in view of the uncertainties he reduced the profit which had been projected by Samson for each of these years for the purposes of his award, and he increased the amount of the reduction year by year. The implication of his judgment was that

after the end of the fourth year Samson's chance of obtaining repeat business was so speculative as not to sound in damages."[64]

In a transferable credit, which was used in the back-to-back business, the name of the supplier was revealed, which did not amount to breach whereas the profit made should have been kept confidential.

> "I would hold that Mr Hapgood's submission that the second and third functions of the transferable letter of credit go hand in hand does not fit the facts. They may go hand in hand in some cases, but in this case they did not. The documents which Samson had to produce to draw on its portion of the credit revealed the identity of the supplier. *But this did not release the bank from their duty to preserve the confidentiality which attached to Pet Products' invoice to Samson.* The nature and extent of that duty was not lessened in any way by the fact that Economy Bag could have discovered the amount of the mark-up because it knew the seller's identity. As it happens, there was no evidence that the bank was aware that Mr Taylor in fact knew the name of the supplier or that he had been introduced to Mr Veerachai. But even if it had been aware of these facts, the bank was not entitled to assume that it was inevitable that the prices which Pet Products were charging to Samson would have been revealed also. *This information remained confidential to Samson, and it was the duty of the bank not to disclose it.*"[65]

---

[64] 2005 WL 62249 (HL), [2005] 2 All E.R. 71, [2005] 1 Lloyd's Rep. 366, (2005) 149 S.J.L.B. 146, [2005] 1 W.L.R. 377, [2005] 1 All E.R. (Comm) 337, (2005) 102(11) L.S.G. 29, 2-02-2005 Times 62,249, [2005] UKHL 3. Jackson and another v. Royal Bank of Scotland plc [2005] UKHL 3, House of Lords, HL, Lord Nicholls of Birkenhead, Lord Hoffmann, Lord Hope of Craighead, Lord Walker, of Gestingthorpe and Lord Brown of Eaton-under-Heywood, 2004 Dec 13, 14: 2005 Jan 27.

[65] Id.

CHAPTER IV

Fraud

IV.1 Fraud ("abuse") or *"fraus omnia corrumpit"*, generally

The fraud exception is globally well-established, but what constitutes fraud for the purposes of these instruments? There is both a criminal and a civil dimension in what we call fraud.

Fraud is hard to define under many laws as are abuse, unreasonableness, unfairness and unconscionability.[1] There is no international standard, nor

---

[1] Quentin Loh and Tang Hang Wu in "Injunctions restraining calls on performance bonds – is fraud the only ground in Singapore?":
"As can be seen from the discussion above, the ambit of the notion of "unconscionability" is far from settled and some confusion has been thrown on the standard of proof required. In particular, the *Min Thai* case suggests a relaxation of the court's attitude in granting injunctive relief to restrain the call on the performance bond."
Charles Proctor, "Enron, Letters of Credit and the Autonomy Principle", *Butterworths Journal of International Banking & Financial Law* (2004 19(6), 204-209):
"What conclusions can be drawn from the above analysis of the *Mahonia* decision? First of all, it may be concluded that the *fraud exception' is not limited to cases in which the applicant for the credit or the issuing bank is the victim of the fraud. The exception may apply if the request for the credit is made as part of a scheme to deceive the public by preparing misleading accounts or in some similar way. To this extent, the ambit of the fraud exception may perhaps be broader than previously thought. The courts must however, be astute to keep the exception within its proper limits, to ensure that the utility of documentary credits in international transactions is not undermined."
Anthony Pugh-Thomas, "Performance Guarantees and Unconscionable Conduct - An Australian Perspective", Case Comment, *J.I.B.L.* (1997, 12(10), 414-417):
"Referring to earlier cases, the judge felt that the word" "unconscientious" caught better the flavour of the evil to which the TPA was directed than" "unconscionable" and he referred in particular to Logue v. Shoalhaven Shire Council where" "it is said that what is involved is a situation or conduct unconscionable so as to invoke the intervention of the court that from the beginning regarded itself as a court of conscience."""
Dong-heon Chae, "Letters of Credit and the Uniform Customs and Practice for Documentary Credits: The Negotiating Bank and the Fraud Rule in Korea Supreme Court CASE 96 DA 43713", *12 Fla. J. Int'l L. 23*, (Spring, 1998):
"The concept of "fraud (Sagi)" in Korea in legal activities is expressed in Article 110 of the Korean Civil Code, which provides that "a declaration of intention induced by fraud or duress

are there internationally agreed criteria, either. We are told by commentators that:

> "The fraud rule is "the most controversial and confused area" in the law governing letters of credit, mainly because the standard of fraud is hard to define. The divergent views expressed by courts and commentators with respect to the essence of the standard of fraud reflect the tension between two different policy considerations: "the importance to international commerce of maintaining the principle of the autonomy of documentary credits ... and the importance of discouraging or suppressing fraud in the letter of credit transaction." "[2]

In *Montrod v. Grundkötter* the court reiterated the position of English law on this issue. Besides the policy considerations discussed above, the rule may be deemed to reflect the fundamental principles of law merchant. The further one goes from these fundamentals, the less certainty there is as to where the fraud concept common to all trading nations ends and where the domain of national law begins. The last sentence, stating clearly that courts refuse to be used for unlawful purposes or illegal activities, is another legal doctrine and principle which overlaps with the general purposes (public policy / ordre public) of law.[3]

> "As already made clear, Montrod's original allegation of fraud on the part of GK as beneficiary has not been pursued before us. There is no issue between the parties that, so far as the state of the authorities is concerned, *no English court has yet held an issuing bank entitled to withhold payment under a letter of credit, against documents which on their face conform with the requirements of the credit, save on the ground of fraud of the beneficiary himself, or the person seeking payment.* Nor is it in dispute that in England the fraud exception is part of the common law and that it is apt to apply despite the fact that *UCP 500 makes no reference to, nor makes allowance for, such an exception.* As was made clear by Lord Diplock in *United City Merchant*

---

may be voidable." Fraud is established when a deceitful act by one party causes a mistake to be made by the other and induces the mistaken party to make a declaration of intention. ....In this case, the Supreme Court used the good faith principle, which in Article 2 of the Civil Code provides that "the exercise of rights and performance of duties shall be in good faith and in accordance with the principles of trust.""

[2] Gao Xiang and Ross P. Buckley, "A Comparative Analysis of the Standard of Fraud Required under the Fraud Rule in Letter of Credit Law", *Duke Journal of Comparative and International Law*, (Spring 2003).

[3] See, e.g., Matti S. Kurkela, Due Process in International Commercial Arbitration, New York, 2005.

Bank (Investments) Ltd v Royal Bank of Canada [1983] 1 AC 168, 184: "The exception for fraud on the part of the beneficiary seeking to avail himself of the credit is a clear application of the maxim *ex turpi causa non oritur actio or*, if plain English is to be preferred, 'fraud unravels all'. *The courts will not allow their process to be used by a dishonest person to carry out a fraud."* [4]

The main exception to the substantive independence of credits and of genuine on-demand instruments is fraud, sometimes expressed in Latin in the maxim of *"fraus omnia corrumpit"*, or, fraud corrupts all.[5] Besides the diversity of definitions of

---

[4] 2001 WL 1479862 (CA (Civ Div)), [2002] 3 All E.R. 697, [2002] C.L.C. 499, [2002] 1 W.L.R. 1975, [2002] 1 All E.R. (Comm) 257, [2001] EWCA Civ 1954.

See also Montrod Ltd v. Grundkötter Fleischvertriebs GmbH [2001] EWCA Civ 1954, Court of Appeal, CA (Civ Div), Thorpe, Potter LJJ and Sir Martin Nourse, 2001 Oct 16, 17; Dec 20.

[5] 171 F.3d 739, 38 UCC Rep.Serv.2d 181, United States Court of Appeals, Second Circuit. 3COM CORPORATION, Plaintiff-Appellee, v. BANCO DO BRASIL, S.A., Defendant-Appellant. Docket No. 98-7658.:

"The doctrine, however, authorizes dishonor only where "a drawdown would amount to an outright fraudulent practice by the beneficiary." *Id.* at 858 (internal quotation marks omitted). For example, if a draft is accompanied by documents evidencing shipment of goods under a contract of sale, the doctrine permits dishonor not where a legitimate dispute exists concerning whether the goods conform to the underlying contract, but only where the goods are so obviously defective that the representation of shipment is plainly false. *See, e.g., United Bank Ltd. v. Cambridge Sporting Goods Corp.*, 41 N.Y.2d 254, 256, 392 N.Y.S.2d 265, 360 N.E.2d 943 (1976) (seller "had shipped old, unpadded, ripped and mildewed gloves rather than the new gloves to be manufactured as agreed upon");

Sztejn v. J. Henry Schroder Banking Corp., 177 Misc. 719, 720, 31 N.Y.S.2d 631 (1941) (beneficiary allegedly shipped not bristles contracted for but rather

"cowhair, other worthless material and rubbish with intent to simulate genuine merchandise and defraud the plaintiff"). Similarly, if a draft is accompanied by a beneficiary's statement that the issuer's customer has materially breached the underlying contract, dishonor is permissible only where the beneficiary's claim of breach is clearly untenable. *See, e.g., Recon/Optical*, 816 F.2d at 858 (draft not fraudulent because "[w]hether or not [the beneficiary's] view of the merits of these disputes is correct, there is no evidence [of] bad faith");

Ground Air Transfer, Inc. v. Westates Airlines, Inc., 899 F.2d 1269, 1272-73 (1st Cir.1990) (draft not fraudulent because claim of default at least "colorable"); *Roman Ceramics Corp. v. Peoples Nat'l Bank*, 714 F.2d 1207, 1214 (3d Cir.1983) (draft fraudulent where claim of nonpayment "has no basis in fact" and thus drawer "has no bona fide claim to payment at all"). In this case, it is undisputed that 3Com's drafts strictly complied with the terms of the Credit by including the statement that "[t]he amount of the draft which this statement accompanies will be applied by us to indebtedness due and owing by Comp Service Ltd a for invoices which Comp Service Ltda defaulted on the payment terms to 3Com Corp." Banco contends only that these statements were fraudulent because the invoices at issue were in the name of, and for goods shipped to, Techtrade rather than Comp Service itself. As discussed above, however, (1) Techtrade was Comp Service's U.S. purchasing agent, (2) Techtrade had assumed the obligations of Expasa, which had been a party to the distributorship agreement with 3Com, and (3) Comp Service had unconditionally

relevant fraud the weight of evidence required to prove its existence is unclear and may vary between jurisdictions.

Unidroit Art. 3.8 tells us that:

> "A party may avoid the contract when it has been led to conclude the contract by the other party's fraudulent representation, including language or practices, or fraudulent non-disclosure of circumstances which, according to reasonable commercial standards of fair dealing, the latter party should have disclosed."

IV.2 Establishing that fraud exists – the necessary sequence

Fraud must be established *prior* to payment to the beneficiary in order to constitute a cause of action. As a leading decision from the U.S. tells us:

> "*The relevant date for establishing knowledge of fraud.* It seems to us clear that, where payment has in fact been made, the bank's knowledge that the demand made by the beneficiary on the performance bond was fraudulent *must exist prior to the actual payment to the beneficiary* and that its knowledge at that date must be proved. Accordingly, if all a plaintiff can establish is such knowledge *after* payment, then he has failed to establish his cause of action. *The bank would not have been in breach of any duty in making the*

---

guaranteed payment of Techtrade's obligations to 3Com, and had waived any right to require 3Com to proceed against Techtrade rather than Comp Service directly. Viewing these facts in the light most favorable to Banco, we conclude that a reasonable finding of "fraud in the transaction" could not be reached in this case. A legitimate dispute exists concerning the meaning of the required statement--that is, the statement is arguably ambiguous with respect to whether it contemplates invoices issued to a third party but for which Comp Service is liable. Consequently, 3Com's presentment of the statements under the circumstances was by no means an "outright fraudulent practice," *Recon/Optical*, 816 F.2d at 858, and we affirm summary judgment for 3Com on this issue."

Christina Teng, "Bank guarantees – Counter Guarantees, Case Comment", *Journal of International Banking Law*, (13 (5),1998): "Comment: The Court of Appeal has reiterated that a bank must honour its guarantee unless there is obvious fraud to the knowledge of the bank. The bank's obligation to pay is independent of the primary contract between supplier and customer. These rules are necessary to maintain trust and certainty in international commerce. However, this case fails to provide an indication as to what constitutes fraud. It is still unclear what sort of evidence should be provided to a bank of fraud and to what extent a bank should take notice and deny payment."

payment without the requisite knowledge. We doubt that this is really open to contest."[6]

Fraud is defined under New York law in *Hyosung America v. Sumagh Textile* as follows:

> "The Agreement provides that disputes arising thereunder shall be governed by the laws of the state of New York.
>
> "Under New York law, the essential elements of a common law fraud claim include 'a material, false representation, an intent to defraud thereby, and reasonable reliance on the representation, causing damage to the plaintiff.' " Turtur v. Rothschild Registry Int'l, Inc., 26 F.3d 304, 310 (2d Cir.1994) (quoting Katara v. D.E. Jones Commodities, Inc., 835 F.2d 966, 970-71 (2d Cir.1987)).

In order to constitute fraud the injured party should have taken all reasonable measures to protect himself ("due diligence"):

> It has been held that where a plaintiff " 'has the means of knowing, by the means of ordinary intelligence, the truth, or the real quality of the subject of the representation, he must make use of those means, or he will not be heard to complain that he was induced to enter into the transaction by misrepresentations,' " Mallis v. Bankers Trust Co., 615 F.2d 68, 80-81 (2d Cir.1980) (quoting *Schumaker v. Mather, 133 N.Y. 590, 596, 30 N.E. 755, 757 (N.Y.1892)),* and that justifiable reliance will not be found in "cases in which plaintiff was placed on guard or practically faced with the facts," *id.* at 81.

If relevant facts are disclosed and warning signals are raised, there is no such reliance as is required to constitute fraud:

> We do not believe that Hyosung was "placed on guard or practically faced with the facts" as a matter of law, or that Hyosung had the means to become aware of the facts by such "ordinary" measures. We have also previously

---

[6] United Trading Corporation S.A. and Murray Clayton Ltd. v. Allied Arab, Bank Ltd. and Others, Court of Appeal, CA (Civ Div), July 17, 1984.

held that " '[w]here sophisticated businessmen engaged in major transactions enjoy access to critical information but fail to take advantage of that access, New York courts are particularly disinclined to entertain claims of justifiable reliance.' "*Keywell Corp. v. Weinstein*, 33 F.3d 159, 164 (2d Cir.1994) (quoting *Grumman Allied Industries, Inc. v. Rohr Industries, Inc.*, 748 F.2d 729, 737 (2d Cir.1984)). However, in the absence of a showing that the "plaintiff was placed on guard or practically faced with the facts," that principle is more relevant in cases, like *Grumman Allied Industries* and *Keywell*, that involve the purchase of a business. In such cases, the "critical information" relating to the misrepresentation is often more discoverable "by the means of ordinary intelligence" through the performance of due diligence. Here, the duty to inquire was more remote and depended on notice."[7]

To what extent the law protects reliance or "reasonable" reliance as compared to and over due diligence is unclear. The level of diligence required from a merchant or banks in general in ordinary circumstances when no warning signals are present may be on a certain level but the level of diligence is remarkably heightened when the circumstances or parties should cause particular concern or set off an alarm. Finally, in case of fraud, one needs to identify the party who carries the risks and should suffer the consequences of fraud.

IV.3 Duty (right) to refrain from paying

Fraud may not just release a party (the issuer or payor) from its obligation to effect payment but may actually establish a duty to refrain from payment.[8] While it is clear that a bank may have the right to refrain from paying, the issue of whether or not a duty to pay exists may be considerably more critical and may expose the bank to liability to the account party if the tender, nevertheless,

---

[7] 137 F.3d 75, 34 UCC Rep.Serv.2d 930. United States Court of Appeals, Second Circuit. HYOSUNG AMERICA, INC., Hyosung America, Inc., as Assignee of Orkid Tex, Inc., Plaintiff-Counter-Defendant-Appellant, v. Sumagh Textile CO., LTD., Defendant-Counter-Claimant-Appellee, Docket No. 96-9408, Argued May 20, 1997, Decided Feb. 13, 1998.

[8] Bertrams, *Bank Guarantees*, at 395-396, writes: "Case law and legal writing in all jurisdictions concerned confirm the principle that if fraud by the beneficiary is evident to the bank it owes a duty to the account party to refrain from payment. If the bank disregards this duty, it incurs liability towards the account party, which for all practical purposes means that it forfeits its right of reimbursement and that the bank is not allowed to debit the customer's accounts. The bank's knowledge of fraud must exist at the time of payment."

is accepted and payment made.[9] If the bank refuses, however, to pay, it may face the beneficiary's claim for wrongful dishonor.

Wunnicke, Wunnicke and Turner write on p. 165:

> "The majority opinion in *Roman Ceramics* holds that the issuer *may dishonor* when fraud is alleged, but the majority opinion does not discuss the issue. A footnote in the majority opinion, however, refers to Comment 2 to § 5-114, which states *that the risk of fraud is borne by the applicant, but when no innocent third parties are involved, "the issuer is no longer under a duty to honor."*
>
> *Boston Hides & Furs v. Sumitomo Bank* acknowledged that a court may enjoin honor or uphold dishonor by an issuing bank that has been informed of fraudulent documents in a presentment and then declared: "If sufficient evidence exists on which a court of appropriate jurisdiction could enjoin honor, the issuing bank, on its own initiative, may refuse payment.""

According to the Hong Kong court, the test is "clear and obvious" fraud, which causes the bank's liability to arise in the event of wrongful payment leading to loss of its right to reimbursement. What is "clear and obvious" is not necessarily "clear and obvious" in commercial reality and therefore the court's additional requirement when "standing in the shoes of paying bank" is highly persuasive excluding *most ex post facto* second-guessing by courts.

> "It is well-established law that the test is whether, standing in the shoes of the paying bank at the time of payment, the fraud was clear and obvious to it (Turkiye Is Bankasi AS v Bank of China [1998] 1 Ll LR 250 at 253, quoting Geoffrey Lane LJ in *Edward Owen Engineering Ltd v*

---

[9] See, e.g., Opinions of the ICC Banking Commission 1984-1986, R 103, p. 23: "In the discussion the following comments were made:

- that the questions involved were largely legal issues, the resolution of which depended on the law applicable
- that the question of jurisdiction on the sales contract was not relevant to jurisdiction on the documentary credit, which was a legally separate instrument
- that banks had a duty to oppose injunctions which restrained them from honouring their irrevocable undertakings.

The Commission decided it could not give an opinion on the question."

> *Barclays Bank International Ltd (CA) [1978] 1 QB 159 at 175F). If fraud was clear and obvious, then the bank pays the beneficiary at its own peril and it is not entitled to reimbursement. But if fraud was not clear and obvious, then it is not for a banker to question why the businessmen involved in the underlying transaction had chosen to conduct their business in any particular way."*[10]

Fraud has been considered to be an exception to the doctrine of independence. It does not have to be so. Fraud could be invoked when the demand for payment constitutes fraudulent use of the letter of credit itself and it does not have to be fraud "borrowed" from the main agreement. An independent transaction, like a letter of credit, may be independently abused in a fraudulent way. It is, however, clear that when the credit, as a commercial one, is only independent in its justification aspect, the fraud under the credit is necessarily fraud under the main agreement. But fraud under the main agreement is not necessarily fraud under the credit, because the credit is independent and it has its independent purpose and scope.[11] Where the border lies is unclear, and it is also unclear whether for instance fraud in the inducement of the underlying agreement would constitute fraud which could be invoked under the credit. It would be recommendable to keep the two transactions separate to the extent possible even in this respect. On the other hand the main purpose in having the facility constituted and the instrument thereunder issued may have been to defraud the banks or the account party.

Standby credits are often used as independent collaterals not guaranteeing a specific performance under the main agreement (like for example repayment of advances). In such cases, fraud under them should clearly be fraud in the sense that its purpose of collateral is abused, although no reason whatsoever to resort to them is visible when analyzing the main agreement. The concept of fraud is narrower when such 'doubly' independent standbys are in question.

The remedy for fraudulent abuse is an injunction. Its availability may depend on lex fori or on the applicable law.

---

[10] [2002] HKLRD (Yrbk) 30. RE GUANG XIN ENTERPRISES LTD, 21 March 2002, Court of First Instance, CFI, HCMP No 3003 of 2001.

[11] For instance delivering defective material or concealing and covering grossly dangerous inferior works may constitute fraud under the underlying construction contract but would not necessarily taint l/c opened by the employer to pay for machinery delivered to the site by contractor.

IV.4 Fraud and good faith

The fraud rule is part of international *ordre public* (public policy) and cannot be contracted away. (That is, parties cannot avoid application of the fraud rule by merely reciting in their contract that it does not apply.) It is an implicit part of every transaction. The rule overlaps to some extent with another rule of international *ordre public* and *lex mercatoria*, namely that of good faith.[12] Fraud in the transaction is *contagious* and may taint everything, including accessory and even substantively independent instruments like, e.g., credits and guarantees and render them void or unenforceable. [13] On the other hand, good faith may collide with the fraud rule if the party entitled to payment or reimbursement under the facility has been in good faith although fraud in the transaction or under the instrument or facility has been established.

UCC provides in Section 5-109 (a):

> (a) If a presentation is made that appears on its face strictly to comply with the terms and conditions of the letter of credit, but a required document is forged or materially fraudulent, or honor of the presentation would facilitate a material fraud by the beneficiary on the issuer or applicant:
> (1) the issuer shall honor the presentation, if honor is demanded by:
>   (i) a nominated person who has given value *in good faith* and without notice of forgery or material fraud,
>   (ii) a confirmer who has honored its confirmation *in good faith*,
>   (iii) *a holder in due course* of a draft drawn under the letter of credit which was taken after acceptance by the issuer or nominated person, or
>   (iv) an assignee of the issuer's or nominated person's deferred obligation that was taken for value and *without notice of forgery or material fraud* after the obligation was incurred by the issuer or nominated person; and
> (2) *the issuer, acting in good faith, may honor or dishonor the presentation in any other case.*

---

[12] Bona fide–rule is more limited referring usually to lack of knowledge only whereas good faith rule is proactive. See URDG Art. 15.

[13] It is unclear to what extent this applies to other crimes like bribery, money laundering, tax evasion, coercion, usury etc

Chapter IV

As fundamental as the strict compliance doctrine is, the fraud exception is of no less legal force and value. Sometimes the two may collide if the beneficiary is in good faith but the issuer is in bad faith.[14] It relates to the role of the judiciary and the legal system as instruments of law enforcement *inherently hostile to and unavailable for the purposes of enforcing criminal or illegal bargains*.[15]

UNC Article 19(3) tells us:

> "In the circumstances set out in subparagraphs (a), (b) and (c) of paragraph (1) of this article, the principal/applicant is entitled to provisional court measures in accordance with article 20."

Since the position of fraud is so paramount, what then constitutes fraud? Fraud has both a criminal and general legal definition in many jurisdictions.[16] Under law merchant, the fraud rule, in order to be effectively invoked by an account party, must be deemed to meet some general requirements in order not to dilute the fundamental principles of the substantively independent *instruments*.[17]

UNC Art. 19 (2) provides:

> "For the purposes of subparagraph (c) of paragraph (1) of this article, the following are types of situations in which a demand has no conceivable basis: (a) The contingency or risk against which the undertaking was designed to secure

---

[14] See, e.g., Dolan, *The Law of Letters of Credit*, 1993 Cumulative Supplement No. 2, p. 6.03.
[15] ILA Resolution on Public Policy as a Bar to Enforcement of International Awards (2002).
[16] Black's Law Dictionary:
"1. A knowing misrepresentation of the truth or concealment of a material fact to induce another to act to his or her detriment. 2. A misrepresentation made recklessly without belief in its truth to induce another person to act. 3. A tort arising from a knowing misrepresentation, concealment of material fact, or reckless misrepresentation made to induce another to act to his or her detriment. 4. Unconscionable dealing; esp., in contract law, the unconscientious use of the power arising out of the parties' relative positions and resulting in an unconscionable bargain." Reprinted from Black's Law Dictionary (7 th ed. 1999) with permission of Thomson West.
[17] Bertrams, *Bank Guarantees*, at 353, writes:
"It is, nonetheless, clear that Continental and English law share four common features. First, all jurisdictions agree that, whatever the notion of fraud might entail, it can be determined by reference to the underlying relationship. Secondly, evidence of actual, as opposed to constructive fraudulent intent on the part of the beneficiary to inflict harm is not required. This explains why the terms 'fraud' and 'abuse' are used interchangeably and why there is no real need to distinguish clearly between them. Thirdly, no distinction is made between 'simple' demand guarantees and demand guarantees which require the submission of a statement from the beneficiary concerning the account party's default. Lastly, no distinction is made between domestic and crossborder cases."

the beneficiary has undoubtedly not materialized; (b) The underlying obligation of the principal/applicant has been declared invalid by a court or arbitral tribunal, unless the undertaking indicates that such contingency falls within the risk to be covered by the undertaking; (c) The underlying obligation has undoubtedly been fulfilled to the satisfaction of the beneficiary; (d) Fulfilment of the underlying obligation has clearly been prevented by wilful misconduct of the beneficiary; (e) In the case of a demand under a counter-guarantee, the beneficiary of the counter-guarantee has made payment in bad faith as guarantor/issuer of the undertaking to which the counterguarantee relates."

IV.5 Clear proof

The *Rionda* case demonstrates two tests: one easier to meet at the pre-trial stage (interim measures) and another more demanding at the trial stage. When granting injunction, another test referred to as "balance of convenience" is applied. It is difficult to say whether it is a procedural test or a material test or both.

> "This case is also the locus classicus for the elucidation of the standard of proof required to make good a case of fraud, both at trial and at the stage of requesting a pre-trial injunction (at p. 561).
>
> At trial the test is this: If the Court considers that on the material before it the only realistic inference to draw is that of fraud, then the seller would have made out a sufficient case of fraud.
>
> At the pre-trial stage the test therefore becomes: Have the plaintiffs established that it is seriously arguable that, on the material available, the only realistic inference is that [the beneficiary] could not honestly have believed in the validity of its demands on the performance bonds? This is later (at p. 565) glossed as "a good arguble case". In the result, the plaintiff failed to obtain an injunction on two separate grounds: first, it failed to establish a good arguable case so that the only realistic inference was that the beneficiary's demand was fraudulent (at p. 565); and secondly, *it failed on balance of convenience* (at p. 566).[18]"

---

[18] 1999 WL 250018 (QBD (Comm Ct)), [1999] C.L.C. 1148, [1999] 2 Lloyd's Rep. 187, [1999] Lloyd's Rep. Bank. 197, [1999] 1 All E.R. (Comm) 890, 6-14-1999 Independent 250,018. Czarnikow-Rionda Sugar Trading Inc. v. Standard Bank London Ltd. and Others, Queen's Bench Division (Commercial Court), QBD (Comm), May 6, 1999.

CHAPTER IV

Clear proof, which allows a bank to refuse to pay, is generally memorialized in a court decision or a temporary injunction or other protective order, which, however, need not be final.[19] This is not a problem at all, but the "guessing" that the bank needs to do in the absence of such a court order may be very painful and expose the bank to liability. Sometimes a pending criminal investigation, a court decision or other evidence may establish fraud beyond any doubt. The banks may not necessarily have to be judges in this respect and should rather avoid it, since court systems often provide interim measures to parties to accomplish an attachment or other court intervention by obtaining injunctive temporary relief or by resorting to other such measures or remedies.[20] If the parties fail to do this,

---

[19] UCC 5-109 (official comment):
"4. The standard for injunctive relief is high, and the burden remains on the applicant to show, by evidence and not by mere allegation, that such relief is warranted. Some courts have enjoined payments on letters of credit on insufficient showing by the applicant. For example, in *Griffin Cos. v. First Nat'l Bank*, 374 N.W.2d 768 (Minn. App. 1985) the court enjoined payment under a standby letter of credit, basing its decision on plaintiff's allegation, rather than competent evidence, of fraud. There are at least two ways to prohibit injunctions against honor under this section after acceptance of a draft by the issuer. First is to define honor (see Section 5- 102(a)(8)) in the particular letter of credit to occur upon acceptance and without regard to later payment of the acceptance. Second is explicitly to agree that the applicant has no right to an injunction after acceptance/whether or not the acceptance constitutes honor. 5. Although the statute deals principally with injunctions against honor it also cautions against granting "similar relief" and the same principles apply when the applicant or issuer attempts to achieve the same legal outcome by injunction against presentation (see *Ground Air Transfer Inc. v. Westates Airlines, Inc.*, 899 F.2d 1269 (1st Cir. 1990)), interpleader, declaratory judgment, or attachment. These attempts should face the same obstacles that face efforts to enjoin the issuer from paying. Expanded use of any of these devices could threaten the independence principle just as much as injunctions against honor. For that reason courts should have the same hostility to them and place the same restrictions on their use as would be applied to injunctions against honor. Courts should not allow the "sacred cow of equity to trample the tender vines of letter of credit law.'"

[20] UCC 5-109 (official comment):
"This recodification makes clear that fraud must be found either in the documents or must have been committed by the beneficiary on the issuer or applicant. See *Cromwell v. Commerce & Energy Bank*, 464 So. 2d 721 (La.1985). Secondly, it makes clear that fraud must be "material". Necessarily courts must decide the breadth and width of "materiality." The use of the word requires that the fraudulent aspect of a document be material to a purchaser of that document or that the fraudulent act be significant to the participants in the underlying transaction. Assume, for example, that the beneficiary has a contract to deliver 1,000 barrels of salad oil. Knowing that it has delivered only 998, the beneficiary nevertheless submits an invoice showing 1,000 barrels. If two barrels in a 1,000 barrel shipment would be an insubstantial and immaterial breach of the underlying contract, the beneficiary's act, though possibly fraudulent is not materially so and would not justify an injunction. Conversely, the knowing submission of those invoices upon delivery of only five barrels would be materially fraudulent. The courts must examine the underlying transaction when there is an allegation of material fraud, for only by examining that transaction can one determine whether a document is fraudulent or the beneficiary has committed fraud and, if so, whether the fraud was material. Material fraud by the beneficiary occurs only when the beneficiary has no colorable right to expect honor and where there

it should reduce or eliminate the bank's exposure to liability for wrongful payment.

UNC Art 20 provides some shelter:

> "(1) Where, on an application by the principal/applicant or the instructing party, it is shown that there is a high probability that, with regard to a demand made, or expected to be made, by the beneficiary, one of the circumstances referred to in subparagraphs (a), (b) and (c) of paragraph (1) of article 19 is present, the court, on the basis of immediately available strong evidence, may: (a) Issue a provisional order to the effect that the beneficiary does not receive payment, including an order that the guarantor/issuer hold the amount of the undertaking, or (b) Issue a provisional order to the effect that the proceeds of the undertaking paid to the beneficiary are blocked, taking into account whether in the absence of such an order the principal/applicant would be likely to suffer serious harm.
>
> (2) The court, when issuing a provisional order referred to in paragraph (1) of this article, may require the person applying therefor to furnish such form of security as the court deems appropriate. (3) The court may not issue a provisional order of the kind referred to in paragraph (1) of this article based on any objection to payment other than those referred to in subparagraphs (a), (b) and (c) of paragraph (1) of article 19, or use of the undertaking for a criminal purpose."

---

is no basis in fact to support such a right to honor. The section indorses articulations such as those stated in *Intraworld Indus. v. Girard Trust Bank.* 336 A.2d 316 (Pa. 1975), *Roman Ceramics Corp. v. People's Nat'l Bank.* 714 F.2d 1207 (3d Cir.1983), and similar decisions and embraces certain decisions under Section 5-114 that relied upon the phrase "fraud in the transaction".

Some of these decisions have been summarized as follows in *Ground Air Transfer v. Westates Airlines*, 899 F.2d 1269, 1272-73 (1st Cir. 1990): We have said throughout that courts may not "normally" issue an injunction because of an important exception to the general 'no injunction' rule The exception, as we also explained in *Itek*. 730 F.2d at 24-25 concerns "fraud" so serious as to make it obviously pointless and unjust to permit the beneficiary to obtain the money. Where the circumstances "plainly" show that the underlying contract forbids the beneficiary the beneficiary of even a "colorable' right to do so, *id.*, at 25; where the contract and circumstances reveal that the beneficiary's demand for payment has "absolutely no basis in fact" *id* see *Dynamics Corp. of Am.* 356 F. Supp. at 999; where the beneficiary conduct has "so vitiated the entire transaction that the legitimate purposes of the independence of the issuers obligation would no longer he served," *Itek*, 730 F.2d at 25 (quoting *Roman Ceramics Corp. v. Peoples Nat'l Bank*, 714 F.2d 1207, 1212 n.12, 1215 (3d Cir. 1983) (quoting *Intraworld Indus.*, 336 A.2d at 324-25)); then a court may enjoin payment."

CHAPTER IV

The criteria applied to establish fraud before a bank must be even stricter than those applied by courts. Banks do not need to be, and should not be, active in establishing fraud.

> "It is simply not for a bank to make enquiries about the allegations that are being made one side against the other. If one side wishes to establish that a demand is fraudulent, it must put the *irrefutable evidence in front of the bank*. It must not simply make allegations and expect the bank to check whether those allegations are founded or not . . .[I]t is not the role of a bank to examine the merits of allegations of breach of contract. To hold otherwise would place banks in a position where they would in effect have to act as Courts in deciding whether to make payment or not. Of course, if a beneficiary were to admit to the bank that it had no right to make the demand, then a totally different situation would arise.

Rionda applied also "the balance of convenience test":

> In the light of these authorities, it seems to me that, even if I assume for the sake of argument that Rionda has otherwise brought itself within the fraud exception, its claim against Standard for a pre-trial injunction must fail on the balance of convenience alone. I would seek to put the matter in the following way. (1) The interest in the integrity of banking contracts under which banks make themselves liable on their letters of credit or their guarantees is so great that not even fraud can be allowed to intervene unless the fraud comes to the notice of the bank (a) in time, i.e., in any event before the beneficiary is paid, and (b) in such a way that it can be said that the bank had knowledge of the fraud. Whether that interest is viewed in terms of the importance that must be attached to the honouring of banking commitments, or in terms of the lifeblood of commerce and in particular international commerce, it has been amply recognized in case after case. Unless the banking commitment can be insulated from disputes between merchants, international trade would become impossible."[21]

---

[21] Czarnikow-Rionda Sugar Trading Inc. v. Standard Bank London Ltd, 1999 WL 250018 (QBD (Comm Ct)), [1999] C.L.C. 1148, [1999] 2 Lloyd's Rep. 187, [1999] Lloyd's Rep. Bank. 197, [1999] 1 All E.R. (Comm) 890, 6-14-1999 Independent 250,018 . . .

IV.6 Whose fraud is relevant?

Can one limit the relevance of fraud to the beneficiary only? Traditionally, starting from the landmark case of *Sztejn*, the fraud exception was considered only in the context of the fraud committed by the beneficiary himself, as was analyzed in *United City Merchants*:

> "A large number of English and American authorities were considered by the Court of Appeal. But, as all three members of the Court of Appeal concluded, there is no English or American authority directly deciding the point now being considered, since it was never an issue. It is very important to bear this in mind since dicta in certain cases state the "fraud exception" in terms of the fraud of the beneficiary, commonly the seller, and the buyers placed much reliance upon them: see, for example, *Edward Owen Engineering Ltd. v. Barclays Bank International Ltd.* [1978] Q.B. 159 and *Sztejn v. J. Henry Schroder Banking Corporation* (1941) 31 N.Y.S. 2d 631.[22]

The fraud may, however, have been committed by a third party with or without the knowledge of the beneficiary and with more or less direct causal or other links to the instrument and the tender thereunder:

> But Stephenson L.J. observed [1982] Q.B. 208, 234A, fraud on the part of the beneficiary was all that the court was concerned with in both of those cases; it never directed its mind in either case to the question of the effect of fraud of a third party. Nor do the Uniform Customs and Practice for Documentary Credits, 1974, which were expressly incorporated into the credit, assist in determining the scope of the fraud exception, since they do not contain any article providing what is to happen as between banker and beneficiary if fraudulent documents are presented.

The drafters of the UCC seem to have had even this unfortunate event in their minds:

> By contrast, the United States Uniform Commercial Code does expressly provide for this situation; the relevant provision (section 5-114 (2)) is set out in the judgment of Stephenson L.J. [1982] Q.B. 208, 236G-237A and

---

[22] See Bertrams, *Bank Guarantees*, at 426.

> *the only words referring to a "forged or fraudulent" document are clearly wide enough to cover cases where the fraud is of a party other than the seller-beneficiary. The decision of the Court of Appeal on this issue is, therefore, entirely consistent with that section given that in this case it is accepted by the appellants that they are in no better position than the sellers. For these reasons, the Court of Appeal were right to conclude that the Royal Bank of Canada were not obliged to make payment under the credit because the bill of lading was a fraudulent document."*[23]

In *United City Merchants* the fraud of a third party, *but known by the beneficiary* at the time of tender, was treated as the beneficiary's own fraud:

> "My Lords, if the broad proposition for which the confirming bank has argued is unacceptable for the reasons that I have already discussed, what rational ground can there be for drawing any distinction between apparently conforming documents that, unknown to the seller, in fact contain a statement of fact that is inaccurate where the inaccuracy was due to inadvertence by the maker of the document, and the like documents where the same inaccuracy had been inserted by the maker of the document with intent to deceive, among others, the seller/beneficiary himself? *Ex hypothesi we are dealing only with a case in which the seller/beneficiary claiming under the credit has been deceived*, for if he presented documents to the confirming bank with knowledge that this apparent conformity with the terms and conditions of the credit was due to the fact that the documents told a lie, *the seller/beneficiary would himself be a party to the misrepresentation made to the confirming bank* by the lie in the documents and the case would come within the fraud exception, as did all the American cases referred to as persuasive authority in the judgments of the Court of Appeal in the instant case."[24]

As illustrated by the above case, fraud committed by others may also be relevant.

Unidroit Article 3.11 tells us:

> "(1) Where fraud, threat, gross disparity or a party's mistake is imputable to, or is known or ought to be known by, a third person for whose acts the

---

[23] United City Merchants (Investments) Ltd. v. Royal Bank of Canada, [1982] 2 W.L.R. 1039, House of Lords.
[24] Id.

other party is responsible, the contract may be avoided under the same conditions as if the behaviour or knowledge had been that of the party itself. (2) Where fraud, threat or gross disparity is imputable to a third person for whose acts the other party is not responsible, the contract may be avoided if that party knew or ought to have known of the fraud, threat or disparity, or has not at the time of avoidance reasonably acted in reliance on the contract."

The fraud must, however, be *in the transaction or in the facility* as vague and indefinite these words may be.[25] Fraud committed by a third party to induce the account party into the transaction without the knowledge of the beneficiary and in the absence of collusion or conspiracy cannot, as a general rule, constitute relevant fraud. Such a "constructive fraud" may, however, be treated as fraud by the courts since the outcome to the account party is equally unfair.[26]

In a multiparty facility the issue as to collusive behaviour and "sham" proceedings with true conflict of interest may arise.

The *Rionda* case illustrates the difficulties when fraud is established in the facility before the facility has been dismantled:

"In my view the independence of Rionda and Standard in the proceedings to date is seriously in question. Of course, by holding that no injunction should be maintained against Standard I suspect that I create a situation where a real gulf may well open up between those parties, since *Standard may then feel obliged to pay the Swiss banks*, which Rionda plainly would not want, and *Rionda may then press its claim against Standard to the effect that Standard has acted outside its mandate and in breach of its obligations to Rionda*. No doubt it is in part Standard's fear of being embroiled in such litigation that has informed its present tactics. None of that, however, is to say that in the bringing of this action and in the argument to date there has been any real issue between them.

---

[25] The UCC provided for "fraud in the transaction as a ground instead of simple fraud". The transaction comes close to the word "facility" as used in this work if combined with the underlying agreement.

[26] Conspiracy often refers to an agreement or understanding made to the detriment of, or to defraud or harm, a third party as opposed to an agreement for the benefit of third party.

CHAPTER IV

The parties may have interests in common ("collusion"), which are not necessarily disclosed, and they may choose not to bring action against parties (whether they are indispensable or not under the applicable procedural rules) who might jeopardize their interests in common:

> In my judgment, while Standard has not been willing formally to consent to any acknowledgment of a situation where the fraud exception applies, it has as I am inclined to infer indicated to Rionda that it would not oppose Rionda's seeking of an injunction against it - as it has not. On the contrary, while saying that it is for present purposes neutral on all substantive issues raised before me, it has argued strongly in favour of maintaining the injunction against it on the balance of convenience, provided I am sufficiently persuaded of a good arguable case (which it does not itself advance) that Rionda brings itself within the fraud exception.
>
> Given also the background to these proceedings, and the leading role that Standard among other banks has played in supporting Rionda through its troubles, and, as I have learned from the evidence before me, given also *the extent to which Standard is unsecured in its transactions with Rionda, I would infer for the purposes of this pre-trial hearing that Standard wanted to have an injunction granted against it, to prevent it from paying under its letters of credit.* That is consistent with the letter written by its solicitors immediately prior to Rionda's launching of these proceedings and is certainly the position it has demonstrated to me, and I think I am entitled to view it as likely to have been the position that it *indicated to Rionda before the action began.*

Legal action to enforce the interests in common, in particular in the absence of parties who may have opposing interests under the same facility, may constitute an abuse of process and may be "sham" proceedings aimed at misleading the court and third parties:

> It follows also that in my view the true nature of the co-operation or at any rate the common ground between Rionda and Standard has not been disclosed in circumstances where it ought to have been. In effect, Standard has continued to support Rionda, whether under the standstill agreement or not, both generally and in relation to its strategy of litigation, both in this country and abroad. Indeed, in his New York deposition,

Mr. Barg accepted that the banks including Standard receive reports on the progress of the litigation from time to time. As Mr. Strauss submitted, none of this is surprising or in the least reprehensible: what is, however, well arguable is that it is an abuse of process to seek indirectly to implicate other foreign parties in litigation which, at any rate at the ex parte stage, Standard had no interest in opposing, and to do so without making a clean breast of the mutual and supporting role being given by Standard, as defendant, to the claimant Rionda."[27]

IV.7 Links required and risks assumed

In order for the fraud committed to affect the viability of the transaction, it must have a sufficient causal link to the transaction. In addition, it would seem justified to require that the fraud will expose the account party to a risk of loss or damage he has not assumed, if no legal protection is granted or equivalent measures are taken. In this area, procedural aspects and material principles are not easy to keep apart. The risk of loss, damage or harm, should perhaps be irreparable in the absence of intervention. "Irreparable" may include final loss, lack of effective remedy or unreasonably lengthy legal proceedings, overly burdensome and uncertain legal remedies, or unavailability or impossibility of execution of the court decision or arbitral award in the ordinary course of proceedings available to the injured party.[28] Most of these risks are often assumed by the parties and the underlying agreement contains the legal weaponry to safeguard the account party's interests. In *Hyosung America*, above, we saw the disinclination of courts to intervene if "the plaintiff was placed on guard and faced with the facts" and that disinclination applies here, too.

One should also remember that a bank involved has a duty to effect payment and a right to do so in most, if not all, cases in the absence of a court order to the contrary.[29]

---

[27] Czarnikow-Rionda Sugar Trading Inc. v. Standard Bank London Ltd, 1999 WL 250018 (QBD (Comm Ct)), [1999] C.L.C. 1148, [1999] 2 Lloyd's Rep. 187, [1999] Lloyd's Rep. Bank. 197, [1999] 1 All E.R. (Comm) 890, 6-14-1999 Independent 250,018.
[28] See Bertrams, *Bank Guarantees*, at 434.
[29] See, however, Bertrams, *Bank Guarantees*, at 395-396.

CHAPTER IV

UCC 5-109 states this principle:

> "2. Subsection (a)(2) makes clear that the issuer may honor in the face of the applicant's claim of fraud. The subsection also makes clear what was not stated in former Section 5-114 that the issuer may dishonor and defend that dishonor by showing fraud or forgery of the kind stated in subsection (a). Because issuers may be liable for wrongful dishonor if they are unable to prove forgery or material fraud, presumably most issuers will choose to honor despite applicants claims of fraud or forgery unless the applicant procures an injunction. Merely because the issuer has a right to dishonor and to defend that dishonor by showing forgery or material fraud does not mean it has a duty to the applicant to dishonor. The applicant's normal recourse is to procure an injunction, if the applicant is unable to procure an injunction, it will have a claim against the issuer only in the rare case in which it can show that the issuer did not honor in good faith."

One could also require that a security, sufficient to cover any and all loss or damage, be submitted by the beneficiary before any court order intervening in the payment process is being enforced.

As to withholding payment, UNC Art 19 (1) provides as follows:

> "(1) If it is manifest and clear that: (a) Any document is not genuine or has been falsified; (b) No payment is due on the basis asserted in the demand and the supporting documents; or (c) Judging by the type and purpose of the undertaking, the demand has no conceivable basis, the guarantor/issuer, acting in good faith, *has a right*, as against the beneficiary, *to withhold payment.*"

UNC addresses the right to withhold payment but omits to create any rule on a duty to do so. In some instances payment by the bank may expose it to liability to the true beneficiary as provided in UCC:

UCC 5-109 (official comment) says:

> "The last clause of Section 5-108(i)(5) deals with a special case in which the fraud is not committed by the beneficiary, but is committed by a stranger to the transaction who forges the beneficiary's signature, If the issuer pays

against documents on which a required signature of the beneficiary is forged, it remains liable to the true beneficiary."

IV.8 Who bears the loss?

If fraud or abuse has been committed and the damage or loss can no more be avoided, one could allocate the loss to the party who may be deemed to have assumed the risk, i.e., the one who did contract with the party who then proved to be dishonest or unreliable.[30] The defrauded account party may have rights and remedies under the transaction and cannot be deemed to have lost those rights. The instruments do not in general replace or substitute any rights but are in addition to them:

> "It is clear that one of the cases principally relied upon by the claimants before the arbitrators was the decision of the Court of Appeal in *W.J. Alan & Co. Ltd. v. L. Nasr Export and Import Co. Ltd.*, [1972] 1 Lloyds Rep. 313; [1972] 2 Q. B. 189, and in particular the obiter dicta of Lord Denning, M. R., at pp. 321 and 210 where he said:
>
> In my opinion a letter of credit is not to be regarded as absolute payment, unless the seller stipulates, expressly or impliedly, that it should be so. He may do it impliedly if he stipulates for the credit to be issued by a particular banker in such circumstances that it is to be inferred that the seller looks to that particular banker to the exclusion of the buyer. There are some cases in the United States which are to be explained in this way, such as *Vivacqua Irmaos S.A. v. Hickerson*, (1939) 190 S. 657 and *Ornstein v. Hickerson* (1941) 40 F. Supp. 305. and in the Sopromacase [1966] 1 Lloyd's Rep. 367 there was a stipulation for a particular banker, which may account for Mr. Justice McNair's observation. The arbitrators specifically found that: . . . the Claimants did not either expressly or impliedly stipulate that the drafts or the Letters of Credit were to be regarded as absolute payment.

---

[30] URDG Art. 11 provides:
"Guarantors and Instructing Parties assume no liability or responsibility for the form, sufficiency, accuracy, genuineness, falsification or legal effect of any document presented to them or for the general and/or particular statements made therein, nor for the good faith or acts or omissions of any person whomsoever."

In this case the arbitrators had found that there was no such stipulation. The respondents did, however, argue that from the agreement on a specific bank as an issuing bank it can be inferred that this was the purpose ("waiver").

> Mr. Evans does not, on behalf of the respondents, criticise the finding that there was no express stipulation but he does attack the finding that there was no implied stipulation that the drafts or letters of credit were to be treated as absolute payment. It seems to be clear, particularly since the arbitrators were apparently quoting part of the language used by Lord Denning, M.R. set out above, that they were satisfied that *the claimants did not stipulate for the credit to be issued by Merchant Swiss Ltd. in such circumstances that it was to be inferred that they looked to that particular bank to the exclusion of the respondents*. This seems to me to be a clear finding of fact, fully open to the arbitrators on the material set out in their award and is therefore unassailable by the respondents. Mr. Evans sought to submit as a proposition of law, that where the identity of the bank is agreed between the parties, and not left to the choice of the buyers, it must follow that the sellers impliedly agree that the liability of the issuing bank has been accepted by them in place of that of the buyers. I do not think that this is correct. *The fact that the sellers have agreed on the identity of the issuing bank is but one of the factors to be taken into account when considering whether there are circumstances from which it can be properly inferred that the sellers look to that particular bank to the exclusion of the buyer*. It is in no way conclusive. In this case, unlike the United States case of Ornstein v. Hickerson referred to by Lord Denning, M. R., which was the basis of Mr. Evans's submission, there were other circumstances which clearly supported the presumption that *the letters of credit were not given as absolute payment but as conditional payment*.
>
> It follows from the finding that the letters of credit were given only as conditional payment, that if they were not honoured, the respondents' debt has not been discharged. This is because the buyers promised *to pay* by letter of credit, not to provide by a letter of credit the source of payment which did not pay. See *W.J. Alan & Co. v. L. Nasr Export*, [1972] 1 Lloyd's Rep. 313 per Lord Justice Stephenson at p.329. *The sellers' remedy in such circumstances is to claim from the buyers either the price agreed in the contract of sale or damages for breach of their contractual promise to pay by letter of credit*. Mr. Evans, however, submits, with his characteristic force and lucidity,

that the buyers' liability was discharged by the claimants and Merchant Swiss Ltd. treating the letters of credit as mere formalities with the result that the drafts presented by the claimants were never formally accepted, although the dates on which they were to be payable was agreed. This, it was contended, amounted to a departure from the variations agreed between the claimants and the respondents in March, referred to above, that payment was to be made by 90-day drafts drawn on Merchant Swiss Ltd. and to this departure the claimants never obtained the respondents' consent. There is an air of unreality about this submission, since the procedure adopted by the claimants and Merchant Swiss Ltd. was one which had been adopted in their previous transactions with the respondents. Because of the close relationship between the respondents and Merchant Swiss Ltd., a fact specifically referred to by the arbitrators in their findings, the very informal way in which the letters of credit were handled and the documents and drafts presented is unlikely to have been unknown to the respondents. However, as Mr. Evans points out, there is no express finding to this effect.

In order to support his submission that the conduct of the claimants and Merchant Swiss Ltd., referred to above, resulted in a discharge of the respondents' obligation to pay the price of the goods, Mr. Evans was obliged to rely heavily upon the proposition that *the respondents were in the position of guarantors of Merchant Swiss's limited liability and that the letters of credit had the essential characteristics of a bill of exchange and were to be treated as such.* On this basis he invoked the well-known lines of authority relating to the discharge of the guarantor's liability when indulgence is shown to the principal debtor and the need to give notice of dishonour prior to enforcing a bill of exchange. *There is in my judgment no justification for so treating the respondents or the letters of credit.* The respondents' liability to the sellers was a primary liability. This liability was suspended during the period available to the issuing bank to honour the drafts and was activated when the issuing bank failed. The respondents were in no respect guarantors of Merchant Swiss Ltd. Further, the suggestion that the letters of credit should be treated as possessing all the main characteristics of a bill of exchange, seems to be derived from the fact that its position was described in the W.J. Alan & Co. v. L. Nasr case as being analogous to a bill of exchange, which is presumed when given under a contract of sale, to be given not as absolute payment but conditional payment. The existence of this analogy does not to my mind provide any warrant for treating letters of credit in the manner suggested. *I therefore see no justification either in*

CHAPTER IV

> law or in fact for holding that the conduct of the claimants and Merchant Swiss Ltd. discharged the buyers' primary liability to pay the purchase price of the goods."[31]

In most cases the account party must bear the loss since he chose the "fraudulent" beneficiary and relied on him in vain.[32] If another party to the facility proved fraudulent causing loss or damage to the other parties, the party to bear the loss should be the one who introduced, retained or relied on the fraudulent party or was in a position to eliminate or reduce the exposure. The same rules of allocation of risks may apply in case of bankruptcy, subject, however, to disclaimers in UCP and other applicable rules.

> "Where, as here, a plaintiff establishes in the first stage of the inquiry that fraud occurred, a defendant "has the full burden of proof by a preponderance of the total evidence on this issue. The burden must be sustained by affirmative proof...." *Scarsdale Nat'l Bank & Trust Co. v. Toronto-Dominion Bank*, 533 F.Supp. 378, 386 n. 12 (S.D.N.Y.1982) (citations omitted).
>
> In *Scarsdale*, a standby letter of credit required certificates stating that the seller had performed certain duties required by the underlying contract. See *Scarsdale*, 533 F.Supp. at 379-80. Shortly after the letter was issued and before performance was complete, the seller submitted the certificates along with a demand under the letter to a bank in exchange for financing.

---

[31] E.D. & F. Man Ltd. v. Nigerian Sweets & Confectionery Co. Ltd.,1977 WL 59840 (QBD (Comm Ct)), [1977] 2 Lloyd's Rep. 50

[32] The risk of fraud seems to pass at the moment of death of the instrument and a discounting of one's own deferred payment undertaking does not change this. See, e.g., *Banco Santander Sa v. Bayfern Limited*,1999 WL 250019 (QBD (Comm Ct)), [1999] C.L.C. 1321, [1999] Lloyd's Rep. Bank. 239, [1999] 2 All E.R. (Comm) 18, (1999) 96(26) L.S.G. 27, 6-29-1999 Times 250,019, 6-21-1999 Independent 250,019:

"The Question. This judgment relates to the trial of certain preliminary issues arising only between the Plaintiff, Banco Santander, and the Third Defendant, Banque Paribas in these proceedings. In a nutshell the question is whether the risk of fraud on the part of the beneficiary of a confirmed deferred payment letter of credit is to be borne by the issuing bank (and so possibly the applicant for the credit) or by the confirming bank where the confirming bank has discounted its own payment obligations to the beneficiary and paid over the discounted sum to it and the fraud is discovered only after it has done so but before the maturity date of the letter of credit. "Santander" was the Confirming Bank and "Paribas" the Issuing Bank. The applicant was Napa Petroleum Trade Inc and the Beneficiary, Bayfern Limited. The Answers to the Issues. I will hear the parties on the form of Order to be made in the light of this judgment and the fact that both have sought to refine the specific questions which were referred to the court. My essential conclusion is that on the assumption that Bayfern was guilty of fraud in the manner alleged and that was known to Santander before November 27, 1998 the risk of that fraud falls on Santander and not Paribas."

By the time the bank submitted the last of the certificates to the issuing bank, the seller had defaulted on his obligations and the issuing bank refused to pay. The court found that the bank that released funds based on the certificates "had actual knowledge" that "the performance required by the certificates had not yet occurred" at the time it paid value. *Because of this knowledge, the court held that the bank's attempt to hide behind the "technical compliance with the paper requirements" amounted to "willful ignorance."*

Because the bank accepted documents it knew to be false, the court concluded that *it had acted in bad faith*, was not a holder in due course, and was not entitled to be reimbursed for the money it had paid to its client.

Similarly, in *Andina Coffee, Inc. v. National Westminster Bank*, 160 A.D.2d 104, 560 N.Y.S.2d 1 (1990), a negotiating bank accepted post-dated documents from the beneficiary, including bills of lading dated six weeks into the future, to finance the payment of goods that were never shipped. When the negotiating bank claimed that it was a holder in due course and was entitled to payment regardless of any fraud in the underlying transaction, the issuing bank countered that the negotiating bank was aware of the fraud. Holding that the post-dated documents were "not only a departure from the requirements of the letters of credit but also ... a form of fraudulent practice," the court concluded that unless the post-dating was expressly allowed under the letters of credit, the documents did not comply with the terms of the letter, and the bank was not entitled to payment.

BOI knew that the undated Default Letter could not have reflected the actual condition it purported to certify. Nothing in the present record contradicts the earlier finding, *see Brenntag*, 9 F.Supp.2d at 344, that Banerjee, the head of the BOI letter of credit department, admitted that when BOI accepted the undated Default Letter from Petro Pharma on March 22, 1996, the statement contained in the Default Letter— that "payment was due 360 days after completion of loading has not been received and is due and owing from Brenntag"—*was not true and could not have been true.* There is no provision in the LOC nor any authorization from Petro Pharma permitting BOI to date stamp the Default Letter when the due date arrived. Under these circumstances, the practice of Singapore bankers, if such it be, cannot constitute good faith. *Were it otherwise, local banking practice could alter the terms of the instruments, and BOI has not advanced any authorities which so hold. Because BOI is not a holder in due course it bears the risk of*

CHAPTER IV

Petro Pharma's fraud. See Brenntag, 175 F.3d at 250; *KMW Int'l v. Chase Manhattan Bank*, 606 F.2d 10, 16 (2d Cir.1979); *United Bank Ltd. v. Cambridge Sporting Goods Corp.*, 41 N.Y.2d 254, 392 N.Y.S.2d 265, 360 N.E.2d 943, 948 (1976)."[33]

IV.9 Nullity exception

Does the nullity of the underlying transaction constitute another defence as to substantively independent letters of credit or bank guarantees?[34]

Nullity is a legal consequence of a failure to comply with law, or a violation of law (e.g., ultra vires). The failure may relate to the formation of the transaction or formalities (e.g., written form) required to accomplish the desired objective, the failure may relate to the absence of a legal requirement (e.g., the legal capacity of a party). Nullity or unenforceability may be a consequence of violation of *bonos mores*, criminal acts, unclean hands, antitrust laws, etc., but it is a legal consequence only, not the ground in itself. There seems to be no reason or rule justifying a conclusion that nullity of the underlying transaction, irrespective of its ground, would result in general in nullity or unenforceability of the accessory financial instruments, whether substantively independent or not. Nor does the well-established fraud rule impose a nullity consequence that would allow legal intervention in the accessory instrument. It would be an exaggeration to contend that the "automatic" effect of fraud would be nullity or unenforceability of the instrument. The fraud rule allows a court investigation and scrutiny of the facts beyond the letter of the instrument in order to determine what legal protection is warranted and to prevent fraud.

---

[33] Brenntag Int'l Chemicals, Inc. v. Norddeutsche Landesbank GZ & Bank of India, 70 F Supp 2d 399 (S.D.N.Y., 1999).

[34] Jason C.T. Chuah, *Is there a nullity in documentary credits?*. Finance & Credit Law 2002, 1(Jan), 3-4; Allen & Overy, Clifford Chance and Ashurst Morris Crisp: *Refusal of documents under a letter of credit*, Butterworths Journal of International Banking & Financial Law, (2002), 17(7), 307-308:
"Further, it was submitted on Fibi Bank's behalf that, in addition to the fraud exception, there was also a 'nullity exception' relating to documents which were nullities to the bank's knowledge at the time of payment notwithstanding that the beneficiary was not involved in any deception. It was held that such exception did not form part of English law, that it lacked authority and that it was contrary to principle. Therefore, Fibi Bank had no defence to SCB's claim for reimbursement."

In the *Montrod v. Grundkötter* case, the judge had this to say:

> *"In my view there are sound policy reasons for not extending the law by creation of a general nullity exception. Most documentary credits issued in the United Kingdom incorporate the UCP by reference.* Various revisions of the UCP have been widely adopted in the USA and by United Kingdom and Commonwealth banks. They are intended to embody international banking practice and to create certainty in an area of law where the need for precision and certainty are paramount. The creation of a general nullity exception, the formulation of which does not seem to me susceptible of precision, involves making undesirable inroads into the principles of autonomy and negotiability universally recognised in relation to letter of credit transactions.
>
> In the context of the fraud exception, the courts have made clear how difficult it is to invoke the exception and have been at pains to point out that banks deal in documents and questions of apparent conformity. In that context they have made clear that it is not for a bank to make its own inquiries about allegations of fraud brought to its notice; if a party wishes to establish that a demand is fraudulent it must place before the bank evidence of clear and obvious fraud: see *Edward Owen Engineering Ltd v Barclays Bank International Ltd [1978] QB 159*; cf Turkiye Is Bankasi AS v Bank of China [1996] 2 Lloyd's Rep 611, 617 per Waller J.
>
> If a general nullity exception were to be introduced as part of English law, it would place banks in a further dilemma as to the necessity to investigate facts which they are not competent to do and from which UCP 500 is plainly concerned to exempt them. Further such an exception would be likely to act unfairly upon beneficiaries participating in a chain of contracts in cases where their good faith is not in question. Such a development would thus undermine the system of financing international trade by means of documentary credits.
>
> I have concluded that there is and should be no general nullity exception based upon the concept of a document being fraudulent *in itself* or devoid of commercial value. I would only add, with reference to Lord Diplock's reservation, that I would not seek to exclude the possibility that, in an individual case, the conduct of a beneficiary in connection with the creation and/or presentation of a document forged by a third party might, though

itself not amounting to fraud, be of such character as not to deserve the protection available to a holder in due course. In this connection, I note the reference by Mocatta J in the *United City Merchants case [1979] 1 Lloyd's Rep 267* to "personal fraud" or "*unscrupulous conduct*" on the part of the seller presenting documents for payment, a remark upon which Lord Diplock made no adverse comment when approving the original judgment on the documentary credit point.

In this connection, we have had brought to our attention the decision of the *High Court of Singapore in Lambias (Importers and Exporters) Co Pte Ltd v Hong Kong and Shanghai Banking Corpn [1993] 2 SLR 751*, in which the defendant bank rejected documents tendered under a letter of credit which included a quality and weight inspection certificate required to be countersigned by a named individual. The court held that the certificate contained discrepancies which entitled the bank to refuse the documents tendered and went on to find that the inspection certificate was in any event a nullity in that, not only did it fail to state the particulars of the goods and their quality and weight, but that, having been issued by the beneficiary instead of the applicant, it had been countersigned by an impostor. Having considered the observations, and in particular the reservation, of Lord Diplock in the *United City Merchants case [1983] 1 AC 168* and the particular facts before the court in relation to the plaintiffs, who had themselves introduced the counter-signatory to the bank as the person named, Goh Phai Cheng JC observed [1993] 2 SLR 751, 765-766: "The law cannot condone actions which, although not amounting to fraud per se, are of such recklessness and haste that the documents produced as a result are clearly not in conformity with the requirements of the credit. The plaintiffs in the present case are not guilty of fraud, *but they were unknowingly responsible for having aided in the perpetration of the fraud. In such a case where the fraud was discovered even before all other documents were tendered, I think it is right and proper that the plaintiffs should not be permitted to claim under the letter of credit.*"[35]

---

[35] *Montrod Ltd v. Grundkötter Fleischvertriebs GmbH*, [2001] EWCA Civ 1954, Court of Appeal, CA (Civ Div.)

IV.10 Illegality

Recently there have been discussions as to the effects of illegality and to what extent it may taint the accessory instruments. There is no right answer to this issue.[36]

In general, illegality in the underlying transaction may result in unenforceability, nullity or voidability of the whole or a part thereof depending on the closeness and material links between the parts. Fraud in the inducement, coercion, bribery and many other crimes have in general such consequences, but even then certain parts of agreement may survive like, e.g., an arbitration clause. However, since both criminal law and contract law are to a great extent covered by national laws and national policies, it is not possible to give extensive guidance in this respect.

One may, however, draw a significant distinction between substantively independent and materially linked accessory instruments and at least draw some presumptions, that in the case of an independent instrument, illegality of the underlying transaction or related agreement in the facility does not affect the enforceability of the instrument except perhaps in cases violating (transnational) *ordre public*. One should, however, bear in mind that there is established law and practice that fraud has such consequences even as to independent instruments, which exception should not be lightly extended to other crimes.

When it comes to substantively dependent instruments like bonds and sureties, the presumption should be the reverse: the illegality of the underlying agreement or related agreement should, unless there are strong reasons to the contrary, extend to the accessory instrument likewise.

International treaties and conventions, which are superive norms, may have provided for such consequences as reflected in *United City Merchants*:

> "*The Bretton Woods Point* The Bretton Woods point arises out of the agreement between the buyers and the seller collateral to the contract of sale of the goods between the same parties that out of the payments in U.S. dollars

---

[36] Jason Chuah, Documentary credit – derogation from principle of autonomy on the basis that terms of illegal underlying transactions, Finance & Credit Law (2003, Nov) 6-7). Jason Chuah, Documentary credits and illegality in the underlying transaction, J Int'l Maritime L (2003, 9(6)) 518-521.

received by the sellers under the documentary credit in respect of each instalment of the invoice price of the goods, they would transmit to the account of the buyers in America one half of the U.S. dollars received.

The Bretton Woods Agreements Order in Council 1946, made under the Bretton Woods Agreements Act 1945, gives the force of law in England to article VIII section 2 (b) of the Bretton Woods Agreement, which is in the following terms: "Exchange contracts which involve the currency of any member and which are contrary to the exchange control regulations of that member maintained or imposed consistently with this agreement *shall be unenforceable in the territories of any member . . .* "

My Lords, I accept as correct the narrow interpretation that was placed upon the expression "exchange contracts" in this provision of the Bretton Woods Agreement by the Court of Appeal in *Wilson, Smithett & Cope Ltd. v. Terruzzi [1976] Q.B. 683.* It is confined to contracts to exchange the currency of one country for the currency of another; it does not include contracts entered into in connection with sales of goods which require the conversion by the buyer of one currency into another in order to enable him to pay the purchase price. As was said by Lord Denning M.R. in his judgment in the *Terruzzi* case at p. 714, the court in considering the application of the provision should look at the substance of the contracts and not at the form. It should not enforce a contract that is a mere "monetary transaction in disguise."

I also accept as accurate what was said by Lord Denning M.R. in a subsequent case, as to the effect that should be given by English courts to the word "unenforceable." The case, Batra v. Ebrahim, is unreported, but the relevant passage from Lord Denning's judgment is helpfully cited by Ackner L.J. in his own judgment in the instant case: [1982] Q.B. 208, 241F-242B.

The unenforceability based on violation of treaties must be taken into account *ex officio* or *sua sponte* by the court.

If in the course of the hearing of an action the court becomes aware that the contract on which a party is suing is one that this country has accepted an international obligation to treat as unenforceable, *the court must take the point itself, even though the defendant has not pleaded it, and must refuse to lend its aid to enforce the contract.* But this does not have the effect of making an exchange contract that is contrary to the exchange control regulations of a member state other than the United Kingdom into a contract that is "illegal" under English law or render acts undertaken in this country in performance of such a contract unlawful. Like a contract of guarantee of which there is no note or memorandum in writing it is unenforceable by the courts and nothing more."[37]

Very rarely has this issue come before the courts. *In Mahonia v. JP Morgan* and the case referred to in the motivations (namely a reinsurance related dispute) the interconnection was discussed in some length. The illegality and fraud were held to be too remote to have any effect on the independent letter of credit issued in cause of the otherwise tainted transactions. The policy aspect as to whom the statutory protection was meant to give legal protection was taken into account in this analysis.

> "The only English case in which illegality has been considered as affecting payment under a letter of credit is Group Josi Re v. Walbrook Insurance Co. Ltd. and Others, [1996] 1 Lloyd's Rep. 345. In that case an underwriting agency, Weavers, wrote primary risks on the London market for a pool of overseas insurers. Weavers also arranged and managed reinsurance of its pool members by outside reinsurers. The plaintiffs, Group Josi, *one of the reinsurers, agreed with Weavers that the latter would pay over to them loss reserves held in respect of the reinsurers in exchange for a letter of credit under which Weavers would be entitled to draw down against debit notes stating that Group Josi were liable for the amounts claimed under the reinsurances.*
>
> Group Josi brought proceedings against Weavers and the reassured companies to restrain them from drawing down under the letters of credit. Amongst the grounds for this claim were: i) Group Josi was not authorized to carry on insurance business in Great Britain under the Insurance Companies Acts 1974-82 and as the contracts of reinsurance were made in London, *they and the letter of credit were illegal and unenforceable*; (ii) the chairman, deputy chairman and managing director of Weavers *were party to a fraud to divert from Weavers and the reassured pool members commissions* which should have been credited to them and Group Josi were induced to enter into the contracts of reinsurance by false and fraudulent

---

[37] United City Merchants (Investments) Ltd. v. Royal Bank of Canada, [1982] 2 W.L.R. 1039, House of Lords.

representations that the commissions would be duly paid or credited to those to whom they were due and that there was a failure to disclose the fraudulent purpose when the reinsurances were placed, that Group Josi had to Weaver's knowledge validly avoided the reinsurances for that reason and that there would therefore be a fraud if Weavers presented the debit notes against the letter of credit.

I had granted an interlocutory injunction restraining the reinsured and Weavers from presenting a claim for payment under the letters of credit. Mr. Justice Clarke held that the reinsurance contracts were illegal but that the letters of credit were not thereby rendered illegal or tainted with illegality and Mr. Justice Phillips held that the reinsurance contracts had not been avoided for non-disclosure. On appeal it was held that there was no evidence that either Weavers or the reassured companies knew of the alleged representation or relied on them and that there was therefore no basis for the argument that it would be dishonest for Weavers to present debit notes to obtain payment under the letters of credit. It was also held that the effect of s. 132(6) of the Financial Services Act, 1986 on s. 2 of the Insurance Companies Act, 1982 was retrospectively to render contracts of reinsurance illegally entered into on the grounds of lack of authorization unenforceable only at the suit of the reinsurers and not by the reassured. *Accordingly, operation of the letter of credit by or on behalf of the reassured would involve no illegality."*[38]

The court continued its analysis by raising the policy issues which lie behind all transactions, national and international, and pointed out that fraud cannot be the only exception to the independence principle. One may thus distinguish between the strengthened force of the policy and the issue of closeness or remoteness of the "evil" and the enforceability of the undertaking or the instrument in question.

"However, there is a real conflict between on the one hand the well-established principle that contracts lawful on their face which are entered into in furtherance of an illegal purpose will be unenforceable at the suit of the party having knowledge of that purpose at the time of contracting and on

---

[38] Mahonia Ltd. v. JP Morgan Chase Bank, 2003 WL 22827091 (QBD (Comm Ct)), [2003] 2 Lloyd's Rep. 911, [2003] EWHC 1927.

the other hand the policy of the law reflected in all the letter of credit cases of preserving the impregnability of the letter of credit save, where the bank has clear evidence of an ex turpi causa defence such as fraud.

This conflict is not, in my judgment, a matter which can be resolved simply by postulating the separate nature of the letter of credit and applying reasoning similar to that in the *Bowmakers case*. Thus, like Lord Justice Staughton in Group Josi, sup. at p. 362, I find it almost incredible that a party to an unlawful arms transaction would be permitted to enforce a letter of credit which was an integral part of that transaction even if the relevant legislation did not on its proper construction render ancillary contracts illegal. *To take an even more extreme example, I cannot believe that any Court would enforce a letter of credit to secure payment for the sale and purchase of heroin* between foreign locations in which such underlying contracts were illegal. On the other hand, there is much to be said for the view that the public policy, in superseding the impregnability of letters of credit where there is an unlawful underlying transaction defence, may not be engaged where the nature of the underlying illegal purpose is relatively trivial, at least where the purpose is to be accomplished in a foreign jurisdiction.

The problems which arise from attempting to reconcile conflicting considerations of public policy may well give rise to uncertain consequences, as illustrated in relation to the finality of New York Convention arbitration awards in *Westacre Investments Inc. v. Jugoimport-SDPR Holding Co., [1999] Q.B. 740*. It would, however, be wrong in principle to invest letters of credit with a rigid inflexibility in the face of strong countervailing public policy considerations. If a beneficiary should as a matter of public policy (ex turpi causa) be precluded from utilizing a letter of credit to benefit from his own fraud, it is hard to see why he should be permitted to use the courts to enforce part of an underlying transaction which would have been unenforceable on grounds of its illegality if no letter of credit had been involved, however serious the material illegality involved. *To prevent him doing so in an appropriately serious case such as one involving international crime could hardly be seen as a threat to the lifeblood of international commerce.*"[39]

---

[39] Id.; Dolan writes on illegality on pp. 9-17 and 9-18 in The Law of Letters of Credit, 1992 Cumulative Supplement No 2:
"Issuers have sometimes argued that because law other than letter of credit law renders payment under the credit illegal, the issuer should have a defense to the beneficiary's complaint when the

CHAPTER IV

As to the issue of *ordre public* and public policy, national or international, and its effects on the transaction or facility and their enforceability, see discussions above.

IV.11 Observations and remarks

Fraud may be deemed constituted, e.g., when

> - the beneficiary has himself falsified the documents or has caused them to be falsified by someone else or when he is aware of the fact that they have been falsified by someone else and submits them to the bank concealing this in order to receive the benefit (funds) under the credit or guarantee;[40]

---

issuer dishonors. The Export Administration Act, for example, specifically provides such a defense to issuers or confirmers of credits that violate that statute; and while some courts have held that the illegality of the underlying transaction will justify an injunction against payment of the credit obligation, a majority have rejected that approach."

[40] UCC 5-109 (official comment) provides:
"Whether a beneficiary can commit fraud by presenting a draft under a clean letter of credit (one calling only for a draft and no other documents) has been much debated. Under the current formulation it would be possible but difficult for there to be fraud in such a presentation. If the applicant were able to show that the beneficiary were committing material fraud on the applicant in the underlying transaction, then payment would facilitate a material fraud by the beneficiary on the applicant and honor could be enjoined. *The courts should be skeptical of claims of fraud by one who has signed a "suicide" or clean credit and thus granted a beneficiary the right to draw by mere presentation of a draft.*"

UCC 5-109 (official comment) provides:
"4. The standard for injunctive relief is high, and the burden remains on the applicant to show, by evidence and not by mere allegation, that such relief is warranted. Some courts have enjoined payments on letters of credit on insufficient showing by the applicant.

For example, in *Griffin Cos. v. First Nat'l Bank*, 374 N.W.2d 768 (Minn. App. 1985) the court enjoined payment under a standby letter of credit, basing its decision on plaintiff's allegation, rather than competent evidence, of fraud. There are at least two ways to prohibit injunctions against honor under this section after acceptance of a draft by the issuer. First is to define honor (see Section 5-102(a)(8)) in the particular letter of credit to occur upon acceptance and without regard to later payment of the acceptance. Second is explicitly to agree that the applicant has no right to an injunction after acceptance/-whether or not the acceptance constitutes honor. 5. Although the statute deals principally with injunctions against honor it also cautions against granting "similar relief" and the same principles apply when the applicant or issuer attempts to achieve the same legal outcome by injunction against presentation (see *Ground Air Transfer Inc. v. Westates Airlines, Inc.*, 899 F 2d 1269 (1st Cir. 1990)), interpleader, declaratory judgment, or attachment. These attempts should face the same obstacles that face efforts to enjoin the issuer from paying. Expanded use of any of these devices could threaten the independence principle just as much as injunctions against honor. For that reason courts should have the same hostility to them and place the same restrictions on their use as would be applied to injunctions against honor. Courts should not allow the "sacred cow of equity to trample the tender vines of letter of credit law."

- the beneficiary is aware of the fact that the documents submitted, although formally genuine, state material facts which are *grossly erroneous* or misleading or *totally untrue*, but submits them to the bank concealing the truth in order to receive the benefit (funds) under the credit or guarantee.

UCC defines the right of court intervention in Section 5-109 b:

"If an applicant claims that a required document is forged or materially fraudulent or that honor of the presentation would facilitate a material fraud by the beneficiary on the issuer or applicant, a court of competent jurisdiction *may temporarily or permanently enjoin the issuer from honoring a presentation or grant similar relief against the issuer or other persons* only if the court finds that:

(1) the relief is not prohibited under the law applicable to an accepted draft or deferred obligation incurred by the issuer;
(2) a beneficiary, issuer, or nominated person *who may be adversely affected is adequately protected* against loss that it may suffer because the relief is granted;
(3) *all of the conditions* to entitle a person to the relief *under the law of this state have been met*; and
(4) on the basis of the information submitted to the court, the applicant *is more likely than not to succeed* under its claim of forgery or material fraud and *the person demanding honor does not qualify* for protection under paragraph (1) of subsection (a) of this section."

In continental Europe the word *abuse* is often used instead of or as a synonym to fraud.[41] There are perhaps a number of reasons for this. Firstly, fraud is often understood as a serious and deliberate criminal offence and, as such, the word fraud may imply an allegation of such a crime having been committed, which is not necessarily the case. The "civil" meaning of fraud is broader and fraud may exist even when the facts do not constitute fraud as a criminal offence but simply

---

[41] Markus Heidinger, Bank Guarantees, Letters of Credit and Similar Instruments under Austrian Law, J Int'l Banking L 12(11), 450-453, (1997):
"It is obvious that banks are reluctant in the exercise of their own discretion to refuse payment unless strong evidence is at hand that the demand is evidently abusive or even fraudulent. However, Austrian courts will interfere by granting temporary injunctions against the beneficiary and the bank if there is strong prima facie evidence at hand that the call is either abusive or even fraudulent."

indicate dishonesty.[42] The word abuse has hardly any criminal-law connotation, so its use is less offensive and, in many jurisdictions, does not expose one to liability for libel or slander. Secondly, there is a classic and well-established doctrine of *"abus de droit"* in law, which seems particularly well adapted to the world of these independent instruments. This is particularly true in international banking, where the main concern often is, in particular in the domain of letters of credit and bank guarantees characterized by the strict compliance doctrine, the impeccable efforts by banks to honor their commitments. The best banks are keen on or obsessed by protecting primarily their own creditworthiness, and secondarily they seek to protect the credit or guarantee instrument as a product of international banking and exchange, and finally they seek the health, the financial polity, of the marketplace. Finally, abuse is perhaps broader as a concept and one may attempt to expand the scope of the applicability of the very narrow (or strict) fraud exception.

The liability for fraud may extend to non-parties as is demonstrated by case law:

> "This reasoning cannot in my opinion apply to liability for fraud. No one can escape liability for his fraud by saying:
>
> "I wish to make it clear that I am committing this fraud on behalf of someone else and I am not to be personally liable."
>
> Evans LJ [2000] 1 Lloyd's Rep 218, 230 framed the question as being "whether the director may be held liable for the company's tort". But Mr Mehra was not being sued for the company's tort. He was being sued for his own tort and all the elements of that tort were proved against him. Having put the question in the way he did, Evans LJ answered it by saying that the fact that Mr Mehra was a director did not in itself make him liable. That of course is true. He is liable not because he was a director but because he committed a fraud. Both Evans and Aldous LJJ treated the *Williams* case

---

[42] Bertrams, *Banking Guarantees*, at 391 writes:
"The survey of case law and legal writing suggests that a call could be fraudulent, in particular, a) in the event of completion of the contract by the account party, b) in the event of breach of fundamental obligations or serious misconduct on the part of the beneficiary, c) in the event that the guarantee has been called in relation to contracts which are not covered by the guarantee, d) in the case of a clear judgment of a competent judicial or arbitral court on the merits against the beneficiary and e) in respect of tender guarantees where the contract has not been awarded to the account party."

[1998] 1 WLR 830 as being based upon the separate legal personality of a company. Aldous LJ [2000] 1 Lloyd's Rep 218, 233 referred to *Salomon v A Salomon & Co Ltd [1897] AC 22*. But my noble and learned friend, Lord Steyn, made it clear [1998] 1 WLR 830, 835 that the decision had nothing to do with company law. It was an application of the law of principal and agent to the requirement of assumption of responsibility under the *Hedley Byrne* principle. Lord Steyn said it would have made no difference if Mr Williams's principal had been a natural person. So one may test the matter by asking whether, if Mr Mehra had been acting as manager for the owner of the business who lived in the south of France and had made a fraudulent representation within the scope of his employment, he could escape personal liability by saying that it must have been perfectly clear that he was not being fraudulent on his own behalf but exclusively on behalf of his employer."[43]

"At the heart of the Court of Appeal's decision is the view that, because Mr Mehra was a director of Oakprime and acted as such when cheating Standard Chartered, his acts must be regarded solely as the acts of Oakprime and he should have no personal civil liability for them.

As Mr Cherryman acknowledged, no man could escape the clutches of the criminal law by the simple device of showing that he had carried out his frauds in his capacity as a director of a company and in circumstances where his acts were to be attributed to the company: *Meridian Global Funds Management Asia Ltd v Securities Commission [1995] 2 AC 500*. In *R v ICR Haulage Ltd [1944] KB 551, 559*, for example, both the managing director and, through him, the haulage company were convicted of conspiracy to defraud. His acts "were the acts of the company and the fraud of that person was the fraud of the company"."

In the world of tort, however, all was said to be more happily arranged for the fraudster. He could use the device of acting as a director to escape any liability to his victims: they were to be regarded not as his victims but

---

[43] Standard Chartered Bank v. Pakistan Nat'l Shipping Corp., 2002 WL 31452047 (HL), [2003] 1 A.C. 959, [2003] 1 All E.R. 173, [2002] B.C.C. 846, [2003] 1 B.C.L.C. 244, [2002] C.L.C. 1330, [2003] 1 Lloyd's Rep. 227, (2002) 146 S.J.L.B. 258, [2002] 3 W.L.R. 1547, [2002] 2 All E.R. (Comm) 931, (2003) 100(1) L.S.G. 26, 11-07-2002 Times 31452,047, [2002] UKHL 43. [2002] UKHL 43; [2002] 3 W.L.R. 1547.

just as the victims of the company's fraud. His fraud might be the fraud of the company but, somehow or other, it was not his own fraud. *My Lords, the maxim culpa tenet suos auctores may not be the end, but it is the beginning of wisdom in these matters.* Where someone commits a tortious act, he at least will be liable for the consequences; whether others are liable also depends on the circumstances. Here, as the facts make plain and as Cresswell J specifically found, "all the ingredients of the tort of deceit are made out against Mr Mehra (and Oakprime)". In other words Standard Chartered have proved all that is required to make Mr Mehra—and through him Oakprime—liable in deceit. That being so, there is no conceivable basis upon which Mr Mehra should not indeed be held liable for the loss that Standard Chartered suffered as a result of his deceit. If he had been a mere employee of Oakprime and had done the same things and written the same letters on behalf of the company in that capacity, it could never have been suggested that Mr Mehra was not personally liable for his fraudulent acts. His status as a director when he executed the fraud cannot invest him with immunity."[44]

---

[44] Id.

CHAPTER V

Interpretation of Instruments

V.1 General

Credits and guarantees are credits and guarantees and not traditional contracts although contracts and their interpretation are perhaps the closest reference. They are very close to ordinary *service contracts* except that the services as a whole constitute "a facility". Sometimes the interpretation of an instrument or contract relates to its classification: is it a credit or something else?[1]

UCC 5-102 (official comment):

> "The adjective "definite" is taken from the UCP. It approves cases that deny letter of credit status to documents that are unduly vague or incomplete. See, *e.g. Transparent Prods. Corp. v Paysaver Credit Union*, 864 F.2d 60 (7th Cir. 1988). Note, however, that no particular phrase or label is necessary to establish a letter of credit. It is sufficient if the undertaking of the issuer shows that it is intended to be a letter of credit, In most cases the parties' intention will be indicated by a label on the undertaking itself indicating that it is a "letter of credit," but no such language is necessary."

Since the enforceability of these instruments is beyond doubt, it would be a waste of time to create a theory as to their exact character. Traditionally when phenomena which do not fully fit into the structure of academic concepts are concerned,

---

[1] UCC 5-104 (official comment) provides:
"Parties should generally avoid modifying the definitions in Section 5-102. The effect of such an agreement is almost inevitably unclear. To say that something is a "guarantee" in the typical domestic transaction is to say that the parties intend that particular legal rules apply to it. By acknowledging that something is a guarantee, but asserting that it is to be treated as a "letter of credit," the parties leave a court uncertain about where the rules on guarantees stop and those concerning letters of credit begin."

we have grown used to, or have been educated in, defining them as *sui generis*.[2] In reality this often means: "I don't fully understand and nor do others, but it does not matter, since it seems to function in any case", an easy and pragmatic way out of a dilemma. Issues of interpretation do arise both with respect to general classification, the kind of instrument in question, whether the conditions precedent are substantive, whether the documents tendered comply or is the claim compatible with the conditions, how are the UCP or other reference rules to be understood, etc.

The very limited need for interpretation and the surrounding commercial reality of the instrument was broadly described in *Glencore v. Bank of China*:

> "The issue in this appeal is simply stated: was the Bank of China, as issuer of two letters of credit, entitled to refuse payment under the credits on the ground that the documents presented did not comply with the terms of the credits? Although documentary credits are very widely used as a medium of payment in international sales transactions, *issues of this kind come before the Courts relatively infrequently.* There are a number of reasons for this. The parties to these transactions (buyers, sellers, issuing and advising banks) are *seasoned professionals*, not inexperienced consumers.
> *The banks are not required to familiarize themselves with any of the infinitely various terms, conventions or esoteric understandings of the sales transactions themselves*: their role is limited to the demanding, but essentially clerical, task of scrutinizing the documents tendered under the credit to establish that they conform to the terms of the credit.
> *Banks, rightly jealous of their reputation in the international market-place,* are generally careful not to refuse payment on grounds of non-conformity unless the non-conformity is clear. Practice is generally governed by the Uniform Customs and Practice for Documentary Credits ("the UCP "), a code of rules settled by experienced market professionals and kept under review to ensure that the law reflects the best practice and reasonable expectations of experienced market practitioners. *When Courts, here and abroad, are asked to rule on questions such as the present they seek to give effect to the international consequences underlying the UCP.*"[3]

---

[2] Gao Xiang and Ross P. Buckley in "The Unique Jurisprudence of Letters of Credit: Its Origin and Sources": "Therefore, whenever dealing with letters of credit, lawyers are best advised to start from the position that a letter of credit is unlike any other commercial instrument."

[3] Glencore Int'l v. Bank of China, 1995 WL 1083922 (CA (Civ Div)), [1996] 5 Bank. L.R. 1, [1996] C.L.C. 111, [1996] 1 Lloyd's Rep. 135, [1998] Masons C.L.R. Rep. 78, 11-27-1995 Times 1083, 922.

INTERPRETATION OF INSTRUMENTS

The court quite rightly emphasized the expectations of the parties to the facility and the central role played by UCP as a source of best practices and the importance of giving effect to the international character of the instruments.

UNC Art 13 gives the following general guidance as to interpretation:

> "(1) The rights and obligations of the guarantor/issuer and the beneficiary arising from the undertaking are determined by the terms and conditions set forth in the undertaking, including any rules, general conditions or usages specifically referred to therein, and by the provisions of this Convention.
>
> (2) In interpreting terms and conditions of the undertaking and in settling questions *that are not addressed* by the terms and conditions of the undertaking or by the provisions of this Convention, *regard shall be had to generally accepted international rules and usages of independent guarantee or stand-by letter of credit practice.*"[4]

UNC gives a paramount role to international rules and trade usages when issues arise which are not expressly covered by the instruments or their reference rules.

The interpretation of credits or guarantees is often said to be subject to traditional rules of interpretation of contract.[5] This is both right and wrong. The general rules of contract interpretation apply to the extent the particular characteristics of these instruments do not dictate another solution.

---

[4] Unidroit Art. 4.3 tells us: "(e) the meaning commonly given to terms and expressions in the trade concerned; (f) usages."

Dolan writes in *The Law of Letters of Credit* at 4-27:
> "This distinction correctly assumes that those bank employees who examine documents and decide whether to honor or dishonor a draft submitted under a credit must know banking practice. It also assumes that they cannot possibly know the usage and customs of those thousands of trades and industries that employ letters of credit."

[5] Dolan writes in *The Law of Letters of Credit* at 4-25:
> "There are strong indications in letter-of-credit law that trade usage, course of dealing, and course of performance will supplement a credit's terms. It is the general view that credits are contracts subject to contract rules of construction including the rules on custom."

See Bertrams, *Bank Guarantees*, at 213-214.

Chapter V

These rules have been defined in case law, e.g., as follows:

(i) The objective interpretation or understanding by a reasonable "outside" person:
"The settlement contained in the Tomlin order must be construed as a commercial instrument. *The aim of the inquiry is not to probe the real intentions of the parties but to ascertain the contextual meaning of the relevant contractual language. The inquiry is objective: the question is what a reasonable person, circumstanced as the actual parties were, would have understood the parties to have meant by the use of specific language.* The answer to that question is to be gathered from the text under consideration and its relevant contextual scene.

(ii) The objective interpretation or meaning should be compatible with that of the commercial community in question:
There has been a shift from literal methods of interpretation towards a more commercial approach. In *Antaios Compania Naviera SA v Salen Rederierna AB [1985] AC 191*, 201, Lord Diplock, in an opinion concurred in by his fellow Law Lords, observed: "if detailed semantic and syntactical analysis of a word in a commercial contract is going to lead to a conclusion that flouts business common sense, it must be made to yield to business common sense." In *Mannai Investment Co Ltd v Eagle Star Life Assurance Co Ltd [1997] AC 749*, 771, I explained the rationale of this approach as follows: "In determining the meaning of the language of a commercial contract . . . the law . . . generally favours a commercially sensible construction. The reason for this approach is that *a commercial construction is more likely to give effect to the intention of the parties. Words are therefore interpreted in the way in which a reasonable commercial person would construe them.* And the standard of the reasonable commercial person is hostile to technical interpretations and undue emphasis on niceties of language."

(iii) The rule against simple literal interpretation:
The tendency should therefore generally speaking be against literalism. What is literalism? It will depend on the context. But an example is given in *The Works of William Paley* (1838 ed), vol III, p 60. The moral philosophy of Paley influenced thinking on contract in the 19th century. The example is as follows: the tyrant Temures promised the garrison of Sebastia that no blood would be shed if they surrendered to him. They surrendered. He shed no blood. He buried them all alive. This is literalism. If possible it should be resisted in the interpretative process.

This approach was affirmed by the decisions of the House in *Mannai Investment Co Ltd v Eagle Star Life Assurance Co Ltd [1997] AC 749, 775e-G*, per Lord Hoffmann and in *Investors Compensation Scheme Ltd v West Bromwich Building Society [1998] 1 WLR 896, 913D-E*, per Lord Hoffmann."[6]

(iv) The suitable test person may be an experienced bank:
"In my judgment, there is nothing in this point. I have to construe the words used in the context of the commercial arrangement into which the parties had entered. I must avoid a semantic construction which flouts business common sense. I rely upon the evidence of Mr. Cannon which I accept, that he, as an experienced banker dealing with credits of this sort would understand that reference was being made to the set of documents and not merely to the bill. I therefore conclude that on this ground the plaintiff's submission fails and to the extent there has been compliance with Article 16(d)."[7]

The above general rules do not cover all the ground.

However, the *sui generis* character of the instruments, as unilateral undertakings of international character, must be taken into account.[8]

---

[6] Sirius Int'l Insurance Co v. FAI General Insurance Ltd, 2004 WL 2714105 (HL), [2005] 1 All E.R. 191, [2005] 1 C.L.C. 451, [2005] Lloyd's Rep. I.R. 294, [2005] 1 Lloyd's Rep. 461, (2004) 148 S.J.L.B. 1435, [2004] 1 W.L.R. 3251, [2005] 1 All E.R. (Comm) 117, (2004) 101(48) L.S.G. 25, 12-03-2004 Times 2714,105, [2004] UKHL 54

[7] Hing Yip Hing Fat Co. Ltd. v. Daiwa Bank, 15-17 January and 11 February 1991, High Court, (Commercial List No. 22 of 1989).

[8] Bertrams, *Bank Guarantees*, at 68, writes:
"Notwithstanding occasional subsumptions under such open-ended concepts as delegation, the German *abstraktes Schuldversprechen* and the German *Garantievertrag*, at present case law and doctrine view the modern independent bank guarantee, as employed in domestic and international trade and which forms part of a multi-party relationship, as a contract *sui generis*."

Compare with United Nations Convention on the Assignment of Receivables in International Trade Article 7:
"1. In the interpretation of this Convention, regard is to be had to its object and purpose as set forth in the preamble, to its international character and to the need to promote uniformity in its application and the observance of good faith in international trade."

And with that Convention's Article 11:
"3. In an international assignment, the assignor and the assignee are considered, unless otherwise agreed, implicitly to have made applicable to the assignment a usage that in international trade is widely known to, and regularly observed by, parties to the particular type of assignment or to the assignment of the particular category of receivables."

Chapter V

There are various levels in the interpretation which often are overlapping or so closely interrelated that keeping them apart seems difficult and hardly productive. One can, however, attempt to distinguish these levels, e.g., as follows:

> (i) Interpretation of messages, statements and acts and omissions of the parties within the framework of the instrument and the facility;
> (ii) Interpretation of the tender or claim in the examination exercise by the bank;
> (iii) interpretation of the rules expressly referred to or, if not so referred to, their role as a trade usage;
> (iv) interpretation of the applicable law when there is one;
> (v) interpretation in the light of the particular circumstances of the case;
> (vi) interpretation in the light of the interests of global banking and international trade.

Most of these aspects were referred to by the court in *Hing Yip v. Daiwa Bank*, as follows:

> "1. The use of the word "Industrial" is an obvious typographical error from the word "Industries" and is not a discrepancy upon which the defendant can rely. (See p.45A.) 2. If the "Industrial" point was a good one, the defendant would be precluded from relying upon it by virtue of Articles 16(e) & (d) of the Uniform Customs and Practice for Documentary Credits (1983 Revision) since it was not in the advice of discrepancies.
> The whole purpose behind Article 16 is that the beneficiary should know precisely his position at the earliest opportunity. *The court has to bear in mind that it is construing a set of rules which are designed to cover an important commercial activity and commercial documents have to be considered in the light of those rules.* (See pp.50A, I, and 51B.). Cockburn v. Alexander (1848)6 CB 791 and The Antaios 1985] 1 AC 191 followed. 3. One of the main reasons why Article 16(d) refers to "without delay" and why there is a preclusion in 16(e) if there is delay, is that as a result of delay in notifying a discrepancy, *the plaintiff is forever prevented from attempting to rectify the matters complained of*. (See p.57A.). 4. It is not necessary for the advice of discrepancies to be treated like a pleading. It is sufficient that it refers to the document which they say does not comply and they need not adumbrate further. (See p.52E.) 5.

The period from 11:38 a.m. on Friday, 9th September to the afternoon of Wednesday, 14th or to the morning of the 15th is not excessive in all the circumstances. It was a very busy month and 20 sets of letters of credit were registered by the defendant on the relevant day. *In assessing what time is reasonable the Court should take into account the size of the bank. For a smaller bank with smaller resources a reasonable time limit might be longer.* On the evidence the defendant bank was not a large bank.
It is also important to bear in mind that most checkers of documentary credits in Hong Kong will not have English as their mother tongue. (See pp.58C-D, G-H.). Bankers Trust Co. v. State Bank of India The Times, 4.9.1990 and 13.6.1991 (C.A.) considered. 6. If telecommunication of the discrepancies whether by phone, fax or telex is possible, then it ought to be used so that *the beneficiary knows as soon as possible that a problem exists and has as much time as possible before the expiration of the credit to get the alleged discrepancies accepted or to consider giving an indemnity.* This could be followed up by sending the original fax or a letter containing the same information by hand, courier or post. (See pp.59E and 60A.) 7. The defendant did not give notice by telecommunication, which, in one form or another, was possible. (See p.59G.)"[9]

V.1.1 Multi-party understanding and interpretation?

Traditional rules of interpretation of contracts are based on the intention of the parties, which prevails over the wording when demonstrated and shared by them at the time of contracting.

Unidroit Article 4.1

> "(1) A contract shall be interpreted according to the common intention of the parties. (2) If such an intention cannot be established, the contract shall be interpreted according to the meaning that reasonable persons of the same kind as the parties would give to it in the same circumstances."

---

[9] Hing Yip Hing Fat Co. Ltd. v. Daiwa Bank Ltd., 15-17 January and 11 February 1991, High Court, HC, (Commercial List No. 22 of 1989).

CHAPTER V

The instruments subject to this study are, however, in general the creation of a will and intention common to at least three parties: the account party, the issuer and the beneficiary. The instrument must, in the absence of clear wording, be interpreted to be in line with the intention of all these parties. It is not sufficient that the account party and the beneficiary agree on what they meant if the issuer disagreed or is unaware of such intentions.[10]

ISBP Preliminary considerations 1 instructs:

> "The terms of a credit are independent of the underlying transaction even if a credit expressly refers to that transaction. To avoid unnecessary costs, delays, and disputes in the examination of documents, however, the applicant and beneficiary should carefully consider which documents should be required, by whom they should be produced, and the time frame for presentation."

Furthermore, it is highly improbable that such a meaning and intention in common would not become part of the conditions precedent and wording of the instrument. This "multiparty intention" test, together with other characteristics of these instruments, exclude in most cases the relevance of intentions or meanings not common to all of them if not expressed in the wording of the instrument.[11] Should they all, however, agree, they should amend or could have amended the wording of the instrument. If all the parties including the issuer have omitted to draft the instrument to reflect such an understanding, it is rather an issue of negligence establishing perhaps a liability, rather than an issue of interpretation or reformation of the instrument.

---

[10] In theory the two parties could otherwise act in collusion or conspire to cause the issuer to effect payment, e.g., if the account party is in financial difficulties.

[11] ISBP Preliminary Considerations 2-3 provides:
"2. The applicant bears the risk of any ambiguity in its instructions to issue or amend a credit. Unless expressly stated otherwise, a request to issue or amend a credit authorizes an issuer to supplement or develop the terms in a manner necessary or desirable to permit the use of the credit. 3. The applicant should be aware that the UCP contains Articles such as Articles 13, 20, 21, 23, 24, 26, 27, 28, 39, 40, 46 and 47 that define terms in a manner that may produce unexpected results unless the applicant fully acquaints itself with these provisions. For example, a credit requiring presentation of a marine bill of lading and containing a prohibition against transhipment will, in most cases, have to exclude UCP subarticle 23(d) to make the prohibition against transhipment effective."

V.1.2 The substantive independence should not lead to disregard of the "facility"

In the interpretation of the instrument the function of the facility may override or pierce the independence of a contractual relationship. This applies in particular to instruments which have been confirmed. In confirmed credits there may be several parties who all focus on the same wording: the account party, the issuing bank, the confirming bank and the beneficiary. In such a network of functional dependence, the giving of value to intentions or conduct of just one or two parties in the interpretation of the wording of the instrument is not acceptable or well-founded, no matter how clear or unambiguous such intentions or such conduct may have been to one party, if not to all of them. The parties in the network establishing the facility may rely and must rely that the wording, as objectively understood, takes all parties "prima facie" to allow examination of the conformity of the demand or tender without uncertainty as to what may have or may not have been meant or implied.[12]

In Harlow and Jones v. American Express Bank the issues were

(i) Was there a rejection?
(ii) What does "on a collection basis" mean?
(iii) Was the credit extended for acceptance by the beneficiary or had it expired?

The Court applied a test comprising the following elements:

(i) objective basis;
(ii) reasonable banker as reference person;
(iii) with knowledge of the factual background;
(iv) common practice v. unique arrangement.

---

[12] See Dolan in *The Law of Letters of Credit* at 7-41 as to "credit or not credit". Rules like, e.g., Unidroit Article 4.2:
"(1) The statements and other conduct of a party shall be interpreted according to that party's intention if the other party knew or could not have been unaware of that intention. (2) If the preceding paragraph is not applicable, such statements and other conduct shall be interpreted according to the meaning that a reasonable person of the same kind as the other party would give to it in the same circumstances."

do not really apply; neither do rules like Unidroit 4.3:
"(a) preliminary negotiations between the parties; (b) practices which the parties have established between themselves; (c) the conduct of the parties subsequent to the conclusion of the contract."

Chapter V

The court said:

> "The principal difficulty facing this defence is that the expert witnesses for all parties were agreed that the words "on a collection basis" or "for collection" are equivocal and must take their meaning from their context. The experts were also agreed that it is common practice that documents which are discrepant, including documents presented after the expiry date of a letter of credit, are sent to the issuing bank for collection or on a collection basis under the letter of credit which will be expressly or impliedly extended if, after inspection, the opener and his bank decide to accept the documents and thus waive the discrepancies. In this event, in the strict analysis, it is probably a renegotiation of the credit in which the opener may, but will not necessarily, require allowances.
>
> So the telex from Creditanstalt to the defendants' Poole office on Feb. 17, read in conjunction with Poole's telex to Creditanstalt of Feb. 10, could support either construction if one were to ignore the letter from Poole to Calcutta and to Creditanstalt of Feb. 17, which is what Mr. Mukherjee in Calcutta did. His understanding was that the phrase: "on a collection basis", and "under the Letter of Credit" were mutually exclusive. He assumed, no doubt, that his telex to Poole of Feb. 10, would be passed on verbatim to the beneficiary's bank. *He took the view that he has made it plain in that telex that the opener had finally rejected the documents, and he thought that the letter of credit was dead and that the bank had no further liability but would act as a mere collecting agent.* He was not familiar with the common practice of forwarding discrepant documents under an expired letter of credit for examination and a final decision by the opener. Having thus convinced himself that his bank was henceforth a mere collecting agent, Mr. Mukherjee regarded the letter of Feb. 17, as entirely inappropriate and he ignored it.
>
> Although on its face it was plainly a tender of the documents under the letter of credit, contradicting his understanding of the position and although his evidence was that, in his experience, it was unique for a transaction under a letter of credit to change over to a simple collection, he sought no elucidation.
>
> *But I have to interpret the scope of the defendants' authority on an objective basis*: namely, what interpretation would be placed on the contractual documents *by reasonable bankers in the position of the parties at the time,* having regard to the factual background known to both of them, or which must be taken to have been known to them. They would know, for example, that the plaintiffs' purchase from Ensidesa would very probably, if not

certainly, have been under a letter of credit, *on essentially back to back terms except for* a price margin, and that the plaintiffs would have been financed by their bank and that neither the plaintiffs nor their bank would be in the least likely to release their security — their commercial documents — to a sub-purchaser against his mere acceptance of 180 days bills of exchange. This would be to transform completely the standard method of financing sales and sub-sales between foreigners and to destroy the whole purpose of letter of credit transactions. It is not surprising that Mr. Mukherjee regarded *this transformation as unique*: namely, a tender of documents under a letter of credit being transformed into a collection outside the letter of credit.

The reasonable bankers would also be aware of *the common practice* of tendering discrepant documents "on a collection basis" after expiry of the letter of credit in order that the opener might consider the actual discrepancies on examination of the documents so as to decide whether to accept or reject. They would also be familiar with the UCP. On this basis, it seems to me that the letter of Feb. 17, must be taken to have meant what it said: that the documents were tendered under the letter of credit, notwithstanding its expiry, and the defendants were obliged either to reject the documents or to accept them in accordance with its terms. They acted contrary to their instructions, and they are, in my judgment, accordingly liable."[13]

The strict compliance doctrine does not leave much room for interpretation of the express terms and conditions of the instrument itself. Beyond its boundaries, the *è contrario* principle governs and eliminates most of implicit terms and conditions or the introduction, by way of interpretation, of new conditions or "hidden" meanings or presumptions.[14]

"We do not understand that to be the law. In *Midland Bank Ltd. v. Seymour, [1955] 2 Lloyd's Rep. 147* Mr. Justice Devlin accepted that a document must contain enough particulars to make it a valid document of its kind but

---

[13] Harlow & Jones Ltd. v. American Express Bank and Creditanstalt-Bankverein, (Third Party), 1990 WL 755029 (QBD (Comm Ct)), [1990] 2 Lloyd's Rep. 343.

[14] Howard N. Bennett, in *Unclear or ambiguous instructions in the world of documentary credits*, Lloyd's Maritime and Commercial Law Quarterly, (2001, 1(Feb)), 24-26, says:
"The Court of Appeal reasoned that, since Art. 5(b) required credits to state "precisely" against which documents payment was to be made, any ambiguity in the terms of the credit should be resolved against inclusion within the category of stipulated, Art. 5(b) documents."

Chapter V

rejected the suggestion that, in the absence of express stipulation, every document should contain all the particulars called for. At p. 152 he said: Having to choose between those two constructions, in my judgment the one that construes the letter of credit as requiring merely that the set should contain all the particulars is the preferable one and the right one, and I arrive at that conclusion mainly on two grounds. The first is that that is the construction which, in my judgment, best fits the language that is used in the letter of credit. The letter of credit quite plainly treats the documents as a set and not as an individual document. It is "against delivery of the following documents", then they are set out, and then it goes on, "evidencing shipment". Strictly speaking, of course, the only document that evidences it is the bill of lading. Quite plainly what the defendants in their letter of credit have in mind is that the documents that they there specify are, as a set of documents, the ordinary shipping documents - the invoice, the bill of lading and the insurance certificate - which are ordinarily and collectively treated as evidencing shipment.

That seems to me to point to the view that they are considering the shipping documents as a set of documents; and dealing with them, therefore, as a set of documents they say that the set must contain the particulars under the heading "Description Quantity and Price". Nothing would have been simpler than to have provided for a particular document containing a special part of those particulars if that had been thought necessary. I think, therefore, that the construction which I am adopting fits in better with the language of the document.

That was a case decided under the common law and not on construction of the UCP. But we find nothing in UCP 500 which contradicts it, and it is relevant that the credit did specify the particulars which the packing lists were to contain. *We do not accept the submission made by Mr. Neville Thomas, Q.C. on behalf of the Bank of China that each of the specified documents listed in the credit had to contain all the details which were specified in the credit after the words "covering shipment of"."*[15]

The role of the banks and the requirement or principle of expediency does not allow profound teleological analysis of "inner or true meanings" of the parties by the examiner of the documents. Much less does it allow hearing of witnesses,

---

[15] Glencore Int'l A.G. v. Bank of China, Court of Appeal, CA, Oct. 23; Nov. 8, 1995.

parties, experts or counsels and as to the purpose or meaning of the parties.[16] In addition, the commercial expediency in international banking eliminates even most of the potential for a sophisticated analysis of the instrument in daily letter of credit practice, which must be carried out within reasonable time-frames.

Further, the unilateral character of the instruments or commitments thereunder and in particular the *policy interests*, in protecting the strategic purpose of effecting payment, and thereby the functioning of the instruments as expected and relied on in the marketplace, tend to lean towards minimum interference by law and courts (the "non-intervention principle").[17]

ISP 1.03 gives "bold" guidance on interpretation as follows:

> "These Rules shall be interpreted *as mercantile usage* with regard for:
> a. integrity of standbys as *reliable* and *efficient* undertakings to pay;
> b. practice and terminology of banks and businesses in day-to-day transactions;
> c. *consistency* within the *worldwide* system of banking operations and commerce; and
> d. *worldwide uniformity* in their interpretation and application."[18]

And case law is very much on the same wavelength, as the court makes clear:

> "In *Bank of Cochin, Ltd. v. Manufacturers Hanover Trust Company*, 808 F.2d 209 (2d Cir.1986), the Second Circuit interpreted Article 8(d) of the UCP according to its plain meaning and the policy underlying the operation of letters of credit. *See id.* at 213. Similarly, in *Alaska Textile*, cited by BOI, the court construed the meaning of "reasonable time" under Article 16(c) of the UCP according to its plain meaning and the interpretations given to

---

[16] Bertrams, *Bank Guarantees*, at 64-65.
[17] UNC Art 5 says:
"In the interpretation of this Convention, regard is to be had to its international character and to the need to promote uniformity in its application and the observance of good faith in the international practice of independent guarantees and stand-by letters of credit."
[18] United Nations Convention on the Assignment of Receivables in International Trade Article 3 provides: "A receivable is international if, at the time of conclusion of the original contract, the assignor and the debtor are located in different States. An assignment is international if, at the time of conclusion of the contract of assignment, the assignor and the assignee are located in different States."

Unidroit 4.4 provides: "Terms and expressions shall be interpreted in the light of the whole contract or statement in which they appear."

it by other courts. *See Alaska Textile*, 982 F.2d at 821-22. Although the court relied on "law from foreign jurisdictions" and "expert testimony," the single case from a foreign jurisdiction interpreted the UCP without reference to actual practices, and the expert testimony was noted only insofar as the experts at issue agreed with the court's interpretation. *See id.; see also 3Com Corp. v. Banco de Brasil*, 2 F.Supp.2d 452, 457 (S.D.N.Y.1998), *aff'd*, 171 F.3d 739 (2d Cir.1999) (interpreting the UCP according to "general principles and policies which underlie the UCP's express terms"). *Nothing in the UCP supports BOI's contention that accepting facially false documents is not bad faith under the UCP.* BOI has cited no case in this Circuit where a court has abandoned the plain meaning of the UCP to examine specific banking practices. *The stated purpose of the UCP is to facilitate international trade by providing a uniform set of rules accepted around the world.* It has been characterized as a "compilation of internationally accepted commercial practices." *Semetex Corp. v. UBAF Arab Am. Bank*, 853 F.Supp. 759, 769 (S.D.N.Y.1994), *aff'd*, 51 F.3d 13 (2d Cir.1995); *Sempione v. Provident Bank*, 75 F.3d 951, 960 (4th Cir.1996) ("The UCP is a formulation of standard international banking practice."), *dismissed on other grounds*, 85 F.3d 615 (4th Cir.1996). *The analysis urged by BOI would alter the UCP and the standards governing letters of credit into a fragmented patchwork of local customs and practices*, the very problem letters of credit and the UCP were designed to avoid. BOI cited *Sempione* as considering evidence of banking practices, but the court made no inquiry into any practice prevalent in the location of the confirming bank, *i.e.*, any *local* practice. In the other case upon which BOI relies heavily, *Alaska Textile*, the court interpreted the term "reasonable time" as used in the UCP. *See Alaska Textile*, 982 F.2d at 820-25. There, our Circuit refused to interpret a reasonable time as the three-day limit customary in New York because the drafters had refused to articulate a fixed time. Among other sources, the court cited an article attributing the absence of a specific limit in the UCP to "a disparity of opinion on the question of what is a 'reasonable time' which precluded international consensus of a particular period." *Id.* at 822 (*quoting* Robert M. Rosenblith, *Lawyer Robert M. Rosenblith Looks at UCC Provisions Against UCP Rule*, 6 Letter of Credit Update 11 (Feb.1990)). BOI concedes a similar disparity of opinion in the practice at issue, which it claims is "standard in Asian and other international markets, but not in New York." The plain language of the UCP does not suggest deference to such disparity."[19]

---

[19] Brenntag International Chemicals, Inc. v. Norddeutsche Landesbank GZ and Bank of India, No. 97 Civ. 2688(RWS).

The banks may, however, in most cases do right and be wiser by effecting payment than by way of adopting the role of courts of law in the interests of "justice". By this way, the excessive exercise of interpretation is avoided.

Some complexities may, however, arise if the beneficiary has no expertise, or if the beneficiary has less expertise in handling these instruments than the banks involved. Often, of course, this is the case. This applies in particular to the limitations of the liability of the banks in the event of that transaction fails in one or another respect.[20] There may be some very limited space for a *contra proferentem* rule in the bank-beneficiary or the bank-account party relationship, since the banks possess or should possess the expertise and should proactively consult the account party when the conditions precedent are being drafted or negotiated and avoid words or expressions which may be misleading to the beneficiary.[21]

Letters of credit as contracts may be interpreted against the issuer to facilitate trade and because the issuer has the obligation and the possibility to actively participate in the drafting and make conspicuous and clear the essential terms and conditions. No additional terms may be implied or inferred from unclear or vague wording or the circumstances. The underlying agreement is irrelevant.

The following case deals with an issue of interpretation between the issuing bank ("MCB") and the confirming bank ("CAI").

> "This appeal gives rise to *a short point of construction of a letter of credit*, one which Mr. Justice David Steel aptly described as "a fine nice point".

---

[20] The standardization of the terms and conditions may appear to be a restraint on competition but the benefits seem to outweigh most of the drawbacks.

[21] Unidroit 4.6 says:
"If contract terms supplied by one party are unclear, an interpretation against that party is preferred."; The banks have a duty to advise the parties. Whether or not this duty imposes a legal liability must be assessed in casu. URDG Art. 3 provides:
"All instructions for the issue of Guarantees and amendments thereto and Guarantees and amendments themselves should be clear and precise and should avoid excessive detail. Accordingly, all Guarantees should stipulate: a. the Principal; b. the Beneficiary; c. the Guarantor; d. the underlying transaction requiring the issue of the Guarantee; e. the maximum amount payable and the currency in which it is payable; f. the Expiry Date and/or Expiry Event of the Guarantee; g. the terms for demanding payment; h. any provision for reduction of the guarantee amount."
Dolan writes in *The Law of Letters of Credit* at 4-38 – 4-39:
"The law remains unsettled. Some courts prefer to invoke a rule construing the ambiguous credit against the drafter; some courts construe it against the issuer."

Chapter V

By common consent that document is badly drafted, though no doubt the commercial men who drafted it must have thought it adequate for its purpose. It is in part due to its infelicities but in greater part due to the advocacy skills of Mr. Jarvis, Q.C. *for the issuing bank ("MCB") and Mr. Males, Q.C. for the confirming bank ("CAI")* that in the course of argument my mind, I confess, has wavered as to the outcome of the appeal. Mr. Jarvis submitted that there was in truth no difficulty of construction, and that, if there was, *CAI should have made enquiry before paying the beneficiary*, as suggested by Lord Justice Robert Goff in European Asian Bank A.G. v. Punjab & Sind Bank (No. 2), [1983] 1 Lloyd's Rep. 611 at pp. 617-618; [1983] 1 W.L.R. 642 at pp. 655-656. He pointed to the difference in wording between special conditions (8) and (9), the former referring to "Non-negotiable documents", which he said meant documents not required to be presented but to be sent to the applicant, and, by way of contrast, the documents specified in (9) which were to be sent to "us [i.e. MCB] by Courier". He relied on the printed "Directions for Nominated Bank" [i.e. CAI] and in particular the instruction, which had been marked with "X", "Please send original and duplicate sets of documents direct to us by successive 'Registered Courier' ", and suggested that the direction to CAI to send original and duplicate sets of documents "to us" by courier at least covered the original and copy documents required by special condition (9) to be sent "to us" by courier. Mr. Jarvis submitted that to the extent that the Judge relied on special condition (10) requiring the beneficiary to furnish a certificate of compliance, as supporting the construction which he favoured, the Judge was using a "bootstraps" argument which did not assist.

In response to the argument on behalf of CAI that *it was entitled to act on a reasonable understanding of what the letter of credit,* if ambiguous, meant, he argued that *that principle should be confined to a case where there is true ambiguity*, that is to say where, after construing the document, it was equally capable of two meanings. I agree with Mr. Jarvis that special condition (10) does not assist. But subject to that, and attractively though the arguments were advanced, I am not persuaded by them.

The letter of credit was expressly made subject to the Uniform Customs and Practice (1993 Revision) ("UCP"). The beneficiary's right to payment under the credit was conditional on the presentation of the "stipulated documents" to the issuing bank and the confirming bank, as the case may be (art. 9(a) and (b)). Accordingly the stipulated documents must be the same for both banks. By art. 5(b) they are "the documents against which payment, acceptance or negotiation is to be made" *and they must be precisely stated. I take that to be the obligation of the issuing bank, which produces the letter of credit.* The UCP contemplates both that documents may be received by a confirming bank which are not stipulated in the credit and need not be examined (art. 13(a)) and that the credit may contain conditions which may be disregarded by the bank (art. 13(c)).

In the letter of credit there are certain documents which unquestionably can be said to be stipulated documents. They include those marked "X" in the "Documents Required" box and those which are identified in the special conditions as required, or otherwise indicated by the language used as being of a similar category. They include the beneficiary's draft, a declaration of shipment, the beneficiary's certificate of compliance, a cotton ginning certificate, a phytosanitary certificate and the shipping line's certificate. None of those documents is mentioned in special condition (9), which on no basis could be said to provide a complete list of the stipulated documents.

In so poorly drafted a letter of credit, it would be unsafe to infer from the reference to non-negotiable documents in special condition (8) that the documents referred to in special condition (9) and not described as "non-negotiable" must be negotiable. Nor do I think that it is clear that the instruction in the directions for nominated banks to send documents to MCB by courier must be read as covering the documents in special condition (9). That instruction does not identify the documents referred to. The requirement in special condition (9) for delivery is that the documents be delivered "to us", i.e., to the issuing bank, and on its face that condition imposes no obligation to deliver the documents to the confirming bank. I am left in real uncertainty as to whether the documents in special condition (9) are stipulated documents.

There has, in my view, been a failure to comply with the requirement of art. 5(b) of precise statement. In those circumstances *I think that the letter of credit must be construed against MCB.* The relevant principle was stated by Lord Diplock in Commercial Banking Co. of Sydney v. Jalsard Pty. Ltd., [1972] 2 Lloyd's Rep. 529 at p. 533; [1973] A.C. 279 at p. 283 in the passage cited by Sir Christopher Staughton. That shows that *even though a Court might arrive at a different construction, the banker can safely act upon a reasonable construction of ambiguous or unclear terms. I cannot say that CAI's construction of the letter of credit was unreasonable, nor do I think it should be held liable because it did not make enquiry before payment.*"[22]

---

[22] Credit Agricole Indosuez v. Muslim Commercial Bank Ltd.,1999 WL 1048266 (CA (Civ Div)), [2000] C.L.C. 437, [2000] 1 Lloyd's Rep. 275, [2000] Lloyd's Rep. Bank. 1, [2000] 1 All E.R. (Comm) 172.

Chapter V

Interpretation may bear on availability of remedies or summary judgement as demonstrated by *Glencore v. Chase* because, "when the relevant terms are determined to be unambiguous, the court may construe the legal meaning of those terms without resort to extrinsic evidence":

> "When a motion for summary judgment centers on the interpretation of contractual terms, the Court's ability to grant the motion turns on whether the relevant terms are ambiguous. The threshold determination as to ambiguity is one of law based solely upon the Court's reading of the terms at issue. *See* United States Fire Ins. Co. v. General Reins. Corp., 949 F.2d 569, 571 (2d Cir.1991); Care Travel Co. v. Pan American World Airways, 944 F.2d 983, 988 (2d Cir.1991); Garza v. Marine Transport Lines, 861 F.2d 23, 27 (2d Cir.1988).
>
> A court will deem contract language unambiguous when "it has ' "a definite and precise meaning, unattended by danger of misconception in the purport of the [contract] itself, and concerning which there is no reasonable basis for a difference of opinion." ' *Care Travel Co.*, 944 F.2d at 988 (quoting *Hunt Ltd. v. Lifschultz Fast Freight*, Inc., 889 F.2d 1274, 1277 (2d Cir. 1989) (in turn quoting *Breed v. Insurance Co. of North America*, 46 N.Y.2d 351, 355, 413 N.Y.S.2d 352, 355, 385 N.E.2d 1280, 1282 (1978)). If the relevant contract terms are determined to be unambiguous, the Court may construe the legal meaning of those terms without resort to extrinsic evidence. *Care Travel Co.*, 944 F.2d at 988; *Metropolitan Life Ins. Co. v. RJR Nabisco, Inc.*, 906 F.2d 884, 889 (2d Cir.1990); *Arcadian Phosphates, Inc. v. Arcadian Corp.*, 884 F.2d 69, 73 (2d Cir.1989); *Rothenberg v. Lincoln Farm Camp, Inc.*, 755 F.2d 1017, 1019 (2d Cir.1985). Where, conversely, the Court determines that "contract language is susceptible of at least two fairly reasonable interpretations, there is a triable issue of fact and summary judgment is inappropriate." *American Home Assur. Co. v. Baltimore Gas & Elec. Co.*, 845 F.2d 48, 51 (2d Cir.1988); accord *Rothenberg*, 755 F.2d at 1019; *Heyman v. Commerce & Industry Ins. Co.*, 524 F.2d 1317, 1320 (2d Cir.1975)."[23]

---

[23] Glencore, Ltd., v. Chase Manhattan Bank & State Bank of Saurashtra, Not Reported in F.Supp., 1998 WL 101734 (S.D.N.Y., 1988).

V.1.3 Interpretation of other instruments

The interpretation of other instruments follows *mutatis mutandis* the same rules. This applied to general characterization as well, and what the instrument is called or how it is captioned is not decisive.

Dolan writes in *The Law of Letters of Credit* on the issue of classification p. 2-11:

> "The court reasoned that the undertaking strayed "too far from the basic purpose of letters of credit, namely, providing a means of assuring payment cheaply by eliminating the need for the issuer to police the underlying contract." The court concluded that "it would hamper rather than advance the extension of the letter of credit concept to new situations if an instrument such as this were held to be a letter of credit"."

The meaning and purpose need to meet the understanding of all parties to the instrument if the interpretation arrived at deviates from what would be the objective understanding by a reasonable outsider.[24] Experience, practice, and legal commentators all agree that often the ambiguity relates to a compromise as to wording reached between the parties involved, one requiring an on-demand type of strong instrument and the other requiring a substantively linked "weak" one.

---

[24] Lars Gorton, *On demand –garanti I svensk rätt – ett rättsfall*, Juridisk tidskrift vid Stockholms universitet, number 3 (2000-2001):
> En garanti måste ses både i ljuset av dess funktion och den ordalydelse som den fått i det enskilda fallet. De inblandade parterna förhandlar ofta mot bakgrund av att den ena parten kräver en "on demand-garanti" medan garantiutställaren eller den som lämnar uppdraget åt garantisten endast är beredd att gå med på en mera inskränkt garanti. I praktiken kan därmed en dispyt mellan parterna vara orsakad av det som Ramberg kallat medveten avtalsotydlighet. Det finns ett samspel mellan det underliggande avtalet och garantin, som dock beroende på vad det är för slag av garanti skall tillmätas eller icke tillmätas betydelse. Garantitexten är därmed av stor betydelse. Härigenom är såväl garantins funktion som dess ordalydelse avgörande."

Richard Bethell-Jones, *Guarantees and Indemnities: Some Important Differences*, J Int'l Banking L & Reg (2006, 21(3)), 156-161:
> "A document which hovers somewhere between a true guarantee and a "clean" standby LC can be difficult to deal with. It is not necessarily a muddle (the document may simply reflect what the parties agreed); but understanding the nature and effect of the document can be challenging (as witness the Marubeni case). You simply have to construe the document—applying the principles summarised by Lord Hoffman in ICS Limited v West Bromwich Building Society—to find out what the parties agreed."

CHAPTER V

"From the above it is clear that we are traveling in a legal area where much law has had to be developed in court practice and will gradually have to be developed against the background of general principles of law. It is obvious that the wording of the undertaking is of great importance. A certain wording has an implication recognized by and in law, whereas there are still other expressions which do not seem quite familiar to the courts. Furthermore there may also be instances where the wording is confused by the use of terminology which is not unambiguous. *The points of outlook are different if one starts from the local domestic area where the traditional suretyship developed than if instead the outlook is from the international point where the letter of credit developed as well as the on demand guarantee.* That being said it is still necessary to keep in mind that there may be different arrangements with several similarities and where we may actually have to fall back on the actual and precise wording of the undertaking."[25]

"Extract from the judgment of Lord Hoffman in ICS Limited v West Bromwich Building Society: "I do not think that the fundamental change which has overtaken this branch of the law, particularly as a result of the speeches of Lord Wilberforce in Prenn v Simmonds [1971] 3 All ER 237 at 240-242, [1971] 1 WLR 1381 at 1384-1386 and Reardon Smith Line Ltd v Hansen-Tangen, Hansen-Tangen v Sanko Steamship Co [1976] 3 All ER 570, [1976] 1 WLR 989, is always sufficiently appreciated. The result has been, subject to one important exception, to assimilate the way in which such documents are interpreted by judges to the common sense principles by which any serious utterance would be interpreted in ordinary life. Almost all the old intellectual baggage of 'legal' interpretation has been discarded. The principles may be summarised as follows.

(1) Interpretation is the ascertainment of the meaning which the document would convey to a reasonable person having all the background knowledge which would reasonably have been available to the parties in the situation in which they were at the time of the contract.

(2) The background was famously referred to by Lord Wilberforce as the 'matrix of fact', but this phrase is, if anything, an understated description of what the background may include. Subject to the requirement that it should have been reasonably available to the parties and to the exception to be mentioned next, it includes absolutely anything which

---

[25] Lars Gorton, *Suretyship and guarantees – some Swedish viewpoints*, Juridiska Föreningens Tidskrift, number 6 (2001).

would have affected the way in which the language of the document would have been understood by a reasonable man.

(3) The law excludes from the admissible background the previous negotiations of the parties and their declarations of subjective intent. They are admissible only in an action for rectification. The law makes this distinction for reasons of practical policy and, in this respect only, legal interpretation differs from the way we would interpret utterances in ordinary life. The boundaries of this exception are in some respects unclear. But this is not the occasion on which to explore them.

(4) The meaning which a document (or any other utterance) would convey to a reasonable man is not the same thing as the meaning of its words. *The meaning of words is a matter of dictionaries and grammars; the meaning of the document is what the parties using those words against the relevant background would reasonably have been understood to mean.* The background may not merely enable the reasonable man to choose between the possible meanings of words which are ambiguous but even (as occasionally happens in ordinary life) to conclude that the parties must, for whatever reason, have used the wrong words or syntax (see Mannai Investment Co Ltd v Eagle Star Life Assurance Co Ltd [1997] 3 All ER 352, [1997] 2 WLR 945.

(5) The 'rule' that words should be given their 'natural and ordinary meaning' reflects the commonsense proposition that we do not easily accept that people have made linguistic mistakes, particularly in formal documents. On the other hand, if one would nevertheless conclude from the background that something must have gone wrong with the language, the law does not require judges to attribute to the parties an intention which they plainly could not have had. Lord Diplock made this point more vigorously when he said in Antaios Cia Naviera SA v Salen Rederierna AB, The Antaios [1984] 3 All ER 229 at 233, [[1985] AC 191 at 201: '... if detailed semantic and syntactical analysis of words in a commercial contract is going to lead to a conclusion that flouts business common sense, it must be made to yield to business common sense.'

If one applies these principles, it seems to me that the judge must be right and, as we are dealing with one badly drafted clause which is happily no longer in use, there is little advantage in my repeating his reasons at greater length. The only remark of his which I would respectfully question is when he said that he was 'doing violence' to the natural meaning of the words. This is an over-energetic way to describe the process of interpretation. Many people, including politicians, celebrities and Mrs Malaprop, mangle meanings and syntax but nevertheless communicate tolerably clearly what they are using the words to mean. If anyone is doing violence to natural meanings, it is they rather than their listeners."[26]

V.1.4 Interpretation of applicable rules

There is a considerable difference in the task of interpretation when it relates to the meaning of words in a document drafted and agreed to by the parties themselves and when the meaning of UCP, ISP or another set of similar rules is being interpreted. The latter exercise often covers both aspects, i.e., what this particular wording means in the light of the applicable reference rules, but both issues may emerge separately and independently, e.g., what does reasonable time mean under UCP. The interpretation of such rules should be very global and universal and should avoid parochial concepts and meanings.

ISP 1.03:

> "These Rules shall be interpreted as mercantile usage with regard for: a. integrity of standbys as reliable and efficient undertakings to pay; b. practice and terminology of banks and businesses in day-to-day transactions; c. consistency within the worldwide system of banking operations and commerce; d. and worldwide uniformity in their interpretation and application."

The practice of international banking may be a relevant extrinsic source of information. In many respects interpreting the UCP is a process similar to interpreting laws and statutes or landmark cases, excluding, however, everything relating to one jurisdiction only. Besides these reference rules, national laws and statutes may need to be interpreted. This should preferably be done showing respect to the international character of the instrument itself. To the extent the issues deal with the (more) domestic relationships of the facility, i.e., non–cross-border infrastructure, the international aspect may be reduced or disregarded.

---

[26] Richard Bethell-Jones, *Guarantees and Indemnities: Some Important Differences*, J Int'l Banking L & Reg, (2006) 21(3), 156-161.

Southland Rubber v. BOC:

"f. Although these names physically appear on the bill of lading, I do not consider that they indicate the name of the carrier within art. 23a for the following reasons: The bill of lading presented (No. SST-01) does not indicate on its face the name of the carrier (i.e., PT.Kemah Nusasemesta not identified as carrier and cannot be assumed to be). The party, PT.Bahtera Bintang Selatan Ujong Pandang, the name appearing on the stamped chop in the shipped on board box does not indicate:
-.his capacity
-.the party on whose behalf he is acting
-.the capacity of the party on whose behalf he is acting
g. *In my experience, bills of lading in this form are treated as non-compliant with art.23a and from my experience it is standard practice to reject documents in this form for such a discrepancy.*
In his report Mr. Castro referred to Position Paper No.4 published on 1.September 1994 which contains the collective views of the group of experts of the ICC. On the interpretation of sub-paragraph.(a)(i) of art. 23 their view is:
1 The name of the carrier must appear as such (my emphasis) on the front of the document. The expression, the front of the document means the side showing the details of the goods, vessel and voyage. Banks will therefore reject documents which fail to comply with the requirement set out in 1' above, ie.which fail to indicate the name of the carrier on the front of the document, even though the identity of the carrier may be indicated on the back of the document. *The overriding concern in the minds of the panel of experts must be that the institution that has been presented with the bill of lading must not be placed in a position whereby they had to speculate or to make an educated guess of the identity of the carrier.* The key words are "the name of the carrier must appear as such" so that in my view, anything short of using the actual word "carrier" to identify the party acting as carrier would not have complied with the provisions of art.23(a)(i) of the UCP.
I consider one of the fundamental principles in any transaction involving documentary credit to be that of certainty of the identity of the parties involved in the contract of carriage. The approach by this court in the construction of the article is therefore not inconsistent with the views expressed by Lord.Diplock in The Antaios. Turning now to the bill of lading in question, I cannot say that on reading the document I am able to say that it appears, on the face of it, to indicate the name of the carrier although the

name of PT.Kemah Nusasemesta appeared twice on the front of the document. The bill of lading does not comply with art. 23(a)(i) of the UCP and I so find. For the reasons given, the plaintiff's claim is dismissed with costs with certificate for two counsel."[27]

V.2 Waiver doctrine: express and implied waivers

Waiver may become applicable in the facility primarily in the bank-beneficiary relationship and in the beneficiary-bank-account party chain likewise with the account party playing there the key role.

The waiver doctrine plays an important but very limited role in credit transactions except for *express* waivers by a beneficiary, which are very common in the daily transactions but rarely lead to legal disputes. There are many estimates that over 50% of documents presented are discrepant and that the discrepancies are waived by the beneficiary.[28] The beneficiary's waiver does not *per se* expand the issuer's duties.[29]

UCP 600 provides in Article 16:

> "b. When an issuing bank determines that a presentation does not comply, it may in its sole judgment approach the applicant for a waiver of the discrepancies. This does not, however, extend the period mentioned in sub-article 14(b)"

---

[27] Southland Rubber Co Ltd v Bank of China, 1997 WL 1911180 (CFI), [1997] HKLRD 1300..

[28] Waiver comes relatively close to preclusion. Preclusion is usually an absolute and legal consequence of an act or omission by force of law regardless of a party's will or intention. Waiver is an act or omission of a party which is to be given or presumed a certain intention or expression of his will. Unidroit 1.8 tells us: "A party cannot act inconsistently with an understanding it has caused the other party to have and upon which that other party reasonably has acted in reliance to its detriment."

[29] ICC Banking Commission Collected Opinions 1995-2001, p. 83:
"ANALYSIS AND CONCLUSION Article 9 of UCP SOO states: "An irrevocable credit constitutes a definite undertaking conclusion of the issuing bank, provided that the stipulated documents are presented to the nominated hank or to the issuing bank and that the terms and conditions for the credit are complied with" and that the issuing bank will pay or accept and pay. In the event that discrepancies are observed in a presentation of documents and the issuing bank complies with the requirements of sub-Article 14(d), the issuing bank is under no obligation to take up the documents, even if a proper waiver of the discrepancies is received from the applicant."

Once again the role of the strict compliance rule and its rationale do not allow to question the significance of what has been expressly stipulated or to replace it by conduct, behaviour or promissory estoppel.[30] The often "one shot" type of operation hardly leaves any room for *implicit waiver* or *waiver by conduct*.[31] On the other hand, in a large percentage of credit transactions there are discrepancies and deviations. This could lead to a justified but unproductive refusal of honor in the absence of express waiver by the account party.[32]

Wunnicke, Wunnicke and Turner write on p. 422:

> "Discrepancy rates of 60 to 90 percent are cited for presentations under commercial letters of credit. But most of the discrepancies are somehow

---

[30] Dolan writes in *The Law of Letters of Credit* at 4-30:
"In *Courtaulds North America, Inc. v. North Carolina National Bank*, the issuer had received a number of drafts with nonconforming invoices, but it always sought and received its customer's approval of payment, notwithstanding the nonconformity. It also never advised the beneficiary of the practice. The trial court found that it was not customary for banks to notify beneficiaries of such waiver by their customers. When the customer filed in bankruptcy, there was no one to waive the nonconformity; and the bank rejected a noncomplying invoice. The Court of Appeals for the Fourth Circuit refused to estop the bank, whose duties were "graven in the credit," and who, therefore, might face liability to the customer's trustee by departing from the credit's terms."

[31] UCC 5-107 provides:
"A person can consent to an amendment by implication. For example, a beneficiary that tenders documents for honor that conform to an amended letter of credit but not to the original letter of credit has probably consented to the amendment. By the same token an applicant that has procured the issuance of a transferable letter of credit has consented to its transfer and to performance under the letter of credit by a person to whom the beneficiary's rights are duly transferred. If some, but not all of the persons involved in a letter of credit transaction consent to performance that does not strictly conform to the original letter of credit, those persons assume the risk that other nonconsenting persons may insist on strict compliance with the original letter of credit. Under subsection (b) those not consenting are not bound. For example, on issuer might agree to amend its letter of credit or honor documents presented after the expiration date in the belief that the applicant has consented or will consent to the amendment or will waive presentation after the original expiration date. If that belief is mistaken, the issuer is bound to the beneficiary by the terms of the letter of credit as amended or waived, even though it may be unable to recover from the applicant."

[32] Dole concludes his article:
"The Independence Principle, the cornerstone of letter-of-credit law, dictates the treatment of applicant ad hoc waiver of known documentary discrepancies. The Independence Principle requires that the issuer make an independent determination as to the apparent facial conformity of the documents presented with the letter of credits terms and conditions. Whether or not the presenter requests that the applicant be approached for a waiver, the approach should not be made until the issuer has identified apparent documentary discrepancies."

Richard F. Dole, Jr., *Applicant ad hoc waiver of discrepancies in the documents presented under letters of credit*, SMU L Rev, Fall 2005.

CHAPTER V

> resolved and the letters of credit get paid. Solutions to discrepancies include correcting the presentation and the issuer's obtaining a waiver of discrepancies from its applicant/customer."

There is a widespread practice among banks to consult the account party as to his position with respect to discrepancies found and even to allow him to review the documents as described in *Bankers Trust v. State Bank of India*:

> "The relevant facts appearing on the evidence have been summarized in the judgments of Lord Justice Lloyd and Lord Justice Farquharson. *It is beyond doubt on the evidence that the practice of issuing banks in London* in respect of import credits (this was an import credit), when they have found discrepancies in the documents, *is commonly, if not universally, to consult the applicant* as to whether, on those discrepancies, it would or would not wish the issuing bank nevertheless to accept the documents. *Under the practice, the issuing bank may, if it sees fit, allow the applicant also to see the documents.*

Should the consultation not result in express waiver by the beneficiary, the issuing bank must determine within the time stipulated whether or not to refuse the documents and give notice of the decision to the remitting bank or the beneficiary.

> Mr. Procter's evidence, accepted by the Judge, was (Evidence D. 3, p. 75H) that: "In the vast majority of cases" the applicant, when consulted, expressed the wish that the issuing bank should accept the documents. Another witness said that this occurred in about 90 per cent of the cases when the applicant was consulted. *If, for any reason, the issuing bank had not received from the applicant the so-called "waiver"* - the request that the issuing bank should accept the documents - *by the end of the time which the issuing bank regarded as a reasonable time for making its determination*, it would notify the remitting bank (or, where applicable, the beneficiary of the credit, the seller) that the documents were refused.
> I need not stress the obvious advantages to the parties, the banks, as well as to their respective customers, which derive from the exercise of this practice. I agree with Lord Justice Lloyd's view that it must be in the interest of *all parties*. As Mr. Procter said (Evidence D. 3, p. 76G): "It saves everyone a lot of time and trouble". On that evidence it has to be accepted that the practice of consultation is reasonable as between the issuing and the remitting bank. For example, as a result, in nine cases out of 10 the documents

will be accepted; whereas, without this practice, in all those cases the probability is that the documents would be rejected, with, at best, an indication from the issuing bank that it might, at some time in the future, seek the consent of the remitting bank, or the seller, to change its decision and to accept the documents.

Does the time which is required for this consultation in the interests of all parties concerned is to be included in the reasonable time reserved for the examiner for review of the documents or does it violate UCP to do so?

> Why, then, should the time reasonably taken for such consultations (which, on the evidence to which I shall refer later, is treated by at least one London clearing bank as being reasonably taken as the by no means insignificant time of 24 hours) not be included in the "reasonable time" which art. 16 permits for the examination and determination by the issuing bank? The contrary conclusion, as it appears to me, in Lord Diplock's words, "flouts business common sense". The defendants' answer, as I understand it, involves acceptance that, as it is put by Lord Justice Lloyd: "Of course there is nothing in the Code to prohibit consultation". *If the Code were to be construed as containing such a prohibition, it would inevitably upset the whole of the existing practice of London banks.* That is because, as a result, any "determination" under art. 16(b) by an issuing bank, however timeously made, would make the refusal of the documents vulnerable to the invocation by the remitting bank of art. 16(e), invalidating the rejection, on the simple and unanswerable ground: "In your determination you took into account that which you are prohibited by the Code from taking into account — consultation as to your customer's wishes".
>
> As I understand it, then, it is accepted that consultation by the issuing bank with the applicant as to whether the applicant would or would not wish to take up the documents, having regard to the discrepancies found by the issuing bank, is not prohibited, expressly or impliedly, by any provision of the Code; including in particular, the words "on the basis of the documents alone". As I understand it, also, it is accepted that the practice of undertaking such consultation is in the interest of both parties to the relevant contract. Once those two propositions are accepted, I am, with all respect, unable to see any valid ground supporting the contention that time reasonably spent in carrying out that consultation, in order to assist the issuing bank in the determination which it is required by art. 16(b) to make, is to be excluded from the assessment of the reasonable time prescribed by art. 16(c).

Chapter V

> *The reasonable time on its express terms includes the examination of the documents and the determination. The time reasonably taken in the determination whether to take up or to refuse the documents is no less a proper element in the assessment of the art. 16(c) reasonable time than is the time reasonably spent in the examination of the documents.* Both factors equally come into the account, because both equally are required to be undertaken by the issuing bank in the fulfilment of its contractual obligations under art. 16. It has been argued by the defendants that, while the issuing bank is not prohibited by the contract from consulting the applicant, nevertheless its right to do so does not arise from the Code: hence any time occupied in this exercise does not come within the scope of the reasonable time visualized or prescribed by art. 16(b) and (c). Its right to consult the applicant, it is said, if I have understood the argument correctly, arises from the general right of waiver: a general, non-contractual, right whereby anyone is entitled to ignore — to place no legal reliance on — *an infringement of a legal right.*

The court distinguishes between two issues: on the one hand, the right to consult the applicant and the inclusion of that time in the definition of reasonable time and, on the other hand, a true common law waiver. Further, one may emphasize the independence aspect by making a clear distinction between a bank's waiver and a beneficiary's waiver although the two should go, and usually do go, usually hand-in-hand.

> I must confess that I do not understand how any question of the common law right of waiver is of any relevance. *The applicant cannot waive a breach of the autonomous contract between the banks, though its wish as to whether the issuing bank should take up or refuse the documents may be highly relevant to the banks' determination.* So far as waiver by the issuing bank is concerned, the provisions of the contract — art. 16 of the Code — are intended to provide for the circumstances in which what may be described as a "deemed waiver" by the issuing bank will arise. It will arise if the issuing bank does not complete its task of examining the documents, making its determination and notifying the remitting bank in the prescribed form within a reasonable time.
>
> There is nothing that I can see *in the general law of non-contractual waiver* which has the slightest bearing on the question whether consultation with the applicant is or is not properly to be taken into account in deciding

whether, under the terms of art. 16, the reasonable time for the carrying out by the issuing bank of its duties under that article has or has not been complied with. I have said that in my opinion the consequences as affecting the existing practice of at least the majority of London banks would be substantial, and possibly serious, if the defendants' submissions were right on this question of principle."[33]

Express waivers by beneficiaries are common and they should preferably be in writing, as, in practice, they are in most cases, as is required by best banking practices.[34]

However, a bank's failure to give notice of dishonor may constitute waiver under ISP Art. 5.03:

"a. *Failure to give notice* of a discrepancy in a notice of dishonour within the time and by the means specified in the standby or these rules *precludes assertion of that discrepancy* in any document containing the discrepancy that is retained or represented, but does not preclude assertion of that discrepancy in any different presentation under the same or a separate standby.

---

[33] Bankers Trust Co. v. State Bank of India, Court of Appeal, CA, May 13, 14, 15 and 16, 1991; June 13, 1991.

[34] ISP 5.05 provides:
"If the issuer decides that a presentation does not comply and if the presenter does not otherwise instruct, the issuer may, in its sole discretion, request the applicant to waive non-compliance or otherwise to authorise honour within the time available for giving notice of dishonour but without extending it. Obtaining the applicant's waiver does not obligate the issuer to waive non compliance."

ISP 5.06 provides:
"If, after receipt of notice of dishonour, a presenter requests that the presented documents be forwarded to the issuer or that the issuer seek the applicant's waiver: a. no person is obligated to forward the discrepant documents or seek the applicant's waiver; b. the presentation to the issuer remains subject to these Rules unless departure from them is expressly consented to by the presenter; and c. if the documents are forwarded or if a waiver is sought: i. the presenter is precluded from objecting to the discrepancies notified to it by the issuer; ii. the issuer is not relieved from examining the presentation under these Rules; iii. the issuer is not obligated to waive the discrepancy even if the applicant waives it; and iv. the issuer must hold the documents until it receives a response from the applicant or is requested by the presenter to return the documents, and if the issuer receives no such response or request within ten business days of its notice of dishonour, it may return the documents to the presenter."

CHAPTER V

> b. *Failure to give notice* of dishonour or acceptance or acknowledgment that a deferred payment undertaking has been incurred obligates the issuer to pay at maturity."

Under the ordinary course of matters, there is no factual room for constituting waiver by way of continuous forbearance or silent acceptance in the beneficiary–bank relationship even in the case of a series of similar credit transactions between the same parties in same kind of goods or in otherwise similar transactions.[35]

In *Banco General v. Citibank*, the role of the waiver doctrine was described as follows:

> "The text of the UCP does not support the application of common law equitable doctrines such as waiver in letter of credit cases. Although we have observed that "equitable doctrines such as waiver and estoppel apply to these types of [letter of credit] transactions" under the Uniform Commercial Code (UCC), Pro-Fab. 772 F.2d at 851, courts have been reluctant to accept claims of waiver in such cases. See Courtaulds N. Am, Inc. v. North Carolina Nat'l Bank. 528 F.2d 802, 807 (4th Cir. 1975) ("Obviously, the previous acceptances of truant invoices cannot be construed as a waiver in the present incident."); Texpor Traders, Inc. v. Trust Co. Bank, 720 F. Supp. 1100, 1115 (S.D.N.Y. 1989) (holding that merely because the account party "in one instance chose to waive discrepancies in the letter of credit, does not require that it do so again, nor does it authorize the issuing bank to similarly waive such discrepancies"); Alpargatas, S.A. v. Century Business Credit Corp., 183 A.D.2d 491, 493. 583 N.Y.S.2d 441, 442 ("The fact that defendant [applicant] may have waived strict compliance in the past does not justify an inference of a waiver of any discrepancies that might arise at some future point under another such letter. . . ."), *appeal dismissed*, 80 N.Y.2d 925, 589 N.Y.S.2d 312, 602 N.E.2d 1128 (1992), *appeal denied*, 82 N.Y.2d 655, 602 N.Y.S. 2d 804, 622 N.E.2d 305 (1993). Against this background, there is no need for us to determine whether common

---

[35] Promissory estoppel in Unidroit Article 2.1.4:
"(1) Until a contract is concluded an offer may be revoked if the revocation reaches the offeree before it has dispatched an acceptance. (2) However, an offer cannot be revoked (a) if it indicates, whether by stating a fixed time for acceptance or otherwise, that it is irrevocable; or (b) if it was reasonable for the offeree to rely on the offer as being irrevocable and the offeree has acted in reliance on the offer."

law equitable doctrines such as waiver are applicable under letters of credit governed by the UCP, because even were we to so find, the facts of this case simply would not support a waiver. Indeed, *nothing in the UCP obligates or even permits a bank to examine documents presented under a letter of credit in relation to similar documents previously examined under a different letter of credit*. Such a practice would undermine the UCP goals of certainty, promptness and finality in the context of an international banking system. See Alaska Textile, 982 F. 2d at 815-16.[36]

One could almost say that no behaviour other than express consent constitutes waiver, and that there is an implicit non-waiver "effect" or rule in credit and guarantee instruments.[37]

Parties other than the account party can in no case give express or create implicit waivers for and on behalf of him without appropriate authorization or power, which authorization or power may, however, be created by "waiver" or by legal position of an agent *de jure* or *de facto*.[38]

---

[36] Banco General Runinahui, S.A. v. Citibank Int'l, (97 F.3d 480)

[37] UCC 5-108 (official comment):
"Waiver of discrepancies by an issuer or an applicant in one or more presentations does not waive similar discrepancies in a future presentation. Neither the issuer nor the beneficiary can reasonably rely upon honor over past waivers as a basis for concluding that a future defective presentation will justify honor. The reasoning of *Courtaulds Of North Am. Inc. v. North Carolina Nat'l Bank*, 528 F.2d 802 (4th Cir. 1975) is accepted and that expressed in *Schweibish v. Pontchartrain State Bank*, 389 So. 2d 73 1 (La. App. 1980) and *Titanium Metals Corp. v. Space Metals, Inc.* 529 P.2d 431 (Utah 1974) is rejected."

See however ISP 3.11:
"In addition to other discretionary provisions in a standby or these Rules, an issuer may, in its sole discretion, without notice to or consent of the applicant and without effect on the applicant's obligations to the issuer, waive the following Rules and any similar terms stated in the standby which are primarily for the issuer's benefit or operational convenience: i. treatment of documents received, at the request of the presenter, as having been presented at a later date (Rule 3.02); ii. identification of a presentation to the standby under which it is presented (Rule 3.03(a)); iv. treatment of a presentation made after the close of business as if it were made on the next business day (Rule 3.05(b)). b. the following Rule but not similar terms stated in the standby: i. a required document dated after the date of its stated presentation (Rule 4.06); or the requirement that a document issued by the beneficiary be in the language of the standby (Rule 4.04). The following Rule relating to the operational integrity of the standby only in so far as the bank is in fact dealing with the true beneficiary: acceptance of a demand in an electronic medium (Rule 3.06(b)). Waiver by the confirmer requires the consent of the issuer with respect to paragraphs (b) and (c) of this Rule."

[38] Negotiorum gestio belongs to this category, meaning, according to Black's Law Dictionary:
"A quasi-contractual situation in which an actor (negotiorum gestor) manages or interferes in the business transaction of another person (dominus negotii) in that person's absence, done without

CHAPTER V

There seems to be no room for the beneficiary's waiver either, since a non-complying presentation by the beneficiary cannot amount to a waiver of the benefit under the instrument: another attempt is permissible until the expiry of the instrument.[39] Another issue is a release by the beneficiary, which has similar effects but is clearly another concept: an expression of will, not a consequence of passivity. The failure to put the documents at the disposal of the presenter may result in waiver as demonstrated by *Credit Industriel et Commercial v. China Merchants Bank* Case No: 2000/738 Neutral citation number: [2002] EWHC 973 (Comm), High Court of Justice Queen's Bench Division Commercial Court, QBD (Comm Ct):

> "The defendants relied upon the decision in The Royan [1998] 2 Lloyd's Rep 250, where the relevant comment from the bank read: "Please consider these documents at your disposal until we receive our principal's instructions concerning the discrepancies mentioned in your schedules. . . .". The observations of Lloyd LJ on that telex were as follows: "The effect of that telex . . . was that the documents were being held unconditionally at the disposal of the sellers. The reference to "until we receive our principal's instructions" was no doubt reflecting the hope that the buyers and sellers might come to some agreement, either by amending the credit or by tendering fresh sanitary certificates. I cannot read that expression of hope as meaning that the documents were not at the disposal of the sellers." This to my mind is wholly different from the present case. It merely concludes that, where the contracting parties are in negotiation, a statement by the bank that it will hold the documents at the disposal of the sellers pending a resolution of the dispute is not a conditional rejection. The claimant's

---

authority but out of concern or friendship. By such conduct, the actor was bound to conduct the matter to a conclusion and to deliver the transaction's proceeds to the person, who likewise was bound to reimburse the actor for any expenses incurred. A negotiorum gestio did not exist if the gestor acted self-interestedly or if the owner expressly forbade the gestor from acting on the owner's behalf."

Reprinted from *Black's Law Dictionary* (7th ed. 1999) with permission of Thomson West.

[39] ISP 3.07 provides:
"Making a non-complying presentation, withdrawing a presentation, or failing to make any one of a number of scheduled or permitted presentations does not waive or otherwise prejudice the right to make another timely presentation or a timely re-presentation whether or not the standby prohibits partial or multiple drawings or presentations. Wrongful dishonour of a complying presentation does not constitute dishonour of any other presentation under a standby or repudiation of the standby. Honour of a non-complying presentation, with or without notice of its non-compliance, does not waive requirements of a standby for other presentations."

submission is further fortified in three ways. First, the ICC Commission on Banking Technique and Practice produced a paper in November 2000 which discussed the steps prescribed for examination, waiver and notice under UCP and contained this passage: *Bank practices outside the scope of UCP*. The process outlined above and on Attachment A outlines the specific steps prescribed under the UCP for examination, waiver and notice. Unfortunately various practices have been implemented which are not in full compliance with the requirements of UCP. *Issuing banks should be cautioned that practices of refusing documents, stating that they are seeking waiver and that if that waiver is received they will release the documents unless they have received instructions to the contrary does not comply with the UCP.*

Once documents are presented to the bank, those documents belong to the presenter until the documents are taken up. Should the presenter choose to dispose of the documents through other means once refusal is received and the issuing bank releases the documents, it may place itself at risk since the documents belong to the presenter. Issuing banks perform when documents are presented in numerous ways. *First, in total compliance with the UCP and secondly, based on business decisions made by the issuing bank.* When issuing (or confirming) banks make business decisions to deviate from the rules it should do so only understanding the risks that it may be assuming." Secondly, a similar notice was tendered in Voest-Alpine (supra). The Bank of China's telex notifying the discrepancies concluded: "we are contacting the applicant of the relative discrepancies. Holding documents at your risks and disposal". The claimant asserted that the notice was ineffective; a) Because there was no clear statement of refusal; and b) Because notification of intention to seek a waiver rendered the communication ambiguous. The judge concluded: "Here, the Bank of China's notice is deficient because nowhere does it state that it is actually rejecting the documents or refusing to honour the letter of credit or any words to that effect. Whilst it is true that under UCP 500 the notice must contain a list of discrepancies and the disposition of the documents and the Bank of China's telex of August 11, 1995 does indeed contain these elements, this only addresses the requirement of Article 14(d)(ii). A notice of refusal, by its own terms, must actually convey refusal as defined in Article 14(d)(i). This submission is only compounded by the statement that the Bank of China would contact the applicant to determine if it would waive the discrepancies. As the Plaintiff's expert, Professor James Byrne testified, within the framework of Article 14, this additional piece of information holds open the possibility of acceptance upon waiver of the discrepancies by JFTC and indicates the Bank of China has not refused the documents." This view was endorsed by the Court of Appeal for the 5th Circuit in an opinion handed down after the hearing before me:—

"We find ample evidence supporting the district court's decision. The court's determination that the August 11 telex did not reject the letter of credit is based primarily on the Bank of China's offer to obtain waiver from JTFC. The offer to solicit waiver, the district court reasoned, suggests that the documents had not in fact been refused but might be accepted after consultation with JFTC.""

V.3 Conditions subsequent

V.3.1 General

In order for the instrument to become payable, *conditions precedent* must be met. That is, the instrument establishes contingent liability, i.e., a liability which matures into a debt when a conforming call has been made by the beneficiary.[40] It goes almost without saying that the instrument expires and the "debt" thereunder is consumed upon payment or similar action. When honor or payment has taken place ("the moment of death"), the instrument has been consummated and executed and cannot be drawn or called anymore and the "clearing" will start among other parties to the facility.

On the other hand, a contingent liability which has *not* matured into debt is terminated when specific *conditions subsequent* have been met. The most important is the running or expiration of a fixed period of time.[41]

---

[40] In the Finnish language "vastuu" and "velka" may well be the right definitions and draw the right distinction.

[41] See Dolan in *The Law of Letters of Credit* at 5-10.; Nico Oelofse, *South Africa: Letters of Credit - Demand Guarantee, Case Comment*, J Intl Bus L. (1997) 12(12), N229-230:
"Comment: The respondent bank obviously interpreted the guarantee to mean that a claim had to be made before the expiry date. The court interpreted the guarantee to mean that a claim could be made even after the expiry date, provided that it was made in respect of transactions concluded before such expiry date. The lesson for banks is that they should make their intention clear, for example by incorporating the ICC's Uniform Rules for Demand Guarantees (ICC Publication No. 458). Article 19 of the URDG makes it clear that any claim or demand must be made before or on the expiry date of the guarantee."

Reasonable time for examination: the Avery Dennison case.

The beneficiary may present the document just a day or two before the expiry of the instrument. The examiner will then have up to a maximum of 5 or 7 days to examine the documents but must give notice as soon as practically possible under the circumstances including, perhaps, contacting the account party for acceptance should there be discrepancies in the document. Should the reasonable time required for examination be longer than the time remaining until the expiry in case of refusal, the beneficiary will not have an opportunity to remedy the tender since the instrument has expired.

> "In the case at bar, Avery presented its demand shortly before the letter of credit was to expire on August 12, 2001. The Bank had seven business days from its receipt of Avery's demand before it was required to honor or dishonor the demand. *See* Iowa Code § 554.5108(2) ("An issuer has a reasonable time after presentation, but not beyond the end of the seventh business day of the issuer after the day of its receipt of documents: (a) to honor, . . . or (c) to give notice to the presenter of discrepancies in the presentation"). The Court concludes that Avery's demand was not in strict compliance with the terms of the letter of credit because the demand did not comply with the required certification and statements expressly set forth in the letter of credit. The Bank accordingly gave Avery written notice of dishonor on Tuesday, August 21, 2001. Avery could not have cured the defects because any subsequent presentment would have come after the letter of credit had expired. The Court thus finds that *by presenting its demand so close to the expiry date, Avery assumed the risk that it would not have time to cure any defects in the presentment before the expiry date.* The Court notes that permitting a beneficiary to enjoy an unrestricted right to cure

---

URDG Art. 19 provides:
"A demand shall be made in accordance with the terms of the Guarantee before its expiry, that is, on or before its Expiry Date and before any Expiry Event as defined in Article 22. In particular, all documents specified in the Guarantee for the purpose of the demand, and any statement required by Article 20, shall be presented to the Guarantor before its expiry at its place of issue; otherwise the demand shall be refused by the Guarantor."

URDG Art. 22 provides:
"Expiry of the time specified in a Guarantee for the presentation of demands shall upon a specified calendar date ("Expiry Date") or upon presentation to the Guarantor of the document(s) specified for the purpose of expiry "Expiry Event". If both an Expiry Date and an Expiry Event are specified in a Guarantee, the Guarantee shall expire on whichever of the Expiry Date or Expiry Event occurs first, whether or not the Guarantee and any amendment(s) thereto are returned."

Chapter V

deficiencies after the presentation deadline would render the expiry date virtually meaningless and would effectively subvert the strict compliance standard. Avery's demand did not contain a statement signed by an authorized official of the beneficiary certifying that "AN EVENT HAS OCCURRED UNDER THE CREDIT AGREEMENT BY AND AMONG FASSON/ AVERY DENNISON CORPORATION AND VERITEC, INC., WHICH ALLOWS THE BENEFICIARY TO DRAW ON LETTER OF CREDIT NUMBER 104." Further, Avery's demand did not contain the required draft language: "DRAWN UNDER MATTHEWS GROUP, LLC STANDBY LETTER OF CREDIT NUMBER 104, DATED MAY 12, 2000." The Court finds that the Bank provided written notice of dishonor within seven business days of presentment, whether calculated from Friday, August 10, 2001 or Monday, August 13, 2001."[42]

In the absence of a stated expiration date UCC provides for an implicit term of one year after issuance. A credit issued as perpetual will expire five years after issuance, as is provided in UCC 5-106::

"(c) If there is no stated expiration date or other provision that determines its duration, a letter of credit expires one year after its stated date of issuance or, if none is stated, after the date on which it is issued. (d) A letter of credit that states that it *is perpetual expires five years* after its stated date of issuance, or if none is stated, after the date on which it is issued."

A release is a particular form of expiry.[43]

---

[42] Avery Dennison Corp v. The Home Trust & Savings Bank, Not Reported in F.Supp.2d, WL 22697175 (N.D. Iowa, 2003).

[43] UNC Art. 12 provides:
"The validity period of the undertaking expires: (a) At the expiry date, which may be a specified calendar date or the last day of a fixed period of time stipulated in the undertaking, provided that, if the expiry date is not a business day at the place of business of the guarantor/issuer at which the undertaking is issued, or of another person or at another place stipulated in the undertaking for presentation of the demand for payment, expiry occurs on the first business day which follows; (b) If expiry depends according to the undertaking on the occurrence of an act or event not within the guarantor/issuer's sphere of operations, when the guarantor/issuer is advised that the act or event has occurred by presentation of the document specified for that purpose in the undertaking or, if no such document is specified, of a certification by the beneficiary of the occurrence of the act or event; (c) If the undertaking does not state an expiry date, or if the act or event on which expiry is stated to depend has not yet been established by presentation of the required document and an expiry date has not been stated in addition, when six years have elapsed from the date of issuance of the undertaking."

Only the beneficiary may release the issuing or confirming bank from their contingent liability under the instrument, but no one else may cause such an expiry. For all other parties the instrument is irrevocable and will expire on payment or at the end of its term.

V.3.2 "Evergreen clauses" and expiry clause

As discussed above, there is a "law against perpetuities". At least under the UCC, perpetual commitments expire at the end of a five-year period. Letters of credit and other instruments may provide for an automatic extension or they may be revolving. Evergreen credits and automatic extensions need to be narrowly construed. That is, in case of ambiguity, one should choose the interpretation which creates the least extensive obligation (a "*de minimis* rule"). However, if the wording is unambiguous, the maxim of *pacta sunt servanda* shall control as is illustrated by *Molter v. Amwest*.

> "The original letter contains an expiration date of November 5, 1990. The letter of credit also provides *an automatic extension* "for one year from the present or any future expiration date hereof * * *," unless the Bank provides notice to Amwest that it will not be renewed. The fourth paragraph of the letter promises to honor drafts if presented before November 5, 1990, "or *any* automatically extended date." (Emphasis added.) On October 25, 1990, the Bank sent Amwest the extension notice which fixed the letter of credit's new expiration date at January 5, 1991. However, the Bank has *not* provided Amwest with any notice that the letter will not be renewed. Based on these facts, we conclude that January 5, 1991, the expiration date set forth in the extension notice, was the *present* expiration date. The references in the evergreen clause to future expiration dates and to "any automatically extended date" contemplate the existence of several possible expiration dates. *The unambiguous language of the entire letter of credit indicates that it will remain in effect until the Bank chooses not to renew it and notifies Amwest of that fact.* As a consequence, we conclude that the letter automatically

---

URDG Art. 25 provides:
  "Where to the knowledge of the Guarantor the Guarantee has terminated by payment, expiry, cancellation or otherwise, or there has been a reduction of the total amount payable thereunder, the Guarantor shall without delay so notify the Principal or, where applicable, the Instructing Party and, in that case, the Instructing Party shall so notify the Principal."

renews itself every January 5 until the Bank notifies Amwest that it will not renew the letter of credit. Therefore, it will expire on the first January 5 following proper notice of nonrenewal. *See Sports, Inc.*, 14 Kan.App.2d at 143-44, 783 P.2d at 1320; see also *B.E.I.*, 978 F.2d at 442, citing *National Surety Corp. v. Midland Bank (3d Cir.1977)*, 551 F.2d 21, 23. Accordingly, the trial court erred when it held that the letter of credit expired on January 4, 1992. Moreover, we conclude that the letter of credit remains in effect until the Bank gives Amwest proper notice of cancellation. For the reasons indicated, the decision of the trial court is reversed. Pursuant to *Supreme Court Rule 366(a)(5) (134 Ill.2d R. 366(a)(5))*, judgment in the sum of $100,000 plus costs will be entered for Amwest. In light of our decision, we find it unnecessary to review the other contentions raised by the parties."[44]

Another evergreen clause, in AXA v. Chase Manhattan

This case also deals with an evergreen clause and wrongful dishonor. The evergreen clause and the expiry clause were *prima facie* incompatible with each other. The Appellate Division of the New Jersey Superior Court held that the expiry clause controlled over the evergreen or automatic extension clause:

> "Borrower filed complaint against bank alleging wrongful dishonor of letter of credit. The Superior Court, Law Division, Morris County, granted summary judgment to bank. Borrower appealed. The Superior Court, Appellate Division, *Carchman*, J.A.D., held that evergreen clause of letter of credit was limited by expiry provision.
> The opinion of the Court was delivered by CARCHMAN, J.A.D. This appeal requires us to reconcile two assertedly disparate clauses contained in a letter of credit (the letter). *The first clause, referred to as an "evergreen" clause, provides for annual automatic renewal of the letter of credit without notice. The second clause, referred to as the "expiry" clause, provides a fixed termination date for the letter.*
> Judge Stephen F. Smith, Jr., in the Law Division, held that the expiry clause governed and granted summary judgment in favor of defendant Chase Manhattan Bank (the bank). We agree with his conclusion, and

---

[44] Molter Corp v. Amwest Surety Ins Co & First Nat'l Bank of Joliet, 267 Ill. App.3d 718, 642 N.E.2d 919, 205 Ill. Dec. 54, 25 UCC Rep.Serv.2d 892.

affirm. The letter was originally issued by Chemical Bank New Jersey, N.A., which thereafter merged with Chase Manhattan Bank. The underlying facts are not in dispute. On June 3, 1992, the bank issued an irrevocable letter of credit in the principal amount of $355,000 to Hankin Environmental Systems, Inc., naming *Laurentian Casualty Company of Canada as beneficiary. Laurentian was thereafter acquired by plaintiff AXA Assurances, Inc., which succeeded Laurentian as beneficiary under the letter.* The letter contains two separate clauses which frame the issue on this appeal. The evergreen clause provides: IT IS A CONDITION OF THIS LETTER OF CREDIT THAT IT SHALL BE DEEMED AUTOMATICALLY EXTENDED WITHOUT AMENDMENT FOR ONE YEAR, FROM THE EXPIRATION DATE HEREOF, OR ANY FUTURE EXPIRATION DATE, UNLESS AT LEAST 30 DAYS PRIOR TO SUCH DATE WE SHALL NOTIFY YOU IN WRITING BY REGISTERED MAIL OR OVERNIGHT COURIER THAT WE ELECT NOT TO EXTEND THIS LETTER OF CREDIT FOR ANY SUCH ADDITIONAL PERIOD. UPON RECEIPT OF SUCH NOTICE YOU MAY DRAW HEREUNDER BY MEANS OF YOUR SIGHT DRAFT ON OURSELVES FOR AN AMOUNT NOT EXCEEDING THE AVAILABLE AMOUNT OF THIS LETTER OF CREDIT.

The expiry clause, however, provides a specific expiration date: WE HEREBY AGREE WITH YOU THAT DRAFTS DRAWN UNDER AND IN ACCORDANCE WITH THE TERMS OF THIS CREDIT WILL BE DULY HONORED UPON PRESENTATION AND DELIVERY OF THE DOCUMENTS AS SPECIFIED IF PRESENTED AT CHEMICAL BANK COMMERCIAL LETTER OF CREDIT DEPT, 55 WATER STREET NEW YORK, N.Y. 10041, **ON OR BEFORE JUNE 02, 1993 BUT NOT BEYOND JUNE 2, 1994**. [.]

The bank took no action under the evergreen clause. On March 9, 1998, plaintiff requested a draw on the letter. The bank refused the request, claiming the letter had expired.

Plaintiff then filed a complaint alleging wrongful dishonor of the letter, and theorizing that the evergreen clause supported the continued validity of the letter. On cross-motions for summary judgment, Judge Smith determined that the clauses were not inconsistent with one another and that *the more general evergreen clause was limited by the expiry provision*. He granted defendant's motion for summary judgment and dismissed the complaint. This appeal followed. A letter of credit is "a bank's agreement to honor written demands for payment at the request of another upon compliance with specified conditions." New Jersey Bank v. Palladino, 77 N.J. 33, 40, 389 A.2d

Chapter V

> 454 (1978). *See also Chase Manhattan Bank v. Equibank, 550 F.2d 882, 885 (3d Cir.1977)* (defining letters of credit generally). An "evergreen clause" is defined "as a '[t]erm in a letter of credit providing for automatic renewal of the credit.'" *Molter Corp. v. Amwest Surety Ins. Co., 267 Ill.App.3d 718, 205 Ill.Dec. 54, 642 N.E.2d 919, 921 (1994)* (quoting J. Dolan, *The Laws of Letters of Credit*, at G-15 (2d ed.1984)). "An evergreen clause in a letter of credit reflects the parties' intent to make credit available for an indefinite period of time." *Ibid.* (citing *B.E.I. Int'l, Inc. v. Thai Military Bank, 978 F.2d 440, 442 (8th Cir.1992)*).

The somewhat misguided belief that letters of credit must be interpreted as contracts is the prevailing rule applied by many American courts.

> *General rules of contract construction apply with equal force in interpreting letters of credit.* See Palladino, supra, 77 N.J. 33, 46, 389 A.2d 454. Other jurisdictions have adopted a similar rule. *See, e.g.,* United Shippers Co-op. v. Soukup, 459 N.W.2d 343, 345 (Minn.Ct.App.1990); Sports, Inc. v. Sportshop, Inc., 14 Kan.App.2d 141, 783 P.2d 1318, 1319 (1989); Willow Bend Nat. Bank v. Commonwealth Mortgage Corp., 722 S.W.2d 12, 13 (Tex.App.1986); First Nat. Bank of Atlanta v. Wynne, 149 Ga.App. 811, 256 S.E.2d 383, 386 (1979); New York Life Ins. Co. v. Hartford Nat. Bank & Trust Co., 173 Conn. 492, 378 A.2d 562, 565 (1977). *Several federal courts have also applied general contract principles in construing the terms of letters of credit. See, e.g.,* Mutual Export Corp. v. Westpac Banking Corp., 983 F.2d 420, 423 (2d Cir.1993); Bank of North Carolina, N.A. v. Rock Island Bank, 570 F.2d 202, 207 (7th Cir.1978); Data General Corp. v. Citizens Nat'l Bank, 502 F.Supp. 776, 784-85 (D.Conn.1980); West Virginia Housing Dev. Fund v. Sroka, 415 F.Supp. 1107, 1109-10 (W.D.Pa.1976).

The instrument must be construed as a whole. This does not, however, refer to the facility or other parts thereof, but to the text of the instrument only:

> Particularly relevant here is the admonition that contracts must be read as a whole without focus on an isolated phrase. *Wheatly v. Sook Suh, 217 N.J.Super. 233, 239, 525 A.2d 340 (App.Div.1987).* "'Individual clauses and particular words must be considered in connection with the rest of the agreement, and all parts of the writing and every word of it, will, if possible, be given effect.'" *Krosnowski v. Krosnowski, 22 N.J. 376, 387- 88, 126 A.2d 182 (1956)* (quoting 9 *Williston on Contracts* § 46 (rev. ed.1945)).

Against this basic framework, we examine the provisions in issue here. The evergreen clause provides for automatic renewal of the letter "for one year, from the expiration date hereof, or any future expiration date," provided that defendant did not give 30 days notice of non-renewal. If this were the sole provision in issue, we would have little difficulty concluding that this letter was renewable on an annual basis without limit absent notification by defendant of its intention not to renew. Such a reading, however, suggests no significance to the expiry provision, which provides that plaintiff may draw upon the credit line "on or before June 2, 1993 but not beyond June 2, 1994." *Reconciling these provisions to give effect to both is not a difficult task. The evergreen clause identifies the term of the letter in one-year increments.* The letter, issued June 3, 1992, thus expired by its terms, subject to the evergreen renewal, on June 2, 1993. Absent any action by defendant as required by the clause, *the letter was automatically renewed for another one-year term. At that point, however, the expiry provision became paramount, as by its terms the letter expired "June 2, 1994." This interpretation gives meaning to both clauses by allowing for the automatic extension of the letter from June 3, 1993 to June 2, 1994, and by terminating defendant's obligation under the letter on June 2, 1994.*

The expiry clause prevails over the evergreen clause:

> Plaintiff relies on two out-of-state cases, *Molter Corp. v. Amwest Surety Insurance Co.*, supra, 267 Ill.App.3d 718, 205 Ill.Dec. 54, 642 N.E.2d 919, and *Sports, Inc. v. Sportshop, Inc.*, supra, 14 Kan.App.2d 141, 783 P.2d 1318, for the proposition *that the letter's evergreen clause prevails* over its expiry provision. Neither case applies to the facts presented here. In *Molter*, the letter of credit at issue contained an evergreen clause which provided: It is a condition of this Letter of Credit that it shall be deemed automatically extended without amendment for one year from the present or any future expiration date hereof, unless forty-five (45) days prior to any such date we shall notify you in writing . . . that we elect not to consider this Letter of Credit renewed for any such additional period. . . . We engage with you that all drafts drawn under and in compliance with the terms of this credit will be duly honored if presented at this office on or before November 5, 1990 or any automatically extended date, as hereinbefore set forth. *[Molter, supra, 205 Ill.Dec. 54, 642 N.E.2d at 921* (emphasis omitted).] The court interpreted the wording of the letter to indicate "the Bank's intent to extend the credit to Amwest for an indefinite period of time." *Id.* at 921-22.

The court further found that the letter renewed itself every year "until the Bank sent notice to Amwest that the letter would not be renewed." *Id.* at 922. The court determined that the letter contemplated the possibility of multiple expiration dates because the clause extended the credit for "one year from the present or any future expiration date" and the bank promised to honor drafts presented before November 5, 1990 or "any automatically extended date." *Id.* at 922-23. In essence, the termination date was modified by the language "or any automatically extended date." Although the letter in the present case contains an evergreen clause similar to the clause at issue in *Molter*, there was no independent expiry date provision in the *Molter* letter. Not only did the Molter letter not contain the "but not beyond" language present in this case, it did contain additional language that supported an interpretation that the original expiration date would be automatically extended absent written notice to the contrary. *Id.* at 921. In this case, the phrase *"but not beyond June 2, 1994" evidences the parties' intent to set forth a specific and definite expiration date for the letter regarding further notice. Sports, Inc., supra, 14 Kan.App.2d 141, 783 P.2d 1318*, is also inapplicable because, as in *Molter*, the letter at issue *did not contain an independently operative expiry provision. See id. at 1319.*

We perceive no conflict between our decision and those of the Illinois and Kansas courts addressing this issue. In the latter instances, the dependent expiry provisions were modified by evergreen language evincing a clear intent to permit indefinite future extensions. Neither case involved the unique expiry language at issue here which reflects an intent to establish a termination date beyond which no extension would be permitted. Consistent with the mandate that we give full effect to "all parts of the writing and every word of it, if possible," *Krosnowski, supra*, 22 N.J. at 387, 126 A.2d 182 (internal quotation marks omitted), we conclude that the expiry provision here specifically modified the evergreen clause so as to impose no liability on defendant past June 2, 1994.

Since there is no ambiguity, the *contra proferentem* rule does not apply:

> *Having determined that the expiry provision controls, we reject plaintiff's alternative argument that the letter was ambiguous and must be construed against the drafter. See New York State Higher Educ. Servs. Corp. v. Lucianna, 284 N.J.Super. 603, 608, 666 A.2d 173 (App.Div.1995). See also In re Kennedy Mortgage Co., 23 B.R. 466, 473-74 (Bankr.D.N.J.1982); In re Miller's Estate, 90 N.J. 210, 221-22, 447 A.2d 549 (1982); Terminal Constr. Corp. v. Bergen*

County Hackensack River Sanitary Sewer Dist. Auth., 18 N.J. 294, 302, 113 A.2d 787 (1955); *Jennings v. Pinto*, 5 N.J. 562, 569, 76 A.2d 669 (1950). We perceive no ambiguity warranting application of this principle. Affirmed. 339 N.J.Super. 22, 770 A.2d 1211, 45 UCC Rep.Serv.2d 854."[45]

V.4 "Pay or extend" claims

The position of the beneficiary under an on-demand instrument or standby credit requiring only a demand as a condition precedent or something as easy to obtain and present is very strong: pulling the trigger or pushing the button is simple and should result in an almost immediate cash flow into the beneficiary's treasury. No doubt the calling is subject to the duty of good faith, but what this duty means in practice is subject to many assessments.

When the beneficiary's call "to pay or extend" is received, the account party may, right or wrong, feel strongly that the call is wholly unjustified, if not fraudulent.[46] The alternative to payment is extension, which may appear as an undesirable option, too, in particular if the account party or principal was rather expecting the expiry with no demands at all and the parties had not agreed on a "revolving" instrument or an extension in advance. Under such circumstances, the call appears coercive or, in case of pending disputes or disagreements, as undue pressure or unscrupulous tactics.[47] The beneficiary, perhaps, having a totally different view of facts or the purpose of the instrument, may deem the call to be justified or even generous, because a considerably softer alternative of extension

---

[45] 339 N.J.Super. 22, 770 A.2d 1211, 45 UCC Rep.Serv.2d 854. Superior Court of New Jersey, Appellate Division. AXA ASSURANCE, INC., Plaintiff-Appellant, v. The Chase Manhattan Bank, f/k/a Chemical Bank New Jersey, N.A., Defendant/Third-Party Plaintiff-Respondent, v. Hankin Environmental Systems, Inc., Third-Party Defendant.

[46] Bertrams, *Bank Guarantees*, at 244:
"Beneficiaries and second issuing banks sometimes lodge shortly before the expiry date a request with the (instructing) bank to 'Please block the amount of the (counter-) guarantee and do not consider the period of validity as expired'. These requests are known as 'hold for value' requests and they are common phenomenon in the Gulf area. Variants include 'extend or hold for value' or 'pay or hold for value' requests and these should be treated in the same way. The general idea of such requests is to avoid making a cash call on the guarantee and counter-guarantee which might have to be refunded later and, at the same time, to avoid the lapse of the (counter-)guarantee. The underlying motives and circumstances may vary."

[47] There are very few calls under these instruments. According to a leading Nordic bank the number of calls per year, on average, may be counted on your fingers.

is offered to the bank and the account party. In some business and legal cultures such a calling may be fully natural and consistent with the ordinary way of conducting one's business.

From the strictly legal point of view, unless fraud is established, the call must be honored if the conditions precedent are met. There is nothing shocking or abusive in the beneficiary doing so no matter how unexpected or unanticipated it may be from the account party's point of view. Should the call be unjustified, the parties are to settle the matter, if not amicably out of court, in accordance with arbitration or other mechanism agreed under the underlying transaction. The financial institutions should not be involved and forced to participate in the perhaps very lengthy and complex litigation and be caught in the crossfire.

Under ISP, payor extend claims have been treated with wisdom and maturity and such a demand is broken down into various elements, which may, in the great majority of cases truly reflect the reasoning behind such a call.

ISP 3.09:

> "A beneficiary's request to extend the expiration date of the standby or, alternatively, to pay the amount available under it:
> a. is a presentation demanding payment under the standby, to be examined as such in accordance with these Rules; and
> b. implies that the beneficiary:
>   i. consents to the amendment to extend the expiry date to the date requested;
>   ii. requests the issuer to exercise its discretion to seek the approval of the applicant and to issue that amendment;
>   iii. upon issuance of that amendment, retracts its demand for payment; and
>   iv. consents to the maximum time available under these Rules for examination and notice of dishonour."

V.5 Contractual patterns

There are three agreements in a simple letter of credit or bank guarantee transaction, namely

> (i) the instrument itself;

INTERPRETATION OF INSTRUMENTS

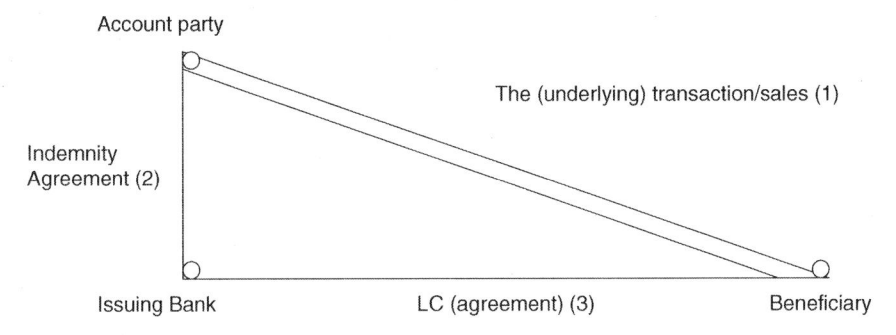

Figure V.1. (Simple) letter of credit or bank guarantee

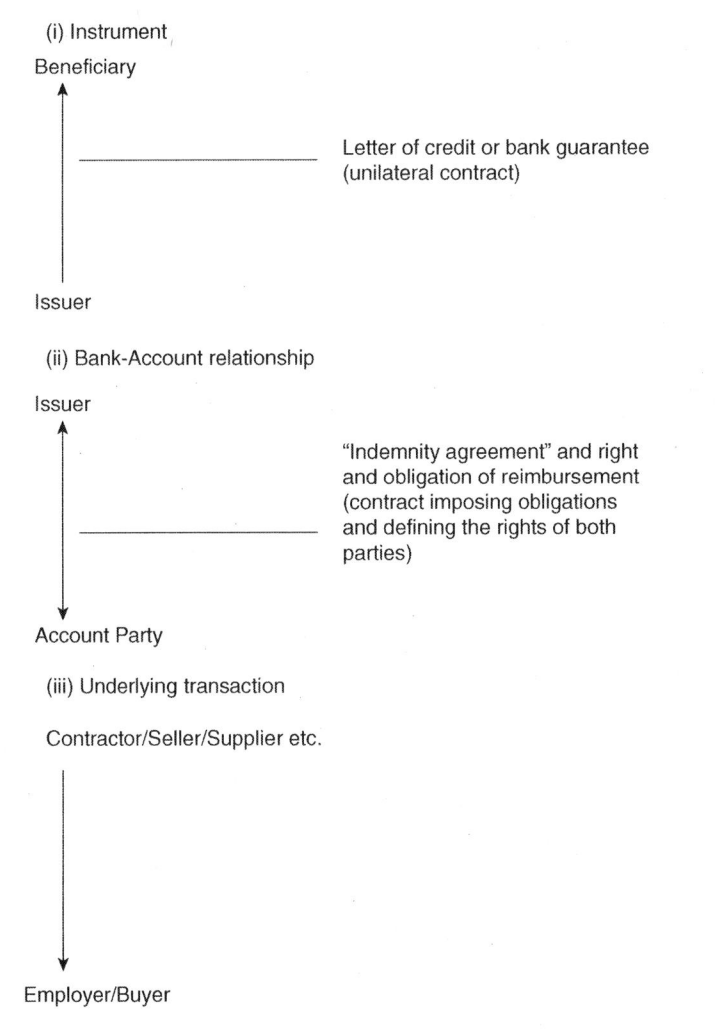

Figure V.2. Instrument, Bank-Account Relationship, Underlying Transaction

LETTERS OF CREDIT AND BANK GUARANTEES UNDER INTERNATIONAL TRADE LAW 255

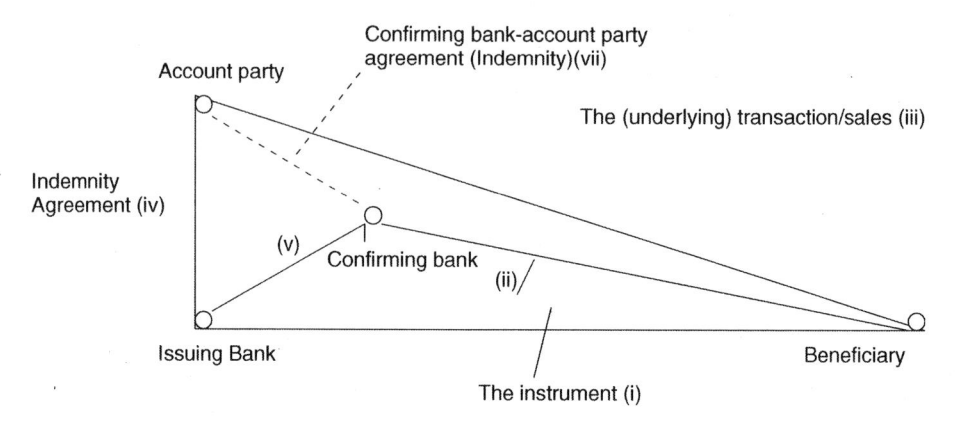

Figure V.3. Confirmed Letter of Credit or Bank Guarantee

(ii) the bank-account party relationship; and
(iii) the underlying ("main") transaction.

All are "formally" accessory but substantively independent *or* dependent from each other according to the type of instrument agreed and issued, as the case may be.

Contracts created in Figure V.3

(i) The instrument (issuer-beneficiary);
(ii) The confirmation of the instrument (confirming bank-beneficiary);
(iii) The underlying agreement;
(iv) Issuing bank–account party agreement (Indemnity);
(v) The issuing bank–confirming bank agreement (Indemnity and/or possibility);
(vi) Three-party agreement between the two banks and the beneficiary under the instrument;[48]

---

[48] ICC Banking Commission Collected Opinions 1995-2001, R 397:
"Who is the formal debtor in the event of a confirmed L/C, the applicant or the confirming bank? .... ANALYSIS AND CONCLUSION Sub-Article 9(a) states that an irrevocable credit constitutes a definite undertaking of the issuing bank, provided that documents are presented to the nominated bank or the issuing bank in conformity with the credit terms. In addition, sub-Article 9(b) refers to the adding of confirmation constituting a definite undertaking of the confirming bank, in addition to that of the issuing bank. In a confirmed L/C situation, the confirming bank would

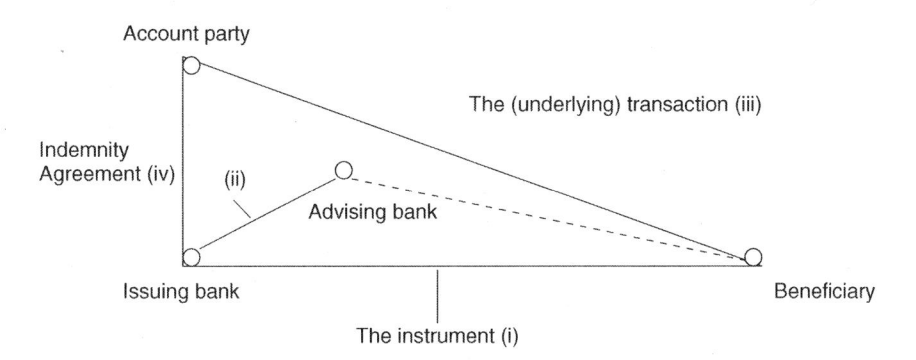

Figure V.4. Advised Letter of Credit

(vii) Confirming bank-account party agreement (Indemnity);
(viii) The indemnity in (v) and (vii) may form a three-party agreement.

Contracts created in Figure V.4:

(i) The instrument (issuer–beneficiary);
(ii) The issuing bank–advisory bank agreement;
(iii) The underlying agreement;
(iv) The issuing bank-account party agreement.

---

be the principal debtor but in the underlying contract for the supply of the goods, the applicant would be the legal debtor. Depending on the specific circumstances of a transaction, the answer to your question may be a subject of local law."

Czech Republic (DCL) Art 687(1) says:
"If an irrevocable credit was confirmed by another bank upon the issuing bank's instruction the beneficiary's claim to performance against such bank arises at the time such bank confirms the credit to the beneficiary. The issuing bank and the bank which confirms the credit are jointly and severally liable to the beneficiary."

Guatemala (DCL) Art 760 says:
"The bank which notifies the issuance of the credit to the beneficiary will not be obliged by the mere notification. If such bank confirms a credit such bank shall be jointly and severally liable."

CHAPTER V

V.6 Sample of use of credits and guarantees in a construction contract

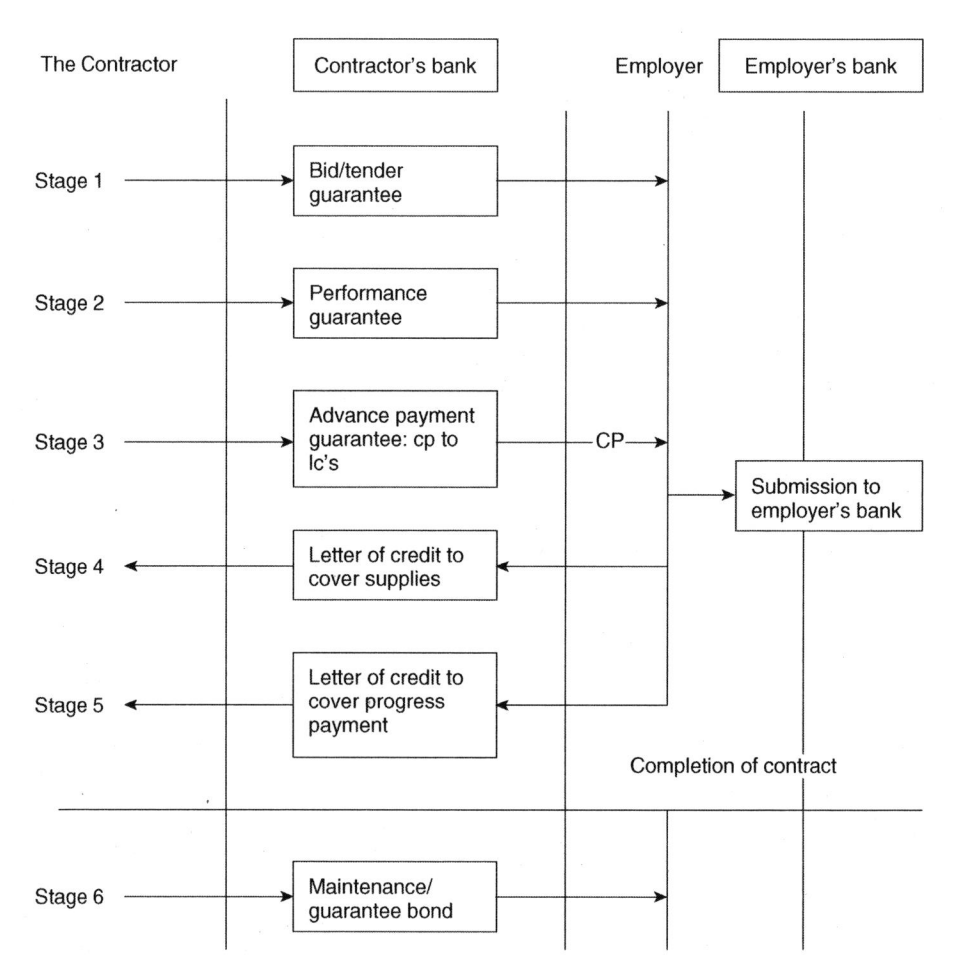

The Contractor	Contractor's bank	Employer	Employer's bank
Stage 1 →	Bid/tender guarantee →		
Stage 2 →	Performance guarantee →		
Stage 3 →	Advance payment guarantee: cp to lc's	—CP→	Submission to employer's bank
Stage 4 ←	Letter of credit to cover supplies ←	←	
Stage 5 ←	Letter of credit to cover progress payment ←	←	
		Completion of contract	
Stage 6 →	Maintenance/ guarantee bond →		

Figure V.5. Sample of use of credits and guarantees

CHAPTER VI

REFUSAL, DISHONOUR, AND REMEDIES

VI.1 What constitutes refusal? – Teachings from *Bank of China*

The *Bank of China* case deals with two issues that commonly arise in international trade, first, fluctuating prices, and second, another issue typical of letter of credit disputes: discrepancies in the documents. The two collide when prices fall and the documents presented are discrepant. Here, additional spice is added by jurisdictional issues.

To quote from the opinion of Circuit Judge Clement of the U.S. Court of Appeals for the Fifth Circuit:

> "The Bank of China appeals an adverse judgment in its dispute with Voest-Alpine Trading USA Corporation regarding the validity of a letter of credit. After conducting a bench trial, the district court concluded that the bank improperly refused payment on the letter and awarded Voest-Alpine damages and attorney's fees. We affirm the district court's judgment.
>
> I. FACTS AND PROCEEDINGS In June 1995, Jiangyin Foreign Trade Corporation ("JFTC"), a *Chinese company, agreed to purchase 1,000 metric tons of styrene monomer from Voest-Alpine Trading USA Corporation ("Voest-Alpine"),* an American company. At Voest-Alpine's insistence, JFTC obtained a letter of credit from the Bank of China for the purchase price of $1.2 million. The letter of credit provided for payment to Voest-Alpine after it delivered the monomer and presented several designated documents to the Bank of China in accordance with the Uniform Customs and

CHAPTER VI

> Practice for Documentary Credits of the International Chamber of Commerce, Publication No. 500 ("UCP 500").
>
> By the time Voest-Alpine was ready to ship its product, the market price of styrene monomer had dropped significantly from *the original contract price. JFTC asked for a price concession, but Voest-Alpine refused.* After shipping the monomer to JFTC, Voest-Alpine presented the documents specified in the letter of credit to Texas Commerce Bank ("TCB"), which would forward the documents to the Bank of China. *TCB noted several discrepancies between what Voest-Alpine presented and what the letter of credit required.* Because it did not believe any of the discrepancies would warrant refusal to pay, Voest-Alpine instructed TCB to present the documents to the Bank of China "on approval," meaning that JFTC would be asked to waive the problems.

The Bank of China did not clearly refuse the documents but held them seeking waiver from the buyer. The buyer refused to waive, whereafter the Bank of China returned the documents and made no payment.

> *The Bank of China received the documents on August 9, 1995.* On August 11 the bank notified TCB that the documents contained seven discrepancies and that it would contact JFTC about acceptance. *On August 15, 1995, TCB, acting on behalf of Voest-Alpine, responded that the alleged discrepancies were not adequate grounds for dishonoring the letter of credit and demanded payment.* On August 19, the Bank of China reiterated its position that the documents were insufficient and stated, "Now the discrepant documents may have us refuse to take up the documents according to article 14(B) of UCP 500." *JFTC refused to waive the discrepancies, and the Bank of China returned the documents to TCB on September 18, 1995.*

The Seller filed action in Texas courts and the defendant Bank of China moved for dismissal for lack of jurisdiction.

> In October 1995, Voest-Alpine filed the instant action for payment on the letter of credit. The Bank of China initially filed a motion for judgment on the pleadings *seeking dismissal for lack of jurisdiction and improper venue, which the district court denied.* We affirmed the district court's jurisdictional decision and held that the venue order was not yet appealable, and the case proceeded to trial. *See Voest-Alpine Trading USA Corp. v. Bank of China,*

142 F.3d 887 (5th Cir.1998) ("*Voest-Alpine*"). After conducting a bench trial, the district court ruled in favor of Voest-Alpine, finding that the Bank of China's August 11, 1995 telex failed to provide notice of refusal and that the discrepancies noted in that telex were not sufficient to allow rejection of the letter of credit.

II. DISCUSSION A. Venue.
As an initial matter, the Bank of China argues that the district court erroneously determined venue to be proper in the Southern District of Texas. We disagree. *A substantial number of the events giving rise to the instant dispute occurred in Texas.*

First, although the letter of credit was initiated in China, it was negotiated in both China and Houston and was sent to Voest-Alpine for acceptance at its headquarters in Houston.

Second, Voest-Alpine presented the allegedly discrepant documents to TCB in Houston.

Finally, payment was to be made to TCB in Houston. Accordingly, the district court correctly held that venue in the Southern District of Texas was proper. *See* 28 U.S.C. § 1391.

The parties to the dispute argued on the status of UCP and whether or not it should be given the status of law or trade usage or both.

B. Notice of Refusal.
The Bank of China's primary contention on appeal is that the district court erroneously concluded that the bank failed to provide proper notice of refusal to Voest-Alpine. In order to reject payment on a letter of credit, an issuing bank must give notice of refusal to the beneficiary "no later than the close of the seventh banking day following the day of receipt of the [presentation] documents." UCP 500 art. 14(d). If the Bank of China did not provide timely notice, it must honor the letter of credit despite any questions as to Voest-Alpine's compliance. *See Heritage Bank v. Redcom Lab., Inc.*, 250 F.3d 319, 327 (5th Cir.2001)(stating that an issuing bank waives its right to reject a letter of credit if it does not give notice of refusal within the time allotted by Article 14(d) of the UCP 500). The parties first dispute the applicable standard of review for this issue. In a bench trial,

findings of fact are reviewed for clear error and legal issues are reviewed de novo. *See Kona Technology Corp. v. Southern Pacific Transportation*, 225 F.3d 595, 601 (5th Cir.2000). Voest-Alpine submits that adequacy of refusal is a factual determination subject to clear error review, *because the UCP 500 is a set of trade usages and not law*. The Bank of China concedes that the UCP 500 is not law, but it argues that de novo review is appropriate because the *UCP 500 has acquired the function and status of law with respect to letters of credit which incorporate its terms*. This circuit has long held that "[u]sage of trade is a question of fact." *Pennzoil Co. v. F.E.R.C.*, 789 F.2d 1128, 1143 (5th Cir.1986). Accordingly, the district court's finding that the Bank of China's letter did not comply with the usages of trade set forth in the UCP 500 is a factual conclusion subject to review for clear error.

Was there a refusal?

The Bank of China received Voest-Alpine's documents on August 9, 1995. Since August 12 and 13 were Chinese banking holidays, the deadline for giving notice of dishonor was August 18, 1995. The Bank of China's only communication before the deadline was its telex of August 11, 1995. Accordingly, the issue is whether that telex provided notice of refusal.

The telex quoted lists a number of discrepancies but fails to draw a definitive conclusion with respect to them. The telex leaves the fate of the tender open: the two last sentences seem to be contradictory although the emphasis is perhaps on the bank's contemplated action to obtain the account party's waiver.

The bank's August 11 telex stated: UPON CHECKING A/M DOCUMENTS, WE NOTE THE FOLLOWING DISCREPANCY: 1. LATE PRESENTATION. 2. BENEFICIARY'S NAME IS DIFFER (sic) FROM L/C. 3. B/L SHOULD BE PRESENTED IN THREE ORIINALS (sic) I/O DUPLICATE, TRIPLICATE. 4. INV. P/L. AND CERT. OF ORIGIN NOT SHOWING "ORIGINAL." 5. THE DATE OF SURVER (sic) REPORT LATER THAN B/L DATE. 6. WRONG L/C NO. IN FAX COPY. 7. WRONG DESTINATION IN CERT. OF ORIGIN AND BENEFICIARY'S CERT. *WE ARE CONTACTING THE APPLICANT FOR ACCEPTANCE OF THE RELATIVE DISCREPANCY. HOLDING DOCUMENTS AT YOUR RISK AND DISPOSAL.*

The district court found that the telex failed to provide notice of refusal because

(1) the bank did not explicitly state that it was rejecting the documents;
(2) the bank's statement that it would contact JFTC about accepting the documents despite the discrepancies "holds open the possibility of acceptance upon waiver" and "indicates that the Bank of China has not refused the documents"; and (3) the Bank of China did not even mention refusal until its August 19 telex in which it wrote: "Now the discrepant documents may have us refuse to take up the documents according to article 14(B) of UCP 500." In light of these circumstances, the district court concluded that the August 11 telex was merely a status report, that the bank would not reject the documents until after it consulted JFTC, and that the bank did not raise the possibility of refusing payment on the letter of credit until August 19. *Accordingly, the district court held that the Bank of China forfeited its right to refuse the documents and was obligated to pay Voest-Alpine.*

Concerning the expert testimony by Professor Byrne, the Fifth Circuit said:

> We find ample evidence supporting the district court's decision. The court's determination that the August 11 telex did not reject the letter of credit is based primarily on the Bank of China's offer to obtain waiver from JFTC. The offer to solicit waiver, the district court reasoned, suggests that the documents had not in fact been refused but might be accepted after consultation with JFTC. In reaching this conclusion, the district court relied heavily on the testimony of *Professor James Byrne* ("Byrne"), Voest-Alpine's expert witness on international standard banking practice and the UCP 500. *Byrne testified that the bank's telex would have given adequate notice had it not contained the waiver clause. The waiver clause, he explained, deviated from the norm and introduced an ambiguity that converted what might otherwise have been a notice of refusal into nothing more than a status report.* Faced with this evidence, the district court correctly decided that the Bank of China noted discrepancies in the documents, and, instead of rejecting the letter of credit outright, contacted JFTC for waiver.

The three-step procedure under UCP was described as follows by Professor Byrne:

> Byrne further explained that the Bank of China's actions, viewed in light of standard banking practices, were ambiguous. The UCP 500 contemplates a three-step procedure for dishonoring letters of credit.

Chapter VI

First, the issuing bank reviews the documents presented for discrepancies.

Second, if the bank finds problems, it contacts the purchaser for waiver.

Finally, after conferring with the purchaser, the bank may issue its notice of refusal. This sequence ensures the issuing bank's independence in making its decision *while also giving the purchaser an opportunity to waive discrepancies*, thus promoting efficiency in a field "where as many as half of the demands for payment under letters of credit are discrepant, yet, in the vast majority of cases, the account party waives the discrepancies and authorizes payment." *Alaska Textile Co., Inc. v. Chase Manhattan Bank, N.A.*, 982 F.2d 813, 824 (2d Cir.1992). In light of the generally accepted procedure outlined by Byrne, we agree with the district court that the Bank of China's notice of refusal was ambiguous and inadequate.

The Fifth Circuit also considered whether the seller bank's employees understood the telex as refusal:

> The Bank of China also contends that the district court improperly accepted Byrne's expert opinion because TCB employees Sherry Mama ("Mama") and Deborah Desilets ("Desilets") both testified that *they understood the bank's August 11 telex to be a notice of refusal*. However, in contrast to Byrne's reasoned explanation of why the waiver clause deviates from standard banking practice, Mama and Desilets, who were both fact witnesses, offer nothing more than their subjective beliefs. Moreover, *the determinative question is not whether the Bank of China provided adequate notice of refusal to TCB, but whether it gave notice to Voest-Alpine; and the bank presented no evidence of Voest-Alpine's interpretation of the telex.*

According to the Fifth Circuit, the telex was ambiguous and failed to comply with UCP leaving final "fate" of the tender open:

> Viewed in the context of standard international banking practices, the Bank of China's notice of refusal was clearly deficient. *The bank failed to use the standard language for refusal, failed to comply with generally accepted trade usages, and created ambiguity by offering to contact JFTC about waiver, thus leaving open the possibility* that the allegedly discrepant documents might have been accepted at a future date. Accordingly, the district court properly found that the August 11 telex was not an adequate notice of refusal.

Since we agree with the district court that the bank failed to provide timely notice, we need not reach the question of whether the alleged discrepancies warranted refusal.

Finally, the issue of damages was discussed. The actual measure of damages was the face value of the credit to be reduced by resale revenues and by what may be recovered under the underlying agreement. The Fifth Circuit said this about damages:

> C. Damages and Attorney's Fees.
>
> Finally, the Bank of China argues that the district court erred in its award of damages and attorney's fees. "A district court's damages award is a finding of fact, which this court reviews for excessiveness using the clear error standard." *Lebron v. U.S.*, 279 F.3d 321, 325 (5th Cir.2002). "The factual findings supporting an award of attorney's fees are reviewed for clear error; the conclusions of law underlying the award are reviewed de novo." *Volk v. Gonzalez*, 262 F.3d 528, 533 (5th Cir.2001). Both parties admit that *East Girard Sav. Ass'n v. Citizens Nat. Bank and Trust Co.*, 593 F.2d 598, 603 (5th Cir.1979), *allows a plaintiff in a wrongful dishonor case to recover the face value of a letter of credit*. The Bank of China contends that the *East Girard* rule should be rejected in the instant case. First, it argues that Voest-Alpine's damages should be reduced by the amount it received on resale of the styrene monomer. However, even if the bank had authority for this proposition, it cannot overcome the trial testimony that Voest-Alpine has not recovered any money by reselling the monomer. Second, the Bank of China argues that its liability to Voest-Alpine should be reduced by the amount it may receive *through a judgment against JFTC in a Chinese court*. However, the district court has already entered an order providing for such a reduction. Accordingly, we affirm the district court's damages award.

The Fifth Circuit discussed attorney's fees at some length and, although the issue relates to Texas law, it does have some general interest:

> The district court also awarded Voest-Alpine $266,453.46 in attorney's fees, with an additional $25,000.00 for fees incurred on appeal. Attorney's fees may be awarded in letter of credit cases only when the "underlying contract provides for their recovery or there is a statute permitting attorney's fees to be awarded." *Id.* at 604. Since there is no contractual provision

for fees in the instant case, the question is whether a statutory basis for recovery exists.

Voest-Alpine contends that fees are appropriate under § 38.001 of the *Texas Civil Practice and Remedies Code*, which generally permits recovery of attorney's fees. The Bank of China argues that § 38.001 is inapplicable to letter of credit lawsuits and, even if it did apply, Voest-Alpine waived its right to relief under the statute. Both prongs of the bank's argument fail. First, the bank cites *East Girard*'s 1979 holding for the proposition that "no statutory provision awards attorney's fees in letter of credit cases." *Id.* at 604. However, the bank ignores *Temple-Eastex, Inc. v. Addison Bank*, 672 S.W.2d 793, 798 (Tex.1984), which held that attorney's fees in letter of credit cases are permitted under § 38.001's predecessor, article 2226 of the Texas Statutes. Accordingly, contrary to the Bank of China's position, a statutory basis for attorney's fees does exist.

Second, the Bank of China argues that Voest-Alpine waived its right to attorney's fees under § 38.001 by failing to specifically cite that statute in either its complaint or the pre-trial order. The bank points to our decision in *Ralston Oil and Gas Co. v. Gensco, Inc.*, 706 F.2d 685, 696 (5th Cir.1983), which held that the plaintiff waived its claim to attorney's fees under article 2226 by failing to plead entitlement to fees under that article "at least with some specificity." However, in *Enserch Corp. v. Shand Morahan & Co., Inc.*, 952 F.2d 1485, 1500-01 (5th Cir.1992), we held that despite *Ralston*'s suggestion that "a party must plead entitlement to [§ 38.001] fees at least with some particularity," all the statute really requires is that the defendant be put on notice that the plaintiff is seeking attorney's fees. In the instant case, Voest-Alpine pled for recovery of "attorney's fees payable under all applicable statutes...." The bank also points to our decision in *Elvis Presley Enterprises, Inc. v. Capece, 141 F.3d 188, 206 (5th Cir.1998)*, for the proposition that a claim or issue omitted from the pre-trial order is waived, even if it appeared in the complaint. However, Voest-Alpine alleged in the pre-trial order that the Bank of China "is liable for the face amount of the Letter of Credit plus attorney's fees, interest, and all costs." Accordingly, since the Bank of China was on notice of Voest-Alpine's intent to seek fees, Voest-Alpine did not waive its entitlement, and we uphold the district court's award.

The first notice, the August 11 notice discussed by the court above, did not constitute refusal. The second (August 19) notice of the Bank of China did constitute refusal, but it was sent too late.

> III. CONCLUSION *The Bank of China failed to provide Voest-Alpine with adequate notice that it was refusing payment on the letter of credit.* Without a valid excuse for nonpayment, the bank is liable for the full amount of the letter of credit and for Voest-Alpine's legal fees. Accordingly, we affirm the judgment of the district court. AFFIRMED. 288 F.3d 262, 47 UCC Rep. Serv.2d 693 "[1]

VI.2 Dishonor

Dishonor means rejection of the tender and refusal to make payment, to accept or to negotiate: after examination of the documents tendered or claim made, the payor may expressly declare that the tender or claim does not meet the conditions precedent.

When the beneficiary submits the documents as a tender or makes a demand in an attempt to meet the conditions precedent of the instrument, the examiner has a reasonable time to verify the conformity or compliance of the tender with the requirements set forth. A failure to tender complying document does not operate as a condition subsequent terminating the availability of the facility. A new attempt or attempts are permissible until expiry or cancellation of the instrument on the basis of condition subsequent. A conforming tender and honor does, however, operate as such as a condition subsequent terminating the existence of the instrument by payment, acceptance or negotiation and in most cases also the facility as a whole, if the domino effect follows as originally contemplated.

No waiver is constituted by a tender or by a refusal or acceptance of a tender or claim as to subsequent tenders.

In fact, ISP 3.07 reads as follows:

> "a. Making a non-complying presentation, withdrawing a presentation, or failing to make any one of a number of scheduled or permitted

---

[1] *Voest-Alpine Trading Corp v Bank of China*, 288 F.3d 262 (5th Cir 2002), 47 UCC Rep.Serv.2d 693

presentations does not waive or otherwise prejudice the right to make another timely presentation or a timely re-presentation whether or not the standby prohibits partial or multiple drawings or presentations.

b. Wrongful dishonour of a complying presentation does not constitute dishonour of any other presentation under a standby or repudiation of the standby.

c. Honour of a non-complying presentation, with or without notice of its non-compliance, does not waive requirements of a standby for other presentations."

The results of the examination should be *given to the* beneficiary without undue delay, by means of a notice of discrepancy.[2] Under ISP the failure to do so constitutes honor:

ISP 5.03:

"a. Failure to give *notice of a discrepancy* in a notice of dishonour within the time and by the means specified in the standby or these rules precludes assertion of that discrepancy in any document containing the discrepancy that is retained or represented, but does not preclude assertion of that discrepancy in any different presentation under the same or a separate standby.

b. *Failure to give notice of dishonour or acceptance or acknowledgment that a deferred payment undertaking has been incurred obligates the issuer to pay at maturity.*"

---

[2] Ebenezer O. I. Adodo, *Conformity of Presentation Documents and a Rejection Notice in Letters of Credit Litigation: A Tale of Two Doctrines*, 36 Hong Kong L J 309, (2006):
"As has been argued, if there is a finding that an alleged discrepancy justifies dishonour, it then becomes necessary to consider the question whether the dishonour was appropriately advised to the party requesting payment. In *Hanil Bank*, the failure of the negotiating bank's attorney to explore this question most probably turned the scale. In contrast, in *Bank of Cochin*, the confirming bank who inadvertently, and perhaps without want of professional diligence, negotiated discrepant documents succeeded because the issuing bank failed to appropriately advise its rejection of the tendered documents."

Under UCC, however, failure to act constitutes dishonor:

UCC 5-108 (official comment) 2:

> "Failure of the issuer to act within the time permitted by subsection (b) constitutes dishonor. Because of the preclusion in subsection (c) and the liability that the issuer may incur under Section 5-111 for wrongful dishonor, the effect of such a silent dishonor may ultimately be the same as though the issuer had honored, i.e., it may owe damages in the amount drawn but unpaid under the letter of credit."

> Although the practical consequences of this difference in approach may be insignificant in practice, the consistency and uniformity of the two major codes, UCC and UCP, in this respect would be desirable.

In case of express dishonor, *all discrepancies* are to be identified as provided in ISP 5.02:

> "A notice of dishonour shall state all discrepancies upon which dishonour is based."

and in UCC 5-108 (3) (c) and (d):

> "(c) to give notice to the presenter of discrepancies in the presentation. Except as otherwise provided in subsection (d) of this section, an issuer is precluded from asserting as a basis for dishonor any discrepancy if timely notice is not given, or any discrepancy not stated in the notice if timely notice is given.

> (d) failure to give the notice specified in subsection (b) of this section or to mention fraud, forgery, or expiration in the notice does not preclude the issuer from asserting as a basis for dishonor fraud or forgery as described in subsection (a) of Section 5-109 or expiration of the letter of credit before presentation."

The notice must list *all* discrepancies with the exception of fraud or forgery.

Failure to indicate a discrepancy constitutes a waiver and the examiner is precluded from raising objections on the basis of that discrepancy later on basis for refusal.

CHAPTER VI

Notice of dishonour must be given without undue delay. The time frame is roughly between 3 and 7 days *calculated from receipt thereof* in order for the examiner to be on the safe side under ISP 5.01:

> "a. Notice of dishonour must be given within a time after presentation of documents which is not unreasonable. i. Notice given within three business days is deemed to be not unreasonable and beyond seven business days is deemed to be unreasonable. ii. Whether the time within which notice is given is unreasonable does not depend upon an imminent deadline for presentation. iii. The time for calculating when notice of dishonour must be given begins on the business day following the business day of presentation. iv. Unless a standby otherwise expressly states a shortened time within which notice of dishonour must be given, the issuer has no obligation to accelerate its examination of a presentation.

Notice must be given by means which allows prompt communication *to the person from whom* the documents were received, as ISP 5.01 makes clear:

> b. i. The means by which a notice of dishonour is to be given is by telecommunication, if available, and, if not, by another *available means which allows for prompt notice*. ii. If notice of dishonour *is received within the time permitted* for giving the notice, then it is deemed to have been given by prompt means. c. Notice of dishonour must be given to the person from whom the documents were received (whether the beneficiary, nominated person, or person other than a delivery person) except as otherwise requested by the presenter."

Upon refusal and dishonor, the documents must be held at the disposal of the presenter, as is provided in ISP 5.07:

> "Dishonoured documents must be returned, held, or disposed of as reasonably instructed by the presenter. Failure to give notice of the disposition of documents in the notice of dishonour does not preclude the issuer from asserting any defense otherwise available to it against honour."

When the payor then submits the tendered documents to the applicant to cause "the dominos to fall", the latter must give prompt notice if he deems that the acceptance and honor was unjustified and that the tendered documents were discrepant.

The criterion is "appearance on their face". Failure to give notice precludes the applicant's right to raise such an objection and constitutes an acceptance. An acceptance does not, however, constitute a waiver for subsequent tenders under the same or other instruments. As ISP 5.09 says:

> "a. An applicant must timely object to an issuer's honour of a noncomplying presentation by giving timely notice by prompt means. b. An applicant acts timely if it objects to discrepancies by sending a notice to the issuer stating the discrepancies on which the objection is based within a time after the applicant's receipt of the documents which is not unreasonable. c. *Failure to give a timely notice of objection by prompt means precludes assertion by the applicant against the issuer of any discrepancy or other matter* apparent on the face of the documents received by the applicant, but *does not preclude* assertion of that objection to any different presentation under the same or a different standby."

VI.3 Remedies – a substantive or procedural issue?

VI.3.1 General

What are the legal consequences of a breach of an undertaking?[3] What action is the aggrieved party entitled to take? Who bears the burden of proof?[4] Who bears the "burden of education"?[5] Which *remedies* are available in a particular case is to

---

[3] Is acceleration a right or remedy? Sample clause:
Upon and any time after the occurrence of any Event of Default which is continuing, the Bank may by written notice: (i) declare any amounts that may be owing hereunder by any Principal to be immediately due and payable; (ii) declare that the Facility shall be cancelled; (iii) take whatever steps the Bank may deem warranted or to enforce any security governed by the terms thereof; and/or (iv) require full cash cover in respect of the Guarantees to be immediately provided.

[4] Dolan writes in *The Law of Letters of Credit* at 11-14:
"Whether the beneficiary or the negotiating bank bears the burden of proving that documents comply with the terms of the credit, however, is a different question. Article 8(e) of the Uniform Customs and Practice for Documentary Credits (Uniform Customs) and the estoppel rules fashioned by many courts suggest that a presenter bears the burden of proving the conformity only of those documents to which the issuer makes timely objection."

[5] ICC Banking Commission Collected Opinions 1995-2001, R 305:
"Which will prevail, the provisions of UCP or the decision of a local court? Is UCP applicable when SWIFT message types do not refer to it? ANALYSIS AND CONCLUSION CASE No.1 1) The query does not make clear whether the court prohibited the issuing bank from making payment under the credit or ordered it to repay the money to the applicant. It is possible, not just in

CHAPTER VI

be determined primarily on the basis of national laws.[6] The process of determining the applicable law and the proper forum has been discussed elsewhere in this book. Are remedies procedural law or substantive law issues? This may relate to issues like who are the indispensable parties to the process procedurally and materially and what is the right or most convenient forum.[7]

In *Harbottle*, the remedy of injunction was at stake. The remedy would require established fraud to allow court interference. The enforcement of claims under the transaction was held to be a commercial risk of no concern to the courts:

> "I cannot accept any of these submissions. First, this is not a case of an established fraud at all. The plaintiffs may well be right in contending that the buyers have no contractual right to payment of any part, let alone the whole, of the guarantee in any of these cases. In the third case the bank concedes that this may be so, because no valid guarantee may be in existence. But all these issues turn on contractual disputes. *They are a long way from fraud, let alone established fraud.* Secondly, the authorities are strongly

---

Country F, for a court acting at the instigation of an applicant to prevent a bank from fulfilling its obligations under a documentary credit. The issue of whether a court can also order the beneficiary to pay a certain amount as a fine is one that cannot be answered by ICC. This is a matter between the applicant, beneficiary and the court. 2) Faced with an order from a court, the issuing bank cannot ignore this and fulfil its obligations under the credit. This applies even where the bank may previously have given a notice of acceptance. 3) You are correct in saying that UCP (Article 4) states: "In Credit operations all parties concerned deal with documents and not with goods, services and or other performances to which the documents may relate. See the answer under 2. as to the action the issuing bank must take. Given that the court order was given on the basis of quality of goods, the issuing bank could have chosen to revert to the court and could have sought the lifting of the order on the basis of the principles of UCP 500. However, there is no requirement for it to do so. 4) Local law will prevail over the obligations and responsibilities detailed in UCP. This applies to all parts of the world not just Country F. 5) This is a problem and the solution would seem to be in the hands of the banks that receive court orders covering quality of goods issues Educating the judicial system in the principles of UCP may decrease the number of these instances"

[6] Bertrams, *Bank Guarantees*, at 446:
"the English technique of a freezing (Mareva) injunction serves the same purpose as the Continental conservatory attachment, namely the preservation of the debtor's assets pending litigation. When granted, a freezing injunction enjoins the debtor from removing his assets from the court's jurisdiction."

[7] Dolan writes in *The Law of Letters of Credit* at 11-12:
"The court added that even if the account party was an indispensable party under Rule 19 (a), the court would have exercised its prerogative under Rule 19 (b) to deny dismissal of the suit rather than force the beneficiary to litigate its claim in a forum whose courts do not understand credit law. The court had noted earlier in its opinion that the beneficiary had obtained the protection of a credit reimbursable in U.S. dollars from a U.S. bank precisely because the beneficiary did not want to litigate in other forums."

against the plaintiffs' contentions. *It is only in exceptional cases that the courts will interfere with the machinery of irrevocable obligations assumed by banks. They are the life-blood of international commerce.* Such obligations are regarded as collateral to the underlying rights and obligations between the merchants at either end of the banking chain. Except possibly in clear cases of fraud of which the banks have notice, the courts will leave the merchants to settle their disputes under the contracts by litigation or arbitration as available to them or stipulated in the contracts. *The courts are not concerned with their difficulties to enforce such claims; these are risks which the merchants take.* In this case the plaintiffs took the risk of the unconditional wording of the guarantees. The machinery and commitments of banks are on a different level. They must be allowed to be honoured, free from interference by the courts. Otherwise, trust in international commerce could be irreparably damaged."[8]

To the extent remedies are substantive, they may also be covered by law merchant. Further, a remedy may be created or founded in law (a "statutory remedy") or it may rests solely on an agreement of the parties. If the remedy is based on agreement only, it has a material element in it, but a legal system may refuse to enforce it.[9]

Procedural laws are to a great extent subject to national law and national *ordre public* and they may include rules of substantive nature which affect the contemplated function of the instrument making room for forum shopping.[10] One may distinguish international due process which, however, may be hard or impossible to be directly implemented in national courts of law due to a lack of i nternational control over sovereign powers of nations and their courts. In international arbitration, due process and *ordre public* play a more visible and concrete role. National procedural law and remedies may bring new or

---

[8] R. D. Harbottle (Mercantile) Ltd. v Nat'l Westminster Bank Ltd, 1976 R. No. 3861][1976 R. No. 4314][1976 H. No. 7364]; [1977] 3 W.L.R. 752, QBD.
[9] See Dolan, *The Law of Letters of Credit*, 1992 Cum Supp No. 2, at S7-8 and S7-9.
[10] Wunnicke, Wunnicke and Turner at 175:
"The court must also find under § 5-109(b)(3) that all of the conditions to injunctive relief under state law have been met. To satisfy the conditions to injunctive relief under state law the applicant may have to show: 1. That there will be irreparable harm if the injunction is not issued or that the applicant does not have an adequate remedy at law 2. Why the status quo should be preserved 3. Whether the threatened injury to the applicant outweighs the injury that will be sustained by the beneficiary if the injunction is granted 4. That granting the injunction will not disserve the public interest."

CHAPTER VI

substantive issues as to the immediate enforceability of "honor" with reference discussion on interpretation the remedy of reformation is rarely relevant.[11]

The main issues in enforcing these instruments are:

> (i) availability of ordinary or *ex parte* protective or temporary measures to enforce a right, to enjoin payment or to attach funds after the death of the instrument;
> (ii) the availability of summary judgment;
> (iii) the time required to enforce a right;
> (iv) the respect of the "parole evidence" rule;
> (v) the availability of specific performance and damages as remedy, and

(i) availability of ordinary or ex parte protective or temporary measures to enforce a right, to enjoin payment or to attach funds after the death of the instrument.[12]

---

[11] Dolan, *The Law of Letters of Credit*, 1992 Cum Supp No. 2, at S4-7 and S4-8:
"Cases for reformation of the credit to conform to the intent of the parties are more persuasive when they rest on a contract between the account party/plaintiff and the issuer, rather than on a contract between the plaintiff/beneficiary and the account party."

[12] See Herbert A. Getz, *Enjoining the International Standby Letter of Credit: The Iranian Letter of Credit Cases*, 21 Harvard Int'l L J, (Winter 1980), and Charles Debattista, *Performance Bonds and Letters of Credit: A Cracked Mirror Image*, J Busn L, (1997):
"In conclusion, it is suggested that the solution to the problem of unfair calls on bonds governed by English law lies in the hands of the English courts and on a new analysis of the relationship between letters of credit and performance bonds. International initiatives, though laudable, are unlikely to bring about a clear and practicable resolution of the problem, given the opposing nature of commercial and political interests and motives. A greater readiness to grant injunctive relief in our courts, based on a greater emphasis on the word "performance" than on the word "bond" and on a fair and practical allocation of the burden of proof, is more likely to succeed."

Bolivinter Oil S.A. v. Chase Manhattan Bank, 1984 WL 281697 (CA (Civ Div)), [1984] 1 Lloyd's Rep. 251, [1984] 1 W.L.R. 392, (1984) 128 S.J.153.:
"Judges who are asked, often at short notice and ex parte, to issue an injunction restraining payment by a bank under an irrevocable letter of credit or performance bond or guarantee should ask whether there is any challenge to the validity of the letter, bond or guarantee itself. If there is not or if the challenge is not substantial, prima facie no injunction should be granted and the bank should be left free to honour its contractual obligation, *although restrictions may well be imposed upon the freedom of the beneficiary to deal with the money after he has received it.* The wholly exceptional case where an injunction may be granted is where it is proved that the bank knows that any demand for payment already made or which may thereafter be made will clearly be fraudulent. But the evidence must be clear, both as to the fact of fraud and as to the bank's knowledge. It would certainly not normally be sufficient that this rests upon the uncorroborated statement of

In *Rionda*, a U.K. case, the court put the (non)-availability of injunction was put into some historical perspective in a summary of the development of the law starting from a leading U.S. case decided in 1941, *Sztejn*:

> "As far as I am aware the fraud exception first makes its appearance on the English stage in Discount Records Ltd. v. Barclays Bank Ltd., [1975] 1 Lloyd's Rep. 444. There Mr. Justice Megarry referred to what Lord Diplock in United City Merchants (Investment) Ltd. v. Royal Bank of Canada at p. 6, col. 2; p. 183G later called the "landmark" American case of Sztejn v. J. Henry Schroeder Banking Corporation, (1941) 31 N.Y.S. 2d 631. Mr. Justice Megarry noted the distinction between the mere allegation of fraud in his case and the establishment of fraud (as a matter of assumption) in *Sztejn*; as well as the assumption in *Sztejn* that the bank was merely an agent for the fraudulent seller. On the facts before Mr. Justice Megarry, however, it appeared as possible as not that the allegedly fraudulent sellers had already been paid by discounting of a draft not yet due, so that (at p. 447) — All that the injunction would do would be to prevent the banks concerned from honouring their obligations. The claim to an injunction appears to have been premised on a breach of contract by the bank, for Mr. Justice Megarry remarked that the plaintiff would in any event have

---

the customer, for irreparable damage can be done to a bank's credit in the relatively brief time which must elapse between the granting of such an injunction and an application by the bank to have it discharged. The appeal will be dismissed.".

Re Guang Xin Enterprises LTD, 21 March 2002, Court of First Instance, CFI, HCMP No 3003 of 2001: "23. On 22 February 2002, the liquidators issued the present summons for a further or better list, and further or alternatively, for specific discovery of 11 classes of documents included in a schedule to the summons, which included the Bank's internal procedures on banking facilities, the Bank's credit files in relation to the Company from 1993, the Bank's internal records regarding approval of the applications for the two letters of credit in question and checking for compliance with them, all correspondence between the Bank and the Company 'regarding acceptance of import documents' and the Bank's letters of credit and document files in relation to the 22 previous letters of credit. The liquidators have alleged that these documents are relevant to the issue whether the Bank had been 'reckless' or 'had turned a blind eye' in making payment under the letters of credit. 24. The Bank has subsequently disclosed the worksheets used by its Bills Checker and Bills Officer which showed that no discrepancies were found. 25. Other than these further documents, the Bank has objected to the application for discovery, first on the ground that it has been made late, but more importantly, on the ground that on the principle of the autonomy of documentary credits, unless fraud was clearly established at the time of payment, it was obliged to pay against the documents and it was entitled to reimbursement. Since the liquidators have not alleged on the evidence that the Bank had knowledge of, or was party to, any fraud at the time it made payment, the documents sought are irrelevant to any issue between the parties and the application for discovery is a 'fishing' exercise."

> his claim against the bank (at p. 448). An injunction was refused. An injunction was again refused in R. D. Harbottle Mercantile Ltd. v. National Westminster Bank Ltd., [1978] Q.B. 146. The only relief claimed against the bank was an injunction. Mr. Justice Kerr doubted the jurisdictional propriety of using such a claim against an English bank in order to bring in as necessary or proper parties an Egyptian bank and the Egyptian sellers (at p. 154). There then followed the passage regarding the "insuperable difficulty", which I have already cited. Mr. Justice Kerr concluded (at pp. 155H-156A) with this: Except possibly in clear cases of fraud of which the banks have notice, the courts will leave the merchants to settle their disputes under the contracts by litigation or arbitration as available to them or stipulated in the contracts. The courts are not concerned with their difficulties to enforce such claims; these are risks which the merchants take. In this case the plaintiffs took the risk of the unconditional wording of the guarantees. The machinery and commitment of banks are on a different level. *They must be allowed to be honoured, free from interference by the courts. Otherwise trust in international commerce could be irreparably damaged.*"[13]

An injunction may be denied even in case of established fraud, on the basis of the "the balance of convenience test", as occurred in *Tukan Timber Ltd.*:

> "In Tukan Timber Ltd. v. Barclays Bank Ltd., [1987] 1 Lloyd's Rep. 171 the plaintiff sought an injunction against its own bank to prevent payment out under a letter of credit. The bank had already twice rejected a demand on the ground of forgery. Mr. Justice Hirst was therefore prepared on the evidence to accept that the beneficiary's fraud to the knowledge of the bank had been sufficiently proved. Even so, he refused an injunction on two grounds. The first was that he did not consider there to be any danger that the bank would pay out at any third attempt by the beneficiary. The second was *on the basis of the balance of convenience considerations* referred to in the Harbottle and United Trading Corporation cases.

---

[13] Czarnikow-Rionda Sugar Trading Inc v Standard Bank London Ltd, Queen's Bench Division (Commercial Court), May 6, 1999.

Mr. Justice Hirst said (at p. 177) that the plaintiff would have "a cast-iron claim .... for breach of contract" against the bank, if it did pay."[14]

As the *Rionda* court explained, established fraud and the status of the (non)-payment to beneficiary may warrant court interference:

"In Themehelp Ltd. v. West, [1996] Q.B. 84, on the other hand, an injunction was granted against the beneficiary of a performance guarantee on the grounds first, that a *clear case of fraud had been sufficiently shown* for pre-trial purposes, and secondly, that the *beneficiary had not yet made a demand under the guarantee*. The majority of the Court, Lord Justice Balcombe and Lord Justice Waite regarded the fact that the defendant was the beneficiary, together with this second ground, as entitling them to step outside the previous cases and their limitations. Thus at p. 97A-B Lord Justice Waite said this: The present case [in the opinion of the learned judge at first instance] was exceptional, in that here the relief was sought at an earlier stage, that is to say a restraint against the beneficiary alone in proceedings to which the guarantor is not a party, *to prevent the exercise by the beneficiary of his power to enforce the guarantee by giving notice of the other party's alleged default* in discharging the liability which was the subject-matter of the guarantee. Before him, as before this court, it was common ground that there is no authority deciding whether an application of that nature is one which the court has power to grant by law, and if so what principles should be applied to it. Then at pp. 98H-99A Lord Justice Waite addressed the minority view of Lord Justice Evans saying - The assumption upon which this argument proceeds is that the autonomy of a performance guarantee is threatened if the beneficiary is placed under a temporary restraint from enforcing it. That is not an assumption, however, which appears to me to have any validity. *In a case where fraud is raised as between the parties to the main transaction at an early stage, before any question of the enforcement of the guarantee*, as between the beneficiary and the guarantor, *has yet arisen at all*, it does not seem to me that the slightest threat is involved to the autonomy of the performance guarantee if the beneficiary is injuncted from enforcing it in proceedings to which the guarantor is not a party."[15]

---

[14] Id.
[15] Id.

and

(ii) *the availability of summary judgment*[16];

What should the substantive independence or other less radical term limiting defenses mean procedurally in case of a dispute? Materially the issue is clear, but do the procedural rules abide by material law?[17] May allegations of fraud, or defenses raised despite the limitations, be heard and examined? Will evidence be admitted? These are crucial issues relating to admissibility of evidence under the "parole evidence" or "extrinsic evidence" rule.[18] Some procedural laws provide a special vehicle for the same purpose: they allow decision-making on the basis of relevant facts only, presuming in case of disputed facts a position most favourable to the party against whom the motion for summary judgment is filed. If under this favorable presumption the claimant (one who moves for the judgment) will prevail, the summary judgment is granted with no need or necessity to delve into more elaborated pleadings or full-fledged trial. The original purpose and effectiveness of the instrument is often based on documents only, and the legitimate interests of the parties in enforcing them "as issued" may be protected. Summary judgment is not available in all jurisdictions but interim protection or other

---

[16] See, e.g., *Grant of Summary judgment and foreign law*, J Int'l Maritime L 2003, 9 (6), 509; *3Com Corp v. Banco Di Brasil*:
"We review *de novo* a district court's entry of summary judgment. *See, e.g., Bogan v. Hodgkins*, 166 F.3d 509, 511 (2d Cir.1999). "Summary judgment is appropriate '[w]here the record taken as a whole could not lead a rational trier of fact to find for the non-moving party.' " *Id.* (quoting *Matsushita Elec. Indus. Co. v. Zenith Radio Corp.*, 475 U.S. 574, 587, 106 S.Ct. 1348, 89 L.Ed.2d 538 (1986)). In determining whether a genuine factual issue exists, courts must resolve all ambiguities and draw all inferences in favor of the non-movant. *See id.* [2] Because subject matter jurisdiction in this case is predicated on diversity of citizenship, we would ordinarily be guided by the choice-of-law principles of the forum state, which in this case is New York, *see Klaxon Co. v. Stentor Elec. Mfg. Co.*, 313 U.S. 487, 496, 61 S.Ct. 1020, 85 L.Ed. 1477 (1941); *Krock v. Lipsay*, 97 F.3d 640, 645 (2d Cir.1996), and in turn these principles might, under some circumstances, direct us to apply the substantive law of a jurisdiction other than New York. However, the parties rely exclusively on New York substantive law, and "where the parties have agreed to the application of the forum law, their consent concludes the choice of law inquiry." *American Fuel Corp. v. Utah Energy Dev. Co.*, 122 F.3d 130, 134 (2d Cir.1997)."

[17] Dolan writes in *The Law of Letters of Credit* at 11-15: "Summary judgment is appropriate only in the absence of factual disputes on matters that are relevant to the ultimate liability question."

[18] Dolan writes in *The Law of Letters of Credit* at 7-42:
"These efforts notwithstanding, there remains the danger that the account party's charge of fraud will result in a full-blown trial in the credit transaction of the ultimate dispute between the account party and the beneficiary—the very result that the independence principle is designed to avoid. In every case there will be delay, and because of the delay the credit's efficiency will suffer."

measures may overlap in protection with the summary judgment proceedings. However, summary judgment proceedings usually lead to a final and enforceable decision, whereas interim measures are temporary subject to other proceedings already pending or yet to be filed. Those other proceedings may then take years to be finalized.

Dolan writes in *The Law of Letters of Credit* on p. 11-25 to 11-26:

> "Courts have often held that disputes arising out of letters of credit present solely legal issues and are ripe for summary judgment. In *Banco De Vizcaya, S.A. v. First National Bank*, the negotiating bank sought payment from the issuer's Chicago correspondent, and the defendant moved for summary judgment. The court, relying on Rule 54(c), held that the defendant's motion was without merit and should be denied. It held further that the plaintiff was entitled to summary judgment even though it had not filed a motion. The court then entered judgment for the plaintiff. Similar impatience with litigation delay in the credit setting is evident in *Bank of Canton, Ltd. v. Republic National Bank*, where the Court of Appeals for the Second Circuit awarded double costs and other damages against a party that appealed from the trial court's award of summary judgment."

(iii) the time required to enforce a right

The time element is an important one. How long does it take to have an enforceable decision or award? Will the decision be enforceable in all the jurisdictions where legal protection may be needed? These issues arose in the *United Trading* case among others:

> "The grant of an injunction would not be upon the basis that they had established fraud, but only on the basis that on the available evidence it was seriously arguable that fraud had occurred. Such a finding does not indicate success in the final action, nor does the failure to obtain an interim injunction predicate failure when the case is ultimately heard. The plaintiffs' position must be contrasted with that of the banks, and in particular with that of Rafidain. If this Court were to grant an injunction which was recognized by the Iraqi Courts, then, if the plaintiffs subsequently failed in the action, the damage would consist of the loss of interest which Rafidain would have to pay to Agromark and injury to its reputation as a bank. The loss of interest on its own could amount to a very large figure — several

CHAPTER VI

million dollars — and the damage to its reputation would be very difficult to quantify. *But the possibility that the Iraqi Courts will not recognize the injunction, with the result that Agromark will obtain a judgment against Rafidain, must be considered as a very real one.* If the positions were reversed and the sale contracts were governed *by English law with an English sole jurisdiction clause,* supported by performance bonds to provide security to the English buyers for the fulfilment in England of the sellers' obligations under the contract, *we can readily appreciate the force of the argument that English Courts would not recognize an interim Iraqi injunction.* (*Cf.* Power Curber International Ltd. v. National Bank of Kuwait SAK, [1981] 2 Lloyd's Rep. 394; [1981] 1 W.L.R. 1233.) If Rafidain suffered such a judgment in the Iraqi Courts, its remedy down the line, if an injunction had been granted, would have to await the outcome of the plaintiffs' claim. *It would inevitably have to run the risk that a different jurisdiction might produce a different result.* Rafidain could thus fall between two stools. As has been made clear at the outset of this judgment, there is no hint of any dishonesty on the part of Rafidain. Why should they, who have merely acted on instructions passed down the line from the plaintiffs' own bank, be put in this perilous situation? There is the further consideration that the plaintiffs, in the light of evidence which has been put before this Court by Rafidain, have been obliged to concede that they have inadequate assets within the jurisdiction to back their cross-undertaking as to damages. Rafidain provided the clearest possible evidence that although the size of the plaintiffs' turnover carried with it the suggestion that they would be undoubtedly good for such an undertaking, on closer examination the reverse was the true position. Mr. Yorke was obliged to concede that any order made in his favour would have to be conditional upon the plaintiffs providing bank or other guarantees within the jurisdiction, and he suggested that the sum of £1,000,000 would be adequate. Even if the potential damages that Rafidain might suffer was limited to the loss of interest on the U.S. $34,000,000, such a sum would be clearly inadequate. Rafidain on the other hand has filed evidence which demonstrates satisfactorily that there is no substance in the suggestion that there is any real risk in the plaintiffs failing to recover as against Rafidain, because of an alleged inability to meet their obligation in U.S. dollars. The difficulties referred to in obtaining confirmation of letters of credit issued by Rafidain has been satisfactorily explained. Thus, even if we had concluded that the plaintiffs had established a good arguable case on the issue of liability and had decided this appeal purely on the issue of the balance of convenience, we would have found against the plaintiffs in the result."[19]

(iv) the respect of the "parole evidence" rule[20]

To what extent may a court allow bringing evidence which is substantively beyond the agreement or instrument or put the proceedings on hold?[21] Presumably most, if not all, legal systems allow courts to exclude or not to admit *irrelevant* evidence. The difficulty in applying this rule in most cases is that irrelevance or relevance may often not be determined until after the evidence has been submitted. In addition, refusal to admit relevant evidence may amount to violation of due process and *ordre public*.[22]

As to substantively independent instruments, this difficulty is considerably less significant. The relevance or irrelevance of evidence may be determined in advance and by not admitting irrelevant evidence the court may protect the expeditious enforceability and commercial value of the instrument as well as the often-referred-to trust in these instruments of international commerce.

---

[19] United Trading Corp v Allied Arab Bank Ltd, CA (Civ Div), July 17, 1984.

[20] Credit Industriel et Commercial v. China Merchants Bank, Case No: 2000/738, Neutral citation number: [2002] EWHC 973, QBD (Comm Ct):
"Before turning to the reactions of the ICC, it is desirable to seek to apply the principles to be derived from these two cases to the present case. Notably, as already observed, there was evidence before the court in both those cases as to how the relevant documents had been produced. In the present case, there is no such evidence. Indeed it might be arguable that such evidence is inadmissible since the standards of care imposed on the bank is to exercise reasonable care to ascertain compliance 'on the face' of the document. It would be a rare case where a checker will have knowledge as to how a document was prepared or any source for extracting information in that regard. Somewhat surprisingly, the relevance of evidence as to how the document was in fact created was not an issue in either decision."

[21] Dolan writes in *The Law of Letters of Credit* at 11-17:
"Although the various jurisdictions state the rule differently, most require the party seeking an injunction to show that he has a substantial probability of success on the merits, that he will suffer irreparable injury without an injunction, or stated differently, that he does not have an adequate remedy at law. It is always difficult for the account party to satisfy these threshold requirements because, if the issuer honors a presentation that is not proper, the account party will have an action at law against the issuer. If there is fraud in the transaction, then the account party will have an action at law against the beneficiary."

[22] Dolan, *The Law of Letters of Credit*, 1990 Cum Supp, at S7-33:
"As a consequence of the Paccar International ruling, the beneficiary of the credit had to await, without the funds, the results of the arbitration between the commercial parties—a result it presumably sought to guard against when it bargained for the letter of credit."

CHAPTER VI

In Unidroit it is given effect as a contractual clause at 2.1.1:[23]

> "A contract in writing which contains a clause indicating that the writing completely embodies the terms on which the parties have agreed cannot be contradicted or supplemented by evidence of prior statements or agreements. However, such statements or agreements may be used to interpret the writing."

If the courts allow the parties to bring evidence on issues which are not directly relevant or relate to the underlying agreement in violation of the substantive independence of an instrument this may turn a credit or on-demand guarantee into a traditional substantive by-dependent one depriving the parties of the very benefits they agree to provide under the facility.[24] In litigation relating to these instruments the courts should pay particular attention to not admitting irrelevant evidence and in case of lengthy proceedings – the procedural system allowing this – require a security or collateral in favour of the defendant to ensure that he may recover fully if the plaintiff fails in his attempts to interfere in the payment process.

---

[23] Official comment:
"If the conclusion of a contract is preceded by more or less extended negotiations, the parties may wish to put their agreement in writing and declare that document to constitute their final agreement. This can be achieved by an appropriately drafted "merger" or "integration" clause (e.g. "This contract contains the entire agreement between the parties"). However, the effect of such a clause is not to deprive prior statements or agreements of any relevance: they may still be used as a means of interpreting the written document. See also Art. 4.3(a). A merger clause of course covers only prior statements or agreements between the parties and does not preclude subsequent informal agreements between them. The parties are, however, free to extend an agreed form even to future amendments. See Art. 2.1.18. This article indirectly confirms the principle set out in Art. 1.2 in the sense that, in the absence of a merger clause, extrinsic evidence supplementing or contradicting a written contract is admissible."

[24] Dolan writes in *The Law of Letters of Credit* at 11-15:
"In *Far Eastern Textile, Ltd. v. City National Bank & Trust Co.*, the credit called for a purchase order signed by Larry Fannin. The beneficiary presented a purchase order signed "Larry Fannin by Paul Thomas" and attempted to introduce evidence that Thomas was authorized to sign Fannin's name. The court held the purchase order to be noncomplying and ruled that the evidence was improper. Finally, in *Board of County Commissioners v. Colorado National Bank*, the issuer of a standby credit sought to introduce evidence to show the intent of the parties in causing the credit to issue and evidence to show that the beneficiary did not sustain any damages as a consequence of the account party's breach of the underlying transaction. The court held the evidence irrelevant."

(v) the availability of specific performance and damages as remedy[25]

Unidroit 7.4.1 reads:

> "Any non-performance gives the aggrieved party a right to damages either exclusively or in conjunction with any other remedies except where the non-performance is excused under these Principles."

Finally the availability of damages and/or specific performance will be discussed although, as a consequence of latest amendments of UCC and commercial realities, the issue is perhaps more theoretical than practical.

VI.3.2 Damages as a remedy

The availability of specific performance may also be an issue although there are cases where *de facto* the same protection may be obtained by action for damages as by action for specific performance.[26] If one is ordered to pay one million Euros in damages or the same amount by specific performance, there is no real difference for the parties except perhaps as to the burden of proof. The right to specific performance entitles one to the amount agreed, with perhaps reduction for loss avoided or mitigated, but an action for damages requires proof of the damage or loss suffered.

In continental Europe specific performance is generally available as the primary remedy. However, in the practice of law, and amid the realities of life, specific performance is seldom a preferred choice of claimants. This is due, mainly, to the time factor. In common law specific performance is an exception and recovery of

---

[25] Unidroit 7.4.2:
"(1) The aggrieved party is entitled to full compensation for harm sustained as a result of the non-performance. Such harm includes both any loss which it suffered and any gain of which it was deprived, taking into account any gain to the aggrieved party resulting from its avoidance of cost or harm. (2) Such harm may be non-pecuniary and includes, for instance, physical suffering or emotional distress."
and Unidroit 7.4.4:
"The non-performing party is liable only for harm which it foresaw or could reasonably have foreseen at the time of the conclusion of the contract as being likely to result from its non-performance."

[26] Anthony Corsi, "Transferable letters of credit: clarification of damages", *Practical Law Companies* (2005), 16(3), 16-17.

damages is the prime remedy sought. Generally, only when money damages do not give sufficient legal redress will specific performance be available.

A key question as to damages is how they are to be measured. In this respect the legal systems do not seem to differ or, if they do, they differ only marginally.[27] In common law the key role is still played by the evergreen rules of the venerable *Hadley v. Baxendale*, supra.

Unidroit 7.4.1.–7.4.4 represents the position in European and many other jurisdictions:

> "7.4.1 *(Right to damages)* Any non-performance gives the aggrieved party a right to damages either exclusively *or in conjunction with any other* remedies except where the non-performance is excused under these Principles.

The remedies available are in many cases cumulative. Even a specific performance action may be complemented by an action for damages.

> 7.4.2 *(Full compensation)* (1) The aggrieved party is entitled to *full compensation* for harm sustained as a result of the non-performance. Such harm includes *both any loss* which it suffered and *any gain of which it was deprived*, taking into account any gain to the aggrieved party resulting from its avoidance of cost or harm. (2) Such harm may be non-pecuniary and includes, for instance, physical suffering or emotional distress.
>
> 7.4.3 *(Certainty of harm)* (1) Compensation is due only for harm, including future harm, that is established with a reasonable degree of certainty. (2) Compensation may be due for the loss of a chance in proportion to the probability of its occurrence. (3) *Where the amount of damages cannot be established with a sufficient degree of certainty, the assessment is at the discretion of the court.*

---

[27] Gerard McMeel, *Contract damages: the interplay of remoteness and loss of a chance*, Lloyd's Maritime and Commercial Law Quarterly, (2004, 1(Feb)), 10-14. For the relevance of foreseeability see also discussion elsewhere in this book on mitigation and contributory negligence.

The *Hadley v. Baxendale* rule is expressed in Unidroit by reiterating the foreseeability test at the time of contracting.

> 7.4.4 (*Foreseeability of harm*) "The non-performing party *is liable only for harm which it foresaw or could reasonably have foreseen at the time of the conclusion of the contract as being likely to result from its non-performance.*"

In *Jackson v. RBS* the rules of *Hadley v. Baxendale* were described in an almost perfect summary as follows:

> "The way in which the Court of Appeal dealt with the case suggests it misunderstood the effect of the rules that were identified in Hadley v Baxendale (1854) 9 Exch 341, 354. They are very familiar to every student of contract law. Most would claim to be able to recite them by heart. But it may be helpful, as background to the discussion that follows, if I were to set out the rules again here: "Where two parties have made a contract which one of them has broken, the damages which the other party ought to receive in respect of such breach of contract should be such as may fairly and reasonably be considered either arising naturally, i e according to the usual course of things, from such breach of contract itself, or such as may reasonably be supposed to have been in the contemplation of both parties, at the time they made the contract, as the probable result of the breach of it." The first rule, prefaced by the word "either", is the rule that applies in this case. It is the ordinary rule. Everyone is taken to know the usual course of things and consequently to know what loss is liable to result from a breach of the contract if things take their usual course. But the way the second rule is expressed, prefaced by the word "or", shows the principle that underlies both limbs. It refers to what was in the contemplation of the parties at the time they made their contract."[28]

> "This point was very clearly explained by Lord Reid in C Czarnikow Ltd v Koufos [1969] 1 AC 350, 383-385. He said at p 385: "I do not think that it was intended that there were to be two rules or that two different standards or tests were to be applied." He continued: "The crucial question is whether, on the information available to the defendant when the contract was made,

---

[28] *Jackson v Royal Bank of Scotland*, [2005] UKHL 37.

he should, or the reasonable man in his position would, have realised that such loss was sufficiently likely to result from the breach of contract to make it proper to hold that the loss flowed naturally from the breach or that loss of that kind should have been within his contemplation." The common ground of the two limbs is what the contract-breaker knew or must be taken to have known, so as to bring the loss within the reasonable contemplation of the parties: see para (4) in the summary by Asquith LJ (giving the judgment of the Court of Appeal) in *Victoria Laundry (Windsor) Ltd v Newman Industries Ltd [1949] 2 KB 528, 539*. (That judgment received a mixed reception from this House in *C Czarnikow v Koufos [1969] 1 AC 350*: Lord Morris of Borth-y-Gest, at p 399, found it "a most valuable analysis" but Lord Upjohn, at p 423, described it as a "colourful interpretation" of Hadley v Baxendale and Lord Reid, at pp 388-90, criticised some aspects of it, but not para (4) of Asquith LJ's summary.) The common ground between the two limbs of the rule has also been noted by Evans LJ (with whom Waite LJ and Sir John May agreed) in *Kpohraror v Woolwich Building Society [1996] 4 All ER 119*. Evans LJ said, at pp 127-128: "I would prefer to hold that the starting point of any application of Hadley v Baxendale is the extent of the shared knowledge of both parties when the contract was made (see generally *Chitty on Contracts*, 27th ed (1994), vol 1, para 26-023, including the possibility that knowledge of the defendant alone is enough). When that is established, it may often be the case that the first and second parts of the rule overlap, or at least that it seems unnecessary to draw a clear line of demarcation between them. This seems to me to be consistent with the commonsense approach suggested by Scarman LJ in *H Parsons (Livestock) Ltd v Uttley Ingham & Co Ltd [1978] QB 791, 813*, and to be applicable here." "[29]

Like Unidroit 7.4.4., the English law leaves the assessment of the amount of damage ultimately to the court. These issues are very difficult indeed both as to the ex post assessment of loss and damage already suffered and in particular as to the loss and damage to be suffered due to loss of profits or premature termination of a business relationship. There seems to be no way to avoid the element of speculation and, on the other hand, one doubt raised in this respect should not result in favoring

---

[29] Id.

the party in breach at the expense of the aggrieved party. *Jackson v. RBS* continues along these lines:

> "In my opinion the cost and delay that would be involved in sending the matter back to the judge are so out of proportion to the amounts involved as to make that course unacceptable. There is on the other hand, much to be said for the broad view. Mr Keith said that the calculations ought to be done properly and that it was desirable to achieve mathematical accuracy. But this expects too much of a calculation that had inevitably to proceed on various broad assumptions. As the judge put it, he had to assess damages on the basis of many possibilities which could not be individually evaluated, some of which might, if they became realities, increase the likelihood of others. I am not persuaded that, if he had appreciated he was making the various mistakes that have now been identified, he would have arrived at a result which was materially different from that which he reached when he made his award. In this situation the second alternative seems to me to be the best way of doing justice between the parties in the disposal of this appeal. I would hold that the award which the judge made, on a reducing basis extending over a four year period, is as good an estimate as can now be made of the effect on Samson's profits of the bank's breach of contract."[30]

UCC 5-111 (official comment):

> "4. Consequential damages for breach of obligations under this article are excluded in the belief that these damages can best be avoided by the beneficiary or the applicant and out of the fear that imposing consequential damages on issuers would raise the cost of the letter of credit to a level that might render it uneconomic. *Fortiori* punitive and exemplary damages are excluded, however, this section does not bar recovery of consequential or even punitive damages for breach of statutory or common law duties arising outside of this article."

---

[30] Id.

VI.3.3 Dynamics Corporation of America v. The Citizens and Southern National Bank and injunction

This case has a simple basic structure, sketched out in Figure VI.1:

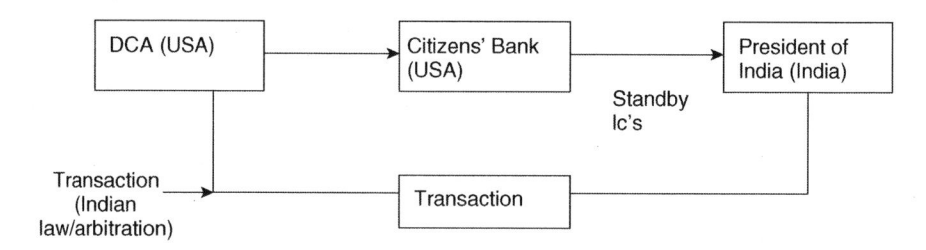

Figure VI.1. Structure of the *Dynamics* Case

The court applied two basic tests when considering whether an injunction could be granted. Because the embargo announced by the United States did not prevent performance under the transaction was the calling of the instrument on this ground fraudulent? The two tests applied under Georgia (U.S.) law, which was applicable, were:

(i) First, did India, the purchaser-defendant, take unconscionable advantage of the situation on a *pro forma* declaration with absolutely no basis in fact?

(ii) Second, a three-part test: (a) the hardships that would result if protection was denied or granted, (b) the probability of ultimate success, and (c) the public interest.

This analysis from 1984 has perhaps not lost all its freshness:

The letters of credit were issued by the defendant bank in favor of the *President of India, intervenor in the proceedings.* The plaintiff had made a contract to supply equipment related to military purposes to India. *The standby letters* of credit were payable to India on demand by sight drafts upon presentation of certain accompanying documents. The document required to be presented was a certificate signed by the President of India in an agreed form stating that Dynamics had failed to carry out certain of its obligations under the main contract. A war broke out between India and Pakistan and *President Nixon announced a partial embargo on military supplies to India,* which covered the equipment to be supplied under the main agreement. *Dynamics filed an action to enjoin India from drawing on the credit*, and India presented a sight draft drawn on the Bank accompanied by the required certificate. The court analyzed the letters of credit as follows: As can be seen, the present case is the reverse of the ordinary. Here, the seller... DCA... rather than the buyer... India... procured the letter of credit from the Bank. It did so not for the purpose of obtaining prompt payment but for the apparent purpose of providing India with additional security as to DCA's performance. Dynamics argued that the certificate presented was fraudulent because it had not failed in its performance under the contract and although the embargo may have prevented India from shipping the equipment from the U.S.A., it had not prevented Dynamics from supplying the equipment FOB its plant in USA as agreed between the parties. India responded naturally that this issue was an issue related to the underlying contract and thus irrelevant as to the letter of credit. *The underlying contract was subject to Indian law and all disputes were to be resolved in arbitration in New Delhi, India*. Dynamics pleaded further that the certificate was not conforming, because it had not been signed by the President of India himself but by someone else for and on behalf of him. *The court applied Georgia law.*

As to the process required to draw on the credit, the court stated: "Since, as India correctly points out, this court has no business making an ultimate adjudication regarding compliance with the provisions of the underlying sales Agreement, India will not be required to prove that DCA 'failed to carry out certain obligations of theirs' under the Agreement in order to get payment from the Bank. Rather, the court views its task in this case as merely guaranteeing that India not be allowed to take *unconscionable advantage* of the situation and run off with the plaintiff's money on *a pro forma declaration which has absolutely no basis in fact*. If it should turn out that there is a legal and factual basis for India's certification, the court will leave plaintiff to its remedy at law."

Although this statement makes sense as a reasonable standard of behavior, it is inconsistent in light of letter of credit law, because it says at the same time that the underlying agreement is and is not relevant. It does not draw a distinction between the purpose of the letter of credit and the purpose of and performance under the main contract, although the statements seem to be made in this meaning. In considering the granting of preliminary injuction to the plaintiff pending the outcome of the prayer for permanent injunction, the court, with reference to *King v. Saddleback Junior College District, 425 F.2nd 426*, took into account "*the relative importance of the rights asserted, the nature of the acts to be enjoined, the relative hardships that would result if the application would be granted or denied, the applicant's probability of ultimate success, and the public interest".*

The *"probability of ultimate success" can be considered to be anything other than a summary proceeding as to the justifiability of the claims based on the main agreement.* It can also be seen as a rough and unsophisticated test of fraud. In this case the plaintiff, had the injunction been denied, would have been obligated to initiate arbitration proceedings in India. Taking into account the enforceability of arbitral awards on the basis of the New York convention, the nature of the defendant as a foreign sovereign ultimately capable of paying its debts and the fact that Dynamics had voluntarily assented to such a method of resolving disputes, it could only with some difficulty be said that to initiate such proceedings would cause severe hardship to Dynamics. On the other hand the hardship caused to the beneficiary in enjoining the payment could perhaps be considered to be even less severe.

The standby letter of credit as a legally trustworthy performance bond can, however, suffer the worst blows in such suits if injunction is granted without proper ground. The proper ground is the fraudulent abuse of the instrument, which can only be determined in the light of the purpose of the instrument itself, not that of the underlying transaction.

The "public interest" seems to enter into letter of credit law in connection with some injunctions. The public interest or public policy is to some extent an alien ingredient in letter of credit law, the influence of which may sometimes be of benefit, but more often harmful or constituting a threat to the smooth flow of transactions in the realm governed by lex mercatoria.

VI.3.4 United Technologies Corporation v. Citibank N.A. and the availability of injunction

The *United Technologies* case is a good introduction to actions filed in connection with the Iranian revolution to stop payment under standby letters of credit. The claimant, a US corporation, attempted to enjoin the payment under a "blended facility" where the actual performance bond was issued to *Telecommunication Company of Iran* (TCI) as beneficiary by the Iranian banks backed up by the letters of credit issued by Citibank in the banks' favor. The case also deals with the applicable law: The American parties (UTI and Citibank) had agreed that New York law applied.

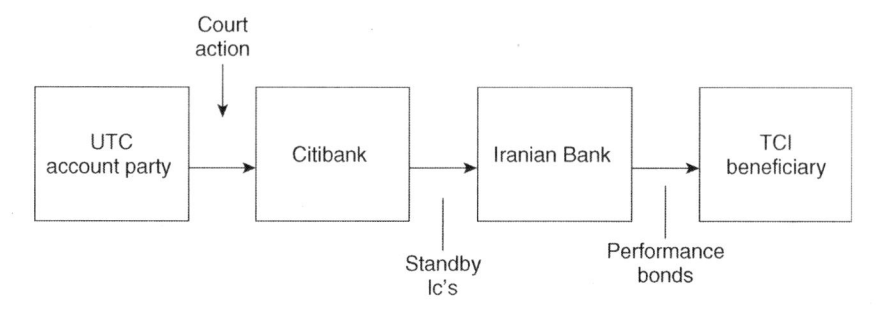

Figure VI.2 Unified Case Structure for *United Technologies*

This analysis of the case and the structure of the facility was given in the first edition of this book, in 1985:

This was an action by the customer to enjoin payment on letters of credit issued by Citibank in favor of Iranians' Bank, a codefendant with Citibank. *The letters of credit were issued to induce Iranians' Bank to issue performance bonds in favor of Telecommunication Company of Iran* (TCI). The performance bonds were required as a security to guarantee the proper carrying out of the obligations undertaken by United towards TCI under certain supply contracts. *The two Iranian codefendants had not been summoned. The parties were in agreement that New York law would govern the issues.* One could hardly have expected them to argue for the application of Iranian law. The court stated that "unlike the usual pattern, the seller [United] procured the issuance of the letter of credit as a guarantee of its contractual performance". The letter of credit issued by Citibank was never advised or confirmed by Iranians' Bank. The performance bonds issued by Iranians' Bank in favor of TCI were separate guarantees backed or secured by letters of credit. No relationship was established between TCI and Citibank and TCI had no claim or right directly against Citibank. A contractual relationship between United, a U.S. corporation, and Citibank, another U.S. corporation, was established as well as a contract between the two banks. *The UCP was not applicable on the letters of credit.* It seems that a three-party customer contract was not created or intended to be created between the customer, the issuing bank, and the issuer of the bonds (Iranians' Bank) nor a three-party contract between the banks and TCI. *The relationship between United and Citibank, a contract between U.S. parties, was most probably to be governed by New York law.* The letter of credit between Citibank and Iranians' Bank is more problematic. The Iranians' Bank as a beneficiary had the right to draw on the letter of credit by notifying Citibank by cable. There was no traditional tender of the documents. The place of receipt of the cable is, however, "analogous" with the place of tender. This was New York, which possibly was also the place of payment. On one hand, one might be strongly tempted to consider New York law applicable to the customer-issuing bank as well to the issuing bank-beneficiary relationship (the beneficiary in this case being the correspondent on mentioned grounds).

On the other hand, one could argue that the intention of all the parties involved, and the purpose of the whole transaction, was the issuance of the bonds by the Iranians' Bank in Iraq, which was the ultimate place of performance and that Iranian law definitely governed the bonds issued by the Iranians' Bank in Iran in favor of TCI. One should, however, draw a clear distinction between letters of credit used as guarantees and letters of credit used as a means or method of payment under the sales contract. *In standby-letter or guarantee arrangements the customer does not request or authorize the issuing bank to issue the letter of credit. The issuing bank is only requested to engage the intermediary bank to issue the "bonds" and not to advise or confirm the credit.* Here lies the main difference between the two arrangements. The issuing bank is actually requested to act as a security or collateral towards the issuer of the final bonds and not to act as a party to the contract with the beneficiary. *The whole transaction is intended to function as collateral and not as substitute performance or subcontract of the customer.* The banks only "stand by", selling their reputation and lending their creditworthiness as liquid collateral to support a client's financial or commercial transactions.

In the present case, Citibank was acting only in its own name. Citibank and Iranians' Bank did not jointly and severally undertake to make the payment to the TCI or the customer. The contract between Citibank and Iranians' Bank was actually a guarantee. The bonds issued were separate from the underlying letter of credit. No contract between the "issuer" and TCI was formed. In the ordinary course of things no "tender" of documents would have been made and no examination would have been carried out by the banks. The making and demanding of payment was extraordinary and exceptional and was not specifically intended and contemplated by the parties. *The letter of credit operated only as a kind of collateral or liquid assets.* The letter of credit was meant and was established as a guarantee and not as a means of making the payment. A guarantee is presumably governed either by the place of anticipated performance or by the law of the guarantor's place of business. *Since no multi-party relationships were, or were meant to be, established, the doctrine of separateness and independence of these three contracts should be maintained in material respects and also for the purpose of choice of law.* No facts beyond the actual scope of each separate contract should be taken into account when determining the applicable law.

The action by United to enjoin payments under the letters of credit seems, however, to cross the contractual borderlines defined above. If the doctrine of strict separateness and independence of these contracts was maintained, United would not be a party to the contract and would have no status or right to make such a demand against Iranians. UCC §5-114(2), however, expressly allows such an action. The customer's right to an injunction when there is fraud in the transaction originated in the area of traditional letters of credit, but seems to find its application in the area of letter of credit "guarantees" as well. *The availability of the remedy of injunction is based on public policy reasons and there seems no reason to limit its application to traditional letters of credit.* As a policy, the prevention of fraud is not more applicable to commercial letters of credit than to standby credits. Under the present facts, it would seem, however, less justifiable to allow the customer to try to enjoin the Iranians' Bank from making the payments. Under irrevocable and confirmed commercial letters of credit, the basic presumption, where the UCP is applicable, should be in favor of a three–party contract between the customer, the issuing bank, and the intermediary bank. In such circumstances the injunction should be available, without doubt, both with regard to payment by the issuing bank as well as the intermediary bank. Under the UCP, direct support for allowing such action cannot be found. *The guarantee undertakings could, however, be regarded as strictly separate and independent contracts not allowing action by the customer against the "intermediary" issuer* of the guarantees. One can, however, argue, invoking established letter of credit law, that there is an implied condition in the customer–issuing bank relationship that no payment will be made if there is fraud in the transaction. The action to enjoin payment would clearly be within the scope of the contract concluded between the customer and the issuing bank. It is evident that if such a condition is implied in letters of credit in customer–bank relationships, the same implied condition in favor of the customer as a third party can be implied in the beneficiary–bank contracts. The word transaction would include the whole arrangement of issuing the performance bonds. This interpretation is both logical and consistent with the conclusions of this work. The implied condition can be regarded as implied on the force of lex mercatoria.

CHAPTER VI

VI.3.5 Remedies under the UCC

It would seem that the liability under letters of credit is primarily for the face amount thereof. There is, however, a general duty to mitigate. On the other hand the liability could be extended to special damages or positive contract interest where the circumstances justify it in accordance with *Hadley v. Baxendale*. If anticipatory breach is in issue, it would seem that civil law would allow an action for the face amount and common law would allow only an action for damages. The common law should, however, allow specific performance to maintain trust in the instrument and to conform to the requirements of uniformity in this field. Any acceptable reason could hardly be presented to deny the availability of such action.

The UCC has recognized the problem of the "right remedy" and expressly allows action for specific performance. As to damages, under the UCC recovery is limited. Recovery does not extend to consequential damages except in cases of breach of common law or statutory duties, in which cases even punitive damages may be recovered. On the other hand, the beneficiary's duty to mitigate has been abolished altogether but damage avoided may reduce recovery. Where damage avoided does reduce recovery, the defendant carries the burden of proof.

Also attorney's fees are recoverable even in an action for injunctive relief. Sometimes it may be somewhat unclear who prevailed, but this issue has quite rightly been left to the discretion of the courts. UCC 5-111 (Official Comment) 6:

> "The *court must award attorney's fees to the prevailing party*, whether that party is an applicant, a beneficiary, an issuer, a nominated person, or adviser. Since the issuer may be entitled to recover its legal fees and costs from the applicant *under the reimbursement agreement*, allowing the issuer to recover those fees from a losing beneficiary may also protect the applicant against undeserved losses. *The party entitled to attorneys' fees has been described as the "prevailing party."* Sometimes it will be unclear which party "prevailed," for example, where there are multiple issues and one party wins on some and the other party wins on others. *Determining which is the prevailing party is in the discretion of the court.* Subsection (e) authorizes attorney's fees in all actions where a remedy is sought "under this article." *It applies even when the remedy might be* an injunction under Section 5-109 or when the claimed remedy is otherwise outside of Section 5-111 Neither an issuer nor a confirmer should be treated as a "losing" party when an

REFUSAL, DISHONOUR, AND REMEDIES

injunction is granted to the applicant over the objection of the issuer or confirmer; accordingly neither should be liable for lees and expenses in that case. *"Expenses of litigation" is intended to be broader than "costs."* For example, expense of litigation would include travel expenses of witnesses, fees for expert witnesses, and expenses associated with taking depositions."

Under UCC, damages may be liquidated, but the formula must be reasonable reflecting the general hostility to undertakings with no or only nominal liability under the terms thereof.

UCC 5-111:

"(a) If an issuer wrongfully dishonors or repudiates its obligation to pay money under a letter of credit before presentation, the beneficiary, successor, or nominated person presenting on its own behalf may recover from the issuer *the amount that is the subject of the dishonor or repudiation*. If the issuer's obligation under the letter of credit is not for the payment of money, the claimant may obtain *specific performance* or, at the claimant's election recover an amount equal to the value of performance from the issuer. In either case, the claimant may also recover incidental *but not consequential damages. The claimant is not obligated to take action to avoid damages that might be due from the issuer under this subsection. If, although not obligated to do so*, the claimant avoids damages, the claimant's recovery from the issuer must be reduced by the amount of damages avoided. *The issuer has the burden of proving the amount of damages avoided*. In the case of repudiation the claimant need not present any document. (b) If an issuer wrongfully dishonors a draft or demand presented under a letter of credit or honors a draft or demand in breach of its obligation to the applicant, the applicant may recover damages resulting from the breach, including incidental but not consequential damages, *less any amount saved as a result of the breach*. (c) If an adviser or nominated person other than a confirmer breaches an obligation under this article or an issuer breaches an obligation not covered in subsection (a) or (b) of this section, a person to whom the obligation is owed may recover damages resulting from the breach, including incidental but *not consequential damages*, less any amount saved as a result of the breach. To the extent of the confirmation, a confirmer has the liability of an issuer specified in this subsection and subsections (a) and (b) of this section. (d) An issuer, nominated person, or adviser who is found liable under subsection (a), (b) or (c) of this section *shall pay interest* on the amount owed thereunder from the date of wrongful dishonor or other appropriate date. (e) *Damages that would otherwise be payable by a party for breach of all obligation under this article may be liquidated by agreement or undertaking, but only in an amount or by a formula that is reasonable in light of the harm anticipated."*

VI.3.6 Equitable relief

Equity represents another arm of justice, or another parallel legal system, which is resorted to when the ordinary remedies do not give protection to meet the criteria of justice or produce harsh or even shocking end results.[31] Equity under some legal systems represents a formal, acknowledged, traditional and distinguished part of the powers of the court to administer justice whereas in many continental European systems equity has been a general but vague principle of justice incorporated into the general principles of law and not always expressly acknowledged in the statutory law. In the 1900s it was introduced to many codes in statutory form as a general clause giving wide-reaching powers to courts to interfere in unreasonable contracts in the interests of equity. It was more and more often resorted to in practice and in theory as the ultimate instrument or vehicle to strike the proper balance when the "mechanical" application of law as such produced an unacceptable outcome. Equity and equitable relief should be conservatively used.

The *United Trading* case

In this case the plaintiff sought relief on the basis of equity against alleged fraudulent or coercive practices although he had knowingly and repeatedly exposed himself to the same practices and risks complained of in the action. The "acceptance" of these practices – as commented on by the court – should have been taken into account as an increased risk in pricing. The issues concern the effects of waivers in commercial transactions. The action was shadowed by concealment of material facts, which was presumed, however, to have been unintentional. The court said:

> "There is, however, a further matter which is relevant to the exercise of our jurisdiction to give equitable relief. It is the plaintiffs' own case that,

---

[31] See Dolan in *The Law of Letters of Credit* at 11-16 – 11-17.

since 1980, they have been subjected to fraud, duress and blackmail by Agromark. Every time a bond came up for renewal there was a telex requiring the plaintiffs either to renew the bond or face the bond being called in. Such a call, according to the plaintiffs, would be a wholly fraudulent one because Agromark knew that the contracts in respect of which the performance bonds had been provided had been fully performed. Thus the plaintiffs were, on their own account, being threatened with fraudulent claims. The plaintiffs took a commercial risk that the performance bonds might well be called in dishonestly by Agromark. When the plaintiffs gave the banks instructions to extend the time limits of the performance bonds, the plaintiffs, as was conceded, intended to claim that any call on the performance bonds during such extended period or periods would be fraudulent. Needless to say, the plaintiffs did not disclose their intentions to the bank. Moreover, on at least five occasions since this course of conduct by Agromark, the plaintiffs involved the banks in the following new transactions: (1) A performance bond supporting the billion egg contract in the sum of U.S. $8.8 million; (2) a performance bond in June, 1981, in the sum of U.S. $3.1 million, increased to $4.6 million; (3) a performance bond in February, 1982, in the sum of U.S. $950,000; (4) a performance bond in March, 1984, in the sum of U.S. $2.3 million involving Fidelity; (5) a further performance bond, also in March, 1984, in the sum of U.S. $305,000. If, as is apparent, the plaintiffs were prepared to run the obvious risks, then they should have provided for those risks in the contract prices. *We do not consider that it would be equitable that they should use the banks' service in the full knowledge of what the risk was, but without disclosing that risk to the banks, and then seek the equitable relief of an interim injunction against those banks when the risk did not pay off.* We have also considered Mr. Strauss's submission that the plaintiffs in their ex parte application to the Court failed in their obligation to make the fullest disclosure of all material facts within their knowledge. Mr. Strauss in particular relied upon the two documents E210 and E212 to which we have made some detailed reference. *We take the view, however, that there was no intentional suppression by the plaintiffs of any material* — one of their main problems, enhanced by Mr. Samrai's inability to speak Arabic, was to appreciate the potential significance of some of the material which was genuinely thought unequivocally to support the plaintiffs' case. There were also undoubtedly problems arising out of the urgency with which the evidence had to be produced. We have inevitably concentrated in giving this judgment on what we have described as the main action. What we have said in that regard makes it clear that the plaintiffs must equally fail in their application for a Mareva injunction."[32]

VI.3.7 Ex parte temporary restraining orders or other protective measures

What kind of interim measures may be available depends primarily on the procedural law of *lex fori* but may also be supplemented by the applicable material law or the agreement. The borderline between procedural law and material law is not clear when available remedies are analyzed. For instance, is fraud a procedural or a material issue or both? Is proof of fraud sufficient or does the plaintiff have to demonstrate in addition to this a favorable balance of drawbacks and benefits for granting an injunction? Is a collateral a must?

Interim or other procedural measures may also be available *ex parte*. In order to enforce *ex parte* other interim measures, due process may (does?) require submission of sufficient security or collateral by the claimant to protect the defendant's interests. Multiple venues may be available allowing forum shopping or even parallel actions in several courts. Such measures, even when granted, do not necessarily constitute *res judicata* or *lis pendens* which could bar bringing other identical or similar actions in other courts or arbitration. Nor does rejection necessarily bar the filing of another application or petition with the same court.

A special kind of measure is *the attachment of the proceeds* of the instrument after due tender and immediately after or in connection with payment to the beneficiary or his assignee.[33] The interests of assignees and the claimant may then

---

[32] United Trading Corp v. Allied Arab Bank Ltd, Court of Appeal, CA (Civ Div), July 17, 1984.
[33] Dolan writes in *The Law of Letters of Credit* at 7-14:
"While these cases appear to resolve the attachment issue on procedural points, all of them reflect the fundamental point that the letter of credit is independent of the underlying contract. If the account party were able to attach the credit or its proceeds in furtherance of rights growing out of the underlying transaction, the independence of the credit would suffer. The issue here is no different from the question that arises when the account party resorts to equitable relief for fraud. Thus, the courts are correct in resisting these attempts to weaken the independence of the credit."
Wunnicke, Wunnicke and Turner at 142-143:
"Traditionally, *attachment* is a seizure by legal process of the property of a debtor. *Garnishment* is a species of attachment whereby property of a debtor held by a third party may be made subject

collide. English law recognizes also the so-called *Mareva injunction*, which, e.g., prohibits or enjoins moving assets outside the jurisdiction.

Interim protection may be available in arbitration, too. Such a clause in the arbitration rules does not necessarily bar access to the same kind of protection in courts of law ("double or multiple jurisdiction"). In arbitration, the instruments and measures available may be even more flexible depending on the rules and on the discretion of the panel, but in general expeditious *ex parte* orders may be difficult to obtain in arbitration except perhaps with the support of a declaratory order by a court backed up with a fully pledged security covering liability to loss or damage to the defendant.

Use of an Injunction: The *Rionda* case

In *Rionda*, a *Mareva* injunction was granted in *ex parte* proceedings to restrain disposal of funds and enjoining making of claims under the letters of credit for the purposes of rescission (cancellation) of the underlying transaction or alternatively to restrain an action for damages. The action was backed up by affidavits and a damages undertaking, without security. The contents of the affidavits concealed the risk of insolvency of the claimants. Mitigation of damage was resorted to. The *Rionda* court said:

> "On July 31, 1998, a few days before the maturity date of Aug. 3, 1998 under L/Cs 213 and 221 and more comfortably before the maturity date of Nov. 17, 1998 under L/C 260, *Rionda obtained two ex parte orders* from Mr. Justice Tuckey. One was an order restraining Standard from paying out under the three letters of credit. *The other was a world-wide Mareva injunction* restraining the second to eighth defendants to these proceedings, namely Grupo Dine and other members of the Dine Group such as in particular Vivalet and USR, *from disposing of or dealing with their assets up to a value of U.S.$50 m.* and, it is to be noted, *from seeking payment out under*

---

to payment of a creditor's claim. . . . Since the landmark decision of the United States Supreme Court in *Harris v. Balk*, the well-settled rule is that a contract may give rise to a debt so as to be subject to an attachment. In letter of credit context, the applicant may seek to attach the issuer's obligation to pay the beneficiary."

CHAPTER VI

the three letters of credit. BCGe and UEB were not made defendants to Rionda's action, however, and no relief was claimed against them.

Those orders were obtained on the basis of *an affidavit* of Mr. Roger Spencer of Rionda's solicitors and of draft affidavits from Mr. Matthew Scott, Rionda's senior vice president and from Mr. Miguel Barg, Rionda's executive vice president. Those draft affidavits were finally sworn a month later on Aug. 31, 1998. *Rionda gave an undertaking in damages* in the usual way, save that it was expressed to be in favour of third parties as well as the defendants. Mr. Justice Tuckey *did not require any security to be provided for that undertaking.* In this connection Mr. Spencer stated (in par. 29 of his affidavit) that Rionda is . . . . an established and active trading house and the financing undertaken in the circumstances of this case demonstrate[s] their creditworthiness with several major banks. He then referred to the accounts for the year ending Sept. 30, 1997 for both Rionda and its major U.K. based subsidiary, saying that these accounts showed Rionda's ability to comply with its undertaking in damages. Of course those accounts would not have dealt with the transactions which are the subject matter of these proceedings, but *there was nothing in the rest of the affidavit material put before the Court to suggest that the troubles over such transactions might have had a devastating or even material effect on Rionda's ability to respond to its undertaking if it had to.* In Rionda's points of claim, endorsed on the writ issued on the same day as Mr. Justice Tuckey made his orders, Rionda pleaded that it had entered into the 003 and 004 contracts on June 12, 1997 and into the 005 contract on Aug. 7, 1997, in each case as financial intermediary, *on the basis of fraudulent misrepresentations* on the part of the Dine Group inter alia regarding the cane and alcohol pledges. In the prayer, for the first time, *rescission (or damages in lieu)* of the 003/005 contracts was claimed - albeit par. 20(iv) of the pleading also stated, as I have mentioned above, that Rionda had intervened in reasonable *mitigation* of its loss to sell the alcohol under contracts 003 and 004. The cause of action pleaded against Standard (see pars. 18 and 28) was an implied term as follows: It was a term of the contract between [Rionda] and [Standard] for the opening of the letters of credit that [Standard] would not pay out under the letters of credit if they became aware that the financing they were intended to provide to the Dine Defendants *was induced by the fraud* of the Dine Defendants.

Rionda accepted before me that the term there pleaded was alleged as an implied term ("the implied term") and was intended to reflect the fraud exception. It may be noted that there is no reference in the pleaded formulation to the need for the fraud to be either clear or established, nor as to the quality of the bank's awareness."[34]

VI.3.8 Declaratory relief

Although declaratory relief would seem to have no or very limited significance, it may play a role as a remedy.[35] A declaration by a court cannot be enforced to stop payment or fraudulent action, but it may cause a party about to make payment, accept a tender or reimburse a party under the facility to reconsider his own position and the interests of justice and perhaps persuade him to refrain from doing so even in a country where any other order of the court having given the declaration could not be enforced, all this provided, that the respect for the court in question is well-founded due to its impeccable reputation and the motivations of the declaration given are convincing, leaving no or very little doubt as to its justification. Such a declaration may prove its value in subsequent proceedings between the same parties or other parties in related actions in courts of law or in resulting arbitration.

The account party or another party may seek such a declaration from the court. The declaration may establish that a payment or a tender would be fraudulent or that the claim or the tender does not meet the conditions precedent of the facility. A mere declaration does not carry very far, perhaps only half way at the best, but it may be useful even as such, as discussed above. In most cases a declaration combined with some other remedies may effectively cover more ground and eliminate or reduce abuse or fraudulent practices.

Declaratory relief and the *Harbottle* case

In the famous *Harbottle* case, declaratory relief was sought and used in combination with other relief. The *ex parte* action was innovated, but failed. As the court explained:

---

[34] Czarnikow-Rionda Sugar Trading Inc v Standard Bank London Ltd, Queen's Bench Division (Commercial Court), May 6, 1999.

[35] Dolan writes in *The Law of Letters of Credit* at 11-30 – 11-31:
"In a few cases, it has been the issuer itself that initiates litigation through a declaratory judgment action, and sometimes the account party will fortify his injunction efforts with attachment proceedings."

"The English plaintiffs entered into three contracts of sale with Egyptian buyers and each contract provided that the plaintiffs would establish a guarantee confirmed by a bank in favour of the buyers. The terms of the guarantees were very wide and the amounts secured were payable on the buyers' demand. *They were established with Egyptian banks and confirmed by* the defendant English bank ("the bank") at which the plaintiffs had an account. The buyers demanded payment under the guarantees. The plaintiffs, who contended that the buyers had no justification for demanding payment, brought three actions against the bank and, in each action, the other defendants were the relevant Egyptian bank and buyers. *They sought a declaration against each defendant that the buyers had no right to draw on the guarantees and injunctions restraining all the defendant banks from making, and all the buyers from demanding, payment under the guarantees.* The plaintiffs applied ex parte for, and were granted, interlocutory injunctions against each defendant. The Egyptian defendants did not enter an appearance and took no part in the subsequent proceedings."[36]

VI.3.9 Various types of injunctions

Once the facility is in place and the beneficiary may pull the trigger, alarming information or facts may emerge which may cause the account party (or an issuing, confirming or paying bank) to consider legal action to interfere with the payment mechanism constituted by the facility. In most cases this relates to suspected or apparent fraud or abuse, or threat of bankruptcy of a party in the facility, exposing another party to risk of losing *de facto* its right to reimbursement or recovery. The legal action to be considered in many cases is stopping the payment or "freezing" of the facility by way of injunction or other interim measures. There are various ways and parts of the facility which may be targeted for such an action.

(i) In most common cases the plaintiff may seek legal protection by having the court enjoin a bank from paying the beneficiary. This is an action taken by the account party (or rarely by his agent or bank). The banks

---

[36] R. D. Harbottle (Mercantile) Ltd. v. National Westminster Bank Ltd, 1977 WL 59355 (QBD), [1978] Q.B. 146, [1977] 2 All E.R. 862, [1977] 3 W.L.R. 752, (1977) 121 S.J. 745.

are often unwilling to take action. They simply refuse to pay, should the circumstances warrant this.

(ii) Another alternative is to enjoin the beneficiary from submitting a tender or making a claim. This injunction is more innovative, hitting perhaps more accurately the "roots of evil".

(iii) A third variation of injunction is an order by the court to the issuing or confirming bank to give immediate notice to the account party in the event of tender or claim. This notice may set off an alarm and enable the plaintiff to seek interim protection or take such protective measures as, e.g., attachment of the funds.

The court speaks on injunctions

The *Harbottle* case deals with *ex parte* orders and the discretionary powers of the court to grant them and to release them even in the absence of the defendant. It distinguishes in a remarkable way "the effects doctrine", i.e., the limits of the enforceability of its order or other ruling. It further points out that the effects of the order when given and where enforceable extend to third parties, who may be guilty of contempt of court if they assist the party against whom it was issued, i.e., the effects have an "erga omnes" dimension not limited to the "inter partes" relationship only, but, however, only within those jurisdictions where legally enforceable. The reader will, besides the brilliant legal analysis, be enlightened and delighted by the reiteration of the fundamental role of courts of law and the bold statement of upholding the reputation of the courts. The court said:

> "Looking at this submission from the point of view of principle I find it entirely unacceptable. Having heard full argument, and having had the opportunity of considering the whole position for the first time inter partes, I feel bound to say that I doubt whether I should ever have granted any of these injunctions in the first place, even ex parte. If the bank had opposed their continuation I should have discharged them. I have already given my reasons for this conclusion in relation to the bank. As regards the Egyptian defendants there is the additional consideration that they are outside the jurisdiction, that their procedural connection with these actions is tenuous and unconvincing, and that the injunctions have no legal force in Egypt. Why then should this court not have power to discharge all the injunctions, now that these actions are again before it? *Injunctions, as here, are*

frequently granted ex parte on the basis of hurried applications against persons before they have any notice of the application. They are not bound to enter an appearance when they are served, but they would be guilty of a contempt of court if they disobey the injunction. When the matter then comes back before the court to continue the order and can be fully considered and at greater leisure, why should the court not have inherent jurisdiction to discharge its prior discretionary order if it appears to it right to do so, even though the persons concerned have not entered an appearance and therefore do not themselves apply for the discharge of the injunction? Why should the court be bound to leave its discretionary order in force when it considers that the order should not have been made, or should not have been continued, and when disobedience to the order is a contempt of court? I cannot believe that this can be right. *Moreover, it is settled law that an injunction may be enforced against third parties if, with knowledge of its existence, they assist the party against whom it has been issued to contravene it.* Conversely, if a third party is adversely affected by the terms of an injunction, our procedure permits him to apply to have it discharged: see Bourbaud v. Bourbaud (1864) 10 L.T. 781. All this shows the flexibility of the procedure concerning these important orders. Why must the Egyptian defendants come to this court and either apply to have the service upon them set aside, with the necessary consequence that the injunctions would be lifted if their application succeeds, or submit to the jurisdiction and apply for their discharge? *I cannot see the slightest reason why the maintenance of inappropriate injunctions should be dependent on the acts of the Egyptian defendants, particularly when the injunctions have no legal force in their country. On the contrary, to maintain them in such circumstances would tend to lower the reputation of our courts."*[37]

"I ought to deal with some of the matters which Mr. Hapgood, Q.C. suggests that TIB knew as at the time when they were about to pay, and from which he suggests inferences should have been drawn. (i) It is alleged that TIB knew that the advance payment was a pre-condition to the obligation of CSC to perform. The answer to that is that TIB did not know that, but even if it did, the fact that CSC was performing indicated that there may have been some variation or waiver as between CSC and ETA. (ii) It is alleged that TIB knew of the financial difficulties of ETA and its difficulties

---

[37] Id.

in making advance payments. There is no doubt that TIB did know that ETA had cashflow problems as a result of non-payment by the Libyan authorities. That led to problems in making the advance payments. That again is no answer to the possibility that CSC were still bound to perform by virtue of some waiver or variation. (iii) It is asserted that ETA had assumed onerous payment obligations when it did not have the funds to discharge those obligations. Again, if that is an assertion of dishonesty from the outset, it is far from clear that ETA did not expect to be able to pay provided funds could be obtained from the Libyan authorities. (iv) Reliance is placed on ETA's serious financial position. It is obvious that ETA were having financial difficulties. Certain promissory notes valued at about U.S.$6868 were dishonoured. They had to borrow from BCCI and it may well be that they could earmark less to materials from that loan than they had originally envisaged. That loan had to be repaid. But, TIB could not be certain as to where the blame lay for the problems that ETA was suffering. ETA had employed CSC to provide the labour force; the labour force had apparently commenced and the assertion of ETA was that that labour force had not got on with the contract as CSC had promised. (v) Reliance is also placed on the fact that TIB knew that ETA had not dealt with any of the specific facts and matters alleged by CSC i.e., the lack of funding, the failure to supply materials etc., and had ETA's mere assertion of a total failure to start for some 11 months. As I have indicated, the wording of performance bonds, and in particular the wording in this case, demonstrates that it is not for a bank to get into those sort of details. If the fraud exception is to apply, the bank must have irrefutable evidence that the claimant is dishonest so that it can establish that dishonesty if it were sued by the beneficiary. If one contemplates TIB being sued by ETA and TIB putting up a defence that inferences should be drawn from the above facts so as to establish ETA's fraud, one can immediately see the problems that a bank such as TIB would have had.

Conclusion

In my view this case is very similar to those cases in which applications for interlocutory injunctions have failed. In this case, BOC itself made only the faintest suggestion that a fraud was being committed and was not prepared to apply for an injunction to so assert. Even now I am uncertain in my own mind that it would be right to draw the inference that ETA were acting dishonestly. That being so, on the material that was before TIB, I am quite clear that they would not have so concluded and that thus they were bound to pay and are entitled to succeed under their counter-guarantees."[38]

VI.3.10 Unjust enrichment

Unjust enrichment is a doctrine acknowledged in many jurisdictions, but its exact contents and theories may vary and they tend to be vague.[39] The purpose is often to prevent unearned windfall profits at the expense of another party's mistake or misfortune.[40] The doctrine has limited use in general and in particular in the field of these instruments, but it may well be applicable in circumstances where the absence of privity of contract (e.g., in the event of bankruptcy of a party to the facility) may bar another action of recovery or if the outcome would otherwise be manifestly wrong (unjust).[41]

Unjust enrichment in the *Glencore* case

This case dealt *inter alia* with unjust enrichment and the right to summary judgment.

> "2. *Glencore's Unjust Enrichment Claim*. SBS also argues that it is entitled to summary judgment on Glencore's third claim that SBS was "unjustly enriched" by having received from SSIL sufficient funds to satisfy SBS's obligations to Glencore under either the L/C or a collection order. (Compl. 55-57). To establish a claim for unjust enrichment, Glencore must demonstrate

---

[38] *Turkiye Is Bankasi v. Bank of China*, Queen's Bench Division (Commercial Court), Feb. 8, 1996.

[39] Troy L. Harris, *Good Faith, Suretyship and the IUS Commune*, 53 Mercer L Rev 581 (Winter 2002): "Whereas the theoretical basis of the duty of reimbursement is implied contract, the theoretical basis of the duty of restitution is unjust enrichment."

[40] Russell McVeagh McKenzie, *New Zealand: Letters of Credit – Liability*, Case Comment, J Int'l Banking L & Reg 18(11), N123, (2003):
"Interestingly, the Judge comments that unjust enrichment may be stated as a cause of action in its own right, if it is related to an accepted cause of action and meets certain criteria. Secondly, the High Court held that ASB Bank could recover $200,000 from Mr. Davidson personally for breach of a warranty in ASB Bank's general terms and conditions that he had power to enter into all documents."

[41] Ellinger comments:
"Issues respecting restitution of an amount paid by error were dealt with by Gavin Kealey Q.C., sitting as judge of the Commercial Court of the Queen's Bench Division in Gulf International Bank BSC v Albaraka Islamic Bank."

that (1) SBS was enriched at Glencore's expense; and (2) the circumstances show that SBS's enrichment was unjust. *See Reprosystem B.V. v. SCM Corp., 727 F.2d 257, 263 (2d Cir.), cert. denied, 469 U.S. 828, 105 S.Ct. 110, 83 L.Ed.2d 54 (1984).* The Court finds that there are disputed issues of material fact precluding the granting of summary judgment on this claim. Determining whether the circumstances under which SBS retained funds received from SSIL show that SBS' retention of the funds was unjust is inextricably linked to the Court's determination of the parties' rights under either L/C law or collection rules. Therefore, summary judgment on the claim at this juncture would be inappropriate. *See Dorlexa Co. v. Barclay's American Business Credit, Inc.*, No. 90 Civ. 6450(LBS), *1992 WL 75133, at * 8 (S.D.N.Y. Mar.30, 1992)* (denying summary judgment on unjust enrichment claim on grounds that resolution of claim depended on interpretation of contract terms which court found to be capable of two reasonable interpretations)."[42]

The *Niru* court speaks on unjust enrichment.

This case deals, among other things, with the right of restitution and unjust enrichment. Enrichment may take the form of the unjustly enriched party being released from its obligation under the facility.

> "As the judge observed in paragraph 28 of his judgment, this argument depends, at least in part, on the proposition that CAI continued to be unjustly enriched as a result of receiving the funds transferred to it by Bank Sepah. Mr Bloch resisted the submission on several bases but the judge ultimately accepted Miss Andrews' submissions after considering a number of authorities, notably *Banque Financière de la Cité v Parc (Battersea) Ltd [1999] 1 AC 221*. He expressed his conclusions in this way in paragraph 54: "If SGS were denied relief in the present case CAI would in my view be unjustly enriched at its expense, CAI was unjustly enriched by the receipt of the money from Bank Sepah and as a result became liable to restore it, CAI did not cease to be liable when it parted with the money: on the contrary, it remained liable because it had received a benefit which it was bound to restore. That liability merged in the judgment and came to an end only when, and by reason of the fact that, the judgment was satisfied in full

---

[42] Glencore v. Chase Manhattan Bank & State Bank of Saurashtra, No. 92 Civ. 6214 JFK., Feb. 23, 1998.

by SGS. SGS was not responsible for CAI's decision to part with the money: that was the result of a combination of Mr Mahdavi's insistence that the bank follow his instructions and its own failure to act in good faith. *CAI has been relieved of liability at the expense of SGS and as a party liable to make restitution on the grounds of unjust enrichment* I do not think that in relation to SGS it can be treated as if it did not receive the benefit on which its liability was based, any more than it could in relation to Niru." That reasoning seems to me to be compelling and, for my part, absent any authority to the contrary, I would follow it. Moreover, I agree with the view expressed by the judge in paragraph 55 of his judgment that the point can be tested by reference to the position which would have arisen if CAI had retained the money which it had received from Bank Sepah instead of paying it away in accordance with Mr Mahdavi's instructions."[43]

Unjust enrichment was defined in the *Niru* case by setting forth four criteria to be met.

"Mance LJ observed in paragraph 22 that it was common ground, based on the Banque Financière case per Lord Steyn at page 227A and The Queen on the application of Charles Rowe v Vale of White Horse DC [2003] EWHC (Admin) per Lightman J at paragraphs 10-11, that four questions arise when considering a claim for unjust enrichment as follows.

(1) Has the defendant benefited or been enriched?

(2) Was the enrichment at the expense of the claimant?

(3) Was the enrichment unjust?

(4) Is there any specific defence available to the defendant (such as change of position)? Those questions seem to me to cover essentially the same ground as the three questions posed by Lord Hoffmann set out above.

---

[43] Niru Battery Mf'g Co v. Milestone Trading, Case No: A3/2003/1167, Neutral Citation Number: [2004] EWCA Civ 487, Court of Appeal (Civil Division).

On the facts of McDonald v Coys the court answered the first three questions yes and the fourth no. As part of his discussion of benefit Mance LJ said this in paragraph 37: "Looking at the matter generally, I *have no doubt that justice requires that a person, who (as a result of some mistake which it becomes evident has been made in the execution of an agreed bargain) has a benefit or the right to a benefit for which he knows that he has not bargained or paid, should reimburse the value of that benefit to the other party if it is readily returnable* without substantial difficulty or detriment and he chooses to retain it (or give it away to a third party) rather than to re-transfer it on request. Even if realisable benefit alone is not generally sufficient, the law should recognise, as a distinct category of enrichment, cases where a benefit is readily returnable. A person who receives another's chattel must either return it or pay damages, commonly measured by reference to its value. . . . However, Mr McDonald's insistence on keeping the mark and the absence of any obvious means of compelling its re-transfer are reasons for analysing this case in terms of unjust enrichment. Mr McDonald knew that he had not bargained or paid for the mark. The mark or its benefit was in practice easily returnable. If Mr McDonald chose to keep it, then I see every reason for treating him as benefited.'"[44]

VI.4 Duty to mitigate and contributory negligence

Along with the rule of *pacta sunt servanda* the *duty to mitigate* the damage forms part of international contract law. Unidroit provides in Article 7.4.8:

"(1) The non-performing party is not liable for harm suffered by the aggrieved party to the extent that the harm could have been reduced by the latter party's taking reasonable steps. (2) The aggrieved party is entitled to recover any expenses reasonably incurred in attempting to reduce the harm."

While the duty to mitigate as such makes common sense and reflects the same ideologies as unenforceability of disclaimers in the case of gross negligence and

---

[44] Id.

CHAPTER VI

willful acts, the scope of the duty is not very extensive.[45] No special measures or efforts need to be taken.[46]

In letter of credit law there are even some express limitations of the duty to mitigate and shift the burden of proof in favor of beneficiary as provided in UCC 5-111 (a).

The duty to mitigate encourages active but only reasonable measures to limit or eliminate the damage, loss or harm *foreseeable* as a consequence of the breach. In most cases the duty is breached by passivity or by omission to take appropriate commercial or legal measures to avoid harmful consequences.

While the duty to mitigate relates to the period of time after breach of another party, contributory negligence reflects the same principles but on a general level: one who by his acts or omissions has been causing a loss to arise is liable with others for that loss in proper proportion to his "contribution" or fault. The contributory negligence doctrine relates to causing the damage or loss to arise while the duty to mitigate encourages action or (sanctions passivity) in the limitation or elimination of the consequences of breach of duty or agreement by someone else.

To some extent it all boils down to the issue of *foreseeability*. If one foresees that an accident is probable or very probable to arise, or that damage or loss is likely to grow as a consequence of a breach of duty of a contracting party or even a third

---

[45] Dolan writes in *The Law of Letters of Credit* at 9-14:
"Whether a beneficiary must show that he attempted to mitigate damages is a question that turns on the independence principle as modified by the rule of Section 5-115. Since the provision reduces the damages of the beneficiary of a commercial credit to the extent of any sum received on resale, it might be argued that the provision hints that the normal damages rules for a disappointed seller apply. Generally, although not always, disappointed sellers must mitigate damages. On the other hand, it might be argued that Section 5-115, being a unique departure from the independence principle, should be applied strictly."

[46] **Sample clause:** If any circumstances arise, which result, or would on the giving of notice result, in a Principal having to make a payment to or for the account of the Bank then without in any way limiting, reducing or otherwise qualifying any of the obligations of a Principal: (i) the Bank shall notify the Parent promptly after the Bank becomes aware of the relevant circumstances and their results, and (ii) in consultation with the Parent, the Bank shall take such steps as it determines are reasonably open to it and as are acceptable to the Bank to mitigate the effect of those circumstances (such as changing the office through which the Bank is acting, novating some or all of its rights or obligations under this Agreement to another person acceptable to the Principal). However, the Bank shall not be obliged to take any such steps which in its reasonable opinion could have an adverse effect on the Bank.

party, one may be under a general or contractual duty to take appropriate action to reduce or eliminate the risk, to warn those concerned thereof, or to take measures to limit the loss or damage. If one fails to do so, one may be partly or even wholly liable for the damage or loss which arises, or one may be prevented from recovering one's own loss or damage from the one who in principle is liable therefore. The standard of behavior of a diligent, reasonable person (*bonus pater familias*) or the risk or liability one is assuming when contracting is determined by the *foreseeability* of the consequences of one's failure to act under a duty or to fulfill one's undertakings or commitments made. Here the rules of *Hadley v. Baxendale*, the doctrine of mitigation and the doctrine of contributory negligence shake hands.

> "My Lords, I shall consider first the defence of contributory negligence. The relevant provisions of the 1945 Act are sections 1(1) and the definition of "fault" in *section 4*: "1(1) Where any person suffers damage as the result partly of his own fault and partly of the fault of any other person or persons, a claim in respect of that damage shall not be defeated by reason of the fault of the person suffering the damage, but the damages recoverable in respect thereof shall be reduced to such extent as the court thinks just and equitable having regard to the claimant's share in the responsibility for the damage..." "4... 'fault' means negligence, breach of statutory duty or other act or omission which gives rise to a liability in tort or would, apart from this Act, give rise to a defence of contributory negligence."
>
> In my opinion, the definition of "fault" is divided into two limbs, one of which is applicable to defendants and the other to plaintiffs. In the case of a defendant, fault means "negligence, breach of statutory duty or other act or omission" which gives rise to a liability in tort. In the case of a plaintiff, it means "negligence, breach of statutory duty or other act or omission" which gives rise (at common law) to a defence of contributory negligence. The authorities in support of this construction are discussed by Lord Hope of Craighead in *Reeves v Comr of Police of the Metropolis [2000] 1 AC 360, 382*. It was also the view of Professor Glanville Williams in Joint Torts and Contributory Negligence (1951), p 318."

The *Standard Chartered Bank* case deals with contributory negligence and attempts to conceal one's own failure. In that case the court said:

> "It follows that conduct by a plaintiff cannot be "fault" within the meaning of the Act unless it gives rise to a defence of contributory negligence at

common law. This appears to me in accordance with the purpose of the Act, which was to relieve plaintiffs whose actions would previously have failed and not to reduce the damages which previously would have been awarded against defendants. *Section 1(1)* makes this clear when it says that "a claim in respect of that damage shall not be defeated by reason of the fault of the person suffering the damage, but [instead] the damages recoverable in respect thereof shall be reduced . . ."

The question is therefore whether at common law SCB's conduct would be a defence to its claim for deceit. Sir Anthony Evans thought that it would. He said that although the conduct of SCB in making a false statement about when the documents had been presented was intentional or reckless, the House of Lords had decided in *Reeves's case [2000] 1 AC 360* that an intentional act could give rise to a defence of "contributory negligence" at common law and therefore count as "fault" for the purpose of the Act. I am not sure that it was necessary to rely upon *Reeves* for this purpose, because the Act requires fault in relation to the damage which has been suffered. That damage was SCB's loss of the money it paid Oakprime. In *Reeves*, the plaintiff's husband had intended to cause the damage he suffered. He intended to kill himself. But SCB did not intend to lose its money. It would be more accurate to say that *it was careless in making payment against documents which, as it knew or ought to have known, did not comply with the terms of the credit, on the assumption that it could successfully conceal these matters from Incombank. In respect of the loss suffered, SCB was in my opinion negligent.*"[47]

VI.5 What remains or may remain to be governed by national laws

Although the uniformity achieved on the international level is remarkable, there is still plenty of territory to be covered by national laws.[48] The core concept of

---

[47] Standard Chartered Bank v. Pakistan National Shipping Corp, [2002] UKHL 43; [2002] 3 W.L.R. 1547, House of Lords.

[48] Bertrams, *Bank Guarantees*, at 453:
"In conclusion, case law shows that the issue of private international law and the possible applicability of foreign law is of little significance in matters concerning guarantees and counter-guarantees. This finding tallies with the view of this study that the technique of independent guarantees and

fraud is not defined by law merchant and maybe it never will be.[49] The same applies to *ordre public* and public policy as well as good faith and unreasonableness, abuse and unconscionability. This leaves room for national laws to apply and to influence results.

Bertrams lists some of these, mentioning expiry dates, extent of damages, interests, set-off, assignment and pledge. As discussed creation of a security interest belongs to this category, as do formation of binding contracts and/or commitments, bad faith v. good faith, duty to disclose information, the liability of an expert as opposed to a layman, enforceability of disclaimers, proscription, interruption of statute of limitation or proscription, waiver and rules of procedure or of mixed nature i.e., those in between procedure and contract law like, e.g., remedies available.

As to fraud, Buckley and Gao observe:

> "At present, however, the fraud rule is still a developing area and the most important source of jurisprudence with respect to the rule is to be found in Article 5 of the U.C.C. and the cases decided thereunder. The most regrettable fact in the course of development of the fraud rule is that the rule is not included in the Uniform Customs and Practice for Documentary Credits—the influential rules for letters of credit that are incorporated by reference into virtually all credits issued worldwide."[50]

---

counter-guarantees, as well as the relevant rules of law, have developed on a transnational level, away from domestic concepts and structures, and that it is a fallacy to think in terms of significant divergence of national laws. The transnational character of the law of independent guarantees is especially reflected in *CA The Hague, 8 June 1993*, where the Court of Appeal observed that the meaning of an 'extend or pay 'request had to be determined in accordance with internationally accepted notions and that the applicable law of Yemen was assumed to adhere to these notions."

[49] ICC Banking Commission Collected Opinions 1995-2001, R202:
"Rights of recourse to the beneficiary in the event of fraud.... However there is an exception to these provisions in many jurisdictions, namely abuse of rights, or fraud. The ambit of this exception and the ensuing consequences for the beneficiary and or the nominated bank may differ from one local jurisdiction to another. It is up to the courts to fairly protect the interests of all bona fide parties concerned. CONCLUSION The conclusion follows from the analysis."

[50] Ross P. Buckley and Xiang Gao, *The Development of the Fraud Rule in Letter of Credit Law: The Journey So Far and the Road Ahead*, U Penn J of Int'l Economic Law (Winter 2002).

CHAPTER VI

What constitutes fraud and whose fraud is relevant as to the effects and enforceability of the instrument issued to the beneficiary may in practice carry such a diversity of facts that drawing the right borderlines or defining what constitutes relevant fraud as distinguished from fraud which is not relevant for the purposes of enforcing these instruments may be not just difficult, but even harmful.

This applies also to the infrastructure necessary to establish the payment mechanism, the credit or the credit facility (beyond the instrument issued to the beneficiary) and their validity.[51] The "infrastructure" begins where the instrument itself (payor-beneficiary) is not in question, i.e., the indemnity agreements and the bank-to-bank relationships. This includes effects of the bankruptcy of a party to the infrastructure.[52] Bankruptcy, insolvency, reorganization (*redressment judiciaire*) and the protection of creditors and third parties often carry the earmarks of national *ordre public*. Attempts to expand the coverage of law merchant to these areas of law appears neither wise nor desired. These instruments are commercial specialities of international exchange whereas the areas mentioned belong to the realm of strong national and economic interests.[53] Nevertheless, there are and there will be situations where these areas of law are in touch or collide and where

---

Dong-heon Chae in *Letters of Credit....*, 12 Fla J Int'l L 23 (Spring, 1998) observed:
"U.C.P. 500 has provided and will continue to provide a useful standard for this goal. On the problem of the fraud exception in letters of credit, U.C.C. Article 5 also provides good guidelines for the courts in other jurisdictions. However, due to the diversity of legal systems and the increasing complexity of letter-of-credit transactions, the effectiveness of U.C.P. 500 will be threatened."

[51] ICC Banking Commission Collected Opinions 1995-2001, R394:
"Where an L/C was issued under conditions contrary to national law..... ANALYSIS AND CONCLUSION UCP 500 comes into effect at the point where the letter of credit is either signed or transmitted by the issuing bank. On that basis the beneficiary, advising/confirming bank and any nominated bank must rely on the letter of credit having been issued in accordance with the issuer's own internal procedures and any local or national directives. There should be no reason to question the validity of such issuance. The question as to whether this credit was validly issued and whether the beneficiary is entitled to any form of compensation is one that cannot be answered by the UCP. The answer lies in the local legal requirements for the issuing bank in its role as issuer, or in the requirements in respect of the goods for which the issuance has been made."

[52] See, e.g., Steven R. Berger, *The Effects of Issuing Bank Insolvency on Letters of Credit*, 21 Harv Intl L J, (Winter 1980).

[53] ICC Banking Commission Collected Opinions 1995-2001, R336:
"Effect of government sanctions on a bank's ability to pay under an L/C.....ANALYSIS AND CONCLUSION The wording of Article 19 UCP 400 (Article 17 UCP 500) has not changed materially through a number of publications of UCP. Given that the issue of sanctions is a relatively new concept, the previous drafters of UCP would not have had this in mind when drafting the Rules. If the documents conformed to the credit, the action is mandated by regulation and the applicant's account must be debited and the funds frozen."

Refusal, Dishonour, and Remedies

a resolution is necessary as to which rules govern and which rules prevail. This may relate in particular to situations where a party appears to have been unjustly enriched or where the interests of the parties involved relate to the priority amongst them and their claims to security or collateral given or the funds being transferred under the facility. As desired as uniformity in those areas of law might be, they remain to be covered by national laws.

The following diagram, Figure VI.3, illustrates the infrastructure of the facility and the instrument ("the paramount contract"):

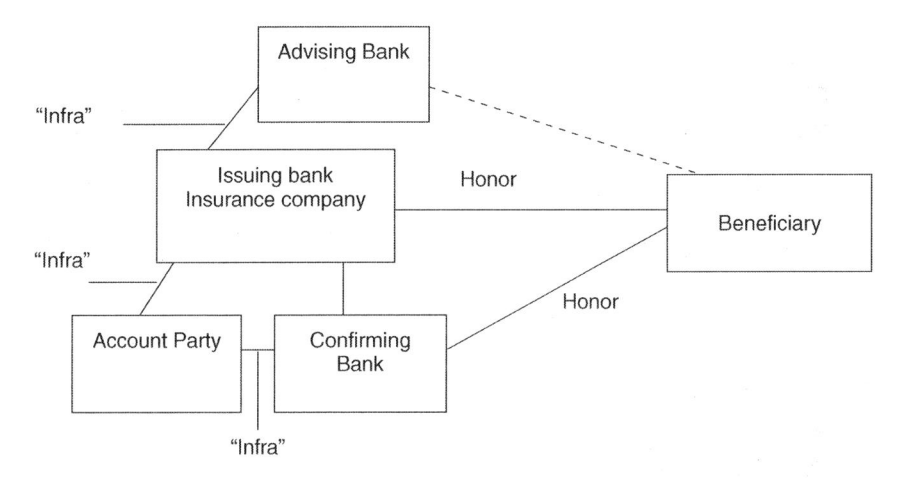

Figure VI.3. The Infrastructure of the Facility and the Instrument

The "honor relationship" is the core of law merchant coverage whereas the influence and coverage of law merchant is reduced, the further away from this core one is.

Where the borderline between national laws and law merchant goes in any individual case depends to a great extent on the applicable national law and its approach to trade usage and customs of the trade and law merchant itself. It may also depend whether the issue is before domestic or international arbitration or before courts of law which are used to handling such disputes or courts of law further away from the heart of circulation of international exchange.

Chapter VI

Since letters of credit are contracts, although *sui generis*, and as such covered to a great extent by contract law, one may find support in emerging law merchant of contracts and also procedurally in due process rules. There is, however, no exact general guide to draw the line between these areas, but a trend of growing influence and acceptance of law merchant may be distinguished. One can give at least one general rule of thumb: the tender or claim, the examination and the honor and dishonor and their consequences, i.e., "the moment of death" (or survival), is to a very large extent to be covered by law merchant.[54]

After the death of the facility and beyond the honor-relationship, the role of national law tends to grow. However, in inter-bank or inter-institutional relationships law merchant remains very strong as to rules and commercial pressure, and as to ethics or moral duty.

The law of these instruments overlaps with other laws and rules. Sometimes there is no conflict at all. Sometimes a similar issue is governed by different rules. A breach or discrepancy under the strict compliance doctrine does not have to be material like under traditional contract law to justify refusal, but, on the other hand, a document to be tendered under a letter of credit does not have to meet strict criteria, but certain tolerance is permissible.[55]

---

[54] ICC Banking Commission Collected Opinions 1995-2001, R253:
"Effect of a subsequent embargo on payment for the goods. . . . ANALYSIS AND CONCLUSION This is not an issue for UCP but one for local law. Having provided a commitment to pay at a future date the confirming bank has complied with the requirements of sub-Article 9(h) (payment to follow on the due date). The consequences of not honouring the commitment on the due date would depend upon the nature of the embargo, with the associated consequences that have been imposed on the confirming bank, and the manner in which local law addresses such circumstances. If an embargo or injunction is placed on a bank due to the nature or type of goods imported, then this should be contested on the grounds of Article 4 of UCP 500 and/or in conjunction with the provisions of local law."

[55] UCP 600 Article 30:
"a. The words "about" or "approximately" used in connection with the amount of the credit or the quantity or the unit price stated in the credit are to be construed as allowing a tolerance not to exceed 10% more or 10% less than the amount, the quantity or the unit price to which they refer. b. A tolerance not to exceed 5% more or 5% less than the quantity of the goods is allowed, provided the credit does not state the quantity in terms of a stipulated number of packing units or individual items and the total amount of the drawings does not exceed the amount of the credit. c. Even when partial shipments are not allowed, a tolerance not to exceed 5% less than the amount of the credit is allowed, provided that the quantity of the goods, if stated in the credit, is shipped in full and a unit price, if stated in the credit, is not reduced or that sub-article 30 (b) is not applicable. This tolerance does not apply when the credit stipulates a specific tolerance or uses the expressions referred to in sub-article 30 (a)."

In general one may distinguish an emergence of hard law in various areas of international law, contract law and procedural law. This is not necessarily a reduction of the freedom to contract, but a result of a growing consensus of what cannot be compromised. This is a result of developing identification of the hard core of rules in common in various legal systems in line with a similar trend in identifying the body of soft rules (law merchant) common to all trading nations. This is reflected *inter alia* in the development of wide equitable powers of courts to interfere as is demonstrated in particular by the "hostility" of legislation and courts to unconscionable disclaimers or (gross) abuse of market power or superior knowledge.

UCC has made a clear distinction between mandatory law and dispositive non-mandatory law.[56] The past freedom to exclude the applicability of UCC altogether is gone.

UCC 5-117 (official comment):

> "3. This section does not permit what is now authorized by the nonuniform Section 5-102(4) in New York. Under the current law in New York a letter of credit that incorporates the UCP is not governed in any respect by Article 5. *Under revised Section 5-116 letters of credit that incorporate the UCP or similar practice will still be subject to Article 5 in certain respects.* First, incorporation of the UCP or other practice does not override the nonvariable terms of Article 5. Second, where there is no conflict between Article 5 and the relevant provision of the UCP or other practice, both apply. Third, practice provisions incorporated in a letter of credit will not be effective if they fail to comply with Section 5-103(c). *Assume, for example, that a practice provision purported to free a party from any liability unless it were "grossly negligent" or that the practice generally limited the remedies that one party might have against another. Depending upon the circumstances, that disclaimer or limitation of liability might be ineffective because of Section 5-103(c)."*

UCC attempts to draw the lines, but the issues and rules overlap.

---

[56] Bertrams, *Bank Guarantees*, at 457:
"Irrespective of the law governing the guarantee or counter-guarantee, courts must apply the public mandatory law of the forum, such as regulations concerning the licence to issue guarantees and currency exchange regulations. Some foreign banks require the instructing bank to confirm that the necessary approvals have been obtained."

UCC 5-117 (official comment):

> "4. in several ways Article 5 conflicts with and overrides similar matters governed by Articles 3 and 4. For example, "draft" is more broadly defined in letter of credit practice than under Section 3-104. The time allowed for honor and the required notification of reasons for dishonor are different in letter of credit practice than in the handling of documentary and other drafts under Articles 3 and 4."

ISP clearly indicates its subsidiary role as to mandatory material law. Thus, ISP 1.02 tells us:

> "a. These Rules supplement the applicable law to the extent not prohibited by that law. b. These Rules supersede conflicting provisions in any other rules of practice to which a standby letter of credit is also made subject."

The frequency of legal disputes relating to these instruments is remarkably low in relation to their overall number and volume. When disputes arise, they relate in most cases to the beneficiary's claims based on refusal of payment against the issuer, claims by account party against the banks for negligence or failure to abide by instructions or by banks against other banks or the account party for reimbursement and of course injunction. The relevant remedy in most cases is primarily damages and secondarily specific performance. The liability for damages, the extent of this liability and the limits thereof are not at all covered by the codified law merchant of these instruments. Damages have, however, well-rooted traditions in contract law and contract law is in the process of developing its own law merchant as strongly demonstrated by the "codifications" of Unidroit, Lando and others. In this area it is not easy to find any reason not to apply these well established principles of traditional contract law perhaps even as such, or at least *mutatis mutandis*, to these instruments as to liability and remedies. It is equally difficult to find any reason for developing different material rules as to the liability of the parties under these instruments. The material rules appear to be the same in practice and in theory.

Letter of credit law seeks support and makes reference to other rules of commercial law, in particular to sales and contract, as is demonstrated by UCC's official comments as to damages. For example, UCC 5-110 (official comment) says:

> 3. The damages for breach of warranty are not specified in Section 5-111. Courts may find *damage analogies* in Section 2-714 in Article 2 and in

warranty decisions under Articles 3 and 4. Unlike wrongful dishonor cases—where the damages usually equal the amount of the draw — the damages for breach of warranty will often be much less than the amount of the draw, sometimes zero. Assume a seller entitled to draw only on proper performance of its sales contract. Assume it breaches the sales contract in a way that gives the buyer a right to damages but no right to reject. The applicant's damages for breach of the warranty in subsection (a)(2) are limited to the damages it could recover for breach of the contract of sale. Alternatively assume an underlying agreement that authorizes a beneficiary to draw only the amount in default. Assume a default of $200,000 and a draw of $500,000. The damages for breach of warranty would be no more than $300,000"

The usages of trade are limited to a particular geographic area or certain goods or services and are not necessarily known beyond that community or by tradesmen operating in other fields of trade, industry or finance. What is referred to as trade usage, custom of trade, trade practice or the like may vary. On the top of this hierarchy one finds a trade usage applied globally in a particular industry, perhaps even codified in a set of rules or practices. Besides banking and bank guarantees and letters of credit, such industry-wide global practices may be identified in insurance, construction and in other engineering industries and transportation. Areas where practices in various countries resemble one another may be found in the automotive industry, and in electronics industries, in which layers of supply-chains are often covered by risk-sharing and "partnership" type of arrangements acknowledging the mutual interdependence in the best cases and reflecting unbalanced market power at the other end. Distribution of goods, trading in commodities, investment banking and commercial agency all demonstrate similarities of various degrees.

Many usages are known in a geographically limited area only in a particular industry, but most usages appear rather to be industry-specific than area-specific for natural reasons. On the other hand, geography plays a role; usages in trade of reindeer meat cannot be globally known or in global use. At the low end of the hierarchy are rules applied and known by two parties only or a handful of tradesmen in the field. In some industries there may be only "a few" tradesmen or companies operating in the same field globally and this trend of consolidation and growth of industry leaders is apparent, e.g., in pharmaceuticals as well as in many other fields. Trade usage or custom of the trade may thus be something of

CHAPTER VI

equal force as law itself or sometimes even stronger. It may, at its weakest, have no significance whatsoever beyond a particular legal relationship or community.

Banks are specialists in their own business and some of them possess unmatched expertise in letters of credit and bank guarantees. However, the documents tendered and their contents may relate to hundreds of thousands of specialized industries in which only those involved know the rules and possess the required understanding of terms, specifications and quality-related issues.

Since trade usages and practices play an important role, an issue may arise as to which usages may be expected to be known by banks involved in financing and payments of practically taken all trades. UCC 5-109 (official comment) gives the following guidance in this respect

> "10. Subsection (f) condones an issuer's ignorance of "any usage of a particular trade"; that trade is the trade of the applicant, beneficiary, or others who may be involved in the underlying transaction. The issuer is expected to know usage that is commonly encountered in the course of document examination. For example, an issuer should know the common usage with respect to documents in the maritime shipping trade but would not be expected to understand synonyms used in a particular trade for product descriptions appearing in a letter of credit or an invoice."

VI.6 De lege ferenda

There are quite a few sets of reference rules covering bank guarantees and letters of credit. Most of them focus on the issuer-beneficiary relationship and the conditions precedent thereof. Some reference rules relate to other relationships of the facility. UCP and UCC cover a lot of common ground. Letters of credit are to a considerable extent covered by uniform rules worldwide, whereas in the area of guarantees and bonds the field is at least in a superficial analysis considerably messier, and much more of substantive law is left to national laws than as is the case with letters of credit. One could perhaps set an ambitious goal to have all these instruments constituting the facility and all relationships thereunder as a whole, covered by one single set of rules.

One could also consider strengthening the independence doctrine by provisions excluding certain remedies or ousting court powers to intervene in performance under the beneficiary–issuer relationship. But this could render this delicate instrument simply too radical.

Docdex is a magnificent new device. It could perhaps be developed into a global documentary credit forum. It could also be elaborated to provide, under the same framework, an arbitration alternative and even a referral service for courts of law when they struggle with these issues. One could perhaps consider optional provisions as to exclusive arbitration under special "docdex" rules.

The coverage of the rules could also be extended to choice of law rules, jurisdictional issues including multiparty proceedings and "extrinsic evidence rule" and proper rules of interpretation.

To arrive at such an ideal world is not as utopian as one might think, when the users and practitioners acknowledge the fact that, in the final analysis we are dealing with one and the same instrument, under which only conditions precedent may vary.

CHAPTER VII

JURISDICTION AND CHOICE OF LAW

VII.1 Interplay of Lex Mercatoria, Conflict of laws and National law

Lex mercatoria has become an evergreen topic of discussion and there is not very much one can say about it which would not have already been said or commented on a number of times in literature and articles.[1] Despite criticism it continues to emerge, continues to gain force, and increasingly takes a written form. Increasingly, also, it is being codified.[2] Supranational law is emerging.

---

[1] Roy Goode, *Rule, Practice, and Pragmatism in Transnational Commercial Law*, International & Comparative Law Quarterly, (July 2005):
 "As law the *lex mercatoria* consists of binding usage and depends in the last resort on recognition by national law. As observed practice the *lex mercatoria* is not dependent on external legal recognition at all, for it is not truly *lex*."
 See, e.g., Filip de Ly: *International Business Law and Law Mercatoria* (Amsterdam, 1992). Tom Pifer, *The ICC Publication of International Standard Banking Practice (ISBP) and the Probable Effect on United States Letter of Credit Law*, Texas Wesleyan Law Review (Spring 2006) writes:
 "The law surrounding LCs [Letters of Credit] is sui generis, developing from the law merchant, separate from the law of contract or suretyship. LC law was mainly established through the confirmation of the customary practices of bankers in dealing with applicants, beneficiaries and various other participants and intermediaries in international transactions. . . .The UCP has been updated about every 10 years and, though it is not the law in any country, it has developed almost to a "supranational code" status, particularly in countries that have not legislated their own code regarding LCs."

[2] See, e.g., the Preamble to the International Institute for the Unification of Private Law (UNIDROIT) Principles of International Commercial Contracts (Rome, 2004) (hereinafter, UNIDROIT):
 "These Principles set forth general rules for international commercial contracts. They shall be applied when the parties have agreed that their contract be governed by them. They may be applied when the parties have agreed that their contract be governed by general principles of law, the *lex mercatoria* or the like. They may be applied when the parties have not chosen any law to govern their contract. They may be used to interpret or supplement international uniform law instruments. They may be used to interpret or supplement domestic law. They may serve as a model for national and international legislators."

Dalhuisen[3] writes:

> "This development is characterized, at least in commerce and finance, by the creation of a distinct international legal order between professional participants that maintains its own transnational legal system. This order I call the "international commercial and financial legal order," and its law is the modern law merchant or the new "lex mercatoria".

One has started to distinguish different levels in *lex mercatoria* ranging from international *ordre public* (or "public policy") to national policies.[4] There are rules which will apply regardless of contract or the will of the parties, and there are also rules of lesser force which the parties may contract out of.[5] The hard core of *lex mercatoria* may include international treaties.[6]

---

[3] Jan H. Dalhuisen, *Legal Orders and their manifestation: the operation of the International Commercial and Financial Legal Order and Its Lex Mercatoria*, 24 Berkeley Journal of International Law 129 (2006).

[4] Yongping Xiao, Zhengxin Huo, *Ordre Public in China's Private International Law*, 53 Am. J. Comp. L. 653, (Summer 2005):
> "In this light, we put forward the following framework for application of the doctrine of ordre public: A foreign law that is applicable pursuant to the conflict rules of China is disregarded if its application would manifestly violate the ordre public of China. In its stead, courts should apply the relevant Chinese law or the law of whichever forum has the most significant relationship with either the litigants or the cause of action."

[5] ILA Resolution on Public Policy as a Bar to Enforcement of International Awards, 2002, New York Convention. See also, *e.g.*, URDG Art 15:
> "Guarantors and Instructing Parties shall not be excluded from liability or responsibility under the terms of Articles 11, 12 and 14 above for their failure to act in good faith and with reasonable care."

See also URCB Art 1 (a):
> "These Rules shall be known as the 'Uniform Rules for Contract Bonds' and shall apply to any Bond which states that these Rules shall apply, or otherwise incorporates these Rules by reference and, for such purposes, it shall suffice that the Bond incorporates a reference to these Rules and the publication number."

and URCG Art 1(2):
> "Where any of these Rules is contrary to a provision of the law applicable to the guarantee from which the parties cannot derogate, that provision prevails."

See also Roeland F Bertrams, *Bank Guarantees in International Trade* (2003) at 378-379:
> "It is generally accepted that the beneficiary cannot claim payment if the underlying contract violates (international) public order. In that event, under the laws of most jurisdictions the guarantee itself will probably be invalid or unenforceable, regardless of its independent nature."

[6] David J. Kalson, *The International Monetary Fund Agreement and Letters of Credit: A Balancing of Purposes*, 44 U. Pitt. L. Rev. 1061 (Summer, 1983):
> "Whichever definition a court chooses to ascribe to the term "exchange contracts," it is clear that Article VIII(2)(b) is not meant to be read in isolation, but rather is to be applied in accordance

Dalhuisen describes the hierarchy of lex mercatoria rules possibly applicable to transnational legal transactions as follows[7]:

"(a) fundamental legal principle;
(b) mandatory custom;
(c) mandatory uniform treaty law (to the extent applicable under its own scope definition and in its own territory);
(d) the contract (or party autonomy in matters at the free disposition of the parties);
(e) directory custom;
(f) directory uniform treaty law (to the extent applicable under its own scope definition and in its own territory);
(g) general principles largely derived from comparative law, uniform treaty law (even where not directly applicable or not sufficiently ratified), ICC Rules and the like; and
(h) residually, domestic laws found through conflict of laws rules."

Many principles of *lex mercatoria* are codified or non-codified trade usages.[8]

---

with the goals of the entire IMF Agreement. Given the twofold purpose of the Agreement, the furtherance of both international trade and international monetary cooperation, a court faced with a dispute under its terms should attempt to balance both concerns. *United City Merchants*, considered with these concerns in mind, correctly stands for the proposition that Article VIII(2)(b) of the IMF Agreement may apply to a letter-of-credit dispute where the letter of credit constitutes an exchange contract. The Court of Appeals and House of Lords arrived at this decision without disturbing either international monetary cooperation, or England's domestic commercial law upon which its lawyers and businesses arrange their activities."

[7] Jan H. Dalhuisen, *Legal Orders and their Manifestation: the Operation of the International Commercial and Financial Legal Order and Its Lex Mercatoria*", 24 Berkeley Journal of International Law 129 (2006).

[8] UCC Section 5-108 official comment:
"8. The standard practice referred to in subsection (e) includes (i) international practice set forth in or referenced by the Uniform Customs and Practice, (ii) other practice rules published by associations of financial institutions, and (iii) local and regional practice. It is possible that standard practice will vary from one place to another. Where there are conflicting practices, the parties should indicate which practice governs their rights. A practice may be overridden by agreement or course of dealing. See Section 1-205(4)."
See also Honduras (DCL) Art 910: "National and international customs shall apply to every issue that

CHAPTER VII

Goode writes:

> "Uncodified usages are inherently more difficult to establish, for they generally depend on expert evidence. It is hard enough to satisfy a court of the existence of a local usage, let alone a usage prevalent on an international market."[9]

Trade usages may be national or local creating an expectation in the trading community that the usage will be complied with unless expressly otherwise agreed. Some trade usages are international in their character, applied to transactions of international character only. Letters of credit in particular and also bank guarantees are often international in their character and often accessory to an underlying transaction of international character to the extent that to submit them to one or another national law may be done only with some violence to their nature. In essence they "float" over all national legal systems, detached therefrom in substance but dependent on them for the purpose of enforcement except when subject to international arbitration.[10]

---

has not been covered by the parties' agreement or by the foregoing provisions."; see also Hungary (DCL) Art. 14(5): "The provisions of the Uniform Customs and Practice for Documentary Credits issued by the International Chamber of Commerce, Paris shall be binding for documentary credits."

[9] Roy Goode, *Rule, Practice, and Pragmatism in Transnational Commercial Law*, International & Comparative Law Quarterly, (July 2005).

[10] Matti Kurkela, *Letters of Credit Under International Trade Law: UCC, UCP and Law Merchant*, (Oceana Publications Inc.,1985), 15; Stoufflet in 24 Arizona Law Review 2, (1982) at 267-268 supports strongly the *lex mercatoria* approach by stating:
"The documentary letter of credit is so completely identical with the UCP that it may be said to belong to an autonomous legal system and that its doctrine is the first manifestation of a lex mercatoria; an international commercial law distinct from any national legal systems."
Carlo Croff, in *The Applicable Law in an International Commercial Arbitration: Is it still a conflict of laws problem?* 16 The International Lawyer 613 (1982), at 643, says:
"In the comparison of the constituent elements of international society with those of merchants' society, one can draw several analogies. The limits and weaknesses of lex mercatoria and of "denationalised' arbitration are often similar to those of public international law. Therefore it can be argued that from a legal point of view there is no fundamental theoretical opposition to the existence of lex mercatoria. It exists in the same way that international law exists."
To some extent similar characterizations were used in Maharanee of Baroda v. Wildenstein, 2 All E.R. 689, (1972). The main issue in that case was *forum non conveniens*. (For other recent cases in England concerning *forum non conveniens*, see: *The owners of the Atlantic Star v. The Owners of the Bona Spes* 2 All E.R. 175, (1973) and MacShannon v. Rockware Glass Ltd. 1 All E.R. 625, (1978) see also *Olympic Corporation v. Societe Generale*, 462 F. 2nd 376 (1972) and 17 Texas Int. L.J. 242 (1982).) In arriving at a decision, the justices made the following statements as to the international character of the issue: The art world is so international in character today that the issue has itself something of an international character.

In the latter case they seem to float freely. In international arbitration these instruments are also often free from the formal rules of national private international law as demonstrated by express rules of some leading arbitration institutes and developing case law. The choice of applicable conflict rules is thus of supranational character. [11]

In order for a trade usage to be applied one may need to bring evidence to prove that it is so commonly used and generally known in a particular trading community as to create a reasonable expectation of being complied with if not expressly otherwise agreed.[12] Trade usage is an implicit condition of the instrument and the transaction.[13] The trade usages applicable in international trade, which apply to instruments or transactions of international or supranational character, may equally create such an expectation, and such an implicit condition. When trade usages are widely recognized and followed by the international trading community for a long period of time, the burden of proof may shift, creating a presumption that trade usages apply unless otherwise proved: it is only consistent to apply supranational trade usages to transactions of supranational character. To do otherwise would do violence to the true character of the transaction.[14] Some rules of *lex mercatoria* are of

---

The parties on either side are citizens of the world. (Lord Denning, M. R.) The nature of the contract, the circumstances in which it was made, the supranational nature of the dispute to which it has given rise, the internationally peripatetic habits of the parties . . . (Lord Edmund, L.J.)

[11] International Chamber of Commerce (hereinafter ICC) Rules Art. 17, Swiss Rules Article 33. See *Tag Heuer*, Supreme Court of France, June 7, 2006 and *Dalico* of the same court Cass civ. 1st, December 20, 1993, J.D.I 1994,432. Note *Gaillard* where the validity issue was delocalized.

[12] Uniform Commercial Code (New York) (hereinafter UCC) Section 5-108 official comment:
"10. Subsection (f) condones an issuer's ignorance of 'any usage of a particular trade'; that trade is the trade of the applicant, beneficiary, or others who may be involved in the underlying transaction. The issuer is expected to know usage that is commonly encountered in the course of document examination. For example, an issuer should know the common usage with respect to documents in the maritime shipping trade but would not be expected to understand synonyms used in a particular trade for product descriptions appearing in a letter of credit or an invoice."

[13] Unidroit 1.9 provides:
"(1) The parties are bound by any usage to which they have agreed and by any practices which they have established between themselves. (2) The parties are bound by a usage that is widely known to and regularly observed in international trade by parties in the particular trade concerned except where the application of such a usage would be unreasonable."

[14] ICC Rules Art. 17. See also *Mahonia Ltd v JP Morgan Chase Bank (No.2) Mahonia Ltd v West LB AG*, (QBD (Comm)) Queen's Bench Division (Commercial Court) 3 August 2004:
"Summary: Held, giving judgment for the claimant, that (1) although the transactions taken together had some of the characteristics of a loan, each Swap agreement had different legally enforceable obligations on the parties to it and on the evidence it had been permissible for E to account for the

such legal force that they cannot be contracted out of. They apply even in the face of an agreement to the contrary, so that they form an *ordre public* of transnational or supranational character.[15]

The only point of real attachment of supranational instruments or transactions to a national jurisdiction may be the place of execution of an arbitral award. If an arbitral award is being sought to be enforced, it will be subject to court control as to its compliance with *ordre public*.[16] There are both substantive and procedural

---

transactions as it had. There had been no breach of US Securities law or of GAAP. Further, there was no evidence that C had believed that E would account for the transaction other than in accordance with the law. The suggestion that C had deliberately misled W as to the nature of the transactions was unfounded. Had there been a conspiracy between C, M and E to devise a transaction which would be falsely accounted for, W could not show that it had been entered into with the intention of injuring W, nor that any damage suffered had arisen from unlawful means. An essential ingredient of the tort of conspiracy to injure by unlawful means was that the unlawful means should be actionable at the suit of the victim against at least one of the co conspirators, *Lonrho Plc v Al-Fayed [1992] 1 A.C. 448, Lonrho Ltd v Shell Petroleum Co Ltd (No.2) [1982] A.C. 173 and Michaels v Taylor Woodrow Developments Ltd [2001] Ch. 493* followed. (2) (Obiter) Had the facts been as W alleged and the letter of credit been part of a scheme to mislead by false accounting contrary to s. 10 of the 1934 Act, it would not have been enforced by the court for public policy considerations. The courts would not enforce security for a contract which had been entered into for a purpose contrary to the law of a friendly foreign state, *Mahonia Ltd v JP Morgan Chase Bank (No.1) [2003] EWHC 1927* considered."

[15] Dalhuisen writes:
"I believe that it is no exaggeration to say that there is a widespread feeling amongst those who think about these matters that domestic laws can no longer adequately deal with the immense increase in the international flow of goods, services, payments, and capital and that as a consequence, the conflict of laws rules as we still know them—oriented as they are towards always finding a domestic, national, or statist law to be applied—have run their course."
ILA Resolution on Public Policy as a Bar to Enforcement of International Awards (2002). Unidroit Article 1.4 provides:
"Nothing in these Principles shall restrict the application of mandatory rules, whether of national, international or supranational origin, which are applicable in accordance with the relevant rules of private international law. "

[16] *Mitsubishi Motors Corporation v. Soler Chrysler-Plymouth Inc.*, 473 U.S. 614, 87 L.Ed. 2d 444 (1985), *Eco Swiss China Time Ltd v. Benetton International NV*, ECJ 1.6.1999 C-126/97, New York Convention Article V; Matti Kurkela: *Letters of Credit under International Trade Law*, p. 272:
"The irrevocable letter of credit was issued by Banco Continental, S.A. of Peru in favor of Glass Fibres and Equipments Ltd., an English company which had agreed to sell equipment to a Peruvian buyer, Vitrorefuerzos, S.A., of Lima. The letter of credit was confirmed by the Royal Bank of Canada, International Centre, Montreal and was negotiable by the London branch of the Royal Bank. Fraud was alleged in the transaction, and the bank refused to honor the credit. In addition, it was alleged that the main agreement was illegal and/or unenforceable as contrary to public policy having been entered into in violation of the Peruvian Exchange Control Regulations and thus unenforceable in England by reason of the Bretton Woods Agreement. This latter issue of Peruvian law was left for subsequent consideration in the judgment. In all other respects English law was applied."

elements in this control. Even this attachment to a national legal system may be superficial, because there may be multiple places and countries where the enforcement may be sought, depending on where the defendant is domiciled, resident, doing business or may have assets.

When seeking out the relevant policies or rules or points of attachment to apply, the policies or rules may need to be determined on the basis of where the transaction has its "effects". In addition to substantive material law merchant, there seems to be an emergence of supranational procedural rules as well.[17]

The freedom of the parties remains extensive, but it is limited by the interests of the trading nations and public policy.[18] The duty of good faith cannot be contracted out of.[19] Comparative law research has been pursued to increase the

---

[17] ALI/Unidroit: Principles of Transnational Civil Procedure, New York (2004), New York Convention. Gabrielle Kaufmann-Kohler, "Globalization of Arbitral Procedure", *Vanderbilt Journal of Transnational Law*, Vol. 36: 1313 (2003).

[18] Wunnicke, Wunnicke, and Turner, *Standby and Commercial Letters of Credit*, (Wiley Law Publications, 1989), at 153:
"On February 5, 1996, the OCC issued its final revised Interpretive Ruling § 7.7016, which authorizes national banks to issue and commit to issue letters of credit and "other independent undertakings" to pay against documents—such as bank guarantees—that are within the scope of applicable law or legally recognized rules of practice. . . . . . . The revised Ruling includes a nonexclusive list of sample laws and rules of practice under which a national bank may issue independent undertakings: UCC Article 5, UCP 500, and United Nations Commission on International Trade Law Convention on Independent Guarantees and Standby letters of Credit (UNCITRAL)."

[19] The UCC (pp. 672-673) provides:
"Good faith" continues in revised Article 5 to be *Observance of reasonable standards of fair dealing has not been added to the definition. The narrower definition of 'honesty in fact' reinforces the 'independence principle' in the treatment of 'fraud' 'strict compliance' 'preclusion', and other tests affecting the performance of obligations that are unique to letters of credit. This narrower definition — which does not include 'fair dealing' — is appropriate to the decision to honor or dishonor a presentation of documents specified in a letter of credit. The narrower definition is also appropriate for other parts of revised Article 5 where greater certainty of obligations is necessary and is consistent with the goals of speed and low cost. It is important that U.S. letters of credit have continuing vitality and competitiveness in international transactions.defined as 'honesty in fact.'*
For example, it would be inconsistent with the 'independence' principle if any of the following occurred: (i) the beneficiary's failure to adhere to the standard of 'fair dealing' in the underlying transaction or otherwise in presenting documents were to provide applicants and issuers with an 'unfairness' defense to dishonor even when the documents complied with the terms of the letter of credit; (ii) the issuer's obligation to honor in 'strict compliance in accordance with standard practice' were changed to 'reasonable compliance' by use of the 'fair dealing' standard, or (iii) the preclusion against the issuer (Section 5-108(d)) were modified under the 'fair dealing' standard to enable the issuer later to raise additional deficiencies in the presentation. The rights and obligations arising from presentation, honor, dishonor and reimbursement are independent and strict, and thus honesty in

understanding between different legal cultures and their representatives, and to build bridges over the gaps. In addition to certain rules that are exclusively supranational, most of *lex mercatoria* is not anything new which is being imposed on, or is alien to, national legal systems. Rather *lex mercatoria* is the nucleus of rules that are common to all or most of the trading nations and are already incorporated in them. *Lex mercatoria* is increasingly codified even though it is not always ratified by a legislature.[20] Instead of concentrating on understanding what is different, and is it really different taking the whole into account (i.e., are we creating a false conflict), it seems much more productive to concentrate on identifying what we have in common. Sometimes what appears to be very different may at the end produce identical results. In the final analysis the conflict is often false.[21]

Although letters of credit and bank guarantees are members of the same family, the rules applicable to commercial letters of credit have enjoyed the benefits of a long-standing tradition in the codification of law merchant as reflected in the ICC's New Rules on Documentary Credits, 2007 Revision, ICC Publication No. 600LF (2006 ed.) (hereinafter UCP 600). On the other hand, the codification of law merchant of bank guarantees is clearly at a more primitive stage, and the influence of national laws is at least *prima facie* considerably greater.[22]

---

fact is an appropriate standard. The contract between the applicant and beneficiary is not governed by Article 5, but by applicable contract law, such as Article 2 or the general law of contracts. 'Good faith' in that contract is defined by other law, such as Section 2- 103(1)(b) or Restatement of Contracts 2d. § 205, which incorporate the principle of 'fair dealing' in most cases or a State's common law or other statutory provisions that may apply to that contract. The contract between the applicant and the issuer (sometimes called the 'reimbursement' agreement) is governed in part by this article (*e.g.*, Sections 5-108(i), 5-111 (b) and 5-103(c)) and partly by other law (*e.g.*, the general law of contracts). The definition of good faith in Section 5-102(a)(7) applies only to the extent that the reimbursement contract is governed by provisions in this article; for other purposes good faith is defined by other law."

[20] Unidroit, International Institute for the Unification of Private Law (UNIDROIT) Principles of International Commercial Contracts 2004; Lando; Beale, *Principles of European Contract Law–Part I And II* (Aspen Publishers, 1999), and Lando; Clive; Prum; Zimmerman, *Principles of European Contract Law–Part III*, (Aspen Publishers, 2003); UCP etc. UCP has been incorporated in national law in New York, and has been incorporated into their law by some other states by reference, which is a formal and exceptional acknowledgement of its force as trade usage or law merchant.

[21] *E.g.*, specific performance is a primary remedy in many civil law countries but its availability is limited. In common law, specific performance is available only in exceptional cases and recovery of damages is the primary remedy. If you analyze the exceptions what finally remains is very similar.

[22] Roy Goode, *Rule, Practice, and Pragmatism in Transnational Commercial Law*, International & Comparative Law Quarterly, (July 2005):

"Take as an example the widely adopted Uniform Customs and Practice for Documentary Credits. These *may* be evidence of pre-existing usage but this will not be true of all the terms, since there will

Kozolchyk writes:

> "The success of the UCP in creating a world wide letter of credit market is due largely to its "living law" status. It is a living law because the conduct it prescribes is indistinguishable from everyday international banking practice. In other words, what the UCP "preaches," the banks practice world wide."[23]

Standby credits seem to fall somewhere between the two categories, being partly comparable to commercial letters of credit, and partly comparable to bank guarantees. Letters of credit have gained recognition also in statutory law in particular in the USA and recently also in China. Most of this statutory law makes reference in one way or the other to trade usages or customs of trade and UCP.[24] Likewise, courts of law tend to recognize the legal force of UCP:

> "5. Conclusion. Based upon the comments received from ICC national committees, members of the ICC Banking Commission and other interested parties, the statements in clauses 3 and 4 above reflect international standard banking practice in the correct interpretation of UCP 500 sub-article 20(b)." It is of course common ground that, if it is appropriate to apply this decision to the documents that are at issue in the present case, they were not discrepant on the ground of lack of originality. But it was the defendant's submission that, despite the express recognition of the limitations or the consultation exercise, the decision did in fact purport to amend Article 20 or, in any event, the decision did not reflect existing standard

---

inevitably be some departures in order to improve current practice; indeed, some of the 'rules' are merely precatory indications of desirable practice, such as the avoidance of excessive detail in a credit."

[23] Boris Kozolchyk, The *"Best Practices" Approach to the Uniformity of International Commercial Law: The UCP 500 and the Nafta Implementation Experience*, 13 Ariz. J. Int'l & Comp. L. 443, (Fall 1996).

[24] Ross P. Buckley and Gao Xiang. *The Unique Jurisprudence of Letters of Credit: Its Origin and Sources*, 4 San Diego Int'l L.J. 91, (2003):

"Due to the highly international character of letters of credit, few individual countries in the world have introduced special legislation governing letters of credit. Where there is any, with the exception of Article 5 of the U.C.C. in the United States, "[i]t tends to consist of only a few provisions often of a general nature." In some jurisdictions, court decisions have constituted an important part of the law of letters of credit. Legal writings or "doctrinal materials" are also considered as supplementary to the law of letters of credit."

Dolan writes:

"This exercise of comparing UCP 500 and Revised Article 5 should be reassuring. While Article 5 is municipal law, it takes generous account of UCP 500; and, in all events, the striking feature of the two regimes is their compatibility." John F. Dolan, *Letters of Credit: A Comparison of UCP 500 and the New U.S. Article 5*, Journal of Business Law, 521-537, (Nov 1999).

banking practice, but merely sought to establish it for the future. I am unable to accept the defendant's submission: a) UCP is a code produced and published by the ICC. b) It is entirely legitimate for the ICC to seek to resolve any ambiguities in, or difficulties of interpretation of, the code. c) The decision in 1999 involved discussion with local banking commissions throughout the world (to which all banks, including CIC and CMB were able to contribute). d) When applied to the facts of the present case, the outcome of the consultation is not inconsistent with the decision on Glencore or Kredietbank, at least if my earlier analysis is correct. e) The decision expressly states that it reflects international standard banking practice: at the least, no bank in following the decision could be said to be acting without reasonable care. f) The consultation exercise began in earnest some 9 months prior to the presentation of the documents in the present case and the decision was promulgated some 2 months prior. This conclusion is consistent with the commercially beneficial aim of reinforcing standard banking practice in regard to the "appearance" of documents and consequent reduction in the risk of inconsistent decisions, all in a field crying out for international consistency. Further, the conclusion I have reached receives some degree of support from the decision of United States District Court for the 5th Circuit in Voest-Alpine Trading USA Corps v Bank of China 167 F Supp 2nd 940 (FD text 2000), where the ICC policy statement was accepted as determinative:— "Third, the Bank of China claimed that the failure to stamp the packing list documents as an "original" was a discrepancy. Again, these documents are clearly originals on their face as they have three slightly differing signatures in blue ink there was no requirement in the letter of credit or the UCP 500 that original documents be marked as such. The ICC's policy statement on the issue provides that, "banks treat as original any document that appears to be hand signed by the issuer of the document . . . the failure to mark obvious originals is not a discrepancy." Whether or not there was any argument on the issue, it follows that the judge must have treated the decision as reflecting international standard banking practice." "[25]

---

[25] *Credit Industriel et Commercial v. China Merchants Bank*, Case No: 2000/738 Neutral citation number: [2002] EWHC 973 (Comm) High Court of Justice Queen's Bench Division Commercial Court.

There may, however, be more similarity in the national laws and practice than what appears to be the case in a superficial analysis.[26] As discussed above, applying a national law to something supranational may be necessary, but may do injustice. Often enough one could just as well apply one or another national law and each choice would seem just as justified or unjustified as another. Sometimes one could apply even several laws simultaneously to a single case and sometimes be even forced to do so.

One should, however, note on one hand that all rules of UCP do not have the same status of supranational law or *lex mercatoria* and, on the other hand, that certain rules of UCP may equally apply as such or *mutatis mutandis* to bank guarantees. On the side of UCP, a new codification has been adopted to cover standby letters of credit, which may indeed follow the path of UCP in success or perhaps finally lead to a merger of all these various rules.[27]

---

[26] UCC Section 5-103 official comment provides:
"2. Like all of the provisions of the Uniform Commercial Code, Article 5 is supplemented by Section 1-103 and, through it, by many rules of statutory and common law. Because this article is quite short and has no rules on many issues that will affect liability with respect to a letter of credit transaction, law beyond Article 5 will often determine rights and liabilities in letter of credit transactions. Even within letter of credit law, the article is far from comprehensive: it deals only with "certain" rights of the parties. Particularly with respect to the standards of performance that are set out in Section 5-108, it is appropriate for the parties and the courts to turn to customs and practice such as the Uniform Customs and Practice for Documentary Credits, currently published by the International Chamber of Commerce as I.C.C. Pub. No. 500 (hereafter UCP). Many letters of credit specifically adopt the UCP as applicable to the particular transaction. Where the UCP are adopted but conflict with Article 5 and except where variation is prohibited, the UCP terms are permissible contractual modifications under Sections 1-102(3) and 5-103(c). See Section 5-116(c). Normally Article 5 should not be considered to conflict with practice except when a rule explicitly stated in the UCP or other practice is different from a rule explicitly stated in Article 5."
Bolivia (DCL) Art 1408:
"Any issue not covered by this paragraph shall be governed by the Uniform Customs and Practices for Documentary Credits in their prevailing version."
Egypt (DCL) Art 341 (3):
"The Uniform Customs and Practice for Documentary Credits by the International Chamber of Commerce shall apply unless the articles of this section contain special provisions."

[27] International Standby Practices, ICC Publication No 590, Paris (1998) reads:
"The formulation of standby letter of credit practices in separate rules evidences the maturity and importance of this financial product. The amounts outstanding of standbys greatly exceed the outstanding amounts of commercial letters of credit. While the standby is associated with the United States where it originated and where it is most widely used, it is truly an international product. Non-U.S. bank outstandings have exceeded those of U.S. banks in the United States alone. Moreover, the standby is used increasingly throughout the world."

Chapter VII

Some of the rules of *lex mercatoria* are in essence, and were originally, trade usages. Trade usages are an important source of law sometimes stronger in force than written law itself.[28] Trade usages are formed by merchants themselves by the necessities of life, plus common sense.[29] Some of *lex mercatoria* has a moral connotation: everyone acknowledges that it is simply right, and other solutions would not provide justice. In order for such trade usages to develop, there must be a market of sufficient size for the issues of conflict or misunderstanding to arise frequently enough to lead to the adoption of common behavior, behavior aiming to act with reason and to eliminate the friction. The trading community thus acts for the common good: a trading community representing diverse cultures, and having no dominant players who could dictate the applicable conditions (either unilaterally or in collusion with each other), is bound to create fair and reasonable usages or customs.[30]

Goode writes:

> "This paper has examined some of the more important concepts underlying the UCP, the URDG and the UNCITRAL Convention. What significance do these instruments have for the general development of transnational commercial law? I believe that they provide a further demonstration of the enormous influence of trade practice and the needs of legitimate business on the development of commercial law. So strong is this influence that sooner or later evolving business practice will always break free from the shackles

---

[28] ICC Arb. Rules Art. 17 (2).

[29] Roy Goode *A New International Lex Mercatoria*, Lloyd's Maritime and Commercial Law Quarterly (3 (Aug) 2000):
"It is evident that, in some quarters at least, there is a growing dissatisfaction with national law as a means of resolving international disputes, and an increasing pressure to look to international trade usage and general principles of commercial law, including those evidenced by international restatements by groups of scholars from different legal families and systems. I welcome this trend, provided that decisions - and particularly those of arbitral tribunals - are disciplined and not self-indulgent and that findings of fact as to trade usage are supported by proper evidence, whether expert or documentary."

[30] Some of the rules applied to these instruments could be argued to be products of the banking industry, and as such they could be argued to be restraints on trade and incompatible with free competition. This line of thinking, as correct as it might appear to be in some respects, could, if enforced, do great harm to these instruments and the international exchange, and in most cases would result in chaos. The benefits clearly outweigh the harm, and, applying the "rule of reason", it would seem that no action would be warranted. The uniformity of laws or legal rules is in most cases a legitimate objective supported by government and trade policies which cannot, in general, be deemed to be harmful to competition. However, in individual cases the rules may present unreasonable results.

of doctrine and jurisprudence and demand acceptance by the courts or the legislature. Typically, the process of harmonisation begins not with any international instrument but with conscious or unconscious judicial parallelism as the courts in each country respond to the needs of that country's business community. So by the time work is begun on uniform rules, a considerable measure of international consensus on law and practice will already have developed, despite major divergences in the general contract law of the legal systems involved. The extent to which these divergences can be reconciled or cast aside is a striking testimony to the pressure for a new lex mercatoria which, as in the Middle Ages, will transcend national boundaries and bring different systems of law into harmony through the usages of trade."[31]

VII.2 Applicable law

VII.2.1 Uniform law merchant

One of the main purposes of this work is to demonstrate that a considerable part of letter of credit or bank guarantee law applicable to such instruments of international character is uniform law merchant.

---

[31] Roy Goode, *Abstract Payment Undertakings in International Transactions, Symposium New Developments in the Law of Credit Enhancement: Domestic and International,* 22 Brook. J. Int'l L. 1, (1996).

ICC Opinions R 248:
"Is a credit subject to UCP 500 if this fact is not mentioned in the SWIFT credit advice?. . . . ANALYSIS Despite the content of Article 1 of UCP 500, which reads "The Uniform Customs and Practice for Documentary Credits, 1993 Revision, ICC Publication No. 500, shall apply to all Documentary Credits (including to the extent to which they may be applicable, Standby Letter(s) of Credit) where they are incorporated into the text of the Credit. They are binding on all parties thereto, unless otherwise expressly stipulated in the Credit", SWIFT message types 700 and 701 invariably do not make reference to the fact that the credit is subject to UCP 500. The SWIFT user handbook does state that credits issued using the SWIFT transmission are automatically subject to the UCP in operation on the date of issuance. CONCLUSION Whilst credits issued using the SWIFT system (without mention of UCP) would seem to be inconsistent with Article 1, it has long been accepted that these types of credits are subject to the UCP in operation on the day of issue. This has become a recognized practice. An ICC opinion given in Publication No. 434 R. 101 states: 'The Commission considered that banks advising credits issued through SWIFT should ensure in accordance with SWIFT rules that the appropriate UCP incorporation clause was included in the credit advice sent to the beneficiary'. The silence in the original SWIFT credit advice as to whether the credit was subject to UCP 500 does not imply that the credit is not subject to the rules, The advising bank should adhere to the opinion given in R. 101."

Chapter VII

> "It may well be uncontroversial to state that the governing law of the L/C is French law. However, not only is there no evidence of any difference between French Law and English Law, it also hardly needs saying that this field affords a paradigm example of the need for avoidance of any difference in approach to UCP 500 as between different jurisdictions." [32]

This applies in particular to material law applicable to the bank-beneficiary relationship and, although in a lesser degree, to the bank-to-bank relationship and issuer account party (applicant) relationship.[33] Regardless of such uniformity, a process of analysis of conflict of laws may be necessary.[34]

It is well established law that the parties have the freedom to agree on the law applicable to their contractual relationship and it's binding and in most cases respected and enforced by the courts of law. Such a choice does not, however, extend to third parties and has no effect *erga omnes* as opposed to enforceability *inter partes*.

The freedom to agree on the applicable material law is, however, not unlimited in the *inter partes* relationship either. Rules of other laws or national or international *ordre public* may apply despite the express choice by the parties.

Letters of credit and bank guarantees do often even in their simplest structures cross national borders. Should the instrument form a more sophisticated facility with more than three parties more than just two or three jurisdictions may be involved or touched upon by the facility? At the outset this would seem to raise the profile or increase the importance of conflict-of-laws rules. In practice the role

---

[32] Credit Industriel et Commercial v. China Merchants Bank, Case No: 2000/738. Neutral citation number: [2002] EWHC 973, QBD (Comm Ct) (44); Heinrich Ferreira, *Choice of law and letters of credit – Articles 4(2), (5), Rome Convention*, Finance and Credit Law 2005, Oct, 1-4.

[33] Luca G. Radicati Di Brozolo, *International Payments and Conflicts of Laws*, American Journal of Comparative Law, (Spring 2000): "Clearly contractual arrangements are incapable of solving all problems, and particularly those falling outside the scope of the lex contractus (typically the effects of insolvency, of blocking orders, and such like)."

[34] Bertrams, *Bank Guarantees*, at 451-2; Luca G. Radicati Di Brozolo, *International Payments and Conflicts of Laws*, American Journal of Comparative Law, (Spring 2000):
"They may have to do with the consequences of a failure to carry out the instructions correctly (what remedies are available in case of late or erroneous payment such as underpayment, payment to the wrong beneficiary: entitlement only to interest or also to damages, and the amount thereof, etc.)."
See also Jason C.T.Chuah, *Choice of Law and Letters of Credit*, Student L Rev (2005, 45 (sum)), 46-47.

of conflict of laws has remained astonishingly low or insignificant. This is naturally a consequence of the paramount role played by UCP and other such rules and the law merchant itself. Should problems relating to choice of law appear more frequently another problem would emerge: which conflict rules are applicable?

Although the freedom to choose the applicable law in a contractual relationship is a blessing it does not solve all the issues under a facility since a credit facility comprises a number of more or less independent contracts. The choice of law made by the parties in one of these relationships does not as such extend to the other contractual relationships which may in turn be governed by another substantive law chosen by the parties thereto or determined by applicable conflict rules. Parts of one facility may thus be governed by different law endangering at least in theory the consistency and uniformity of decisions in case of disagreement or dispute.

The choice of law made by the parties to govern their contractual relationship does not and cannot extend to issues where third parties have interests which are not derivatives of the agreement. This applies in particular to bankruptcy and insolvency of a party to the facility. Bankruptcy, insolvency, reorganization and other related laws are in most cases part of a jurisdiction's *ordre public* and public policy, and will often be applied despite choice-of-law clauses in the interests of equal treatment of the bankrupt's creditors.

While banks and other financial institutions are well equipped and possess sophisticated methods to address these issues in lending transactions and in security transactions, it is not at all as common to find these issues expressly addressed to or governed by a sophisticated clause in letter of credit or bank guarantee facilities as is traditionally the case in other finance transactions. This seems to be further evidence of the blessings of uniformity in the field and the benefits of generally adopted rules like UCP. Occasionally, although rarely, the emerging issues of applicable laws may present problems not covered by the provisions of the facility compelling the courts to have recourse to conflict-of-laws rules. Should such issues be more frequent and problematic they would be regularly covered by express clauses. In many international finance transactions the parties choose either English law or New York law as the applicable law and English courts or New York courts as primary venue. The former choice as to letter of credit would rather be a reference to and incorporation of UCP and the applicable national law would have only a secondary role in importance.

Chapter VII

Should there be a dispute in a cross-border facility which cannot be settled out of court the parties will submit the dispute to courts of law. The plaintiff, in the absence of a choice-of-court agreement, may have a multiple choice as to the court where he may bring the action. This relates to bringing the proper action itself but even more so to protective or interim measures. The requirements as to contacts or presence in the jurisdiction in question with respect to the latter are often more relaxed than to an ordinary action. The plaintiff's choice ("forum shopping") may have significant consequences as to the conflicts rules to be applied (*lex fori*), remedies available and the cost of litigation and access to evidence by way of discovery or other such means.

When a dispute arises under a cross-border facility it will often taint or involve other parties to the facility, too. The dispute tends to cross the borders as well and the parties to the original dispute may find it necessary, beneficial or useful to have the other parties to the facility involved in the same proceedings or the latter may have a direct or indirect interest in doing so even on their own initiative. This may complicate and multiply the jurisdictional aspects resulting in questions of "may, must, should or should not" as to the role of those other parties in the legal proceedings initiated by one party against another but not all parties of the facility in question. The applicable rules or commercial necessity may require that the other parties are summoned, too, or just heard or given an opportunity to be heard.

If the court where the action is pending comes to the conclusion that a foreign law is to be applied to the dispute or a part thereof another issue is to be raised: how and by whom should the substance of that law be proved? In most cases the "burden of education" rests with the parties but occasionally a court may or must play a role in this "fact finding" task. In general the parties bear the risk as to the sufficiency of evidence as to the content of the foreign law to be applied.

The complexity of the choice-of-law process when no agreement exists is demonstrated in case law, e.g., as follows:

> "It was and is common ground between the parties that the correct approach for the purposes of identifying the governing law is to look at how the contract was intended by its terms to operate at the time it was made, rather than to look at what in fact occurred. That is what the judge did in coming to his conclusions. He dealt with the matter on the basis that, under the terms of the contract, it was anticipated that vis-a-vis the

issuing bank (Hastin) and the confirming bank (Panin), the beneficiary (Marconi) would deal with, and be entitled to receive, payment from SCB as advising and negotiating bank making payment to Marconi in England and itself receiving reimbursement here. Further, it was and is common ground that under a Letter of Credit it is desirable that the same system of law should govern the co-existing contracts between (a) the issuing bank and the beneficiary, (b) the confirming bank and the beneficiary, (c) the issuing bank and the confirming bank: see Bank of Baroda (supra) and *Bank of Credit and Commerce Hong Kong Ltd v Sonali Bank [1995] 1 Lloyds Rep 227* at 237(col.1). Since the instant letter of credit was a negotiation credit, it is also relevant to consider the contracts between the issuing/confirming banks and the negotiating bank."[35]

There are also many issues which are not covered by law merchant, some issues which are in a grey area and issues which, in the network of legal relationships, are undoubtedly covered by national laws – as of domestic character or due to lack of law merchant.[36] This work also demonstrates that, when applying the choice law rules, you will in many cases end up applying law merchant i.e., there is no true conflict.[37]

---

[35] PT Pan Indonesia Bank Ltd v. Marconi Communications Int'l Ltd, 2005 WL 936857 (CA (Civ Div)), [2005] 2 All E.R. (Comm) 325, 5-18-2005 Times 936,857, [2005] EWCA Civ 422. A3/2004/0684, Neutral Citation Number: [2005] EWCA Civ 422,.

[36] ICC Banking Commission Collected Opinions 1995-2001, R 385:
"Can an issuing bank issue its letters of credit subject to UCP 500 and to matters not governed therein, to the laws of the country of issuance?.... ANALYSIS AND CONCLUSION An issuing bank is perfectly at liberty to issue their letters of credit which are subject to UCP 500 and to matters not governed therein, to the laws of the country of issuance."
ICC Banking Commission Collected Opinions 1995-2001, R 386:
"Is it mandatory that all documentary credits be made subject to UCP 500? If a bank acts in violation of UCP interpretation on transferable credits, is it accountable to compensate? CONCLUSION In answer to the questions you have posed: it is not mandatory that all documentary credits be made subject to UCP 500. Provided all parties are in agreement, a documentary credit could be issued subject to some other form of rules or law. If the UCP 500 is incorporated into the wording of the credit (or is issued using the SWIFT MT700 series message without specific reference to UCP500 see ICC Opinion R.248 in Publication No. 596), then it is binding on all parties to the extent that none of the provisions is overridden within the terms and conditions of the credit."

[37] Bertrams, *Bank Guarantees*, at 421-2:
"German doctrine in particular expresses the view that the issue of the beneficiary's fraud, in the case of indirect guarantees, must be determined in accordance with foreign law, namely the local law governing the relationship between the foreign issuing bank and the foreign beneficiary. This view seems sound and logical. . . . . It is even more significant that those courts which perfunctorily noted that the primary guarantee was governed by foreign law, evidently applied their own, but not necessarily

Chapter VII

It is further worthwhile to point out that conflict rules are being delocalized and becoming part of international law and practice and as such forming a *lex mercatoria* of conflict of laws. Certain material issues are also becoming delocalized like, e.g., the validity of the agreement when submitted to international arbitration. Nevertheless, it is important to know the rules and to realize that rules looking *de jure* different on their face may well end up being *de facto* similar or identical. (This situation is called a "false conflict".)

Also, as discussed, the parties may agree on the law applicable to their relationship. This is a well-established and commonly accepted principle and needs no argumentation.

UCC 5-116 (a):

> "The liability of an issuer, nominated person, or adviser for action or omission is governed by the law of the jurisdiction chosen by an agreement in the form of a record signed or otherwise authenticated by the affected parties in the manner provided in Section 5-104 or by a provision in the person's letter of credit, confirmation, or other undertaking. The jurisdiction whose law is chosen need not bear any relation to the transaction."

UNC Art. 21:

> "The undertaking is governed by the law the choice of which is: (a) Stipulated in the undertaking or demonstrated by the terms and conditions of the undertaking; or (b) Agreed elsewhere by the guarantor/issuer and the beneficiary."

---

provincial, notions of fraud. The explanation is, no doubt, that the law with respect to independent (demand) guarantees is very much characterised by its transnational nature and that the principles of fraud in relation to such guarantees are strikingly similar. The application of foreign law in respect of fraud may also be dispelled on the grounds of public. Moreover, litigation in cases of (alleged) fraud predominantly turns on evidence, and the standards in this respect also display a striking uniformity."
Razeen Sappideen, *International Commercial Letters of Credit: Balancing The Rights of Buyers and Sellers in Insolvency*, J Busn L (2006, March) 133-156:
"First, in the United Kingdom, there has been an insistence of a level of proof far in excess of that normally required in civil cases. Secondly, and what has caused its demise, has been the subordination of the fraud exception to the third-party priority rule and as the Montrod case shows, this priority extends even to fraud by the buyer over the financier. The alternative to the judicial remedy is for buyers to resort to some self help through a contractual provision giving them priority over those of a holder, though this may not be free of difficulty. Better still, would be for buyers to opt for a New York choice of law and forum!"

In the absence of express choice of law, the classic approach in conflict-of-laws analysis is to determine the law applicable to an international transaction or act or omission (tort) by way of rigid or formal rules.

While this method has to some extent been abandoned,[38] the problems remain and have in fact multiplied: several laws may be applicable to one single instrument or transaction at the same time in the absence of express choice of law or even despite it.[39] In addition, there seems to be a recognition of a variety in "layers" of these rules having different degrees of binding force and of penetration.

ISP Art. 1.05 provides expressly acknowledging the realm of national law:

> "These Rules do not define or otherwise provide for: a. power or authority to issue a standby; b. formal requirements for execution of a standby (e.g. a signed writing); or c. defenses to honour based on fraud, abuse, or similar matters. *These matters are left to applicable law.*"

As to these instruments of international banking and finance, there seem to be certain special or almost unique features:

(i) the instruments are often wholly or essentially unilateral;
(ii) they relate to or are accessory to an international transaction which may in itself be supranational or cross-border;

---

[38] This applies in particular in international arbitration. See, e.g., ICC Rules Art 17 (1); Swiss Rules Art. 33 (2).

[39] UCC 5-102 (official comment):
"The subject matter in Article 5, letters of credit, may also be governed by an international convention that is now being drafted by UNCITRAL, the draft Convention on Independent Guarantees and Standby Letters of Credit. The Uniform Customs and Practice is an international body of trade practice that is commonly adopted by international and domestic letters of credit and as such is the law of the transaction by agreement of the parties. Article 5 is consistent with and was influenced by the rules in the existing version of the UCP. In addition to the UCP and the international convention, other bodies of law apply to letter of credit. For example, the federal bankruptcy law applies to letters of credit with respect to applicants and beneficiaries that are in bankruptcy; regulations of the Federal Reserve Board and the Comptroller of the Currency lay out requirements for banks that issue letters of credit and describe how letters of credit are to be treated for calculating asset risk and for the purpose of loan limitations. In addition there is an array of anti-boycott and other similar laws that may affect the issuance and performance of letters of credit. All of these laws are beyond the scope of Article 5, but in certain circumstances they will override Article 5."

CHAPTER VII

(iii) the instruments cross national borders and even legal and commercial cultures and are often rather supranational than national in their character.

UNC Art 4:

"(1) An undertaking is international if the places of business, as specified in the undertaking, of any two of the following persons are in different States: guarantor/issuer, beneficiary, principal/applicant, instructing party, confirmer. (2) For the purposes of the preceding paragraph: (a) If the undertaking lists more than one place of business for a given person, the relevant place of business is that which has the closest relationship to the undertaking; (b) If the undertaking does not specify a place of business for a given person but specifies its habitual residence, that residence is relevant for determining the international character of the undertaking."

(iv) there are significant national or international policy interests in the background like, e.g., maintaining confidence in these instruments to ensure the benefits they bring to international exchange and promotion of national and international banking (London, New York, Frankfurt);

(v) The instruments often together with other functionally linked agreements constitute "one (credit) facility".

VII.2.2 The *Zeevi* case and policy interests

The policy interest may play a very important role – in particular in a financial metropolis as demonstrated in this almost hair-raising case of *Zeevi & Sons*.

The case of J. Zeevi and Sons, Ltd. v. Grindlays Bank (Uganda) Ltd. is one of the most interesting cases in this field of law. First of all, it is interesting because it was pleaded by Henry Harfield for and on behalf of the defendant bank. Secondly, a very interesting choice of law issue was raised which may have to some extent been influenced by two considerations: *ordre public* and the *interests of New York City as a monetary center of the world.*

The freely negotiable letter of credit:

The defendant, an Ugandan banking corporation, issued an irrevocable letter of credit in favor of the plaintiff, an Israeli partnership. The letter of credit was valid until January 31, 1973 "for presentation of drafts in Kampala". It contained the following additional stipulations: "We *guarantee the payment of drafts* drawn in conformity with the terms and conditions stated. The negotiating bank must send drafts direct to us by air-mail." "The negotiating bank is authorized to claim reimbursement for their payment on the due dates listed above from (First National City Bank, 399 Park Avenue, New York) to the debit of our account with them together *with a certificate to the effect that all terms of the credit have been complied with* and the drafts have been air-mailed to us." *The letter of credit was a commercial one and freely negotiable by any bank*. Although the irrevocable letter of credit originated from Uganda and was (secondarily) "finally" payable in Kampala, Uganda, it was primarily payable in New York by a correspondent bank of the issuing bank. The correspondent bank (Citibank) did, however, undertake no independent obligation towards the beneficiary. New York was the place of reimbursement between two banks, the negotiating bank (Chemical Bank) and Citibank, neither of which was independently liable under the letter of credit.

The Ugandan government introduced laws blockading all foreign exchange payments in 1972

In March 1972 the officials of Uganda, obviously using their statutory powers in accordance with Ugandan law, notified defendant not to make foreign exchange payments with regard to this letter of credit. The defendant informed its correspondent New York Bank (Citibank), cancelling previous instructions and the credit and ordering it not to "effect payment . . . due to be paid on or after 15th April 1972." The defendant bank also informed the plaintiff of the cancellation of the credit.

Presentation of drafts by Chemical Bank and dishonor by Citibank

On December 28, 1972 Chemical Bank presented to Citibank for reimbursement the drafts under the credit, but the drafts were returned unpaid to Chemical.

Zeevi & Sons takes legal action in New York

The action was commenced by the beneficiary (not by Chemical) attaching the funds of defendant on deposit with Citibank, and defendant was served by publication.

The defendant contended, among other things, that the court lacked subject matter jurisdiction and that the law of Uganda (under which the payment would have been illegal) was applicable and the obligation to effect payment void and unenforceable.

Choice of law: Uganda or New York – The interest analysis

The court concluded that New York law applies and the decision is worth while quoting as a whole with regard to this issue: (5) We come now to the question of the choice of law '(The) rule which has evolved clearly in our most recent decisions is that *the law of the jurisdiction having the greatest interest in the litigation will be applied and that the facts or contacts which obtain significance in defining State interests are those which relate to the purpose of the particular law in conflict'"* (Intercontinental Planning v. Daystrom, Inc., 24 N.Y. 2nd 372, 382, 300 N.Y.S.2nd 817, 825, 248 N.E.2nd 576, 582). New York *has an overriding and paramount interest in the outcome of this litigation. It is a financial capital of the world, serving as an international clearinghouse and market place for a plethora of international transactions,* such as to be so recognized by our decisional law (Intercontinental Planning v. Daystrom, Inc., supra at pp. 383-384, 300 N.Y.S.2nd at pp. 826-827, 248 N.E.2nd at pp. 582-583). A vast amount of international letter of credit business is customarily handled by certain New York banks whose facilities and foreign connections are particularly adaptable to this field of operation (34 N.Y.Jur., Letters of Credit, § 10, p. 427). *The parties, by listing United States dollars as the form of payment, impliedly accepted these facts and set up procedures to implement their trust in our policies. In order to maintain its pre-eminent financial position, it is important that the justified expectations of the parties to the contract be protected (cf. Kossick v. United Fruit Co.,* 365 U.S. 731, 741, 81 s. Ct. 886, 6 L.Ed.2nd 56).

Since New York has the greatest interest and is most intimately concerned with the outcome of this litigation, its laws should be accorded paramount control over the legal issues presented (cf. Auten v. Auten, 308 N.Y. 155,161,124 N.E. 2nd 99, 102).

Some conclusions

The law of the place of payment was thus applied. The place of payment in this case had the least possible contacts with the parties and the letter of credit except the fact that it was designated as the place of reimbursement. The Ugandan bank was not doing business in New York; it had no branch or subsidiary there. Citibank as the correspondent bank undertook no independent obligation under the letter of credit and was only acting as an advising bank. The plaintiffs' contacts with New York seem to be nonexistent. The drafts were presented by Chemical Bank which was obviously acting as a correspondent bank to the plaintiff's bank. *The court did not, however, decide the case on the ground of place of payment but by using the theory (adopted in Auten v. Auten) of the importance of the jurisdiction which has the greatest interest in the litigation.*

Although some consideration must be given to the discriminatory character of the action undertaken by the Ugandan authorities (apparently forced to do so by president Idi Amin) and the express 'policy' argumentation of the court, the case can and must be considered as having established the exceptional weight to be given to the place of payment as a contact to be valued for choice of law purposes.

The decision does, however, also indirectly indicate that any place of payment may not necessarily always have an equal importance in this respect. The choice of place of payment like New York or London must be considered as a matter of great convenience and importance to the parties, especially if the currency used is the national currency of the place of payment. The possible effect of these considerations may, however, be only marginal. In the present case the courts of New York would not have had in personam jurisdiction over the Ugandan bank. The necessary jurisdiction was created by attaching the defendant's funds in New York. Most international banks operate branches, representative offices or maintain bank accounts in New York.

It is in the interest of the international banking community as well as in the interest of the financial centers of the world that claims relating to international banks may be brought in its court and that reliance on such policies is maintained. To adopt another kind of a policy might undermine the popularity of such places as a banking center.

One could also very strongly argue that since these centers greatly benefit from the business transacted they should also carry the burdens thereof. These arguments would mainly apply to jurisdictional and especially *forum non conveniens* issues.

CHAPTER VII

VII.3 A Preference for English Law

VII.3.1 General

Why is English law given such an eminent position in this kind of project with the emphasis on law merchant? There are various obvious reasons, and less apparent reasons, for this. The role played by London and England as a capital of international trade, exchange, banking and insurance has been and remains exceptional. This has led to a development of law, practice and usage and an accumulation of know-how. At the same time the court system and the law have continued to inspire confidence despite the cost and delay. After all, these elements are of lesser importance than the outcome (although they matter too). The openness of the marketplace and economy and the transparency created by the language known to many of us have accelerated this development aided by the devotion of the people to independence, freedom and democracy: all these elements appeal also to the business community. No wonder there is plenty of easily accessible case material even in the most exotic areas, areas where disputes arise, proportionally taken, very seldom, as in this area of letters of credit. London and New York are unmatched in the length of tradition, the education of courts in financial law, and the clarity and elegance of legal writing easily understandable to any business person (not just lawyers). This is why English law plays an eminent role even in the study of letters of credit.

English law takes a position in favor of applying the law of the place of performance (as opposed to the law of the place of performer). In terms of international banking, the place of payment or tender may, indeed, often be the very center of gravity.

> "English courts and authors take the view that the applicable law of a credit be determined by the place of performance of the bank. This is not to be confused with the place of the bank's domicile. The place of performance is deemed to be the location at which the beneficiary shall present the documents in order to obtain payment and, thus, the applicable law is often determined to be the law of the confirming or paying bank."[40]

---

[40] DCL (UK) p. 119; UCC 5-111 (official comment):
"1. The right to specific performance is new. The express limitation on the duty of the beneficiary to mitigate damages adopts the position of certain courts and commentators. Because the letter of credit depends upon speed and certainty of payment, it is important that the issuer not be given an incentive to dishonor. The issuer might have an incentive to dishonor if it could rely on the burden of mitigation falling on the beneficiary, (to sell goods and sue only for the difference between the

VII.3.2 Choice of Law and the *Offshore International* Case

This is one of the first cases dealing in some length with choice of law issues. The summary written in the first edition in 1985 still serves, with some comments as an introduction to the case. The case deals with an advance payment "guarantee" which was issued by a Spanish bank in favor of a Panamian beneficiary and advised but not confirmed by a New York bank.

Offshore International[41] is of the utmost importance and interest. It has been referred to by many authorities as one of the leading cases, or perhaps the leading English case, with regard to choice of law. One of the main issues was the determination of the law applicable to the irrevocable letter of credit issued by the defendant Spanish bank, Banco Central, in favor of the plaintiff. The plaintiff, *Offshore International*, was incorporated in Panama. The irrevocable letter of credit was advised but not confirmed by Chase Manhattan N.A. of New York as agent for the Spanish bank. It covered the repayment of an advance payment made by the plaintiff to the second defendant, a Spanish contractor, under a contract between the plaintiff and the second defendant. Thus the letter of credit was meant to operate as a guarantee, not as a method of paying. Credit was to be available in New York by the plaintiff's drafts on Chase Manhattan at sight when accompanied by a document signed by the plaintiff and the second defendant evidencing cancelling of the contract between them or an arbitral award to such effect.

---

price of the goods sold and the amount due under the letter of credit). Under the scheme contemplated by Section 5-111(a), the beneficiary would present the documents to the issuer. If the issuer wrongfully dishonored, the beneficiary would have no further duty to the issuer with respect to the goods covered by documents that the issuer dishonored and returned. The issuer thus takes the risk that the beneficiary will let the goods rot or be destroyed. Of course the beneficiary may have a duty of mitigation to the applicant arising from the underlying agreement, but the issuer would not have the right to assert that duty by way of defense or setoff. See Section 5- 117(d). If the beneficiary sells the goods covered by dishonored documents or if the beneficiary sells a draft after acceptance but before dishonor by the issuer, the net amount so gained should be subtracted from the amount of the beneficiary's damages — at least where the damage claim against the issuer equals or exceeds the damage suffered by the beneficiary. If, on the other hand, the beneficiary suffers damages in an underlying transaction in an amount that exceeds the amount of the wrongfully dishonored demand (e.g., where the letter of credit does not cover 100 percent of the underlying obligation), the damages avoided should not necessarily be deducted from the beneficiary's claim against the issuer. In such a case, the damages would be the lesser of (i) the amount recoverable in the absence of mitigation (that is, the amount that is subject to the dishonor or repudiation plus any incidental damages) and (ii) the damages remaining after deduction for the amount of damages actually avoided."

[41] Offshore International S.A. v. Banco Central S.A. and Another <1977> 1 W.L.R. 399

CHAPTER VII

The amount of the letter of credit was stated in USD. The fact pattern of the case for the purpose of choice of law is the following:

- Issuing bank (Banco Central) operating and incorporated in Spain;
- Beneficiary (Ofshore International) incorporated in Panama;
- Customer incorporated in Spain and operating there;
- Advising bank (Chase) operating in New York;
- First tender of documents in New York and payment at sight in the same place;
- Currency stated in U.S. dollars; and
- Language used was evidently English.

The court outlined the problem and held as follows:

Spanish or New York law?

The contest here is between New York and Spanish law. What are the relevant factors in favour of each? As regards New York, the credit was opened through a New York bank — payment was to be made in U.S. dollars. Further, such payment was only to be made against documents presented in New York. *In favour of Spanish law being the proper law, is the fact that the letter of credit was opened by a Spanish bank, the first defendants.* Thus, on the side of New York law are all matters of performance, whereas, in relation to Spanish law, Spain and Spanish bank was *the source of obligation*. In my judgment, it is with New York law that the transaction has its closest and most real connection. (Emphasis added.)

The situs of debt or source of obligation?

The comment as to Spain and the Spanish bank being the *source of the obligation* is most interesting. The court pointed out further, agreeing with counsel, that a " ... very great inconvenience would arise, if the law of the issuing bank were to be considered as the proper law. The advising bank would have constantly to be seeking to apply a whole variety of foreign laws." The court applied the law of the place of performance to the beneficiary–issuing bank relationship.

It is not clear why the proceedings were instituted in England and not in Spain or New York. This may have been because of the arbitration pending in England in accordance with the main contract or it may have been due to an express agreement of the parties. The Spanish bank may have been subject to the *in personam* jurisdiction of English courts and the plaintiff may have preferred English courts in lieu of the defendants' national courts in Spain. As to the availability of precedents in the field, the court stated, "There is no decided case dealing precisely with the point. The two cases to which I have been referred, each heard over 100 years ago, I have found of no real assistance."

The argument as to the inconvenience caused to the advising bank is not too convincing. Why should the inconvenience of the advising bank outweigh that of the issuing bank or anyone else participating in the facility?

VII.3.3 Very Little To Do With England: *Power Curber International Ltd. v. National Bank of Kuwait S.A.K.* (Or, The Stay Must Go)

This case is fascinating both as to facts and to the motivations of the decision. Thus it could speak for itself, and it would need only to be quoted. But I dare to add some interim and introductory comments.

The part of the decision that I present here begins with a somewhat bold or surprising comment: "This case has nothing to do with England except that the plaintiff chose to bring his action here". This reflects the value of the "brand" of the English courts as well as procedural problems of international transactions

As the court said in its Judgment:

> "Lord DENNING, M.R.: This case raises an important point in international trade. *It has nothing to do with England except that an action has been brought here.* It is brought by American sellers who exported goods from the U.S.A. to buyers in Kuwait. They were to be paid by a letter of credit issued by the National Bank of Kuwait. The bank wish to honour their obligations. They wish to pay the sums due under the letter of credit. But *the Courts in Kuwait have forbidden the bank to pay*. What is the bank to do?"

CHAPTER VII

After having introduced the dilemma of the honorable Kuwaiti bank, the court introduces the true litigants:

> "The plaintiff company's name is Power Curber International Ltd. You might think that it was an English company seeing that its name ends with "Ltd." But it is in fact an American corporation which carries on business at Salisbury in Northern [sic] Carolina. I will call it "Power Curber". It exports machinery to countries in the Middle East.
>
> *It operates through a firm of distributors in Kuwait* called Hammoudeh & Al Fulaij General Trading & Contracting Company WLL. I will call the firm 'Hammoudeh'. *The directors have close contacts with America and spend their time between that Country and the Middle East. They are the "distributors" for Power Curber in the Middle East. By which I take it they buy goods on their own account from Power Curber and resell them on a commission or other basis in the Middle East.*
>
> About July, 1979, Power Curber agreed to supply machinery to Hammoudeh to be shipped from the U.S.A. not later than Mar. 1, 1980, on c.i.f. terms and paid as to 25 per cent on presentation of documents and the remaining 75 per cent one year after date of shipment. The buyers (Hammoudeh) were to give usance drafts (that is, bills of exchange payable at a later date) for this remaining 75 per cent. In order to be sure of payment, Power Curber required Hammoudeh to open a letter of credit in their favour. *Hammoudeh went to their bank, the National Bank of Kuwait, and asked them to issue a letter of credit. No doubt Hammoudeh put the bank in funds or otherwise secured the bank so that the bank would be indemnified against their liability under the letter of credit.*
>
> **The letter of credit**
>
> The letter of credit is dated "Kuwait 6 Sept. 1979". *It was issued by the National Bank of Kuwait (the issuing bank) to the Bank of America, Florida, Miami, U.S.A. (the advising bank)* through the North Carolina National Bank in Charlotte, North Carolina. It was an irrevocable credit but not a confirmed credit. It is so important that I will set out most of it."

Jurisdiction and Choice of Law

Proceedings in Kuwaiti courts brought by Hammoudeh resulted in an injunction against the issuing bank:

> "It appears that early in November, 1980, Hammoudeh filed a claim in the Courts of Kuwait against Power Curber for 50,000 *Kuwait dinars. That is about $180,000*. We do not know the nature of the claim but it is thought it may be a claim for commission. Following on that claim, *Hammoudeh applied to the Court in Kuwait for an order for "provisional attachment" of the sums payable by the National Bank of Kuwait under the letter of credit* to Power Curber. *On Nov. 5, 1980, the Court in Kuwait ordered the "provisional attachment"*. This order prevented the bank from making any further payment under the letter of credit in Kuwait or outside Kuwait: and made the bank accountable to the Court for the amount involved. *The bank lodged a protest against the attachment: and applied to the Court in Kuwait to set aside the order for "provisional attachment". But the Court refused to set it aside. And its refusal has been upheld by the Court of Appeal in Kuwait."*

Proceedings were then initiated in England by Power Curber against the issuing bank:

> "*On Jan.27, 1981,* Power Curber issued a writ in the High Court in England against the National Bank of Kuwait *(which was trading here and had a registered address in London)*. They claimed $75,794.46 and applied for judgment under R.S.C., 0.14. On Mar. 27, 1981, *Mr. Justice Parker gave judgment in favour of Power Curber* against the National Bank of Kuwait for that amount *but stayed execution on it until further order*. There is now an appeal by Power Curber against the stay and by the bank against the judgment. The questions debated before us were these:
>
> i. Should Power Curber be granted summary judgment?
>
> ii. *Even if granted summary judgment, should execution be stayed?* By our English law a plaintiff is entitled to have summary judgment given for him if the defendant has no arguable defence to the claim. The Judge (Mr. Justice Parker) gave summary judgment for the plaintiffs. But he stayed execution on it until further order. *Each side appeals*. I will deal first with summary judgment."

The court's conclusion, which begins here, represents law at its best and merits attention in its maturity and vision:

> "The striking fact is that the Courts here in London are asked to enforce a letter of Credit opened by buyers in Kuwait in favour of sellers in the U.S.A. for payment in the U.S.A. *But this is because London is an important Centre of international trade. Merchants from all over the world come here to settle their disputes. Banks from all over the world have branches here to receive and make payments. So far as we can be of service to international trade, we will accept the task and fulfil [sic] it to the best of our ability.* I would approve the judgment of Mr. Justice Parker in favour of the sellers. I would not grant a stay of execution. "

The discussion on the law applicable begins between the choice of North Carolina and Kuwaiti law.

> "Lord Justice GRIFFITHS: I will deal first with the Cross-appeal. The bank submit that the Judge should give leave to defend because payment of the sums due under the letter of Credit is unlawful according to the proper law of the contract. This submission depends upon the proper law of the letter of Credit being Kuwaiti law. *In my view the proper law of the letter of credit was the law of the state of North Carolina.* Under the letter of credit the bank accepted the obligations of paying or arranging the payment of the sums due in American dollars *against presentation of documents at the sellers' bank in North Carolina.* The bank could not have discharged its obligation by offering payment in Kuwait. Furthermore the bank undertook to reimburse the advising bank if they paid on their behalf in dollars in America. In *Offshore International S.A. v. Banco Central S.A.* (1976) 2 Lloyd's Rep. 402, Mr. Justice Ackner held that the place at which the bank must perform its obligation under a letter of credit determines the proper law to be applied to the letter of credit. In my view that case was correctly decided.
>
> Secondly, it was submitted that payment was unlawful according to the lex situs of the debt which is said is Kuwait. But this is a debt that is owed in American dollars in North Carolina. I do not regard the fact that the bank that owes the debt has a residence in Kuwait as any reason for regarding Kuwait as the lex situs of the debt. *The lex situs of the debt is North Carolina* and this ground for giving leave to defend cannot be supported.

No other grounds were advanced for resisting judgment under R.S.C. 0. 14 and I agree that the cross-appeal should be dismissed."

Next the court addressed the question of whether or not the stay was justified:

"Now as to the appeal: Should the Judge have granted a stay of the judgment? At the time the case was before Mr. Justice Parker the order of the Kuwait Court *was under appeal to the Kuwait Court of Appeal.* In those circumstances, I think I should have been very tempted to grant a short stay to await the outcome of the decision of the Court of Appeal, because I fear that *I should have thought it highly unlikely that the Court of Appeal would uphold an order that interfered so seriously with the well recognized international obligation of a bank under an irrevocable letter of credit. By granting the stay I should have been relieved of the disagreeable obligation to refuse to recognize the order of a Court of a friendly state.*

But now we know the result of the Court of Appeal hearing in Kuwait and must face the choice between enforcing the obligation upon the bank to pay under its irrevocable letter of credit or recognizing the order of the Kuwait Court. *I have no doubt that we should uphold the obligation to pay under the irrevocable letter of credit and remove the stay.* Letters of credit have become established as a universally acceptable means of payment in international transactions. *They are regarded by merchants the world over as equivalent to cash; they have been rightly described by that most distinguished commercial lawyer Mr. Justice Kerr as the life blood of international commerce,* see *Harbottle Ltd. v. National Westminster Bank Ltd.,* (1978) 1 Q.B. 146. The bankers' promise to pay the seller is wholly independent of the underlying contract of sale between the seller and the buyer, or of any other contractual dispute that may arise between them. The whole purpose of this form of payment is that a seller should not be kept out of his money by litigation against him at the suit of the buyer. In the absence of fraud the seller is entitled to be paid on presentation of genuine documents."

The Kuwaiti order given in *ex parte* proceedings:

"In the present case we do not even know with certainty the nature of the buyer's claim in Kuwait because *he obtained his provisional attachment order at an ex parte hearing* and has never served the American seller with any documents specifying the claim. It may be in respect of commission,

Chapter VII

or it may arise in respect of the goods in respect of which the letter of credit was issued. There is no suggestion of fraud and in the absence of fraud an English Court would not have interfered with the banker's obligation to pay under the letter of credit, see *Discount Records Ltd. v. Barclays Bank Ltd.*, <1975> 1 Lloyd's Rep. 444; <1975> 1 W.L.R. 315; *Harbottle (Mercantile) Ltd. v. National Westminster Bank Ltd.*, <1978> 1 Q.B. 146 and *Edward Owen Engineering Ltd. v. Barclays Bank International Ltd.*, <1978> 1 Lloyd's Rep. 166; <1978> 1 Q.B. 159."

Concerning protection of the "brand" or credibility of the bank in dilemma, the court said:

"We should do the Bank of Kuwait a grave disservice if we were not to remove this stay for it would undoubtedly seriously damage their credibility as an international bank if it was thought that their paper was not worth holding because an ex parte application to their domestic Courts could prevent payment under an expressly irrevocable obligation."

Does an English court have to respect a ruling or order of a foreign court?

"There is no recognized rule of international law that compels this Court to recognize this ex parte order of the Kuwait Court. It is of course entitled to be treated with respect and wherever possible this Court will in the interests of comity seek to recognize and uphold the order of the Court of a friendly state. But unhappily in this case the approach of the Kuwait Court appears to be so out of step with that of our own Courts and the Courts of other trading nations that I fear we cannot recognize it. The choice lies between upholding the world-wide practices of international commerce or the order of the Kuwait Court. I choose the first option and would remove the stay.

Lord DENNING, M.R.: Mr. Justice Waterhouse cannot be here this afternoon, and I will ask Lord Justice Griffiths to read his judgment. Mr. Justice WATERHOUSE: I agree that this appeal should be allowed and that the cross-appeal should be dismissed.

Despite the forceful argument of Counsel for the bank, I am unable to accept that leave to defend the action should have been granted. On the issue as to the proper law of the letter of credit, I respectfully agree with what has been said by Lord Denning, M.R., and Lord Justice Griffiths about the correctness and application to the instant case of the reasoning of Mr. Justice Ackner if *Offshore International S.A. v. Banco Central S.A.*, <1976> 2 Lloyd's Rep. 402; <1977> 1 W.L.R. 399. The more difficult issue for me has been that relating to the lex situs of the debt."

As to the question of what is the situs of a debt (under Kuwaiti law), Mr. Justice Waterhouse said:

"A debt is generally to be looked upon as situate in the Country where it is properly recoverable or can be enforced and it is noteworthy that the sellers here submitted voluntarily to the dismissal of their earlier proceedings against the bank in North Carolina. We have been told that they did so because of doubts about the jurisdiction of the North Carolina Court, which was alleged in the pleadings to be based on the transaction of business by the bank there, acting by itself or through another named bank as its agent. *As for the question of residence, the bank has been silent about any residence that it may have within the United States of America.* In the absence of any previous binding authority on the question, *I have not been persuaded that this debt due under an unconfirmed letter of credit can be regarded as situate in North Carolina merely because there was no provision* for payment at a branch of a bank used by the sellers in Charlotte, and I do not regard the analogy of a bill of exchange or a security transferable by delivery as helpful. Nevertheless, Mr. Justice Parker was right, in my judgment, to refuse the bank leave to defend because the Kuwaiti provisional order of attachment did not affect the existence of the debt. Counsel for the bank has submitted that the effect of that order was to alter the debt from one due to the sellers to a debt due to the Court or held to the order of the Court awaiting a decision as to whom it should be paid. I agree with Mr. Justice Parker that this submission is based upon a single sentence in an affidavit and that it does not bear that weight. *There is no acceptable evidence that, according to the law of Kuwait, the debt has ceased to be due to the sellers.* There is no ground, therefore, for granting leave to defend and Counsel for the bank has not sought to argue that a stay of proceedings is justified if leave to defend was properly refused."

Mr. Justice Waterhouse considered whether the action would have been tried in England although the case had nothing to do with England:

"If there had been an arguable defence, *I would have held that the action should be tried in England because there is a legitimate juridical advantage*

CHAPTER VII

> *to the sellers in proceeding here, which outweighs any disadvantage to the bank.*
>
> The sellers' appeal against the stay of execution granted by Mr. Justice Parker has to be considered in the changed circumstance that the bank's appeal to the Court of Appeal in Kuwait against the provisional order of attachment has failed. Although *a further appeal to the Cour de Cassation* there is proceeding, we have been told that it will not be heard until the end of the year. I agree, therefore, that *the overwhelming balance of the argument now is in favour of removal of the stay of execution.* Part of the argument for the bank on this issue has been that it is expedient for the Court to permit execution to proceed pending resolution of the dispute between Hammoudeh and the sellers: it is suggested that the bank may be exposed to the risk of proceeding for contempt in Kuwait or of double payment. One has sympathy with the bank in its dilemma, and its good faith is not in doubt, not least because it has already paid to the plaintiffs $82,546.80 due earlier on Nov. 7, 1980, in respect of the same letter of credit, despite the provisional attachment order."

Mr. Justice Waterhouse concluded that the stay must "go" as violating the foundation of international letter of credit law:

> "However, *the action of the opener, Hammoudeh, and the reasoning of the Kuwait Court of Appeal appears to me to strike at the essential foundations of the international acceptability of letters of credit so that the stay ought not to continue.* <Order: Appeal allowed with costs. Cross-appeal dismissed with costs. Appln. leave to appeal to the House of Lords refused>."

VII.3.4 False conflict?

At first glance there seem to be two major streams with respect to the law applicable: the law of *the place or location of the party* rendering the most characteristic performance on the one hand or the law of the *place of payment or performance* on the other. By "the place of payment" English law refers to the place where the beneficiary shall present the documents to meet the conditions precedent and to obtain honor, i.e., payment in immediately available funds ("cash"), or a deferred payment undertaking, or acceptance. This is where "the death" of the instrument takes place and the dismantling of the facility begins, causing the dominos to fall across borders. In the great majority of commercial real-world cases this place is at the same time the location or domicile of the issuing or conforming bank, i.e., their physical banking offices.[42] Generally, the payment is effected at this location.

The most characteristic performance under these instruments is the performance of the paying bank to the beneficiary, i.e., the examination of the tender, or demand and honor, or refusal thereafter. All this happens at "the place of payment". In great majority of cases, this happens at the location, i.e., at the bank's offices. The law of the location leads to the application of the same law as the English rule of "place of payment". We cannot but conclude that the two approaches, although different in name and in principle, lead in most cases to the application of the same material law: the place of payment is, in general, the same as the place or location of performer, i.e., where the most characteristic performance, payment against tender, is made. It is the core and the main purpose of the instrument and the facility, and it hardly ever is effected anywhere else than at the location of the bank's own office or branch. Are we not dealing with a false conflict or a "*quasi*-problem" created by formal rules only?

The place-of-payment approach is further reinforced if the place of payment is a financial center of the world. This may be presumed to express or indicate a confidence of the parties in the proper functioning of that marketplace, including due enforcement of possible claims, and appropriate legal protection when and if needed. These policy aspects may, indeed, weigh more heavily the more paramount the financial center is in our global economy. Such centers include New York, London, Hong Kong, Singapore and Frankfurt.

Complexities may arise with letters of credit. In particular complexities may arise with freely negotiable letters of credit. In the latter case there is no predetermined place of payment, where "the moment of death" occurs. This may take place almost anywhere. One may presume that in such a case the place of business of

---

[42] Stuart Dutson, *A Dangerous Proposal - The European Commission's Attempt to Amend the Law Applicable to Contractual Obligations*, Legislative Comment, J Busn L, (2006):
"613. In the case of letters of credit, the presumption would usually be displaced as a result of the more closely connected test where the documents were to be presented to, and payments made by, an advising bank in another jurisdiction. It is common ground that under a letter of credit it is desirable that the same system of law should govern the co-existing contracts between: (i) the issuing bank and the beneficiary; (ii) the confirming bank and beneficiary; and (iii) the issuing bank and the confirming bank. Letters of credit often contain no express choice of law as a result of an assumption that this is true and will be respected by the courts."

Chapter VII

the confirming or issuing bank, in lieu of the place of business of the negotiating bank, would prevail as being the place where the party who renders the most characteristic performance is situated. The place of payment remains undetermined except as to payment (reimbursement) to the negotiating bank. In a freely negotiable letter of credit, the negotiation may be deemed not to be of paramount importance, whereas the issuing or the confirming of such a "movable" instrument is the most characteristic significant performance inspiring the desired confidence in the instrument issued.

If these rules are applied to the confirming bank transaction, there are two places where the "moment of death" may take place. Is one to apply the law of the place of the confirming bank to its confirmation and the law of the issuing bank to the issuing bank or should one or the other law apply to both relationships?[43] And if one single law is chosen, which one is to prevail? The answer is not self-evident, and it may depend on whether (a) there is a three-party agreement is between the two banks and the beneficiary, or (b) there are two separate bank-beneficiary agreements. In case "(a)", applying just one law would seem consistent since the instrument issued is being confirmed as it is. If, however, the confirmation is anticipated or agreed to be by a nominated bank in a financial center, the law of the confirming bank, for policy reasons and as a presumed expression of the will of the parties, forms perhaps the heaviest connection of the instrument to national jurisdictions and the law of the financial center should thus prevail. It is possible, as well, to apply two laws at the same time, and to do so is unlikely to produce different results. The following case, *Sonali*, sheds light on these issues.

VII.3.5 Seeking the closest and most real connection: the *Sonali* case

This case illustrates at the outset how the infrastructure or facility is built and the instrument is issued and utilized in commerce:

> "The governing law of the contracts between BCCHK and Sonali:

---

[43] Stuart Dutson, "A Dangerous Proposal — The European Commission's Attempt to Amend the Law Applicable to Contractual Obligations", Legislative Comment *Journal of Business Law*, (2006): "The English courts have also suggested that the more closely connected test may well be satisfied where the place of performance of the contract differs from the place of business of the party whose performance is characteristic of the contract."

Sonali contends that seven claims under five letters of credit are barred by limitation under the law of Bangladesh, which Sonali contends to be the proper law of the relevant contracts. Sonali confirmed at the hearing that it was common ground in the case of each of the five credits that:

(i) the Bangladeshi importer agreed to purchase goods from the Hong Kong seller;
(ii) payment was to be effected by letter of credit;
(iii) the Bangladeshi buyer applied to Sonali to open a letter of credit;
(iv) Sonali issued a letter of credit in favour of the Hong Kong seller;
(v) the letter of credit was expressed to be subject to the UCP 1983 Revision and was a negotiation credit;
(vi) the confirming bank, BCCHK, agreed to add its confirmation to the credit;
(vii) the Hong Kong seller/beneficiary presented documents to BCCHK;
(viii) either: (a) the documents conformed with the credit; or (b) the documents did not conform with the credit but Sonali advised BCCHK that the non-conforming documents were acceptable;
(ix) BCCHK negotiated the documents and presented them to Sonali;
(x) Sonali either: (a) expressly advised BCCHK of its (Sonali's) acceptance of the documents; or (b) failed within a reasonable time to give notice of refusal of the documents and return them or hold them at the disposal of BCCHK, so as to be precluded from claiming that the documents did not conform pursuant to art. 16(e) of the UCP 1983 Revision;
(xi) reimbursement to BCCHK was to be from an account maintained by Sonali at one of its branches in England;
(xii) Sonali failed to reimburse BCCHK on the due date for payment under the credit."[44]

The dispute arose due to Sonali's failure to reimburse BCCHK. The following chapter illustrates the rich flora of facts reflecting the commercial reality of trading:

> I refer to the documents exhibited to *Miss Kinloch's affidavit* relating to the seven claims/five credits (8, 10/11, 31, 32/33 and 37). I will take claim 11

---

[44] Bank of Credit & Commerce Hong Kong Ltd v. Sonali Bank,1994 WL 1063048 (QBD (Comm Ct)), [1994] C.L.C. 1171, [1995] 1 Lloyd's Rep. 227, 10-20-1994 Independent 1063,048.

CHAPTER VII

(U.S.$69,224.47) under credit 10/11-BBA/1/89/166/DP as an example. *The issuing bank was Sonali, Dhaka.* The credit was dated Dec. 12, 1989 (p. 242). *The buyer/opener/applicant was Smart Apparels* (PTE) Ltd., Dhaka. *The seller/beneficiary was Cheong Wor Textiles Co. Ltd.*, Hong Kong. The amount was U.S. $123,000. The credit provided:

Negotiation: 15 days from the date of shipment . . . Payment Stipulation. Against submission of the following documents. (1) Beneficiary's draft payable at 120 days sight showing our credit number drawn on openers . . . Other Terms and Conditions . . . (5) This L/C is opened against export L/C Number. . . dated 13.10.1989 of First Fidelity Bank, U.S.A . . . (7) Bill of Exchange must be presented to the negotiating bank not later than 15 days from the date of bill of lading and on scrutiny if documents are found correct and drawn as per terms of L/C . . . and conveying due date of payment to them which will be fallen due after 120 days from the date of negotiation of documents and on that due date of payment *negotiating bank will claim reimbursement to our Sonali Bank, 29-33 Osborn Street, London E1 for the 100% invoice value plus interest* from the date of negotiation of documents to the date of payment maximum 120 days. (8) *Interest at 9.5% p.a.* should be paid from the date of negotiation of documents for "usance period" i.e., up to the date of our payment if made earlier than maturity date of drafts with maximum 120 days . . . *Instruction To Negotiating Bank* - Negotiating Bank will reimburse themselves by drawing upon negotiation of documents in strict compliance with credit terms. Negotiating bank is authorised to claim their reimbursement after 120 days from the date of negotiation of documents to our head office U.S.$ Regular Account No. . . . *maintained with Sonali Bank, 29-33 Osborn Street, London E1 with a certificate that all terms of this credit have been complied with. . .* This credit *is subject to (UCP)* . . . (1983 Revision) . . . At p. 242 BCCHK added its confirmation (on Jan. 30, 1990) stating: We hereby confirm that we will honour the bill drawn in strict compliance with the terms of this credit for USD 123,000 (BCCHK) *BCCHK notified the beneficiary of amendments* on the following dates. Dec. 29, 1989 (please add your confirmation); Jan. 2, 1990 (payment of import bill including interest at LIBOR but not exceeding 12 per cent. p.a. will be made 150 days from the date of negotiation of documents); Jan. 10, 1990 (value decreased - quantity); Jan. 17, 1990 (pre-shipment inspection; words deleted from paragraph (7); shipment date); Feb. 2, 1990 (shipment date extended); Mar. 6, 1990 "the enclosed amendment bears our confirmation" (L/C value; shipment date extended; L/C transferable; export L/C of First Fidelity Bank must appear in all invoices; please add your confirmation to this credit).

On Apr. 24, 1990 (p. 257) *BCCHK sent to Sonali a form entitled* "Local/ foreign bills purchased (documentary) with/without discrepancies) stating: . . . negotiation has been effected in accordance with your telex authorization . . . advise acceptance by tested telex . . . Reimbursement: at maturity we shall claim reimbursement from your Head Office USD Regular A/C No. . . . with your London/UK office for the proceeds plus interest at 12% p.a. from date of negotiation to date of payment as instructed . . . *this negotiation has been effected* according to (UCP) 1983 (Revision).

On May 31, 1990 (p. 260) *Sonali telexed BCCHK: . . . your bill . . . for USD69,224.47 accepted and will mature for payment on 20.9.90. Please claim your reimbursement accordingly.*

Later on Sonali changed its earlier position referring to instructions and to disputes under the transaction:

On July 30, 1990 (p. 262) Sonali Bank London Ltd. telexed BCCHK as follows: We have been instructed *by the L/C opening bank not to honour your claim* for USD . . . 69,224.47 . . . until their further specific instruction is received by us on 3.7.90. It may be mentioned that payment will be released by them *after settlement of dispute between supplier and the opener* as advised by the opener to them.

This was a plain contravention of art. 3 of the UCP 1983 Revision which states the fundamental principle that: . . . credits, by their nature, are separate transactions from the sales of other contracts on which they may be based and banks are in no way concerned with or bound by such contracts, even if any reference whatsoever to such contracts is included in the credit.

On Aug. 7, 1990 (p. 263) Sonali Dhaka telexed BCCHK: . . . we have been requested by the opener. . . to instruct beneficiary of L/C that payment of

CHAPTER VII

> their bills for . . . 69,224.47 will be paid from the export proceeds after export of readymade garments under relative export L/C no. . . . dated 13.10.89. . . . On Aug. 21, 1990 (p. 266) BCCHK telexed Sonali Dhaka: . . . we have related your message to the beneficiary regarding payment of the above bills will be paid from the import proceeds after export of readymade garments under export L/C and was replied by the beneficiary via their letter that they do not have any agreement or commitment with L/C opener. You are requested to . . . authorise your London Office to honour our claim under the bill reference . . . upon maturity i.e., 20.9.90.

BCCHK was in a confusing situation, caught in a crossfire with an open credit position:

> On Nov. 16, 1990 (p. 269) *BCCHK telexed Sonali Dhaka: . . . we have claimed reimbursement on maturity date from Sonali Bank, London but payment was refused by them. In reply to our telex reminders your branch advised that the opener of L/C imposed temporary injunction on them . . . to stop payment. It is very abnormal under international trade to have a bill drawn under an irrevocable letter of credit bearing acceptance, unpaid upon maturity. . . .*

Court proceedings in Dhaka were commenced by the account party:

> On Dec. 12, 1990 (p. 271) Sonali Dhaka telexed BCCHK: - . . . opener . . . has filed a suit to . . . Court of First Sub-Judge Court Dhaka for imposing injunction on our payment against your above bills. Accordingly we have been served with show cause by notice the court and *our reply which is being prepared by our legal adviser opposing the injunction to be submitted to court on 12.1.91 fixed for hearing.* Meanwhile our legal adviser advised us not to proceed for settlement of above payment until court decision since suit has already been filed and accepted by the . . . court for hearing. *We therefore request you to please wait for court decision which we will convey you in due course.*

The importer submits a settlement proposal and the proceeding continues without BCCHK being a party:

> On June 15, 1991 (p. 273) Bank of Credit and Commerce International (Overseas) Ltd. Dhaka telexed BCCHK: . . . the importer of the above L/C have *submitted a written proposal in settlement of the above L/C* requesting

to compensate their losses or to accept 30% discount from the invoice value under the above L/C and interest will be paid for 120 days only on such discounted value and send a fresh draft along with the revised invoice to the opening bank i.e., Sonali Bank . . .

As to the proceedings referred to in the above correspondence Miss Kinloch states in par. 27 of her affidavit: . . . *this action was commenced before the First Munsiff Court, Dhaka by . . . the applicant . . . against . . . the beneficiary . . . and Sonali Bank. BCCHK are not party to the action* but were informed by Sonali Bank in September 1990 that the plaintiff had obtained an injunction to restrain payment under the L/C by Sonali Bank. It is thought that there was a hearing in this action in February 1991, but the nature of the hearing and its outcome are unknown.

I have in addition carefully considered the documents exhibited to Miss Kinloch's affidavit relating to the remainder of the seven claims/five credits (8, 10 of 10/11, 31, 32/33 and 37). Mr. Hossain did not suggest in the course of the hearing that there were material distinctions between the seven claims/five credits as to governing law and I was only referred to sample claims/credits in the course of the hearing. I do not consider that the result differs as between the seven claims/five credits, all of which are subject to the common features set out above.

After describing the traditional steps to create the facility and traditional dismantling thereof until the dominos stopped falling, the court described the contractual network as follows:

It is necessary to distinguish between five contractual relationships that arise in respect of the five credits:

1. The contract of sale between the buyer in Bangladesh and the seller in Hong Kong.

2. The contract between the buyer/applicant and the issuing bank (Sonali) containing the terms upon which a letter of credit was to be opened in favour of the seller/beneficiary.

3. The contract between the issuing bank (Sonali) and the confirming bank (BCCHK) constituting the confirming bank's mandate as to advice and confirmation of the credit and negotiation.

4. The contract between the issuing bank (Sonali) and the seller/beneficiary in Hong Kong containing the issuing bank's undertaking to pay without recourse to drawers and/or bona fide holders, drafts drawn by the beneficiary under the credit.

5. The contract between the confirming bank (BCCHK) and the seller/beneficiary containing the confirming bank's additional undertaking to pay without recourse to drawers and/or bona fide holders, drafts drawn by the beneficiary under the credit.

The authorities recognize that there are strong commercial reasons why contracts 3, 4 and 5 should be governed by the same system of law. In the present case I am concerned in particular with the law governing the contracts between BCCHK and Sonali (contract 3 above) in the case of the five credits.

The issue of conflict of laws arose and the court gave an analysis that is quite meritorious:

In the light of the above authorities I turn to consider the question - what was the governing law of the contracts between BCCHK and Sonali in the case of the five credits (8, 10/11, 31, 32/33 and 37) referred to above. The letters of credit in question predated Apr. 1, 1991 so the question has to be decided not by application of the 1990 Act but by application of common law principles and in particular by asking the question - *with which system of law have the contracts their closest and most real connection*? In my view the contract between BCCHK and Sonali was in each case governed by the law of Hong Kong for the following reasons:

(i) It is common ground that in each case BCCHK (in Hong Kong) agreed to add its confirmation to the credit.

(ii) When Sonali requested BCCHK to confirm Sonali's irrevocable credit and BCCHK added its confirmation, such confirmation constituted a definite undertaking of BCCHK (the confirming bank), in addition to that of Sonali (the issuing bank), provided that the stipulated documents were presented and the terms and conditions of the credit were complied with, to negotiate without recourse to drawers and/or bona fide holders, drafts drawn by the beneficiary, at a tenor, on the applicant for the credit (art. 10(b)(iv) UCP 1983 Revision).

(iii) By requesting BCCHK to add its confirmation, Sonali authorized BCCHK to negotiate against documents which appeared on their face to be in accordance with the terms and conditions of the credit, and undertook to reimburse BCCHK in accordance with the provisions of the UCP 1983 Revision (art. 11(d) and see also art. 16(a)).

(iv) Having confirmed the credit BCCHK was *obliged* to negotiate the documents (see Jack, Documentary Credits (2nd ed.) p. 122 par. 6.17(6)).

(v) The credits contemplated that negotiation of documents presented by or on behalf of the Hong Kong beneficiary *would take place in Hong Kong* (and this is what happened with resulting payment by BCCHK to the beneficiary).

Reimbursement in each case was to be claimed from a Sonali London branch (but this does not affect the conclusion that Hong Kong law was the law with which the contract had its closest and most real connection). I add the following footnotes. *In my view the governing law is the law of Hong Kong* (a) whether or not the beneficiary presented direct or through a presenting bank; and (b) whether or not a presenting bank negotiated/discounted the documents; and (c) whether or not the documents presented to BCCHK conformed with the credit or did not conform (but Sonali advised BCCHK that the non-conforming documents were acceptable or Sonali is precluded by art. 16(e) UCP 1983 Revision from claiming that the documents were not in accordance with the terms of the credit)."[45]

---

[45] Bank of Credit & Commerce Hong Kong Ltd v. Sonali Bank, 1994 WL 1063048 (QBD (Comm Ct)), [1994] C.L.C. 1171, [1995] 1 Lloyd's Rep. 227, 10-20-1994 Independent 1063,048..

VII.3.6 Were Performance Bonds Really So New? *Edward Owen Ltd. v. Barclays Bank*

The following summary of this landmark case is from the first edition of this book written when the problems or issues which had emerged appeared more dramatic than they do now, when we can analyze them with the neutrality that distance in time gives us. Many events of the 1970s were dramatic, but perhaps more so politically, culturally and emotionally than legally. It is difficult but important to keep these areas of human and social life apart, but only to a certain extent: equity must be given its proper place.

This case is perhaps one of the first, if not the first, time the close relationship and the similarity of the basic mechanism of performance bonds and letters of credit is clearly expressed. A performance bond is described as a new creature, which it really was, but in essence it is the same old structure in a new "fancy" costume: "very similar" and "stands on a similar footing". The case dealt with injunction and English law was applied. The actual performance bonds were issued by a Libyan bank and were subject to Libyan law.

This was a typical case of guarantee arrangement *analogous with standby letters of credit*. The plaintiff, an English engineering company, made a contract with the Agricultural Development Council of Libya for the supply of and installation of glasshouses in Libya. *The main contract was subject to Libyan law and disputes between the parties were to be referred to the exclusive jurisdiction of the competent Libyan court.*

The English sellers instructed their bankers to give the necessary guarantee in favor of Umma Bank (the state bank of Libya), which in turn issued a similar on-demand guarantee in favor of the Libyan buyers. The relationships established were described by the court as follows:

"So there was a string of guarantees. The English suppliers guaranteed Barclays Bank International, Barclays Bank International guaranteed the Umma Bank in Libya, and the Umma Bank guaranteed the Libyan buyers." The court described in a most accurate way the close relationship between letters of credit and guarantees:

(Lord Denning, M.R.) *The law as to performance bonds. A performance bond is a new creature so far as we are concerned. It has many similarities to letter of credit, with which of course we are very familiar.* It has been long established that when a letter of credit is issued and confirmed by a bank, the bank must pay it if the documents are in order and the terms of the credit are satisfied. Any dispute between buyer and seller must be settled between themselves. The bank must honour the credit. That was clearly stated in *Hamzeh Malas & Sons v. British Imex Industries Ltd.* <1958> 2 Q.B. 127. Jenkins, L.J., giving the judgment of this court, said, at p. 129: ". . . .it seems to be plain enough that the opening of a confirmed letter of credit constitutes a bargain between the banker and the vendor of the goods, which imposes upon the banker an absolute obligation to pay, irrespective of any dispute there may be between the parties as to whether the goods are up to contract or not. An elaborate commercial system has been built up on the footing that bankers' confirmed credits are of that character, and in my judgment, it would be wrong for this court in the present case to interfere with the established practice."

(BROWNE L.J.) I agree that this appeal should be dismissed for the reasons given by Lord Denning M.R. Kerr J. in *Harbottle (Mercantile) Ltd. v. National Westminster Bank Ltd.* <1977> 3 W.L.R. 752 and this court in *Howe Richardson* case, June 23, 1977: Bar Library Transcript No. 270 treated a bank's position under a guarantee or performance bond of the type given by Barclays Bank to the Umma Bank as being very similar to the position of a bank which has opened a confirmed irrevocable letter of credit, and I have no doubt that this is right.

The conclusion as to the material law applicable to these guarantees was the following:

"All this leads to the conclusion that the performance guarantee stands on a similar footing to a letter of credit. A bank which gives a performance guarantee must honour that guarantee according to its terms. It is not concerned in the least with the relations between the supplier and the customer; nor with the question whether the supplier has performed his contracted obligation or not; nor with the question whether the supplier is in default or not. The bank must pay according to its guarantee, on demand, if so stipulated, without proof or conditions. The only exception is when there is a clear fraud of which the bank has notice."

Browne, L.J., also made a most interesting statement as to the applicable law:

"*The performance bond is presumably also governed by Libyan law.* We do not know what the position of Libyan law may be between the plaintiffs and the

Executive Authority or between the Executive Authority and the Umma Bank. It seems to me therefore that we cannot exclude the possibility that there may be a genuine dispute between the plaintiffs and the Executive Authority as to matters arising under the underlying contract."

The statement concerns the performance bond issued by Umma Bank in favor of the Libyan buyers and not the interbank guarantees, not to mention the relationship between the plaintiff and Barclays Bank. In any case the court applied English law to the case where the issue was the discharge of an interim injunction obtained by the customer. This case illustrates in an excellent way the problems that may be encountered in defining whether remedies are procedural law or part of a public policy or material law. *If the availability of injunction belongs to the realm of procedural law or to public policy, and is to be determined by lex fori, it does not ultimately matter what law is applicable to the contract in question because the court will in any case follow its own procedural rules or ordre public. If, on the other hand, the remedies are considered to be part of material law, their availability should be determined on the basis of the applicable law arrived at after the application of the choice of law rules of the lex fori.*

VII.3.7 The Uniform Commercial Code (UCC) – An American Creature

The UCC adopts the prevailing main principles as to choice of law. The freedom of the parties to agree on the law applicable is expressly acknowledged adding that *there need to be no contact with the law so chosen*. UCC expressly acknowledges the submission of the instrument to UCP or other such "private" rules. Such reference cannot, however, replace the nonvariable or "mandatory" rules of UCC.[46] A choice of law made in bad faith to avoid the applicability of certain mandatory

---

[46] Compare to UNC Article 23: "1. The application of a provision of the law of the State in which the assignor is located may be refused only if the application of that provision is manifestly contrary to the public policy of the forum State. 2. The rules of the law of either the forum State or any other State that are mandatory irrespective of the law otherwise applicable may not prevent the application of a provision of the law of the State in which the assignor is located. 3. Notwithstanding paragraph 2 of this article, in an insolvency proceeding commenced in a State other than the State in which the assignor is located, any preferential right that arises, by operation of law, under the law of the forum State and is given priority over the rights of an assignee in insolvency proceedings under the law of that State may be given priority notwithstanding article 22. A State may deposit at any time a declaration identifying any such preferential right."

rules may not be successful. In modern private international law such rules may, in any case, be applied if important enough policies lie behind them, not to mention transnational *ordre public*.[47]

The following sentences deal with the autonomy or freedom of the parties to agree on the applicable law:

UCC 5-116:

> "(a) The liability of an issuer, nominated person or adviser for action or omission is governed by the law of the jurisdiction chosen by an agreement in the form of a record signed or otherwise authenticated by the affected parties in the manner provided in Section 5-104 or by a provision in the person's letter of credit, confirmation, or other undertaking. *The jurisdiction whose law is chosen need not bear any relation to the transaction.*

---

[47] Stuart Dutson, *A Dangerous Proposal - The European Commission's Attempt to Amend the Law Applicable to Contractual Obligations*, Legislative Comment, J Busn L, (2006).:
"Foreign mandatory laws intervening Article 8 of the proposal provides: "Article 8—Mandatory rules 1. Mandatory rules are rules the respect for which is regarded as crucial by a country for safeguarding its political, social or economic organisation to such an extent that they are applicable to any situation falling within their scope, irrespective of the law otherwise applicable to the contract under this Regulation. 2. Nothing in this Regulation shall restrict the application of the rules of the law of the forum in a situation where they are mandatory. 3. Effect may be given to the mandatory rules of the law of another country with which the situation has a close connection. In considering whether to give effect to these mandatory rules, courts shall have regard to their nature and purpose in accordance with the definition in paragraph 1 and to the consequences of their application or non-application for the objective pursued by the relevant mandatory rules and for the parties. . . . . While English courts are likely to give speculative attempts to rely on Art. 8(3), short shrift, foreign mandatory laws (which would appear to fall within the definition in Art. 8(1)) do not irregularly arise in international disputes. . . . . In the Explanatory Memorandum to the proposed Art. 8(3), the Commission attempts to justify its inclusion on the basis that: "the Brussels I Regulation sometimes provides for alternative grounds of jurisdiction; it is therefore essential in a genuine European justice area for the courts to be able to have regard to another Member State's mandatory provisions"." "
UNC Article 31:
"1. Nothing in articles 27 to 29 restricts the application of the rules of the law of the forum State in a situation where they are mandatory irrespective of the law otherwise applicable. 2. Nothing in articles 27 to 29 restricts the application of the mandatory rules of the law of another State with which the matters settled in those articles have a close connection if and insofar as, under the law of that other State, those rules must be applied irrespective of the law otherwise applicable."

The secondary rule applies if no such express choice has been made: what constitutes "location" is defined as a factual place of operation, not a place of legal domicile or incorporation or registration:

> (b) Unless subsection (a) of this section applies, the liability of an issuer, nominated person, or adviser for action or omission is governed *by the law of the jurisdiction in which the person is located.* The person is considered to be located at the address indicated in the person's undertaking. If more than one address is indicated, the person is considered to be located at the address from which the person's undertaking was issued.

For choice of law or jurisdiction purposes, each branch is treated as a legal entity:

> For the purpose of jurisdiction, choice of law, and recognition of interbranch letters of credit, but not enforcement of a judgment, all branches of a bank are considered separate juridical entities and a bank is considered to be located at the place where its relevant branch is considered to be located under this subsection.

UCP will be applied by express choice or reference only, not by way of trade usage or custom. The UCC mandatory rules are "hard" material laws, which cannot be contracted away:

> (c) Except as otherwise provided in this subsection, the liability of an issuer, nominated person, or adviser *is governed by any rules of custom or practice, such as the uniform customs and practice for documentary credits,* to which the letter of credit, confirmation, or other undertaking *is expressly made subject.* If (1) this article would govern the liability of an issuer, nominated person, or adviser under subsection (a) or (b) of this section, (2) the relevant undertaking incorporates rules of custom or practice, and (3) there is conflict between this article and those rules as applied to that undertaking, *those rules govern except to the extent of any conflict with the nonvariable provisions* specified in subsection (c) of Section 5-103.(d) If there is conflict between this article and article 3, 4, 4A or 9, this article governs."

UCC seems to take a step away from favoring the law of the place of performance, which has played a decisive role in some important cases. This might change the outcome in the rare instances where the two rules do not result in the application of the same law (as is the case in the great majority of instruments), because the place of payment is the place of the location of the paying bank.[48]

VII.3.8 Educating the Adjudicator – the "Burden of Education"

In international litigation as well as in arbitration, the judge or the arbitrator is not necessarily at all educated in the applicable substantive law. An arbitrator may not be a lawyer by education. At the outset this may be shocking but such a reaction is not well founded. The arbitrators need to be educated in the law and in the facts of the case just like judges in cases which are beyond the beaten path. "Jura novit curia" does not necessarily carry you any further than "jura novit arbiter".

A judge knows his or her "own" procedural law to be applied as *lex fori*. Procedural law may well contain material elements as demonstrated in this work. The judge does not necessarily, however, have the vaguest idea about the material foreign law to be applied to the dispute, and very few legal systems impose upon the judge a duty to study, do research or investigate the foreign law. The maxim *jura novit curia* does not and cannot apply to the substance of foreign law. There are areas of cases in which such duties of investigation and research are imposed on judges, but they are exceptions.[49]

In international arbitration, the arbitrators are often in the same position: they have not been educated in the substantive law to be applied. Such a situation is very common and is no reason for panic. The procedural rules applied in international arbitration provide for more flexibility than national laws, which is meant

---

[48] George P. Graham, *International Commercial Letters of Credit and Choice of Law: So Whose Law Should Apply Anyway?* 47 Wayne L Rev 201 (Spring, 2001):
"While Article 5's choice of law provision may work well for domestic letter of credit transactions, until all contracting nations reach the level of commercial maturity countries such as the United States and England enjoy, it represents an unwise addition to international letter of credit transactions. Without intervention by the U.S. courts, foreign courts and governments may now have more leeway than ever to enter orders manipulating the independence principle. For now, American lawyers, to protect their beneficiaries' interests, better heed the clear command of U.C.C. section 5-116(b), and negotiate, with the applicant, a choice of law provision full of teeth. American lawyers should insist on an express provision commanding the courts to apply U.S. law with regard to the issuer's payment obligations under the letter of credit. This is to say, American lawyers must make it clear that U.S. law governs with regard to the independence principle and its narrowly tailored fraud exception."

[49] Matti S. Kurkela, *Jura Novit Curia and the Burden of Education in International Arbitration – A Nordic Perspective*, ASA Bulletin 3/2003 (Septembre).

CHAPTER VII

to allow the panel "to tailor-make" the proceedings, but may confuse those inexperienced in the tools and instruments available and the due process requirements of arbitration. Although the arbitrators are by no means acting in a legal vacuum, there is plenty of room for action and seeking accurate and appropriate procedural and material solutions. Although *lex mercatoria*, the uniformity of substantive law and that of conflict rules, is making progress, *lex mercatoria* can neither materially, procedurally nor formally be the sole source of law unless the parties have so agreed.

All this often boils down to the conclusion that it is up to the parties to educate the judge or the panel as to the rules and principles of applicable material law. The "burden of education" comes close to the traditional rule of "burden of proof". In both areas of burden, the arbitrators often have wider powers than the judiciary to fill in the gaps by various actions as the case may require and as they may see fit for the purposes of promoting justice and the overall interests of the parties in dispute.

The burden of education may be heavy both in courts as well as in arbitration as to the law merchant and in particular with respect to the special rules applicable to letters of credit and bank guarantees. In the case of some decision makers, their attitude may prevent them from learning. And, for some, efforts of learning new things causes so much pain that even the most eloquent of advocates may "fail to be heard".

Dolan writes:

> "The standby letter of credit is indeed the invention of the goldsmith's successors. It is a marvelous, efficient device; but it *works successfully only in the light of the law merchant*. It is on the independence principle that the success of the standby rests. If courts permit account parties to dilute the principle with fraud claims, the merchants will lose their latest invention."[50]

If the burden of education has not been met by the parties, the courts tend to apply their own law. Some statutes put it bluntly: "if no sufficient evidence is presented", domestic law will be applied. Some legal systems are more elegant "presuming that the foreign law and *lex fori* are similar in content." The end result is

---

[50] John F. Dolan, *Standby letters of credit and fraud (is the standby only another invention of the Goldsmiths in Lombard Steet?* Cardozo Law Review, (Fall 1985).

the same, but the latter expression is more diplomatic leaving the impression that foreign law is being applied and that there is a false conflict only. The following section of the *PT Pan Indonesia* case does describe the burden in an almost exhaustive manner and with impeccable clarity:

> "In deciding issues raised before the court which are asserted to be governed by foreign law, *the court proceeds upon the basis that such law is to the same effect as English law unless material is provided which demonstrates the contrary. Mere assertion is insufficient unless it is supported by credible evidence as to the foreign law*. This is a necessary rule if proceedings are not to be stultified or unduly delayed, particularly in the interlocutory stages, in any case where the answer to a claim with a foreign element is clear so far as English law is concerned. It will often be the case that *the material provided as to foreign law will be of an incomplete or provisional nature unsupported by detailed authority or by materials of the weight or complexity suitable to a final disposal*, but nonetheless sufficient to satisfy the court that an arguable defence or other relevant issue has been established for the purposes of a decision at that stage of the proceedings. Nonetheless, the party who asserts that the application of foreign law would provide a different result *bears the burden of satisfying the court that that is so. If the evidence proffered is of such incomplete, inconsistent or unconvincing character that it is insufficient for its purpose, it is not necessary for the opposing party to adduce his own contradictory evidence from an expert in the relevant foreign law.*"[51]

In the *Turkiye Is Bankasi* case also there was some lack of clarity as to whether English law or Turkish law would be applicable. The parties did, after having heard authorities and referred to them, agree that there would not be any difference in the material rules to be applied regardless of which of the two laws would be applied and that the outcome under either English or Turkish law would be same. The issue at hand was fraud, in particular how to demonstrate the existence of fraud by evidence, and the availability of injunction or interlocutory relief. English (or Turkish) law was applied and the ruling reiterated the traditional principles set forth in the landmark cases of English law. The court said:

> "At one stage it seemed as though there might be *a debate about Turkish law and whether that achieved any different result from that which would flow*

---

[51] PT Pan Indonesia Bank Ltd v. Marconi Communications Int'l Ltd, A3/2004/0684, Neutral Citation Number: [2005] EWCA Civ 422, CA (Civ Div).

from English law, but, following the evidence of Professor Ozsunay, both sides accepted that the right course for me to adopt was to take the law as the law of England. Both sides relied on the well-known authorities in this area: *Edward Owen Engineering Ltd. v. Barclay's Bank International Ltd.*, [1978] 1 Lloyd's Rep. 166; [1978] 1 Q.B. 159; United Trading Corporation and Murray Clayton Ltd. v. Allied Arab Bank Ltd., [1985] 2 Lloyd's Rep. 554 and *Bolivinter Oil S.A. v. Chase Manhattan Bank N.A.*, [1984] 1 Lloyd's Rep. 251; [1984] 1 W.L.R. 392. The three cases above referred to were all cases concerned with the obtaining of an injunction preventing payment under a performance bond. *In those cases the plaintiff was unsuccessful in obtaining an interlocutory injunction.* I do not think there is any material difference between them as to what the appropriate test is as to whether a bank has a defence to a demand on a performance bond. In my view the reason that the plaintiffs were unsuccessful in all the cases is that they were unable to show that they had an arguable case, that the only realistic inference that a bank could draw was that the demands were fraudulent. In the United Trading case Lord Justice Ackner (as he then was) concluded: . . . that, although the plaintiffs have provided, on the available material, a seriously arguable case that there is good reason to suspect, certainly in regard to some of these contracts, that the demands on the performance bonds have not been honestly made, they have not established a good arguable case that the only realistic inference is that the demands were fraudulent and that the respondents to this appeal should now be acting on this footing.

That passage identifies the difficulty that a plaintiff has in succeeding in stopping payment on a performance bond. *He may show an arguable case that the demand is not honest, but, that is not sufficient.* He must also establish that 'the only realistic inference is that the demands were fraudulent.' What Lord Denning said in *Edward Owen* was: . . . these performance guarantees are virtually promissory notes payable on demand. So long as the Libyan customers make an honest demand, the banks are bound to pay: the banks will rarely, if ever, be in a position to know whether the demand is honest or not. At any rate they will not be able to prove it to be dishonest. So they will have to pay. The facts of that case itself illustrate the difficulty for a plaintiff. What Lord Justice Geoffrey Lane (as he then was) said at p. 174, col. 2; p. 175G, in relation to the submission of Counsel for the plaintiff, was as follows: . . . the way he [Counsel] seeks to establish fraud is this. He points to the undoubted fact that the buyers in Libya have failed to reply to any of the requests for a proper confirmed letter of credit according, Mr. Ross-Munro submits, to the terms of the contract and, moreover, have failed to produce any suggestion of any default or breach of contract on the part of the sellers in England which would possibly justify a demand that the performance guarantee would be implemented. I disagree that that amounts to any proof or evidence of fraud. *It may be suspicious, it may indicate the possibility of sharp practice, but there is nothing in those facts remotely approaching true evidence of fraud or anything which makes fraud obvious or clear to the bank.* Thus there is nothing, it seems to me, which casts any doubt upon the bank's prima facie obligation to fulfil its duty under the two tests which I have set out."[52]

VII.4 Jurisdiction

In case of a dispute or the bankruptcy of a party to the network of agreements i.e., the facility, it is necessary to establish the right venue.[53] Unfortunately there is no one single global place of jurisdiction or arbitral or other body to adjudicate on all disagreements relating to these instruments.[54] Therefore one needs to do a proper analysis on the basis of the facts of each individual case and on the basis of the contract in question.

The "right venue" in international transactions and as to instruments of international, transnational or supranational character may be approached from various

---

[52] Turkiye Is Bankasi AS v. Bank of China,1996 WL 1093298 (QBD (Comm Ct)), [1996] 5 Bank. L.R. 241, [1996] 2 Lloyd's Rep. 611, 3-08-1996 Times 1093,298.

[53] In many banking transactions the financial institutions reserve to themselves a unilateral right and option to choose one of several alternative venues and jurisdictions whereas the obligor is tied to one single exclusive venue. Here is a sample clause designed to accomplish this:
"For the exclusive benefit of the Surety and for the purpose of enforcement of this Deed: each of the Indemnitors hereby agrees to submit to the non-exclusive jurisdiction of the Courts of England and Wales and that any judgment or order of an English Court made in this respect is conclusive and binding on it and may be enforced against it in the courts of any other jurisdiction; and without prejudice to and without limiting the effect of what is provided herein, each of the Indemnitors hereby further agrees to submit to the nonexclusive jurisdiction of the courts of any and all other jurisdictions in which (a) surety may sustain or pay any loss for which the Principal *Indemnitor and/or any Other Indemnitor may be liable* hereunder and/or (b) the Surety may be sued or be subject to suit or arbitration as a consequence of having issued any Bond; and/or (c) any construction project may be located which is the subject of any contract referred to in any Bond; and/or (d) any assets of the Principal Indemnitor and/or any Other Indemnitor may be located, and that any judgment or order of any such court made in this respect is conclusive and binding on it and may be enforced against it in the courts of any other jurisdiction; each of the Indemnitors hereby waives any objections on the grounds of venue or forum non conveniens or any similar grounds in respect of proceedings by the Surety in any jurisdiction selected by the Surety."

[54] To establish such a forum wouldn't be as utopian a quest as one might think at the outset.

angles. One is, of course, the plaintiff's subjective interest. Another is *lex fori's* rules as to its jurisdiction *in rem* and *in personam* relating primarily as to its *prima facie* or *pro forma* jurisdiction over the parties involved and the subject matter. Multiple parties in the dispute may raise issues as to indispensable parties to the process, and public interests, such as, e.g., the bankruptcy of a party in the venue, may eliminate any discretion as to the dismissal of the case on any ground. Finally the choice of forum agreement made by the parties may or may not be a factor binding on the court as well and in some instances the choice may be challenged as overly burdensome or unreasonable.[55]

Finally the *forum non conveniens* doctrine may produce results which eliminate courts which in the overall analysis are formally competent (have jurisdiction) but are not the best or most rational or purposeful choice in the interests of justice. To add spice in the "minestrone-soup" of transnational litigation, one should keep in mind that interim or protective measures are often available to parties regardless of even exclusive choice-of-forum clauses.[56] Further, the rules as to *lis pendens* may vary from country to country both as to claims made in courts and in arbitration, allowing parallel and "competing" proceedings on similar or closely related matters and parties.

The parties may, of course, agree on a place of jurisdiction or refer to a set of rules providing for a venue. One needs to keep in mind that the action brought may regardless of such an agreement be dismissed by a court, e.g.,on the basis of the *forum non conveniens* doctrine, which takes into account not just the interests of

---

[55] See, e.g., draft Hague Convention on Choice of Court Agreements, 30.6.2005 art 6:
"Obligations of a court not chosen. A court of a Contracting State other than that of the chosen court shall suspend or dismiss proceedings to which an exclusive choice of court agreement applies unless -a) the agreement is null and void under the law of the State of the chosen court; b) a party lacked the capacity to conclude the agreement under the law of the State of the court seised; c) giving effect to the agreement would lead to a manifest injustice or would be manifestly contrary to the public policy of the State of the court seised; d) for exceptional reasons beyond the control of the parties, the agreement cannot reasonably be performed; or e) the chosen court has decided not to hear the case."
and *The Bremen v. Zapata Off-Shore Co.*, 407 U.S. 1 (1972).

[56] Convention on Choice of Court Agreements, 30.6.2005, Article 7:
"Interim measures of protection are not governed by this Convention. This Convention neither requires nor precludes the grant, refusal or termination of interim measures of protection by a court of a Contracting State and does not affect whether or not a party may request or a court should grant, refuse or terminate such measures."

the parties but also those of the court system and jurisdiction in question. English law endorses this doctrine:

> "The forum selection is treated more delicately by English courts. The domicile of the defendant is considered to be the general forum for a litigation. If the facts of a case show a great number of characteristics that link the case to a foreign jurisdiction, a court will refuse to hear the case owing to the existence of a more appropriate jurisdiction, provided that the defendant can present evidence that a more appropriate jurisdiction exists and that a trial in the United Kingdom is not more beneficial for the plaintiff than a trial in such other jurisdiction."[57]

In *Johann Prutscher v. Fidelity International Bank,* as to jurisdiction, the court held that the defendant had *in personam* jurisdiction in New York., Similarly, the three cement contracts were effectively amended to provide for payment thereunder in New York by Nigeria's unilateral establishment of the letters of credit with CBN, all of which were payable in New York. Under these circumstances, the locus of injury was in New York. Since defendants chose New York as the place of payment, the burden of litigating in this forum should not be overly burdensome.[58]

In *Texas Trading Mining Corp. v. Federal Republic of Nigeria and Central Bank of Nigeria,* where "all negotiations of the contract and subsequent settlement agreement between the parties were carried on outside the United States and the contract is governed by Nigerian law", the court held that the fact that "the letter of credit was payable in New York to plaintiff, a New York corporation, through a correspondent bank of the Central Bank" did not constitute sufficient connections to assume jurisdiction over the issuing bank, a foreign government agency.

In *Verlinden B.V. v. Central Bank of Nigeria* a Dutch corporation sued CBN for anticipatory repudiation of an irrevocable letter of credit issued by CBN and advised and payable by its correspondent in New York. Establishment of the

---

[57] DCL (UK). UCC 5-117 (official comment):
"If the parties choose a forum under subsection (e) and if — because of other law — that forum will not take jurisdiction, the parties' agreement or undertaking should then be construed (for the purpose of forum selection) as though it did not contain a clause choosing a particular forum. That result is necessary to avoid sentencing the parties to eternal purgatory where neither the chosen State nor the State which would have jurisdiction but for the clause will take jurisdiction — the former in disregard of the clause and the latter in honor of the clause."

[58] *Johann Prutscher v. Fidelity International Bank, 502 F. Supp. 535 (1980).*

correspondent bank relationship between the U.S. banks and CBN did not create personal jurisdiction over CBN in U.S. courts. The traditional jurisdiction test of "doing business" is not applicable under the Foreign Sovereign Immunities Act.[59]

In *BCCHK (in liquidation) v. Sonali Bank* the court pointed out that there are cases where no particular forum can be described as "the natural" forum. In order for a court to dismiss an action on the grounds of forum convenience, one should need to establish that

(i) there is a more appropriate court where the case can be tried more suitably; and
(ii) the alternative court has jurisdiction (competence, kompetenz).

In addition, the defendant must show that the alternative forum is clearly or distinctly more appropriate. Here, there were parallel proceedings pending in Bangladesh and the law of Hong Kong applied. The court concluded that "Nothing is gained by any discussion of the relative merits of various different procedures" The BCCHK court went on to say:

> "(2) Stay on the ground of forum non conveniens? The authorities
> In *Spiliada Maritime Corporation v. Cansulex Ltd.*, [1987] 1 Lloyd's Rep. 1 at p. 10, col. 1 to p. 12, col. 1; [1987] 1 A.C. 460 at pp. 476B to 478E Lord Goff summarized the relevant principles. In particular he said:
>
> The basic principle is that a stay will only be granted on the ground of forum non conveniens where the court is satisfied that there *is some other available forum, having competent jurisdiction, which is the appropriate forum for the trial of the action, i.e., in which the case may be tried more suitably for the interests of all the parties and the ends of justice* ... The question being whether there is some other forum which is the appropriate forum, for the trial of the action, it is pertinent to ask whether the fact that the plaintiff has, ex hypothesi, founded jurisdiction as of right in accordance with the law of this country, of itself gives the plaintiff an advantage in the sense that the English court will not lightly disturb jurisdiction so established ...

---

[59] *Verlinden B.V. v. Central Bank of Nigeria*, 488 F. Supp. 1284 (1980).

Furthermore, *there are cases where no particular forum can be described as the natural forum for the trial of the action.* Such cases are particularly likely to occur in commercial disputes, where there can be pointers to a number of different jurisdictions (see e.g. *European Asian Bank A.G. v. Punjab and Sind Bank [1982] 2 Lloyd's Rep. 356*), or in Admiralty, in the case of collisions on the high seas. I can see no reason why the English Court should not refuse to grant a stay in such a case, where jurisdiction has been founded as of right. It is significant that, in all the leading English cases where a stay has been granted, there has been another clearly more appropriate forum - in *The Atlantic Star [1974] A.C. 436* (Belgium); in *MacShannon's case [1978] A.C. 795* (Scotland); in *Trendtex [1982] A.C. 679* (Switzerland); and in *The Abidin Daver, [1984] A.C. 398* (Turkey). In my opinion, *the burden resting on the defendant is not just to show that England is not the natural or appropriate forum for the trial, but to establish that there is another available forum which is clearly or distinctly more appropriate than the English forum. In this way, proper regard is paid to the fact that jurisdiction has been* founded in England as of right and there is the further advantage that, on a subject where comity is of importance, it appears that there will be a broad consensus among major common law jurisdictions. I may add that if, in any case, the connection of the defendant with the English forum is a fragile one (for example, if he is served with proceedings during a short visit to this country), it should be all the easier for him to prove that there is another clearly more appropriate forum for the trial overseas. See further European Asian Bank A.G. v. Punjab and Sind Bank sup. at pp. 363 to 366 per Lord Justice Stephenson. In Adria Services Y.U. v. Grey Shipping Co. Ltd. July 30, 1993 unreported Mr. Justice Clarke said: . . . if the plaintiffs satisfy me that the defendants have no arguable defence then, save in an exceptional case, the right course would be to refuse a stay and to give judgment, because there would then be no real issues between the parties which should be tried either here or elsewhere.

Applying the principles in The Spiliada sup. in my view it would be wholly inappropriate to grant a stay on the ground of forum non conveniens inter alia for the following reasons:

(i) The plaintiff founded jurisdiction as of right in accordance with the law of England.

(ii) Sonali has not shown that Bangladesh is clearly or distinctly more appropriate than the English forum. Sonali has no presence in

Hong Kong and has declined an invitation to accept service of Hong Kong proceedings.

(iii) Sonali concedes that (apart from the alleged counter-claims) there is no defence to any of the claims save in seven instances where Sonali contends that the claims *under five letters of credit are barred by limitation under the law of Bangladesh.*

(iv) For the reasons set out above I do not consider that Sonali has any triable defence to the claims under the five letters of credit. *The relevant contracts are not governed by the law of Bangladesh but by the law of Hong Kong.*

(v) I have had regard to the fact that BCCHK is plaintiff in an action in Bangladesh in respect of credit 37 and a defendant in proceedings in Bangladesh in respect of credit 31. In my view these matters are not of sufficient weight to justify a stay (see Dicey & Morris, The Conflict of Laws (12th ed.) p. 405 as to lis alibi pendens). Mr. Templeman reserved a detailed argument to the effect that the plaintiff would not obtain substantial justice in Bangladesh. I make clear that I have had no regard to these (reserved) submissions in reaching my decision not to grant a stay. Every court has different procedures. *Nothing is gained by any discussion of the relative merits of various different procedures.* Furthermore, there is of course authority binding on me which deplores any discussion or entertainment of those types of argument. (Mr. Justice Hobhouse cited with approval in New Hampshire Insurance Co. v. Strabag Bau [1992] 1 Lloyd's Rep. 361 at p. 371 per Lord Justice Lloyd)."[60]

In European Asian Bank the court set forth a three-pronged analysis, namely:

1) Is there an alternative jurisdiction which is more appropriate?
2) If there is, do proceedings in England offer the plaintiff a real advantage?
3) If not, then the balance must be struck by the court.

---

[60] Bank of Credit & Commerce Hong Kong Ltd v. Sonali Bank, QBD (Comm Ct), Aug. 3, 1994.

"(1) The Court has first to consider whether there is another jurisdiction which is clearly more appropriate than England for the trial of the action. The burden of proving the existence of such other jurisdiction rests on the defendant (i.e., in the present case on the Punjab Bank). *In considering whether there is another such jurisdiction, the Court will consider all the circumstances of the particular case.*

(2) If the Court concludes that there is another clearly more appropriate jurisdiction, *the burden remains on the defendant to show that trial in England will afford the plaintiffs no real advantage.* If he can do so, it must be unjust to refuse a stay.

But, if trial in England will afford the plaintiff a real advantage, then a balance must be struck and the Court must decide in its discretion whether justice demands a stay. Now, in the affidavit sworn by Mr. Lee in support of the Punjab Bank's application, there are many suggestions that England is not the natural forum for this action. But I must make clear from the outset that what the Punjab Bank has to prove is *not* that England is not the natural forum, but that another jurisdiction is clearly more appropriate for the trial of the action — what in MacShannon's case was called the "natural forum" or the "natural or appropriate forum". It often happens that cases are tried in this country when it cannot be said that England is the natural forum; this is particularly true of cases tried in the Commercial Court or in the Admiralty Court. But it does not follow that in those cases the defendant could, if he wished to do so, have successfully applied for a stay. *For there are many cases, of which collisions at sea and international commercial transactions provide typical examples, where there is no particular jurisdiction which can be classed as the natural forum*; in such cases, if jurisdiction is founded here by means of personal service or by means of service out of the jurisdiction pursuant to O. 11 of the Rules of the Supreme Court, there is no reason why the action should not be allowed to proceed in this country."[61]

The alternative jurisdictions were India or Singapore. The letters of credit were governed by the law of Singapore, which is identical with the law of England. The breach or cause of action arose in New York. The parties were Indian and German.

---

[61] European Asian Bank A.G. v. Punjab and Sind Bank, 1981 WL 187765 (QBD (Comm Ct)), [1981] 2 Lloyd's Rep. 651, [1981] Com. L.R. 246.

CHAPTER VII

(The German party had a branch in Singapore). There was simply no venue which would not cause considerable inconvenience to the parties or to the proceedings or would cause considerably less inconvenience than English court where the action was already pending.

> "Be that as it may, I have simply to apply the principles in MacShannon's case, and I have first to consider whether the Indian jurisdiction is clearly more appropriate for the trial of the action. First of all reference was made to the parties to the action. Of these, one is Indian; the other is West German, the relevant branch being in Singapore. Second, reference was made to the letter of credit contract, and it was submitted by the Punjab Bank that that contract was governed by Indian law. That submission I am unable to accept. True, the letter of credit was issued by an Indian bank; but it was notified through a correspondent bank in Singapore, which later confirmed the credit, and was issued in favour of sellers in Singapore, who were advised of it through another bank in Singapore. The letter of credit was payable against documents; it contemplated negotiation of documents through certainly one bank in Singapore (A.B.N.), in which event payment to the beneficiary would have been made in Singapore, though it was provided that "in negotiation please claim reimbursement from Irving Trust Co., 1 Wall Street" — no doubt as a matter of convenience because this was a dollar credit. At all events, payment would not have been made in India. In these circumstances, I do not consider that the governing law of the letter of credit was Indian law; most probably it was the law of Singapore — c.f. *Offshore International S.A. v. Banco Central S.A.*, [1976] 2 Lloyd's Rep. 402; [1977] 1 W.L.R. 399. *I should add that the evidence before the Court is that the law concerning letters of credit in Singapore is identical to the law concerning letters of credit in this country.* I should also add that since, under the letter of credit, the European Asian Bank, if entitled to payment, was entitled to be paid in New York, the breach occurred and so the cause of action arose in New York; but neither party has contended that New York has more than an incidental connection with this case."[62]

> "Having regard to all these facts, I find it impossible to conclude that, for the present action, India is a clearly more appropriate forum for the trial of the action. This is not a case like *The Atlantic Star,* [1973] 2 Lloyd's Rep. 197;

---

[62] Id.

[1974] A.C. 436, or MacShannon's case, or the *Trendtex* case, where in each case there was held to be an overwhelming connection with another jurisdiction — with Belgium, Scotland and Switzerland, respectively. In each of these other cases, it was held that another country was the natural forum for the trial of the action; it cannot, in my judgment, be said of the present case that the natural forum is India. Nor, in my judgment, can it be said that the Punjab Bank's second string, Singapore, is the natural forum. *It is true that the proper law of the letter of credit is, in my judgment, the law of Singapore, and that (ignoring for the moment the issue of fraud) a substantial proportion of the evidence is likely to come from Singapore*. But, apart from fraud, *the oral evidence is unlikely to be substantial* (and in any event the evidence from Singapore is for the most part likely to be called by the European Asian Bank, rather than by the Punjab Bank); *other evidence will have to be called from India;* and the evidence before this Court is that, in all material respects, the law of Singapore is identical to English law. Furthermore the Punjab Bank, which has no branch in Singapore, *is under no obligation to submit to the jurisdiction of the Singapore Courts*; and if regard is had to the plea of fraud, then the Punjab Bank, if it did submit itself to the Singapore jurisdiction, would be faced with *the same difficulty as it is faced with in England in seeking to join Jain* as a third party; and in any event the evidence relating to the alleged fraud, if it has to be called, will come not only from Singapore, but from other countries including India. In these circumstances I cannot see that Singapore is, any more than India, a clearly more appropriate forum than England for the trial of the action."[63]

URDG and jurisdiction

URDG provides for an exclusive place of venue with no alternative or discretionary forum for the banks. The choice is for the guarantor's or Instructing Party's place of business, which is a natural place of venue from the point of view of the banks, which are involved in this business on a daily basis. From the Beneficiary's point of view it may well be a foreign forum with some inconvenience involved. In any case a clear choice is to be preferred, eliminating lengthy disputes as to the appropriateness of one venue over another, which is not objectively productive but may well serve subjective interests or have value in litigation tactics or promote dilatory practices.

---

[63] Id.

URDG provides the following as to forum rules in its Art. 28:

> "Unless otherwise provided in the Guarantee or Counter-Guarantee, any dispute between the Guarantor and the Beneficiary relating to the Guarantee or between the Instructing Party and the Guarantor relating to the Counter-Guarantee shall be settled *exclusively* by the competent court of the country of the *place of business of the Guarantor or Instructing Party* (as the case may be), or, if the Guarantor or Instructing Party has more than one place of business, by the competent court of the country of the branch which issued the Guarantee or Counter-Guarantee."

URCB and jurisdiction

In URCB *multi-party arbitration* is said to be the primary choice. Art. 8 (b):

> "All disputes arising between *the Beneficiary, the Principal* and *the Guarantor* or any of them in relation to a Bond governed by these Rules shall, unless otherwise agreed, be finally settled under the Rules of Conciliation and Arbitration of the International Chamber of Commerce by one or more arbitrators appointed in accordance with the said Rules."

If the parties have contracted out the arbitration clause, URCB provides, in the absence of express choice of forum by the parties, the venue to be the court in the place of the Guarantor's principal place of business.[64]

The UCC and jurisdiction

UCC (5-116) subjects choice of forum to the same principles as choice of law, as follows.

> "(e)The forum for settling disputes arising out of an undertaking within this article may be chosen in the manner and with the binding effect that governing law may be chosen in accordance with subsection (a) of this section."

---

[64] URCB Art.8 provides also for an option allowing the beneficiary to bring action instead in the courts of the place of the branch of which issued the Bond. In principle these are the same rules as those that appear in URCG Art.11(3)

Special choice-of-law considerations in the banking business

Banking is a special business. This applies in particular to lending and credit. It is customary for the banks to use *asymmetrical choice-of-forum clauses*, whereby the bank as lender reserves various options as venue at its choice and in its sole discretion whereas the borrower or the customer has only one exclusive venue for bringing legal action. As unreasonable as such clauses could be in business-to-consumer relationships or even in some business-to-business relationships (e.g., dominant position or monopoly power), in lending or credit exposure they are in most cases fully acceptable or even necessary.

Such asymmetrical clauses are not in use in the rules often referred to, but presumably very common in indemnity agreements. If the choice-of-forum clause is asymmetrical, providing for one exclusive forum only for the customer or borrower, the available venue must, however, represent something convenient and meet the criteria of due process.

In most cases the exclusive forum is courts of law in England or New York, which unquestionably does not cause any concern. Arbitration, as popular as it otherwise is (for example in the construction industry, in international business transactions and in investment disputes), has not fully been accepted by the banking industry. A good international institutional arbitration, however, combined with access to courts for protective measures, is an alternative worth considering[65] as promoted by some authorities:

> "In summary, we suggest that when parties contemplate a letter of credit for financing an international sale of goods or services they should include an arbitration provision in the underlying contract. The provision could specify that where a seller's demand under a letter of credit has no conceivable basis, or involves material, egregious, willful, or intentional fraud, an arbitrator may award attorneys' fees, compensatory and consequential damages. The clause could also provide that if the case involves conduct that the arbitrator finds particularly outrageous, punitive damages may be awarded, limited to twice the compensatory and consequential damages."[66]

---

[65] See Swiss Arbitration Association (ASA) Special Series No 2, *Arbitration in Banking and Financial Matters*, Geneva (2003).

[66] Mark S. Blodgett and Donald O. Mayer, *International Letters of Credit: Arbitral Alternatives to Litigating Fraud*, 35 Am. Bus L J 443, (Spring, 1998).

The reason for the somewhat reserved position of the financial services industry may well be at least partly in the flavor of compromise often attached to arbitration. In monetary transactions there is very little room for equity or "besserwissers". The undertakings are to be strictly enforced in line with *pacta sunt servanda* since a dollar is a dollar.

VII.4.1 Forum non conveniens and forum shopping?

Forum shopping is a classic issue of private international law. It refers to the choice a potential plaintiff or claimant has as to the country or court where it is the most favourable to bring action ("venue") either procedurally or materially, i.e., where the choice-of-law rules lead to the application of the most favourable material law maximizing the plaintiff's chances to prevail. The choice may relate to the freedom to make the choice after the cause of action arose or the choice made at the time an agreement is concluded.[67] In the event of having such a choice, the plaintiff may try to analyze in advance what benefits and what drawbacks a choice of a particular venue may bring with it, e.g., in the following respects:

   (i)   choice of law rules and applicable material laws;
   (ii) enforceability of the decision where the defendant has assets;
   (iii) procedural rules; availability of interim or protective measures or summary judgment; rules as to discovery, access to evidence and witnesses;
   (iv) cost of litigation; standards applied to assessing damages;
   (v)   anticipated length of proceedings;
   (vi) the expertise of the courts in question.

In the world of letters of credit or bank guarantees, both the facility in question and the transaction often cross many borders. This applies to the underlying transaction as well as to the forming of the financial back up for the transaction ("facility"). This may offer for the plaintiff a multitude of choices as to whom to sue and where. The fact that the financial instruments, even when substantively fully independent, are interlinked may enable the claimant to choose a preferred venue and force one or several defendants to answer in a forum which would not necessarily have

---

[67] In the latter case one can challenge the choice made, *e.g.*, if it is unduly burdensome to a party as to costs, lack of enforceability or otherwise in particular if the clause comes close to denial of access to justice.

been their choice at all. Forum shopping relates to the convenience and benefits of the plaintiff whereas the *forum non conveniens* doctrine attempts to draw a balance between the private interests of all parties and the public good.

In *First National Bank* forum shopping issues were at the forefront. The main choice as to venue was between the two financial capitals, London and New York, and their material law. The choice led to bringing an action in New York because in *Banco Santander* the English Court of Appeal held that fraud defence and other defences are available to the issuing bank if the confirming bank discounts a deferred payment credit before its maturity and becomes thereby an assignee of the beneficiary. The New York court said:

> "There has been extensive activity in London concerning this situation for almost two years. Indeed, until shortly before these actions were commenced, it was assumed among the English counsel for these parties that this litigation would be brought in London. On February 25, 2000, however, the English Court of Appeal decided *Banco Santander, S.A. v. Banque Paribas*, in which it held that a confirming bank that discounts a deferred payment letter of credit in advance of maturity becomes the assignee of the claim of the beneficiary against the issuing bank and therefore is subject to whatever defenses the issuer may have against the beneficiary. This suggests that the issuing banks would be entitled to assert Simetal's alleged fraud as a defense to the claims of the confirming banks with respect to the LCs. *In consequence, plaintiff rapidly shifted ground and brought these actions in New York, where it argues that New York law should govern and seeks to avoid the impact of the Banco Santander case. Defendants move to dismiss on the ground, among others, of forum non conveniens.*"[68]

As discussed, forum shopping may relate to both obtaining optional chances for success under procedural laws as well as material laws (conflict rules). In procedural aspects the issue goes hand in hand with the rules relating to jurisdiction over persons and causes of action, i.e., matters *in rem*. Should there be more than one defendant or claimant, the analysis may become quite complicated, in particular if the *forum non conveniens* doctrine is to be applied *ex officio* or

---

[68] First Union Nat'l Bank v Paribas, 135 F Supp 2d 443 (SD NY 2001)..

CHAPTER VII

by motion of a party. In the U.S. one of the landmark cases is *Piper Aircraft*, cited infra.

The *forum non conveniens* doctrine attempts to balance "a series of private and public interests". When the choice is to be made between two of the leading courts in commercial matters, it simplifies the choice by reducing some elements of inconvenience. Should the court retain the case and apply foreign law, this will bring up the issue of the "burden of education", i.e., who has the duty and bears the risk of bringing evidence as to the rules and substance of the foreign law to be applied. The court said:

> "The analysis of *forum non conveniens* motions requires consideration of whether there is an adequate alternative forum and, if so, a balancing of "a series of private and public interests in determining whether to retain the case or dismiss it in favor of [the] alternative forum." E.g., Piper Aircraft Co. v. Reyno, 454 U.S. 235, 254 n. 22, 102 S.Ct. 252, 70 L.Ed.2d 419 (1981); DiRienzo v. Philip Servs. Corp., 232 F.3d 49, 56 (2d Cir.2000); see American Dredging Co. v. Miller, 510 U.S. 443, 447-48, 114 S.Ct. 981, 127 L.Ed.2d 285 (1994); Gulf Oil Corp. v. Gilbert, 330 U.S. 501, 506-07, 67 S.Ct. 839, 91 L.Ed. 1055 (1947). Manela v. Garantia Banking Ltd., 940 F.Supp. 584, 590 (S. D.N.Y.1996) (quoting Ioannides v. Marika Mar. Corp., 928 F.Supp. 374, 377 (S.D.N.Y.1996)) (internal quotation marks omitted); accord, e.g., American Dredging Co., 510 U.S. at 447-48, 114 S.Ct. 981 (quoting Gilbert, 330 U.S. at 508-09, 67 S.Ct. 839). A. Private Interest Factors. No one disputes that England is an adequate alternative forum. The Court therefore turns to the so-called "private interest factors," first among them being the often stated principle that a plaintiff's choice of forum is entitled to substantial deference and should not be disturbed lightly."[69]

In *First Union National Bank* the court analyzed the various circumstances starting from the basic rule that the plaintiff's choice may not be disturbed lightly. On the other hand, it is difficult to challenge an English court as a convenient alternative so that the ultimate choice depended on practical issues like the court stated ("intensely practical and fact-bound"). These include, among other things:

(i) access to sources of proof;

---

[69] Id.

(ii) availability of methods to compel unwilling witnesses to testify and the cost thereof;
(iii) other factors making the trial "easy", expeditious and inexpensive.

In two English-speaking countries which both apply common law some of the most serious problems would not arise at all. As the *First Union National Bank* court said:

> "In the last analysis, it always must be borne in mind that there is no algorithm that assigns precise weights to the factors that inform *forum non conveniens* determinations. *The doctrine instead is intensely practical and fact-bound.* The most that may be said is that courts reach informed judgments after considering all of the pertinent circumstances. *While plaintiff's citizenship* surely is a strong factor in its favor, its impact ultimately may be outweighed by a sufficiently robust showing in favor of an alternative forum. And to state the converse of the Second Circuit's recent comment, it simply stands to reason that the weaker the connection between a plaintiff's U.S. activities, even those of a U.S. plaintiff, and the events at issue in the lawsuit, the more likely it is that defendants attacking the plaintiff's choice of a U.S. forum will be able to marshal a successful challenge to that choice. So the Court turns to the remaining private interest factors, which include such matters as the relative ease of access to sources of proof, availability of compulsory process for attendance of unwilling, and the cost of obtaining the attendance of willing witnesses, and other practical considerations that make trial of a case easy, expeditious and inexpensive."[70]

The court analyzed the impacts of the Hague Convention and the benefits, drawbacks and unavailability of depositions instead of live testimony and pre-trial discovery, saying:

> "Plaintiff next argues that the deposition testimony of unwilling witnesses in England could be obtained by compulsory process issued by an English court pursuant to the Hague Evidence Convention, to which the United Kingdom is a party. But plaintiff misses the key point and overstates a subsidiary one. The focus on the availability of compulsory process for

---

[70] Id.

unwilling witnesses reflects a strong preference for live trial testimony. Unwilling English witnesses could be compelled to testify in person only if the trial were held in England. *And even if depositions in theory might be an acceptable substitute for live testimony, adequate depositions of unwilling witnesses would be difficult or impossible to obtain under the Convention.* British reservations to the Convention make it unavailable as a means of obtaining *pretrial discovery as distinct from trial testimony*. It therefore is reasonable to suppose that an unwilling witness would challenge any effort to take the witness' testimony as forbidden discovery. Even if unsuccessful in blocking a deposition altogether, the witness would be entitled to insist upon adherence to English trial procedure, which forbids impeachment by the party calling the witness. *Finally, documents cannot be requested by class*. Individual documents must be described specifically and individually. In sum, insisting on a trial in New York unquestionably would deprive the finder of fact of the live testimony of unwilling English witnesses and quite likely would deprive it of a meaningful substitute in the form of depositions."[71]

The court continued its analysis by referring to the need to "educate" New York counsels of the parties, who had already been working with English counsel on the same issue for some time. There was also parallel and related litigation already pending in London, which would continue in any case. This raised a concern for consistency and efficiency if not litigated in one place. The court said:

"Finally, defendants quite accurately point out that their *English counsel* have been heavily involved in this dispute for over one year as, indeed, appears to be true also of plaintiff's *English counsel*. Plaintiff has foresworn, for itself, any inconvenience of having New York counsel *educate themselves in this complex matter*. But it is perfectly apparent that the retention of this case in New York will subject the defendants to needless expense involved in bringing new attorneys into the intricacies of this complicated transnational litigation. It is apparent also that extensive litigation concerning these matters and involving the plaintiff will go forward in England in any event. Arab Banking Corporation ("ABC"), Bank of Muscat ("BM") and Emirates Bank International ("EBI") have sued plaintiff in England concerning the very same matters. ABC and BM are not parties here,

---

[71] Id.

so those cases will go forward no matter what, and EBI may seek to press its London suit even if these cases proceed here. *Interests in consistency and efficiency argue in favor of having all of this litigation in one place.*"[72]

Then the court addressed some of the public interest issues bringing up congested courts and the burden of "jury duty" imposed on foreign parties. In addition the benefits of having local disputes in local courts in the view of those concerned is a public interest of importance. The problem of choice of law and applying foreign law ("burden of education") was also brought up.

The *Zeevi* case was also discussed at some length by the court in the motivations.

> "As laid out in *Gilbert*, the *public interest* factors are as follows: "[f]actors of public interest also have place in applying the doctrine. Administrative difficulties follow for courts when litigation is piled up in *congested centers* instead of being handled at its origin. *Jury duty* is a burden that ought not to be imposed upon the people of a community which has no relation to the litigation. In cases which touch the affairs of many persons, there is reason for holding the trial *in their view* and reach rather than in remote parts of the country where they can learn of it by report only. There is a *local interest in having localized controversies decided at home.* There is an appropriateness, too, in having the trial of a diversity case in a forum that is at home with the state law that must govern the case, rather than having a court in some other forum *untangle problems in conflict of laws, and in law foreign to itself.*" *Gilbert*, 330 U.S. at 508-09, 67 S.Ct. 839. The chief points of contention concerning the public interest factors are *whether New York or English law governs* the cases and whether the United States has any real interest in providing a forum for this controversy beyond the fact of plaintiff's citizenship.

> Plaintiff contends that 'each defendant had only one explicit obligation to [it]—to pay U.S. dollars to First Union in New York.' Based on this premise, it argues that 'the breach at issue—the failure to reimburse the confirming bank—took place in New York' and, further, that New York law governs here under *J. Zeevi & Sons, Ltd. v. Grindlays Bank (Uganda) Limited* because New York was the place of payment. Contrary to plaintiff's repeated

---

[72] Id.

misstatements, however, none of the LCs required payment in New York, and none limited FUNB-London's claim against its issuer to the specified New York account. Moreover, there are least two significant distinctions between the *Zeevi* case upon which plaintiff places such heavy reliance and this one. . . .

Zeevi involved a letter of credit issued by a Ugandan bank in favor of an Israeli beneficiary. The LC authorized the negotiating bank to claim reimbursement from the issuer's account in New York. The defendant, pursuant to a subsequent Ugandan government directive, then instructed its New York bank not to pay on the LC. The issuer's New York bank in turn rejected a number of drafts on the LC presented to it by another New York bank. The beneficiary then sued the Ugandan issuing bank in New York for breach of contract. The New York Court of Appeals held that the cause of action arose in New York, giving it jurisdiction under New York's Banking Law, because 'New York was the locus of repudiation, whereas it should have been a site of payment.' Applying the familiar New York interest analysis, the court then held that New York law governed the beneficiary's action against the issuer because New York had a great interest in applying its own law to the dispute '[i]n order to maintain its preeminent financial position.' In reaching the first of these conclusions, it focused on the fact that the 'defendant's order countermanding payment by cable and letter took effect upon receipt by Citibank in New York and then gave rise to a cause of action here.'

While New York's interest as "a financial capital of the world" argues for the application of New York law here, and while it is arguable that the "locus of repudiation" in the sense that the *Zeevi* court used the phrase was here as well, these cases involve an additional factor altogether—what appears to be a quite substantial fraud defense. *The alleged fraud, indeed, is the dominant feature of the litigation, and it has no perceptible contacts with New York or the United States. It is arguable that this fraud defense would be governed by the same law* as the LCs. Nonetheless, it is entirely possible that English law either would govern both issues or would govern the fraud defense even if New York law otherwise governed the LCs themselves. . . .

There is another difference. In *Zeevi*, the plaintiff was the beneficiary of the LC, who was injured when the issuer's New York agent refused to pay drafts presented to it in New York. Here, on the other hand, the plaintiff, in any practical sense, is the London branch of the confirming bank, which was injured in the first instance in consequence of the fraud perpetrated on it in London by the English beneficiary. *Thus, while there are similarities here to the Zeevi case that cut in favor of application of New York law to the LC issues, there also are differences that cut in the opposite direction.* In the last analysis, it is premature to make a definitive choice of law ruling both because it is not yet clear that there is a conflict between New York and English law and because the litigation is at a preliminary stage. *What may be said is that there is at least some likelihood that this Court, if it retained the cases, would be obliged to apply English law to part of or to the entire case, a factor that cuts to some degree in defendants' favor. An English court, on the other hand, would apply its own law to the entire dispute.*"[73]

While in *Zeevi* the choice was between courts in Kampala, Uganda and New York, in this case the choice was between London and New York. Despite a number of fact issues in common to *Zeevi*, there were also considerable differences, in particular with respect to justified expectations of the parties and public policy interests. The court concluded:

"Finally, there is the matter of whether the burden of this litigation fairly ought to be imposed on our judges and juries. This Court is quite mindful, as was the New York Court of Appeals in resolving the choice of law issue in Zeevi, of the importance to New York, as a world financial capital, of providing a forum in which "the justified expectations of the parties to" international letter of credit business may be enforced. But that interest is not a trump to be played whenever a party to such a transaction seeks to use our courts for a lawsuit with little or no apparent contact with New York or the United States. As the Appellate Division recently recognized, the existence of a letter of credit with some tangential connection to New York does not alone require the denial of a *forum non conveniens* dismissal, particularly where there is an adequate alternative forum in which related litigation is pending. Here, the litigation and related activity concerning the Simetal fraud is centered in London. *The English courts are eminently capable of dealing with this litigation. The choice here is not between a U.S. District Court and a forum of debatable competence and fairness.*"[74]

---

[73] Id.
[74] Id.

VII.4.2 Forum connexitatis

If the instrument constitutes a multi-party agreement or is regarded to be "a facility" it may be well founded to require that all parties to the multi-party agreement or directly involved parties to the facility are *heard* at the same time in the same proceedings. However, the applicable procedural rules may or may not have jurisdiction over such parties *per se* but their relationship to the agreement or facility may constitute such a close connection that they must be

   (i) summoned;
   (ii) heard;
   (iii) given an opportunity to be heard; or
   (iv) allowed to intervene as party or quasi-party with no direct interest but an indirect one.

Whether such a connection constituting sufficient grounds for jurisdiction ("*forum connexitatis*") in one or several roles or gives parties such right to intervene is an issue of applicable procedural and/or material rules. In some circumstances hearing such an intimately connected party ("indispensable party") may be a must in order to meet the *"audiatur et altera pars"* maxim i.e., the foundation of due process.

The *forum connexitatis* rule may collide with the *forum conveniens* rule but this conflict may prove to be false, since a greater inconvenience, with conflicting decisions and greater costs and loss of time, may follow if all the (indispensable) parties are not heard in the same proceedings. Fundamentally both rules serve to a great extent the same rationale.

VII.4.3 Docdex proceedings

When it comes to documentary credits, a great majority of all disputes can be settled by analyzing the documents only, without resorting to any other facts or evidence. As a matter of fact one should do exactly this. One should refuse to admit evidence relating to subjective intentions or purposes, the underlying transaction and performance thereunder, and other materials which are not apparent on the face of the documents. In principle and as a general rule, all such facts are totally irrelevant (the "parole or extrinsic evidence rule of documentary credit law") for the purposes of analyzing the conformity of the tender and "the moment of death" honor and dishonor. The further one gets from this basic issue of beneficiary–issuer relationship under the instrument itself, the more importance must be given to such extrinsic evidence. This applies in particular to the bank-to-bank relationship and the account party–bank relationship when issues, other than the compliance of the tender, are in question.[75]

What is said above does not have much relevance, if any at all, as to traditional guarantees or bonds or similar materially dependent instruments.

In fact, since 1997, ICC has provided special services to the international community which recognize the above characteristic features of letters of credit. Besides opinions and decisions of the ICC Banking Commission, the Docdex procedure was introduced. A Docdex expert decision, which may be binding if so agreed, can usually be given in 2-3 months compared to years of litigation in courts.[76] More than 50 cases have already been decided under the Docdex procedure. Docdex dispute resolution services may be used to resolve disputes relating to documentary credits, demand guarantees under URDG, and collection under ICC Uniform Rules for Collections.

Superficially, the procedure resembles arbitration, although it does not procedurally or otherwise fully meet the due process or other criteria set forth for arbitration:

Docdex article 1.3:

> "When a dispute is submitted to the Centre in accordance with these rules, the Centre shall appoint three experts from a list of experts maintained by the Banking Commission. These three experts (Appointed Experts) shall make a decision which, after consultation with the Technical Adviser of the Banking Commission, shall be issued by the Centre as a DOCDEX Decision in accordance with these rules. The DOCDEX Decision is not intended to conform with any legal requirements of an arbitration award."

---

[75] In the 1970's I suggested a mini-arbitration body to be established to settle these issues.
[76] http://www.iccwbo.org/drs/english/docdex/all_topics.asp#rules.

CHAPTER VII

Docdex article 2.1:

> "The Initiator shall apply for a DOCDEX Decision by submission of a request (Request). The Initiator may be one of the parties to the dispute applying individually, or more or all parties to the dispute submitting jointly a single Request. The Request, including all documents annexed thereto, shall be supplied to the Centre in Paris, France, in four copies."

Docdex article 3.1:

> "The Respondent may submit an Answer to the Initiator's Request. The Respondent may be one or more of the parties to the dispute named in the Request as Respondent, each submitting an individual Answer or submitting jointly a single Answer. The Answer must be received by the Centre within the period stipulated in the Centre's Acknowledgement of the Request (see Article 5). The Answer, including all documents annexed thereto, shall be supplied to the Centre in Paris, France, in four copies."

Docdex articles 4.1-4.2:

> "4.1. Request, Answers and Supplements shall be final as received.
> 4.2. The Centre may ask the Initiator and Respondent, by way of an Invitation, to submit specific supplementary information, including copies of documents, relevant to the DOCDEX Decision (Supplement)."

The decision is based on the submissions only. Exceptional other submissions or information may be requested (the "parole evidence rule").

Docdex articles 7.2-7.3:

> "7.2 The Appointed Experts shall render their decision impartially and exclusively on the basis of the Request, Answer(s) and Supplement(s) thereto, and the documentary credit and the UCP and/or URR, or the collection and the URC, or the demand guarantee and the URDG.
> 7.3 Where it is deemed necessary by the Appointed Experts, their Chair may ask the Centre to invite the Initiator and Respondent, pursuant to Article 4 of these rules, to provide additional information and/or copies of documents."

There are no oral hearings. The names of experts retained are not disclosed to the parties, and there are no witnesses or experts to be heard.

Docdex article 7.5:

> "Neither the Initiator nor the Respondent shall
>
> - seek an oral hearing in front of the Appointed Experts,
>
> - request ICC to reveal the name of any Appointed Expert,
>
> - seek to have an Appointed Expert or officer of the Banking Commission called as witness, expert or in any similar function to an arbitral tribunal or a court of law hearing the dispute in connection with which such Appointed Expert or officer of the Banking Commission participated by rendering a DOCDEX Decision."

There are some great advantages in the process and it is exceptionally well suited for its purpose. One may predict a great future for the process and the first years have already demonstrated that the concept is sound and working.

APPENDICES

APPENDIX A

United Nations Convention on Independent Guarantees and Stand-By Letters of Credit

This Convention represents a response by the trading community and legal expertise to problems encountered and issues raised as to unconditional guarantees and standby-letters in international exchange. It represents to a great extent an international consensus and a codification of prevailing practice and trends.

© 1995 by UCITRAL. Reproduced with permission.

Contents

Chapter I. Scope of Application

Article 1. Scope of application
Article 2. Undertaking
Article 3. Independence of undertaking
Article 4. Internationality of undertaking

Chapter II. Interpretation

Article 5. Principles of interpretation
Article 6. Definitions

Chapter III. Form and content of undertaking

Article 7. Issuance, form and irrevocability of undertaking
Article 8. Amendment
Article 9. Transfer of beneficiary's right to demand payment
Article 10. Assignment of proceeds

Appendix A

Article 11. Cessation of right to demand payment
Article 12. Expiry

Chapter IV. Rights, obligations and defences

Article 13. Determination of rights and obligations
Article 14. Standard of conduct and liability of guarantor/issuer
Article 15. Demand
Article 16. Examination of demand and accompanying documents
Article 17. Payment
Article 18. Set-off
Article 19. Exception to payment obligation

Chapter V. Provisional court measures

Article 20. Provisional court measures

Chapter VI. Conflict of laws

Article 21. Choice of applicable law
Article 22. Determination of applicable law

Chapter VII. Final clauses

Article 23. Depositary
Article 24. Signature, ratification, acceptance, approval, accession
Article 25. Application to territorial units
Article 26. Effect of declaration
Article 27. Reservations
Article 28. Entry into force
Article 29. Denunciation

Explanatory note by the UNCITRAL Secretariat on the United Nations Convention on Independent Guarantees and Stand-By Letters of Credit

Introduction

I. Scope of application

A. Types of instruments covered
B. Coverage of counter-guarantees and confirmations

C. Instruments outside scope of Convention
D. Definition of "independence"
E. "Documentary" character of undertakings covered
F. Definition of internationality
G. Connecting factors for application of the Convention

II. Interpretation

III. Form and Content of Undertaking

A. Issuance
B. Amendment
C. Transfer and assignment
D. Cessation of right to demand payment
E. Expiry

IV. Rights, Obligations and Defences

A. Determination of rights and obligations
B. Demand by beneficiary
C. Examination of demand and payment
D. Fraudulent or abusive demands for payment

V. Provisional Court Measures

VI. Conflict of laws

VII. Final clauses

Appendix A

United Nations Convention on Independent Guarantees and Stand-By Letters of Credit

Chapter I. Scope of application

Article 1. Scope of application

(1) This Convention applies to an international undertaking referred to in article 2:

   (a) If the place of business of the guarantor/issuer at which the undertaking is issued is in a Contracting State, or

   (b) If the rules of private international law lead to the application of the law of a Contracting State,

   unless the undertaking excludes the application of the Convention.

(2) This Convention applies also to an international letter of credit not falling within article 2 if it expressly states that it is subject to this Convention.

(3) The provisions of articles 21 and 22 apply to international undertakings referred to in article 2 independently of paragraph (1) of this article.

Article 2. Undertaking

(1) For the purposes of this Convention, an undertaking is an independent commitment, known in international practice as an independent guarantee or as a stand-by letter of credit, given by a bank or other institution or person ("guarantor/issuer") to pay to the beneficiary a certain or determinable amount upon simple demand or upon demand accompanied by other documents, in conformity with the terms and any documentary conditions of the undertaking, indicating, or from which it is to be inferred, that payment is due because of a default in the performance of an obligation, or because of another contingency, or for money borrowed or advanced, or on account of any mature indebtedness undertaken by the principal/applicant or another person.

(2) The undertaking may be given:

   (a) At the request or on the instruction of the customer ("principal/applicant") of the guarantor/issuer;

   (b) On the instruction of another bank, institution or person ("instructing party") that acts at the request of the customer ("principal/applicant") of that instructing party; or

(c) On behalf of the guarantor/issuer itself.

(3) Payment may be stipulated in the undertaking to be made in any form, including:

(a) Payment in a specified currency or unit of account;

(b) Acceptance of a bill of exchange (draft);

(c) Payment on a deferred basis;

(d) Supply of a specified item of value.

(4) The undertaking may stipulate that the guarantor/issuer itself is the beneficiary when acting in favour of another person.

Article 3. Independence of undertaking

For the purposes of this Convention, an undertaking is independent where the guarantor/issuer's obligation to the beneficiary is not:

(a) Dependent upon the existence or validity of any underlying transaction, or upon any other undertaking (including stand-by letters of credit or independent guarantees to which confirmations or counter-guarantees relate); or

(b) Subject to any term or condition not appearing in the undertaking, or to any future, uncertain act or event except presentation of documents or another such act or event within a guarantor/ issuer's sphere of operations.

Article 4. Internationality of undertaking

(1) An undertaking is international if the places of business, as specified in the undertaking, of any two of the following persons are in different States: guarantor/issuer, beneficiary, principal/applicant, instructing party, confirmer.

(2) For the purposes of the preceding paragraph:

(a) If the undertaking lists more than one place of business for a given person, the relevant place of business is that which has the closest relationship to the undertaking;

(b) If the undertaking does not specify a place of business for a given person but specifies its habitual residence, that residence is relevant for determining the international character of the undertaking.

Appendix A

Chapter II. Interpretation

Article 5. Principles of interpretation

In the interpretation of this Convention, regard is to be had to its international character and to the need to promote uniformity in its application and the observance of good faith in the international practice of independent guarantees and stand-by letters of credit.

Article 6. Definitions

For the purposes of this Convention and unless otherwise indicated in a provision of this Convention or required by the context:

(a) "Undertaking" includes "counter-guarantee" and "confirmation of an undertaking";

(b) "Guarantor/issuer" includes "counter-guarantor" and "confirmer";

(c) "Counter-guarantee" means an undertaking given to the guarantor/issuer of another undertaking by its instructing party and providing for payment upon simple demand or upon demand accompanied by other documents, in conformity with the terms and any documentary conditions of the undertaking, indicating, or from which it is to be inferred, that payment under that other undertaking has been demanded from, or made by, the person issuing that other undertaking;

(d) "Counter-guarantor" means the person issuing a counter-guarantee;

(e) "Confirmation" of an undertaking means an undertaking added to that of the guarantor/issuer, and authorized by the guarantor/issuer, providing the beneficiary with the option of demanding payment from the confirmer instead of from the guarantor/issuer, upon simple demand or upon demand accompanied by other documents, in conformity with the terms and any documentary conditions of the confirmed undertaking, without prejudice to the beneficiary's right to demand payment from the guarantor/issuer;

(f) "Confirmer" means the person adding a confirmation to an undertaking;

(g) "Document" means a communication made in a form that provides a complete record thereof.

Chapter III. Form and Content of Undertaking

Article 7. Issuance, form and irrevocability of undertaking

(1) Issuance of an undertaking occurs when and where the undertaking leaves the sphere of control of the guarantor/issuer concerned.

(2) An undertaking may be issued in any form which preserves a complete record of the text of the undertaking and provides authentication of its source by generally accepted means or by a procedure agreed upon by the guarantor/issuer and the beneficiary.

(3) From the time of issuance of an undertaking, a demand for payment may be made in accordance with the terms and conditions of the undertaking, unless the undertaking stipulates a different time.

(4) An undertaking is irrevocable upon issuance, unless it stipulates that it is revocable.

Article 8. Amendment

(1) An undertaking may not be amended except in the form stipulated in the undertaking or, failing such stipulation, in a form referred to in paragraph (2) of article 7.

(2) Unless otherwise stipulated in the undertaking or elsewhere agreed by the guarantor/issuer and the beneficiary, an undertaking is amended upon issuance of the amendment if the amendment has previously been authorized by the beneficiary.

(3) Unless otherwise stipulated in the undertaking or elsewhere agreed by the guarantor/issuer and the beneficiary, where any amendment has not previously been authorized by the beneficiary, the undertaking is amended only when the guarantor/issuer receives a notice of acceptance of the amendment by the beneficiary in a form referred to in paragraph (2) of article 7.

(4) An amendment of an undertaking has no effect on the rights and obligations of the principal/applicant (or an instructing party) or of a confirmer of the undertaking unless such person consents to the amendment.

Article 9. Transfer of beneficiary's right to demand payment

(1) The beneficiary's right to demand payment may be transferred only if authorized in the undertaking, and only to the extent and in the manner authorized in the undertaking.

Appendix A

(2) If an undertaking is designated as transferable without specifying whether or not the consent of the guarantor/issuer or another authorized person is required for the actual transfer, neither the guarantor/ issuer nor any other authorized person is obliged to effect the transfer except to the extent and in the manner expressly consented to by it.

Article 10. Assignment of proceeds

(1) Unless otherwise stipulated in the undertaking or elsewhere agreed by the guarantor/issuer and the beneficiary, the beneficiary may assign to another person any proceeds to which it may be, or may become, entitled under the undertaking.

(2) If the guarantor/issuer or another person obliged to effect payment has received a notice originating from the beneficiary, in a form referred to in paragraph (2) of article 7, of the beneficiary's irrevocable assignment, payment to the assignee discharges the obligor, to the extent of its payment, from its liability under the undertaking.

Article 11. Cessation of right to demand payment

(1) The right of the beneficiary to demand payment under the undertaking ceases when:

   (a) The guarantor/issuer has received a statement by the beneficiary of release from liability in a form referred to in paragraph (2) of article 7;

   (b) The beneficiary and the guarantor/issuer have agreed on the termination of the undertaking in the form stipulated in the undertaking or, failing such stipulation, in a form referred to in paragraph (2) of article 7;

   (c) The amount available under the undertaking has been paid, unless the undertaking provides for the automatic renewal or for an automatic increase of the amount available or otherwise provides for continuation of the undertaking;

   (d) The validity period of the undertaking expires in accordance with the provisions of article 12.

(2) The undertaking may stipulate, or the guarantor/issuer and the beneficiary may agree elsewhere, that return of the document embodying the undertaking to the guarantor/issuer, or a procedure functionally equivalent to the return of

the document in the case of the issuance of the undertaking in non-paper form, is required for the cessation of the right to demand payment, either alone or in conjunction with one of the events referred to in subparagraphs (a) and (b) of paragraph (1) of this article. However, in no case shall retention of any such document by the beneficiary after the right to demand payment ceases in accordance with subparagraph (c) or (d) of paragraph (1) of this article preserve any rights of the beneficiary under the undertaking.

Article 12. Expiry

The validity period of the undertaking expires:

(a) At the expiry date, which may be a specified calendar date or the last day of a fixed period of time stipulated in the undertaking, provided that, if the expiry date is not a business day at the place of business of the guarantor/issuer at which the undertaking is issued, or of another person or at another place stipulated in the undertaking for presentation of the demand for payment, expiry occurs on the first business day which follows;

(b) If expiry depends according to the undertaking on the occurrence of an act or event not within the guarantor/issuer's sphere of operations, when the guarantor/issuer is advised that the act or event has occurred by presentation of the document specified for that purpose in the undertaking or, if no such document is specified, of a certification by the beneficiary of the occurrence of the act or event;

(c) If the undertaking does not state an expiry date, or if the act or event on which expiry is stated to depend has not yet been established by presentation of the required document and an expiry date has not been stated in addition, when six years have elapsed from the date of issuance of the undertaking.

Chapter IV. Rights, Obligations and Defences

Article 13. Determination of rights and obligations

(1) The rights and obligations of the guarantor/issuer and the beneficiary arising from the undertaking are determined by the terms and conditions set forth in the undertaking, including any rules, general conditions or usages specifically referred to therein, and by the provisions of this Convention.

Appendix A

(2) In interpreting terms and conditions of the undertaking and in settling questions that are not addressed by the terms and conditions of the undertaking or by the provisions of this Convention, regard shall be had to generally accepted international rules and usages of independent guarantee or stand-by letter of credit practice.

Article 14. Standard of conduct and liability of guarantor/issuer

(1) In discharging its obligations under the undertaking and this Convention, the guarantor/issuer shall act in good faith and exercise reasonable care having due regard to generally accepted standards of international practice of independent guarantees or stand-by letters of credit.

(2) A guarantor/issuer may not be exempted from liability for its failure to act in good faith or for any grossly negligent conduct.

Article 15. Demand

(1) Any demand for payment under the undertaking shall be made in a form referred to in paragraph (2) of article 7 and in conformity with the terms and conditions of the undertaking.

(2) Unless otherwise stipulated in the undertaking, the demand and any certification or other document required by the undertaking shall be presented, within the time that a demand for payment may be made, to the guarantor/issuer at the place where the undertaking was issued.

(3) The beneficiary, when demanding payment, is deemed to certify that the demand is not in bad faith and that none of the elements referred to in subparagraphs (a), (b) and (c) of paragraph (1) of article 19 are present.

Article 16. Examination of demand and accompanying documents

(1) The guarantor/issuer shall examine the demand and any accompanying documents in accordance with the standard of conduct referred to in paragraph (1) of article 14. In determining whether documents are in facial conformity with the terms and conditions of the undertaking, and are consistent with one another, the guarantor/issuer shall have due regard to the applicable international standard of independent guarantee or stand-by letter of credit practice.

(2) Unless otherwise stipulated in the undertaking or elsewhere agreed by the guarantor/issuer and the beneficiary, the guarantor/issuer shall have reasonable time,

but not more than seven business days following the day of receipt of the demand and any accompanying documents, in which to:

(a) Examine the demand and any accompanying documents;

(b) Decide whether or not to pay;

(c) If the decision is not to pay, issue notice thereof to the beneficiary.

The notice referred to in subparagraph (c) above shall, unless otherwise stipulated in the undertaking or elsewhere agreed by the guarantor/issuer and the beneficiary, be made by teletransmission or, if that is not possible, by other expeditious means and indicate the reason for the decision not to pay.

Article 17. Payment

(1) Subject to article 19, the guarantor/issuer shall pay against a demand made in accordance with the provisions of article 15. Following a determination that a demand for payment so conforms, payment shall be made promptly, unless the undertaking stipulates payment on a deferred basis, in which case payment shall be made at the stipulated time.

(2) Any payment against a demand that is not in accordance with the provisions of article 15 does not prejudice the rights of the principal/applicant.

Article 18. Set-off

Unless otherwise stipulated in the undertaking or elsewhere agreed by the guarantor/issuer and the beneficiary, the guarantor/issuer may discharge the payment obligation under the undertaking by availing itself of a right of set-off, except with any claim assigned to it by the principal/applicant or the instructing party.

Article 19. Exception to payment obligation

(1) If it is manifest and clear that:

(a) Any document is not genuine or has been falsified;

(b) No payment is due on the basis asserted in the demand and the supporting documents; or

(c) Judging by the type and purpose of the undertaking, the demand has no conceivable basis, the guarantor/issuer, acting in good faith, has a right, as against the beneficiary, to withhold payment.

Appendix A

(2) For the purposes of subparagraph (c) of paragraph (1) of this article, the following are types of situations in which a demand has no conceivable basis:

    (a) The contingency or risk against which the undertaking was designed to secure the beneficiary has undoubtedly not materialized;

    (b) The underlying obligation of the principal/applicant has been declared invalid by a court or arbitral tribunal, unless the undertaking indicates that such contingency falls within the risk to be covered by the undertaking;

    (c) The underlying obligation has undoubtedly been fulfilled to the satisfaction of the beneficiary;

    (d) Fulfilment of the underlying obligation has clearly been prevented by wilful misconduct of the beneficiary;

    (e) In the case of a demand under a counter-guarantee, the beneficiary of the counter-guarantee has made payment in bad faith as guarantor/issuer of the undertaking to which the counterguarantee relates.

(3) In the circumstances set out in subparagraphs (a), (b) and (c) of paragraph (1) of this article, the principal/applicant is entitled to provisional court measures in accordance with article 20.

Chapter V. Provisional Court Measures

Article 20. Provisional court measures

(1) Where, on an application by the principal/applicant or the instructing party, it is shown that there is a high probability that, with regard to a demand made, or expected to be made, by the beneficiary, one of the circumstances referred to in subparagraphs (a), (b) and (c) of paragraph (1) of article 19 is present, the court, on the basis of immediately available strong evidence, may:

    (a) Issue a provisional order to the effect that the beneficiary does not receive payment, including an order that the guarantor/issuer hold the amount of the undertaking, or

    (b) Issue a provisional order to the effect that the proceeds of the undertaking paid to the beneficiary are blocked, taking into account whether in the absence of such an order the principal/ applicant would be likely to suffer serious harm.

(2) The court, when issuing a provisional order referred to in paragraph (1) of this article, may require the person applying therefor to furnish such form of security as the court deems appropriate.

(3) The court may not issue a provisional order of the kind referred to in paragraph (1) of this article based on any objection to payment other than those referred to in subparagraphs (a), (b) and (c) of paragraph (1) of article 19, or use of the undertaking for a criminal purpose.

Chapter VI. Conflict of Laws

Article 21. Choice of applicable law

The undertaking is governed by the law the choice of which is:

(a) Stipulated in the undertaking or demonstrated by the terms and conditions of the undertaking; or

(b) Agreed elsewhere by the guarantor/issuer and the beneficiary.

Article 22. Determination of applicable law

Failing a choice of law in accordance with article 21, the undertaking is governed by the law of the State where the guarantor/issuer has that place of business at which the undertaking was issued.

Chapter VII. Final Clauses

Article 23. Depositary

The Secretary-General of the United Nations is the depositary of this Convention.

Article 24. Signature, ratification, acceptance, approval, accession

(1) This Convention is open for signature by all States at the Headquarters of the United Nations, New York, until 11 December 1997.

(2) This Convention is subject to ratification, acceptance or approval by the signatory States.

(3) This Convention is open to accession by all States which are not signatory States as from the date it is open for signature.

Appendix A

(4) Instruments of ratification, acceptance, approval and accession are to be deposited with the Secretary-General of the United Nations.

Article 25. Application to territorial units

(1) If a State has two or more territorial units in which different systems of law are applicable in relation to the matters dealt with in this Convention, it may, at the time of signature, ratification, acceptance, approval or accession, declare that this Convention is to extend to all its territorial units or only one or more of them, and may at any time substitute another declaration for its earlier declaration.

(2) These declarations are to state expressly the territorial units to which the Convention extends.

(3) If, by virtue of a declaration under this article, this Convention does not extend to all territorial units of a State and the place of business of the guarantor/issuer or of the beneficiary is located in a territorial unit to which the Convention does not extend, this place of business is considered not to be in a Contracting State.

(4) If a State makes no declaration under paragraph (1) of this article, the Convention is to extend to all territorial units of that State.

Article 26. Effect of declaration

(1) Declarations made under article 25 at the time of signature are subject to confirmation upon ratification, acceptance or approval.

(2) Declarations and confirmations of declarations are to be in writing and to be formally notified to the depositary.

(3) A declaration takes effect simultaneously with the entry into force of this Convention in respect of the State concerned. However, a declaration of which the depositary receives formal notification after such entry into force takes effect on the first day of the month following the expiration of six months after the date of its receipt by the depositary.

(4) Any State which makes a declaration under article 25 may withdraw it at any time by a formal notification in writing addressed to the depositary. Such withdrawal takes effect on the first day of the month following the expiration of six months after the date of the receipt of the notification of the depositary.

Article 27. Reservations

No reservations may be made to this Convention.

Article 28. Entry into force

(1) This Convention enters into force on the first day of the month following the expiration of one year from the date of the deposit of the fifth instrument of ratification, acceptance, approval or accession.

(2) For each State which becomes a Contracting State to this Convention after the date of the deposit of the fifth instrument of ratification, acceptance, approval or accession, this Convention enters into force on the first day of the month following the expiration of one year after the date of the deposit of the appropriate instrument on behalf of that State.

(3) This Convention applies only to undertakings issued on or after the date when the Convention enters into force in respect of the Contracting State referred to in subparagraph (a) or the Contracting State referred to in subparagraph (b) of paragraph (1) of article 1.

Article 29. Denunciation

(1) A Contracting State may denounce this Convention at any time by means of a notification in writing addressed to the depositary.

(2) The denunciation takes effect on the first day of the month following the expiration of one year after the notification is received by the depositary. Where a longer period is specified in the notification, the denunciation takes effect upon the expiration of such longer period after the notification is received by the depositary.

DONE at New York, this eleventh day of December one thousand nine hundred and ninety-five, in a single original, of which the Arabic, Chinese, English, French, Russian and Spanish texts are equally authentic.

IN WITNESS WHEREOF the undersigned plenipotentiaries, being duly authorized by their respective Governments, have signed the present Convention.

* * *

APPENDIX A

Explanatory note by the UNCITRAL secretariat on the United Nations Convention on Independent Guarantees and Stand-by Letters of Credit*

Introduction

1. The United Nations Convention on Independent Guarantees and Stand-by Letters of Credit was adopted and opened for signature by the General Assembly

---

* This note has been prepared by the secretariat of the United Nations Commission on International Trade Law (UNCITRAL) for informational purposes. It is not an official commentary on the Convention.

[1] The draft Convention was prepared by the Working Group on International Contract Practices at its thirteenth to twenty-third sessions. (For the reports of those sessions, see the following volumes of the UNCITRAL Yearbook: *Yearbook, Volume XXI: 1990* (United Nations publication, Sales No. E.91. V.6), document A/CN.9/330; *Yearbook, Volume XXII: 1991* (United Nations publication, Sales No. E.93. V.2), documents A/CN.9/342 and A/CN.9/345; *Yearbook, Volume XXIII: 1992* (United Nations publication, Sales No. E.94.V.7), documents A/CN.9/358 and A/CN.9/361; *Yearbook, Volume XXIV: 1993* (United Nations publication, Sales No. E.94.V.16), document A/CN.9/374 and Corr.1; *Yearbook, Volume XXV: 1994*(United Nations publication, Sales No. E.95.V.20), documents A/CN.9/388 and A/ CN.9/391; and "Yearbook, volume XXVI: 1995" (to be issued subsequently as a United Nations sales publication), documents A/CN.9/405 and A/CN.9/408.) The deliberations of UNCITRAL on the draft Convention are reflected in the report on the work of its twenty-eighth session (1995) (*Official Records of the General Assembly, Fiftieth Session, Supplement No. 17* (A/50/17), paras. 11-201), annex I of which contains the draft Convention as submitted by the Commission to the General Assembly.

[2] UNCITRAL is an intergovernmental body of the General Assembly that prepares international commercial law instruments designed to assist the international community in modernizing and harmonizing laws dealing with international trade. Other legal instruments prepared by UNCITRAL include the following: United Nations Convention on Contracts for the International Sale of Goods (*Official Records of the United Nations Conference on Contracts for the International Sale of Goods, Vienna, 10 March-11 April 1980* (United Nations publication, Sales No. E.82.V.5), part I); Convention on the Limitation Period in the International Sale of Goods, 1974 (New York) (*Official Records of the United Nations Conference on Prescription (Limitation) in the International Sale of Goods, New York, 20 May-14 June 1974* (United Nations publication, Sales No. E.74.V.8), part I); United Nations Convention on the Carriage of Goods by Sea, 1978 (Hamburg) (*Official Records of the United Nations Conference on the Carriage of Goods by Sea, Hamburg, 6-31 March 1978* (United Nations publication, Sales No. E.80.VIII.1), document A/CONF.89/13, annex I); United Nations Convention on the Liability of Operators of Transport Terminals in International Trade (A/CONF.152/13, annex); UNCITRAL Arbitration Rules (*Official Records of the General Assembly, Thirty-first Session, Supplement No. 17* (A/31/17), para. 57); UNCITRAL Notes on Organizing Arbitral Proceedings ("Yearbook, volume XXVIII: 1996" (to be issued subsequently as a United Nations sales publication), document A/CN.9/423); UNCITRAL Conciliation Rules (*Official Records of the General*

by its resolution 50/48 of 11 December 1995.[1] The Convention was prepared by the United Nations Commission on International Trade Law (UNCITRAL).[2]

2. The Convention is particularly designed to facilitate the use of independent guarantees and stand-by letters of credit where only one or the other of those instruments is traditionally in use. The Convention also solidifies recognition of common basic principles and characteristics shared by the independent guarantee and the stand-by letter of credit. In order to emphasize the common umbrella of rules provided for both independent guarantees and stand-by letters of credit and to overcome divergences that may exist in terminology, the Convention uses the neutral term "undertaking" to refer to both types of instruments.

3. Independent undertakings covered by the Convention are basic tools of international commerce. They are used in a variety of situations. For example, they are used to secure performance of contractual obligations including construction, supply and commercial payment obligations; to secure repayment of an advance payment in the event that such repayment is required; to secure a winning bidder's obligation to enter into a procurement contract; to ensure reimbursement of payment under another undertaking; to support issuance of commercial letters of credit and insurance coverage; and to enhance creditworthiness of public and private borrowers. Yet familiarity with one or the other instrument covered by the Convention is not universal; there is an absence of legislative provisions dealing with them, practices concerning the two types of instruments have differed in certain respects, and important questions confronting users, practitioners and courts in the daily life of these instruments are beyond the power of the parties to settle contractually.

4. By establishing a harmonized set of rules for the two types of instruments covered, the Convention will provide greater legal certainty in their use for day-to-day commercial transactions, as well as marshal credit for public borrowers. Also, by making a single legal regime available to both independent guarantees and stand-by letters of credit, the Convention will facilitate the issuance of both instruments in combination with each other, for example, the issuance of a stand-by letter of credit to support the issuance of a guarantee, or the reverse case.

Assembly, Thirty-fifth Session, Supplement No. 17(A/35/17), para. 106); Model Law on International Commercial Arbitration (1985) (Official Records of the General Assembly, Fortieth Session, Supplement No. 17 (A/40/17, annex I); United Nations Convention on International Bills of Exchange and International Promissory Notes (General Assembly resolution 43/165, annex, of 9 December 1988); Model Law on International Credit Transfers (1992) (Official Records of the General Assembly, Forty-seventh Session, Supplement No. 17 (A/47/17); annex I); UNCITRAL Model Law on Procurement of Goods, Construction and Services (1994) (Official Records of the General Assembly, Forty-ninth Session, Supplement No. 17 and corrigendum (A/49/17 and Corr.1), annex I); and UNCITRAL Model Law on Electronic Commerce (Official Records of the General Assembly, Fifty-first Session, Supplement No. 17 (A/51/17), annex I).

APPENDIX A

The Convention will further facilitate "syndications" of lenders, by allowing them to combine more easily both types of instruments. Lenders participating in a syndication can spread credit risk among themselves, which enables them to extend larger volumes of credit.

5. The Convention gives legislative support to the autonomy of the parties to apply agreed rules of practice such as the Uniform Customs and Practice for Documentary Credits (UCP), formulated by the International Chamber of Commerce (ICC), or other rules that may evolve to deal specifically with stand-by letters of credit, and the Uniform Rules for Demand Guarantees (URDG, also formulated by ICC). In addition to being essentially consistent with the solutions found in rules of practice, the Convention supplements their operation by dealing with issues beyond the scope of such rules. It does so in particular regarding the question of fraudulent or abusive demands for payment and judicial remedies in such instances. Furthermore, the deference of the Convention to the specific terms of independent guarantees and stand-by letters of credit, including any rules of practice incorporated therein, enables the Convention to work in tandem with rules of practice such as UCP and URDG.

6. It should be noted that, strictly speaking, an independent guarantee or stand-by letter of credit is an undertaking given to a beneficiary. Accordingly, the focus of the Convention is on the relationship between the guarantor (in the case of an independent guarantee) or the issuer (in the case of a stand-by letter of credit) (hereinafter referred to as "guarantor/issuer") and the beneficiary. The relationship between the guarantor/issuer and its customer (the principal, in the case of an independent guarantee, or the applicant, in the case of a stand-by letter of credit, hereinafter referred to as "principal/applicant") largely falls outside the scope of the Convention. The same may be said of the relationship between a guarantor/issuer and its instructing party (the instructing party being, for example, a bank, requesting, on behalf of its customer, the guarantor/issuer to issue an independent guarantee).

7. Provided below is a summary of the main features and provisions of the Convention.

I. Scope of Application

A. Types of instruments covered

8. The scope of application of the Convention is confined to instruments of the type understood in practice as independent guarantees (referred to as, e.g. "demand", "first demand", "simple demand" or "bank" guarantees) or stand-by letters of credit (article 2(1)). Those instruments can be covered by the umbrella

of the Convention because they share a wide area of common use. Both types of instruments, which are payable upon presentation of any stipulated documents, are used to secure against the possibility that some contingency may occur (e.g. a breach of a contract). It may be noted that another major use in particular of stand-by letters of credit is as an instrument to effectuate payment of mature indebtedness ("financial" or "direct pay" stand-by letters of credit).

9. In the undertakings covered by the Convention the guarantor/issuer promises to pay the beneficiary upon a demand for payment. The demand may, depending upon the terms of the undertaking, be either a "simple" demand or one having to be accompanied by the other documents called for in the guarantee or stand-by letter of credit. The guarantor/issuer's obligation to pay is triggered by the presentation of a demand for payment in the form, and with any supporting documents, as may be required by the independent guarantee or stand-by letter of credit. The guarantor/issuer is not called on to investigate the underlying transaction, but is merely to determine whether the documentary demand for payment conforms on its face to the terms of the guarantee or stand-by letter of credit. Because of this characteristic the instruments covered by the Convention are referred to commonly as being "independent" and "documentary" in nature.

10. Reflecting practice, various types of scenarios are envisaged in which an undertaking may be given, including at the request of the customer ("principal/applicant"), on the instruction of another entity or person ("instructing party") acting at the request of the customer of the instructing party, or on behalf of the guarantor/issuer itself (article 2(2)).

11. Full freedom is given to the parties to exclude completely the coverage of the Convention (article 1), with the result that another law becomes applicable. Since the Convention, if it is applicable, is to a large extent suppletive rather than mandatory, wide breadth is given to exclude or alter the rules of the Convention in any given case.

B. Coverage of counter-guarantees and confirmations

12. The Convention is designed to include coverage of the "counter-guarantee". A counter-guarantee is defined in the Convention (article 6(c)) in the same essential terms as the basic notion of "undertaking", namely, as an undertaking given to the guarantor/issuer of another undertaking by its instructing party and providing for payment upon simple demand or upon demand accompanied by other documents, in conformity with the terms and any documentary conditions of the undertaking (counter-guarantee).

APPENDIX A

13. Apart from this general treatment of counter-guarantees as "undertakings", the Convention provides a specific provision on counter-guarantees in the context of fraudulent or abusive demands for payment; in that context counter-guarantees may raise questions distinct from those raised by other undertakings covered by the Convention (see paragraph 48, below).

14. The Convention also includes in its scope confirmations of undertakings, i.e. an undertaking added to that of, and authorized by, the guarantor/issuer. A confirmation gives the beneficiary an option of demanding payment from the confirmer as an alternative to demanding payment from the guarantor/ issuer. By requiring authorization of the guarantor/issuer, the Convention does not recognize as confirmations "silent" confirmations, i.e. confirmations added without the assent of the guarantor/issuer.

C. Instruments outside scope of Convention

15. The Convention does not apply to "accessory" or "conditional" guarantees, i.e. guarantees in which the payment obligation of the guarantor involves more than the mere examination of a documentary demand for payment. Thus, the Convention does not annul or affect such other instruments in any way, nor does it regulate or discourage their use in any way. Whether it would be preferable to use in any given case an independent undertaking of the type covered by the Convention, or another type of instrument, would depend on the commercial circumstances at play and the particular interests of the parties involved.

16. Letters of credit other than stand-by letters of credit are not covered by the Convention. However, the Convention does recognize a right of parties to international letters of credit other than stand-by letters of credit to "opt into" the Convention (article 1(2)). That provision has been included in particular because the Convention provides a set of rules that parties to commercial letters of credit may wish in their own judgement to take advantage of, in view of the broad common ground between commercial and stand-by letters of credit, and in view of the occasional difficulties in determining whether a letter of credit is of a stand-by or commercial variety.

D. Definition of "independence"

17. While it is widely recognized that undertakings of the type covered by the Convention are "independent", there has been a lack of uniformity internationally in the understanding and recognition of that essential characteristic. The Convention will promote such uniformity by providing a definition of "independence" (article 3). That definition is phrased in terms of the undertaking not

being dependent upon the existence or validity of the underlying transaction, or upon any other undertaking. The latter reference, to other undertakings, clarifies the independent nature of a counter-guarantee from the guarantee that it relates to and of a confirmation from the stand-by letter of credit or independent guarantee that it confirms.

18. In addition, to fall within the scope of the Convention, an undertaking must not be subject to any terms or conditions not appearing in the undertaking. It is specified that, to fall within the Convention, an undertaking should not be subject to any future, uncertain act or event, with the exception of presentation of a demand and other documents by the beneficiary or of any other such act or event that falls within the "sphere of operations" of the guarantor/issuer. That is in line with the notion that the role of the guarantor/issuer in the case of independent undertakings is one of paymaster rather than investigator.

E. "Documentary" character of undertakings covered

19. As an adjunct to being "independent" from the underlying transaction, the undertakings covered by the Convention possess a "documentary" character. This means that the duties of the guarantor/issuer when faced with a demand for payment are limited to examining the demand for payment and any supporting documents to ascertain whether the demand and other documents submitted conform "facially" with what is called for under the terms of the independent guarantee or stand-by letter of credit. The effect of this rule is that undertakings possessing "non-documentary conditions" are outside the scope of the Convention. The only conditions which would not have to be documentary in nature would relate to acts or events within the sphere of operations of the guarantor/issuer. A simple example of the latter would be a determination by the guarantor/issuer as to whether a required monetary deposit had been made in a designated account maintained with that guarantor/issuer.

F. Definition of internationality

20. The Convention limits its application to undertakings that are international. Internationality is determined on the basis of the places of business, as specified in the undertaking, of any two of the following being in different States: guarantor/issuer, beneficiary, principal/applicant, instructing party, confirmer (article 4(1)). Special rules are provided for the case of an undertaking listing more than one place of business for a party, as well as for the case of a party not having a "place of business" as such, but only a habitual residence (article 4(2)).

APPENDIX A

G. Connecting factors for application of the Convention

21. The Convention applies to international undertakings in either one of two ways. The first way is linked to the location of the guarantor/issuer in a State party to the Convention ("Contracting State") (article 1(1)(a)). The second way in which the Convention applies is if the rules of private international law lead to the application of the law of a Contracting State (article 1(1)(b)).

22. The Convention provides an additional layer of harmonization of law in this field, in that its chapter VI (Conflict of laws, articles 21 and 22) supplies the rules to be followed by courts of Contracting States in identifying in any given case the law applicable to an independent guarantee or a stand-by letter of credit. Those rules apply whether or not in a particular case it turns out that the Convention is the applicable substantive law for the independent guarantee or stand-by letter of credit in question (see paragraphs 52 and 53, below).

II. Interpretation

23. The Convention contains a general rule that interpretation of the Convention should be with a view to its international character and the need to promote uniformity in its application (article 5). In addition, interpretation is to have regard for the observance of good faith in international practice. Abstracts of any court decisions or arbitral awards applying and interpreting a provision of the Convention will be included in the case collection system called case law on UNCITRAL texts (CLOUT).

III. Form and Content of Undertaking

24. The Convention provides rules on several aspects of the form and content of undertakings, as summarized below.

A. Issuance

25. On the question of the point of time and place of issuance (i.e. when and where the obligations of the guarantor/issuer to the beneficiary become operative), the Convention promotes certainty in an area traditionally of some uncertainty owing to the existence of differing notions. The Convention rule is that issuance occurs when and where the undertaking leaves the sphere of control of the guarantor/issuer (e. g. when it is sent to the beneficiary)(article 7(1)). In addition,

the Convention defines issuance in terms of its practical effect. Once issued, the undertaking is available for payment in accordance with its terms and is irrevocable.

26. As is customary in legal texts of UNCITRAL, the Convention establishes a flexible and forward-looking form requirement for issuance. By requiring a form that preserves a complete record of the text of the undertaking, rather than referring to "written" form, the Convention accommodates issuance in a non-paper-based medium (e.g. by means of electronic data interchange). It does so by referring to issuance in any form that preserves a complete record of the text of the undertaking and provides a generally acceptable or specifically agreed means of authentication (article 7(2)).

27. The Convention does not deal with the question of capacity to issue undertakings (i.e. who is permitted to be a guarantor/issuer). That question, which raises regulatory or other legal implications that differ from country to country, is left to national law.

B. Amendment

28. Legislative recognition is given by the Convention to the rule of practice that amendment of an undertaking requires acceptance by the beneficiary in order to take effect, unless it is otherwise stipulated (article 8(3)). The Convention takes cognizance of the possibility that an amendment might be authorized in advance by the beneficiary. In such cases, the amendment takes effect upon issuance (article 8(2)).

29. In one of the few provisions of the Convention that directly addresses the relationship between the principal/applicant and the guarantor/issuer, it is made clear that an amendment has no effect on the rights and obligations of the principal/applicant, or for that matter of an instructing party or of a confirmer, unless such other person consents to the amendment (article 8(4)).

C. Transfer and assignment

30. The Convention reflects the distinction drawn in practice between, on the one hand, transfer to another person of the original beneficiary's right to demand payment and, on the other hand, assignment of the proceeds of the undertaking, if payment is made. In the case of assignment of proceeds, as contrasted with transfer, the right to demand payment remains with the original beneficiary, the assignee being given only the right to receive the proceeds of payment if such payment occurs.

Appendix A

31. Regarding transfer, the Convention endorses the dual requirement, found in UCP, that the undertaking itself must state that it is transferable, and that, in addition, any actual transfer must be consented to by the guarantor/issuer (article 9). The rationale is that a change in the person who is to present the demand for payment and any accompanying documents may increase the risk assumed by the guarantor/issuer (e.g. if the guarantor/issuer would feel that the proposed transferee was less reliable or familiar than the originally designated beneficiary). For that reason guarantor/issuers are given the opportunity to consent to any given transfer.

32. Regarding assignment of proceeds, the beneficiary of the undertaking may, unless otherwise stipulated in the undertaking or elsewhere agreed, assign the proceeds (article 10(1)). If the beneficiary assigns the proceeds and if the guarantor/issuer or another person obliged to effect payment has received a notice originating from the beneficiary, payment to the assignee discharges the obligor, to the extent of its payment, from liability under the undertaking (article 10(2)).

D. Cessation of right to demand payment

33. The Convention gives legislative effect to notions of cessation of the right to demand payment that are widely followed in practice, though not yet universally recognized in national laws or judicial precedents. Under the Convention (article 11), the events that trigger cessation include: a statement by the beneficiary releasing the guarantor/issuer; a termination of the undertaking agreed by the guarantor/ issuer; full payment of the amount stipulated in the undertaking, unless the undertaking provided for automatic renewal or increase of the amount available; expiry of the validity period of the undertaking. By affirming that the presentation of the demand for payment has to occur prior to the expiry of the undertaking, the Convention will help to overcome any remaining uncertainty as to that question.

34. A degree of uncertainty still surrounds, in some jurisdictions, the question of the effect of retention of the instrument embodying the undertaking as regards definitive cessation of the right to demand payment. The Convention, in line with what is regarded widely as the best practice, provides that in no case does retention of the instrument prolong the right to demand payment if the amount available has already been paid or if the undertaking has expired (article 11(2)). Apart from those two contexts, the parties remain free to stipulate a requirement of return of the undertaking in order to terminate the right to demand payment.

E. Expiry

35. The Convention provides (article 12) that the validity period of an undertaking expires in the following ways: at the expiry date, which may be a fixed date or the last day of a fixed period stipulated in the undertaking; if expiry is linked to the occurrence of an act or event, upon presentation of the document called for in the undertaking to indicate the occurrence of the act or event, or, if no such document is called for, by presentation by the beneficiary of certification for that purpose; or after six years from issuance, if no expiry date has been stipulated or if a stipulated expiry act or event has not occurred.

IV. Rights, Obligations and Defences

A. Determination of rights and obligations

36. The rights and obligations of the guarantor/issuer and the beneficiary are determined by the terms and conditions of the undertaking (article 13(1)). Express reference is made in the Convention to rules of practice, general conditions or usages (e.g. UCP, URDG) to which the undertaking is specifically made subject. This is in line with a main purpose of the Convention, to give legislative support to the right of commercial parties to incorporate such rules of practice, conditions or usages. That approach ensures that the Convention will remain a living instrument, sensitive to developments in practice, including future revisions of rules of practice such as UCP and URDG and the development of other international rules of practice.

37. The flexible linking of the Convention to the needs and evolving usages and standards of commercial practice is also referred to elsewhere in the Convention. For example, in the interpretation of the terms and conditions of an undertaking and in settling questions not addressed by the Convention, regard is to be had to generally accepted international rules and usages of independent guarantee or stand-by letter of credit practice (article 13(2)).

38. Similarly, the standard of conduct of the guarantor/issuer, based on good faith and the exercise of reasonable care, is to be defined by reference to generally accepted standards of international practice of independent guarantees and stand-by letters of credit (article 14(1)). While the Convention leaves open the possibility of stipulating a standard somewhat lower than the generally applicable standard of care, it clearly prohibits any exemption of the guarantor from liability for lack of good faith or gross negligence.

Appendix A

B. Demand by beneficiary

39. As regards the beneficiary, the process of demanding and obtaining payment involves presenting a demand for payment and any accompanying documents in accordance with the terms of the undertaking. In view of the documentary character of the demand, the form requirements of the Convention applicable to the undertaking itself (see paragraph 27, above) apply to the demand (article 15(1)). The place of presentation is at the counters of the guarantor/issuer at the place of issuance, unless some other place or person is stipulated for payment purposes (article 15(2)).

40. In addition, the Convention provides (article 15(3)) that by virtue of making a demand the beneficiary implicitly certifies that the demand is not made in bad faith and that none of the circumstances exist that would justify non-payment in accordance with the provisions of the Convention on fraudulent or abusive demands for payment (see paragraphs 47 and 48, below).

C. Examination of demand and payment

41. The duty of the guarantor/issuer is to examine the demand and any accompanying documents to determine whether they are in facial conformity with the terms and conditions of the undertaking and consistent with one another (article 16(1)). That determination is to have due regard to the applicable standard of international practice, a formulation that ensures that the Convention takes account of developments in practice as regards the notion of facial conformity.

42. In a provision expressly subject to variation by the terms of the undertaking, the guarantor/issuer is given a "reasonable time", up to a maximum of seven days, to examine the demand and to decide whether to pay (article 16(2)). Thus, what is deemed a "reasonable time" may well be less than seven days, but in no case more than seven days, unless some different period is stipulated. This takes into account that the time needed for examination of the demand would depend upon the nature of each case (e.g. volume and complexity of documents to be examined).

43. If a decision is taken not to pay, the guarantor/issuer is required to promptly so notify the beneficiary, indicating the grounds therefor (article 16(2)). If the demand is determined to be conforming, payment is to be made promptly, or at any later time stipulated in the undertaking.

44. The Convention recognizes that the guarantor/issuer may, unless the undertaking provides otherwise, discharge the payment obligation by exercising a right

of set-off that is generally available under the applicable law (article 18). However, the Convention does not recognize any such right of set-off with respect to claims assigned by the principal/applicant or instructing party, as such a possibility would risk undermining the purpose of the undertaking.

D. Fraudulent or abusive demands for payment

45. A main purpose of the Convention is to establish greater uniformity internationally in the manner in which guarantor/issuers and courts respond to allegations of fraud or abuse in demands for payment under independent guarantees and stand-by letters of credit. That has been a particularly troublesome and disruptive area in practice because allegations of fraud have a tendency to arise when there is a dispute as to the performance of an underlying contractual obligation. That difficulty and the resulting uncertainty have been compounded further because of the divergent notions and ways with which such allegations have been treated both by guarantor/issuers and by courts approached for provisional measures to block payment.

46. The Convention helps to ameliorate the problem by providing an internationally agreed general definition of the types of situations in which an exception to the obligation to pay against a facially compliant demand would be justified (article 19(1)). The definition encompasses fact patterns covered in different legal systems by notions such as "fraud" or "abuse of right". The definition refers to situations in which it is manifest and clear that any document is not genuine or has been falsified, that no payment is due on the basis asserted in the demand or that the demand has no conceivable basis.

47. For additional precision, the Convention provides illustrative examples of cases in which a demand would be deemed to have no conceivable basis (article 19(2); e.g. the underlying obligation has been undoubtedly fulfilled to the satisfaction of beneficiary; the fulfilment of the underlying obligation clearly has been prevented by wilful misconduct of beneficiary; in the case of a demand under a counterguarantee, the beneficiary of the counter-guarantee has made payment in bad faith as guarantor/issuer of the undertaking to which the counter-guarantee relates).

48. The Convention, by entitling but not imposing a duty on the guarantor/issuer, as against the beneficiary, to refuse payment when confronted with fraud or abuse (article 19(1)), strikes a balance between different interests and considerations at play. By allowing discretion to the guarantor/issuer acting in good faith, the Convention is sensitive to the concern of guarantor/issuers over preserving the commercial reliability of undertakings as promises that are independent from underlying transactions.

49. At the same time, the Convention affirms that the principal/applicant, in the situations referred to, is entitled to provisional court measures to block payment (article 19(3)). This recognizes that it is the proper role of courts, and not of guarantors/issuers, to investigate the facts of underlying transactions. Furthermore, the Convention does not annul any rights that the principal/applicant may have in accordance with its contractual relationship with the guarantor/issuer to avoid reimbursement of payment made in contravention of the terms of that contractual relationship.

V. Provisional Court Measures

50. Apart from entitling a principal/applicant or an instructing party to provisional court measures blocking payment or freezing proceeds of an undertaking in the types of cases referred to above, the Convention establishes a standard of proof to be met in order to obtain such provisional measures (article 20(1)). That standard refers to ordering of provisional measures on the basis of immediately available strong evidence of a high probability that the fraudulent or abusive circumstances are present. Reference is also made to consideration of whether the principal/applicant would be likely to suffer serious harm in the absence of the provisional measures and to the possibility of the court requiring security to be posted.

51. While authorizing provisional court measures in the cases concerned, the Convention minimizes the use of judicial procedures to interfere in undertakings by limiting the granting of provisional court measures to those types of cases, with one additional type of case. Provisional court orders blocking payment or freezing proceeds are also authorized in the case of use of an undertaking for a criminal purpose (article 20(3)).

VI. Conflict of Laws

52. As noted above (paragraph 22), the Convention contains in chapter VI conflict of law rules to be applied by the courts of Contracting States in order to identify the law applicable to international undertakings as defined in article 2, regardless of whether in any given case the Convention itself would prove to be the applicable law. Those conflict of laws rules recognize a choice of law stipulated in the undertaking or demonstrated by its terms or conditions, or agreed elsewhere by the guarantor/issuer and the beneficiary (article 21).

53. In the absence of a choice of law as described above, the Convention provides for application to the undertaking of the law of the State where the guarantor/issuer has that place of business at which the undertaking was issued (article 22).

VII. Final Clauses

54. The final clauses (articles 23-29) contain the usual provisions relating to the Secretary-General of the United Nations as depositary and providing that the Convention is subject to ratification, acceptance or approval by those States that have signed it by 11 December 1997, that it is open to accession by all States that are not signatory States and that the text is equally authentic in Arabic, Chinese, English, French, Russian and Spanish.

55. In view of its largely suppletive character, as well as of the right of parties to exclude the Convention in its entirety, no reservations are permitted. The Convention enters into force one year from the date of deposit of the fifth instrument of ratification, acceptance, approval or accession.

* * *

Further information may be obtained from:

UNCITRAL Secretariat Vienna International Centre
P.O. Box 500
A-1400 Vienna
Austria

Telephone: (43-1) 26060-4060 or 4061
Telefax: (43-1) 26060-5813
E-mail: uncitral@uncitral.org

APPENDIX B

Official Comments of Article 5 of the Uniform Commercial Code

UCC Article 5 is the most comprehensive statute on letters of credit in the world. It is to a great extent comparable with UCP (Uniform Customs and Practices) but includes additional elements in the text itself as well as in the official comments which are very helpful in analyzing and understanding these instruments and in particular significant common law practice in this field. UCC is a summary of a long tradition and is not only a derivative of UCP. It reflects admirable sophistication in clarity and drafting and is a great contribution to the further development of these instruments.

Section 5-101. Short title.

This article may be cited as "Uniform Commercial Code—Letters of Credit".

Official Comment

The Official Comment to the original Section 5-101 was a remarkably brief inaugural address. Noting that letters of credit had not been the subject of statutory enactment and that the law concerning them had been developed in the cases, the Comment stated that Article 5 was intended 'within its limited scope' to set an independent heoretical frame for the further development of letters of credit. That statement addressed accurately conditions as they existed when the statement was made, nearly half a century ago. Since Article 5 was originally drafted, the use of letters of credit has expanded and developed, and the case law concerning these developments is, in some respects, discordant.
Revision of Article 5 therefore has required reappraisal both of the statutory goals and of the extent to which particular statutory provisions further or adversely affect achievement of those goals.

Appendix B

The statutory goal of Article 5 was originally stated to be: (1) to set a substantive theoretical frame that describes the function and legal nature of letters of credit; and (2) to preserve procedural flexibility in order to accommodate further development of the efficient use of letters of credit. A letter of credit is an idiosyncratic form of undertaking that supports performance of an obligation incurred in a separate financial, mercantile, or other transaction or arrangement. The objectives of the original and revised Article 5 are best achieved (1) by defining the peculiar characteristics of a letter of credit that distinguish it and the legal consequences of its use from other forms of assurance such as secondary guarantees, performance bonds, and insurance policies, and from ordinary contracts, fiduciary engagements, and escrow arrangements; and (2) by preserving flexibility through variation by agreement in order to respond to and accommodate developments in custom and usage that are not inconsistent with the essential definitions and substantive mandates of the statute. No statute can, however, prescribe the manner in which such substantive rights and duties are to be enforced or imposed without risking stultification of wholesome developments in the letter of credit mechanism. Letter of credit law should remain responsive to commercial reality and in particular to the customs and expectations of the international banking and mercantile community. Courts should read the terms of this article in a manner consistent with these customs and expectations.

The subject matter in Article 5, letters of credit, may also be governed by an international convention that is now being drafted by UNCITRAL, the draft Convention on Independent Guarantees and Standby Letters of Credit. The Uniform Customs and Practice is an international body of trade practice that is commonly adopted by international and domestic letters of credit and as such is the 'law of the transaction' by agreement of the parties. Article 5 is consistent with and was influenced by the rules in the existing version of the UCP. In addition to the UCP and the international convention, other bodies of law apply to letters of credit. For example, the federal bankruptcy law applies to letters of credit with respect to applicants and beneficiaries that are in bankruptcy; regulations of the Federal Reserve Board and the Comptroller of the Currency lay out requirements for banks that issue letters of credit and describe how letters of credit are to be treated for calculating asset risk and for the purpose of loan limitations. In addition there is an array of anti-boycott and other similar laws that may affect the issuance and performance of letters of credit. All of these laws are beyond the scope of Article 5, but in certain circumstances they will override Article 5.

Section 5-102. Definitions.

(a)   In this article:
    (1) "Adviser" means a person who, at the request of the issuer, a confirmer, or another adviser, notifies or requests another adviser to

notify the beneficiary that a letter of credit has been issued, confirmed, or amended.

(2) "Applicant" means a person at whose request or for whose account a letter of credit is issued. The term includes a person who requests an issuer to issue a letter of credit on behalf of another if the person making the request undertakes an obligation to reimburse the issuer.

(3) "Beneficiary" means a person who under the terms of a letter of credit is entitled to have its complying presentation honored. The term includes a person to whom drawing rights have been transferred under a transferable letter of credit.

(4) "Confirmer" means a nominated person who undertakes, at the request or with the consent of the issuer, to honor a presentation under a letter of credit issued by another.

(5) "Dishonor" of a letter of credit means failure to timely honor or to take an interim action, such as acceptance of a draft, that may be required by the letter of credit.

(6) "Document" means a draft or other demand, document of title, investment security, certificate, invoice, or other record, statement, or representation of fact, law, right, or opinion: (i) which is presented in a written or other medium permitted by the letter of credit or, unless prohibited by the letter of credit, by the standard practice referred to in subsection (e) of section 5-108; and (ii) which is capable of being examined for compliance with the terms and conditions of the letter of credit. A document may not be oral.

(7) "Good faith" means honesty in fact in the conduct or transaction concerned.

(8) "Honor" of a letter of credit means performance of the issuer's undertaking in the letter of credit to pay or deliver an item of value. Unless the letter of credit otherwise provides, "honor" occurs: (i) upon payment, (ii) if the letter of credit provides for acceptance, upon acceptance of a draft and, at maturity, its payment, or (iii) if the letter of credit provides for incurring a deferred obligation, upon incurring the obligation and, at maturity, its performance.

(9) "Issuer" means a bank or other person that issues a letter of credit, but does not include an individual who makes an engagement for personal, family, or household purposes.

(10) "Letter of credit" means a definite undertaking that satisfies the requirements of section 5-104 by an issuer to a beneficiary at the request or for the account of an applicant or, in the case of a financial

APPENDIX B

institution, to itself or for its own account, to honor a documentary presentation by payment or delivery of an item of value.

(11) "Nominated person" means a person whom the issuer: (i) designates or authorizes to pay, accept, negotiate, or otherwise give value under a letter of credit, and (ii) undertakes by agreement or custom and practice to reimburse.

(12) "Presentation" means delivery of a document to an issuer or nominated person for honor or giving of value under a letter of credit.

(13) "Presenter" means a person making a presentation as or on behalf of a beneficiary or nominated person.

(14) "Record" means information that is inscribed on a tangible medium, or that is stored in an electronic or other medium and is retrievable in perceivable form.

(15) "Successor of a beneficiary" means a person who succeeds to substantially all of the rights of a beneficiary by operation of law, including a corporation with or into which the beneficiary has been merged or consolidated, an administrator, executor, personal representative, trustee in bankruptcy, debtor in possession, liquidator, and receiver. (b) Definitions in other articles applying to this article and the sections in which they appear are: "Accept" or "acceptance" Section 3—410 "Value" Sections 3-303, 4-209. (c) Article 1 contains certain additional general definitions and principles of construction and interpretation applicable throughout this article.

Official Comment

1. Since no one can be a confirmer unless that person is a nominated person as defined in Section 5-102(a)(11), those who agree to "confirm" without the designation or authorization of the issuer are not confirmers under Article 5. Nonetheless, the undertakings to the beneficiary of such persons may be enforceable by the beneficiary as letters of credit issued by the "confirmer" for its own account or as guarantees or contracts outside of Article 5.

2. The definition of "document" contemplates and facilitates the growing recognition of electronic and other nonpaper media as "documents," however, for the time being, data in those media constitute documents only in certain circumstances. For example, a facsimile received by an issuer would be a document only if the letter of credit explicitly permitted it, if the standard practice authorized it and the letter did not prohibit it, or the agreement of the issuer and beneficiary permitted it. The fact that data transmitted in a nonpaper (unwritten) medium can be recorded on paper by a recipient's computer printer, facsimile machine, or the like does not under current practice render the data so transmitted a "document." A facsimile or S.W.I.F.T. message received directly by

the issuer is in an electronic medium when it crosses the boundary of the issuer's place of business. One wishing to make a presentation by facsimile (an electronic medium) will have to procure the explicit agreement of the issuer (assuming that the standard practice does not authorize it). Where electronic transmissions are authorized neither by the letter of credit nor by the practice, the beneficiary may transmit the data electronically to its agent who may be able to put it in written form and make a conforming presentation.

3. "Good faith" continues in revised Article 5 to be defined as "honesty in fact." "Observance of reasonable standards of fair dealing" has not been added to the definition. The narrower definition of "honesty in fact" reinforces the "independence principle" in the treatment of "fraud," "strict compliance," "preclusion," and other tests affecting the performance of obligations that are unique to letters of credit. This narrower definition — which does not include "fair dealing" — is appropriate to the decision to honor or dishonor a presentation of documents specified in a letter of credit. The narrower definition is also appropriate for other parts of revised Article 5 where greater certainty of obligations is necessary and is consistent with the goals of speed and low cost. It is important that U.S. letters of credit have continuing vitality and competitiveness in international transactions.

For example, it would be inconsistent with the "independence" principle if any of the following occurred: (i) the beneficiary's failure to adhere to the standard of "fair dealing" in the underlying transaction or otherwise in presenting documents were to provide applicants and issuers with an "unfairness" defense to dishonor even when the documents complied with the terms of the letter of credit; (ii) the issuer's obligation to honor in "strict compliance in accordance with standard practice" were changed to "reasonable compliance" by use of the "fair dealing" standard, or (iii) the preclusion against the issuer (Section 5-108(d)) were modified under the "fair dealing" standard to enable the issuer later to raise additional deficiencies in the presentation. The rights and obligations arising from presentation, honor, dishonor and reimbursement, are independent and strict, and thus "honesty in fact" is an appropriate standard.

The contract between the applicant and beneficiary is not governed by Article 5, but by applicable contract law, such as Article 2 or the general law of contracts. "Good faith" in that contract is defined by other law, such as Section 2-103(1)(b) or Restatement of Contracts 2d, Section 205, which incorporate the principle of "fair dealing" in most cases, or a State's common law or other statutory provisions that may apply to that contract.

The contract between the applicant and the issuer (sometimes called the "reimbursement" agreement) is governed in part by this article (e.g., Sections 5-108(i), 5-111(b), and 5-103(c)) and partly by other law (e.g., the general law of contracts). The definition of good faith in Section 5-102(a)(7) applies only to the extent that the reimbursement contract is governed by provisions in this article; for other purposes good faith is defined by other law.

Appendix B

4. Payment and acceptance are familiar modes of honor. A third mode of honor, incurring an unconditional obligation, has legal effects similar to an acceptance of a time draft but does not technically constitute an acceptance. The practice of making letters of credit available by "deferred payment undertaking" as now provided in UCP 500 has grown up in other countries and spread to the United States. The definition of "honor" will accommodate that practice.

5. The exclusion of consumers from the definition of "issuer" is to keep creditors from using a letter of credit in consumer transactions in which the consumer might be made the issuer and the creditor would be the beneficiary. If that transaction were recognized under Article 5, the effect would be to leave the consumer without defenses against the creditor. That outcome would violate the policy behind the Federal Trade Commission Rule in 16 CFR Part 433. In a consumer transaction, an individual cannot be an issuer where that person would otherwise be either the principal debtor or a guarantor.

6. The label on a document is not conclusive; certain documents labelled "guarantees" in accordance with European (and occasionally, American) practice are letters of credit. On the other hand, even documents that are labelled "letter of credit" may not constitute letters of credit under the definition in Section 5-102(a). When a document labelled a letter of credit requires the issuer to pay not upon the presentation of documents, but upon the determination of an extrinsic fact such as applicant's failure to perform a construction contract, and where that condition appears on its face to be fundamental and would, if ignored, leave no obligation to the issuer under the document labelled letter of credit, the issuer's undertaking is not a letter of credit. It is probably some form of suretyship or other contractual arrangement and may be enforceable as such. See Sections 5-102(a)(10) and 5-103(d). Therefore, undertakings whose fundamental term requires an issuer to look beyond documents and beyond conventional reference to the clock, calendar, and practices concerning the form of various documents are not governed by Article 5. Although Section 5-108(g) recognizes that certain nondocumentary conditions can be included in a letter of credit without denying the undertaking the status of letter of credit, that section does not apply to cases where the nondocumentary condition is fundamental to the issuer's obligation. The rules in Sections 5-102(a)(10), 5-103(d), and 5-108(g) approve the conclusion in *Wichita Eagle & Beacon Publishing Co. v. Pacific Nat. Bank*, 493 F.2d 1285 (9th Cir. 1974).

The adjective "definite" is taken from the UCP. It approves cases that deny letter of credit status to documents that are unduly vague or incomplete. See, e.g., *Transparent Products Corp. v. Paysaver Credit Union*, 864 F.2d 60 (7th Cir. 1988). Note, however, that no particular phrase or label is necessary to establish a letter of credit. It is sufficient if the undertaking of the issuer shows that it is intended to be a letter of credit.

In most cases the parties' intention will be indicated by a label on the undertaking itself indicating that it is a "letter of credit," but no such language is necessary.

A financial institution may be both the issuer and the applicant or the issuer and the beneficiary. Such letters are sometimes issued by a bank in support of the bank's own lease obligations or on behalf of one of its divisions as an applicant or to one of its divisions as beneficiary, such as an overseas branch. Because wide use of letters of credit in which the issuer and the applicant or the issuer and the beneficiary are the same would endanger the unique status of letters of credit, only financial institutions are authorized to issue them.

In almost all cases the ultimate performance of the issuer under a letter of credit is the payment of money. In rare cases the issuer's obligation is to deliver stock certificates or the like. The definition of letter of credit in Section 5-102(a)(10) contemplates those cases.

7. Under the UCP any bank is a nominated bank where the letter of credit is "freely negotiable." A letter of credit might also nominate by the following: "We hereby engage with the drawer, indorsers, and bona fide holders of drafts drawn under and in compliance with the terms of this credit that the same will be duly honored on due presentation" or "available with any bank by negotiation." A restricted negotiation credit might be "available with x bank by negotiation" or the like.

Several legal consequences may attach to the status of nominated person. First, when the issuer nominates a person, it is authorizing that person to pay or give value and is authorizing the beneficiary to make presentation to that person. Unless the letter of credit provides otherwise, the beneficiary need not present the documents to the issuer before the letter of credit expires; it need only present those documents to the nominated person. Secondly, a nominated person that gives value in good faith has a right to payment from the issuer despite fraud. Section 5-109(a)(1).

8. A "record" must be in or capable of being converted to a perceivable form. For example, an electronic message recorded in a computer memory that could be printed from that memory could constitute a record. Similarly, a tape recording of an oral conversation could be a record.

9. Absent a specific agreement to the contrary, documents of a beneficiary delivered to an issuer or nominated person are considered to be presented under the letter of credit to which they refer, and any payment or value given for them is considered to be made under that letter of credit. As the court held in *Alaska Textile Co. v. Chase Manhattan Bank, N.A.*, 982 F.2d 813, 820 (2d Cir. 1992), it takes a "significant showing" to make the presentation of a beneficiary's documents for "collection only" or otherwise outside letter of credit law and practice.

APPENDIX B

10. Although a successor of a beneficiary is one who succeeds "by operation of law," some of the successions contemplated by Section 5-102(a)(15) will have resulted from voluntary action of the beneficiary such as merger of a corporation. Any merger makes the successor corporation the "successor of a beneficiary" even though the transfer occurs partly by operation of law and partly by the voluntary action of the parties. The definition excludes certain transfers, where no part of the transfer is "by operation of law" – such as the sale of assets by one company to another.
11. "Draft" in Article 5 does not have the same meaning it has in Article 3. For example, a document may be a draft under Article 5 even though it would not be a negotiable instrument, and therefore would not qualify as a draft under Section 3-104(e).

Section 5-103. Scope.

(a) This article applies to letters of credit and to certain rights and obligations arising out of transactions involving letters of credit.
(b) The statement of a rule in this article does not by itself require, imply, or negate application of the same or a different rule to a situation not provided for, or to a person not specified, in this article.
(c) With the exception of this subsection, subsections (a) and (d) of this section, paragraphs (9) and (10) of subsection (a) of section 5-102, subsection (d) of section 5-106, and subsection (d) of section 5-114, and except to the extent prohibited in subsection (3) of section 1-102 and subsection (d) of section 5-117, the effect of this article may be varied by agreement or by a provision stated or incorporated by reference in an undertaking. A term in an agreement or undertaking generally excusing liability or generally limiting remedies for failure to perform obligations is not sufficient to vary obligations prescribed by this article.
(d) Rights and obligations of an issuer to a beneficiary or a nominated person under a letter of credit are independent of the existence, performance, or nonperformance of a contract or arrangement out of which the letter of credit arises or which underlies it, including contracts or arrangements between the issuer and the applicant and between the applicant and the beneficiary.

Official Comment

1. Sections 5-102(a)(10) and 5-103 are the principal limits on the scope of Article 5. Many undertakings in commerce and contract are similar, but not identical

to the letter of credit. Principal among those are "secondary," "accessory," or "suretyship" guarantees. Although the word "guarantee" is sometimes used to describe an independent obligation like that of the issuer of a letter of credit (most often in the case of European bank undertakings but occasionally in the case of undertakings of American banks), in the United States the word "guarantee" is more typically used to describe a suretyship transaction in which the "guarantor" is only secondarily liable and has the right to assert the underlying debtor's defenses. This article does not apply to secondary or accessory guarantees and it is important to recognize the distinction between letters of credit and those guarantees. It is often a defense to a secondary or accessory guarantor's liability that the underlying debt has been discharged or that the debtor has other defenses to the underlying liability. In letter of credit law, on the other hand, the independence principle recognized throughout Article 5 states that the issuer's liability is independent of the underlying obligation. That the beneficiary may have breached the underlying contract and thus have given a good defense on that contract to the applicant against the beneficiary is no defense for the issuer's refusal to honor. Only staunch recognition of this principle by the issuers and the courts will give letters of credit the continuing vitality that arises from the certainty and speed of payment under letters of credit. To that end, it is important that the law not carry into letter of credit transactions rules that properly apply only to secondary guarantees or to other forms of engagement.

2. Like all of the provisions of the Uniform Commercial Code, Article 5 is supplemented by Section 1-103 and, through it, by many rules of statutory and common law. Because this article is quite short and has no rules on many issues that will affect liability with respect to a letter of credit transaction, law beyond Article 5 will often determine rights and liabilities in letter of credit transactions. Even within letter of credit law, the article is far from comprehensive; it deals only with "certain" rights of the parties. Particularly with respect to the standards of performance that are set out in Section 5-108, it is appropriate for the parties and the courts to turn to customs and practice such as the Uniform Customs and Practice for Documentary Credits, currently published by the International Chamber of Commerce as I.C.C. Pub. No. 500 (hereafter UCP). Many letters of credit specifically adopt the UCP as applicable to the particular transaction. Where the UCP are adopted but conflict with Article 5 and except where variation is prohibited, the UCP terms are permissible contractual modifications under Sections 1-102(3) and 5-103(c). See Section 5-116(c). Normally Article 5 should not be considered to conflict with practice except when a rule explicitly stated in the UCP or other practice is different from a rule explicitly stated in Article 5.

Except by choosing the law of a jurisdiction that has not adopted the Uniform Commercial Code, it is not possible entirely to escape the Uniform Commercial Code.

APPENDIX B

Since incorporation of the UCP avoids only "conflicting" Article 5 rules, parties who do not wish to be governed by the nonconflicting provisions of Article 5 must normally either adopt the law of a jurisdiction other than a State of the United States or state explicitly the rule that is to govern. When rules of custom and practice are incorporated by reference, they are considered to be explicit terms of the agreement or undertaking.

Neither the obligation of an issuer under Section 5-108 nor that of an adviser under Section 5-107 is an obligation of the kind that is invariable under Section 1-102(3). Section 5-103(c) and Comment 1 to Section 5-108 make it clear that the applicant and the issuer may agree to almost any provision establishing the obligations of the issuer to the applicant. The last sentence of subsection (c) limits the power of the issuer to achieve that result by a nonnegotiated disclaimer or limitation of remedy.

What the issuer could achieve by an explicit agreement with its applicant or by a term that explicitly defines its duty, it cannot accomplish by a general disclaimer. The restriction on disclaimers in the last sentence of subsection (c) is based more on procedural than on substantive unfairness. Where, for example, the reimbursement agreement provides explicitly that the issuer need not examine any documents, the applicant understands the risk it has undertaken. A term in a reimbursement agreement which states generally that an issuer will not be liable unless it has acted in "bad faith" or committed "gross negligence" is ineffective under Section 5-103(c). On the other hand, less general terms such as terms that permit issuer reliance on an oral or electronic message believed in good faith to have been received from the applicant or terms that entitle an issuer to reimbursement when it honors a "substantially" though not "strictly" complying presentation, are effective. In each case the question is whether the disclaimer or limitation is sufficiently clear and explicit in reallocating a liability or risk that is allocated differently under a variable Article 5 provision.

Of course, no term in a letter of credit, whether incorporated by reference to practice rules or stated specifically, can free an issuer from a conflicting contractual obligation to its applicant. If, for example, an issuer promised its applicant that it would pay only against an inspection certificate of a particular company but failed to require such a certificate in its letter of credit or made the requirement only a nondocumentary condition that had to be disregarded, the issuer might be obliged to pay the beneficiary even though its payment might violate its contract with its applicant.

3. Parties should generally avoid modifying the definitions in Section 5-102. The effect of such an agreement is almost inevitably unclear. To say that something is a "guarantee" in the typical domestic transaction is to say that the parties intend that particular legal rules apply to it. By acknowledging that something is a guarantee, but asserting that it is to be treated as a "letter of credit," the parties leave a court uncertain about where the rules on guarantees stop and those concerning letters of credit begin.

4. Section 5-102(2) and (3) of Article 5 are omitted as unneeded; the omission does not change the law.

Section 5-104. Formal requirements.

A letter of credit, confirmation, advice, transfer, amendment, or cancellation may be issued in any form that is a record and is authenticated:

(a) by a signature, or
(b) in accordance with the agreement of the parties or the standard practice referred to in subsection (e) of section 5-108.

Official Comment

1. Neither Section 5-104 nor the definition of letter of credit in Section 5-102(a)(10) requires inclusion of all the terms that are normally contained in a letter of credit in order for an undertaking to be recognized as a letter of credit under Article 5. For example, a letter of credit will typically specify the amount available, the expiration date, the place where presentation should be made, and the documents that must be presented to entitle a person to honor. Undertakings that have the formalities required by Section 5-104 and meet the conditions specified in Section 5-102(a)(10) will be recognized as letters of credit even though they omit one or more of the items usually contained in a letter of credit.
2. The authentication specified in this section is authentication only of the identity of the issuer, confirmer, or adviser.

An authentication agreement may be by system rule, by standard practice, or by direct agreement between the parties. The reference to practice is intended to incorporate future developments in the UCP and other practice rules as well as those that may arise spontaneously in commercial practice.

3. Many banking transactions, including the issuance of many letters of credit, are now conducted mostly by electronic means. For example, S.W.I.F.T. is currently used to transmit letters of credit from issuing to advising banks. The letter of credit text so transmitted may be printed at the advising bank, stamped "original" and provided to the beneficiary in that form. The printed document may then be used as a way of controlling and recording payments and of recording and authorizing assignments of proceeds or transfers of rights under the letter of credit. Nothing in this section should be construed to conflict with that practice.

To be a record sufficient to serve as a letter of credit or other undertaking under this section, data must have a durability consistent with that function. Because consideration is not required for a binding letter of credit or similar undertaking (Section 5-105) yet

Appendix B

those undertakings are to be strictly construed (Section 5-108), parties to a letter of credit transaction are especially dependent on the continued availability of the terms and conditions of the letter of credit or other undertaking. By declining to specify any particular medium in which the letter of credit must be established or communicated, Section 5-104 leaves room for future developments.

Section 5-105 Consideration.

Consideration is not required to issue, amend, transfer, or cancel a letter of credit, advice, or confirmation.

Official Comment

It is not to be expected that any issuer will issue its letter of credit without some form of remuneration. But it is not expected that the beneficiary will know what the issuer's remuneration was or whether in fact there was any identifiable remuneration in a given case. And it might be difficult for the beneficiary to prove the issuer's remuneration. This section dispenses with this proof and is consistent with the position of Lord Mansfield in *Pillans v. Van Mierop*, 97 Eng.Rep. 1035 (K.B. 1765) in making consideration irrelevant.

Section 5-106. Issuance, amendment, cancellation, and duration.

(a) A letter of credit is issued and becomes enforceable according to its terms against the issuer when the issuer sends or otherwise transmits it to the person requested to advise or to the beneficiary. A letter of credit is revocable only if it so provides.
(b) After a letter of credit is issued, rights and obligations of a beneficiary, applicant, confirmer, and issuer are not affected by an amendment or cancellation to which that person has not consented except to the extent the letter of credit provides that it is revocable or that the issuer may amend or cancel the letter of credit without that consent.
(c) If there is no stated expiration date or other provision that determines its duration, a letter of credit expires one year after its stated date of issuance or, if none is stated, after the date on which it is issued.
(d) A letter of credit that states that it is perpetual expires five years after its stated date of issuance, or if none is stated, after the date on which it is issued.

Official Comment

This section adopts the position taken by several courts, namely that letters of credit that are silent as to revocability are irrevocable. See, e.g., *Weyerhaeuser Co. v. First Nat. Bank*, 27 UCC Rep. Serv. 777 (S.D. Iowa 1979); *West Va. Hous. Dev. Fund v. Sroka*, 415 F. Supp. 1107 (W.D. Pa. 1976). This is the position of the current UCP (500). Given the usual commercial understanding and purpose of letters of credit, revocable letters of credit offer unhappy possibilities for misleading the parties who deal with them.

2. A person can consent to an amendment by implication. For example, a beneficiary that tenders documents for honor that conform to an amended letter of credit but not to the original letter of credit has probably consented to the amendment. By the same token an applicant that has procured the issuance of a transferable letter of credit has consented to its transfer and to performance under the letter of credit by a person to whom the beneficiary's rights are duly transferred. If some, but not all of the persons involved in a letter of credit transaction consent to performance that does not strictly conform to the original letter of credit, those persons assume the risk that other nonconsenting persons may insist on strict compliance with the original letter of credit. Under subsection (b) those not consenting are not bound. For example, an issuer might agree to amend its letter of credit or honor documents presented after the expiration date in the belief that the applicant has consented or will consent to the amendment or will waive presentation after the original expiration date. If that belief is mistaken, the issuer is bound to the beneficiary by the terms of the letter of credit as amended or waived, even though it may be unable to recover from the applicant.

In general, the rights of a recognized transferee beneficiary cannot be altered without the transferee's consent, but the same is not true of the rights of assignees of proceeds from the beneficiary. When the beneficiary makes a complete transfer of its interest that is effective under the terms for transfer established by the issuer, adviser, or other party controlling transfers, the beneficiary no longer has an interest in the letter of credit, and the transferee steps into the shoes of the beneficiary as the one with rights under the letter of credit. Section 5-102(a)(3). When there is a partial transfer, both the original beneficiary and the transferee beneficiary have an interest in performance of the letter of credit and each expects that its rights will not be altered by amendment unless it consents.

The assignee of proceeds under a letter of credit from the beneficiary enjoys no such expectation. Notwithstanding an assignee's notice to the issuer of the assignment of proceeds, the assignee is not a person protected by subsection (b). An assignee of proceeds should understand that its rights can be changed or completely extinguished

Appendix B

by amendment or cancellation of the letter of credit. An assignee's claim is precarious, for it depends entirely upon the continued existence of the letter of credit and upon the beneficiary's preparation and presentation of documents that would entitle the beneficiary to honor under Section 5-108.

3. The issuer's right to cancel a revocable letter of credit does not free it from a duty to reimburse a nominated person who has honored, accepted, or undertaken a deferred obligation prior to receiving notice of the amendment or cancellation. Compare UCP Article 8.

4. Although all letters of credit should specify the date on which the issuer's engagement expires, the failure to specify an expiration date does not invalidate the letter of credit, or diminish or relieve the obligation of any party with respect to the letter of credit. A letter of credit that may be revoked or terminated at the discretion of the issuer by notice to the beneficiary is not "perpetual."

Section 5-107. Confirmer, nominated person, and advisor.

(a) A confirmer is directly obligated on a letter of credit and has the rights and obligations of an issuer to the extent of its confirmation. The confirmer also has rights against and obligations to the issuer as if the issuer were an applicant and the confirmer had issued the letter of credit at the request and for the account of the issuer.

(b) A nominated person who is not a confirmer is not obligated to honor or otherwise give value for a presentation.

(c) A person requested to advise may decline to act as an adviser. An adviser that is not a confirmer is not obligated to honor or give value for a presentation. An adviser undertakes to the issuer and to the beneficiary accurately to advise the terms of the letter of credit, confirmation, amendment, or advice received by that person and undertakes to the beneficiary to check the apparent authenticity of the request to advise. Even if the advice is inaccurate, the letter of credit, confirmation, or amendment is enforceable as issued.

(d) A person who notifies a transferee beneficiary of the terms of a letter of credit, confirmation, amendment, or advice has the rights and obligations of an adviser under subsection (c) of this section. The terms in the notice to the transferee beneficiary may differ from the terms in any notice to the transferor beneficiary to the extent permitted by the letter of credit, confirmation, amendment, or advice received by the person who so notifies.

Official Comment

1. A confirmer has the rights and obligations identified in Section 5-108. Accordingly, unless the context otherwise requires, the terms "confirmer" and "confirmation" should be read into this article wherever the terms "issuer" and "letter of credit" appear.

A confirmer that has paid in accordance with the terms and conditions of the letter of credit is entitled to reimbursement by the issuer even if the beneficiary committed fraud (see Section 5-109(a)(1)(ii)) and, in that sense, has greater rights against the issuer than the beneficiary has. To be entitled to reimbursement from the issuer under the typical confirmed letter of credit, the confirmer must submit conforming documents, but the confirmer's presentation to the issuer need not be made before the expiration date of the letter of credit.

A letter of credit confirmation has been analogized to a guarantee of issuer performance, to a parallel letter of credit issued by the confirmer for the account of the issuer or the letter of credit applicant or both, and to a back-to-back letter of credit in which the confirmer is a kind of beneficiary of the original issuer's letter of credit. Like letter of credit undertakings, confirmations are both unique and flexible, so that no one of these analogies is perfect, but unless otherwise indicated in the letter of credit or confirmation, a confirmer should be viewed by the letter of credit issuer and the beneficiary as an issuer of a parallel letter of credit for the account of the original letter of credit issuer. Absent a direct agreement between the applicant and a confirmer, normally the obligations of a confirmer are to the issuer not the applicant, but the applicant might have a right to injunction against a confirmer under Section 5-109 or warranty claim under Section 5-110, and either might have claims against the other under Section 5-117.

2. No one has a duty to advise until that person agrees to be an adviser or undertakes to act in accordance with the instructions of the issuer. Except where there is a prior agreement to serve or where the silence of the adviser would be an acceptance of an offer to contract, a person's failure to respond to a request to advise a letter of credit does not in and of itself create any liability, nor does it establish a relationship of issuer and adviser between the two. Since there is no duty to advise a letter of credit in the absence of a prior agreement, there can be no duty to advise it timely or at any particular time. When the adviser manifests its agreement to advise by actually doing so (as is normally the case), the adviser cannot have violated any duty to advise in a timely way. This analysis is consistent with the result of *Sound of Market Street v. Continental Bank International*, 819 F.2d 384 (3d Cir. 1987) which held that there is no such duty. This section takes no position on the reasoning of that case, but does not overrule the result. By advising or agreeing to advise a letter of credit, the adviser assumes a duty to

Appendix B

the issuer and to the beneficiary accurately to report what it has received from the issuer, but, beyond determining the apparent authenticity of the letter, an adviser has no duty to investigate the accuracy of the message it has received from the issuer. "Checking" the apparent authenticity of the request to advise means only that the prospective adviser must attempt to authenticate the message (e.g., by "testing" the telex that comes from the purported issuer), and if it is unable to authenticate the message must report that fact to the issuer and, if it chooses to advise the message, to the beneficiary. By proper agreement, an adviser may disclaim its obligation under this section.

3. An issuer may issue a letter of credit which the adviser may advise with different terms. The issuer may then believe that it has undertaken a certain engagement, yet the text in the hands of the beneficiary will contain different terms, and the beneficiary would not be entitled to honor if the documents it submitted did not comply with the terms of the letter of credit as originally issued. On the other hand, if the adviser also confirmed the letter of credit, then as a confirmer it will be independently liable on the letter of credit as advised and confirmed. If in that situation the beneficiary's ultimate presentation entitled it to honor under the terms of the confirmation but not under those in the original letter of credit, the confirmer would have to honor but might not be entitled to reimbursement from the issuer.

4. When the issuer nominates another person to "pay," "negotiate," or otherwise to take up the documents and give value, there can be confusion about the legal status of the nominated person. In rare cases the person might actually be an agent of the issuer and its act might be the act of the issuer itself. In most cases the nominated person is not an agent of the issuer and has no authority to act on the issuer's behalf. Its "nomination" allows the beneficiary to present to it and earns it certain rights to payment under Section 5-109 that others do not enjoy. For example, when an issuer issues a "freely negotiable credit," it contemplates that banks or others might take up documents under that credit and advance value against them, and it is agreeing to pay those persons but only if the presentation to the issuer made by the nominated person complies with the credit. Usually there will be no agreement to pay, negotiate, or to serve in any other capacity by the nominated person, therefore the nominated person will have the right to decline to take the documents. It may return them or agree merely to act as a forwarding agent for the documents but without giving value against them or taking any responsibility for their conformity to the letter of credit.

Section 5-108. Issuer's rights and obligations.

(a) Except as otherwise provided in section 5-109, an issuer shall honor a presentation that, as determined by the standard practice referred to in subsection (e) of this section, appears on its face strictly to comply with the terms and conditions of the letter of credit. Except as otherwise provided in section 5-113 and unless otherwise agreed with the applicant, an issuer shall dishonor a presentation that does not appear so to comply.

(b) An issuer has a reasonable time after presentation, but not beyond the end of the seventh business day of the issue after the day of its receipt of documents: (1) to honor, (2) if the letter of credit provides for honor to be completed more than seven business days after presentation, to accept a draft or incur a deferred obligation, or (3) to give notice to the presenter of discrepancies in the presentation.

(c) Except as otherwise provided in subsection (d) of this section, an issuer is precluded from asserting as a basis for dishonor any discrepancy if timely notice is not given, or any discrepancy not stated in the notice if timely notice is given.

(d) Failure to give the notice specified in subsection (b) of this section or to mention fraud, forgery, or expiration in the notice does not preclude the issuer from asserting as a basis for dishonor fraud or forgery as described in subsection (a) of section 5-109 or expiration of the letter of credit before presentation.

(e) An issuer shall observe standard practice of financial institutions that regularly issue letters of credit.

(f) An issuer is not responsible for: (1) the performance or nonperformance of the underlying contract, arrangement, or transaction, (2) an act or omission of others, or (3) observance or knowledge of the usage of a particular trade other than the standard practice referred to in subsection (e) of this section.

(g) If an undertaking constituting a letter of credit under paragraph (10) of subsection (a) of section 5-102 contains nondocumentary conditions, an issuer shall disregard the nondocumentary conditions and treat them as if they were not st ated.

(h) An issuer that has dishonored a presentation shall return the documents or hold them at the disposal of, and send advice to that effect to, the presenter.

(i) An issuer that has honored a presentation as permitted or required by this article: (1) is entitled to be reimbursed by the applicant in immediately available funds not later than the date of its payment of funds; (2) takes the documents free of claims of the beneficiary or presenter; (3) is precluded from asserting a right of recourse on a draft under sections 3-414 and 3-415; (4) except as otherwise provided in sections 5-110 and 5-117, is precluded from restitution of money paid or other value given by mistake to the extent the mistake concerns discrepancies in the documents or tender which are apparent on the face of the presentation; and (5) is discharged to the extent of its performance under the letter of credit unless the issuer honored a presentation in which a required signature of a beneficiary was forged.

Official Comment

1. This section combines some of the duties previously included in Sections 5-114 and 5-109. Because a confirmer has the rights and duties of an issuer, this section applies equally to a confirmer and an issuer. See Section 5-107(a).

The standard of strict compliance governs the issuer's obligation to the beneficiary and to the applicant. By requiring that a "presentation" appear strictly to comply, the section requires not only that the documents themselves appear on their face strictly to comply, but also that the other terms of the letter of credit such as those dealing with the time and place of presentation are strictly complied with. Typically, a letter of credit will provide that presentation is timely if made to the issuer, confirmer, or any other nominated person prior to expiration of the letter of credit. Accordingly, a nominated person that has honored a demand or otherwise given value before expiration will have a right to reimbursement from the issuer even though presentation to the issuer is made after the expiration of the letter of credit. Conversely, where the beneficiary negotiates documents to one who is not a nominated person, the beneficiary or that person acting on behalf of the beneficiary must make presentation to a nominated person, confirmer, or issuer prior to the expiration date.

This section does not impose a bifurcated standard under which an issuer's right to reimbursement might be broader than a beneficiary's right to honor. However, the explicit deference to standard practice in Section 5-108(a) and (e) and elsewhere expands issuers' rights of reimbursement where that practice so provides. Also, issuers can and often do contract with their applicants for expanded rights of reimbursement. Where that is done, the beneficiary will have to meet a more stringent standard of compliance as to the issuer than the issuer will have to meet as to the applicant. Similarly, a nominated person may have reimbursement and other rights against the issuer based on this article, the UCP, bank-to-bank reimbursement rules, or other agreement or undertaking of the issuer. These rights may allow the nominated person to recover from the issuer even when the nominated person would have no right to obtain honor under the letter of credit.

The section adopts strict compliance, rather than the standard that commentators have called "substantial compliance," the standard arguably applied in *Banco Español de Credito v. State Street Bank and Trust Company*, 385 F.2d 230 (1st Cir. 1967) and *Flagship Cruises Ltd. v. New England Merchants Nat. Bank*, 569 F.2d 699 (1st Cir.

1978). Strict compliance does not mean slavish conformity to the terms of the letter of credit. For example, standard practice (what issuers do) may recognize certain presentations as complying that an unschooled layman would regard as discrepant. By adopting standard practice as a way of measuring strict compliance, this article indorses the conclusion of the court in *New Braunfels Nat. Bank v. Odiorne*, 780 S. W.2d 313 (Tex.Ct.App. 1989) (beneficiary could collect when draft requested payment on 'Letter of Credit No. 86-122-5' and letter of credit specified 'Letter of Credit No. 86-122-S' holding strict compliance does not demand oppressive perfectionism). The section also indorses the result in *Tosco Corp. v. Federal Deposit Insurance Corp.*, 723 F.2d 1242 (6th Cir. 1983). The letter of credit in that case called for "drafts Drawn under Bank of Clarksville Letter of Credit Number 105." The draft presented stated "drawn under Bank of Clarksville, Clarksville, Tennessee letter of Credit No. 105." The court correctly found that despite the change of upper case "L" to a lower case "l" and the use of the word "No." instead of "Number," and despite the addition of the words "Clarksville, Tennessee," the presentation conformed. Similarly a document addressed by a foreign person to General Motors as "Jeneral Motors" would strictly conform in the absence of other defects.

Identifying and determining compliance with standard practice are matters of interpretation for the court, not for the jury. As with similar rules in Sections 4A-202(c) and 2-302, it is hoped that there will be more consistency in the outcomes and speedier resolution of disputes if the responsibility for determining the nature and scope of standard practice is granted to the court, not to a jury. Granting the court authority to make these decisions will also encourage the salutary practice of courts' granting summary judgment in circumstances where there are no significant factual disputes. The statute encourages outcomes such as *American Coleman Co. v. Intrawest Bank*, 887 F.2d 1382 (10th Cir. 1989), where summary judgment was granted.

In some circumstances standards may be established between the issuer and the applicant by agreement or by custom that would free the issuer from liability that it might otherwise have. For example, an applicant might agree that the issuer would have no duty whatsoever to examine documents on certain presentations (e.g., those below a certain dollar amount). Where the transaction depended upon the issuer's payment in a very short time period (e.g., on the same day or within a few hours of presentation), the issuer and the applicant might agree to reduce the issuer's responsibility for failure to discover discrepancies. By the same token, an agreement between the applicant and the issuer might permit the issuer to examine documents exclusively by electronic or electro-optical means. Neither those agreements nor others like them explicitly made by issuers and applicants violate the terms of Section 5-108(a) or (b) or Section 5-103(c).

2. Section 5-108(a) balances the need of the issuer for time to examine the documents against the possibility that the examiner (at the urging of the applicant or

APPENDIX B

for fear that it will not be reimbursed) will take excessive time to search for defects. What is a "reasonable time" is not extended to accommodate an issuer's procuring a waiver from the applicant. See Article 14c of the UCP.

Under both the UCC and the UCP the issuer has a reasonable time to honor or give notice. The outside limit of that time is measured in business days under the UCC and in banking days under the UCP, a difference that will rarely be significant. Neither business nor banking days are defined in Article 5, but a court may find useful analogies in Regulation CC, 12 CFR 229.2, in state law outside of the Uniform Commercial Code, and in Article 4.

Examiners must note that the seven-day period is not a safe harbor. The time within which the issuer must give notice is the lesser of a reasonable time or seven business days. Where there are few documents (as, for example, with the mine run standby letter of credit), the reasonable time would be less than seven days. If more than a reasonable time is consumed in examination, no timely notice is possible. What is a "reasonable time" is to be determined by examining the behavior of those in the business of examining documents, mostly banks. Absent prior agreement of the issuer, one could not expect a bank issuer to examine documents while the beneficiary waited in the lobby if the normal practice was to give the documents to a person who had the opportunity to examine those together with many others in an orderly process. That the applicant has not yet paid the issuer or that the applicant's account with the issuer is insufficient to cover the amount of the draft is not a basis for extension of the time period.

This section does not preclude the issuer from contacting the applicant during its examination; however, the decision to honor rests with the issuer, and it has no duty to seek a waiver from the applicant or to notify the applicant of receipt of the documents. If the issuer dishonors a conforming presentation, the beneficiary will be entitled to the remedies under Section 5-111, irrespective of the applicant's views.

Even though the person to whom presentation is made cannot conduct a reasonable examination of documents within the time after presentation and before the expiration date, presentation establishes the parties' rights. The beneficiary's right to honor or the issuer's right to dishonor arises upon presentation at the place provided in the letter of credit even though it might take the person to whom presentation has been made several days to determine whether honor or dishonor is the proper course. The issuer's time for honor or giving notice of dishonor may be extended or shortened by a term in the letter of credit. The time for the issuer's performance may be otherwise modified or waived in accordance with Section 5-106.

The issuer's time to inspect runs from the time of its "receipt of documents." Documents are considered to be received only when they are received at the place specified for presentation by the issuer or other party to whom presentation is made.

Failure of the issuer to act within the time permitted by subsection (b) constitutes dishonor. Because of the preclusion in subsection (c) and the liability that the issuer may incur under Section 5-111 for wrongful dishonor, the effect of such a silent dishonor may ultimately be the same as though the issuer had honored, i.e., it may owe damages in the amount drawn but unpaid under the letter of credit.

3. The requirement that the issuer send notice of the discrepancies or be precluded from asserting discrepancies is new to Article 5. It is taken from the similar provision in the UCP and is intended to promote certainty and finality.

The section thus substitutes a strict preclusion principle for the doctrines of waiver and estoppel that might otherwise apply under Section 1-103. It rejects the reasoning in *Flagship Cruises Ltd. v. New England Merchants' Nat. Bank*, 569 F.2d 699 (1st Cir. 1978) and *Wing On Bank Ltd. v. American Nat. Bank & Trust Co.*, 457 F.2d 328 (5th Cir. 1972) where the issuer was held to be estopped only if the beneficiary relied on the issuer's failure to give notice.

Assume, for example, that the beneficiary presented documents to the issuer shortly before the letter of credit expired, in circumstances in which the beneficiary could not have cured any discrepancy before expiration. Under the reasoning of *Flagship* and *Wing On*, the beneficiary's inability to cure, even if it had received notice, would absolve the issuer of its failure to give notice. The virtue of the preclusion obligation adopted in this section is that it forecloses litigation about reliance and detriment.

Even though issuers typically give notice of the discrepancy of tardy presentation when presentation is made after the expiration of a credit, they are not required to give that notice and the section permits them to raise late presentation as a defect despite their failure to give that notice.

4. To act within a reasonable time, the issuer must normally give notice without delay after the examining party makes its decision. If the examiner decides to dishonor on the first day, it would be obliged to notify the beneficiary shortly thereafter, perhaps on the same business day. This rule accepts the reasoning in cases such as *Datapoint Corp. v. M & I Bank*, 665 F. Supp. 722 (W.D. Wis. 1987) and *Esso Petroleum Canada, Div. of Imperial Oil, Ltd. v. Security Pacific Bank*, 710 F. Supp. 275 (D. Ore. 1989).

The section deprives the examining party of the right simply to sit on a presentation that is made within seven days of expiration. The section requires the examiner to examine the documents and make a decision and, having made a decision to dishonor, to communicate promptly with the presenter. Nevertheless, a beneficiary who presents documents shortly before the expiration of a letter of credit runs the risk that it will never have the opportunity to cure any discrepancies.

5. Confirmers, other nominated persons, and collecting banks acting for beneficiaries can be presenters and, when so, are entitled to the notice provided in subsection (b). Even nominated persons who have honored or given value against an earlier presentation of the beneficiary and are themselves seeking reimburse-

ment or honor need notice of discrepancies in the hope that they may be able to procure complying documents. The issuer has the obligations imposed by this section whether the issuer's performance is characterized as "reimbursement" of a nominated person or as "honor."

6. In many cases a letter of credit authorizes presentation by the beneficiary to someone other than the issuer. Sometimes that person is identified as a "payor" or "paying bank," or as an "acceptor" or "accepting bank," in other cases as a "negotiating bank," and in other cases there will be no specific designation. The section does not impose any duties on a person other than the issuer or confirmer, however a nominated person or other person may have liability under this article or at common law if it fails to perform an express or implied agreement with the beneficiary.

7. The issuer's obligation to honor runs not only to the beneficiary but also to the applicant. It is possible that an applicant who has made a favorable contract with the beneficiary will be injured by the issuer's wrongful dishonor. Except to the extent that the contract between the issuer and the applicant limits that liability, the issuer will have liability to the applicant for wrongful dishonor under Section 5-111 as a matter of contract law. A good faith extension of the time in Section 5-108(b) by agreement between the issuer and beneficiary binds the applicant even if the applicant is not consulted or does not consent to the extension.

The issuer's obligation to dishonor when there is no apparent compliance with the letter of credit runs only to the applicant. No other party to the transaction can complain if the applicant waives compliance with terms or conditions of the letter of credit or agrees to a less stringent standard for compliance than that supplied by this article. Except as otherwise agreed with the applicant, an issuer may dishonor a noncomplying presentation despite an applicant's waiver.

Waiver of discrepancies by an issuer or an applicant in one or more presentations does not waive similar discrepancies in a future presentation. Neither the issuer nor the beneficiary can reasonably rely upon honor over past waivers as a basis for concluding that a future defective presentation will justify honor. The reasoning of *Courtaulds of North America Inc. v. North Carolina Nat. Bank*, 528 F.2d 802 (4th Cir. 1975) is accepted and that expressed in *Schweibish v. Pontchartrain State Bank*, 389 So.2d 731 (La.App. 1980) and *Titanium Metals Corp. v. Space Metals, Inc.*, 529 P.2d 431 (Utah 1974) is rejected.

8. The standard practice referred to in subsection (e) includes (i) international practice set forth in or referenced by the Uniform Customs and Practice, (ii) other practice rules published by associations of financial institutions, and (iii) local and regional practice. It is possible that standard practice will vary from one place to another. Where there are conflicting practices, the parties should indicate which practice governs their rights. A practice may be overridden by agreement or course of dealing. See Section 1-205(4).

9. The responsibility of the issuer under a letter of credit is to examine documents and to make a prompt decision to honor or dishonor based upon that examination. Nondocumentary conditions have no place in this regime and are better accommodated under contract or suretyship law and practice. In requiring that nondocumentary conditions in letters of credit be ignored as surplusage, Article 5 remains aligned with the UCP (see UCP 500 Article 13c), approves cases like *Pringle-Associated Mortgage Corp. v. Southern National Bank*, 571 F.2d 871, 874 (5th Cir. 1978), and rejects the reasoning in cases such as *Sherwood & Roberts, Inc. v. First Security Bank*, 682 P.2d 149 (Mont. 1984).

Subsection (g) recognizes that letters of credit sometimes contain nondocumentary terms or conditions. Conditions such as a term prohibiting "shipment on vessels more than 15 years old," are to be disregarded and treated as surplusage. Similarly, a requirement that there be an award by a "duly appointed arbitrator" would not require the issuer to determine whether the arbitrator had been "duly appointed." Likewise a term in a standby letter of credit that provided for differing forms of certification depending upon the particular type of default does not oblige the issuer independently to determine which kind of default has occurred. These conditions must be disregarded by the issuer. Where the nondocumentary conditions are central and fundamental to the issuer's obligation (as for example a condition that would require the issuer to determine in fact whether the beneficiary had performed the underlying contract or whether the applicant had defaulted) their inclusion may remove the undertaking from the scope of Article 5 entirely. See Section 5-102(a)(10) and Comment 6 to Section 5-102.

Subsection (g) would not permit the beneficiary or the issuer to disregard terms in the letter of credit such as place, time, and mode of presentation. The rule in subsection (g) is intended to prevent an issuer from deciding or even investigating extrinsic facts, but not from consulting the clock, the calendar, the relevant law and practice, or its own general knowledge of documentation or transactions of the type underlying a particular letter of credit.

Even though nondocumentary conditions must be disregarded in determining compliance of a presentation (and thus in determining the issuer's duty to the beneficiary), an issuer that has promised its applicant that it will honor only on the occurrence of those nondocumentary conditions may have liability to its applicant for disregarding the conditions.

10. Subsection (f) condones an issuer's ignorance of "any usage of a particular trade"; that trade is the trade of the applicant, beneficiary, or others who may be involved in the underlying transaction. The issuer is expected to know usage that is commonly encountered in the course of document examination. For example, an issuer should know the common usage with respect to documents in the maritime shipping trade but would not be expected to understand

Appendix B

synonyms used in a particular trade for product descriptions appearing in a letter of credit or an invoice.
11. Where the issuer's performance is the delivery of an item of value other than money, the applicant's reimbursement obligation would be to make the "item of value" available to the issuer.
12. An issuer is entitled to reimbursement from the applicant after honor of a forged or fraudulent drawing if honor was permitted under Section 5-109(a).
13. The last clause of Section 5-108(i)(5) deals with a special case in which the fraud is not committed by the beneficiary, but is committed by a stranger to the transaction who forges the beneficiary's signature. If the issuer pays against documents on which a required signature of the beneficiary is forged, it remains liable to the true beneficiary.

Section 5-109. Fraud and forgery.

(a) If a presentation is made that appears on its face strictly to comply with the terms and conditions of the letter of credit, but a required document is forged or materially fraudulent, or honor of the presentation would facilitate a material fraud by the beneficiary on the issuer or applicant: (1) The issuer shall honor the presentation, if honor is demanded by: (i) a nominated person who has given value in good faith and without notice of forgery or material fraud, (ii) a confirmer who has honored its confirmation in good faith, (iii) a holder in due course of a draft drawn under the letter of credit which was taken after acceptance by the issuer or nominated person, or (iv) an assignee of the issuer's or nominated person's deferred obligation that was taken for value and without notice of forgery or material fraud after the obligation was incurred by the issuer or nominated person; and (2) The issuer, acting in good faith, may honor or dishonor the presentation in any other case.

(b) If an applicant claims that a required document is forged or materially fraudulent or that honor of the presentation would facilitate a material fraud by the beneficiary on the issuer or applicant, a court of competent jurisdiction may temporarily or permanently enjoin the issuer from honoring a presentation or grant similar relief against the issuer or other persons only if the court finds that: (1) The relief is not prohibited under the law applicable to an accepted draft or deferred obligation incurred by the issuer; (2) A beneficiary, issuer, or nominated person who may be adversely affected is adequately protected against loss that t may suffer because the relief is granted; (3) All of the conditions to entitle a person to the relief under the law of this state have been met; and (4) On the basis of the information submitted to the court, the applicant is more likely than not to succeed under its claim of forgery or material fraud and the person demanding honor does not qualify for protection under paragraph (1) of subsection (a) of this section.

Official Comment

1. This recodification makes clear that fraud must be found either in the documents or must have been committed by the beneficiary on the issuer or applicant. See *Cromwell v. Commerce & Energy Bank*, 464 So.2d 721 (La. 1985).

Secondly, it makes clear that fraud must be "material." Necessarily courts must decide the breadth and width of "materiality." The use of the word requires that the fraudulent aspect of a document be material to a purchaser of that document or that the fraudulent act be significant to the participants in the underlying transaction. Assume, for example, that the beneficiary has a contract to deliver 1,000 barrels of salad oil. Knowing that it has delivered only 998, the beneficiary nevertheless submits an invoice showing 1,000 barrels. If two barrels in a 1,000 barrel shipment would be an insubstantial and immaterial breach of the underlying contract, the beneficiary's act, though possibly fraudulent, is not materially so and would not justify an injunction. Conversely, the knowing submission of those invoices upon delivery of only five barrels would be materially fraudulent. The courts must examine the underlying transaction when there is an allegation of material fraud, for only by examining that transaction can one determine whether a document is fraudulent or the beneficiary has committed fraud and, if so, whether the fraud was material.

Material fraud by the beneficiary occurs only when the beneficiary has no colorable right to expect honor and where there is no basis in fact to support such a right to honor. The section indorses articulations such as those stated in *Intraworld Indus. v. Girard Trust Bank*, 336 A.2d 316 (Pa. 1975), *Roman Ceramics Corp. v. People's Nat. Bank*, 714 F.2d 1207 (3d Cir. 1983), and similar decisions and embraces certain decisions under Section 5-114 that relied upon the phrase "fraud in the transaction." Some of these decisions have been summarized as follows in *Ground Air Transfer v. Westates Airlines*, 899 F.2d 1269, 1272-73 (1st Cir. 1990):

We have said throughout that courts may not "*normally*" issue an injunction because of an important exception to the general "no injunction" rule. The exception, as we also explained in Itek, 730 F.2d at 24-25, concerns "fraud" so serious as to make it obviously pointless and unjust to permit the beneficiary to obtain the money. Where the circumstances "*plainly*" show that the underlying contract forbids the beneficiary to call a letter of credit, Itek, 730 F.2d at 24; where they show that the contract deprives the beneficiary of even a "*colorable*" right to do so, id., at 25; where the contract and circumstances reveal that the beneficiary's demand for payment has "absolutely no basis in fact," id.; see Dynamics Corp. of America, 356 F. Supp. at 999; where the ben-

Appendix B

eficiary's conduct has "so vitiated the entire transaction that the legitimate purposes of the independence of the issuer's obligation would no longer be served," Itek, 730 F.2d at 25 (quoting *Roman Ceramics Corp. v. Peoples National Bank*, 714 F.2d 1207, 1212 n.12, 1215 (3d Cir. 1983) (quoting Intraworld Indus., 336 A.2d at 324-25)); *then* a court may enjoin payment.

2. Subsection (a)(2) makes clear that the issuer may honor in the face of the applicant's claim of fraud. The subsection also makes clear what was not stated in former Section 5-114, that the issuer may dishonor and defend that dishonor by showing fraud or forgery of the kind stated in subsection (a). Because issuers may be liable for wrongful dishonor if they are unable to prove forgery or material fraud, presumably most issuers will choose to honor despite applicant's claims of fraud or forgery unless the applicant procures an injunction. Merely because the issuer has a right to dishonor and to defend that dishonor by showing forgery or material fraud does not mean it has a duty to the applicant to dishonor. The applicant's normal recourse is to procure an injunction, if the applicant is unable to procure an injunction, it will have a claim against the issuer only in the rare case in which it can show that the issuer did not honor in good faith.

3. Whether a beneficiary can commit fraud by presenting a draft under a clean letter of credit (one calling only for a draft and no other documents) has been much debated. Under the current formulation it would be possible but difficult for there to be fraud in such a presentation. If the applicant were able to show that the beneficiary were committing material fraud on the applicant in the underlying transaction, then payment would facilitate a material fraud by the beneficiary on the applicant and honor could be enjoined. The courts should be skeptical of claims of fraud by one who has signed a "suicide" or clean credit and thus granted a beneficiary the right to draw by mere presentation of a draft.

4. The standard for injunctive relief is high, and the burden remains on the applicant to show, by evidence and not by mere allegation, that such relief is warranted. Some courts have enjoined payments on letters of credit on insufficient showing by the applicant. For example, in *Griffin Cos. v. First Nat. Bank*, 374 N.W.2d 768 (Minn.App. 1985), the court enjoined payment under a standby letter of credit, basing its decision on plaintiff's allegation, rather than competent evidence, of fraud.

There are at least two ways to prohibit injunctions against honor under this section after acceptance of a draft by the issuer. First is to define honor (see Section 5-102(a)(8)) in the particular letter of credit to occur upon acceptance and without regard to later payment of the acceptance. Second is explicitly to agree that the applicant has no right to an injunction after acceptance—whether or not the acceptance constitutes honor.

5. Although the statute deals principally with injunctions against honor, it also cautions against granting "similar relief" and the same principles apply when the applicant or issuer attempts to achieve the same legal outcome by injunction against presentation (see *Ground Air Transfer Inc. v. Westates Airlines, Inc.*, 899 F.2d 1269 (1st Cir. 1990)), interpleader, declaratory judgment, or attachment. These attempts should face the same obstacles that face efforts to enjoin the issuer from paying. Expanded use of any of these devices could threaten the independence principle just as much as injunctions against honor. For that reason courts should have the same hostility to them and place the same restrictions on their use as would be applied to injunctions against honor. Courts should not allow the "sacred cow of equity to trample the tender vines of letter of credit law."

6. Section 5-109(a)(1) also protects specified third parties against the risk of fraud. By issuing a letter of credit that nominates a person to negotiate or pay, the issuer (ultimately the applicant) induces that nominated person to give value and thereby assumes the risk that a draft drawn under the letter of credit will be transferred to one with a status like that of a holder in due course who deserves to be protected against a fraud defense.

7. The "loss" to be protected against—by bond or otherwise under subsection (b)(2) — includes incidental damages. Among those are legal fees that might be incurred by the beneficiary or issuer in defending against an injunction action.

Section 5-110. Warranties.

(a) If its presentation is honored, the beneficiary warrants: (1) To the issuer, any other person to whom presentation is made, and the applicant that there is no fraud or forgery of the kind described in subsection (a) of section 5-109; and (2) To the applicant that the drawing does not violate any agreement between the applicant and beneficiary or any other agreement intended by them to be augmented by the letter of credit.

(b) The warranties in subsection (a) of this section are in addition to warranties arising under articles 3, 4, 7 and 8 because of the presentation or transfer of documents covered by any of those articles.

Official Comment

1. Since the warranties in subsection (a) are not given unless a letter of credit has been honored, no breach of warranty under this subsection can be a defense to dishonor by the issuer. Any defense must be based on Section 5-108 or 5-109

APPENDIX B

and not on this section. Also, breach of the warranties by the beneficiary in subsection (a) cannot excuse the applicant's duty to reimburse.

2. The warranty in Section 5-110(a)(2) assumes that payment under the letter of credit is final. It does not run to the issuer, only to the applicant. In most cases the applicant will have a direct cause of action for breach of the underlying contract. This warranty has primary application in standby letters of credit or other circumstances where the applicant is not a party to an underlying contract with the beneficiary. It is not a warranty that the statements made on the presentation of the documents presented are truthful nor is it a warranty that the documents strictly comply under Section 5-108(a). It is a warranty that the beneficiary has performed all the acts expressly and implicitly necessary under any underlying agreement to entitle the beneficiary to honor. If, for example, an underlying sales contract authorized the beneficiary to draw only upon "due performance" and the beneficiary drew even though it had breached the underlying contract by delivering defective goods, honor of its draw would break the warranty. By the same token, if the underlying contract authorized the beneficiary to draw only upon actual default or upon its or a third party's determination of default by the applicant and if the beneficiary drew in violation of its authorization, then upon honor of its draw the warranty would be breached. In many cases, therefore, the documents presented to the issuer will contain inaccurate statements (concerning the goods delivered or concerning default or other matters), but the breach of warranty arises not because the statements are untrue but because the beneficiary's drawing violated its express or implied obligations in the underlying transaction.

3. The damages for breach of warranty are not specified in Section 5-111. Courts may find damage analogies in Section 2-714 in Article 2 and in warranty decisions under Articles 3 and 4.

Unlike wrongful dishonor cases—where the damages usually equal the amount of the draw—the damages for breach of warranty will often be much less than the amount of the draw, sometimes zero. Assume a seller entitled to draw only on proper performance of its sales contract. Assume it breaches the sales contract in a way that gives the buyer a right to damages but no right to reject. The applicant's damages for breach of the warranty in subsection (a)(2) are limited to the damages it could recover for breach of the contract of sale. Alternatively assume an underlying agreement that authorizes a beneficiary to draw only the "amount in default." Assume a default of $200,000 and a draw of $500,000. The damages for breach of warranty would be no more than $300,000.

Section 5-111. Remedies.

(a) If an issuer wrongfully dishonors or repudiates its obligation to pay money under a letter of credit before presentation, the beneficiary, successor, or nominated person presenting on its own behalf may recover from the issuer the amount that is the subject of the dishonor or repudiation. If the issuer's obligation under the letter of credit is not for the payment of money, the claimant may obtain specific performance or, at the claimant's election, recover an amount equal to the value of performance from the issuer. In either case, the claimant may also recover incidental but not consequential damages. The claimant is not obligated to take action to avoid damages that might be due from the issuer under this subsection. If, although not obligated to do so, the claimant avoids damages, the claimant's recovery from the issuer must be reduced by the amount of damages avoided. The issuer has the burden of proving the amount of damages avoided. In the case of repudiation the claimant need not present any document.

(b) If an issuer wrongfully dishonors a draft or demand presented under a letter of credit or honors a draft or demand in breach of its obligation to the applicant, the applicant may recover damages resulting from the breach, including incidental but not consequential damages, less any amount saved as a result of the breach.

(c) If an adviser or nominated person other than a confirmer breaches an obligation under this article or an issuer breaches an obligation not covered in subsection (a) or (b) of this section, a person to whom the obligation is owed may recover damages resulting from the breach, including incidental but not consequential damages, less any amount saved as a result of the breach. To the extent of the confirmation, a confirmer has the liability of an issuer specified in this subsection and subsections (a) and (b) of this section.

(d) An issuer, nominated person, or adviser who is found liable under subsection (a), (b) or (c) of this section shall pay interest on the amount owed thereunder from the date of wrongful dishonor or other appropriate date.

(e) Damages that would otherwise be payable by a party for breach of an obligation under this article may be liquidated by agreement or undertaking, but only in an amount or by a formula that is reasonable in light of the harm anticipated.

APPENDIX B

Official Comment

1. The right to specific performance is new. The express limitation on the duty of the beneficiary to mitigate damages adopts the position of certain courts and commentators. Because the letter of credit depends upon speed and certainty of payment, it is important that the issuer not be given an incentive to dishonor. The issuer might have an incentive to dishonor if it could rely on the burden of mitigation falling on the beneficiary (to sell goods and sue only for the difference between the price of the goods sold and the amount due under the letter of credit). Under the scheme contemplated by Section 5-111(a), the beneficiary would present the documents to the issuer. If the issuer wrongfully dishonored, the beneficiary would have no further duty to the issuer with respect to the goods covered by documents that the issuer dishonored and returned. The issuer thus takes the risk that the beneficiary will let the goods rot or be destroyed. Of course the beneficiary may have a duty of mitigation to the applicant arising from the underlying agreement, but the issuer would not have the right to assert that duty by way of defense or setoff. See Section 5-117(d). If the beneficiary sells the goods covered by dishonored documents or if the beneficiary sells a draft after acceptance but before dishonor by the issuer, the net amount so gained should be subtracted from the amount of the beneficiary's damages—at least where the damage claim against the issuer equals or exceeds the damage suffered by the beneficiary. If, on the other hand, the beneficiary suffers damages in an underlying transaction in an amount that exceeds the amount of the wrongfully dishonored demand (e.g., where the letter of credit does not cover 100 percent of the underlying obligation), the damages avoided should not necessarily be deducted from the beneficiary's claim against the issuer. In such a case, the damages would be the lesser of (i) the amount recoverable in the absence of mitigation (that is, the amount that is subject to the dishonor or repudiation plus any incidental damages) and (ii) the damages remaining after deduction for the amount of damages actually avoided.

A beneficiary need not present documents as a condition of suit for anticipatory repudiation, but if a beneficiary could never have obtained documents necessary for a presentation conforming to the letter of credit, the beneficiary cannot recover for anticipatory repudiation of the letter of credit. *Doelger v. Battery Park Bank*, 201 A.D. 515, 194 N.Y.S. 582 (1922) and *Decor by Nikkei Int'l, Inc. v. Federal Republic of Nigeria*, 497 F.Supp. 893 (S.D.N.Y. 1980), *aff'd*, 647 F.2d 300 (2d Cir. 1981), *cert. denied*, 454 U.S. 1148 (1982). The last sentence of subsection (c) does not expand the liability of a confirmer to persons to whom the confirmer would not otherwise be liable under Section 5-107.

Almost all letters of credit, including those that call for an acceptance, are "obligations to pay money" as that term is used in Section 5-111(a).

2. What damages "result" from improper honor is for the courts to decide. Even though an issuer pays a beneficiary in violation of Section 5-108(a) or of its contract with the applicant, it may have no liability to an applicant. If the underlying contract has been fully performed, the applicant may not have been damaged by the issuer's breach. Such a case would occur when A contracts for goods at $100 per ton, but, upon delivery, the market value of conforming goods has decreased to $25 per ton. If the issuer pays over discrepancies, there should be no recovery by A for the price differential if the issuer's breach did not alter the applicant's obligation under the underlying contract, i.e., to pay $100 per ton for goods now worth $25 per ton. On the other hand, if the applicant intends to resell the goods and must itself satisfy the strict compliance requirements under a second letter of credit in connection with its sale, the applicant may be damaged by the issuer's payment despite discrepancies because the applicant itself may then be unable to procure honor on the letter of credit where it is the beneficiary, and may be unable to mitigate its damages by enforcing its rights against others in the underlying transaction. Note that an issuer found liable to its applicant may have recourse under Section 5-117 by subrogation to the applicant's claim against the beneficiary or other persons.

One who inaccurately advises a letter of credit breaches its obligation to the beneficiary, but may cause no damage. If the beneficiary knows the terms of the letter of credit and understands the advice to be inaccurate, the beneficiary will have suffered no damage as a result of the adviser's breach.

3. Since the confirmer has the rights and duties of an issuer, in general it has an issuer's liability, see subsection (c). The confirmer is usually a confirming bank. A confirming bank often also plays the role of an adviser. If it breaks its obligation to the beneficiary, the confirming bank may have liability as an issuer or, depending upon the obligation that was broken, as an adviser. For example, a wrongful dishonor would give it liability as an issuer under Section 5-111(a). On the other hand a confirming bank that broke its obligation to advise the credit but did not commit wrongful dishonor would be treated under Section 5-111(c).

4. Consequential damages for breach of obligations under this article are excluded in the belief that these damages can best be avoided by the beneficiary or the applicant and out of the fear that imposing consequential damages on issuers would raise the cost of the letter of credit to a level that might render it uneconomic. *A fortiori* punitive and exemplary damages are excluded, however, this section does not bar recovery of consequential or even punitive damages for breach of statutory or common law duties arising outside of this article.

5. The section does not specify a rate of interest. It leaves the setting of the rate to the court. It would be appropriate for a court to use the rate that would normally apply in that court in other situations where interest is imposed by law.

APPENDIX B

6. The court must award attorney's fees to the prevailing party, whether that party is an applicant, a beneficiary, an issuer, a nominated person, or adviser. Since the issuer may be entitled to recover its legal fees and costs from the applicant under the reimbursement agreement, allowing the issuer to recover those fees from a losing beneficiary may also protect the applicant against undeserved losses. The party entitled to attorneys' fees has been described as the "prevailing party." Sometimes it will be unclear which party "prevailed," for example, where there are multiple issues and one party wins on some and the other party wins on others. Determining which is the prevailing party is in the discretion of the court. Subsection (e) authorizes attorney's fees in all actions where a remedy is sought "under this article." It applies even when the remedy might be an injunction under Section 5-109 or when the claimed remedy is otherwise outside of Section 5-111. Neither an issuer nor a confirmer should be treated as a "losing" party when an injunction is granted to the applicant over the objection of the issuer or confirmer; accordingly neither should be liable for fees and expenses in that case.

"Expenses of litigation" is intended to be broader than "costs." For example, expense of litigation would include travel expenses of witnesses, fees for expert witnesses, and expenses associated with taking depositions.

7. For the purposes of Section 5-111(f) "harm anticipated" must be anticipated at the time when the agreement that includes the liquidated damage clause is executed or at the time when the undertaking that includes the clause is issued. See Section 2A-504.

Section 5-112. Transfer of letter of credit.

(a) Except as otherwise provided in section 5-113, unless a letter of credit provides that it is transferable, the right of a beneficiary to draw or otherwise demand performance under a letter of credit may not be transferred.

(b) Even if a letter of credit provides that it is transferable, the issuer may refuse to recognize or carry out a transfer if: (1) the transfer would violate applicable law; or (2) the transferor or transferee has failed to comply with any requirement stated in the letter of credit or any other requirement relating to transfer imposed by the issuer which is within the standard practice referred to in subsection (e) of section 5-108 or is otherwise reasonable under the circumstances.

Official Comment

1. In order to protect the applicant's reliance on the designated beneficiary, letter of credit law traditionally has forbidden the beneficiary to convey to third parties its right to draw or demand payment under the letter of credit. Subsection (a) codifies that rule. The term "transfer" refers to the beneficiary's conveyance of that right. Absent incorporation of the UCP (which make elaborate provision for partial transfer of a commercial letter of credit) or similar trade practice and absent other express indication in the letter of credit that the term is used to mean something else, a term in the letter of credit indicating that the beneficiary has the right to transfer should be taken to mean that the beneficiary may convey to a third party its right to draw or demand payment. Even in that case, the issuer or other person controlling the transfer may make the beneficiary's right to transfer subject to conditions, such as timely notification, payment of a fee, delivery of the letter of credit to the issuer or other person controlling the transfer, or execution of appropriate forms to document the transfer. A nominated person who is not a confirmer has no obligation to recognize a transfer.

The power to establish "requirements" does not include the right absolutely to refuse to recognize transfers under a transferable letter of credit. An issuer who wishes to retain the right to deny all transfers should not issue transferable letters of credit or should incorporate the UCP. By stating its requirements in the letter of credit an issuer may impose any requirement without regard to its conformity to practice or reasonableness. Transfer requirements of issuers and nominated persons must be made known to potential transferors and transferees to enable those parties to comply with the requirements. A common method of making such requirements known is to use a form that indicates the information that must be provided and the instructions that must be given to enable the issuer or nominated person to comply with a request to transfer.

2. The issuance of a transferable letter of credit with the concurrence of the applicant is *ipso facto* an agreement by the issuer and applicant to permit a beneficiary to transfer its drawing right and permit a nominated person to recognize and carry out that transfer without further notice to them. In international commerce, transferable letters of credit are often issued under circumstances in which a nominated person or adviser is expected to facilitate the transfer from the original beneficiary to a transferee and to deal with that transferee. In those circumstances it is the responsibility of the nominated person or adviser to establish procedures satisfactory to protect itself against double presentation or dispute about the right to draw under the letter of credit. Commonly such a person will control the transfer by requiring that the original letter of credit be given to it or by causing a paper copy marked as an original to be issued where the original letter of credit was electronic. By keeping possession of the original

APPENDIX B

letter of credit the nominated person or adviser can minimize or entirely exclude the possibility that the original beneficiary could properly procure payment from another bank. If the letter of credit requires presentation of the original letter of credit itself, no other payment could be procured. In addition to imposing whatever requirements it considers appropriate to protect itself against double payment the person that is facilitating the transfer has a right to charge an appropriate fee for its activity.

"Transfer" of a letter of credit should be distinguished from "assignment of proceeds." The former is analogous to a novation or a substitution of beneficiaries. It contemplates not merely payment to but also performance by the transferee. For example, under the typical terms of transfer for a commercial letter of credit, a transferee could comply with a letter of credit transferred to it by signing and presenting its own draft and invoice. An assignee of proceeds, on the other hand, is wholly dependent on the presentation of a draft and invoice signed by the beneficiary.

By agreeing to the issuance of a transferable letter of credit, which is not qualified or limited, the applicant may lose control over the identity of the person whose performance will earn payment under the letter of credit.

Section 5-113. Transfer by operation of law.

(a) A successor of a beneficiary may consent to amendments, sign and present documents, and receive payment or other items of value in the name of the beneficiary without disclosing its status as a successor.

(b) A successor of a beneficiary may consent to amendments, sign and present documents, and receive payment or other items of value in its own name as the disclosed successor of the beneficiary. Except as otherwise provided in subsection (e) of this section, an issuer shall recognize a disclosed successor of a beneficiary as beneficiary in full substitution for its predecessor upon compliance with the requirements for recognition by the issuer of a transfer of drawing rights by operation of law under the standard practice referred to in subsection (e) of section 5-108 or, in the absence of such a practice, compliance with other reasonable procedures sufficient to protect the issuer.

(c) An issuer is not obliged to determine whether a purported successor is a successor of a beneficiary or whether the signature of a purported successor is genuine or authorized.

(d) Honor of a purported successor's apparently complying presentation under subsection (a) or (b) of this section has the consequences specified in subsection (i) of section 5-108 even if the purported successor is not the successor of a beneficiary. Documents signed in the name of the beneficiary or of a disclosed successor by a person who is neither the beneficiary nor the successor of the beneficiary are forged documents for the purposes of section 5-109.

(e) An issuer whose rights of reimbursement are not covered by subsection (d) of this section or substantially similar law and any confirmer or nominated person may decline to recognize a presentation under subsection (b) of this section.

(f) A beneficiary whose name is changed after the issuance of a letter of credit has the same rights and obligations as a successor of a beneficiary under this section.

Official Comment

This section affirms the result in *Pastor v. Nat. Republic Bank of Chicago*, 76 Ill.2d 139, 390 N.E.2d 894 (Ill. 1979) and *Federal Deposit Insurance Co. v. Bank of Boulder*, 911 F.2d 1466 (10th Cir. 1990).

An issuer's requirements for recognition of a successor's status might include presentation of a certificate of merger, a court order appointing a bankruptcy trustee or receiver, a certificate of appointment as bankruptcy trustee, or the like. The issuer is entitled to rely upon such documents which on their face demonstrate that presentation is made by a successor of a beneficiary. It is not obliged to make an independent investigation to determine the fact of succession.

Section 5-114. Assignment of proceeds.

(a) In this section, "proceeds of a letter of credit" means the cash, check, accepted draft, or other item of value paid or delivered upon honor or giving of value by the issuer or any nominated person under the letter of credit. The term does not include a beneficiary's drawing rights or documents presented by the beneficiary.

(b) A beneficiary may assign its right to part or all of the proceeds of a letter of credit. The beneficiary may do so before presentation as a present assignment of its right to receive proceeds contingent upon its compliance with the terms and conditions of the letter of credit.

(c) An issuer or nominated person need not recognize an assignment of proceeds of a letter of credit until it consents to the assignment.

(d) An issuer or nominated person has no obligation to give or withhold its consent to an assignment of proceeds of a letter of credit, but consent may not be unreasonably withheld if the assignee possesses and

Appendix B

exhibits the letter of credit and presentation of the letter of credit is a condition to honor.

(e) Rights of a transferee beneficiary or nominated person are independent of the beneficiary's assignment of the proceeds of a letter of credit and are superior to the assignee's right to the proceeds.

(f) Neither the rights recognized by this section between an assignee and an issuer, transferee beneficiary, or nominated person nor the issuer's or nominated person's payment of proceeds to an assignee or a third person affect the rights between the assignee and any person other than the issuer, transferee beneficiary, or nominated person. The mode of creating and perfecting a security interest in or granting an assignment of a beneficiary's rights to proceeds is governed by article 9 or other law. Against persons other than the issuer, transferee beneficiary, or nominated person, the rights and obligations arising upon the creation of a security interest or other assignment of a beneficiary's right to proceeds and its perfection are governed by article 9 or other law.

Official Comment

1. Subsection (b) expressly validates the beneficiary's present assignment of letter of credit proceeds if made after the credit is established but before the proceeds are realized. This section adopts the prevailing usage — "assignment of proceeds" — to an assignee. That terminology carries with it no implication, however, that an assignee acquires no interest until the proceeds are paid by the issuer. For example, an "assignment of the right to proceeds" of a letter of credit for purposes of security that meets the requirements of Section 9-203(1) would constitute the present creation of a security interest in that right. This security interest can be perfected by possession (Section 9-305) if the letter of credit is in written form. Although subsection (a) explains the meaning of "'proceeds' of a letter of credit," it should be emphasized that those proceeds also may be Article 9 proceeds of other collateral. For example, if a seller of inventory receives a letter of credit to support the account that arises upon the sale, payments made under the letter of credit are Article 9 proceeds of the inventory, account, and any document of title covering the inventory. Thus, the secured party who had a perfected security interest in that inventory, account, or document has a perfected security interest in the proceeds collected under the letter of credit, so long as they are identifiable cash proceeds (Section 9-306(2), (3)). This perfection is continuous, regardless of whether the secured party perfected a security interest in the right to letter of credit proceeds.

2. An assignee's rights to enforce an assignment of proceeds against an issuer and the priority of the assignee's rights against a nominated person or transferee beneficiary are governed by Article 5. Those rights and that priority are stated in subsections (c), (d), and (e). Note also that Section 4-210 gives first priority to a collecting bank that has given value for a documentary draft.

3. By requiring that an issuer or nominated person consent to the assignment of proceeds of a letter of credit, subsections (c) and (d) follow more closely recognized national and international letter of credit practices than did prior law. In most circumstances, it has always been advisable for the assignee to obtain the consent of the issuer in order better to safeguard its right to the proceeds. When notice of an assignment has been received, issuers normally have required signatures on a consent form. This practice is reflected in the revision. By unconditionally consenting to such an assignment, the issuer or nominated person becomes bound, subject to the rights of the superior parties specified in subsection (e), to pay to the assignee the assigned letter of credit proceeds that the issuer or nominated person would otherwise pay to the beneficiary or another assignee.

Where the letter of credit must be presented as a condition to honor and the assignee holds and exhibits the letter of credit to the issuer or nominated person, the risk to the issuer or nominated person of having to pay twice is minimized. In such a situation, subsection (d) provides that the issuer or nominated person may not unreasonably withhold its consent to the assignment.

Section 5-115. Statute of limitations.

An action to enforce a right or obligation arising under this article must be commenced within one year after the expiration date of the relevant letter of credit or one year after the cause of action accrues, whichever occurs later. A cause of action accrues when the breach occurs, regardless of the aggrieved party's lack of knowledge of the breach.

Official Comment

1. This section is based upon Sections 4-111 and 2-725(2).
2. This section applies to all claims for which there are remedies under Section 5-111 and to other claims made under this article, such as claims for breach of warranty under Section 5-110. Because it covers all claims under Section 5-111, the statute of limitations applies not only to wrongful dishonor claims against the issuer but also to claims between the issuer and the applicant arising from the reimbursement agreement. These might be for reimbursement (issuer v.

APPENDIX B

applicant) or for breach of the reimbursement contract by wrongful honor (applicant v. issuer).
3. The statute of limitations, like the rest of the statute, applies only to a letter of credit issued on or after the effective date and only to transactions, events, obligations, or duties arising out of or associated with such a letter. If a letter of credit was issued before the effective date and an obligation on that letter of credit was breached after the effective date, the complaining party could bring its suit within the time that would have been permitted prior to the adoption of Section 5-115 and would not be limited by the terms of Section 5-115.

Section 5-116. Choice of law and forum.

(a) The liability of an issuer, nominated person, or adviser for action or omission is governed by the law of the jurisdiction chosen by an agreement in the form of a record signed or otherwise authenticated by the affected parties in the manner provided in section 5-104 or by a provision in the person's letter of credit, confirmation, or other undertaking. The jurisdiction whose law is chosen need not bear any relation to the transaction.

(b) Unless subsection (a) of this section applies, the liability of an issuer, nominated person, or adviser for action or omission is governed by the law of the jurisdiction in which the person is located. The person is considered to be located at the address indicated in the person's undertaking. If more than one address is indicated, the person is considered to be located at the address from which the person's undertaking was issued. For the purpose of jurisdiction, choice of law, and recognition of interbranch letters of credit, but not enforcement of a judgement, all branches of a bank are considered separate juridical entities and a bank is considered to be located at the place where its relevant branch is considered to be located under this subsection.

(c) Except as otherwise provided in this subsection, the liability of an issuer, nominated person, or adviser is governed by any rules of custom or practice, such as the uniform customs and practice for documentary credits, to which the letter of credit, confirmation, or other undertaking is expressly made subject. If (1) this article would govern the liability of an issuer, nominated person, or adviser under subsection (a) or (b) of this section, (2) the relevant undertaking incorporates rules of custom or practice, and (3) there is conflict between this article and those rules as applied to that undertaking, those rules govern except to the extent of any conflict with the nonvariable provisions specified in subsection (c) of section 5-103.

OFFICIAL COMMENTS OF ARTICLE 5 OF THE UNIFORM COMMERCIAL CODE

(d) If there is conflict between this article and article 3, 4, 4-A or 9, this article governs.

(e) The forum for settling disputes arising out of an undertaking within this article may be chosen in the manner and with the binding effect that governing law may be chosen in accordance with subsection (a) of this section.

Official Comment

1. Although it would be possible for the parties to agree otherwise, the law normally chosen by agreement under subsection (a) and that provided in the absence of agreement under subsection (b) is the substantive law of a particular jurisdiction not including the choice of law principles of that jurisdiction. Thus, two parties, an issuer and an applicant, both located in Oklahoma might choose the law of New York. Unless they agree otherwise, the section anticipates that they wish the substantive law of New York to apply to their transaction and they do not intend that a New York choice of law principle might direct a court to Oklahoma law. By the same token, the liability of an issuer located in New York is governed by New York substantive law — in the absence of agreement — even in circumstances in which choice of law principles found in the common law of New York might direct one to the law of another State. Subsection (b) states the relevant choice of law principles and it should not be subordinated to some other choice of law rule. Within the States of the United States *renvoi* will not be a problem once every jurisdiction has enacted Section 5-116 because every jurisdiction will then have the same choice of law rule and in a particular case all choice of law rules will point to the same substantive law.

Subsection (b) does not state a choice of law rule for the "liability of an applicant." However, subsection (b) does state a choice of law rule for the liability of an issuer, nominated person, or adviser, and since some of the issues in suits by applicants against those persons involve the "liability of an issuer, nominated person, or adviser," subsection (b) states the choice of law rule for those issues. Because an issuer may have liability to a confirmer both as an issuer (Section 5-108(a), Comment 5 to Section 5-108) and as an applicant (Section 5-107(a), Comment 1 to Section 5-107, Section 5-108(i)), subsection (b) may state the choice of law rule for some but not all of the issuer's liability in a suit by a confirmer.

2. Because the confirmer or other nominated person may choose different law from that chosen by the issuer or may be located in a different jurisdiction and fail to choose law, it is possible that a confirmer or nominated person may be obligated to pay (under their law) but will not be entitled to payment from the issuer (under its law). Similarly, the rights of an unreimbursed issuer, confirmer,

APPENDIX B

or nominated person against a beneficiary under Section 5-109, 5-110, or 5-117, will not necessarily be governed by the same law that applies to the issuer's or confirmer's obligation upon presentation. Because the UCP and other practice are incorporated in most international letters of credit, disputes arising from different legal obligations to honor have not been frequent. Since Section 5-108 incorporates standard practice, these problems should be further minimized—at least to the extent that the same practice is and continues to be widely followed.

3. This section does not permit what is now authorized by the nonuniform Section 5-102(4) in New York. Under the current law in New York a letter of credit that incorporates the UCP is not governed in any respect by Article 5. Under revised Section 5-116 letters of credit that incorporate the UCP or similar practice will still be subject to Article 5 in certain respects. First, incorporation of the UCP or other practice does not override the nonvariable terms of Article 5. Second, where there is no conflict between Article 5 and the relevant provision of the UCP or other practice, both apply. Third, practice provisions incorporated in a letter of credit will not be effective if they fail to comply with Section 5-103(c). Assume, for example, that a practice provision purported to free a party from any liability unless it were "grossly negligent" or that the practice generally limited the remedies that one party might have against another. Depending upon the circumstances, that disclaimer or limitation of liability might be ineffective because of Section 5-103(c).

Even though Article 5 is generally consistent with UCP 500, it is not necessarily consistent with other rules or with versions of the UCP that may be adopted after Article 5's revision, or with other practices that may develop. Rules of practice incorporated in the letter of credit or other undertaking are those in effect when the letter of credit or other undertaking is issued. Except in the unusual cases discussed in the immediately preceding paragraph, practice adopted in a letter of credit will override the rules of Article 5 and the parties to letter of credit transactions must be familiar with practice (such as future versions of the UCP) that is explicitly adopted in letters of credit.

4. In several ways Article 5 conflicts with and overrides similar matters governed by Articles 3 and 4. For example, "draft" is more broadly defined in letter of credit practice than under Section 3-104. The time allowed for honor and the required notification of reasons for dishonor are different in letter of credit practice than in the handling of documentary and other drafts under Articles 3 and 4.

5. Subsection (e) must be read in conjunction with existing law governing subject matter jurisdiction. If the local law restricts a court to certain subject matter jurisdiction not including letter of credit disputes, subsection (e) does not authorize parties to choose that forum. For example, the parties' agreement

under Section 5-116(e) would not confer jurisdiction on a probate court to decide a letter of credit case.

If the parties choose a forum under subsection (e) and if—because of other law—that forum will not take jurisdiction, the parties' agreement or undertaking should then be construed (for the purpose of forum selection) as though it did not contain a clause choosing a particular forum. That result is necessary to avoid sentencing the parties to eternal purgatory where neither the chosen State nor the State which would have jurisdiction but for the clause will take jurisdiction—the former in disregard of the clause and the latter in honor of the clause.

Section 5-117. Subrogation of issuer, applicant, and nominated person.

(a) An issuer that honors a beneficiary's presentation is subrogated to the rights of the beneficiary to the same extent as if the issuer were a secondary obligor of the underlying obligation owed to the beneficiary and of the applicant to the same extent as if the issuer were the secondary obligor of the underlying obligation owed to the applicant.

(b) An applicant that reimburses an issuer is subrogated to the rights of the issuer against any beneficiary, presenter, or nominated person to the same extent as if the applicant were the secondary obligor of the obligations owed to the issuer and has the rights of subrogation of the issuer to the rights of the beneficiary stated in subsection (a) of this section.

(c) A nominated person who pays or gives value against a draft or demand presented under a letter of credit is subrogated to the rights of:
   (1) the issuer against the applicant to the same extent as if the nominated person were a secondary obligor of the obligation owed to the issuer by the applicant; (2) the beneficiary to the same extent as if the nominated person were a secondary obligor of the underlying obligation owed to the beneficiary; and (3) the applicant to the same extent as if the nominated person were a secondary obligor of the underlying obligation owed to the applicant.

(d) Notwithstanding any agreement or term to the contrary, the rights of subrogation stated in subsections (a) and (b) of this section do not arise until the issuer honors the letter of credit or otherwise pays and the rights in subsection (c) of this section do not arise until the nominated person pays or otherwise gives value. Until then, the issuer, nominated person, and the applicant do not derive under this section present or prospective rights forming the basis of a claim, defense, or excuse.

APPENDIX B

Official Comment

1. By itself this section does not grant any right of subrogation. It grants only the right that would exist if the person seeking subrogation "were a secondary obligor." (The term "secondary obligor" refers to a surety, guarantor, or other person against whom or whose property an obligee has recourse with respect to the obligation of a third party. See Restatement of the Law Third, Suretyship Section 1 (1995).) If the secondary obligor would not have a right to subrogation in the circumstances in which one is claimed under this section, none is granted by this section. In effect, the section does no more than to remove an impediment that some courts have found to subrogation because they conclude that the issuer's or other claimant's rights are "independent" of the underlying obligation. If, for example, a secondary obligor would not have a subrogation right because its payment did not fully satisfy the underlying obligation, none would be available under this section. The section indorses the position of Judge Becker in *Tudor Development Group, Inc. v. United States Fidelity and Guaranty*, 968 F.2d 357 (3rd Cir. 1991).

2. To preserve the independence of the letter of credit obligation and to insure that subrogation not be used as an offensive weapon by an issuer or others, the admonition in subsection (d) must be carefully observed. Only one who has completed its performance in a letter of credit transaction can have a right to subrogation. For example, an issuer may not dishonor and then defend its dishonor or assert a setoff on the ground that it is subrogated to another person's rights. Nor may the issuer complain after honor that its subrogation rights have been impaired by any good faith dealings between the beneficiary and the applicant or any other person. Assume, for example, that the beneficiary under a standby letter of credit is a mortgagee. If the mortgagee were obliged to issue a release of the mortgage upon payment of the underlying debt (by the issuer under the letter of credit), that release might impair the issuer's rights of subrogation, but the beneficiary would have no liability to the issuer for having granted that release.

List of References

See the list of references of *Letters of Credit under International Trade Law: UCC, UCP and Law Merchant*. Oceana Publications, Inc., 1985, not reproduced here.

Adodo, Ebenezer O. I.
"Conformity of Presentation Documents and a Rejection Notice in Letters of Credit Litigation: A Tale of Two Doctrines", 36 HKLJ 309, *Hong Kong Law Journal*, 2006

Aharoni, Daniel and Johnson, Adam
"Fraud and Discounted Deferred Payment Documentary Credits: The Banco Santander Case", J.I.B.L. 2000, 15(1). *Journal of International Banking Law* (2000).

Allen & Overy, Clifford Chance and Ashurst Morris Crisp
"Refusal of documents under a letter of credit", *Butterworths Journal of International Banking & Financial Law*, 2002, 17(7), 307-308

Bennett, Howard N.
"Unclear or ambiguous instructions in the world of documentary credits", *Lloyd's Maritime and Commercial Law Quarterly*, 2001, 1(Feb), 24-26

Berger, Steven R.
"The Effects of Issuing Bank Insolvency on Letters of Credit", *Harvard International Law Journal*, Vol. 21, No. 1 (Winter 1980).

Bertrams, Roeland F.
Bank Guarantees in International Trade, third revised edition, Kluwer Law International, ICC Publishing S.A., 2003.

Bethell-Jones, Richard
"Guarantees and Indemnities: Some Important Differences", J.I.B.L.R. 2006, 21(3), 156-161, *Journal of International Banking Law and Regulation* (2006)

List of References

Blodgett, Mark S. and Mayer, Donald O.
"International Letters of Credit: Arbitral Alternatives to Litigating Fraud", 35 Am. Bus. L.J. 443, *American Business Law Journal* (Spring, 1998).

Buckley, Ross P. and Gao, Xiang
"The Development of the Fraud Rule in Letter of Credit Law: The Journey so far and the Road Ahead", *University of Pennsylvania Journal of International Economic Law* (Winter 2002).

Chae, Dong-heon
"Letters of Credit and The Uniform Customs and Practice for Documentary Credits: The Negotiating Bank and The Fraud Rule in Korea Supreme Court Case 96 DA 43713", 12 Fla. J. Int'l L. 23, *Florida Journal of International Law* (Spring, 1998).

Chuah, Jason C.T.
"Is there a nullity in documentary credits?", F. & C.L. 2002, 1(Jan), 3-4, *Finance and Credit Law* (2002).

"Documentary credit – derogation from principle of autonomy on the basis that terms of illegal underlying transactions", F & C.L. 2003, Nov, 6-7 *Finance & Credit Law* (2003).

"Documentary credits and illegality in the underlying transaction", J.I.M.L. 2003, 9(6), 518-521 *Journal of International Maritime Law* (2003).

"International standard banking practice for the examination of documents under documentary credits", *Student Law Review* 2003, 39(Sum).

"Choice of Law and Letters of Credit", *Student Law Review* 2005, 45 (sum), 46-47

Creed, Nicholas
"The governing law of letter of credit transaction", *Journal of International Banking Law* (2001).

Croff, Carlo
"The Applicable Law in an International Commercial Arbitration: Is it still a conflict of laws problem?" *16 The International Lawyer 613* (1982)

Corsi, Anthony
"Transferable letters of credit: clarification of damages", *Practical Law Companies* 2005, 16(3), 16-17.

Dalhuisen, J.H.
"Legal Orders and their manifestation: the operation of the International Commercial and Financial Legal Order and Its Lex Mercatoria", 24 *Berkley Journal of International Law* 129 (2006).

Debattista, Charles
"Performance Bonds and Letters of Credit: A Cracked Mirror Image", J.B.L. 1997, Jul, 289-305, *Journal of Business Law* (1997).

De Ly, Philip
International Business Law and Law Mercatoria. T.M.C. Asser Instituut North-Holland, 1992.

Di Brozolo, Luca G. Radicati
"International Payments and Conflicts of Laws", *American Journal of Comparative Law*, (Spring 2000)

Dolan, John F.
"Letters of Credit: A Comparison of UCP 500 and the New U.S. Article 5", *Journal of Business Law*, Nov, 521-537 (1999).

"Standby letters of credit and fraud (is the standby only another invention of the Goldsmiths in Lombard Steet?)" *Cardozo Law Review* (Fall 1985).

"A study of subrogation mostly in letter of credit and other abstract obligation transactions", *Missouri Law Review* (Fall 1999).

The Law of Letters of Credit, Commercial and Standby Credits, Warren, Gorham & Lamont, 1984

The Law of Letters of Credit, Commercial and Standby Credits, 1990 Cumulative Supplement, Warren, Gorham & Lamont, 1984

The Law of Letters of Credit, Commercial and Standby Credits, Second Edition, 1993 Cumulative Supplement No. 2, Warren, Gorham & Lamont, 1993

List of References

Dole, Richard F. Jr.
"Applicant ad hoc waiver of discrepancies in the documents presented under letters of credit" *Southern Methodist University Law Review*, (Fall 2005)

Dutson, Stuart Journal of Business Law, 2006, Legislative Comment, A DANGEROUS PROPOSAL - THE EUROPEAN COMMISSION'S ATTEMPT TO AMEND THE LAW APPLICABLE TO CONTRACTUAL OBLIGATIONS.

Ellinger, E.P.
"Important Recent Cases", J.B.L. 2004, Nov, 709-711 *Journal of Business Law*, (2004).

Ferreira, Heinrich
"Choice of law and letters of credit – Articles 4(2), (5), Rome Convention", *Finance and Credit Law* 2005, Oct, 1-4.

Gao, Xiang
"Presenters immune from the fraud rule in the law of letters of credit", *Lloyd's Maritime Commercial Law Quarterly* 2002, 1 (Feb).

Getz, Herbert A.
"Enjoining the International Standby Letter of Credit: The Iranian Letter of Credit Cases", *Harvard International Law Journal*, Volume 21, Number 1 (Winter 1980).

Goode, Roy
"A New International Lex Mercatoria", *Lloyd's Maritime and Commercial Law Quarterly* 2000, 3 (Aug).

"Abstract Payment Undertakings in International Transactions, Symposium New Developments in the Law of Credit Enhancement: Domestic and International", 22 Brook. J. Int'l L. 1, *Brooklyn Journal of International Law* (1996).

"Rule, Practice, and Pragmatism in Transnational Commercial Law", 54 ICLQ 539, *International & Comparative Law Quarterly* (July 2005)

Gorton, Lars
"Remburs, dokumentgranskning och doktrinen om strikt uppfyllelse", *Svensk Juristtidning*, No. 9 (2003).

"Suretyship and guarantees – some Swedish viewpoints", *Juridiska Foreningens Tidskrift*, No. 6 (2001).

Graham, George P.
"International Commercial Letters of Credit And Choice of Law: So Whose Law Should Apply Anyway?" 47 Wayne L. Rev. 201, *Wayne Law Review* (Spring 2001).

Grant of Summary judgment and foreign law. *Journal of International Maritime Law 2003*, 9 (6), 509.

Hague Convention on Choice of Court Agreements, 30.6.2005.

Hare, Christopher
"The Rome Convention and Letters of Credit, Marconi v. Pan Indonesia Bank", *Lloyd's Maritime and Commercial Law Quarterly*, 2005, 4 (Nov), 417-423

Harris, Troy L.
"Good Faith, Suretyship, and The Ius Commune", 53 Mercer L. Rev. 581, *Mercer Law Review*, Winter (2002)

Harvard Law Review
"«Fraud in The Transaction»: Enjoining Letters of Credit During The Iranian Revolution", 93 Harv. L. Rev. 992, *Harvard Law Review*, March (1980). NOTE.

Heidinger, Markus
"Bank Guarantees, Letters of Credit and Similar Instruments under Austrian Law", J Intl Banking L. 1997, 12(11), 450-453, *Journal of International Banking Law* (1997).

Hemmo, Mika
Pankkioikeus, Talentum Media Oy, Jyväskylä, 2001

ICC
Collected Docdex Decisions 1997-2003, Decisions by ICC Experts on documentary credit disputes, Edited by Gary Collyer & Ron Katz, ICC Publication No 665, France 2004.

List of References

Decisions (1975-1979) of the ICC Banking Commission on queries relating to Uniform Customs and practice for Documentary Credits, ICC Publication No 371, France, 1980

ICC Banking Commission Collected Opinions 1995-2001 on UCP 500, UCP 400, URC 522 & URDG 458, Queries and responses edited by Gary Collyer & Ron Katz. Complete listing by Article. Consolidated index with over 200 key words. ICC Publication No. 632, France 2002.

ICC Docdex Rules, ICC Rules for Documentary Instruments Dispute Resolution Expertise, First revision, ICC Publication number 811, 2002

International Standard Banking Practices (ISBP) for the examination of documents under documentary credits, ICC Publication No. 645, 2003

Opinions (1980-1981) of the ICC Banking Commission on queries relating to Uniform Customs and Practice for Documentary Credits, ICC Publication No 399, France 1982.

Opinions of the ICC Banking Commission on queries relating to Uniform Customs and Practice for Documentary Credits 1984-1986, edited by Bernard Wheble ICC Publication No 434, France 1987.

Kalson, David J.
"The International Monetary Fund Agreement and Letters of Credit: A Balancing Of Purposes", 44 U. Pitt. L. Rev. 1061, *University of Pittsburgh Law Review*, Summer (1983).

Kozolchyk, Boris
"The "Best Practices" Approach to the Uniformity of International Commercial Law: The UCP 500 and The Nafta Implementation Experience", 13 Ariz. J. Int'l & Comp. L. 443, *Arizona Journal of International and Comparative Law*, Fall (1996).

Kurkela, Matti S.
Due Process in International Commercial Arbitration. Oceana Publications, Inc., 2005

Letters of Credit under International Trade Law: UCC, UCP and Law Merchant. Oceana Publications, Inc., 1985

"Jura Novit Curia and the Burden of Education in International Arbitration – A Nordic Perspective", *ASA Bulletin*, Vol. 21, No. 3 (September 2003).

Lando, Ole; Beale, Hugh
Principles of European Contract Law- Part I And II, Aspen Publishers, 1999

Lando, Ole; Clive, Eric; Prum, Andre; Zimmerman, Reinhard

Principles of European Contract Law- Part III, Aspen Publishers, 2003.

Lehtinen, Tuomas
First demand -takuu, Tampere, 1994

Loh, Quentin and Wu, Tang Hang
"Injunctions restraining calls on performance bonds – is fraud the only ground in Singapore?" L.M.C.L.Q. 2000, 3(Aug), 348-363, *Lloyd's Maritime and Commercial Law Quarterly* (2000)

McKenzie, Russell McVeagh
"New Zealand: Letters of Credit – Liability", Case Comment, J.I.B.L.R. 2003, 18(11), N123, *Journal of International Banking Law and Regulation*, 2003

McMeel, Gerard
"Contract damages: the interplay of remoteness and loss of a chance", *Lloyd's Maritime and Commercial Law Quarterly*, 2004, 1(Feb), 10-14.

"Pay now, argue later", *Lloyd's Maritime and Commercial Law Quarterly* 1999, 1(Feb), 5-9

Moses, Margaret L.
"Letters of Credit and the Insolvent Applicant: A Recipe for Bad Faith Dishonor", 57 Ala L.Rev. 31, *Alabama Law Review*, Fall 2005

List of References

Oelofse, Nico
"South Africa: Letters of Credit - Demand Guarantee", Case Comment, J.I.B.L. 1997, 12(12), N229-230, *Journal of International Banking Law*, 1997

Pifer, Tom
"The ICC Publication of International Standard Banking Practice (ISBP) and the Probable Effect on United States Letter of Credit Law", *Texas Wesleyan Law Review*, Spring (2006)

Proctor, Charles
"Confirmed Letters of Credit – A New Twist", *Butterworths Journal of International Banking and Financial Law* – April 2000 15(4), 109-114

"Enron, Letters of Credit and the Autonomy Principle", *Butterworths Journal of International Banking & Financial Law* 2004 19(6), 204-209.

Pugh-Thomas, Anthony
"Performance Guarantees and Unconscionable Conduct - An Australian Perspective", Case Comment, J.I.B.L. 1997, 12(10), 414-417, *Journal of International Banking Law* (1997)

Sappideen, Razeen
"International Commercial Letters of Credit: Balancing The Rights of Buyers And Sellers in Insolvency", J.B.L. 2006, MAR, 133-156, *Journal of Business Law* (2006)

Standby and Commercial Letters of Credit, Wiley Law Publications, 1989

Stoufflet, Jean
"Fraud in Documentary Credit, Letter of Credit And Demand Guaranty", 10th Biennial Conference of the International Academy of Commercial and Consumer Law International Banking Development, 106 Dick. L. Rev. 21. *Dickinson Law Review*, Summer (2001)

Teng, Christina
"Bank guarantees – Counter Guarantees", Case Comment, *Journal of International Banking Law*, 13 (5), 1998.

United Nations
United Nations Convention on the Assigned of Receivables in International Trade, New York, 2004 ("UNC")

Wang Corne, Charmian
Rethinking the Law of Letters of Credit, University of Sydney, 2006

Wood, Philip R.
Comparative Law of Security and Guarantees, Law and Practice of International Finance, Sweet & Maxwell, 1995

Wunnicke, Brooke; Wunnicke, Diane; Turner, Paul

Xiang, Gao and Buckley, Ross P.
"The Unique Jurisprudence of Letters of Credit: Its Origin and Sources", 4 San Diego Int'l L.J. 91, *San Diego International Law Journal* (2003)

"A Comparative Analysis of the Standard of Fraud Required under the Fraud Rule in Letter of Credit Law", *Duke Journal of Comparative and International Law*, Spring (2003).

Xiao, Yongping and Huo, Zhengxin
"Ordre Public in China's Private International Law", This Issue is Dedicated to Arthur Taylor von Mehren (1922-2006), 53 Am. J. Comp. L. 653, *American Journal of Comparative Law*, Summer (2005)

CASES

3COM CORPORATION, Plaintiff-Appellee, v. BANCO DO BRASIL, S.A., Defendant-Appellant. Docket No. 98-7658. 171 F.3d 739, 38 UCC Rep.Serv.2d 181, United States Court of Appeals, Second Circuit.

AVERY DENNISON CORPORATION, Plaintiff, v. THE HOME TRUST & SAVINGS BANK, Defendant. No. 02-2007 LRR., Nov. 7, 2003. Not Reported in F.Supp.2d, 2003 WL 22697175 (N.D.Iowa). United States District Court, N.D. Iowa, Eastern Division.

LIST OF REFERENCES

AXA ASSURANCE, INC., Plaintiff-Appellant, v. THE CHASE MANHATTAN BANK, f/k/a Chemical Bank New Jersey, N.A., Defendant/Third-Party Plaintiff-Respondent, v. Hankin Environmental Systems, Inc., Third-Party Defendant. 339 N.J.Super. 22, 770 A.2d 1211, 45 UCC Rep.Serv.2d 854. Superior Court of New Jersey, Appellate Division.

Banco Santander Sa v. Bayfern Limited, Royal Bank of Scotland Plc, Banque Paribas, Racayo Limited, L.O.S.L. Limited, Case No: 1998 folio No. 794, High Court of Justice Queen's Bench Division Commercial Court, QBD (Comm). 1999 WL 250019 (QBD (Comm Ct)), [1999] C.L.C. 1321, [1999] Lloyd's Rep. Bank. 239, [1999] 2 All E.R. (Comm) 18, (1999) 96(26) L.S.G. 27, 6-29-1999 Times 250,019, 6-21-1999 Independent 250,019.

Bank of Credit & Commerce Hong Kong Ltd. (In Liquidation) v. Sonali Bank, Queen's Bench Division (Commercial Court), QBD (Comm Ct), Aug. 3, 1994. 1994 WL 1063048 (QBD (Comm Ct)), [1994] C.L.C. 1171, [1995] 1 Lloyd's Rep. 227, 10-20-1994 Independent 1063,048.

Bankers Trust Co. v. State Bank of India, Court of Appeal, CA, May 13, 14, 15 and 16, 1991; June 13, 1991. 1991 WL 837888 (CA (Civ Div)), [1991] 2 Lloyd's Rep. 443, 6-25-1991 Times 837,888, 8-14-1991 Independent 837,888, 6-28-1991 Financial Times 837,888.

Balfour Beatty Civil Engineering (t/a Balfour Beatty/Costain (Cardiff Bay Barrage) Joint Venture) v Technical & General Guarantee Co Ltd (CA (Civ Div)) Court of Appeal (Civil Division)14 October 1999, [2000] C.L.C. 252, 68 Con. L.R. 180, 1999 WL 852268. 1999 WL 852268 (CA (Civ Div)), [2000] C.L.C. 252, 68 Con. L.R. 180.

Bolivinter Oil S.A. v. Chase Manhattan Bank N.A. and Others, Practice Note, Court of Appeal, CA (Civ Div), Sir John Donaldson M.R. and Griffiths L.J., 1983 Dec. 5; 9. 1984 WL 281697 (CA (Civ Div)), [1984] 1 Lloyd's Rep. 251, [1984] 1 W.L.R. 392, (1984) 128 S.J. 153.

BRENNTAG INTERNATIONAL CHEMICALS, INC., Plaintiff, v. NORDDEUTSCHE LANDESBANK GZ and Bank of India, Defendants. No. 97 Civ. 2688(RWS). Nov. 5, 1999. 70 F.Supp.2d 399, 42 UCC Rep.Serv.2d 1107. United States District Court, S.D. New York.

Credit Agricole Indosuez v. Generale Bank and Seco Steel Trading Inc., and Considar Inc., Queen's Bench Division (Commercial Court), QBD (Comm Ct), Sept. 30, 1999. 1999 WL 1319093 (QBD (Comm Ct)), [2000] C.L.C. 205, [2000] 1 Lloyd's Rep. 123, [1999] 2 All E.R. (Comm) 1016.

Credit Agricole Indosuez v. Muslim Commercial Bank Ltd. Court of Appeal, CA, Nov. 8, 24, 1999; Nov. 24, 1999. 1999 WL 1048266 (CA (Civ Div)), [2000] C.L.C. 437, [2000] 1 Lloyd's Rep. 275, [2000] Lloyd's Rep. Bank. 1, [2000] 1 All E.R. (Comm) 172.

Credit Industriel et Commercial v. China Merchants Bank Case No: 2000/738 Neutral citation number: [2002] EWHC 973 (Comm) High Court of Justice Queen's Bench Division Commercial Court QBD (Comm Ct) 2002 WL 819936 (QBD (Comm Ct)), [2002] C.L.C. 1263, [2002] 2 All E.R. (Comm) 427, [2002] EWHC 973.

Czarnikow-Rionda Sugar Trading Inc. v. Standard Bank London Ltd. and Others, Queen's Bench Division (Commercial Court), QBD (Comm), May 6, 1999. 1999 WL 250018 (QBD (Comm Ct)), [1999] C.L.C. 1148, [1999] 2 Lloyd's Rep. 187, [1999] Lloyd's Rep. Bank. 197, [1999] 1 All E.R. (Comm) 890, 6-14-1999 Independent 250,018.

E.D. & F. Man Ltd. v. Nigerian Sweets & Confectionery Co. Ltd. Queen's Bench Division (Commercial Court), QBD (Comm Ct), Dec. 13 and 14, 1976. 1977 WL 59840 (QBD (Comm Ct)), [1977] 2 Lloyd's Rep. 50.

European Asian Bank A.G. v. Punjab and Sind Bank, Queen's Bench Division (Commercial Court), QBD (Comm), Apr. 29, 30, May 1 and July 15, 1981; July 31, 1981. 1981 WL 187765 (QBD (Comm Ct)), [1981] 2 Lloyd's Rep. 651, [1981] Com. L.R. 246.

FIRST UNION NATIONAL BANK, Plaintiff, v. PARIBAS, f/k/a Banque Paribas, Defendant., First Union National Bank, Plaintiff, v. Anz Grindlays Bank, Defendant. First Union National Bank, Plaintiff, v. Emirates Bank International, Defendant., First Union National Bank, Plaintiff, v. Arab African International Bank, Defendant. Nos. 00 Civ. 5397(LAK), 00 Civ. 5398(LAK), 00 Civ. 5400(LAK), 00 Civ., 5401(LAK)., March 29, 2001. 135 F.Supp.2d 443. United States District Court, S.D. New York.

LIST OF REFERENCES

Gestingthorpe and Lord Brown of Eaton-under-Heywood, 2004 Dec 13, 14: 2005 Jan 27. 2005 WL 62249 (HL), [2005] 2 All E.R. 71, [2005] 1 Lloyd's Rep. 366, (2005) 149 S.J.L.B. 146, [2005] 1 W.L.R. 377, [2005] 1 All E.R. (Comm) 337, (2005) 102(11) L.S.G. 29, 2-02-2005 Times 62,249, [2005] UKHL 3.

GLENCORE, LTD., Plaintiff, v. The CHASE MANHATTAN BANK, N.A. and State Bank of Saurashtra, Defendants., No. 92 Civ. 6214 JFK., Feb. 23, 1998. Not Reported in F.Supp., 1998 WL 101734 (S.D.N.Y.). United States District Court, S.D. New York. Not Reported in F.Supp., 1998 WL 101734 (S.D.N.Y.)

Glencore International A.G. and Another v. Bank of China, Court of Appeal, CA, Oct. 23; Nov. 8, 1995. 1995 WL 1083922 (CA (Civ Div)), [1996] 5 Bank. L.R. 1, [1996] C.L.C. 111, [1996] 1 Lloyd's Rep. 135, [1998] Masons C.L.R. Rep. 78, 11-27-1995 Times 1083,922.

Harlow and Jones Ltd. v. American Express Bank Ltd. and Creditanstalt-Bankverein, (Third Party), Queen's Bench Division (Commercial Court), QBD (Comm), Jan. 16, 17, 18, 22, 23 and 26, 1990; Feb. 12, 1990. 1990 WL 755029 (QBD (Comm Ct)), [1990] 2 Lloyd's Rep. 343.

HING YIP HING FAT CO LTD v THE DAIWA BANK LTD, 15-17 January and 11 February 1991, High Court, HC, (Commercial List No. 22 of 1989). 1991 WL 1124851 (HC), [1991] 2 HKLR 35, [1991] HKLY 70.

HYOSUNG AMERICA, INC., Hyosung America, Inc., as Assignee of Orkid Tex, Inc., Plaintiff-Counter-Defendant-Appellant, v. SUMAGH TEXTILE CO., LTD., Defendant-Counter-Claimant-Appellee., Docket No. 96-9408., Argued May 20, 1997., Decided Feb. 13, 1998. 137 F.3d 75, 34 UCC Rep.Serv.2d 930. United States Court of Appeals, Second Circuit.

Jackson and another v. Royal Bank of Scotland plc [2005] UKHL 3, House of Lords, HL, Lord Nicholls of Birkenhead, Lord Hoffmann, Lord Hope of Craighead, Lord Walker, of Gestingthorpe and Lord Brown of Eaton-under-Heywood, 2004 Dec 13, 14: 2005 Jan 27. 2005 WL 62249 (HL), [2005] 2 All E.R. 71, [2005] 1 Lloyd's Rep. 366, (2005) 149 S.J.L.B. 146, [2005] 1 W.L.R. 377, [2005] 1 All E.R. (Comm) 337, (2005) 102(11) L.S.G. 29, 2-02-2005 Times 62,249, [2005] UKHL 3

Johann Prutscher v. Fidelity International Bank, 502 F. Supp. 535 (1980)

Mahonia Ltd. v. JP Morgan Chase Bank and Another, [2003] EWHC 1927 (Comm), Queen's Bench Division (Commercial Court), QBD (Comm Ct), June 23-25; July 30, 2003. 2003 WL 22827091 (QBD (Comm Ct)), [2003] 2 Lloyd's Rep. 911, [2003] EWHC 1927.

MOLTER CORPORATION, an Illinois corporation, Plaintiff-Appellee, v. AMWEST SURETY INSURANCE COMPANY, Defendant-Appellant, and First National Bank of Joliet, a National Banking Corporation, Defendant. No. 3-94-0236., Nov. 18, 1994. 267 Ill.App.3d 718, 642 N.E.2d 919, 205 Ill.Dec. 54, 25 UCC Rep.Serv.2d 892. Appellate Court of Illinois, Third District.

Montrod Ltd v. Grundkötter Fleischvertriebs GmbH [2001] EWCA Civ 1954, Court of Appeal, CA (Civ Div), Thorpe, Potter LJJ and Sir Martin Nourse, 2001 Oct 16, 17; Dec 20. 2001 WL 1479862 (CA (Civ Div)), [2002] 3 All E.R. 697, [2002] C.L.C. 499, [2002] 1 W.L.R. 1975, [2002] 1 All E.R. (Comm) 257, [2001] EWCA Civ 1954.

Niru Battery Manufacturing Company, Bank Sepah Iran v. Milestone Trading, Limited, Maritime Freight Services Limited, Ali Akhbar Mahdavi, Credit Agricole Indosuez, SGS United Kingdom Limited, Case No: A3/2003/1167, Neutral Citation Number: [2004] EWCA Civ 487, Court of Appeal (Civil Division), CA, Before: The President Lord Justice Clarke and Lord Justice Sedley, Wednesday 28th April 2004, On Appeal from the High Court of Justice Queen's Bench Division Commerical Court, Mr Justice Moore-Bick [2003] EWHC 1032 (Comm). 2004 WL 960993 (CA (Civ Div)), [2004] 1 C.L.C. 882, [2004] 2 Lloyd's Rep. 319, (2004) 148 S.J.L.B. 538, [2004] 2 All E.R. (Comm) 289, [2004] EWCA Civ 487.

NV KONINKLIJKE SPHINX GUSTAVSBERG v COOPERATIEVE CENTRALE-RAIFFEISEN-BOERENLEENBANK BA, 24 November 2005, COURT OF APPEAL, CIVIL APPEAL NO 161 OF 2004 ON APPEAL FROM HCCL NO 188 OF 1997), CA, CACV 161/2004. 2005 WL 3034900 (CA), [2005] HKEC 1929.

Offshore International S.A. v. Banco Cantral S.A. and Another <1977> 1 W.L.R. 399

PT Pan Indonesia Bank Limited TBK v. Marconi Communications International Limited, A3/2004/0684, Neutral Citation Number: [2005] EWCA Civ 422, Court of Appeal (Civil Appeals Division), CA (Civ Div), Before: Lord Justice Potter, Lord Justice Buxton and Lord Justice Hooper, Wednesday 27th April, 2005, On Appeal from the High Court of Justice Queen's Bench Division (Steel J), [2004]

List of References

EWCH 129 (Comm). 2005 WL 936857 (CA (Civ Div)), [2005] 2 All E.R. (Comm) 325, 5-18-2005 Times 936,857, [2005] EWCA Civ 422.

R. D. Harbottle (Mercantile) Ltd. v. National Westminster Bank Ltd. and Others Same v. Same and Others Harbottle Coal Co. Ltd. and Another v. Same and Others [1976 R. No. 3861][1976 R. No. 4314][1976 H. No. 7364]; [1977] 3 W.L.R. 752, Queen's Bench Division, QBD, Kerr J., 1977 Jan. 26, 27, 31 Feb. 3. 1977 WL 59355 (QBD), [1978] Q.B. 146, [1977] 2 All E.R. 862, [1977] 3 W.L.R. 752, (1977) 121 S.J. 745.

RE GUANG XIN ENTERPRISES LTD, 21 March 2002, Court of First Instance, CFI, HCMP No 3003 of 2001. [2002] HKLRD (Yrbk) 30.

Sirius International Insurance Co (Publ) v. FAI General Insurance Ltd and others, [2004] UKHL 54, House of Lords, HL, Lord Bingham of Cornhill, Lord Nicholls of Birkenhead, Lord Steyn, Lord Walker of Gestingthorpe and Lord Brown of Eaton-under-Heywood, 2004 Nov 8, 9; Dec 2. 2004 WL 2714105 (HL), [2005] 1 All E.R. 191, [2005] 1 C.L.C. 451, [2005] Lloyd's Rep. I.R. 294, [2005] 1 Lloyd's Rep. 461, (2004) 148 S.J.L.B. 1435, [2004] 1 W.L.R. 3251, [2005] 1 All E.R. (Comm) 117, (2004) 101(48) L.S.G. 25, 12-03-2004 Times 2714,105, [2004] UKHL 54.

SOUTHLAND RUBBER CO LTD v BANK OF CHINA, 30 October and 6 November 1997, Court of First Instance, CFI, (Commercial List No 208 of 1996). 1997 WL 1911180 (CFI), [1997] HKLRD 1300.

Standard Chartered Bank v. Pakistan National Shipping Corpn and Others (Nos 2 and 4) [2002] UKHL 43; [2002] 3 W.L.R. 1547 House of Lords, HL, Lord Slynn of Hadley, Lord Mustill, Lord Hoffmann, Lord Hobhouse of Woodborough and Lord Rodger of Earlsferry, 2002 May 20, 21; Nov 6. 2002 WL 31452047 (HL), [2003] 1 A.C. 959, [2003] 1 All E.R. 173, [2002] B.C.C. 846, [2003] 1 B.C.L.C. 244, [2002] C.L.C. 1330, [2003] 1 Lloyd's Rep. 227, (2002) 146 S.J.L.B. 258, [2002] 3 W.L.R. 1547, [2002] 2 All E.R. (Comm) 931, (2003) 100(1) L.S.G. 26, 11-07-2002 Times 31452,047, [2002] UKHL 43.

SZTEJN v. J. HENRY SCHRODER BANKING CORPORATION et al. July 1, 1941. Supreme Court, New York County, New York, Special Term. 177 Misc. 719, 31 N.Y.S.2d 631.

List of References

Turkiye Is Bankasi AS v. Bank of China Queen's Bench Division (Commercial Court), QBD (Comm Ct) Jan. 22, 23, 24, 25; Feb. 8, 1996. 1996 WL 1093298 (QBD (Comm Ct)), [1996] 5 Bank. L.R. 241, [1996] 2 Lloyd's Rep. 611, 3-08-1996 Times 1093,298.

United City Merchants (Investments) Ltd. Appellants (First Plaintiffs) and Glass Fibres and Equipments Ltd. Appellants (Second Plaintiffs) v. Royal Bank of Canada (Incorporated In Canada) Respondents (Defendants), Vitrorefuerzos S.A. First Third Party and Banco Continental S.A. Second Third Party, [1982] 2 W.L.R. 1039, House of Lords, HL, Lord Diplock, Lord Fraser of Tullybelton, Lord Russell of Killowen, Lord Scarman and Lord Bridge of Harwich, 1982 March 16, 17, 18, 22; May 20. 1982 WL 221777 (HL), [1983] 1 A.C. 168, [1982] 2 All E.R. 720, [1982] 2 Lloyd's Rep. 1, [1982] 2 W.L.R. 1039, [1982] Com. L.R. 142.

United States Court of Appeals, Eleventh Circuit. Banco General Runinahui, S.A., Plaintiff-Counter-Defendant-Appellant, v. Citibank International, A division of Citibank, N.A., New York, Defendant-Third-Party-Plaintiff-Counter-Defendant-Appellant, R.M. Wade & Co., d.b.a. Wade Mfg. Co., Third-Party Defendant-Counter-Claimant-Appellee. No. 95-4444. Oct. 10, 1996

United Trading Corporation S.A. and Murray Clayton Ltd. v. Allied Arab, Bank Ltd. and Others, Court of Appeal, CA (Civ Div), July 17, 1984. 1985 WL 311451 (CA (Civ Div)), [1985] 2 Lloyd's Rep. 554 (Note).

VOEST-ALPINE TRADING USA CORPORATION, Plaintiff-Appellee, v. BANK OF CHINA; et al., Defendants, Bank of China, Defendant-Appellant. No. 01-20363. April 23, 2002. 288 F.3d 262, 47 UCC Rep.Serv.2d 693. United States Court of Appeals, Fifth Circuit.

Index

A

Abuse
and fraud, 182n. 17, 207–8
loss, who bears, 193–98
Acceptance
letters of credit, 27
Accessory guarantees, 1n. 1, 12
Advised letter of credit
interpretation of instruments, *257*
Affiliates
comfort letters, 8
Agricultural Development Council of Libya, 366
Amendment by implication, 235n. 31
Assignability, 67–71
and bad faith, 67
conforming tender by original beneficiary, 70
documentary credit, 72n. 90
and honor, 67n. 87
negotiable instruments, 68n. 88
principle of debtor protection, 69
proceeds of letter of credit, 70
receivables, assignment of, 68n. 88
right of set-off, 69n. 89
rights transferred, 70–71
substantively independent instruments, 69
Attorney's fees
refusal, 265–267
remedies, 294
Autonomy
indemnity agreements, 102–5
Avery Dennison **case,** 245–47
AXA v. Chase Manhattan, 248–53

B

Back-to-back credit forming chain of commercial letters of credit, *41*
Bad faith
and assignability, 67
and disclaimers, 59
and fraud, 197
Bahrain
security interest in document or goods, 51

Balance of convenience test
fraud, 183, 186
Bangladesh
choice of law, 358–65
jurisdiction, 378–79
Bank guarantees
beneficiari-es, 17n. 28
and commercial letters of credit, 35n. 59
conditions precedent, 14–16
defaults, 16
freedom of contract, 17
function of, 14–18
insolvency of debtor, 15
interpretation of instruments, *255, 256*
lex mercatoria, trade usages, 325
liquidation of debtor, 15
and performance, 16
Bank of China, **259–67**
Bank-to-bank indemnity, 107–71
active discovery, engagement in, 131
balance and underlying agreement, 113–14
bonus pater familias standard, 150
care, duty of, of bank, 147–54
claiming bank, 110, *111*
confidentiality, duty of, 168–71
consistency requirement, 127–32
drafts, 132
cross-border inter-bank relationships, 108–9
death of facility, 115
discrepancies, 160–61
dishonor, notice of, 160n. 56, 161–62
documentation, 134–35
domino effect, 115
duty to whom and for what, 154–58
è contrario rule, 132–37
experts, interviews with, 137–139
Fonck, Mirja, 139
Heino, Pekka, 137–38
Ikävalko, Petri, 138–39
Vainionpää, Matti, 138
facility and instrument, *115*
fraud rule, 117–18
and strict compliance doctrine, 123n. 20

Bank-to-bank indemnity (*cont.*)
   functionally dependent instruments, 114
   generally, 107–13
   honor, 161–62
      described, 114–15
      duty to, 163–64
      and "moment of death" of the instrument, 114–20
      strict compliance doctrine, 121
   international relationships, 108–9
   intra-bank relationships, 113
   liability of banks, 140–71
      bonus pater familias standard, 150
      care, duty of, of bank, 147–54
      confidentiality, duty of, 168–71
      discrepancies, 160–61
      dishonor, notice of, 160n. 56, 161–62
      duty to whom and for what, 154–58
      generally, 140–47
      honor, 161–64
      mixed standard of liability, 151
      notify and refuse, duty to, 158–62
      ordre public character, 168
      parole evidence rule, 152
      payment to beneficiary, duty to notify account party, 161
      placing documents at disposal of the beneficiary, sample clause, 155–56, 165–68
      and public policy, 168–69
      reasonable care standard, 153
      reasonable time, defined, 162–65
      refuse, duty to, 163–64
      results liability, 151–53
      standards of international practice, 148–50
      time needed and available to examiner, 141–42
      "without delay," defined, 142–47
      wrongful dishonor, 164
   mixed standard of liability, 151
   "moment of death" of the instrument, 114–20
   mutatis mutandis, 133
   nondocumentary conditions, 133n. 29
   notify and refuse, duty to, 158–62
   ordre public character, 168
   pacta sunt servanda rule, 133
   parole evidence rule, 133, 152
   payment to beneficiary, duty to notify account party, 161
   placing documents at disposal of the beneficiary, sample clause, 155–56, 165–68
   and public policy, 168–69

Bank-to-bank indemnity (*cont.*)
   reasonable care standard, 153
   reasonable time, defined, 162–65
   refuse, duty to, 163–64
   reimbursement arrangements, 109
   reimbursement authorization, 110
   reimbursing bank, 111–12
   results liability, 151–53
   standards of international practice, 148–50
   strict compliance doctrine, 120–27
      consistency requirement, 127–32
      è contrario rule, 132–37
      liability of banks, 140
      as tendered rule, 132–37
   substantive issues, 108
   supranational relationships, 108–9
   Sztejn opinion, 117–19, 124
   as tendered rule, 132–37
   time needed and available to examiner, 141–42
   underlying agreement, balance and, 113–14
   "without delay," defined, 142–47
   wrongful dishonor, 164
BCCHK, 358–65, 378–79
Beneficiaries
   bank guarantees, 17n. 28
   confirmed letters of credit, 31
   fraud, 187–88
   letters of credit, 24
Black letter law, 26
"Blended" facilities, 40–42
   back-to-back credit forming chain of commercial letters of credit, *41*
   multi-party stand-by, *41*
   stand-by credit facility, *42*
Bonds, 9–11
   limits, 10–11
   underlying contract, link, 9
***Bonus pater familias* standard**
   bank-to-bank indemnity, 150
   duty to mitigate, 311
Brand, protection of
   choice of law, 349, 354
Breach
   indemnity agreements, 101
      duty to inform as to allegation of, 97–98
   of obligations, damages as remedy, 287
   right of set-off, 46
   of warranty, damages, 318–19
***Bretton Woods Point*, 202–3**

Burden of education, 271, 371–75
Burden of proof, 271

C

Cash flow and on-demand guarantees, 18n. 29
Cattaui, Maria, 39
China
  choice of law, 331–32
Choice of law, 323–97. *See also* Jurisdiction
  applicable law, 335–45
    policy interests, 342–45, 391–93
    uniform law merchant, 335–42
    Zeevi case, 342–45, 391–93
  banking business, special considerations, 385–86
  burden of education, 371–75
  commercial letters of credit, 331
  conflict of laws, 323–35
  Edward Owen Ltd. v. Barclays Bank, 366–68, 374
  English law, preference for, 346–75
    brand, protection of, 349, 354
    burden of education, 371–75
    Edward Owen Ltd. v. Barclays Bank, 366–68, 374
    false conflict, 356–58
    generally, 346
    New York law vs., 348–49
    North Carolina law vs. Kwaiti law, 352–53
    Offshore International case, 347–49
    performance bonds, 366–68
    Power Curber International Ltd. v. National Bank of Kuwait, 349–56
    situs of debt, 348–49, 355
    Sonali case, 358–65, 378–79
    source of obligation, 348–49
    Spanish law vs., 348–49
    Uniform Commercial Code (UCC), 368–71
  false conflict, 356–58
  lex mercatoria, 323–35, 340
    applicable rules, 325
    codification, 330
    trade usages, 325–27, 334
  "moment of death," 358
  national law, 323–35
  Offshore International case, 347–49
  ordre public character, 324, 328
    uniform law merchant, 336
  performance bonds, 366–68
  place of payment, 357
  place or location of the party, 356
  policy interests, 342–45, 391–93

Choice of law (*cont.*)
  Power Curber International Ltd. v. National Bank of Kuwait, 349–56
  public policy, 324
  Sonali case, 358–65, 378–79
  standby letters of credit, 331, 333n. 27
  Uniform Commercial Code (UCC), 368–71
  uniform law merchant
    cross-border facility, disputes, 338
    inter partes enforcement, 336
    ordre public character, 336
  Zeevi case, 342–45, 391–93
Collusive elements, disclaimers, 56
Comfort letters, 7–9
  wording, 8
Commercial letters of credit, *29,* 32–36
  back-to-back credit forming chain of commercial letters of credit, *41*
  and bank guarantees, 35n. 59
  choice of law, 331
  doctrine of substantive independence, 103
  "double" security, 35
  functions of, 32–35
  interim payments, 35n. 59
  payment under, 37
  Russia, exports to, 35n. 60
  security interest in document or goods, 33n. 55, 47–52
  Turkey, exports to, 35n. 60
Commission on Banking Technique and Practice, 39
Compliance
  strict compliance doctrine. *See* Strict compliance doctrine
Conditions precedent, 5–7
  bank guarantees, 14–16
  indemnity agreements, 100
  letters of credit, 26
Confidentiality
  bank-to-bank indemnity, 168–71
Confirmed letters of credit, 28–32, *33*
  beneficiaries, 31
  commercial letters of credit, *29*
  freely negotiable credit, 29n. 52
  indemnity agreements, 31
  interpretation of instruments, *256*
  obligation of confirmer, 31
  restricted negotiation credit, 28n. 51

Conflict-of-laws rules
  and jurisdiction, 323–35
  security interest in document or goods, 48–49
Consistency requirement
  bank-to-bank indemnity, 127–32
    drafts, 132
Construction contract, sample of use of credits and guarantees, *258*
Contingent liability
  on-demand guarantees, 23
Contracts
  interpretation, 211
  remedies, 282
***Contra proferentem* rule**
  interpretation of instruments, 252
Contributory negligence, 309–12
Credit Agricole case, disclaimers under, 54–56
Credit facility
  infrastructure, 314, *315*
Credits
  defined, 25–26
  irrevocable, 7n. 11

D

Dalhuisen, Jan H., 324, 325
Damages
  breach of warranty, 318–19
  fault, defined, 311
  liquidation, 295
  refusal, 265–267
  as remedy, 283–87
    breach of obligations, 287
    certainty of harm, 284
    consequential damages, 287
    full compensation, 284
Death of facility
  bank-to-bank indemnity, 115
  and national law, role of, 316
Declaratory relief, 301–2
Default
  bank guarantees, 16
  cross default, 101–2
  indemnity agreements, 101–2
    breach of other obligations, 101
    cross default, 101–2
    duty to inform as to allegation of, 97–98
    events of, 101
    insolvency, 102
    material adverse change, 102

Default (*cont.*)
  non-payment, 101
  remedies, 319
Deferred payment undertaking, 27n. 49
Definite, defined, 211
***De lege ferenda,* 320–21**
Denning, Lord, 366–67, 374
Disclaimers, 52–61
  acceptable versus nonacceptable, 55
  acts or omissions of others, 59
  and bad faith, 59
  burden of education, 59
  collusive elements, 56
  communication errors, 57
  Credit Agricole case, 54–56
  force majeure clause, 58
  and indemnity, 54–55
  "in the absence of negligence," 53
  and joint dominance, 55
  liability, 59, 61
  nature, disasters, 59
  standardized conditions, simple disclaimers, 57–61
  three-party agreements, 59, *60*
  war, 59
Discrepancies
  interpretation of instruments, 235–36, 240, 241n. 37
  notice of, failure to give, 268–69
  refusal, 265
Dishonor, 267–71
  bank-to-bank indemnity
    wrongful dishonor, 164
  discrepancies, failure to give notice of, 268–69
  domino effect, 267, 270
  failure to act, 269
  fraud, 175n. 5
  notice of, 239–40
    bank-to-bank indemnity, 160n. 56, 161–62
    failure to give, 268–71
  and refusal, 270
  wrongful, 268
    interpretation of instruments, 248–53
***Docdex* proceedings, 394–97**
Doctrinal materials, 331n. 24
Doctrine of substantive independence
  indemnity agreements, 102–5
Documentary credit, 24n. 44, 26
Documentation
  bank-to-bank indemnity, 134–35
  standby letters of credit, 134–35

INDEX

Document, defined, 26n. 47
Document or goods, security interest in, 47–52
Dolan, John A., 11–12, 74, 279, 372
Domestic laws
  and international flow of goods, 328n. 15
Domino effect, 72
  bank-to-bank indemnity, 115
  dishonor, 267, 270
Due diligence
  fraud, protection from, 177
Duty of care
  bank-to-bank indemnity, 147–54
Duty of confidentiality
  bank-to-bank indemnity, 168–71
Duty (right) to refrain from paying
  fraud, 178–80
Duty to honor
  bank-to-bank indemnity, 163–64
Duty to mitigate, 309–12
  bonus pater familias standard, 311
Duty to notify and refuse
  bank-to-bank indemnity, 158–62
Duty to refuse
  bank-to-bank indemnity, 163–64
Dynamics Corporation of America v. The Citizens and Southern National Bank, 288–90

E

è contrario rule, 132–37
Education, burden of, 371–75
Edward Owen Ltd. v. Barclays Bank, 366–68, 374
Egypt
  security interest in document or goods, 51
Electronic letter of credit, 137–38
Embargo, 316n. 54
  India, 288–90
Enforcement, remedies, 274–83
  death of instrument, attaching funds after, 274–78
  ordinary or ex parte protective or temporary measures, 274–78
  parole evidence rule, 281–82
  specific enforcement, 283
  summary judgment, availability of, 278–79
  time required to enforce right, 279–81
  uniform law merchant, 336
English law
  burden of education, 371–75
  damages as remedy, 286
  Edward Owen Ltd. v. Barclays Bank, 366–68, 374

English law (*cont.*)
  false conflict, 356–58
  generally, 346, 386
  Jurisdiction and choice of law
    New York law vs., 348–49
    Spanish law vs., 348–49
  North Carolina law vs. Kwaiti law, 352–53
  Offshore International case, 347–49
  performance bonds, 366–68
  Power Curber International Ltd. v. National Bank of Kuwait, 349–56
  situs of debt, 348–49, 355
  Sonali case, 358–65, 378–79
  source of obligation, 348–49
  Uniform Commercial Code (UCC), generally, 368–71
Equitable relief, 296–98
  United Trading case, 296–98
Europe
  remedies, damages as, 283–87
Evergreen clauses
  interpretation of instruments, 247–53
Ex parte protective measures, 274–78, 298–301
Expediency, principle of, 222–23
Experts, interviews with, 139
Expert testimony and refusal, 263
Expert witnesses, 220

F

False conflict, choice of law, 356–58
Fault, defined, 311
Finland
  bank-to-bank indemnity, 139
Force majeure clause
  disclaimers, 58
Foreign law. *See also* Choice of law
  mandatory, 369n. 47
Forgery, 188, 192
Forum connexitatis, 394
Forum non conveniens doctrine, 376, 386–93
Forum shopping, 386–93
Fraud, 173–210
  and abuse, 182n. 17, 207–8
  "automatic" effect of, 198
  and bad faith, 197
  balance of convenience test, 183, 186
  bank-to-bank indemnity, 117–18
    and strict compliance doctrine, 123n. 20
  beneficiary, by, 187–88

Fraud (*cont.*)

Bretton Woods Point, 202–3
"civil" meaning of, 207
clear and obvious fraud, 179
clear proof, 183–86
controversial nature of fraud rule, 174
deemed constituted, 206–7
definitions, 173–74, 177
developing nature of fraud rule, 313
dishonor, 175n. 5
doctrine of independence, exception, 180
due diligence, protection, 177
duty (right) to refrain from paying, 178–80
equitable relief, 296–98
establishing existence of, 176–78, 186, 276–78
forgery, 188, 192
"fraud corrupts all," 175
generally, 173–76
and good faith, 181–83
illegality, 201–6
injunction, 276–79
injunctive relief, 184n. 19
and international treaties and conventions, 202–3
letters of credit, fraud rule, 27n. 50, 174
liability, nonparties, 208–9
links required, 191–93
loss, who bears, 193–98
material fact, concealment, 182n. 16
multiparty facility, 189–90
non-parties, extension of liability to, 208–9
nullity exception, 198–200
ordre public character, 181, 313, 314
    and illegality, 202
proof, 183–86
relevance, 187–91
remedies
    exception, 275–78
    national laws, governed by, 313
right of court intervention, 207
risks assumed, 191–93
standby letters of credit, 38n. 67, 180
and strict compliance doctrine, 182
tort law, 209–10
unconscionability, 173n. 1
withholding payment, 192

Freedom of contract
bank guarantees, 17

Freely negotiable letters of credit, 29n. 52, 226, 343

G

Glencore case
unjust enrichment, 306–7
Goode, Roy, 326, 334–35
Good faith
and fraud, 181–83
indemnity agreements, 88–90
Guarantees, 1–2n. 2
accessory guarantees, 1n. 1, 12
bank guarantees. *See* Bank guarantees
condition precedent to become payable, 12
on-demand guarantees. *See* On-demand guarantees
secondary guarantees, 1n. 1, 12, 13
traditional guarantees, 11–14

H

Hague Evidence convention, 389–9
Harbottle case, 301–2
and injunctions, 303–5
Heino, Pekka, 137–38
Hoffmann, Lord, 78–79
Hong Kong
bank-to-bank indemnity, 116–17, 141–42
choice of law, 358–65
fraud, 179
jurisdiction, 378–79
Honor, 2–3
and assignability, 67n. 87
bank-to-bank indemnity, 161–62
    description of honor, 114–15
    duty to honor, 163–64
    "moment of death" of the instrument, 114–20
    strict compliance doctrine, 121
defined, 3
maturation, 26
non-complying presentation, 268
relationship, 315
Hostage crisis (1979), 22n. 39
Hutton, Lord, 78

I

Ikävalko, Petri, 138–39
Illegality, fraud, 201–6
Indemnity
agreements. *See* Indemnity agreements
and disclaimers, 54–55
Indemnity agreements, 81–105
autonomy, 102–5

Indemnity agreements (*cont.*)
  bank-to-bank indemnity. *See* Bank-to-bank indemnity
  breach, 101
    duty to inform as to allegation of, 97–98
  cash cover, 93–95
  conclusive evidence, 92–93
  conditions precedent, 100
  confirmed letters of credit, 31
  default, 101–2
    breach of other obligations, 101
    cross default, 101–2
    duty to inform as to allegation of, 97–98
    events of, 101
    insolvency, 102
    material adverse change, 102
    non-payment, 101
  defined, 7
  doctrine of substantive independence, 102–5
  duty to inform as to allegation of breach or default, 97–98
  duty to inform as to financial status, 97
  features of, 91–102
  good faith, 88–90
  information, duty to give, 99–100
  insolvency, 102
  introduction to, 81–88
  legal proceedings, duty to inform of, 98
  loan agreements, resemblance, 82–83, 87
  master agreement, 91
  material adverse change, 102
  negative pledge, 95–96
  Pari Passu provision, 95
  procedural independence, 105
  refusal of bank to accept documents timely received, 83
  reimbursement and, 81–88
  representations and warranties, 88–90, 100
  sample clauses, 84
    breach, 101
    cash cover, 93–95
    conclusive evidence, 92–93
    default, 101–2
    duty to inform as to allegation of breach or default, 97–98
    duty to inform as to financial status, 97
    information, duty to give, 99–100
    legal proceedings, duty to inform of, 98
    negative pledge, 96
    Pari Passu provision, 95

Indemnity agreements (*cont.*)
    representations and warranties, 100
    security mechanism, 92
    umbrella indemnity agreements, 91
  security interest in document or goods, 49–50
  security mechanism, 92
  services agreements, 81–88
  umbrella, 91
  unconscionability, 90
  unreasonableness, 90
  use of term, 96
Independence
  fraud, doctrine of independence, exception, 180
  interpretation of instruments, 219–28
Independent guarantor
  subrogation, 73n. 91
India
  bank-to-bank indemnity, 142–47
  embargo, 288–90
  injunctions, 288–90
Information
  indemnity agreements, duty to give, 99–100
Infrastructure
  and payment mechanism, 314, *315*
Injunctions
  availability of, 290–93
  fraud, 276–79
  India, 288–90
  Iranian revolution, 290–93
  types of, 302–6
Injunctive relief
  fraud, 184n. 19
Insolvency
  indemnity agreements, 102
Instruments, 1–78
  amendments of, 42–45
  assignability, 67–71
  bank guarantees, 14–18
  "blended" facilities, 40–42
  bonds, 9–11
  comfort letters, 7–9
  commercial letters of credit, 29, 32–36
  conditions precedent, 5–7
  confirmed letters of credit, 28–32, *33*
  disclaimers, 52–61
  generally, 1–3
  honor, 2–3, 26
  interbank relationships, 45
  interpretation. *See* Interpretation of instruments

Instruments (*cont.*)
  legal structure, 1–7
  letters of credit, generally. *See* Letters of credit
  mechanics of, 1–7
  mezzanine instruments, 3–5, 124
  "no bearer" rights, 65–67
  on-demand, 4, 12
  on-demand guarantees, 18–23
  quasi-instruments, 3–5
  revocable credits, 43
  security interest in document or goods, 47–52
  set-off, right of, 45–47
  standby letters of credit, 36–40
  subrogation, 72–79
  sureties, 11–14
  traditional guarantees, 11–14
  transferability, 61–65
Interbank relationships, 45
International treaties and conventions
  fraud, 202–3
Interpretation of instruments, 211–58
  advised letter of credit, *257*
  ambiguity, 229–30
  amendment by implication, 235n. 31
  applicable rules, interpretation of, 232–34
  Avery Dennison case, 245–47
  AXA v. Chase Manhattan, 248–53
  bank guarantees, *255, 256*
  case law, 223–28
    definition of rules, 214–15
  and commercial reality of the instrument, 212
  conditions subsequent, 244–53
    Avery Dennison case, 245–47
    AXA v. Chase Manhattan, 248–53
    contra proferentem rule, 252
    evergreen clauses, 247–53
    generally, 244–47
    "moment of death," 244
    wrongful dishonor, 248–53
  confirmed letter of credit, *256*
  construction contract, sample of use of credits and guarantees, *258*
  consultation in interests of all parties, 237–38
  contractual patterns, 254–57
  contra proferentem rule, 252
  definite, defined, 211
  discrepancies, 235–36, 240, 241n. 37
  dishonor, notice of, 239–40
  and disregard of facility, 219–28

Interpretation of instruments (*cont.*)
  evergreen clauses, 247–53
  expediency, principle of, 222–23
  and expert witnesses, 220
  express waivers, 234–44
  generally, 211–17
  guidance, 213
  implied waivers, 234–44
  independence principle, 235n. 32
  "industries" and "industrial," 216
  instrument, bank-account relationship, underlying transaction, *255*
  "moment of death," 244
  multi-party understanding and, 217–18
  natural and ordinary meaning of words, 231
  notice of refusal, 243
  "on a collection basis," tendering of discrepant documents, 221
  other instruments, interpretation of, 229–32
  "pay or extend" claims, 253–54
  preclusion, 234n. 28
  previous negotiation of parties, 231
  simple letter of credit, *255*
  strict compliance doctrine, 221–22
  and substantive independence, 219–28
  sui generis character of instruments, 215
  waiver doctrine, 234–44
  wrongful dishonor, 248–53
Iranian revolution (1979), 290–93
  on-demand guarantees, 22n. 39
Irrevocable credits, 7n. 11
ISPs, 39

J

Joint dominance
  and disclaimers, 55
Jurisdiction, 375–97. *See also* **Choice of law**
  alternative venues, 375n. 53
  Docdex proceedings, 394–97
  forum connexitatis, 394
  forum non conveniens doctrine, 376, 386–93
  forum shopping, 386–93
  generally, 375–76
  lex fori, 371, 375
  and refusal, 259
  right venue, determination, 375–76
  and UCC, 384
  and URCB, 384
  and URDG, 383–84

K

Kozolchyk, Boris, 331
Kuwait
    choice of law, 349–56

L

Lane, Geoffrey, 374
The Law of Letters of Credit (Dolan), 11–12, 279
Legal proceedings
    indemnity agreements, duty to inform, 98
Legal succession, transferability, 64
Letter-of-credit law, 26, 28
Letters of credit. *See also* **specific topics**
    acceptance, 27
    amendment, 25
    cancellation, 25
    commercial. *See* Commercial letters of credit
    conditions precedent, 26
    confirmed. *See* confirmed letters of credit
    deferred payment undertaking, 27n. 49
    defined, 24
    duration, 25
    fraud rule, 27n. 50
    generally, 24–28
    issuance, 25
    payment, 27
Lex fori, 371, 375
Lex mercatoria, 323–35, 340
    applicable rules, 325
    codification, 330
    trade usages, 325–27, 334
Liability
    bank-to-bank indemnity, 140–71
        bonus pater familias standard, 150
        care, duty of, of bank, 147–54
        confidentiality, duty of, 168–71
        discrepancies, 160–61
        dishonor, notice of, 160n. 56, 161–62
        duty to whom and for what, 154–58
        generally, 140–47
        honor, 161–64
        mixed standard of liability, 151
        notify and refuse, duty to, 158–62
        ordre public character, 168
        parole evidence rule, 152
        payment to beneficiary, duty to notify account party, 161

Liability (*cont.*)
        placing documents at disposal of the beneficiary, sample clause, 155–56, 165–68
        and public policy, 168–69
        reasonable care standard, 153
        reasonable time, defined, 162–65
        refuse, duty to, 163–64
        results liability, 151–53
        standards of international practice, 148–50
        time needed and available to examiner, 141–42
        "without delay," defined, 142–47
        wrongful dishonor, 164
    disclaimers, 59, 61
    fraud, nonparties, 208–9
Libya
    choice of law, 366–68, 374
Liquidation
    damages, 295
Loan agreements
    indemnity agreements, resemblance, 82–83, 87
Loss
    fraud, who bears loss, 193–98

M

Mandatory law
    national laws, governed by, 317, 318
Material adverse change
    indemnity agreements, 102
Material fact, concealment, 182n. 16
Mezzanine instruments, 3–5
    strict compliance doctrine, 124
Mitigate, duty to, 309–12
"Moment of death"
    bank-to-bank indemnity
        honor and "moment of death" of the instrument, 114–20
    choice of law, 358
    interpretation of instruments, 244
Multi-party stand-by, *41*
Multi-party understanding and interpretation of instruments, 217–18
Mutatis mutandis, 318
    bank-to-bank indemnity, 133

N

National laws
    death of facility, 316
    and jurisdiction, 323–35
    law merchant, borderline between, 315

Index

National laws (*cont.*)
    mandatory law, 317, 318
    non-mandatory law, 317
    remedies, 312–20
Negative pledge, indemnity agreements, 95–96
Negligence
    contributory negligence, 309–12
Netherlands
    indemnity agreements, 81n. 1
New York convention, 290
New York law
    choice of law, 344
    generally, 386
    vs. English law, 348–49
Nigerian law, 377–78
Niru case
    subrogation, 76–79
    unjust enrichment, 307–9
Nixon, Richard M., 288
"No bearer" rights, 65–67
Nondocumentary conditions
    bank-to-bank indemnity, 133n. 29
Nordea Bank, 137–38
North Carolina law vs. Kwaiti law, 352–53
Notice
    discrepancies, failure to give notice, 268–69
    of dishonor, 239–40
    dishonor, failure to give notice, 268–71
    refusal, 261–65
    of refusal, 243
Notify and refuse, duty to
    bank-to-bank indemnity, 158–62
Nullity exception, fraud, 198–200

O

Offshore International case, 347–49
OKO Bank, 139
On-demand guarantees, 18–23
    accessory agreements, 20
    and cash flow, 18n. 29
    contingent liability, 23
    demand-condition, 20–21
    and Iranian revolution (1979), 22n. 39
    trust arrangements, 22
On-demand instruments, 4, 12
Operation of law
    transferability, 64–65
Ordre public character. See also Public policy
    bank-to-bank indemnity, 168

Ordre public character (cont.)
    choice of law, 324, 328
        uniform law merchant, 336
    fraud, 181, 313, 314
    and illegality, 202
    remedies, 273
Ownership, right of, 48
Ozsunay, Professor, 374

P

Pacta sunt servanda rule, 309
    bank-to-bank indemnity, 133
Parent companies
    comfort letters, 8
Pari Passu provision, indemnity agreements, 95
Parole evidence rule, 281–82, 396
    bank-to-bank indemnity, 133, 152
Payment, letters of credit, 27
"Pay or extend" claims, 253–54
Performance bonds, 366–68
Policy interests, choice of law, 342–45, 391–93
Power Curber International Ltd. v. National Bank of Kuwait, 349–56
Principle of debtor protection, 69
Probability of ultimate success, 290
Promisee, 1–2n. 2
Promisor, 1–2n. 2
Proof, 271
    fraud, 183–86
Public interest
    standby letters of credit, 290
Public policy
    and bank-to-bank indemnity, 168–69
    choice of law, 324
    and fraud, 181

Q

Quasi-instruments, 3–5

R

Reasonable care, 126
    bank-to-bank indemnity, 153
Reasonable time, defined
    bank-to-bank indemnity, 162–65
Receivables
    assignment of, 68n. 88
Refusal
    and ambiguity, 264–65
    attorney's fees, 265–267

Refusal (*cont.*)
  damages, 265–267
  discrepancies, 265
  and dishonor, 270
  duty to refuse, bank-to-bank indemnity, 163–64
  and expert testimony, 263
  and jurisdiction, 259
  notice of, 243, 261–65
  venue, 261
  what constitutes, 259–67
Reimbursement
  and indemnity agreements, 81–88
Remedies
  attachment of proceeds, 298
  attorney's fees, 294
  breach of obligations, 287
  contributory negligence, 309–12
  damages as remedy, 283–87
    breach of obligations, 287
    certainty of harm, 284
    consequential damages, 287
    full compensation, 284
  death of instrument, attaching funds after, 274–78
  declaratory relief, 301–2
  default, 319
  de lege ferenda, 320–21
  duty to mitigate, 309–12
  Dynamics Corporation of America v. The Citizens and Southern National Bank, 288–90
  enforcement, 274–83
    damages as remedy, 283–87
    death of instrument, attaching funds after, 274–78
    ordinary or ex parte protective or temporary measures, 274–78
    parole evidence rule, 281–82
    specific enforcement, 283
    summary judgment, availability of, 278–79
    time required to enforce right, 279–81
  equitable relief, 296–98
    United Trading case, 296–98
  ex parte protective measures, 274–78, 298–301
  fault, defined, 311
  fraud, 275–78
    national laws, governed by, 313
  generally, 271–83
  Glencore case, 306–7
  Harbottle case, 301–2
    and injunctions, 303–5
  injunctions, 272–73, 276–79, 288–90

Remedies (*cont.*)
  availability of, 290–93
  types of, 302–6
  mixed nature of procedures, 313
  national laws, governing by, 312–20
  national procedural law, 273–74
  Niru case, 307–9
  ordre public character, 273
  parole evidence rule, 281–82
  prevailing party, 294
  probability of ultimate success, 290
  pro forma declaration, 289
  "right remedy," 294
  Rionda case, 299–301
  set-off, right of, 45–47
  specific enforcement as, 283
  statutory, 273
  substantive versus procedural issue, 271–309
  summary judgment, availability of, 278–79
  under UCC, 294–96
  United Technologies Corporation v. Citibank N.A., 290–93
  United Trading case, 296–98
  unjust enrichment, 306–9
Representations and warranties
  indemnity agreements, 88–90, 100
Restricted negotiation credit, 28n. 51
Results liability
  bank-to-bank indemnity, 151–53
Revocable credits, 43
Right of set-off, 45–47
  assignability, 69n. 89
***Rionda* case, 299–301**
Risks
  fraud, risks assumed, 191–93
Russia, exports to
  commercial letters of credit, 35n. 60

S

Sampo Bank, 138
Secondary guarantees, 1n. 1, 12, 13
Security interest in document or goods, 47–52
  Bahrain, 51
  conflict-of-laws rules, 48–49
  Egypt, 51
  indemnity agreements, 49–50
  ownership, right of, 48
  perfection of, 50–51
Services agreements, 81–88

INDEX

Set-off, right of, 45–47
  assignability, 69n. 89
Simple letter of credit
  interpretation of instruments, *255*
  standby letters of credit, *40*
Situs of debt
  choice of law, 348–49, 355
***Sonali* case,** 358–65, 378–79
Spanish law
  vs. English law, 348–49
Standby letters of credit, 12n. 19, 17
  account party, adverse change, 38
  American versus European, differences, 38
  "blended" facilities, 40–42
  and burden of education, 372
  choice of law, 331, 333n. 27
  and commercial letters of credit, 34n. 57
  diversified use of, 37n. 65
  doctrine of substantive independence, 103–4
  documentation, 134–35
  fraud, 38n. 67, 180
  function of, 36–40
  and Iranian revolution, 290–93
  ISPs, 39
  multi-party stand-by, *41*
  and performance bonds, 366–68
  public interest, 290
  "simple" standby letters of credit, *40*
  stand-by credit facility, *42*
  transferability, 63
Strict compliance doctrine
  bank-to-bank indemnity, 120–27
    consistency requirement, 127–32
    è contrario rule, 132–37
    liability of banks, 140
    as tendered rule, 132–37
  and fraud, 182
  interpretation of instruments, 221–22
Subrogation, 72–79
  domino effect, 72
  effect of, 73–74
  generally, 72–75
  independent guarantor, 73n. 91
  jurisdiction, 73
  Niru case, 76–79
  nominated person, 76
  two sources for, 76–79
  and UCC, 75–76
  unjust enrichment, 76–77

Supranational law
  and arbitral awards, 328
  emergence of, 323
Sureties, generally, 11–14
Suretyship guarantees, 1n. 1
Svenska Handelsbaken, 138–39
SWIFT rules, 335n. 31
***Sztejn* opinion,** 117–19, 124

T

Tender
  acceptance of, 267–68
  bank-to-bank indemnity as tendered rule, 132–37
Three-party agreements
  disclaimers, 59, *60*
Tolerance
  and strict compliance rule, 127
Tort law
  fraud, 209–10
Trade usages
  lex mercatoria, 325–27, 334
Traditional guarantees, 11–14
  and freedom of contract, 13
Transferability, 61–65
  legal succession, 64
  non-independent instruments, 62–63
  operation of law, 64–65
  standby letters of credit, 63
Turkey, exports to
  commercial letters of credit, 35n. 60
Turkish law, 373–74

U

Uganda
  choice of law, 342–45, 391–93
Umbrella indemnity agreements, 91
UNCITRAL, 341n. 39
Unconscionability, 173n. 1, 289
  indemnity agreements, 90
Uniform Commercial Code (UCC), generally, 368–71
  Article 5, Official Comments, 431–72
  and jurisdiction, 383–84
Uniform law merchant, 335–42
United Kingdom
  fraud cases, 202–4
United Nations Convention on Independent Guarantees and Standby Letters of Credit (UNC), 88–89, 401–29

United Trading case, 296–98
Unjust enrichment, 76–77, 306–9
Unreasonableness, indemnity agreements, 90
URCB and jurisdiction, 384
URDG and jurisdiction, 384

V

Vainionpää, Matti, 138
Venue, refusal, 261

W

Waiver doctrine
  interpretation of instruments, 234–44

Warranties
  indemnity agreements. *See* Representations and warranties
White law, 26
Wrongful dishonor, 268
  bank-to-bank indemnity, 164
  interpretation of instruments, 248–53

Z

Zeevi case, 342–45, 391–93